PROTECTING CONSUMER RIGHTS

Tăng Thành Trai Lê
Professor of Law
University of Notre Dame

SHEPARD's/McGRAW-HILL, INC.
P.O. Box 1235
Colorado Springs, Colorado 80901

McGRAW-HILL BOOK COMPANY

New York ● St. Louis ● San Francisco ● Auckland ● Bogotá ● Caracas
Colorado Springs ● Hamburg ● Lisbon ● London ● Madrid ● Mexico ● Milan
Montreal ● New Delhi ● Oklahoma City ● Panama ● Paris ● San Juan
São Paulo ● Singapore ● Sydney ● Tokyo ● Toronto

Library of Congress Cataloging-in-Publication Data

Lê, Tăng Thành Trai, 1928-
    Protecting consumer rights / Tăng Thành Trai Lê.
        p.   cm.
    Includes index.
    ISBN 0-07-034852-9
    1. Consumer protection--Law and legislation--United States.
    2. Consumer credit--Law and legislation--United States.   3. Consumer protection--Law and legislation--United States--States.   4. Consumer credit--Law and legislation--United States--States.   I.   Title.
    KF1609.L4 1987
    343.73'071--dc19
    [347.30371]   87-28867
    ISBN 0-07-034852-9   CIP

OC 1723 3652

For Châu

Acknowledgments

Writing a book to completion and eventual publication requires help and support of many people. Colleagues, students, friends, I thank you all for your assistance, interest and encouragement throughout the entire endeavor.

A few individuals, however, have to be named:

Dean David T. Link of the Notre Dame Law School who facilitated my task tremendously by allowing me a light teaching load in the Spring of 1986;

Assistant Dean William O. McLean who made all the administrative arrangements to accommodate my work;

Professor Roger F. Jacobs, Director of the Notre Dame Law School Library and his dedicated and competent staff. Among this staff, a special thanks goes out to Dwight B. King, Jr., and Carmela R. Kinslow for their relentless effort to provide me with the necessary material;

Edward F. Kelly, J.D. 1987, my research assistant for his invaluable help;

Willa Mae Parker, my secretary, for her impeccable work, dedication, patience and above all her great sense of humor.

Finally, I extend my deepest thanks to my husband Châu Lê, my children, Mimi, Khôi, and their spouses, Douglas and Sue, for their interest and support during the writing of this book.

Notre Dame, Thanksgiving 1987

Contents

3   Extending Credit

4 Credit Disclosures

1

Introduction

§1.01 Historical Background

The term *consumer* generally refers to a natural person who buys goods or services primarily for personal, family, or household purposes. The term thus excludes a corporate entity or an individual who purchases the goods or services for a business purpose such as resale. The class of consumers was expanded to include not only the parties who are privy to the contract of sale between sellers and buyers, but also any natural person who uses the goods, if the use is primarily for personal, family, and household purposes. That there should be special rules carved out of traditional contract and tort theories to protect this class of persons is a new phenomenon. Until the end of the World War I, there was little support in the United States for laws to protect poorer groups or to aid the consumer in the marketplace. Society was rather characterized by the dominance of an egalitarian principle which held that the law should be the same for everyone, whether rich or poor. It was an egalitarian principle characteristic of the Protestant Ethic that so permeated American society. Where the spirit of rugged individualism and self-reliance reigned, self protection and the betterment of one's material conditions were a personal problem, not a societal one.

This individualist, egalitarian philosophy was well-adapted to the demographic conditions of the time. Americans in the pre-World War I period of our history operated most frequently on a small community level, with little mass production or mass consumption. One bought products from a local merchant's store, or borrowed money from the local lender (if one borrowed at all, credit being frowned upon) with whom one was already somewhat familiar. Commercial transactions were personal in many ways.

In such an atmosphere, it is difficult to imagine the passage of laws specifically designed to aid the consumer. But with the birth of mass production and mass consumption brought about by the new automobile industry, the system of marketing was no longer the province of the local merchant's store. The merchants now had at their disposal formidable means of promoting their wares and introducing them into consumers' homes. Consumerism and the "buy now, pay later" plan were no longer the exception but became the rule.

The atmosphere wherein rugged individualism thrived has been replaced by a new system. On one side stands the sophisticated merchant with mass production, saturation advertising, and sales of goods on a national scale; on the other side stands the individual consumer. Traditional legal principles which treat sellers and buyers on the same footing no longer seem right. *Caveat emptor,* or "buyer beware," should no longer be the order of the day. Although a consumer may be wealthy, the term *consumer* is generally associated with the unsophisticated, the poor, the underprivileged. A report issued in 1968 by the National Advisory Commission on Civil Disorders, "On Exploitation of Disadvantaged Consumers by Retail Merchants," found that

> while higher prices are not necessarily exploitive in themselves, many merchants in ghetto neighborhoods take advantage of their superior knowledge of credit buying by engaging in various exploitative tactics— high-pressure salesmanship, bait advertising, misrepresentation of prices, substitution of used goods for promised new ones, failure to notify consumers of legal actions against them, refusal to repair or replace substandard goods, exhorbitant prices, credit charges, and use of shoddy merchandise.[1]

The common law remedies are no longer deemed adequate to respond to the consumer's plight. A new set of rules is needed.

In the 1960s, Ralph Nader capitalized on this nascent sentiment, gave it impetus and organizational support, and managed to influence legislation for the benefit of the consumer. Nader became the foremost consumer crusader, and with his efforts, the doctrine of *caveat emptor* was relegated to history. The courts, even before consumer legislation, spearheaded the legal movement in this direction. For example, in the case of *Unico v Owen,*[2] the court was already saying:

---

[1] National Advisory Commission on Civil Disorders, Riot Commission Report 274-76 (1968), *cited in* D. Rothschild & D. Carroll, Consumer Protection §1.01, at 2 (1973).
[2] 50 NJ 101, 232 A2d 405 (1967).

Just as the community has an interest in insuring (usually by means of legislative process) that credit financing contracts facilitating sales of consumer goods conform to community-imposed standards of fairness and decency, so too the courts, in the absence of controlling legislation, in applying the adjudicating process, must endeavor, whenever reasonably possible, to impose those same standards on principles of equity and public policy. An initial step in that direction of unquestioned need and fortunately of common judicial acceptance, is the view that consumer goods contracts and their concurrent financing arrangements, should be construed most strictly against the seller who imposed the contract on the buyer, and against the finance company which participated in the transaction, directly or indirectly, or was aware of the nature of the seller's consumer goods sales and installment payment operation.[3]

Beginning in the 1970s, a flurry of legislation at the state and federal levels was enacted to protect the consumer. There seem to have been several strands of purpose in this legislation: protection of the underdog, racial equality, economic parity, and a certain anti-establishment sentiment.

Regardless of the undertones, it is clear that nowadays the law perceives the equality gap between the provider of goods, money or credit on one hand, and the acquirer of these amenities on the other hand, and tries to step in to fill that gap.

§1.02 Impact of Consumer Legislation

Whether the law succeeds in fulfilling its goal of filling the equality gap between suppliers and consumers is an open question. For all its effort to serve the unsophisticated consumer, consumer legislation is nonetheless complex, and by its nature, still directs itself to the sophisticated consumer. How many borrowers, for example, are truly able to take advantage of the technical disclosures that the Truth in Lending Act requires from lenders?

The continued upper hand of suppliers of goods and services means that it is not very often that the consumer has the opportunity to use consumer law as a sword in this battle. It is far more likely that the consumer may use it, simply, as a shield, when sued, to execute an obligation under a contract that violates one or more tenets of consumer protection law. Whether consumer law is to be used as a sword or as a shield, however, the lawyer in this latter part of the twentieth century cannot practice effectively in the area of business law without an adequate grasp of consumer legislation.

---

[3] *Id* at 112, 232 A2d at 411.

§1.03   The Federal Trade Commission Act

The most resounding repudiation of the *caveat emptor* doctrine was the enactment and subsequent amendment of §5 of the Federal Trade Commission (FTC) Act.[4] Generally referred to as the FTC Rule, it purports to curb the unfair and deceptive practices in the marketplace, when the interest of the consumer is at stake.

The Federal Trade Commission, established by Congress in 1914, played an important role in protecting consumers at an early date. Originally, however, the primary purpose of the Commission did not concern the protection of consumers, but rather the enforcement of antitrust laws. The Federal Trade Commission Act gave the FTC the power to prohibit *unfair methods of competition,* and no reference was made to consumer protection or deceptive trade practices. Very soon, the courts and the Commission came to realize that one way for honest competition to be hurt was by deceiving consumers. Since consumer deception constituted an unfair method of competition, it came within the FTC's authority to regulate. Thus the Commission, erected as a de facto protector of the consumer, grew stronger and stronger, especially with the subsequent amendments to the Act which extended the authority of the Commission to consumer-related issues.

The Federal Trade Commission Act, prohibiting unfair or deceptive acts or practices in or affecting commerce, served as a model for many of the state laws, the so-called "Little FTCs."

In the 1980s, there has been a trend toward restricting the powers of the FTC and replacing protectionism with a free market approach.[5] However, in spite of this retreat, the FTC remains the leading enforcement agency with respect to unfair or deceptive consumer practices.

§1.04   The Consumer Credit Protection Act

Another important piece of federal legislation designed to protect consumers is the Consumer Credit Protection Act of May 1968.[6] There follows a synopsis of the most important subchapters of the Act and what each subchapter is designed to accomplish.

Subchapter I, usually referred to as the Truth in Lending Act (TILA), deals with consumer credit cost disclosures. TILA requires persons extending credit to disclose to the consumer a number of important credit terms, which many creditors had in the past conveniently failed to reveal or clarify. TILA has been amended several times, and the periodic additions of new subject matters has continually expanded the scope of the Act. For example, the Fair Credit Billing Act was added in 1974, and the Consumer Leasing Act in 1976. The most

---

[4] 15 USC §45(a)(1).

[5] For instance, note the amendment to the FTC Act, the FTC Improvement Act, Pub No 96-252, 94 Stat 374, (1980) (codified at 15 USC §57(a) & (b)).

[6] Pub L No 90-321, 82 Sat 146 (1968) (amended 1980).

dramatic change by far, however, took place in 1980, when TILA was drastically amended by the Truth in Lending Simplification and Reform Act (the Simplification Act), which became fully effective on October 1, 1982. The Simplification Act was more than an amendment; it changed TILA so dramatically that many refer to it as "the new TILA."

Subchapter II concerns "Restrictions on Garnishment," and is designed to prevent excessive credit payments from being extracted from the consumer through the consumer's workplace. It is also intended to protect the consumer's job when creditors use garnishment of wages to collect debts.

Subchapter III deals with consumer credit reporting, and is appropriately entitled the Fair Credit Reporting Act. It is meant to eradicate the abuses of consumer reporting agencies. It regulates the contents, the confidentiality, and the use of credit reports, and gives consumers access to those reports.

Subchapter IV, the Equal Credit Opportunity Act, prevents credit discrimination based on sex, marital status, national origin, and other suspicious bases of discrimination.

Subchapter V, the Fair Debt Collection Practices Act, seeks to abate abusive, deceptive and unfair debt collection practices of debt collectors.

Subchapter VI deals with "Electronic Fund Transfers." It regulates electronic transfer systems such as bank cards and 24-hour banking machines, with a view toward protecting the user of the systems.

§1.05   State Consumer Law

As stated above, the FTC Act gave impetus to the state legislatures in the area of consumer protection. Apart from the "little FTC" statutes dealing with unfair and deceptive practices, states have also enacted consumer protection statutes dealing with truth-in-lending disclosures, and various aspects of consumer transactions such as retail installment sales, door-to-door sales, interest, and rate of credit. The 1970s particularly saw a great deal of legislation in these areas. But these laws are far from uniform. They vary greatly from state to state. There have been several attempts to standardize the law among the states, but only two of these attempts have achieved some success.

First, the National Conference of Commissioners on Uniform State Laws drafted the Uniform Consumer Credit Code (U3C), the original version in 1968 and a revised version in 1974. At the time of this writing, only 14 states have adopted the U3C. The reason for this lack of success was because when the U3C was proposed to the states, the consumer movement was already so far advanced that the model was seen as not progressive enough. Even among the states adopting the U3C, there is much variation in the Codes provisions. Thus, this first effort to achieve uniformity in the area, while important, has met with limited success.

The other effort, which is more progressive and pro-consumer than the U3C, is the 1970 National Consumer Act, revised in 1973 as the Model Consumer Credit Act. The Act was put forth by the National Consumer Law Center at Boston College Law School. The Model Act goes further than the U3C and covers areas that the U3C left out, such as deceptive trade practices and credit bureau abuses. However, neither the National Consumer Act nor its abbreviated version, the Model Consumer Credit Act, were adopted as such by any state. The success of this effort might be measured rather by the influence of the Model Act upon consumer protection legislation in a number of states, notably Wisconsin.

§1.06   Consumer Law and the Practitioner

The practitioner, unless working for a specialized public interest firm that focuses on consumer issues, is usually reluctant to take consumer cases, for two main reasons. First, the stakes are usually quite small. Individual consumer claims are usually modest. Compared to an injury case, actual recovery is often insignificant. Second, unfamiliarity with consumer law is widespread. Consumer law is new, and, even today, not a major subject in law school curricula. Generally, lawyers trained in the case method do not feel comfortable with the volume of legislation on the subject and the amount of statutory and regulatory interpretation that accompanies it.

These inhibitions may be mitigated, however. First, in terms of financial reward, many consumer protection statutes provide for reasonable attorneys' fees to be awarded the successful litigant. It is notable in this connection that attorneys' fees are also awarded to a successful legal aid litigant, where the plaintiff did not personally incur any costs.[7] Furthermore, in an appropriate case, if the legal requirements are met, a class action could be instituted to aggregate individual complaints into a more sizeable case. This allows for greater recovery, and more substantial attorneys' fees. Although federal law places stringent conditions on class actions in addition to those imposed by the specific statutes involved,[8] class action is still an attractive avenue.

Consumers are not the only ones with a stake in consumer cases. On the other side of the fence, creditors and suppliers of goods and services also need competent advice on consumer law. In this case, the financial consideration is no longer a discouraging factor.

Second, on the question of unfamiliarity with consumer legislation, there are now a number of very good publications on consumer law that are of great help to the practitioner in sorting out the profusion of relevant legislation. The foremost is the CCH Consumer Credit Guide, an invaluable source of information on both federal and state consumer law. Rothschild and Carroll's *Consumer Protection Reporting Service* and Fonseca's *Handling Consumer Credit Cases* are also very helpful. Serial Publications of the National Consumer Law Center, with updated supplements each year, are also good sources of information. A truly excellent beginning guide to consumer law is the Nutshell Series' *Consumer Law* by David G. Epstein and Steve H. Nickles. This list, of course, is far from

---

[7] *See* Harris v Tower Loan, Inc, 609 F2d 120 (5th Cir 1980).
[8] An example is Fed R Civ P 23.

exhaustive. These volumes, however, do provide at least a good base from which to develop a workable knowledge of consumer issues.

§1.07   Outline of This Book

The present volume is directed toward the practitioner. It deals with each topic from the perspective of one who is faced with an issue and now needs to go to the applicable law. This approach explains the book's organizational structure. This book is divided into 11 chapters as follows:

Chapter 1

Introduction

Chapter 2

Sales and Consumer Protection: advertising, unfair and deceptive acts and practices, door-to-door sales, referral sales, state and federal warranty law.

Chapter 3

Extending Credit: Who can extend credit, fair credit reporting, and equal credit opportunity.

Chapter 4

Credit Disclosure: The different types of credit and related disclosures under the Truth-In-Lending Act.

Chapter 5

Charge and Rate Regulations: Examining usury laws and the various methods by which a creditor may overcharge and the protections available against abusive credit practices.

Chapter 6

Credit Insurance: The creditor's methods to guarantee the loan by means of insurance paid for by the consumer; abuses and protection.

Chapter 7

Credit Cards: This chapter examines the law regarding issuance of credit cards, disclosure requirements, credit card billing, the problem of lost or stolen cards.

Chapter 8

Electronic Fund Transfers: This chapter deals primarily with the Federal Electronic Fund Transfer Act and applies the provisions of the Act to the problems of issuance, access devices, liability for authorized or unauthorized uses, resolution of disputes, and the consumer's remedies.

Chapter 9

Assignment of Creditors' Claims: How consumer legislation overrides and preempts traditional legal doctrines. This chapter examines the demise of the holder-in-due-course doctrine when the consumer's claims and defenses are at stake.

Chapter 10

Debt Collection: This chapter examines how federal and state law attempt to protect the defaulting consumer by regulating the creditor's various methods of debt collection.

Chapter 11

Real Estate Transactions: This chapter deals with that most important transaction in the consumer's life, the purchase of a home. Besides the TILA provisions applicable to this issue, we will examine the Real Estate Settlement Procedure Act, the Interstate Land Sales Full Disclosure Act, and Real Estate Warranty law.

This book does not purport to be an exhaustive treatment of all the relevant consumer issues. However, we hope that our work will be a useful and practical guide to the practitioner. Our goal has been to introduce some simplicity into a very complex topic.

2 Sales and Consumer Protection

9

§2.01   Introduction

Under the common law, the seller's multifaceted tactics to induce the consumer to buy were deemed to be a fact of life. *Caveat emptor* or *buyer beware* was the order of the day. The law treated all every buyer alike, be it a powerful corporation with a vast legal department or an unsophisticated low-income consumer. The law rarely intervened to affect the rules of the game in favor of any particular group.

Things changed, however, after Ralph Nader and his "Nader's Raiders" broke upon the American scene. As a result of the new social consciousness brought about by the consumer revolution, the legislature, at the state and federal levels, closely scrutinizes the seller's conduct with a view to protecting the consumer. In the area of sales, the legislature's scrutiny concentrates on the various methods the seller uses to induce sales, such as advertising, sales practices, and warranties accompanying the sale of consumer goods.

§2.02   Advertising under the Common Law

The common law does not regulate advertising. It simply offers the consumer a variety of tort and contract theories on which the plaintiff may base an action against *false* advertising.

There are several legal theories affording remedies to the aggrieved plaintiff. The first is the tort action for deceit or misrepresentation. This action requires proof of five elements:

1. A false representation of material fact
2. Scienter, that is, that the defendant knew the statement to be false or failed to inform himself
3. Intent to induce plaintiff's reliance
4. Justifiable reliance
5. Damages proximately caused by the reliance[1]

The law of misrepresentation has not been entirely clarified by the courts. The tort action for damages in deceit is based in some courts on intent and in others on negligence or strict liability. Intent and negligence are not easy to prove. The burden of proof for such elements as scienter and justifiable reliance limits the efficacy of this action from the consumer's point of view.

Another recognized legal theory is the theory of strict liability for defective products causing personal injury. This action dispenses with the burden of proof of the defendant's negligence or intent, but may succeed only in limited circumstances. The product must be defective when sold and the defective condition must be unreasonably dangerous to the consumer or the consumer's property. Furthermore, recovery is limited to physical harm or injury to property. Defective products that cause only economic losses are generally not covered.[2]

Equitable remedies such as rescission or restitution are yet other available legal theories. The objective of these remedies, which are available where the legal remedy would be inadequate to deal with the resulting injury, is to "restore the parties to the *status quo [ante]*" and thereby "prevent the misrepresenter from gaining a benefit from the transaction."[3]

There are important obstacles to the success of such an action, for at least three reasons:

1. The court may deem that the misrepresentation amounts to mere *puffing*, or harmless exaggeration. As a practice acceptable in the commercial world, puffing is considered more as an opinion than a misrepresentation
2. The parol evidence rule prevents the plaintiff from introducing evidence which contradicts a written contract that specifically disclaims all other warranties or oral representations
3. The consumer's right to bring an action against the seller may be barred if the consumer uses the goods after discovery of the defect or fails

---

[1] Prosser & Keeton, the Law of Torts §105, at 729 (5th ed 1984).
[2] *Id* 729-35; Restatement (Second) of Torts §402A (1965).
[3] Prosser & Keeton, *supra* note 1, at 529.

to notify the seller in a timely manner. In these instances, the consumer may be deemed to have accepted the contract

The fourth available legal theory is an action for breach of express warranty, since advertising may be deemed to be a form of express warranty. This action is based on contract and as such does not require proof of scienter. However, the common law still requires proof of the buyer's reliance for recovery. Even if the plaintiff can prove reliance, the reliance must be *reasonable*. Here again, the unclear distinction between warranty and puffing renders the consumer's chances for recovery quite problematic. The additional limitations imposed by the parol evidence rule when there is a written contract, excluding any other extrinsic evidence, including the false advertising, often create insuperable obstacles to recovery.

If the plaintiff, based on one or more of the above legal theories, does succeed, the plaintiff is entitled only to money damages in the amount of the loss incurred by the seller's misrepresentation. If the loss is not great, the action is most often not worth the trouble and the cost. As a practical result, the seller is encouraged to continue the deceptive advertising.

§2.03   False Advertising and State Law

The Printer's Ink Model Statute

The *Printer's Ink* Model Statute was drafted in 1911 for the advertising industry trade journal, *Printer's Ink*. The statute made it a misdemeanor for any person to use an advertisement which contained "any assertion, representation or statement of fact which is untrue, deceptive or misleading."

Approximately 44 states and the District of Columbia adopted the statute, which for many years remained the only statute which offered significant public remedy for false advertising. To implement the statute, many states, through legislation, empowered the attorney general or other public officials to seek an injunction to stop false advertising.

The *Printer's Ink* Statute has not proved to be an effective deterrent to false advertising for several reasons:

1. Some states dilute the statute by adding a scienter requirement or *intent to deceive* element. To be charged under these statutes, the advertiser must know or be charged with knowledge that the representation is untrue, deceptive, or misleading

2. Some forms of deception, such as *bait-and-switch* advertising, are not covered by the statute

3. Due to the criminal nature of the statute, the courts tend to construe the statute restrictively, and prosecutors are reluctant to institute criminal proceedings. Some jurisdictions applied the statute restrictively to exclude radio and television advertising. Others have amended their statutes to apply to both. The statutes, even thus amended, were aimed

only at advertisers, excluding publishers or broadcasters having no knowledge of the false and deceptive advertising.[4] A survey made at the request of the New York Bar Association indicated that most jurisdictions which had the statute never used the statute, and only a handful of prosecutions were ever instituted in the other jurisdictions[5]

Specific Statutes Dealing with Particular Groups of Goods and Commodities

Every state has enacted statutes regulating the advertising in specific commercial areas. Examples of such statutes are:

1. Statutes dealing with bank, insurance, and security advertising. The so-called state Blue Sky Laws provide for cease-and-desist orders and injunctions against the sale of securities promoted by false advertising literature
2. Statutes based on federal legislation dealing with false advertising in food, drugs, and cosmetics
3. Statutes related to farm product advertising[6]

These statutes generally provide a criminal penalty for deceptive advertising, including the revocation of the offender's right to do business. These numerous statues vary from state to state. More often than not, they are arbitrary in scope and infrequent in enforcement.

§2.04   Advertising under Federal Law

Advertising may be included in the general federal proscription of *unfair or deceptive acts or practices in commerce.* In 1914, Congress enacted the Federal Trade Commission Act which created the Federal Trade Commission.[7] Section 5 of the Act prohibited "unfair methods of competition."[8] Originally, the purpose of the Act in creating the FTC and in proscribing unfair methods of competition was not to protect the consumer, but rather to give teeth to the enforcement of antitrust laws by giving the Commission broad powers to act against various forms of anticompetition practices in industries. This focus on industries prompted the Supreme Court to hold in *FTC v Raladam Co*[9] that the statute

---

[4] Note, *The Regulation of Advertising,* 56 Colum L Rev 1018, 1059-60 (1956).

[5] S. Oppenheim & G. Weston, Unfair Trade Practices and Consumer Protection 543-44 (1974).

[6] *See* Note, *The Regulation of Advertising,* 56 Colum L Rev 1018, at 1065-67 and app B, at 1102 (1956).

[7] 15 USC §41.

[8] 15 USC §45.

[9] 283 US 643 (1931).

applied only if the unfair method injured competitors. Injury to the consumer alone was not sufficient.

To afford greater protection to consumers, Congress passed the Wheeler-Lea Amendment in 1938.[10] Section 5, as amended, prohibited not only unfair methods of competition, but also "unfair or deceptive acts or practices in commerce." The FTC was given the authority to proscribe practices that were unfair or deceptive to the public, but not injurious to competitors. The new amendment thus repudiated *FTC v Raladam.*

The term *unfair and deceptive practices in commerce* was interpreted by the Supreme Court to mean that the Act did not apply to wholly intrastate activities. In *FTC v Bunte Brothers, Inc,*[11] the FTC charged the Bunte Brothers with violating §5 of the FTC Act by selling *break and take* packages in Illinois in which the amount received by the purchasers depended on chance. The Supreme Court recognized that the use of such packages was an unfair method of competition prohibited by §5, but held that the term *commerce* in which those methods were barred was interstate and not intrastate commerce. The court explained that to read unfair methods of competition in intrastate commerce as though it meant unfair methods of competition in any way affecting interstate commerce required clearer congressional manifestation of intention.[12]

In 1975, §5 was amended to apply to practices "in or *affecting* commerce."[13] Section 5(a)(1) now provides: "Unfair methods of competition in or affecting commerce, and unfair or deceptive acts or practices in or affecting commerce, is declared unlawful."

§2.05   —*Deceptive* Acts or Practices Defined

Section 5 of the FTC Act does not define the term *deceptive.* The Commission, acting on the broad authority granted by Congress and the federal courts, has forged an extensive body of law interpreting the term *deceptive.* The resulting concept of deception eliminates altogether the proof requirements of scienter, knowledge, actual reliance, or damage of the common law fraud.

A practice is *deceptive* if:

1. It has the tendency or capacity to mislead
2. A substantial number of consumers
3. In a material way[14]

---

[10] Pub L No 447, §§1-5, 52 Stat 111 (amending 15 USC §§41, 44, 45, 52-58).

[11] 312 US 349 (1941).

[12] *Id* 355.

[13] Emphasis added. Pub L No 93-637, §201(a), 88 Stat 2193.

[14] Letter from Patricia P. Bailey and Michael Pertschuk, FTC Commissioners, to John D. Dingell, Chairman, House Comm on Energy and Commerce (Feb 24, 1984) providing statement of law of deception *cited in* Bailey & Pertschuk, *The Law of Deception: The Past as Prologue,* 33 Am UL Rev 849, 850 n4 (1983-84).

The act or practice that has the tendency to mislead may be an affirmative oral or written representation, a failure to perform certain acts, or generally any marketing practices associated with the supply of products, including real property, and services.

Dealing with the first prong of the test, i.e., *the capacity or tendency to mislead,* the commission need not find that actual deception has occurred. Activities with only the potential to mislead may be found deceptive. The United States Court of Appeals for the Third Circuit noted that "[t]he purpose of the Federal Trade Commission Act is to protect the public, not to punish a wrongdoer, . . . and it is in the public interest to stop any deception at its incipiency."[15] As a consequence, any "likelihood or propensity" of deception is enough. The advertiser's good faith or bad faith is immaterial.[16] Even an honorable intent to live up to the promise in spite of a contrary representation still may be deceptive. For example, take the case of *Montgomery Ward & Co v FTC*.[17] In this case, the FTC charged that Montgomery Ward engaged in a deceptive practice because Montgomery Ward in its advertising represented that it guaranteed its merchandise "without condition or limitation." Ward's written warranty, however, was subject to certain limitations. Ward argued that its advertising did not constitute a deceptive practice, because Ward's policy was to honor its guarantees as advertised in spite of the limitations in its written warranty. The FTC contended that the advertising was nonetheless deceptive. The court agreed, stating that the Act does not require false advertising for a finding of violation. It requires simply deceptive advertising, which was present here. Thus, whatever Ward's intentions may have been, these intentions were not conclusive in determining the deceptiveness of the advertising or trade practice. The court said, "assuming Ward has a policy of honoring guarantees as advertised, the issue is yet not one of performance, but one of advertising . . . ."[18]

The second prong of the deceptive test is the finding that the conduct or practice has the capacity to mislead a substantial number of consumers. In *Charles of the Ritz Distributors Corp v FTC*,[19] the Court agreed with the FTC, finding to be deceptive the advertisement of the Charles of the Ritz Rejuvenescence Cream that stated, among other things, that the preparation brings to the user's skin "quickly the clear radiance . . . the petal-like quality and texture of youth," and that "your face need know no drought years . . . ."

The advertiser argued that no deception was involved because "no straight-thinking person could believe that its cream would actually rejuvenate." The court answered that the law was not "made for the protection of

---

[15] Regine Corp v FTC, 322 F2d 765, 768 (3d Cir 1963).

[16] Feil v FTC, 285 F2d 879, 896 (9th Cir 1960).

[17] 379 F2d 666 (7th Cir 1967).

[18] *Id* 670.

[19] 143 F2d 676 (2d Cir 1944).

experts, but for the public—that vast multitude which includes the ignorant, the unthinking and the credulous."[20]

With respect to the third prong, that the misrepresentation must be material, it has generally been interpreted that the deception is material if it affects the consumer's choice of the product.

§2.06   —*Unfair* Acts or Practices Defined

Beside *deceptive* acts or practices, *unfair* acts or practices are also prohibited. There might, for example, be business practices that are not per se deceptive, but which nevertheless might be unfair to consumers.

The Supreme Court case of *FTC v Sperry & Hutchinson Co*[21] lays down the standards for *unfairness* under the Act. Unfairness is determined on the basis of:

1. Whether the practice offends public policy, that is, whether it comes under at least the penumbra of the common-law or statutory law
2. Whether the practice is immoral, unethical, oppressive, or unscrupulous
3. Whether the practice causes substantial injury to consumers (S & H standards)

Thus, the concept of unfairness under the Act is more comprehensive than that of deception.

The FTC has indicated that in determining whether a practice is unfair, the most important factor is whether there is substantial injury to the consumer.[22] The FTC presents three criteria for determining whether injury is *substantial* enough to merit a finding of violation of the Act. Under these criteria, the injury must:

1. Be substantial
2. Not be outweighed by any countervailing benefits to the consumer that the practice produces
3. Be an injury that the consumers themselves cannot reasonably have avoided.[23]

With respect to advertising, the FTC has issued a number of *Guides* applicable to various industries.[24] The two dealing with the sale of goods that are worthy

---

[20] *Id* 679.

[21] 405 US 233 (1972).

[22] Letter from FTC to the Senate Committee on Commerce, Science and Transportation, 97th Cong, 2d Sess 23 (1982).

[23] *Id.*

[24] Some examples of FTC Guides: Title Advertising and Labeling 16 CFR §228; Guide for Advertising Fallout Shelters 16 CFR §229; and Guide for Advertising Shell-Homes 16 CFR §230 etc.

of note are bait-and-switch advertising[25] and deceptive pricing.[26]

§2.07   —Bait-and-Switch Advertising

Bait-and-switch advertising begins with an offer to sell a product or service which in fact the advertiser does not really intend or desire to sell. The insincere advertisement is made very alluring so as to catch the attention and imagination of the consumer, but the intention is to switch products and lure the consumer into buying something else, usually at a higher price or on a basis more advantageous to the advertiser.

The FTC notes that the actual sale of the merchandise advertised does not preclude the existence of a bait-and-switch scheme. If the sale of the originally advertised merchandise is but an incidental by-product of the fundamental sales plan, and is intended really to provide an aura of legitimacy to a sales operation which has a hidden purpose, then it would still be an impermissible instance of bait-and-switch advertising.

Rule 238.3 provides objective standards by which to determine whether an offer is bona fide or a bait-and-switch practice. The following are such indicators:

1. Refusal to show, demonstrate, or sell the product offered in accordance with the terms of the offer

2. The disparagement, by acts or words, of the advertised product or its condition (that it needs repairs, that it has no warranty, etc.)

3. The failure to have available at the outlets listed in the advertisement a sufficient quantity of the advertised product, unless the advertiser sufficiently discloses that the supply is limited, or available only at certain disclosed locations

4. Refusal to take orders for the advertised merchandise to be delivered within a reasonable period of time

5. Showing or demonstrating a product which is defective or unusable

All of these activities are aimed at discouraging the consumer from actually buying the product advertised. In addition, a further indicator is:

6. The advertiser's use of a sales plan or method of penalizing salesmen who sell the product advertised

One case involving bait-and-switch was *In re Leon A. Tashof.*[27] In this case dealing with the sale of eyeglasses, the FTC had no direct evidence of the advertiser's switching customers from the advertised $7.50 pairs of glasses to more expensive ones. However, the records showed that only nine sales, which

---

[25] 16 CFR pt 238.
[26] 16 CFR pt 251.
[27] 74 FTC 1361 (1968), *affd,* 437 F2d 707 (DC Cir 1970).

represented 64/100 of 1 per cent of eyeglasses sales, were made at $7.50. The court concluded that the advertiser had engaged in bait-and-switch advertising because the record leaves unexplained why the (seller's) customers, presumably anxious to purchase at as low a price as possible, would so consistently have bought more expensive glasses if suitable glasses at $7.50 were available. Furthermore, the fact that the seller had continued to advertise the $7.50 glasses for a year and a half despite the scarcity of sales at $7.50 tends to show the seller's purpose was "to bring customers into the store for other reasons."[28]

§2.08   —Deceptive Pricing

An example will illustrate deceptive pricing practices. Suppose a merchant advertises a Fourth of July sale, wherein the price of widgets, ordinarily $20, is reduced to $15. Now, the widgets have sold for $20 only during a short period before the "sale." In effect, the store has inflated the price simply in order to reduce it and declare a 25 per cent off sale. This would constitute deceptive pricing, because $20 is not the regular price at which widgets are sold to the public for any substantial period before the announced "reduction."

Another form of deceptive pricing occurs when the advertiser represents that the price of an item is reduced, or offers "savings" to purchasers, without specifying the amount of reduction in price, while in fact the reduction is minimal, and, thus, the savings insignificant. Such advertising is deceptive because if consumers knew of the true facts, they would not have been influenced sufficiently to come to the store and purchase the product. Deceptive pricing is thus akin to bait-and-switch advertising, except that there is no "switch" of products.

Another type of deceptive pricing involves use of the word *free.* Under the FTC Guide,[29] when the purchaser is told that an article is *free* to the purchaser if another article is purchased, the word *free* must indicate that the purchaser is paying nothing for the one article and that the purchaser is paying nothing more than the regular price for the other. Thus, if the purchaser sees or hears "buy one, get one free," or "50 per cent off with purchase of two," then the purchaser has a right to expect that there are no price-strings attached, that is, that the merchant will not recover in whole or in part the cost of the so-called *free* product or service by marking up the price of the other article or articles, by substituting inferior merchandise, or by any other means.[30]

The FTC also requires disclosure of any terms or conditions of *free offer.*[31] The supplier who promotes a *free offer,* and who knows or should know that the reseller does not pass on such an offer to the buyer or uses it as a deception,

---

28 437 F2d at 710.
29 16 CFR pt 251.
30 16 CFR §251.1(b).
31 16 CFR §251.2(c).

must take appropriate steps to end the reseller's deception, including the withdrawal of the *free offer*.[32]

A supplier, in advertising a *free promotion*, should clearly state the areas in which the offer is not available, if the advertising is likely to be seen in such areas. The supplier should also state clearly the extent to which the offer is available through participating retailers by using terms such as *some, all, a majority,* or *a few*.[33]

To make the *free offer* meaningful, the FTC rule limits the number of *free promotions*. A single product cannot be advertised *free* in a trade area for more than 6 months within a 12 month period. There should be a minimum of 30 days between two *free offers*. There should be no more than three *free offers* in the same trade area within a 12 month period. Additionally, within the same period, the volume of the *free offer* sale should not exceed 50 per cent of the total volume of the sales of the same product in the area.[34] Finally, offers of *free* goods or services which may be deceptive under the above criteria may not be corrected by use of words such as *gift, bonus, given without charge,* or the like.[35]

§2.09 —Remedies for Unfair and Deceptive Practices under Federal Law

Public Action

The Federal Trade Commission has the authority to issue a cease-and-desist order when it discovers an ongoing unfair or deceptive act or practice in commerce.[36] The recipient of the order may then appear before the Commission to show cause why such an order should not be issued. If the Commission is not satisfied after the hearing, it will let the order stand. The person complained of may then obtain review in a United States Court of Appeals.[37] If such review is not sought within the time allowed for filing a petition for review, or upon the denial of a petition for certiorari, or if the order of the Commission has been affirmed, or petition for review dismissed by the Court of Appeals, the cease-and-desist order becomes final.[38] The order also becomes final after 30 days from the date of issuance of the mandate of the Supreme Court affirming the Commission's order or dismissing the petition for review.[39] Any violation of the cease-and-desist order after this time subjects

---

[32] 16 CFR §251.1(d).

[33] 16 CFR §251.1(e).

[34] 16 CFR §251.1(h).

[35] 16 CFR §251.1(i).

[36] 15 USC §45(a)(6), (b).

[37] 15 USC §45(b).

[38] 15 USC §45(g)(1)-(3).

[39] 15 USC §45(g)(4).

the offender to the possibility of a civil penalty, originally up to $5,000 for each violation.[40]

Consumer groups have criticized the FTC's enforcement procedure as too weak, and recommend that more power be given to the FTC. The FTC Act was therefore amended to give the Commission more power, in a bill tagged onto the Trans-Alaska Oil Pipeline Act in 1973.[41] The amendments increased the enforcement and investigative capabilities of the Commission. Section 408 of the Oil Pipeline Act allows the FTC to:

> 1. Seek injunctive relief in federal court if it reasonably believes that a law within its enforcement jurisdiction has been violated
> 2. Represent itself in federal court by its own attorneys if after 10 days notice the Justice Department does not take the court action the Commission desires
> 3. Increase the maximum civil penalty for violation of the cease-and-desist orders from $5,000 to $10,000

The power to issue injunctions is perhaps the most important new attribute to the FTC's power. The injunctive authority will render the cease-and-desist order effective pending the final decision, so that the Commission need not wait until the Court of Appeals decides the case in order to enforce its order—a much more efficient and effective remedy. Unfortunately for this improvement, the FTC's new authority was embedded in a highly controversial piece of energy legislation that became the subject of a procedural quagmire.[42] Consequently, the source of the FTC's strongest enforcement and investigative powers is the Magnuson-Moss/FTC Improvements Act.[43] Title II of that Act expands the jurisdictional reach of the Commission to matters affecting commerce, which increases considerably the Commission's authority. Today, under the Act, the Commission may bring actions for civil penalties in federal courts for the violation of regulations or orders that the Commission has issued with respect to unfair or deceptive acts or practices, without first resorting to a cease-and-desist order and proceeding. The Commission may also bring civil actions in federal or state court to obtain redress on behalf of consumers, or any other persons, who have been injured by unfair or deceptive acts or practices or violations of FTC cease-and-desist orders.[44]

In addition to this enforcement mechanism, which the FTC may use against any party that violates its cease-and-desist order directly, the FTC has additional clout applicable to third parties. Since 1975, the FTC Act permits the FTC to use the cease-and-desist order not only against one person, as the

---

[40] 15 USC §45(1).

[41] Pub L No 93-153, 87 Stat 576 (amending 15 USC §45).

[42] *See* E. Kintner & C. Smith, *The Emergence of the FTC as a Formidable Consumer Protection Agency*, 26 Mercer L Rev 651, 665-70 (1975).

[43] Pub L No 93-637, 88 Stat 2183-2202 (1975); *see* **§2.29.**

[44] 15 USC §45(m)(1)(A).

basis of the usual proceeding, but also against other comparable industries, which are aware of the cease-and-desist order. Thus, any comparable industry that has actual knowledge of the cease-and-desist order, or has knowledge fairly implied from the facts and circumstances, and engages in the act or practice proscribed, is subject to the same civil penalty as the original violator.[45] The FTC makes a practice of sending copies of its cease-and-desist orders to other persons in the industry, in order to put them on notice, and extend, in effect, the application and scope of the order.

Private Action

Consumers injured by deceptive acts or practices have no private cause of action under §5 of the FTC Act. In the leading case of *Holloway v Bristol-Myers Corp,*[46] the United States Court of Appeals for the District of Columbia Circuit one again expressed the federal court's reluctance to grant a private action under §5. In *Holloway,* the plaintiffs claimed to represent the interests of the consumers at large and brought a class action suit against Bristol-Myers Corporation, the manufacturer of Excedrin, a popular nonprescription analgesic compound. The plaintiffs alleged that Bristol-Myers' advertisement that Excedrin was a more effective pain reliever than common aspirin was false, deceptive, and materially misleading, inducing the public at large to purchase Excedrin in preference to other equally effective and less expensive products. The court dealt with the issue of whether consumers and members of the public at large may bring a private action to enforce §5 of the Federal Trade Commission Act. The court, based on a reading of the Act and its legislative history, construed the Act not to confer upon private individuals, either consumers or business competitors, a right of action under the Act.

Congress also seems reluctant to go any further. Attempts to amend the act to encompass a private right of action have failed to win congressional approval. Therefore, any hope that consumers may have of enforcing §5 prohibitions could only be found in state unfair and deceptive acts and practices (UDAP) statutes. The FTC itself encourages such statutes as a means of giving more teeth to its own proscriptions. FTC jurisprudence can be and has been used to support private cause of action under state UDAP statutes.[47]

§2.10   State Unfair and Deceptive Acts or Practices Statutes (UDAP)

Between the mid 1960s and 70s there was an explosion of state statutes that aimed at protecting consumers against abusive commercial practices. Alabama was the last holdout, but finally followed suit, so that by 1981, all the states and the District of Columbia had such consumer protection statutes.

---

[45] 15 USC §45(1)(B)

[46] 485 F2d 986 (DC Cir 1973).

[47] *See* Leaffer & Lipson, *Consumer Actions Against Unfair and Deceptive Acts or Practices: The Private Uses of FTC Jurisprudence,* 48 Geo Wash L Rev 521 (1980).

State UDAP statutes usually adopt one of the several models. The first is the Uniform Trade Practice and Consumer Protection Law, a model statute drafted by the Committee on Suggested State Legislation of the Council of State Governments in collaboration with the Federal Trade Commission. This model legislation offered three alternatives. Alternative 1 is patterned exactly after §5 of the FTC Act prohibiting both unfair methods of competition and unfair or deceptive acts or practices. Fourteen states have adopted this alternative.[48] Alternative 2, which prohibits only false, misleading, or deceptive practices, is enacted in Kentucky and Texas. These states, however, have subsequently amended the original versions substantially.[49] Alternative 3 enumerates a specific number of prohibited practices, but includes "any other practice that is unfair or deceptive." Nine states have enacted this alternative with various modifications.[50] A few states, such as California and Wisconsin,[51] adopted the FTC Act directly, without going through the model state statute.

A second model is the Uniform Consumer Sales Practices Act developed by the National Conference of Commissioners on Uniform State Laws and the American Bar Association.[52] The statute applies only to *consumer transactions* and prohibits deceptive acts or practices. Practices deemed unconscionable, are also prohibited. Ohio, Utah, and Kansas are the three states that have enacted this model legislation. Ohio later amended its original version to proscribe *unfair* practices also.[53]

The Uniform Deceptive Trade Practices Act developed by the National Conference on Uniform State Laws is a third model. The Act was written with

---

[48] Conn Gen Stat §42-110 (1983); Fla Stat Ann §501.201 (West 1979 & Supp 1983); Haw Rev Stat §480 (1976 & Supp 1982); Ill Rev Stat ch 121 1/2, para 261 (Supp 1983-1984) (Consumer Fraud and Deceptive Business Practices Act §1); La Rev Stat Ann §51:1401 (West Supp 1984); Me Rev Stat Ann tit 5, §206 (1979 & Supp 1983-1984); Mass Gen Laws Ann ch 93A (West 1975 & Supp 1984); Mont Code Ann §30-14-101 (1987); Neb Rev Stat §59-1601 (1978 & Supp 1983); NC Gen Stat §75-1 (1981 & Supp 1983); SC Code Ann §66-71 (Law Co-op 1976 & Supp 1983); Vt Stat Ann tit 9, §2451A (1970 & Supp 1983); Wash Rev Code Ann §19.86 (1978 & Supp 1983-1984); W Va Code §46A-6-101 (1980 & Supp 1983).

[49] Ky Rev Stat Ann §367.110 (Baldwin Supp 1982); Tex Bus & Com Code Ann tit 2, §17.41 (Vernon 1968 & Supp 1984).

[50] Alaska Stat §45.50f 471 (1983); Ga Code Ann §106-1201 (Harrison 1968 & Supp 1982-1983); Idaho Code §48-601 (1977); Md Com Law Code Ann §13-101 (1983); Miss Code Ann §75-24-1 (Supp 1983); NH Rev Stat Ann §358A (Supp 1981 & Supp 1983); Pa Stat Ann tit 73, §201-1 (Purdon 1971 & Supp 1983-1984); RI Gen Laws §6-13.1 (1969 & Supp 1983); Tenn Code Ann §47-18-101 (1979 & Supp 1983).

[51] Cal Civ Code §1770 (West 1973 & Supp 1984); Cal Bus & Prof Code §17200 (West 1987); Wis Stat §100.20 (West 1973 & Supp 1983-1984).

[52] 7A ULA 231 (1978).

[53] Ohio Rev Code Ann §1345.01 (Baldwin 1984); Utah Code Ann §13-11-1 (Supp 1983). In addition, Kan Stat Ann §50-624 (1983).

a view to prohibiting unfair methods of competition, but forms the basis of UDAP statutes in some 12 states.[54]

Other models are consumer fraud acts, which prohibit "deception, fraud, false pretense, false promise, misrepresentation or knowing concealment, suppression, or omission of any material fact with intent that others rely." Seven states have followed these models.[55] A number of states did not adopt any particular model but borrowed features from various sources and added their own.[56]

Given this diversity of sources, and the variations enacted, UDAP laws naturally vary considerably from state to state. When examining such a statute, attention should be focused on the scope of transactions which the Act covers, the scope of the practices proscribed, and the persons who are subject to the statute.

§2.11 —Transactions Covered by UDAP Statutes

Most UDAP statutes apply to the sale of land as well as to the sale of goods or services. A number of transactions, although they are transactions involving consumers, are excluded from the scope of UDAP statutes. Generally, the exempted transactions are those involving credit, realty, leases, insurance, and utilities. These are covered by other special statutes or laws specifically designed for them. However, a court may interpret exempted transactions very restrictively, such that a given transaction seemingly excluded may come under the scope of the UDAP statute.

For example, a Vermont court ruled in *Lavinia v Howard Bank*[57] that a bank loan is a service because "anyone supplying money, a need, could be one who serves." A Kansas court found that home mortgages and other forms of credit are also goods or services in *State v Brotherhood Bank & Trust*.[58] Also, the Texas Supreme Court has ruled that an extension of credit in conjunction with a retail sale is covered by the UDAP statute because it is a transaction involving the

---

[54] Colo Rev Stat §6-1-101 (1973 & Supp 1983); Del Code Ann tit 6, §2531 (1974 & Supp 1982); Ga Code Ann §106-701 (Harrison 1968 & Supp 1982-1983); Haw Rev Stat §481A (1976 & Supp 1982); Ill Rev Stat ch 121 1/2, para 311 (Supp 1983-1984); Me Rev Stat Ann tit 10, §1211 (1980 & Supp 1983-1984); Neb Rev Stat §87-301 (1981 & Supp 1982); NM Stat Ann §57-12-1 (1978 & Supp 1983); Nev Rev Stat §598.360 (1983); Ohio Rev Code Ann §4165 (Baldwin 1984); Okla Stat Ann tit 78, §51 (West 1976 & Supp 1983-1984); Or Rev Stat §646.605 (1983).

[55] Ariz Rev Stat Ann §44-1521 (1967 & Supp 1983-1984); Ark Stat Ann §70.901 (1979 & Supp 1983); Del Code Ann tit 6, §2511 (1974 & Supp 1982); Iowa Code §714.16 (West 1979 & Supp 1983-1984); Mo Rev Stat §407.010 (1979 & Supp 1984); NJ Stat Ann §555.8 (West 1964 & Supp 1983-1984); ND Cent Code §51-15 (1974).

[56] DC Code Encycl ch 28 app 11 §1 (West 19__); Ind Code Ann §24-5-0.5 (Burns 1982 & Supp); Mich Comp Laws §445.901 (Supp 1983-1984); NY Gen Bus Law §349 (Consol Supp 1987); SD Codified Laws Ann §37-24 (1977 & Supp 1983); Va Code Ann §59.1-196 (1982 & Supp 1983); Wyo Stat §40-12-101 (1977 & Supp 1983).

[57] No C400-75 Cn C, Clearinghouse No 26,015 (Vt Super Ct Jan 9, 1976).

[58] 8 Kan App 2d 57, 649 P2d 419 (1982).

purchase of goods, even though the lender is not the seller.[59] Thus, in spite of the language of the statutes, a look at the court decisions may reveal a quite liberal interpretation of what transactions are covered under the relevant UDAP.[60]

§2.12   —Scope of the Practices Proscribed

A number of UDAP statutes enumerate specific prohibited practices. Generally, among states that adopt this approach, the "laundry list" is fairly similar. A typical example is the California statute which includes on its list a number of specific practices such as the misrepresenting of the source of the goods, the disparaging of goods of another, bait-and-switch advertising, and unconscionable practices.[61]

Some other UDAP statutes provide a list of specific proscribed practices, but round off the list with a general provision prohibiting "any other unconscionable, false, misleading or deceptive act or practice in the conduct of trade or commerce."[62]

§2.13   —Persons Subject to the UDAP Statutes

UDAP statutes generally apply to sellers, but certain sellers are exempted from the scope of the Act. Usually exempt from their coverage are insurance companies, nonmerchants, wholesalers, printers, and members of the media.

Regarding protected consumers, usually only the consumer who actually contracts with the seller may have a right of action. States vary on the question of whether third-party beneficiaries may sue under the UDAP statutes. They may or may not have rights to bring a UDAP action. In *First National Bank v Hackworth*[63] the Texas Court of Appeals dismissed a UDAP claim because the consumer had died, reasoning that treble damages claims, being punitive, were personal and did not survive the consumer. The consumer's estate did not have a cause of action because it was not a consumer.

§2.14   —Remedies under the UDAP Statutes

State UDAP statutes provide consumers with an array of remedies. Some are specific to UDAP statutes per se; others derive from actions already recognized

---

[59] Knight v International Harvester Credit Corp, 627 SW2d 382 (Tex 1982).

[60] J. Sheldon, Unfair and Deceptive Acts and Practices §2.2 (1986 Supp); The Consumer Credit and Sales Legal Practices Series, National Consumer Law Center.

[61] Cal Civ Code §1770 (West 1985).

[62] Ala Code §8-19-5 (1981).

[63] 673 SW2d 218 (Tex Ct App 1984).

under other state law. Combining these two sources, consumer remedies include recovery for:

1. Actual damages, in the form of loss-of-bargain damages—Under the common-law calculation, this represents the difference between what consumers thought they were getting and what they actually got. Some courts go so far as to allow restitution, although the statutes themselves may limit recovery to actual damages. The consumer may also recover damages which would be considered foreseeable consequences of the deception. These may be labeled either incidental or consequential damages

2. *Statutory damages*—Some UDAP statutes allow recovery of minimum/maximum statutory damages even though no actual damage was proven. For example, the Kansas UDAP statute provides for a minimum of $2,000 for a violation.[64] In *Watkins v Roach Cadillac Inc*,[65] the court awarded $2,000 statutory damages while actual damage was only $200

3. Multiple Damages and Punitive Damages Usually treble damages will be allowed only where the conduct involved is willful. However, in some states, treble damages may be awarded absent bad faith or other willful conduct. One Texas court, for example, without inquiring into willfulness or bad faith, has said treble damages are mandatory once a UDAP violation is proven.[66] Generally, where the state's law allows punitive damages for common law fraud, the courts will also allow punitive damages for violations of the UDAP statute. For example, in *Brown v Lyons*,[67] the court awarded punitive damages for an "unconscionable act and practice" under the Ohio Consumer Sales Practice Act,[68] although the Ohio UDAP already provides for recovery of "three times the amount of actual damages"[69]

4. Injunctive Relief—An overwhelming number of UDAP statutes allow a person likely to be damaged by a deceptive practice to seek injunctive relief. The persons who may seek an injunction may include consumers as well as others, such as the attorney general. When the UDAP statute itself does not create a remedy of private injunctive relief, a court may grant an injunction at its discretion

---

[64] Kan Stat Ann §50-623 (1983).

[65] 7 Kan App 2d 8, 637 P2d 458 (1981).

[66] Woods v Littleton, 554 SW2d 662 (Tex 1977). In Pennington v Singleton, 606 SW2d 682 (Tex 1980) the Texas Supreme Court reversed a lower court's interpretation requiring intent as a precondition for multiple damages.

[67] 43 Ohio Misc 14, 332 NE2d 380 (1974).

[68] Ohio Rev Code §1345.03A (Baldwin 1984).

[69] Ohio Rev Code §1345.01 (Baldwin 1984).

§2.15 —Class Action under the UDAP Statutes

One type of UDAP statute contains provisions specifically providing for class actions. These provisions either supersede or supplement more general class actions allowed under state law.

A second type of UDAP statute contains specific prohibitions against class actions, foreclosing this consumer option altogether.

A third type of statute is silent on class action, so one may resort to the state requirements for class action suits in general. Since UDAP statutes change the common law of misrepresentation, fraud, and deceit, class actions under UDAP statutes are more likely to succeed than suits under traditional law. Under the UDAP statutes, the many subjective elements of proof which the common law requires need not be shown. All that the plaintiffs need to establish is that there is a pattern of conduct on the part of the seller that has a tendency to deceive.

§2.16 —Attorneys' Fees

All UDAP statutes award attorneys' fees to successful consumer litigants, but the court, not the statute, determines when such fees are to be awarded. Many courts grant attorneys' fees only when there is evidence that the consumer is injured by the UDAP violation. Some courts, on the other hand, grant attorneys' fees even when there are no actual damages. For example, in Massachusetts, attorneys' fees were awarded simply on a showing that an unfair act or practice had been committed.[70] The court, granting attorneys' fees in *Trempe v Aetna Casualty & Surety Co*, explained that "there is a benefit to the public where deception in the marketplace is brought to light (and thereby corrected) by an individual who has been deceived even though his actual damages were not proved."[71] Attorneys' fees for appellate proceedings may also be awarded.[72]

Some courts even award attorneys' fees where the seller's counterclaim exceeds or offsets the amount of the consumer's recovery. In a Texas case, *Building Concepts, Inc v Duncan*,[73] the plaintiff sued Building Concepts seeking damages under the Texas Deceptive Trade Practices Act. Building Concepts, Inc. counterclaimed for recovery in *quantum meruit* under the contract for construction of the plaintiffs' home. Building Contracts argued that attorneys' fees should not be awarded the plaintiffs because, since the defendant's counterclaim exceeded the plaintiffs' recovery, there was no net recovery and, therefore, no judgment for actual damages in the plaintiffs' favor.

The court held that a consumer is not required to obtain a net judgment for

---

[70] *See* Shapiro v Public Serv Mut Ins Co, 19 Mass App Ct 648, 657-58, 477 NE2d 146 (1984).

[71] Trempe v Aetna Casualty & Sur Co, 20 Mass App 448, 480 NE2d 670, 676 (1985).

[72] *See* Patsy v Liberty Mobile Home Sales, Inc, 394 Mass 270, 475 NE2d 392 (1985).

[73] 667 SW2d 897 (Tex Ct App 1984).

actual damages or for some other form of relief in order to obtain attorneys' fees and court costs, so long as the consumer prevails on the original claim for damages. The court stated:

> We do not believe the legislature intended to discourage a consumer from filing suit under the Act, and obtaining damages, only to be denied attorney's fees because the sum awarded on the claim . . . has been offset by the other party's counterclaim . . . [I]n order to give real meaning to the Act and to penalize for deceptive trade practices, the consumer must have uninhibited access to the courts.[74]

In this case, the plaintiffs also had to pay Building Concept's attorneys' fees because Texas law provided for attorneys' fees for any prevailing party, and Building Concepts prevailed in its counterclaim. Where a statute specifically grants attorneys' fees only to consumers, it has been held that a court could not interpret the statute so as to grant attorneys fees to the seller.[75]

§2.17 Door-to-Door Sales

Given the presumption among Americans that one's home is one's castle, it is not surprising that many view the high-pressure sales tactics often applied by door-to-door salespeople against unwary consumers as amounting to an invasion of privacy. This door-to-door sales practice presents many dangers to the consumer. Once the salesperson has the foot in the door, it is hard to get rid of the unwanted person.

The very fact that the sales technique is door-to-door presents hazards, almost regardless of the skill of the seller. After all, in a department store, one can browse more or less at will, and walk away when things do not look favorable for a good buy. But in one's home, there is no walking away once the salesperson is inside. Furthermore, while a store permits "shopping around," a one-to-one confrontation with a salesperson in the house presents no such immediate alternative.

Additionally, in a store, contact with a salesperson creates some degree of accountability. The customer with a problem can always go back to the same salesperson or complain to the management. A door-to-door salesperson, on the other hand, is more or less anonymous. Where can a customer go to complain or demand a refund? And while one might express one's dissatisfaction by ceasing to do business at a certain store, door-to-door salespeople are not subject to these coercions. Thus, they have less reason to be honest, both before and after a transaction.

It may be of some further interest here to point out just who is likely to be

---

[74] *Id* 903.

[75] Sato v Century 21 Ocean Shores Real Estate, 101 Wash 2d 599, 681 P2d 242 (1984). A good treatment of the attorneys' fees issue in consumer action is in J. Shelton, Unfair and Deceptive Acts and Practices §8.6 at 183.91 (1986 Supp).

home when a door-to-door salesperson arrives—certainly not the business person in the family. Instead, those consumers who will be home are the elderly, the handicapped, or often others least equipped to deal effectively with someone using the door-to-door sales technique. The consumer is thus often at an even greater disadvantage.

§2.18 —The FTC Rule on Door-to-Door Sales

The FTC adopted in 1974 a trade regulation rule entitled *Cooling-Off Period for Door-to-Door Sales*.[76] The FTC defines a door-to-door sale as:

A sale, lease, or rental of consumer goods or services with a purchase price of $25 or more, whether under single or multiple contracts in which the seller or his representative personally solicits the sale, including those in response to or following an invitation by the buyer, and the buyer's agreement or offer to purchase is made at a place other than the place of business of the seller.[77]

The FTC Rule requires the door-to-door seller to follow the following procedures:

1. The seller must furnish the buyer a notice, at least in 10-point bold type, which must state substantially:
"You the buyer may cancel this transaction at any time prior to midnight of the third business day after the date of this transaction. See the attached Notice of Cancellation form for an explanation of this right."
The notice must be in the same language as that principally used in the oral sales presentation. It must appear on the document in immediate proximity to the place reserved on the contract for the signature of the buyer. If no contract is used, then the notice must be on the front page of the receipt[78]
2. At the time the buyer signs the door-to-door sales contract or otherwise agrees to buy goods or services from the seller, the seller must furnish a *Notice of Cancellation* which must be attached to the contract or receipt, and, must be easily detachable, and written in the same language as that used in the contract.[79] The FTC provides this model form:

NOTICE OF CANCELLATION
[ENTER DATE OF TRANSACTION]
(Date)
YOU MAY CANCEL THIS TRANSACTION, WITHOUT ANY PEN-

---

[76] 16 CFR pt 429.
[77] 16 CFR §429.1, Note 1(a).
[78] 16 CFR §429.1(a).
[79] 16 CFR §429.1(b).

ALTY OR OBLIGATION, WITHIN THREE BUSINESS DAYS FROM THE ABOVE DATE. IF YOU CANCEL, ANY PROPERTY TRADED IN, ANY PAYMENTS MADE BY YOU UNDER THE CONTRACT OR SALE, AND ANY NEGOTIABLE INSTRUMENT EXECUTED BY YOU WILL BE RETURNED WITHIN 10 BUSINESS DAYS FOLLOWING RECEIPT BY THE SELLER OF YOUR CANCELLATION NOTICE, AND ANY SECURITY INTEREST ARISING OUT OF THE TRANSACTION WILL BE CANCELED.

IF YOU CANCEL, YOU MUST MAKE AVAILABLE TO THE SELLER AT YOUR RESIDENCE IN SUBSTANTIALLY AS GOOD CONDITION AS WHEN RECEIVED, ANY GOODS DELIVERED TO YOU UNDER THIS CONTRACT OR SALE: OR YOU MAY IF YOU WISH, COMPLY WITH THE INSTRUCTIONS OF THE SELLER REGARDING THE RETURN SHIPMENT OF THE GOODS AT THE SELLER'S EXPENSE AND RISK.

IF YOU DO MAKE THE GOODS AVAILABLE TO THE SELLER AND THE SELLER DOES NOT PICK THEM UP WITHIN 20 DAYS OF THE DATE OF YOUR NOTICE OF CANCELLATION, YOU MAY RETAIN OR DISPOSE OF THE GOODS WITHOUT ANY FURTHER OBLIGATION. IF YOU FAIL TO MAKE THE GOODS AVAILABLE TO THE SELLER, OR IF YOU AGREE TO RETURN THE GOODS TO THE SELLER AND FAIL TO DO SO, THEN YOU REMAIN LIABLE FOR PERFORMANCE OF ALL OBLIGATIONS UNDER THE CONTRACT.

TO CANCEL THIS TRANSACTION, MAIL OR DELIVER A SIGNED AND DATED COPY OF THIS CANCELLATION NOTICE OR ANY OTHER WRITTEN NOTICE, OR SEND A TELEGRAM, TO [Name of seller], AT [address of seller's place of business] NOT LATER THAN MIDNIGHT OF _____ (date).

I HEREBY CANCEL THIS TRANSACTION.

(Date) _____

_____
(Buyer's signature)

3. The seller is further required to complete the *Notice of Cancellation* by entering the seller's name, address, and the date by which the buyer may give notice of cancellation. This date may not be earlier than the third business day following the date of the transaction.[80]

4. It constitutes an unfair and deceptive act or practice for the seller to fail to inform the buyer orally at the time the buyer purchases the goods of the buyer's right to cancel.[81] The seller may not misrepresent in any

---

[80] 16 CFR §429.1(c).
[81] 16 CFR §429(e).

way the buyer's rights to cancel[82]

Further, the rule requires that upon notice of cancellation, the seller must within 10 business days refund all payment made, *or* return any goods or property traded in, in the same condition as when received, *or* cancel or return any payment instrument furnished by the buyer (such as check, promissory note, etc.).[83] The FTC Rule prohibits the seller from negotiating a transfer or assigning the claim against the buyer to a third party prior to midnight of the fifth business day from the purchase date.[84] The seller must in addition advise the buyer as to what the seller wants to do with the goods in the buyer's possession, such as repossess them or abandon them.[85] The FTC's door-to-door sales rule does not apply in the following situations:

1. Where the seller conducts the transaction entirely by mail or telephone, without contacting the consumer directly[86]
2. Where the transaction involves the sale or rental of real property[87]
3. Where the transaction is a sale of insurance, securities, or commodities by a broker or dealer registered with the Securities and Exchange Commission[88]
4. Where the buyer has initiated the contract and the goods or services are needed for an immediate personal emergency of the buyer. However, the seller is exempted from the rule only if the buyer, in writing, expressly waived the buyer's right to cancel the sale within three business days[89]

§2.19 —State Laws on Door-to-Door Sales

States also passed laws to deal with door-to-door sales tactics under a variety of headings, from *Home Solicitation Sales* to *Unfair and Deceptive Trade Practices* to *Retail and Installment Sales*.[90] Every state except New Mexico requires a three-day cooling-off period similar to the FTC Rule. In all states, the cooling-off period does not begin until the seller has provided formal notice to the consumer that the consumer has the right to cancel within 72 hours or a longer period according to the statute. The statutes each provide the formal notice requirements and other information similar to those required by the FTC Rule.

Like the FTC Rule, most statutes also provide for an "emergency situation."

---

[82] 16 CFR §429(f).

[83] 16 CFR §429(g).

[84] 16 CFR §429(h).

[85] 16 CFR §429(i).

[86] 16 CFR §429.1 Note 1 (a)(4).

[87] 16 CFR §429.1 Note 1 (a)(6).

[88] *Id.*

[89] 16 CFR §429.1, Note 1(a)(3).

[90] A number of these are collected in the Consumer Credit Guide (CCH) at §525.

Under this exception, the consumer has no right to cancel, i.e., there is no cooling-off period, if

    1. The consumer requests the salesperson to provide goods and services at once without delay, and

    2. The seller complies with the request in good faith before the consumer gives notice of cancellation, and

    3. The goods cannot be returned to the seller in substantially the same condition as when they were delivered to the consumer.

§2.20 —Interplay of State Law and the FTC Rule

In adopting its Rule, the FTC was aware of the existence of state statutes treating exactly the same problem, and did not intend to preempt state law entirely. The federal Rule, therefore, only preempts state laws to the extent that they are inconsistent with the provisions of the Rule. Examples of inconsistency in a state statute would be denying the buyer a right substantially the same or greater than the right provided under the Rule to cancel a door-to-door sale, imposing any fee or penalty for cancellation, or not providing for notice to the buyer of the buyer's right to cancel in a manner or form substantially the same as that which the Rule provides.[91]

In an advisory opinion, the FTC has specifically stated that the cooling-off notice provided for in the Uniform Consumer Credit Code (U3C) is inconsistent with the FTC Rule because the U3C notice implies that the buyer must give a specific reason for cancelling the transaction.[92] Another important advisory opinion by the FTC suggested how to handle possible state-federal inconsistencies. The FTC stated that it has no objection to the seller's inclusion of the notice as required by state law *and* the notice required by the FTC Rule on the sale contracts "as long as any language in the state or municipal notice directly inconsistent with the Rule is stricken."[93] Thus, language in a state notice which allows the seller to keep all or part of the cash down payment in case of cancellation is clearly inconsistent with the FTC Rule and must be stricken. Moreover, since the buyer's right to cancel transactions covered by the Rule is not limited to agreements solicited at or near the buyer's residence, and does not require the buyer to furnish any reason for cancellation, and may be exercised by mail or delivery of any written notice or telegram, any language to the contrary in a state notice is similarly directly inconsistent with the Rule.[94]

---

[91] 16 CFR §429, Note 2.

[92] FTC Advisory Op, 87 FTC 1444 (May 20, 1976).

[93] Consumer Credit Guide (CCH) §98583 (July 1, 1975).

[94] *Id.*

§2.21   Referral Sales

A referral sale is one in which the buyer agrees to purchase goods and services, usually at an inflated price, and the seller offers the buyer a commission or discount for each customer whom the buyer refers to the seller. The tactic in essence is the seller's bid to make an inflated price attractive to the buyer by making savings or discounts contingent on future referrals. The abuses of this tactic are such that in many states a referral sales plan is a violation per se of the UDAP statute, no matter how reasonable the seller's representations are. Some states by separate legislation prohibit referral sales altogether. Even if a state does not prohibit referral sales per se, the practice may still be deemed deceptive if the seller's claims are exaggerated or unsubstantiated. For example, the Uniform Consumer Credit Code[95] prohibits the use of referral sales in which the rebate is conditional upon "the occurrence of an event after the time the consumer agrees to buy or lease." Thus, a referral system aimed at inducing the consumer to furnish names of prospective buyers is not prohibited. However, if the consumer is required to furnish names of people who will actually become buyers, the practice is prohibited. Under the U3C, if a seller or lessor violates the Code provisions prohibiting referral sales, the consumer can keep the goods sold without paying for them.[96]

Referral sales are deceptive for several reasons: the prices are generally inflated as stated above; the seller's promises of discount or commission are often oral, and the parol evidence rule precludes the buyer from proving they were made; and the seller's promises, if in writing, are made in a contract separate from the contract of sale. The consumer may be prevented from invoking the referral contract as a defense against a claim pertaining to the sale contract made by the seller, or, more often, by the seller's assignee. In other words, the buyer is still obligated to make good the buyer's promise to pay regardless of the seller's conduct with respect to the referral sale. In *Sherwood & Roberts - Yakima, Inc v Leach*,[97] the court interpreted lottery laws to prohibit referral sales practices, and subjected the seller to criminal penalties and permanent injunctions applicable to prohibited lotteries.

§2.22   Lemon Laws

Given the importance of the automobile in the lives of the American consumer, the existence of "lemon laws," which apply only to purchases of automobiles, is not surprising. Inadequacies of federal and state warranty law when applied to automobile purchases, as well as limitations in remedy under

---

[95] U3C §2.411 (1968); U3C §3.309 (1974).

[96] *Id.*

[97] 67 Wash 2d 630, 409 P2d 160 (1965); *contra* Braddock v Fam Fin Corp, 95 Idaho 256, 506 P2d 824 (1973) (referral sales are not lotteries because not based on chance).

the Uniform Commercial Code,[98] have caused consumers and legislatures to provide specific protection for auto purchasers under a variety of state laws.[99]

The first state lemon laws were passed in Connecticut[100] and California[101] in 1982. In the two years following, more than 30 states also adopted lemon laws, and the movement continues. While there are variations among the lemon laws of the several states, their common feature is to replace individual contracts between the consumer and the merchant with an *objective contract.* In effect, the results of a bargain between industrial representatives and consumer groups have been enacted into law. The lemon laws provide guidelines, more specific than existing law, for determining the conditions requisite to revocation of the contract, the conditions for fixing liability, and proper informal settlement procedures. Variations among state lemon laws pertain to the following:

1. Whether the consumer must provide a manufacturer with *written* notice of the defect
2. Whether the statute applies to defects affecting safety of the vehicle, as opposed to value or use
3. Whether agreements to waive or modify rights under lemon laws are enforceable
4. Applicability of statues of limitations
5. Applicability of state laws in a multistate purchase
6. Who chooses between refund or replacement—the manufacturer or the consumer[102]

In spite of the variations among the states' lemon laws, an examination of the first enacted lemon law from Connecticut yields an idea of the type of protection they afford the consumer generally.[103]

The Connecticut statute applies to:

1. The consumer, defined as a purchaser other than for purposes of resale
2. Any transferee who receives the motor vehicle during the duration of an express warranty
3. Any other person entitled by the terms of the warranty to enforce the obligations of the warranty.

The statute is further limited in its coverage to passenger cars or *passenger*

---

[98] The most potent remedy under the federal Magnuson-Moss Warranty Act is refund or replacement but only where the seller offers a written "full warranty." Most cars, however, are sold under "limited warranty." For remedies under the UCC, see **§2.32.**

[99] *See* Coffinberger & Samuels, *Legislative Responses to the Plight of New Car Purchasers,* 18 UCC LJ 168 (1985).

[100] 1982 Conn Pub Acts 82-287 (amended 1984 Conn Pub Acts 84-338).

[101] Cal Civ Code §1793.2 (West Supp 1983).

[102] Coffinberger & Samuels, *supra* 20 note 99, at 177.

[103] Conn Gen Stat Ann §42-179 (West 1960).

and commercial motor vehicles.[104] If a new[105] motor vehicle does not conform to all applicable express warranties, and the consumer reports the nonconformity to the manufacturer, its agent, or its authorized dealer during the term of such express warranty or during the period of one year following the date of original delivery of the motor vehicle to the consumer, whichever is the earlier date, the law requires the above-named persons to make the necessary repairs to conform the vehicle to such express warranty even after the expiration of the express warranty or the one-year period.[106] If, after a reasonable number of attempts at repair, the defect continues, then the manufacturer shall replace the motor vehicle with a new one, or shall refund the purchase price, less a reasonable allowance for the consumer's use of the vehicle. However, these duties on the part of the manufacturer will only arise if the defect or nonconformity substantially impairs the use and value of the motor vehicle.[107]

The statute defines the meaning of a reasonable number of attempts at repair as four or more made within the term of the express warranty or during the period of one year following the date of original delivery, whichever comes first, providing the defect persists, or, the vehicle is out of service by reason of repair for a period of 30 or more days total, during the period of express warranty or during the first year following delivery, whichever is the earlier date. However, refund or replacement may be obtained only if the consumer has first resorted to informal settlement procedures, if the manufacturer has established such a mechanism.[108]

Lemon laws generally do not affect existing remedies under state laws. Section 2-608 of the Uniform Commercial Code, giving the buyer the right to revoke acceptance for the manufacturer's or seller's failure to cure a warranty defect within a reasonable time, remains in effect. The lemon laws simply supplement existing law by providing more specific guidelines for the conditions of revocation and liability, and for informal settlement procedures. In fact, lemon laws have already come under attack for falling short of their original purpose of consumer protection.[109]

The nonuniformity of state lemon laws, their lack of teeth to protect the consumer, and the great number of consumer complaints sparked a proposal for federal legislation in 1983. The Automobile Consumer Protection Act of

---

[104] Conn Gen Stat Ann §42-179(a) (West 1960).

[105] New York is the first state to enact a lemon law for protection of purchasers of used cars. NY Gen Bus Law §198-b (McKinney 1968).

[106] Conn Gen Stat Ann §42-179(b) (West 1960).

[107] *Id.* The California statute requires only substantial impairment of use, value, *or* safety. About half of the existing lemon statutes adopt the Connecticut version. The other half adopt the California version. Cal Civ Code §1793.2(e)(4)(A) (West 1985). *See* Honigman, *The New "Lemon Laws": Expanding UCC Remedies,* 17 UCC LJ 116, 121 (1984).

[108] Conn Gen Stat Ann §42-179(d) (West 1960).

[109] *See* J. Vergeront, *Minnesota Developments, A Sour Note: A Look at the Minnesota Lemon Law,* 68 Minn L Rev 846 (1984). The author of the article states "[Lemon laws] are more of a placebo than an enhancement of existing remedies," *id* 880.

1983,[110] however, never left committee, and no hearings were held. The Act would have provided a standard statute of limitations period of four years from the original date of delivery, a coverage period of two years or 18,000 miles, whichever came first, an allowance for a court to award reasonable attorneys' fees to a prevailing plaintiff and an incorporation of many of the common features of the state lemon laws which had already begun to appear.[111]

§2.23 Warranty under the Uniform Commercial Code

With respect to the sale of goods, the Uniform Commercial Code (UCC) now embodies state laws on warranties with respect to the sale of goods. Article 2 of the Code on sale of goods has been enacted in every state except Louisiana. Thus, an understanding of the UCC's basic provisions on warranties could be a valuable tool in the hands of consumers' counsel to protect the consumer against the seller when the goods are defective or do not conform to the contract.[112]

There are two types of warranties under the Code: warranties of title and warranties of quality. The warranty of quality is subdivided into express and implied warranties. Implied warranties are further subdivided into the warranty of merchantability, which applies only to merchants, and the warranty of fitness for a particular purpose, which applies to all sellers of goods.

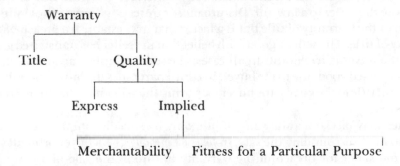

The UCC provisions on warranties are organized as follows:

1. Warranty of title: UCC §2-312
2. Express warranty: §2-313
3. Implied warranty of merchantability: §2-314
4. Implied warranty of fitness for a particular purpose: §2-315
5. Exclusion or modification of warranties: §2-316

---

[110] HR 3827, 98th Cong, 1st Sess (1983).

[111] Coffinberger & Samuels, *supra* note 99, at 173-75.

[112] *See* T. Le & E. Murphy, Sales and Credit Transactions Handbook ch 3 (Shepard's/McGraw-Hill 1985).

6. Cumulation and conflict of warranties: §2-317
7. Third-party beneficiaries and warranty: §2-318

Although the organization of the Code looks simple, the UCC law on warranties is very complex. The practitioner must wind his or her way through a maze of technicalities. Further, the lack of uniformity among the courts in the various jurisdictions in interpreting the Code provisions adds to the complexity of the law.

Technically, the UCC warranty provisions apply only to the sale of goods. Most courts, however, apply by analogy the Code provisions to transactions other than those for the sale of goods to include leases, bailments, and the furnishing of services. However, the analogy cannot go so far as to apply to a real estate transaction. In such cases, the common law on warranty would apply.

Furthermore, one should not lose sight of the fact that the Code provisions can be superseded or supplemented by other statues or federal law. Affording greater protection to the consumer in this area is the Magnuson-Moss Warranty Act.

§2.24   —Warranty of Title

Under §2-312 of the UCC, in any contract for sale made by a professional or amateur seller, the seller warrants that the buyer will receive a clean title that will not expose the buyer to a lawsuit. Disturbance of quiet possession is not by itself a breach of the warranty of title but is a factor that may establish a breach of the warranty of title. The seller's good faith belief that the seller has transferred good title to the buyer is irrelevant. In all cases, the seller simply warrants that the seller has passed good title to the buyer. If a third party sues the buyer, claiming a paramount title to the goods, the buyer may bring the seller into the suit to vouch for the sale.[113]

A seller may disclaim a warranty of title only by specific language or by the circumstances surrounding the sale. In *Jones v Linebaugh*,[114] a buyer brought suit against the seller for breach of the warranty of title in the sale of an antique automobile known as a Bugatti. When the buyer offered to buy the antique car, the seller informed him that he, the seller, did not have title to it, as the car was owned by someone else. The buyer requested, then, that the seller obtain title to the car in the seller's own name. The seller later told the buyer that pursuant to the buyer's request, the seller had set his attorneys to working out the details of obtaining title, and that they were then completing the task. The buyer then paid the purchase price and took possession of the car. Two years later, a third party, claiming paramount title to the automobile, sued the buyer. The buyer settled the claim and then sued his seller for breach of warranty of

---

[113] UCC §2-607(5).
[114] 34 Mich App 305, 191 NW2d 142 (1971).

title. In defense, the seller claimed that he had disclaimed any warranty of title, pointing out that the bill of sale stated:

> The seller sold and assigned to the buyer all of the seller's right, title, and interest to the chattel, and that to the best of his knowledge, there was no title in existence by way of legislation with the state of Michigan, or with any other state or any nation.

The court held that the language was not specific enough to disclaim the seller's warranty of title, and so the buyer succeeded in his claim for breach of warranty.

A strong dissenting opinion in the *Linebaugh* case argued that the court should have paid attention to the circumstances surrounding the sale. These, said the dissenting judge, indicated that the plaintiff not only had reason to know, but that he did know, that the defendant did not take title, and that the defendant was selling only such title as he got from the third party.

The dissenting judge may have had a good point. Under §2-312 of the Code, surrounding circumstances will create a disclaimer if they cause the buyer to believe that the seller does not claim title in himself, or that the seller purports to sell only such right or title as he or a third party may have. The majority might have relied uniquely on the language of the written disclaimer which, of course, was not specific enough to disclaim a warranty of title.

§2.25   —Express Warranties

Express warranties are one division of the warranties of quality, that is warranties which create standards binding upon sellers. Warranties of quality may be express if they are based upon the agreement between the parties, or implied if they arise by operation of law. It is important to remember that express warranties apply not just to merchants, but to all sellers. Thus, your neighbor's affirmation of fact as to the quality of goods at her garage sale may give rise to a breach of express warranty, if your reliance on that affirmation is deemed reasonable.

A seller can create an express warranty, without specifically stating that there is an intent to do so. Such a warranty can be created by an affirmation of a fact or promise, any description of the goods, or the use of any sample or model.[115] For any of the above to create an express warranty, however, it must be a part of the basis of the bargain between the buyer and seller.

Pre-Code law concerning the creation of express warranties was laid out in §12 of the Uniform Sales Act which provided: "Any affirmation of fact or any promise by the Seller relating to the goods is an express warranty if the natural tendency of such affirmation or promise is to induce the buyer to purchase the goods, and if the buyer purchases the goods relying thereon." The buyer's reliance therefore was required before an express warranty could exist. The

---

[115] UCC §2-313 and comment 6.

UCC in §2-313(1), however, does not mention reliance, but talks only about the basis of the bargain. A seller can create an express warranty without any specific intention to do so as long as the seller's affirmation of fact, description of goods, or use of samples or models results in the buyer entering into a contract.[116] The Code thus seems to adopt a purely objective standard. However, reliance still seems to play an important part in the law of express warranty, because Comment 3 to §2-313 states that "any fact which is to take [the seller's] affirmations, once made, out of the agreement [i.e the basis of the bargain] requires affirmative proof." In other words, if the seller denies that an express warranty was made, the seller must prove that the buyer did not rely on the seller's affirmation, description, sample, or model. Reliance thus enters through the back door.

The precise time when an express warranty is made is immaterial. The representation need not be made at the time the sale actually takes place in order to constitute an express warranty. An express warranty can arise from advertisements, catalogues, brochures, pamphlets, signs and the like.

Even postsale statements can qualify as express warranties. In such a case, the sole question is whether the description or affirmation would be regarded as the basis of the bargain. Thus, for example, if the buyer asks for and receives an additional assurance after the sale, the assurance becomes a warranty and is viewed as modification of the contract. Under §2-209 of the UCC, such a modification need not be supported by any new consideration. Thus, postsale oral statements can be an express warranty, as part of the basis of the bargain.[117]

An example of a postsale warranty is provided by the case of *Jones v Abriani*.[118] In this case, the buyer purchased a mobile home. Upon delivery, the buyer complained about defects in the mobile home, and the seller promised to repair them. Although the contract of purchase did not provide for the duty to repair, the court held for the buyer, explaining that the postcontract promise to repair was a modification of the contract, and needed no consideration under UCC §2-209.

§2.26   —Puffing, Commendation, Opinion versus Express Warranty

Section 2-313(2) of the UCC states that "an affirmation merely of the value of the goods or a statement purporting to be merely the seller's opinion or commendation of the goods does not create a warranty." The issue which often arises is whether an affirmation of fact made by the seller is deemed to be an express warranty or simply the seller's opinion of puffing. It has been said that one of the primary tests for determining if an express warranty was created is

---

[116] UCC §2-313 comment 3.

[117] UCC §2-313 comment 7.

[118] 169 Ind 556, 350 NE2d 635, 19 UCC Rep Serv (Callaghan) 1102 (1976).

whether the seller assumed to assert a fact of which the buyer was ignorant or whether the seller merely expressed a judgment about a matter as to which each party could be expected to have an opinion.[119] This test is not easy to apply. The courts usually consider several factors in determining if the seller created an express warranty, such as the buyer's experience regarding the particular sale and the goods involved (e.g., a car dealer as opposed to a homemaker buying a car), the buyer's reliance on the seller's representation, and the reasonableness of the buyer's reliance.

In some cases, the seller's statement is clearly puffing, as in mass advertising wherein one hears such phrases as "tastes great," "you'll love it," "you can't buy a better product." But in some cases, it is not easy to tell the difference between puffing and affirmation of fact. For instance, what is the status of the statement that if a particular machine were operated in a certain way, "there would be no worry about getting hurt?"[120] The court held that this was opinion and no express warranty. Affirmations that a mobile home is "in perfect condition"[121] and that an automobile is in "A-1 shape and mechanically perfect"[122] have yielded contrary results.

§2.27 —Implied Warranty of Merchantability

Implied warranties arise by operation of law. There are two types of implied warranties: warranty of merchantability and warranty of fitness for a particular purpose.

Section 2-314 of the UCC provides that: "Unless excluded or modified, a warranty that the goods shall be merchantable is implied in a contract for their sale if the seller is a merchant with respect to goods of that kind." A warranty of merchantability thus arises only when there is a sale of goods, and the seller is a merchant in goods of that kind.

Sale of Goods

The implied warranty of merchantability applies only to the sale of goods. However, some courts included *lease* and *bailment* in the word *sale*. Furthermore, goods have been interpreted to include services as well.[123]

---

[119] Annot, 94 ALR3d 729-30 (1979).

[120] Neiss v Rockwell Co, 9 Ill App 3d 906, 293 NE2d 375, 12 UCC Rep Serv (Callaghan) 429 (1973).

[121] Performance Motors Inc v Allen, 280 NC 385, 186 SE2d 162, 10 UCC Rep Serv (Callaghan) 568 (1972) (puffing).

[122] Wat Henry Pontiac Co v Bradley, 202 Okla 82, 210 P2d 348 (1948) (express warranty).

[123] *See* WE Johnson Equip Co v United Airlines Inc, 238 So 2d 98, 8 UCC Rep Serv (Callaghan) 53 (Fla 1970) (lease subject to implied warranties); Buckeye Union Fire Ins Co v Detroit Edison Co, 38 Mich App 325, 196 NW2d 316, 10 UCC Rep Serv (Callaghan) 977 (1972) (furnishing of electricity subject to warranty of merchantability).

Merchant

Only merchants are subject to the warranty of merchantability. This is the only warranty for which a nonmerchant is not responsible. A *merchant* is:

> A person who deals in goods of the kind or otherwise by his occupation holds himself out as having knowledge or skill peculiar to the practices or goods involved in the transaction or to whom such knowledge or skill may be attributed by his employment of an agent or broker who by his occupation holds himself out as having such knowledge or skill.[124]

In those states that expand the scope of Article 2 of the Code to apply not only to the sale of goods, but also to other *transactions* in goods such as leases, bailments, or furnishing of services, the term *merchant* will also include lessors, bailees, contractors, and other professional suppliers. Even if it is found that the person is a nonmerchant not bound by the implied warranty of merchantability under the Code, that person must still perform in good faith.[125]

Merchantability

The Code does not define merchantability. It simply lists six examples of merchantability. Goods to be merchantable must be at least such as:

1. Pass without objection in the trade under the contract description
2. In the case of fungible goods, are of fair and average quality within the description
3. Are fit for the ordinary purposes for which such goods are used
4. Run, within the variations permitted by the agreement, of even kind, quality, and quantity within each unit and among all units involved
5. Are adequately contained, packaged, and labeled as the agreement may require
6. Conform to the promises or affirmations of fact made on the container or label if any

This list, however, is not an exhaustive one.[126] An implied warranty of merchantability can also arise from a course of dealing between the buyer and the seller or from the usage of trade.[127]

---

[124] UCC §2-104(1).
[125] UCC §1-103.
[126] UCC §2-314(2) and comments 6-10.
[127] UCC §2-314(3) and comment 12.

§2.28 —Implied Warranty of Fitness for a Particular Purpose

Under §2-315, three conditions must be present for a seller to be held liable for breach of warranty of fitness for a particular purpose:

1. The seller must know the buyer's purpose in buying the goods
2. The seller must know that the buyer is relying on the seller's skill and judgment in selecting or furnishing suitable goods
3. The buyer must in fact rely on the seller's skill and judgment

The seller need not be a merchant to be held liable under this warranty.

Knowledge of Purpose

The difference between an implied warranty of merchantability and an implied warranty of fitness for a particular purpose is that the former simply requires that the goods be fit for the purpose for which the goods of that kind are ordinarily used, whereas the latter focuses on the particular purpose for which the buyer purchases the goods. The buyer's special needs must be properly communicated to the seller, either expressly or by the circumstances surrounding the sale, for this warranty to apply.[128]

Reliance

The law protects a buyer who relies on a seller's judgment, even when there is no explicit agreement between the parties. However, to be liable for breach of warranty of fitness for a particular purpose, the seller must have had reason to know that the buyer was relying on the seller's skill and judgment at the time the sale occurred. The buyer's reliance can be either expressly communicated to the seller or inferred from the circumstances surrounding the transaction. The comparative expertise of the seller and the buyer with respect to the goods sold is a factor to be considered in determining whether the buyer relied on the seller's judgment or on the buyer's own when purchasing the goods. Other factors to consider are whether the buyer furnished precise specifications to the seller as to the quality or character of the goods, and whether the buyer ordered goods using a brand name. However, the mention of a brand name does not by itself exclude the warranty of fitness for a particular purpose.

> If the buyer himself is insisting on a particular brand, he is not relying on the seller's skill and judgment and so no warranty results. But the mere fact that the article purchased has a particular patent or trade name is not sufficient to indicate nonreliance if the article has been recommended by the seller as adequate for the buyer's purpose.[129]

---

[128] UCC §2-315 comment 1.
[129] UCC §2-315 comment 5.

It is possible, however, that the ordinary purpose and the particular purpose are the same. For instance, both the implied warranty of merchantability and the implied warranty of fitness for a particular purpose may apply to the sale of a breeding bull.[130]

§2.29   —Disclaimers of Warranties under the Uniform Commercial Code

A seller may disclaim all or part of the warranties. For warranty law is contract law, and what one contract can do, another can undo. The idea is that if the seller clearly disclaims one, or more, or all warranties, making it clear to the buyer that the seller warrants nothing, then the buyer knows what the buyer is getting, and the transaction is fair. Usually, however, this is not what happens. Among the seller's sale techniques has often been the practice of burying a disclaimer inconspicuously under the prominently displayed warranty or disguising the disclaimer in such circumlocutions or terminology that the consumer is caught off guard as to the nature of the warranty.

Another technique sellers have used to achieve the same purpose is a clause limiting the consumer's remedies, such as: "Seller's obligation if the goods do not meet this warranty is limited solely to replacing or repairing defective parts." Both of these methods, the disclaimer of warranty and the limitation of remedies, achieve the same purpose: to restrict the seller's liability if the products sold are not as good as the buyer expected them to be. However, the law treats disclaimers of warranties and limitations of remedies quite differently.

Section 2-316 of the UCC deals with disclaimers of warranties and Section 2-719 deals with limitations of remedies. These sections, however, are anything but consistent, and are far from being a model of fine drafting. Interpreting them through their opacity and lack of logic is a study in ambiguity. Still, the ambiguity may be to some degree intentional. It is as though the drafters had some difficulty in reconciling the contradictory interests of buyer and seller and so, combining elements of the common law from both sides of the fence, tried to satisfy both at the same time. As a result, a supplier with an able legal department may well be able to use the technicalities of the Code at the expense of the consumer.

§2.30   —Disclaimer of Express Warranties

Section 2-316(1) of the UCC provides:

> Words or conduct relevant to the creation of an express warranty and words or conduct tending to negate or limit warranty shall be construed

---

[130] *See* Torstensen v Melcher, 195 Neb 764, 241 NW2d 103, 19 UCC Rep Serv (Callaghan) 484 (1976).

wherever reasonable as consistent with each other; but subject to the provisions of this Article on parol or extrinsic evidence (Section 2-202) negation or limitation is inoperative to the extent that such construction is unreasonable.

What all this means is that when one creates an express warranty, it is very difficult to disclaim it, because the disclaimer and the warranty are to be construed as consistent with one another if it is reasonable to do so. With an express warranty, such consistency is difficult to achieve reasonably, for "you have this warranty-but you don't" is not easy to state coherently.

Thus, on the fact of it, the Code does not appear to look favorably upon disclaimers of express warranty. However, there is a considerable barrier in the way of a consumer's enforcement of an oral express warranty which the seller cleverly disclaims by a writing which usually states "There are no warranties, express or implied, which extend beyond the description on the face hereby." This barrier is the parol evidence rule which prohibits the use of extrinsic evidence, the oral express warranty in our case, that contradict a writing which purports to be the sole agreement between the parties. For example, suppose a consumer needs an air conditioner appropriate for the size of the consumer's room, and explains this need to a seller of air conditioners. The seller orally warrants that the model sold will answer the consumer's needs, and, based on this assertion, the consumer purchases it. At this time, the seller gives to the consumer a memorandum of sale which states in part: "No oral agreement, guarantee, promise, representation or warranty shall be binding on the parties to this transaction." What then? Section 2-202 of the UCC on the parol evidence rule which limits the parties' bargain to the four corners of the written contract gives the consumer a real problem.

However, courts have mitigated the four-corner rule, and have allowed oral evidence to be admitted based on a variety of rationales, such as: the writing was not intended by both parties to be the final agreement;[131] parol evidence may be admitted to explain or supplement a writing;[132] there was fraud, duress, misrepresentation, or some similar factor going to the issue of contract formation itself. Furthermore, it may be an unfair and deceptive practice for the seller to use a disclaimer not explained to the consumer.

§2.31   —Disclaimers of Implied Warranties

A disclaimer of implied warranties may be made by several methods. A seller may disclaim the implied warranty of merchantability either orally or in writing. In either case, the term *merchantability* must be used, and in the case of a written

---

[131] UCC §2-202 comment 3. *See* Drier v Perfection Inc, 259 NW2d 496, 23 UCC Rep Serv (Callaghan) 323 (SD 1977); Miller v Hubbard Wray Co, 52 Or App 897, 630 P2d 880, 32 UCC Rep Serv (Callaghan) 1378 (1981).

[132] Session v Chartrand Equip Co, 133 Ill App 3d 719, 479 NE2d 376, 41 UCC Rep Serv (Callaghan) 749 (1985).

disclaimer, the writing that disclaims the warranty must be *conspicuous*.[133] The term *conspicuous* is a source of some difficulty. Section 1-201(10) of the UCC defines *conspicuous* as follows:

> A term or clause is conspicuous when it is so written that a reasonable person against whom it is to operate ought to have noticed it. A printed heading in capitals (as: NON NEGOTIABLE BILL OF LADING) is conspicuous. Language in the body of a form is "conspicuous" if it is in larger or other contrasting type or color. But in a telegram any stated term is "conspicuous". *Whether a term or clause is "conspicuous" or not is for decision by the court* [emphasis added].

Given this discretionary power, a Ohio court has held a small print clause to be *conspicuous*.[134]

A disclaimer of a warranty of fitness for a particular purpose cannot be made orally. It must be in writing and must be conspicuous. The term *fitness*, unlike the term *merchantability*, need not be mentioned.[135]

A seller may disclaim all implied warranties by use of certain terms that make clear that the seller warrants nothing. Section 2-316(3) of the UCC states:

> Notwithstanding Subsection (2) (which imposes the formal requisites for disclaimers of implied warranties) (a) Unless circumstances indicate otherwise, all implied warranties are excluded by expressions like "as is," "with all faults," or other language which in common understanding calls the buyer's attention to the exclusion of warranties and makes plain that there is no implied warranty.

The language of the Code is clear. Use of the terms *as is, with all faults*, or the like need not be conspicuous. However, §2-316(3) gives rise to various interpretations.

One interpretation occurs in *Osborne v Genevie*.[136] The dispute arose from a contract for the sale of a mobile home, in which the disclaimer clause stated that "the buyer is buying the trailer 'as is' and no representations or statements have been made by seller except as herein stated so that no warranty, express or implied, arises from this writing." The Florida District Court of Appeals for the Second District asked the question "whether the conspicuous requirement of [UCC §2-316(2)] is applicable to an as is disclaimer . . . ." The court, acknowledging that other courts may hold differently, held that the requirements must be conspicuous since the purpose of the Code provision was to make sure that the "unsophisticated buyer" be forewarned.[137]

---

[133] UCC §2-316(2).
[134] Avenell v Westinghouse Elec Corp, 41 Ohio App 2d 150, 324 NE2d 583 (1974).
[135] UCC §2-316(2).
[136] 289 So 2d 21, 14 UCC Rep Serv (Callaghan) 85 (Fla Dist Ct App 1974).
[137] *Id* at 23, 14 UCC Rep Serv (Callaghan) at 88.

Some courts, however, do not require *as is* or similar terms to be conspicuous. *Gilliam v Indiana National Bank*[138] illustrates this position. The defendants, in a seizure action for failure to make payments on a mobile home, asserted as a defense that the trailer was defective, and that the retailer and manufacturer had breached implied warranties. The bill of sale included the statement: "Sold as is." The court held that the implied warranties were sufficiently disclaimed, and noted that §2-316(3) "does not require that the as is exclusion be conspicuous [and] Section 2-316(3) is to be read 'notwithstanding subsection (2).' "

A seller may disclaim all implied warranties by the buyer's inspection of the goods or refusal to inspect them. Section 2-316(3)(b) provides:

> [W]hen the buyer, before entering into the contract, has examined the goods or sample or model as fully as he desired, or has refused to examine the goods, there is no implied warranty with regard to defects which an examination ought in the circumstances to have revealed to him.

The idea here is that the buyer is entitled to receive what the buyer has contracted for, and that a full inspection before contracting to buy indicates that the buyer is getting just that. On the other hand, not every presale inspection excludes implied warranties. Comment 8 to UCC §2-316 states:

> An examination under circumstances which do not permit chemical or other testing of the goods would not exclude defects which could be ascertained only by such testing. Nor can latent defects be excluded by a simple examination.

A buyer's refusal to examine the goods upon the seller's request to do so also operates as a disclaimer. The seller's request in this case puts the buyer on notice that the buyer is assuming the risk of defects which an examination ought to reveal.[139]

As one might guess, all of this does not always operate to the consumer's advantage. An example is the sad case of the Moluccan Cockatoo, in *Tarulli v Birds in Paradise*.[140] The consumer purchased this rare bird for $400, and signed an agreement which guaranteed the bird's health at the time of sale and for two days following, and urged the consumer to "have the bird checked by a licensed veterinarian" within those two days. The customer did not take the bird to the veterinarian, and the next month it died of anemia. The court concluded that the seller had effectively disclaimed his warranty under §2-316(3)(b) of the UCC because: "the seller by the demand for an examina-

---

[138] 337 So 2d 352, 20 UCC Rep Serv (Callaghan) 307 (Ala Civ App 1976).
[139] UCC §2-316 comment 8.
[140] 99 Misc 2d 1054, 417 NYS2d 854, 26 UCC Rep Serv (Callaghan) 872 (1979).

tion . . . put the buyer on notice that he is assuming the risk of defects which the examination ought to reveal."[141]

§2.32   —Limitation of Remedies

A limitation of remedies achieves the same purpose as a disclaimer: to limit or modify the seller's liability. For instance, a disclaimer might state, "No warranty is extended to cover moving parts of this mechanical widget." A limitation of remedies may read, "Remedy for defects to this mechanical widget is limited to the widget's stationary parts only." Both statements are calculated to achieve the same purpose of releasing the seller's liability with respect to the moving parts. Under the UCC, however, requirements for the effectiveness of disclaimers of warranties are completely different from those for the effectiveness of limitation of remedy clauses. A limitation of remedies need not be conspicuous; it need not mention the term *merchantability;* it requires no "magic words." All the law requires is that the limitation be a part of the agreement between the parties and that the remedy so limited not fail of its essential purpose.[142] Additionally, unless the language of the limitation expressly states that the given remedy is exclusive, a buyer still has recourse to other remedies under the Code.

Usually, a limitation of remedies clause is used to limit or exclude consequential damages. However, limitation of consequential damages for injury to the person in the case of consumer goods is prima facie unconscionable.[143]

A limitation of remedies can be buried in the small print of a contract because there is no legal requirement that it be *conspicuous* as must disclaimers of warranties.[144]

§2.33   Federal Warranty Law: The Magnuson Moss Warranty Act

As we have seen, under the Uniform Commercial Code, a seller or manufacturer can disclaim all liability for the goods and services sold by using the proper technique and language. Congress has long recognized that the consumer is at a disadvantage under existing law.[145] It is often the case that a buyer, having in hand a written warranty, is truly surprised to learn that the warranty does not cover a particular component that is in need of repair, or

---

[141] *Id* at 1057, 417 NYS2d at 856, 26 UCC Rep Serv (Callaghan) at 875.

[142] UCC §2-719(2).

[143] UCC §2-719(3).

[144] *See* Note, *Legal Control on Warranty Liability Limitation Under the UCC*, 63 Va L Rev 791 (1977).

[145] Reports on the House Version of the Magnuson Moss Warranty Act, House Committee on Interstate and Foreign Commerce, HR 1107, 93d Cong, 2d Sess (1974), 4 US Code Cong & Admin News 7702 (1974).

that he or she will have to pay substantial transportation costs to get repair or replacement of a defective part that is covered by the warranty.

In view of an increasing awareness of the consumer's helplessness in an era of mass consumption, it is no surprise that Congress eventually stepped in to grant the consumer more effective protection in the field of warranties. To that effect, the Magnuson-Moss Warranty/Federal Trade Commission Improvements Act was signed into law on January 4, 1975, and became effective six months after that date.[146]

§2.34   —Purpose of the Act

The Magnuson-Moss Warranty Act (Magnuson-Moss) places its primary emphasis upon disclosure requirements. The purpose of the Magnuson-Moss Act is to solve customer warranty problems by:

1. Requiring that the terms and conditions of written warranties in consumer products be clearly and conspicuously stated in simple and readily understood language

2. Prohibiting the proliferation of classes of warranties on consumer products and requiring that such warranties be either a full or limited warranty, with the requirements of a full warranty clearly stated

3. Safeguarding against the disclaimer or modification of the implied warranty of merchantability

4. Providing consumers with access to reasonable and effective remedies when there is a breach of warranty on consumer goods[147]

The law imposes minimum obligations upon suppliers of consumer products when they provide consumers with a written document called a *warranty*. In imposing the disclosure obligation upon suppliers, Congress's aim was to remedy the situation where the consumer is deceived by clever and ambiguous language dealing with implied and express warranties. The Act requires a clear statement of the terms and conditions of the warranty, terms and conditions that are regulated by the Act itself. Thus, warranties can be made more readily comprehensible to the average consumer, who will then be able to make a more informed choice between products. The Act's primary purpose is to change "the rule of the warranty game."[148]

The Magnuson-Moss Warranty Act empowers the Federal Trade Commission to issue rules for implementing the Act within one year after the date of

---

[146] 15 USC §2312(a).

[147] HR 1107, 93d Cong, 2d Sess 1974, 4 US Code Cong & Admin News 7702 (1974).

[148] S Rep No 151, 93d Cong, 1st Sess 2, at 8 (1975); Strasser, *Magnuson-Moss Warranty Act: An Overview and Comparison with UCC Coverage, Disclaimer, and Remedies in Consumer Warranties,* 27 Mercer L Rev 1111 (1976).

enactment.[149] The FTC has issued to date three rules, on (1) disclosure of warranty terms;[150] (2) presale availability of warranty information;[151] and (3) minimum requirements for informal dispute settlement procedures.[152]

§2.35   —Written Warranty Defined

The Act does not require a seller to make any warranty. The Act applies only if the warrantor chooses to offer a written warranty on a consumer product to a consumer.[153] Thus, oral representation and television advertisements do not come under the Act. The Act defines a written warranty as:

> 1. Any written affirmation of fact or written promise made in connection with the sale of a consumer product by a supplier to a buyer which relates to the nature of the material or workmanship by affirming or promising that the product is defect-free or will meet a specified level of performance over a specified period of time.
>
> 2. Any undertaking in writing made in connection with the sale to refund, repair, replace, or take other remedial action, should the product fail to meet the promise and affirmation set forth in the undertaking which written affirmation, promise or undertaking becomes part of the basis of bargain between a supplier and a buyer for purposes other than resale of such product.[154]

Under this definition, statements of general policy in connection with the supplier's products such as *satisfaction guaranteed* are not a written warranty because they do not promise a specified level of performance for a specified period of time.

Certain requirements relating to energy efficiency ratings for electrical appliances, or care-labeling of apparel, which may be considered expressions of warranty under the Uniform Commercial Code, would not be considered written warranties under the Act, because the specified level of performance does not relate to any specified duration of time. Similarly, a product information disclosure is not a written warranty.[155] In addition, under the Act's definition, there is warranty where a seller, by a writing, gives a consumer an unconditional right to revoke acceptance of goods within a certain number of days after delivery, without regard to defects or to any failure to meet a specified level of performance. The FTC points out that a supplier in this case

---

[149] 15 USC §2312(c).
[150] 16 CFR §701.
[151] 16 CFR §702.
[152] 16 CFR §703.
[153] 15 USC §2302.
[154] 15 USC §101(6).
[155] 16 CFR §700.3(a).

should use the term *free trial period* and not *warranty* if there is no intent to give a warranty.[156]

The courts have had occasion to interpret the scope of a written warranty in *Shelton v General Motors Corp.*[157] In this case, purchasers of General Motors automobiles sued GM because GM had substituted THM 200 transmissions for THM 350 transmissions in its vehicles. The plaintiffs contended that GM had expressly represented and warranted that GM automobiles contained THM 350 transmissions, and that these express warranties were given in brochures, manuals, consumer advertising, and other communications which GM distributed. In the case, the written warranty distributed to the purchasers did not mention any particular model of transmission, and therefore GM contended that the other communications were not written warranties, and were therefore not covered by the Magnuson-Moss Warranty Act. The district court found that the term *written warranty* in the Act may cover documents that do not meet all the tests of the formal definition of written warranty under §101(6) of the Act. The court examined the legislative history and concluded that "other written warranties present in connection with the same transaction should also be enforceable as part of the written warranty [to the consumer]."[158] The court further stated that there is little reason to believe that a purchaser will distinguish between written representations made in a formal warranty and those made in the accompanying material.[159]

The Seventh Circuit, however, held otherwise, declaring that the term *written warranty* should have a single, precise meaning, and should not include any "promises, affirmations, or undertakings other than those defined as written warranties by §101(6)."[160] The Supreme Court denied certiorari.

§2.36 —Consumer Product Defined

To qualify as a *consumer product*, the property in question must meet the following statutory criteria:

> 1. The product must be tangible (as opposed to semi-tangibles, such as stocks and bonds)
> 2. The product must be distributed in commerce
> 3. The product must be one normally used for personal, family, or household purposes.[161]

The FTC has interpreted this latter criterion to mean that a product is a

---

[156] 16 CFR §700.3(b).

[157] 500 F Supp 1181 (DC Ill 1980), *revd*, 660 F2d 311 (7th Cir 1981), *cert denied*, 456 US 974 (1982).

[158] 500 F Supp at 1190.

[159] *Id.*

[160] 660 F2d at 322.

[161] 15 USC §101(1).

consumer product if the use of that type of product by consumers is not uncommon.[162] The percentage of sales or the use to which a particular item is put by a particular buyer is thus irrelevant. Products such as typewriters and automobiles, since they are commonly used for personal, family, or household purposes, are therefore consumer products, even though they are used for business as well. In case of ambiguity in the interpretation of this criterion, doubt is to be resolved in favor of the consumer.[163] Thus, *consumer product* under the Act is more comprehensive than the term *consumer goods* under the Uniform Commercial Code. Under the UCC, goods are consumer goods if they are used or bought primarily for personal, family, or household purposes. The focus is on the actual use of the goods by their holder. On the other hand, normal use of the product and not the actual use, is determinative under the Act. The Act intends to cover more than just consumer goods, since it covers uses beyond consumer use. The protection under the Act in effect follows the product itself and not its use in the hands of its user.

§2.37   —The Problem of Fixtures

The FTC has adopted several approaches to determine when tangible products affixed to realty qualify as *consumer products* under the Act.

The Intent of the Parties

The Act's definition of *consumer products* includes "any such property intended to be attached to or installed in any real property without regard to whether it is so attached or installed." Where the consumer's intent is to contract for the realty, e.g., where the consumer contracts with a builder to construct a home, the building materials, although separately identifiable, are not *consumer products*.[164] On the other hand, where the consumer contracts for the purchase of such materials "over the counter" for the purpose of improvement, repair, or modification of a home, the materials are *consumer products*. In this case, the consumer's intent is not to contract for any realty but for the separate items of tangible personalty which will be incorporated in the realty.[165]

Function Separateness

Items of equipment attached to real property, but having a function apart from real property, are included in the definition of consumer products (for example, air conditioners, furnaces, and water heaters). Some equipment, on the other hand, which would seem to have no functional separateness, nevertheless qualifies as consumer product. This includes thermal, mechanical,

---

[162] 16 CFR §700.1(a).

[163] *Id.*

[164] 16 CFR §700.1(f).

[165] 16 CFR §700.1(e).

or electrical equipment. But wiring, plumbing, ducts, and like items are not *consumer products*.[166]

Needless to say, there is some abiguity in this area.[167] In any case, a fixture will still qualify as a consumer product if it meets the Act's criteria, even if under state law it is strictly classified as fixture only.[168]

§2.38   —Consumer

The consumer product must be sold to a consumer for the Act to apply. The Act defines the *consumer* to mean:

> 1. A buyer who buys other than for purposes of resale, i.e., a non-professional buyer of any consumer products
> 2. Any person who buys such a product secondhand during the duration of the warranty or service contract applicable to the product
> 3. Any third party or any other party who can enforce the warranty or service contract against the warrantor under applicable state law.[169]

Thus, the Act broadens the categories of persons who will be entitled to enforce the provisions of the warranty. They include the original buyer, subsequent purchasers, and other persons entitled under state laws to enforce the warranty provisions. Dealing with subsequent purchasers, however, the Act and the FTC rules permit a warrantor to limit any obligation under the warranty to the original buyer only.[170]

Written warranties not intended for consumers are not covered by the Act. For example, a warranty given by a supplier of parts to the manufacturer of the final consumer product does not come under the Act. However, if the component supplier's written warranty is intended for the consumer, then the Act applies. The FTC provides the example in this regard of a supplier's written warranty to the consumer covering a refrigerator that is sold in a boat or a recreational vehicle.[171]

§2.39   —Disclosure Requirements

No seller is required to give a warranty on a consumer product, but if a written warranty is given, it must comply with the disclosure requirements of

---

[166] 16 CFR §700.1(d).

[167] *See* Lester, *The Magnuson-Moss Act: The Courts Begin to Talk*, 16 UCC L.J 119, at 123-24 (1983).

[168] 16 CFR §700.1(d).

[169] 15 USC §2301(a)(3).

[170] 15 USC §2302(a)(2); 16 CFR §701.3(a)(1).

[171] 16 CFR §700.2.

the Act. The disclosure requirements apply to written warranties on consumer goods which cost the consumer more than $15.00.[172]

The Act requires that the warranty be incorporated in a single document, and the language must be simple and readily understandable to the average consumer.[173] The document must provide the following information:

1. The identity of the person or persons to whom the written warranty is extended—whether the warranty is limited only to the original consumer or extends to other persons, transferees of the original purchase

2. A clear description and identification of the products, parts, or components covered by or excluded from the warranty

3. A clear statement of the remedies in the event of defect, malfunction, or failure to conform to the written warranty

4. The event which triggers the warranty obligation if it differs from the purchase date, together with the warranty duration

5. A detailed explanation of the procedure which the consumer should follow in order to obtain performance of the warranty obligation, and where the consumer can obtain such performance. This means the document must include names of the warrantors, mailing addresses, the name or title of the employee or department responsible for the performance, and a telephone number that consumers may use without charge to obtain information on warranty performance

6. Disclosure of availability of any informal dispute settlement mechanism chosen by the warrantor in compliance with the federal regulations

7. Limitations, if any, on the duration of implied warranties (in the case of limited warranty only). The FTC requires that any such limitation must be accompanied by the following statement: "Some states do not allow limitations on how long an implied warranty lasts, so the above limitation may not apply to you"

8. Disclosure as to any exclusions or limitations of remedies such as incidental or consequential damages and the effectiveness of these exclusions or limitations under state law

9. Inclusion of a general statement: "This warranty gives you specific legal rights and you may also have other rights which vary from state to state."

Documents that promise replacement or refund, but which are not strictly deemed to be written warranties, are not subject to the above disclosure requirements provided:

1. The suppliers have already published such disclosures in publications with general circulation, *and*

---

[172] 16 CFR §701.2.
[173] 16 CFR §701.3(a).

2. The disclosures are provided free of charge to any consumer upon written request[174]

Consumers who sue for failure to receive the required disclosures must show that they have suffered damages as a result of such failure.

In *Gates v Chrysler Corp,*[175] the consumer bought an automobile with numerous defects. Her Chrysler dealership worked on the car a number of times, but the defects persisted, and the consumer sued. Her suit succeeded on the first count, for damages and rescission. The second count sought damages and attorneys' fees, alleging a violation of the Magnuson-Moss Warranty Act, for failure to include the required statement: "This warranty gives you special legal rights, and you may also have other rights which vary from state to state." The court was not sympathetic to this claim, stating that while there may have been a violation, it was surely

a most technical one and contributed not at all to appellant's damages. The relief which she sought and received was afforded by state law; obviously, she was not misled to her detriment by Chrysler's failure to advise her of that law's possible existence at the time of the sale.[176]

The fact that mere technical violation of the Act will not give rise, by itself, to a cause of action for damages does not mean that the technicalities may safely be waived. In *FTC v Virginia Homes Manufacturing Corp,*[177] the FTC sought and obtained a permanent injunction against a manufacturer. The manufacturer had refused to send notice to holders of an old warranty that their rights had been expanded under new legislation. The technicalities involved the designation of the warranty (the old warranty was designated *Manufacturer's Warranty and Limitation of Remedy,* thus violating the Act's requirement that a warranty be designated *Full (statement of duration) Warranty* or *Limited Warranty,* and the completeness of the required step-by-step explanation of the procedure a consumer should follow in order to obtain performance of a warranty obligation. The old warranty stated only that Virginia Homes would remedy any substantial defects provided it received written notice within prescribed time, and included a detachable warranty registration card with Virginia Homes' mailing address on the back. Virginia Homes was affirmatively ordered to comply.

§2.40 —Designations of *Full Warranty*

Any warrantor who gives a written warranty on a product that costs more than $15 is obligated to designate the warranty as either *Full (statement of*

[174] 16 CFR §701.3(b).

[175] 397 So 2d 1187 (Fla Dist Ct App 1981).

[176] *Id* 1189.

[177] 509 F Supp 51 (DC Md 1981).

duration) *Warranty* or *Limited Warranty.* There are no other permissible designations.

A warranty can be designated as *Full* only if it complies with the federal minimum standards of §104 of the Act regulating the following:

1. Duration of warranty
2. Persons covered
3. Remedies
4. Warranty registration cards
5. Exclusion of consequential damage

Duration

When duration of warranty in the written warranty is designated as *Full,* no limitation of duration of any implied warranty is allowed.[178]

Persons Covered

A *full* warranty may not expressly restrict the warranty rights of a transferee who is a consumer during its stated duration,[179] except where the terms of the warranty expressly limit the warranty to the first purchaser.[180]

Remedies

In case of defect or malfunction, a supplier who gives a *full* warranty must fix the product within a reasonable time and without charge.[181] Furthermore, the warrantor must permit the consumer to elect a refund or replacement of the warranted product without charge if repeated repair efforts fail to remedy the product.[182]

The warrantor may not impose any duty other than notification upon the consumer as a condition of securing the remedies stated above, unless the warrantor can demonstrate that the duty imposed is reasonable. However, as a condition of refund or replacement, the warrantor may require that the consumer make the product available to the supplier free and clear of liens and encumbrances.[183] The warrantor may also stipulate that the warrantor will not be liable if the defect or malfunction of the product is caused by the consumer's unreasonable use of the product or by damage not due to the defect of the product.[184]

---

[178] 15 USC §2304(a)(2).
[179] 15 USC §2304(b)(4).
[180] 16 CFR §700.6(b).
[181] 15 USC §2304(a)(1).
[182] 15 USC §2304(a)(4).
[183] 15 USC §2304(b)(2).
[184] 15 USC §2304(c).

Warranty Registration Cards

Often upon purchase of a product, the consumer is asked to sign a warranty registration card in order to get the benefit of the warranty. If a *full* warranty is given however, the warrantor is not permitted to require that a consumer return a registration card as a condition of providing the warranty. Language such as "this warranty is void unless a warranty registration card is returned to the warrantor" is not permissible in a *full* warranty. Nor is it permissible to imply such a condition.[185]

Full-warrantors may use such cards as one possible means of proof of the date the product was purchased. However, the warranty must then disclose that failure to return the card will not affect the consumer's right under the warranty, provided the consumer can show in some reasonable manner the date of the purchase.[186]

Exclusion of Consequential Damages

A *full* warranty may not exclude or limit consequential damages unless such exclusion or limitation conspicuously appears on the face of the warranty.[187] The question arises as to whether the Act authorizes a limitation of consequential damages for personal injuries which under state law[188] would be prima facie unconscionable. The answer is no. The Act provides that nothing in the Act shall "supersede any provision of State law regarding consequential damages for injury to the person or other injury."[189]

§2.41   —Designation of *Limited Warranty*

A warranty which does not include the above federal minimum requirements must be designated as *limited.* The act does not clearly specify the content of a *limited* warranty. Thus, a *limited* warranty may avoid the requirements imposed for a *full* warranty with respect to duration, remedies, rights of transferees, and other duties required from the warrantor. However, a giver of a *limited* warranty is not free of all restrictions. A *limited* warranty is subject to:

 1. Disclosure requirements—All the information required by the Act and the federal regulation must be disclosed on its face[190]
 2. Limitations on disclaimers of implied warranties—Under the Act, disclaimers of implied warranties are prohibited, whether the warranty is

---

185 16 CFR §700.7(b).
186 16 CFR §700.7(b)(c).
187 15 USC §2304(a)(3).
188 UCC §2-719(3).
189 15 USC §2311(b)(2).
190 *See* **§2.38.**

full or *limited.*[191] In the case of a *limited* warranty, the Act permits a limitation on the duration of the implied warranties if such limitation is reasonable and is set forth in clear and unmistakable language and prominently displayed on the face of the warranty[192]

3. Prohibition Against Tying Arrangements—Under the Act, "[n]o warrantor of a consumer product may condition his written or implied warranty of such product on the consumer's using, in connection with such product, any article or service (other than article or service provided without charge under the terms of the warranty) which is identified by brand, trade, or corporate name . . ."[193] The Act empowers the FTC to waive this prohibition if the tying arrangement is justified under the circumstances or is in the public interest. Tying arrangements are prohibited with respect to *full* as well as *limited* warranties.

Although the Act does not impose any further restrictions on a *limited* warranty, a writing designated as a *limited* warranty which does not provide any effective remedy for the consumer would constitute an unfair and deceptive act in violation of §5 of the Federal Trade Commission Act.

§2.42 —Pre-Sale Availability of Written Warranty Terms

In order to improve the adequacy of information available to consumers, prevent deception, and thereby improve competition in the marketplace, the Act directs the FTC to prescribe rules requiring that the terms of any written warranty on a consumer product be made available to the prospective consumer prior to the sale of the product.[193]

In compliance with these directives, the FTC developed rules governing pre-sale availability of written warranty terms.[194] There are four methods for making warranty information available before sale, any one of which will satisfy the FTC rules:

1. Displaying the text of the warranty with the product[195]
2. Maintaining, in a location readily accessible to the consumer, a binder or series of binders which contain copies of the warranties for the products sold in each department in which any consumer product with a written warranty is offered for sale[196]

---

[191] 15 USC §2308(a).
[192] 15 USC §2308(b).
[193] 15 USC §2302(c).
[193] 15 USC §2302(c).
[194] 16 CFR §702.
[195] 16 CFR §702.3(a)(1)(i).
[196] 16 CFR §702.3(a)(1)(ii).

3. Placing or displaying the package of any consumer product on which the written warranty is disclosed in a manner visible to prospective consumers at the point of sale[197]

4. Displaying in close proximity to the warranted consumer product a notice which discloses the text of the written warranty[198]

With respect to catalogue and mail-order sales, if a written warranty accompanies the consumer product, the seller must clearly and conspicuously describe the warranted product, either by putting the full text of the written warranty in the catalogue or by stating that the written warranty is in the catalogue or by stating that the written warranty can be obtained free upon written request. If this latter method is chosen, then the seller must disclose the address where the warranty can be obtained, and must provide a copy of the warranty promptly upon a consumer's request.[199]

In a door-to-door sale, disclosure of such warranty information is also required prior to consummation of the sale. The sales representative must disclose to the prospective buyer that the representative has copies of the product warranties and that the buyer may inspect such warranties at any time during the sales presentation.[200]

§2.43   —Informal Dispute Settlement Procedures

The rules governing settlement procedures were promulgated "to encourage warrantors to establish procedures whereby disputes are fairly and expeditiously settled through informal dispute settlement mechanisms."[201] In contrast to the FTC Rules on disclosure and on pre-sale availability of written warranty, this is an optional rule not required from the warrantor.

If the warrantor chooses to adopt such a dispute settlement mechanism, it must disclose clearly and conspicuously all the information necessary for the consumer to resort to the mechanism. This includes the following disclosures:

1. Availability of the procedure

2. The relevant name, address, and telephone number related to the procedure which the consumer may use without charge

3. A statement of the procedure that the consumer must go through prior to seeking remedies in court. The statement must also disclose that if the consumer seeks redress under state law, the consumer is not required to go through the settlement procedure[202]

---

[197] 16 CFR §702.3(a)(iii)

[198] 16 CFR §702.3(a)(iv).

[199] 16 CFR §702(c).

[200] 16 CFR §702(d).

[201] 15 USC §230(a)(1).

[202] 16 CFR §703(b)(3).

The warrantor is required to act in good faith in determining whether it will abide by a decision reached through the informal dispute settlement mechanism.[203] It appears few warrantors have used this procedure, even though it may be more beneficial to them. This may be attributable to the many requirements imposed by the rule.

§2.44   —Consumer Remedies for Noncompliance with the Act

Public Enforcement

The Attorney General of the United States or the FTC may restrain warrantors from making deceptive warranties covering a consumer product or from violating the provisions of the Act.[204] The FTC may exercise its power with respect to such violations and treat them as unfair and deceptive practices or acts under §5(a)(1) of the FTC Act. A cease-and-desist order or a temporary injunction may be issued against the warrantor where the court finds it appropriate, weighing the equities, the likelihood of ultimate success, and the public interest.[205]

Private Action

The most important feature of the Magnuson-Moss Act is to confer on the consumer private enforcement rights. Under the Act, consumers have a federal cause of action for breach of warranty as well as the right to sue for noncompliance with the provisions of the Act.[206] Thus warranty law is no longer purely state law, but is now federal law as well, and encompasses an expanded array of enforceable rights. The interplay between federal and state law is often complex, however.[207] No small part of the complexity is due to the poor drafting of the Act. Nevertheless, by making available the award of attorneys' fees and expenses in a warranty action, the federal law has greatly increased a consumer's realistic chances for worthwhile suit and recovery for violations of the Act.

A consumer damaged by a warrantor's violation of the Act may bring suit in state or federal court for legal and equitable relief.[208] Federal jurisdiction requires the amount in controversy to be at least $25 per plaintiff, and $50,000 in the aggregate. In a class action suit, the number of plaintiffs must not be

---

[203] 16 CFR §703(2)(g).

[204] 15 USC §2310(c)(1).

[205] *Id.*

[206] 15 USC §2310(d)(1).

[207] *See* Schroeder, *Private Actions Under the Magnuson-Moss Warranty Act,* 66 Calif L Rev 1 (1978).

[208] 15 USC §2310(d)(1).

less than 100.[209] The consumer's private right of action is in addition to warranty rights already existing under state law. For example, a written warranty under the Act also constitutes an express warranty under §2-313 of the Uniform Commercial Code. Thus, quite apart from the Act, the consumer would have the remedies available under the UCC.

The courts have usually interpreted strictly the jurisdictional requirements for bringing action in a federal court. Consequently, most Magnuson-Moss Act cases have been brought in state courts. This seems to have been the intention of the drafters of the Act in the first place.

Barnett v Chrysler Corp[210] provides an example. The consumer brought action in the United States District Court of Nebraska for relief in the amount of $7,000, because Chrysler allegedly repossessed a defective automobile without refunding the consumer. The court rejected the claim on jurisdictional grounds and returned it to state courts for adjudication:

> While there is no express limitation that actions brought in a federal court must be class actions, the requirement that a minimum of $50,000 be in controversy limits the availability of a federal forum for individual consumer actions. The claim before the court now does not meet the jurisdictional amount . . .[211]

Given these requirements, and the fact that consumer goods are usually inexpensive items, it is difficult for individual plaintiffs to meet the minimum requirement for federal court jurisdiction. This explains why, in a number of cases, plaintiffs have tried to add punitive damages or attorneys' fees to the amount in controversy. In *Novosel v Northway Motor Car Corp*,[212] a plaintiff seeking compensatory damages in the amount of $9,638 tried to gain federal jurisdiction by seeking $50,000 in punitive damages.

The court noted that the Act is "virtually silent as to the amount and type of damages which may be awarded for breach of warranty," and therefore looked to the Supreme Court case of *St. Paul Mercury Indemnity Co v Red Cab Co*.[213] That case allows for including punitive damages in the amount of controversy, if the claim is apparently made in good faith. It must appear to be a legal certainty that the claim is really for less than the jurisdictional amount to justify dismissal.[214] The *Novosel* court noted that this standard made it difficult in general to dismiss a case on jurisdictional grounds by reason of the amount in controversy, but then continued:

> Nevertheless, the legal certainty standard is clearly applicable in those

---

[209] 15 USC §2310(d)(3).
[210] 434 F Supp 1167 (D Neb 1977).
[211] *Id* 1168.
[212] 460 F Supp 541 (NDNY 1978).
[213] 303 US 283 (1938).
[214] *Id* 288-89.

cases where recovery is limited by the terms of a contract . . . where the governing law places limits upon the damages recoverable, . . . and, where the amount demanded is merely *colorable* for the purpose of obtaining jurisdiction.[215]

Thus, although the court held that both actual and punitive damages must be considered in determining the amount in controversy for actions in a federal court, the court dismissed the plaintiff's case on three bases: (1) that state law did not allow for punitive damages in contract or breach of warranty cases; (2) that no allegations of intentional or tortious conduct appeared on the complaint; and (3) that the plaintiff failed to make a preliminary showing that it could possibly recover punitive damages.[216] Therefore, the jurisdictional amount requirement was not met.

Another case on the same issue allowed punitive damages to be included in the jurisdictional amount. In *Schafer v Chrysler Corp,*[217] the court looked to state law and found that Indiana allowed punitive damages in contract cases where the defendant's conduct was tantamount to a tort, and said, "The Court cannot conclude to a legal certainty that the claim is really for less than the jurisdictional amount."[218] Thus, in spite of the fact that the use of punitive damages to satisfy the amount in controversy "triggers special jurisdictional scrutiny,"[219] the defendant's motion to dismiss was denied.

In *Saval v BL Ltd,*[220] five consumers attempted to bring one claim for breaches of warranty concerning their respective automobiles. Together, with costs, attorneys' fees, and punitive damages, their suit would have cleared the jurisdictional amount barrier. However, the court decided that no common defect or other common grounds for the complaints existed sufficient to allow joinder of claims into one suit, that attorneys' fees are not to be included in the amount of controversy for jurisdictional purposes, for if they were, the $25 amount requirement would be rendered meaningless, and that under applicable state law, no punitive damages were allowed in contractual disputes without a showing of actual or implied malice. The case was dismissed from the federal court although state statutes of limitation had already run their course.

From these cases, it appears that under the Magnuson-Moss Act, the jurisdictional amount requirement must be strictly met, complaints seeking relief in the form of punitive damages will trigger special scrutiny, the federal jurisdiction does not create broad new opportunities for joinder of suits, and

---

[215] 460 F Supp at 544.
[216] *Id* 546.
[217] 544 F Supp 182 (ND Ind 1982).
[218] *Id* 186.
[219] *Id* 185.
[220] 710 F2d 1027 (4th Cir 1983).

attorneys' fees may not be included for the purpose of determining whether the $50,000 federal jurisdictional requirement has been met. Consequently, even though the Magnuson-Moss Act creates new federal rights for consumers, these rights will most often be enforced in the courts of their respective states.

§2.45 —Equitable Relief

The Magnuson-Moss Act authorizes consumers to sue warrantors "for damages and other legal and equitable relief" for failure to comply with any written or implied warranty.[221] Equitable relief could include repair, replacement, and refund. In addition, rescission and specific performance may also be available. There is nothing specific in the Act to clarify the availability of these latter two remedies. However, rescission of the contract must be within the purpose of the Act because, among other remedies, the Act specifies refund, a rescissionary right. The option of replacement or refund is available where repeated efforts at repair have failed.[222]

Specific performance is not a significant remedy when the subject matter is consumer products. Consumer products are not unique, and are easily replaceable. Thus refund and replacement will nearly always be more appropriate than specific performance.

A case that treats the equitable remedy issue is *Lieb v American Motors Corp*,[223] in which the court stated, "The language authorizing consumer actions contains no qualification concerning the type of equitable relief available and it would be a misuse of court's power to write such restrictions into the statute."[224] The case was dismissed for lack of the proper jurisdictional amount, but the court acknowledged the availability under the proper circumstances of all types of equitable relief, including injunction.[225]

§2.46 —Attorneys' Fees

Perhaps the most significant right the Act gives the aggrieved consumer is the right to recover litigation costs, including attorneys' fees.[226] This right is available even to a consumer who essentially sues under state law. For example, if a consumer sues for breach of an implied warranty of merchantability, the consumer will have a cause of action under state[227] as well as federal law if a written warranty is involved. The consumer can recover damages and litigation costs, including attorneys' fees.

---

[221] 15 USC §2310(d)(1).

[222] 15 USC §2304(a)(4).

[223] 538 F Supp 127 (SDNY 1982).

[224] *Id* 134.

[225] *Id.*

[226] 15 USC §2310(d)(2).

[227] UCC §2-314.

As *Hanks v Pandolfo*[228] shows, the judge is granted considerable discretion in the award of attorneys' fees. In *Pandolfo,* the plaintiffs appealed the judgment awarding counsel fees of $450 because, the plaintiffs contended, the court was bound to grant attorneys' fees based on actual time expended, the court failed to grant reasonable attorneys' fees (the plaintiff was asking for $2,825) and the court reduced the fees on an improper basis. The Superior Court of Connecticut rejected these contentions. The court pointed out that the Act provides:

> If a consumer finally prevails in any action brought under paragraph (1) of this subsection, he *may* be allowed by the Court to recover as part of the judgment a sum equal to the aggregate amount of cost and expenses (*including attorney's fees based on actual time expended*) determined by the court to have been *reasonably incurred* by the plaintiff . . . *unless the court shall determine that such an award of attorney's fees would be inappropriate* [court's emphasis].[229]

Therefore, said the court, the determination made in the case by the trial court to reduce the requested attorneys' fees from $2,825 to $450 was not unreasonable or improper.

The Act imposes three restrictions on recovery of attorneys' fees and litigation costs:

    1. The litigation costs and attorneys' fees are recoverable only if the consumer prevails in his warranty claim and brings the action under the Magnuson-Moss Act[230]

    2. The warrantor must first be afforded a reasonable opportunity to cure[231]

    3. The consumer must first exhaust the informal settlement mechanism for the case, if there is one, before seeking judicial redress[232]

If the consumer wishes to sue under state law without being subject to such restrictions, the consumer may do so, but the action will no longer be under the Act, and therefore, litigation costs and attorneys' fees could no longer be recovered under the Act.

---

[228] 38 Conn Supp 447, 450 A2d 1167 (1982).
[229] *Id* 1169 (quoting 15 USC §2310(d)(2)).
[230] 15 USC §2310(d)(2).
[231] 15 USC §2310(e).
[232] 15 USC §2410(a)(3).

§2.47 —Applicability of Other Federal and State Laws

Nothing in the Magnuson-Moss Warranty Act is to be construed so as to affect warranties governed by other federal laws.[233] Thus, warranties under federal laws relating to certain specified goods remain unaffected.

The Act however, does affect state laws, by preempting any such law which:

1. Relates to labeling or disclosure on written warranties or performance thereunder

2. Lies within the scope of the provisions of the Act, dealing with contents of warranties, designation of written warranties, federal minimum standards for warranty and

3. Is not identical to such provisions[234]

Notice that the criteria for preemption by the Magnuson-Moss Act are not the criteria which are usually applied. Ordinarily, the question is not whether the state statute is identical, but whether it affords more or less protection to the consumer than the federal law. Under Magnuson-Moss, the requirement is that the state statute be identical to the federal statute, otherwise it is preempted.

On the other hand, the Act does not invalidate or restrict any right or remedy by which the consumer is protected under other state law, and state law still determines the conditions of recovery for a breach of implied warranty. Thus, whether vertical privity is required for recovery,[235] or what constitutes the basis for emotional distress,[236] are matters resolved by state law. Furthermore, causes of action for personal injuries arising out of the sale of allegedly defective products remain generally a matter of state law.[237] In other words, the Act provides federal standards of recovery, but the individual states may still determine the conditions for such recovery.

---

[233] 15 USC §2311(d).

[234] 15 USC §2311(c)(1).

[235] See Mendelson v General Motors Corp, 105 Misc 2d 346, 432 NYS2d 132 (1980).

[236] See Sie v General Motors Corp, 588 F Supp 1207 (DC Va 1984).

[237] See Bush v American Motors Sales Corp, 575 F Supp 1581 (DC Colo 1984).

3

Extending Credit

§3.01 Introduction

There is well-documented evidence that credit was present in primitive society and was extensively regulated.[1] Existence of credit was shown in the Hammurabi's Code in 1800 B.C. and reached sophisticated forms during the Greek period of 700 B.C. The Romans' Twelve Tables in 443 B.C. allowed personal slavery and imprisonment for debt. Security accompanying existence of credit in the form of pledges and other devices was recognized and regulated by Roman law in the Code of Justinian.

Credit has also always existed in the United States. The image of settlers always paying in cash was not completely accurate.[2] However, the explosion of consumer credit really began between 1950 and 1971. During this period, consumer credit outstanding rose from $21.5 billion to $137.2 billion. At the end of 1983, the total had reached $396 billion.[3] The growth resulted from the consumer's ability and willingness to incur debts and the mass production of consumer goods, especially the automobile.

§3.02 Who Can Extend Credit

In the United States, there are three types of lending institutions: depository institutions, nondepository institutions, and sellers. Usually, one does not refer

---

[1] *See* E. Hoebel, The Law of Primitive Man, chs 6 & 9 (1954).

[2] *See* Report of the National Commission on Consumer Finance, Consumer Credit in the United States 5 (1972).

[3] P. Rasor, Consumer Finance Law 6 (1985).

to *extenders* of credit but rather to *holders* of credit. The Federal Reserve Board classifies amounts of customer credit by holders rather than originators. For example, the foremost extenders of credit are automobile dealers, but the commercial paper is then assigned to banks and finance companies. Although the dealers originally extend the credit, the credit is in reality held by the financial institutions.

§3.03 —Depository Institutions

The most common type of depository institution is the commercial bank. Its principal business is to accept deposits, make loans, and collect commercial paper. But besides commercial banks, depository institutions also include savings institutions such as savings and loans, credit unions, and savings banks.

Prior to the enactment of the Depository Institution and Regulatory Control Act of 1980,[4] savings institutions were strictly limited as to the type of deposits they could accept and the types of loans they could make. These restrictions prevented savings and loans from competing with commercial banks in their banking activities. For example, the law did not allow depositors in savings and loans to draw checks on their accounts. However, under the 1980 Act, savings institutions now engage in a wide range of activities in competition with commercial banks.

Depository institutions and savings institutions may be governed by state or federal law or both. Where the charter establishing the organization, usually a corporation, is issued by the federal government, the bank is known as a national bank governed by federal law. The related federal agency, the Federal Reserve Board, carries out the law through extensive regulations and interpretations. These, originally published in the Federal Register, are subsequently codified in the Code of Federal Regulations (CFR).

When the charter is issued by the state, the bank is a state bank supervised by the state banking commissioner. All national banks are members of the Federal Reserve System and must be insured by the Federal Deposit Insurance Corporation (FDIC). State banks are not required to become members of the Federal Reserve System, but may choose to do so. Even nonmember state banks are to a certain extent subject to the regulatory authority of the Federal Reserve Board.

§3.04 —Commercial Banks

Commercial banks are the most common type of financial institution. They engage in common commercial functions such as accepting deposits, making loans, and collecting commercial paper. They may also engage in other activities such as investment banking, which underwrites securities for large corporations. They also may be specialized, such as trade banks. Many

---

[4] Pub L No 96-221, 94 Stat 132 (codified in scattered sections of §§12, 15 USC).

commercial banks have small loan departments that extend credit.[5] Commercial banks account for over 40 per cent of the outstanding consumer credit in the United States.

§3.05 —Savings Institutions

Savings and loan associations may be chartered under either state or federal law. They were developed to meet the increasing consumer demand for home financing that commercial banks were unable to meet. The first savings and loan was the Oxford Provident Building Association of Philadelphia, organized in 1841. The organization was patterned after the English building societies which included a number of voluntary members who pooled savings in order to extend loans to other members.

Savings and loans are regulated by the Federal Home Loan Bank Board. Originally, 90 per cent of their funds were tied up in real estate mortgages, but this has not been the case in recent years. All federal savings and loans must be members of the Federal Home Loan Bank System. State institutions may elect to join if they so desire.

§3.06 —Credit Unions

Credit unions are usually organized among persons with some common bond, such as common employment. As the Federal Credit Union Act specifies, "It is a requirement to the establishment of a Federal Credit Union that the membership be limited to groups having a common bond of occupation or association, or to a group within a well-defined neighborhood, community or rural district."[6]

Credit unions first appeared in Germany in 1848. In the United States, they did not appear until 1934. They currently account for 14 per cent of outstanding consumer credit except for automobile and home improvement loans. The Federal Credit Union system is administered by the National Credit Union Administration, an independent agency of the executive branch of the government.

§3.07 —Savings Banks

The concept of a savings bank originated with Daniel Defoe in 1767, who suggested the organization of "friendly societies for provident habits in general."[7] These institutions were formed to encourage savings at a time when

---

[5] 12 USC §85. *See* Rockland-Atlas Natl Bank v Murphy, 329 Mass 755, 110 NE2d 638 (1953).

[6] 12 USC §1759.

[7] G. Munn, Encyclopedia of Banking and Finance 665 (1962).

commercial banks did not serve this function. The Federal Home Loan Bank is authorized to approve charters for federal mutual savings banks. Federal legislation governing savings and loans apply also to mutual savings banks.

§3.08   —Morris Plan Banks (or Industrial Banks)

This is a creation of a clever lawyer, Arthur J. Morris, to get around state usury laws. The first Morris bank was chartered in 1910. In those days, loans were usually in a lump sum form and installment loans were rare, because the mechanics of installment loans were complex, requiring the constant adjustment of interest rates and principal and sophisticated methods of bookkeeping.

The Morris Plan allowed banks to provide loans at higher than the normal rate of interest by deducting the legal interest in advance and then requiring the borrower to make monthly or weekly deposits with the bank in non-interest earning accounts during the period of the loan. The bank would use the deposits, reaping profits on them, and as a result could collect interest which went beyond the state usury limits.

Morris Plan banks have the power to accept deposits, issue investment certificates, and make installment loans. Morris Plan banks fulfilled a need and flourished in the 1920s and 1930s until the enactment of installment loan legislation which allowed other institutions and lenders to enter the installment loan field. Morris banks are created by special law in the states in which they operate and are state-incorporated.

The question arises as to whether a Morris Plan bank is truly a bank, because deposits are not payable upon demand.[8] At any rate, they are eligible for membership with the FDIC and the Federal Reserve System.[9]

§3.09   —Nondepository Institutions

There are many institutions that are in the business of lending money, but which are not allowed to take or solicit deposits, issue checks, or conduct other banking operations. They are, therefore, subject to controls different from those applied to depository institutions. The loans involved are obtained from investors or the institution's own resources. These institutions include pawn shops, small loan companies, and finance companies. Most states have special statutes regulating the licensing and operation of finance companies that make consumer loans. Small loan companies and finance companies are often permitted an interest rate higher than that allowed by state usury laws so as to attract legitimate lenders into the consumer credit field. As long as the usury ceiling was low, legitimate businesses would not enter the field, and consumers would go to "loan sharks." By allowing a higher interest rate, the law has helped remedy that situation. Finance companies, originally extensively regulated by

---

[8] *See* Heller, Handbook of Federal Bank Holding Company Law 6-7 (1976).
[9] 12 USC §321.

state law, are now more and more subject to federal legislation through the extension of the Consumer Credit Protection Act, especially the Truth-in-Lending Act, and the great power it gave to the Federal Reserve Board and the Federal Trade Commission. Finance companies now hold great quantities of commercial paper generated by consumer credit transactions. The paper then is discounted and collected by commercial banks. Finance companies account for approximately 27 per cent of outstanding consumer loans.

§3.10 —Sellers

Retailers are also extending credit to the consumer, through installment sales contracts and purchase money transactions. The funds rarely come from the seller, except the large retailers, such as Sears Roebuck and the like. Large retailers, as well as gas companies, are permitted to issue credit cards.

Retailers usually assign the commercial paper to other banks or finance companies on a recourse or nonrecourse basis. Retailers may also direct the consumer to a lender who will extend the credit for the consumer to purchase from the retailer. Traditionally, the law treated sellers and lenders differently, but the distinction has become blurred pursuant to new legislation enacted in recent years, although it has not completely disappeared.[10]

§3.11 Obtaining Information for Extending Credit: The Credit Reporting Industry

In order to avoid getting stuck with a bad debt, a creditor wants information about the consumer's past behavior in order to determine if the consumer is a good credit risk. In the past, this information was gathered through a face-to-face interview with the consumer and, perhaps, a requirement that the consumer fill out an application detailing the consumer's financial status. This simple system worked in its time, but the modern explosion of credit transactions made this system obsolete. In order to fill the void created by the demise of this system, creditors have turned for information to the professionals of the credit reporting industry. There are four major institutions in the credit reporting industry: credit bureaus, investigative reporting agencies, credit card authorization services, and bad check lists.

§3.12 —Credit Bureaus

Credit bureaus are the most popular members of the credit reporting industry. The credit bureaus gather credit and financial information on nearly every adult American.

Each file contains data identifying the individual: name, alias, address, social

---

[10] For example, the U3C continues to treat them differently. *See* §1.301(12),(15) and U3C act 2, pts 2 & 3.

security number, spouse's name. It will also contain financial information on the individual: employment history, sources and amount of income, lines of credit, amounts, due dates, payment habits, billing disputes, and other relevant data. In addition, the file will include public record information: arrests, detentions, bankruptcies, and tax and other liens.

The information for such files comes from the credit grantors themselves, but also from other sources such as newspapers and public records. The information is fed into either a central source, to which automated credit bureaus have access, or to local credit bureaus directly. Manual credit bureaus receive the information through a microfiche service offered by Associated Credit Bureaus, Inc, the credit bureau trade association also known as the "Trade Verification Service." The five largest agencies, of which TRW Inc is the leader, together maintain 150 million files.

Of all of the information released to them, credit grantors pay particular attention to two items: *payment habit* and *amount owing.* How credit grantors rate a consumer's payment habit is illustrated below:

0   Too new to rate; approved but not used
1   Pays (or paid) within 30 days of billing; pays accounts as agreed
2   Pays (or paid) in more than 30 days, but not more than 60 days, or not more than one payment past due
3   Pays (or paid) in more than 60 days, but not more than 90 days, or two payments past due
4   Pays (or paid) in more than 90 days, but not more than 120 days, or three or more payments past due
5   Account is at least 120 days overdue but is not yet rated "9"
7   Making regular payments under Wage Earner Plan or similar arrangement
8   Repossession (indicate if it is a voluntary return of merchandise by the customer)
9   Bad debt; place for collection; skip

Credit grantors use the information on *amount owing* to avoid extending credit to overburdened consumers.

Without leaving the office, credit grantors can now have almost instantaneous information on a consumer by use of direct computer tie-ins with credit bureaus files. The loan officer need only feed in certain identifying information on the applicant, and the applicant's file will appear before the loan officer in a matter of minutes.

Consumer reports are not always error-free. The system presents dangers. As the Privacy Protection Study Commission reports:

> Correctly identifying an individual is chief among the problems that the automated (credit) bureaus have had to address. With information from hundreds of sources on literally millions of individuals being compiled and collated in one place, identification methods, some of which partially rely on the Social Security number, must be improved over methods that

are adequate in smaller operations. Proper matching of information in existing files with information coming from outside sources is especially important. . . .[11]

§3.13 —Investigative Reporting Agencies

Insurers, employers, and, less often, lenders frequently want to have an even more thorough and detailed collection of information on the consumer than a regular consumer report. What they want in this type of special report is not simply the financial history of the subject, but also information about the subject's character, way of life, and any other general information pertaining to the subject's personal life, ranging from yard care and housekeeping proficiency to drinking and sexual habits. Indeed, there sometimes seems to be no limit to the type of information collected by information gatherers for the use of investigative agencies.

Equifax Services, Inc, based in Atlanta, is one of the largest of these agencies. It alone maintains files on over 50 million Americans and issues more than 20 million reports a year. Investigators are trained to gather information from the consumer's friends, neighbors, co-workers, and the like. One can well imagine the type of information that might be gathered from these sources.[12] Many of the investigators seem to enjoy this kind of investigative digging, and some of their reports read like scandal sheets.

§3.14 —Credit Card Authorization Services

These services allow credit card issuers and merchants who honor such cards to detect stolen cards, expired cards, cardholders who have exceeded their credit limits, and other problems. A merchant is usually required to get authorization before honoring the credit card for transactions over a certain limit specified by the card issuer. The merchant usually calls the authorization service over the telephone and gets information from the latter on the status of the card. The authorization service system may be an in-house system operated by the card issuer itself, such as that used by Sears and American Express, or it can be an independent organization which provides authorization services on a worldwide basis, such as that used by Mastercard and Visa. Another type of authorization service provides information on credit card accounts to restaurants, hotels, and airlines. These services usually get their information from the credit card issuers themselves.

---

[11] Congress enacted the Privacy Act in 1974, 5 USC §552(a). §5 of that Act created the Privacy Protection Study Commission. In 1977, the Commission submitted its report, Personal Privacy in an Information Society. Most of the materials used to describe the credit report agencies are from this report and from P. Rasor, Consumer Finance Law 17-22 (1985).

[12] Privacy Protection Study Commission Report, Personal Privacy in an Information Society 60 (1977).

§3.15 —Bad Check List Services

These services gather lists of bad checking accounts of consumers and funnel the information to subscribing merchants. The merchants in turn supply information to the agencies.

Greenway v Information Dynamics Ltd [13] is a case dealing with bad check list and collecting agencies, and describes the mechanics of how those organizations operate. In the case, Information Dynamics Ltd (IDL) provided services to businesses in a wide area covering Arizona, New Mexico, Colorado, Utah, and Wyoming. The organization's data base was gathered through reports from merchants who subscribed to IDL's services. The merchants reported the names of individuals whose checks had bounced, and also provided other information including the individuals' checking account numbers, their driver's license numbers, and the reasons for return of the checks. IDL distributed to subscribers microfilm or microfiche lists, as well as Holoscan Film and bulletins, and each subscribing merchant was given a machine with which to read the information set down on the list. The purpose of all this was to enable a merchant cashing a check to know the check-cashing history of the consumer. Clearly, these services fit the definition of credit reporting agencies.

Besides the above agencies, there is another provider of information known as the Lender's Exchange. This is an index maintained by finance companies. It is a nonprofit, cooperative organization which serves as a clearing house for information among members.

The Lender's Exchange exists mainly to assist lenders in identifying individuals who already have existing obligations, so that lenders will not lend to borrowers who are otherwise over extended. But it does not keep records of indebtedness, nor does it contain information on the consumers' paying habits.

A common thread running through all the components of the credit reporting industry is their pervasiveness, comparable to a web stretching out over the whole of society. It is obvious that such a large system would have to have its flaws, and inaccurate information could surely find its way into the consumer files. The devastating effect that such information can have on an individual's life requires that some safeguards be provided to insure the accuracy of the information to the extent possible, and, failing that, to allow the consumer to check and correct the error. Furthermore, the intrusive nature of the credit reporting industry, especially the investigative reporting agencies, poses serious threats to the consumer's right to privacy and, as such, should be regulated so as to curb the threat.

---

[13] 399 F Supp 1092 (D Ariz 1974), *affd*, 524 F2d 1148 (4th Cir 1975).

§3.16   —Common Law Remedies for False Credit Reporting

Under the common law, a consumer may have some remedies for publication of false credit or other information. These remedies would take the form of causes of action for defamation or invasion of privacy. However, these remedies are inadequate to protect the consumer.

With respect to defamation, the prospects for recovery are grim, in view of the privilege that the courts accord to credit bureaus. This privilege protects persons who make honest but false statements about third persons to another person who could be affected by the third person's behavior.[14] Courts consistently hold that credit bureaus have that privilege.[15]

Actions for invasion of privacy do not hold up good prospects either, because an essential element in such an action is proof of *unreasonable* public exposure of private facts. The release of a consumer report to a few subscribers is not sufficient public exposure to sustain the publication element on the level necessary to establish a claim. Moreover, the plaintiff often is required to bring the report itself to present it in court. Under the common law, such a report can be obtained only in discovery, and only if the plaintiff can show actual malice.[16] Thus, the common law remedies are obviously inadequate since, as a practical matter, the average consumer could not effectively bring such an action. Special statutory measures are thus necessary in order to provide anything approaching adequate consumer protection.

§3.17   —The Fair Credit Reporting Act

In 1970, Congress responded to the consumer's plight with the passage of the Fair Credit Reporting Act (FCRA).[17] About a dozen states have also enacted legislation seeking to protect the consumer by regulating the consumer's relationship with credit reporting agencies and the users of the reports. Congress realized that legislation was necessary "to insure that credit reporting agencies exercised their grave responsibilities with fairness, impartiality, and a respect for the consumer's right to privacy."[18]

The Act is very short and is written in very general terms. By attempting to strike a balance between the need to protect the consumer and the efficient and speedy execution of the industry's needs, the Act's provisions are usually

---

[14] *See* Note, *Judicial Construction of the Fair Credit Reporting Act: Scope and Civil Liability,* 76 Colum L Rev 458 461-64 (1976).

[15] *See, e.g.,* Barker v Retail Credit Co, 8 Wis 2d 664, 100 NW2d 391 (1960); *see also* W. Prosser, Law of Torts 817 (4th ed 1971).

[16] *See* Note, *supra* Note 14, at 458; *see also* Tureen v Equifax Inc, 571 F2d 411 (8th Cir 1978).

[17] The Act is codified at 15 USC §1681 *et seq,* and became Title VI of the Consumer Credit Protection Act.

[18] 15 USC §1681(a)(4).

couched in general and vague terms. Accordingly, the exact scope of the Act has been determined mostly by judicial interpretations. In dealing with the FCRA, the practitioner should consult the FTC's Compliance Manual, which is reproduced in 5 CCH Consumer Credit Guide, ¶11,305.

§3.18   —Consumer Report Defined

The FCRA applies only to consumer reports. This term is defined to mean:

> Any written, oral or other communication of any information by a consumer reporting agency bearing on a consumer's credit worthiness, credit standing, credit capacity, character, general reputation, personal characteristics, or mode of living which is used or expected to be used or collected in whole or in part for the purpose of serving as a factor in establishing the consumer's eligibility for: 1) credit or insurance to be used primarily for personal, family or household purposes, 2) employment purposes, or 3) other purposes authorized under §1681(b) of this title.

Section 1681(b) enumerates a number of permissible purposes of consumer reports. After giving a limiting list of these purposes, e.g., employment, insurance, credit, it contains a general provision in §1681(b)(E) which provides that a consumer reporting agency may furnish a consumer report to a person who "otherwise has a legitimate business need for the information in connection with a business transaction involving the consumer." This catchall sentence is where most of the litigation arises, since one part of the list seems limiting, but the catchall provision seems to indicate a contrary intent.

An argument has been made that if a consumer report is released not for a permissible purpose, then it is not a consumer report which is governed by the Act. This was the holding in *Henry v Forbes*.[19] In this case, the defendants requested a report for background information in connection with a political purpose. Therefore, the purpose was not for employment, not for insurance, nor for a commercial transaction. No consumer relationship existed between the user and the person who was the object of the report. The court held that the FCRA did not apply because "[T]he Act clearly does not provide a remedy for all illicit or abusive use of information about consumers."[20] This interpretation seems unduly restrictive. In effect, the more reprehensible the use, the less subject to the Act.

The trend in recent years has been to adopt a more liberal view of what constitutes a consumer report. In *Heath v Credit Bureau, Inc,*[21] an active union reformer asserted in his complaint that the union had requested from the credit

---

[19] 433 F Supp 5 (D Minn 1976).

[20] *Id* 10.

[21] 618 F2d 693 (10th Cir 1980).

bureau a consumer report in order to embarrass and discredit him in the eyes of the public, especially those of his coworkers and brother union members, in violation of the Act. The district court dismissed the complaint for failure to state a claim, reasoning that the Act applies only if the relationship between the person requesting information from a credit reporting agency and the individual subject of the report is a consumer relationship. Since there was no *consumer relationship,* there was no *consumer report.* The Tenth Circuit reversed the district court's decision. The court did not focus, as did the district court, on the purpose of the party requesting the information. Citing the Act's definition of a consumer report, which stated that the relevant information must be "used or expected to be used *or collected* in whole or in part for the purpose of serving as a factor" in the extension of credit, the Tenth Circuit focused on the beliefs of the Credit Reporting Agency, the party that *collects* the information, and not on the *user* of the report. If, at the time the information was collected, the agency expected or believed it to be used for a permissible purpose, the release of the information would be a consumer report, even if the request for information was made under a false pretense of a proper purpose. In short, as one can see, when the information on an individual consumer is released by a credit reporting agency on the expectation or belief that the information will be used for a proper purpose under the Act, then the information is a consumer report, regardless of whether the report *is* so used or not.

Prior to *Heath,* the Ninth Circuit in *Hansen v Morgan* [22] already had held that a consumer report under the FCRA existed if four conditions were met:

1. It was a written communication of information
2. By a consumer reporting agency
3. Bearing on the person's creditworthiness, credit standing, or credit capacity, and
4. Which was used or *expected* to be used or collected in whole or in part for the purpose of establishing the person's credit eligibility for credit transactions

As the court pointed out: "Since the credit bureau knew nothing of the requesting party's purpose, it must have supplied this information with the expectation that it would be used for purposes consistent both with the Act (FCRA) and with the credit bureau's membership contract."[23]

§3.19 —Obligations of Credit Reporting Agencies to Maintain Reasonable Procedures

The main obligation imposed upon credit reporting agencies is phrased in procedural terms. Section 1681a of the Act requires that consumer reporting

---

[22] 582 F2d 1214 (9th Cir 1978).
[23] *Id* 1218.

agencies "maintain reasonable procedures designed to avoid violation of section 1681c (prohibiting the reporting of obsolete information) and to limit the furnishing of consumer reports to the purposes listed under section 1681b (concerning permissible purpose for consumer reports) of this title." These procedures also require that "prospective users of the information identify themselves and certify the permissible purpose and use for which the information is sought. If the consumer reporting agency has reasonable grounds for believing that the report will not be used for a proper purpose then it may not supply the report."[24] Section 1681e(b) also requires that "[w]henever a consumer reporting agency prepares a consumer report it shall follow reasonable procedures to assure maximum possible accuracy of the information concerning the individual about whom the report relates."

This section has been vigorously litigated because plaintiffs alleging false statements in a consumer report usually claim a violation of this section despite its being phrased in strictly procedural terms. The plaintiff's contention is that the violation of the section by failing to maintain reasonable procedures directly resulted in the false information being included in the consumer report.[25]

One case on this issue reads like a horror story. In *Thompson v San Antonio Retail Merchants Association*,[26] the plaintiff, William Douglas Thompson III, was denied credit by Gulf Oil Corporation and Montgomery Ward because of an inaccurate credit report released by San Antonio Retail Merchants Association (SARMA). The defendant, SARMA, used a computerized system that depended heavily upon information fed into SARMA's files by subscribers. Through the use of a computerized automatic capturing feature, SARMA would capture information fed by the subscriber from its own computer terminals into SARMA's central computer. In order to gain access to the credit history of a particular consumer, the subscriber had to feed the consumer's identifying information from its own computer terminal into SARMA's central computer. SARMA's computer then searched its own records and displayed on the subscriber's terminal the credit history file that matched the consumer's identity. When the subscriber accepted the information, SARMA's central computer automatically captured into the consumer's file any information from the subscriber's terminal that the central file did not have.

The social security number is the most important identifying item. The automatic capturing feature may accept erroneous information fed in by subscribers if no adequate auditing procedures are built into the system. In *Thompson*, the computer erroneously reported to the subscribers inquiring about the plaintiff the bad credit history of another consumer, a William Daniel Thompson, Jr. (the plaintiff's name being William Douglas Thompson III).

The file became a potpourri of information on both Thompsons. The social

---

[24] 15 USC §1681e(a).

[25] P. Rasor, Consumer Finance Law 33 (1985).

[26] 682 F2d 509 (5th Cir 1982).

security number of one Thompson became that of the other, and so with the wives' names and those of their respective employers.

All the time the plaintiff was denied credit, he thought that it was because of a previous felony conviction for burglary. He became very depressed, as he had been trying to straighten out his life. Not until almost a year later did his wife learn that the reason for the plaintiff's adverse credit rating was a bad debt at a jewelry store with which the plaintiff never had done business. The credit bureau promised to straighten the file, but continued to mail letters intended for the plaintiff in the name of William David Thompson, Jr. The court found that the defendant violated §1681e(b) of the Act for negligent failure to maintain reasonable procedures to insure maximum possible accuracy of the information.

The court pointed out that the Act does not impose strict liability for inaccuracy in credit reporting, but only a reasonable procedure standard. Under this standard, the court found that the defendant committed two acts of negligence: first, failure to exercise reasonable care in programming the computer to capture information into a file automatically without an adequate procedure to foster accuracy; and second, failure to employ a system which would recognize the disparity in social security numbers between the two Thompsons. Thus, the court affirmed the district court's award of $10,000 for humiliation and mental distress to the plaintiff, although no out-of-pocket actual damages were incurred.

The determination of what constitutes *reasonable procedure to assure accuracy* involves a balancing test. This balancing test requires a court to weigh the inaccuracy of the information against the availability of more accurate information and the burden of providing such information. As a court pointed out, "the statute does not require maximum possible accuracy, only that the consumer reporting agency must follow *reasonable procedure* to assure such accuracy [emphasis in original]."[27]

A mere showing of inaccuracy is not enough to shift the burden of proof to the defendant on the issue of the reasonableness of procedures to insure accuracy. The plaintiff must at least "present some evidence from which a trier of facts can infer that the consumer reporting agency failed to follow reasonable procedures in preparing a credit report."[28] In other words, the credit reporting agencies are not strictly liable for inaccurate reports. *McPhee v Chilton Corp* [29] illustrates this point. In this case, the plaintiff filed a petition in bankruptcy. Two months later, the plaintiff asked the bankruptcy court to dismiss the petition after the plaintiff fully paid all the creditors. Two years after these events took place, the plaintiff applied for a loan, and the creditor asked for a consumer report. The report did mention the petition in bankruptcy, but failed to note the dismissal of the petition and the payment of debts.

The court held that the agency was not liable. The court had this to say: "To

---

[27] Alexander v Moore & Assocs, Inc, 553 F Supp 948, 952 (D Haw 1982).

[28] Stewart v Credit Bureau, Inc, 734 F2d 47, 51 (DC Cir 1987).

[29] 468 F Supp 494 (D Conn 1978).

require an agency independently to update information after receipt and verification would burden commercial dealings beyond any currently required legislative mandate."[30]

On the other hand, in *Miller v Credit Bureau, Inc,*[31] the plaintiff was denied credit because the consumer report indicated that the plaintiff had failed to pay a bill. The report, however, failed to disclose that the bill was only $12, and that the plaintiff disputed that amount. The court maintained that the defendant violated the Act. "The Fair Credit Reporting Act itself does not attempt to set forth any specific elements of a reasonable procedure. If the Act is to have any meaning at all, however, it must be read to require credit agencies to do more than merely collect and distribute credit information." The court then took issue with the procedure the defendant used to gather and check information. No checking was done as to the accuracy of the information until a consumer complained. Thus, the court seems to impose a duty to verify information whenever possible.

Under some circumstances, the methods of gathering information are so outrageous that they by themselves establish a prima facie case of unreasonable procedures. *Millstone v O'Hanlon Reports, Inc,*[32] involves the methods used by an investigative reporting agency.

The evidence showed that employees of the defendant usually spent anywhere from 10 minutes to one-half hour gathering the information. In this particular case, the agent contacted four neighbors of the plaintiff in Washington. One refused to speak to the agent, and two said they knew of nothing firsthand and did not want to get involved. Thus, all the data in the report was gathered from one single neighbor, who was now deceased. All told, about one-half hour was spent preparing the report for which the agent was entitled to, and did receive, $1.85. The evidence also showed that an average agent in the defendant's firm prepared 140 to 160 reports every two weeks. The court concluded that the procedures mentioned were not reasonable.

> Defendant's methods of reporting on consumers' credit backgrounds as shown at trial were so slipshod and slovenly as to not even approach the realm of reasonable standards of care as imposed by the statute. Defendant's reporting methods were so wanton as to be clearly willful non-compliance with the Fair Credit Reporting Act in the eyes of this court.[33]

---

[30] *Id* 498.

[31] [1969-1973 Transfer Binder] Consumer Credit Guide (CCH) ¶99,173 (DC Sup 1972).

[32] 383 F Supp 269 (ED Mo 1974), *affd,* 528 F2d 829 (8th Cir 1976).

[33] *Id* 275.

§3.20 —Duty of Disclosure to Consumers

One of the purposes of the Act is to keep consumers informed about the information being used to prepare credit reports concerning them. In order to accomplish this purpose, the Act contains three sections which outline the information that consumer reporting agencies must disclose to consumers.

First, §1681g requires that, upon request by the consumer, the consumer reporting agency must disclose the contents of the consumer's file. The disclosure is not total, however. It need only encompass "the nature and substance of the information in the file," leaving out medical information.[34]

The reason medical information is left out is because there is fear that the consumer would not understand the medical terms. California has remedied this problem by allowing release of medical information to a doctor named by the consumer.[35] The credit reporting agency must also disclose the source of all the information appearing on the consumer report, unless the information was acquired for, and used in, an investigative report. Even in the latter case, the source of the information may be obtained in discovery.

Disclosure of the recipients of any consumer report is also required.[36] If the reports were for employment purposes, then every report supplied in the two years preceding the request must be furnished, while credit reports for any other reason supplied in the previous six months must be provided.[37] In any event, information obtained or reports supplied prior to the enactment of the Act do not fall under the requirements of this section.[38]

Second, §1681d deals exclusively with disclosure concerning investigative consumer reports. Subsection (a) of §1681d requires that a consumer be informed that an investigative consumer report is being prepared concerning his character, general reputation, personal characteristics, and mode of living. This information must be provided not more than three days after the report is first requested.[39] This information is not necessary if the report is to be used for employment purposes for which the consumer has not specifically applied.[40] Furthermore, the Act requires that the *procurer* of the investigative consumer report, or someone who causes the report to be produced, disclose to the consumer the nature and scope of the investigation requested upon written request by the consumer.[41]

Finally, §1681h stipulates the conditions for compliance with the Act's disclosure requirements. The disclosures must be made during normal

---

[34] 15 USC §1681g(a)(1).

[35] Cal Civ Code §1786.10 (West 1985).

[36] 15 USC §1681g(a)(2).

[37] 15 USC §1681g(a)(3).

[38] 15 USC §1681g(b).

[39] 15 USC §1681d(a)(1).

[40] 15 USC §1681d(a)(2).

[41] 15 USC §1681d(b).

business hours and on reasonable notice.[42] The consumer may receive the disclosure in person after showing proper identification, or by telephone if the consumer has already made a written request containing proper identification and has prepaid, or been charged directly for, the cost of the call.[43] The consumer reporting agency is required to have trained personnel on duty to explain the disclosure information to the consumer,[44] and in receiving the disclosure, the consumer may be accompanied by one other person. The agency may require the consumer to furnish a written statement which grants the agency permission to discuss the consumer's file in this person's presence.[45]

§3.21   —Obligations of the Credit Reporting Agency in Case of Disputed Accuracy

The agency must reinvestigate and make any necessary correction if the consumer asserts that the information in the report is inaccurate.[46] If the reinvestigation does not resolve the disputed accuracy, the consumer may file a brief statement to set forth the nature of the dispute. The agency may limit the consumer to 100 words if it assists the consumer in writing a clear summary of the dispute.[47] The disputed item must be incorporated in any report released to a user.[48] If the reinvestigation yields inaccurate information, or an information item whose accuracy can no longer be verified, the agency must delete that information.[49] The consumer has the right to request the agency to inform any recipient who already has received the report within two years for purpose of employment, or six months for any other purpose, of the deletion or of the explanatory statement.[50]

§3.22   —Obligations of Users of Consumer Reports

The term *user* is not defined in the Act. The absence of the definition has caused litigation over whether a given individual or institution is subject to the obligations and liabilities the Act imposes upon *users.*

In most cases, the *user* is the ultimate recipient of the credit report who needs the data provided by the reporting agency. The courts, however, have

---

[42] 15 USC §1681h(a).

[43] 15 USC §1681h(b)(1) and (2).

[44] 15 USC §1681h(c).

[45] 15 USC §1681h(d).

[46] 15 USC §1681i(a).

[47] 15 USC §1681i(b).

[48] 15 USC §1681i(c).

[49] 15 USC §1681i(a).

[50] 15 USC §1681i(d).

expanded the scope of the definition to cover persons who obtain the consumer report, not necessarily the persons who need it.

The court in *Hansen v Morgan*, [51] applied the term *user* to an intermediary who obtained a consumer credit report for use by another person. Likewise, in *Booth v TRW Credit Data*,[52] the court held that the term *user* refers not only to the ultimate destination of a credit report, but also includes the person who acquires it for another.

The law treats users of general consumer reports and users of investigative consumer reports differently. Since an investigative consumer report might be more damaging to the consumer's character and general reputation, and because it digs more into the private life of the consumer, the law singles out the investigative consumer report for special treatment.

Dealing with consumer reports generally, the obligations of the user arise only when the user, based on the adverse information in the report, either denies credit or increases the cost of credit to the consumer. In such a case, the user of the consumer report must advise the consumer of the adverse information and supply to the consumer the name and address of the consumer reporting agency making the report.[53]

If the user requests an investigative consumer report, the user must disclose to the consumer that such report was requested. The user must inform the consumer of the consumer's right to request disclosure of the nature and scope of the investigation.[54] If the report sought is to be used for employment purposes, these disclosures need not be made.

In *Carroll v Exxon Co, USA*,[55] the user did not make the required disclosures to the consumer when denying credit. The defendant contended that it did not violate the Act, since denial of credit was not based on information contained in the report. Rather, credit was denied because of the lack of information regarding the consumer's credit. The court held that, still, the user must disclose, contemporaneously upon notification of denial of credit, the name and address of the reporting agency. Similarly, in *Fischl v General Motors Acceptance Corp*,[56] the Fifth Circuit reversed the district court's holding that the defendant did not violate the Act because credit was not refused based on information in the report but simply for what was *not* in the report. The Fifth Circuit decided that the user's disclosure duty is triggered whenever credit for personal purposes is denied, based either wholly or partly upon information, whether or not wholly derogatory, that is traceable to the credit report. Thus, even if the consumer has an excellent credit report, though not meeting the user's own standard, the user still has to comply with the mandated disclosures.

---

[51] 582 F2d 1214 (9th Cir 1978).

[52] 557 F Supp 6 (ED Pa 1982).

[53] 15 USC §1681m(a).

[54] 15 USC §1681d(a)(b).

[55] 434 F Supp 557 (ED La 1977).

[56] 708 F2d 143 (5th Cir 1983).

§3.23   —Civil Liability

Consumer reporting agencies and report users who fail to comply with the provisions of the Fair Credit Reporting Act may be subject to civil liability, discussed in this section, and criminal liability, covered in **§3.24.** Civil liability may be imposed for willful noncompliance or negligent noncompliance. A consumer who is successful in a cause of action against a consumer reporting agency or user of information for willful noncompliance may recover:

> 1. Actual damages sustained by the consumer as a consequence of the defendant's failure
> 2. Punitive damages as the court may allow
> 3. Costs of the action and reasonable attorneys' fees as determined by the court[57]

If noncompliance is simply negligent, the plaintiff can recover actual damages, attorneys' fees, and costs of the action, but not punitive damages.[58]

The line between *willful* and *negligent* is not always clear. In *Carrol v Exxon Co,*[59] the court found the noncompliance *willful* simply because the user, when denying credit to the plaintiff, did not observe the procedures outlined in the Act. Specifically, the oil company failed to disclose the reasons for its denial and the name and address of the credit reporting agency.

However, the court in *Collins v Retail Credit Co*[60] seems to require more for *willfulness.* In this case, the court awarded $50,000 punitive damages for "willful" conduct not simply because the defendant engaged in "haphazard" investigation procedures, but because it also failed to disclose to the plaintiff the nature and substance of all the adverse information on file on the plaintiff. Further, it refused to honor the plaintiff's request to reinvestigate. Under *Collins,* nonobservance of the required procedures is not enough for a finding of "willful" conduct.

Actual damages covers anything from recovery for out-of-pocket losses to recovery for mental anguish, sleeplessness, and nervousness,[61] and even future damages.[62] Punitive damages may be ordered even without proof of actual damages.[63]

Only consumer reporting agencies and users are subject to civil liability. A person who provides information on a consumer's credit rating may not be a consumer reporting agency governed by the Act. It has been held that an FBI agent who provides incorrect information on a consumer to a bank, when, on

---

[57] 15 USC §1681n.

[58] 15 USC §1681o.

[59] 434 F Supp 557 (DC La 1977).

[60] 410 F Supp 924 (ED Mich 1976).

[61] Millstone v O'Hanlon Reports, Inc, 383 F Supp 269 (ED Mo 1974), *affd,* 528 F2d 829 (8th Cir 1976).

[62] Bryant v TRW, Inc, 487 F Supp 1234 (DC Mich 1980).

[63] Ackerley v Credit Bureau, Inc, 385 F Supp 658 (DC Wyo 1974).

the basis of such information, the bank denies credit to the consumer, is not liable under the Act because the FBI is not a *consumer reporting agency*.[64] Also, a department store which supplies wrong information on a consumer to a credit bureau is neither a *user* nor a *consumer reporting agency* liable under the Act.[65]

§3.24 —Criminal Liability

The Act imposes criminal liability in two situations. First, any officer or employee of a consumer reporting agency who knowingly and willingly provides information concerning the consumer from the agency's file to a person not authorized to receive that information shall incur a maximum fine of $5,000 or a maximum of one year's imprisonment or both.[66] Second, a person who knowingly and willfully obtains information on a consumer from a consumer reporting agency under false pretenses shall also be fined a maximum of $5,000 or imprisoned for not more than one year or both.[67]

The wording of these sections does not seem to indicate that they provide a civil cause of action for the consumer. However, the Ninth Circuit has held that violations of these sections give rise to a civil cause of action. In *Hansen v Morgan*,[68] the defendants argued that §1681q, penalizing the person who obtains information on the consumer under false pretenses, was intended to protect the consumer reporting agency required by statute to institute reasonable reporting procedures to protect the privacy of the consumer and, therefore, the consumer has no standing to sue under it. The Ninth Circuit rejected this argument as a misreading of the Act. The court reasoned that the FCRA was designed to protect not consumer reporting agencies, but consumers themselves. The prohibition against obtaining a consumer report under false pretenses is a provision of the Act, and the violation of it forms a basis for civil liability under the Act.

§3.25 —Administrative Enforcement

Unless enforcement of the Act is specifically committed to some other federal agency, the Federal Trade Commission has primary responsibility for enforcing the Act. Violation of any provision of the Act constitutes an unfair or deceptive act or practice under §5(a) of the Federal Trade Commission Act. The FTC has procedural, investigative, and enforcement powers with respect to any consumer reporting agency or person subject to the provisions of the Act. To enforce the Act, the FTC may:

---

[64] Ricci v Key Bancshares, Inc, 768 F2d 456 (1st Cir 1985).
[65] Rush v Macy's, Inc, 596 F Supp 1540 (DC Fla 1984).
[66] 15 USC §1681r.
[67] 15 USC §1681q.
[68] 582 F2d 1214 (9th Cir 1978).

1. Issue procedural rules to enforce compliance with the requirements of the Act
2. Require the filing of reports and the production of documents
3. Demand the appearance of witnesses

Again, it is important for the practitioner to consult the FTC's interpretation of the Act as well as its statement of the rules of compliance set forth in 5 CCH Consumer Credit Guide, ¶11,301.

§3.26 —Preemption of State Laws

State laws are preempted in two ways. First, in order to encourage consumer reporting agencies to comply with the disclosure provisions of the Act, §1681h(e) of the Act provides that any information disclosed to the consumer could not serve as a basis for an action under state law for defamation, invasion of privacy, or negligence against consumer reporting agencies, users of information, or persons who furnish information to consumer reporting agencies. Thus, the consumer's substantive rights created by the Act are controlled by federal law and not by state law. Federal preemption does not apply, however, to a consumer's action for false information furnished with malice or willful intent to injure the consumer.[69] In other words, in a defamation action based on information disclosed under the Act, the defendant enjoys a qualified immunity which the plaintiff can overcome only by a showing of the defendant's malice or willful intent to injure the plaintiff.[70]

Second, state laws concerning collection, distribution, or use of information on consumers are preempted by the provisions of the Act if they are inconsistent with any provision of the Act, and then only to the extent of that inconsistency.[71] Thus, state laws still apply if they are not inconsistent. As in most federal consumer protection statutes, *inconsistency* should be interpreted as affording less protection to the consumer.

§3.27   Against Discrimination in Granting Credit: The Equal Credit Opportunity Act (ECOA)

It is a fact that applicants for credit often are denied credit based on considerations unrelated to creditworthiness. Those considerations pertain to sex, race, marital status, age, national origin, and other similar factors.[72]

---

[69] 15 USC §1681h(e).

[70] Thorton v Equifax, Inc, 619 F2d 700 (8th Cir), *cert denied*, 449 US 835 (1980).

[71] 15 USC §1681t.

[72] *See* S Rep No 589, 94th Cong, 2d Sess 6 (1976), *reprinted in* 96 US Code Cong & Admin News 403.

In 1974, Congress enacted the Equal Credit Opportunity Act[73] (ECOA) with the express purpose that consumers should be evaluated in a nondiscriminatory manner when applying for credit. Originally, the Act aimed at ending discrimination by creditors against credit applicants based on sex and marital status only. Two years later, in 1976, Congress passed an amendment to ECOA effective March 23, 1977,[74] which expanded the scope of prohibited discriminatory criteria. Besides sex and marital status, the prohibited bases now include race, color, religion, national origin, age, receipt of public assistance, or good faith exercise of rights under the Consumer Credit Protection Act.[75] The Act grants authority to the Federal Reserve Board to implement the Act by enacting appropriate regulations.[76]

Accordingly, the Federal Reserve Board has enacted Regulation B[77] to implement and supplement the Act. Any practitioner should pay particular attention to Regulation B as well as to the Act itself.

§3.28   —Scope of the ECOA

The Act applies to "any aspect of a credit transaction."[78] In spite of the seemingly broad terminology, the Act, and particularly Regulation B, focus not upon all aspects of credit transactions, but upon the extending of credit only.

Credit is a right, granted by a creditor, to:

1. Defer payment of the debt
2. Incur debt and defer its payment
3. Purchase property or services and defer payment[79]

The term *creditor* means "a person who, in the regular course of business, regularly participates in the decision of whether or not to extend credit."[80]

Exactly what constitutes a credit transaction has been subject to some dispute and contrary interpretations. In *Brothers v First Leasing*,[81] the Ninth Circuit held that a consumer lease is within the definition of a credit transaction. The court based its decision to broadly interpret the Act on the overriding national policy against discrimination. One week after the decision in *Brothers*, in an informal staff opinion, the FTC indicated that the ECOA did not cover consumer

---

[73] The Act is codified at 15 USC §1691 *et seq* and became Title VII of the Consumer Credit Protection Act.

[74] Pub L No 94-239, §§7, 8, 90 Stat 255 (Mar 23, 1976).

[75] 15 USC §1691(a).

[76] 15 USC §1691b(a).

[77] 12 CFR §202.

[78] 15 USC §1691(a).

[79] 12 CFR §202.2(j).

[80] 12 CFR §202.2(1).

[81] 724 F2d 789 (9th Cir), *cert denied*, 469 US 835 (1984).

leases.[82] Since the FTC's staff opinions are not binding upon the courts, disputes may arise in the future as to what types of credit transactions are covered by the Act.

The scope of the ECOA, however, is clearly broader than the Truth in Lending Act (TILA) in defining the term *creditor*.[83] The ECOA does not require, as does the TILA, that the credit transaction consist of more than four installments, nor that it carry a finance charge. Additionally, the TILA protects only those persons who have been extended *consumer credit*, i.e., credit for "personal, family, household, or agricultural purposes."[84] The ECOA's coverage is broader. It includes credit transactions for other purposes, such as business loans. Thus, a person who applies for a loan to buy a pick-up truck to start a hauling business is not protected by the TILA, but may be protected by certain provisions of the ECOA.[85]

§3.29   —Transactions Exempted from the ECOA

The Federal Reserve Board has excluded, wholly or partially, certain credit transactions from the ECOA's scope. These are:

1. Public utility credit
2. Securities credit
3. Incidental credit defined as extensions of credit which are not made pursuant to the terms of a credit card account, not subject to a finance charge, and not payable by agreement in more than four months
4. Business credit, i.e., extension of credit primarily for business or commercial, including agricultural, purposes
5. Credit extended to a government[86]

Note that the above exempt transactions are not completely outside of the scope of the Act. They may be nearly totally exempt, such as credit involving government, but they can be simply partly exempted, with certain provisions of the Act still applying. The practitioner in this field should consult Regulation B to get a more exact view of the precise character of the exempt transactions, to see what kind of inquiry a creditor should undertake when dealing with a particular exempt transaction.

---

[82] FTC Staff Op (Feb 1, 1984), *cited in* P. Rasor, Consumer Finance Law 107 (1985).

[83] 15 USC §1602(f); Regulation Z, 12 CFR §226.2(a)(17).

[84] 15 USC §1602(h); Regulation Z, 12 CFR §226.2(a).

[85] *See* National Consumer Law Center, Consumer Credit and Sales Legal Practice Series, Equal Credit Opportunity Act 9 (1982).

[86] 12 CFR §202.3.

§3.30 —Persons Protected under the ECOA

The Act applies to any applicant for credit.[87] *Applicant* is defined as "any person who applies to a creditor directly for an extension, renewal, or continuation of credit, or applies to a creditor indirectly by use of an existing credit plan for an amount exceeding a previously established credit limit."[88]

Regulation B given an even broader definition. *Applicant* includes "any person who requests or who has received an extension of credit."[89] Thus, a person may have a cause of action under the ECOA, even though that person has not made a formal request for credit according to the creditor's usual procedures.[90]

Under Regulation B, an applicant must be a person who is primarily liable for repayment. Persons secondarily liable, such as a guarantor, surety, or endorser, are not applicants having a cause of action under the Act except with respect to the Act's prohibition against requiring the signature of the spouse of a qualified applicant.[91]

The ECOA and Regulation B's requirements may be examined with relation to the taking of applications for credit, the evaluation of the applications for credit, the creditor's rules in extending credit, and notification of the action taken by the creditor.

§3.31 —The Taking of Applications for Credit

The ECOA and Regulation B state that a creditor cannot use the *prohibited bases* when considering an application for credit. As stated above, *prohibited bases* include race, color, religion, national origin, sex, marital status, or age, provided that the applicant has the capacity to enter into a binding contract.[92] The *prohibited bases* include further the fact that all or part of the applicant's income derives from any public assistance program, or the fact that the applicant has in good faith exercised any right under the Consumer Credit Protection Act or any state law upon which an exemption has been granted by the Federal Reserve Board.[93] When taking an application for credit, a creditor may not make any oral or written statement with a prohibited basis that would have the effect of discouraging applicants for credit.[94]

---

[87] 15 USC §1691(a).

[88] 15 USC §1691a(b).

[89] 12 CFR §202.2(e).

[90] *See* Cragin v First Fed Savs & Loans Assoc, 498 F Supp 379 (D Nev 1980).

[91] 12 CFR §§202.2(e), .7(d).

[92] 15 USC §1691(a)(1)(2) & (3); 12 CFR §202.2(3).

[93] 15 USC §1691(a)(1)(2) & (3); 12 CFR §2022(3).

[94] 12 CFR §202.5(a).

Marital Status

A creditor may not request any information concerning the spouse or former spouse of an applicant unless:

1. That spouse will be permitted to use the account
2. The spouse will be contractually liable on the account
3. The applicant is relying on the spouse's income as the basis for repayment of the credit requested
4. The applicant resides in a community property state, and community state laws are involved
5. The applicant is relying on alimony, child support, or separate maintenance payments from a spouse or former spouse, as the basis for repayment of the credit requested.[95]

Sex

The Act prohibits a creditor from inquiring into the sex of the applicant. However, a creditor may request a title (Mr., Mrs., Ms.), provided that the credit application discloses that the designation of such a title is optional.[96]

Child Bearing or Child Rearing

A creditor may not inquire about the applicant's birth control practices or the applicant's intention concerning child bearing or rearing. However, the creditor may inquire as to the number and ages of the applicant's dependents, provided that such request is made without reference to any other prohibited basis.[97]

Race, Color, Religion, National Origin

Except for the applicant's permanent residence or immigration status, there is a complete ban on inquiry about the applicant's race, color, religion, or national origin.[98]

Summary

All these rules are not easy to interpret in practice. The complexity of the rules stems from the fact that Congress has to strike a balance between the need to protect the consumer against discriminatory practices and the legitimate needs of the creditor to bring in the relevant factors in order to determine the applicant's creditworthiness. As an example, inquiry about marital status may be discriminatory per se, but it *would* be a legitimate inquiry if the marital status

---

[95] 12 CFR §202.5(c)(i) & (2).
[96] 12 CFR §202.5(d)(3).
[97] 12 CFR §202.5(d)(4).
[98] 12 CFR §202.5(d)(5).

has an impact on the applicant's ability to pay, as exists in a community property jurisdiction.

§3.32 —The Evaluation of Credit

As a general rule, a creditor, in evaluating the application for credit, may consider any information relevant to the applicant's creditworthiness. However, the creditor may not use the information to discriminate against an applicant on a prohibited basis.

In interpreting this general rule, Regulation B indicates that Congress intended to apply the *effects test* concept,[99] enunciated by the Supreme Court when dealing with employment cases such as *Griggs v Duke Power Co,*[100] and *Albemarle Paper Co v Moody.*[101] The *effects test* is a judicial doctrine developed by the Supreme Court under Title VII of the Civil Rights Act of 1964.[102]

In *Griggs v Duke Power Co,* black employees of the defendant Duke Power Company challenged the company's requirement of a high school diploma or passing of an intelligence test as a condition of employment or transfer to other jobs at the defendant's plant. Section 703(a) of Title VII of the Civil Rights Act of 1964, similar to the ECOA, makes it unlawful to consider race, color, religion, sex, or national origin as a basis for employment. Section 703(h) authorizes the use of any professionally developed ability test, provided that it is not designed or used to discriminate.

The Supreme Court held that the diploma or intelligence test requirement, though neutral on its face, had the *effect* of excluding blacks at a substantially higher proportion than whites. Furthermore, the test was not substantially related to satisfactory performance. As a result, such requirements are prohibited, regardless of the employer's lack of discriminatory intent.[103]

In *McDonnell Douglas Corp v Green,*[104] the court clarified the problem of burden of proof in a Title VII action. The complainant in order to succeed in an employment case must establish a prima facie case of discrimination. In *McDonnell,* the plaintiff, a black mechanic, established a prima facie case by showing that he belonged to the protected class, that he was qualified for the job and that his performance was satisfactory, and that he was rejected in spite of his qualifications. Once the prima facie case is made, the burden of proof then shifts to the defendant to show that the reason for rejection was legitimate, i.e., nondiscriminatory, and that people in a nonprotected class, such as whites, would likewise be discharged for engaging in the same conduct.

Applying this test in the credit area will be more complex than applying it

---

[99] 12 CFR §202.6 Note 2.
[100] 401 US 424 (1971).
[101] 422 US 405 (1975).
[102] 42 USC §2000e *et seq.*
[103] 401 US at 429-33.
[104] 411 US 792 (1973).

in the employment area. Different creditors may have different standards of qualification for credit. The test therefore cannot be as cleanly objective.[105]

The Federal Reserve Board has tried to explain how the *effects test* could be used in the case of credit extension as follows:

> The Board interprets the application of an "effects test" to the credit area to mean that the use of certain information in determining creditworthiness, even though such information is not specifically proscribed by proposed 202.6(b), may violate the amended Act if the use of that information has the effect of denying credit to a class of persons protected by the amended act at a substantially higher rate than persons not of that class, unless the creditor is able to establish that the information has a manifest relationship to creditworthiness. Even then, if an aggrieved applicant could show that a creditor could have used a less discriminatory method which would serve the creditor's need to evaluate creditworthiness as well as the challenged method, a violation may be found.[106]

The FRB's Official Staff Commentary explains further:

> The Act and Regulation may prohibit a creditor practice that is discriminatory in effect because it has a disproportionately negative impact on a prohibited basis even though the creditor has no intent to discriminate, and the practice appears neutral on its face, unless the creditor practice meets a legitimate business need that cannot reasonably be achieved as well by means that are less disparate in their impact.[107]

The FBR's staff provides this example: Requiring a minimum income which is neutral on its face could have the effect of discriminating against women and minority applicants. However, if the creditor can demonstrate that there is a relationship between the income requirements and creditworthiness for the level of credit involved, the use of *that* income requirement would be legitimate. This test, even as formulated, is not always easy to apply when it is complicated by a creditor's scoring system.

§3.33   —Scoring Systems

When evaluating an applicant's creditworthiness, the creditor may use the judgmental system, based on human judgment, or a scoring system. Using the judgmental system, the creditor will analyze a credit application in light of the creditor's own prior experience and institutional guidelines. Judgmental systems may have flaws, including imperfect recollection of past experience,

---

[105] *See* Baer, *The Equal Credit Opportunity Act and the "Effects Test"*, 95 Banking LJ 241, 256-57 (1978).

[106] 41 Fed Reg 29874 (July 20, 1976).

[107] 12 CFR §202.6(a) and Official Staff Commentary.

and the institutional guidelines may not be always valid without extensive research and verification.

A credit scoring system purports to provide an objective analysis of creditworthiness based on a variety of factors. The various data pertaining to creditworthiness are stored in computer banks and used to project repayment or creditworthiness probabilities. The projections are formulated into a point system which is individually applied to each piece of information supplied on the credit application. The system is based on an analysis of the performance of the creditor's past applicants.

Each factor, (e.g., age, time at present address, age of auto, bank accounts, references, major credit cards, etc.) is given a score, and the total of the scores either meets or fails to meet a predetermined cutoff point, on the basis of which the creditor will either accept or reject the application for credit.[108]

Regulation B accepts the scoring system as a legitimate method for evaluating creditworthiness, provided such a system qualifies as "an empirically derived, demonstrably and statistically sound, credit scoring system."[109] Regulation B gives the following requirements for a scoring system to qualify under the above test:

> 1. The system must be based on data that are derived from an empirical comparison of sample groups or other populations of creditworthy and noncreditworthy applicants within a reasonable preceding period of time.
> 2. It must be developed for the purpose of evaluating the creditworthiness of applicants with respect to the legitimate business interests of the creditor
> 3. It must be developed and validated objectively and scientifically according to accepted statistical principles and methodology[110]

The effects test and the credit scoring system were at issue in *Cherry v Amoco Oil Co.*[111] In this case, Amoco Oil utilized a computerized scoring system to evaluate credit applications. The Amoco system uses 38 factors in scoring each application. One of them is the United States Postal Service zip code area. The plaintiff was a white woman residing in a predominantly nonwhite residential area of Atlanta. Her zip code area was given the lowest rate in the Amoco System. The evidence showed that had she lived in an area whose zip code was accorded a higher score, she would have been granted a credit card. The plaintiff asserted that Amoco's use of zip code ratings was the use of information based on a prohibited basis (race).

The court held that under the *effects test* rule, the plaintiff failed to make out a prima facie case. The court found that she failed to show that the zip code ratings tend to adversely affect black applicants disproportionately. All that it

---

[108] *See* Hsia, *Credit Scoring and the Equal Credit Opportunity Act*, 30 Hastings LJ 371 (1978).

[109] 12 CFR §202.2(p).

[110] *Id.*

[111] 490 F Supp 1026 (ND Ga 1980).

shows is that the system used, taking into account the zip code, tends to reject a disproportionate number of persons living in some predominantly black areas. The court took judicial notice of the housing pattern in Atlanta, and concluded that the low-rated zip codes in the Amoco system were not all predominantly black, and, therefore, the zip code factor was not suspect per se.

For the plaintiff to have made a case, she would have had to have shown a pool of qualified black applicants who fared differently from equally qualified white applicants due solely to the zip code ratings. This is almost impossible for the plaintiff to prove, because race does not appear on the face of any creditor's scoring system.

§3.34 —Role of *Prohibited Bases* in Credit Evaluation

Age

A creditor may not take into account an applicant's age, provided that the applicant is old enough to enter into a binding contract. In a credit scoring system which is valid under Regulation B, a creditor may use an applicant's age as a predictive variable, provided that the age of an elderly applicant, who is defined as 62 or older,[112] is not assigned a negative value in the scoring system. In particular, it is permissible to use the age of an elderly applicant when such age is used as a positive factor determining creditworthiness.

In a judgmental system, a creditor may not take age directly into account in any aspect of the credit transaction. For example, the creditor may not reject an application because the applicant is 60 years old. However, age may be used with other information in order to determine the applicant's creditworthiness. For example, the creditor may consider the applicant's length of time to retirement in order to ascertain whether the applicant's retirement income will support the extension of credit and its repayment schedule.[113] Additionally, a creditor may consider the applicant's age and life expectancy to evaluate the adequacy of any security offered, to see whether the term of the credit would exceed the life expectancy of the applicant, and to determine the cost of realizing on the collateral with respect to the applicant's equity.[114]

Receipt of Public Assistance

In evaluating the credit application, the creditor may not reject an application simply because the applicant's income derives from public assistance. However, public assistance income may be a pertinent element of creditworthiness. For example, the creditor may consider the length of time an applicant will

---

[112] 12 CFR §202.2(o).

[113] 12 CFR §202.6(b)(2) and Official Staff Commentary.

[114] *Id.*

remain eligible for public assistance, or whether the creditor can attach or garnish the applicant's income in case of default.[115]

Child Bearing/Child Rearing

In evaluating creditworthiness, a creditor is prohibited from considering statistics or making assumptions about the likelihood that a person like the applicant or the applicant's spouse will have a certain number of children, and, for that reason, receive diminished or interrupted income in the future.[116]

Telephone Listing

A creditor may not take into account whether there is a telephone listing in the name of the applicant. This is due to the fact that this would result in discrimination against certain protected classes of persons, for example, a wife whose phone is listed under the husband's name. Regulation B, however, allows the creditor to take into account whether there is a telephone in the person's residence.[117]

Income Sources

In evaluating the application, Regulation B prohibits a creditor from excluding or discounting certain incomes such as income derived from part-time employment, annuities, pensions, alimony, child support, or public assistance, which are deemed to be *protected income*. The creditor may, however, evaluate all such incomes as to whether they are consistently made. In evaluating all types of protected income, the creditor must deal with them on an individual basis, by analyzing the individual applicant's actual circumstances, and not on the basis of aggregate statistics derived from a group.[118]

Credit History

If the creditor considers credit history in evaluating the applicant's creditworthiness, the creditor must consider any account in the name of both spouses, and if the applicant so requests, the account report in the name of the applicant's spouse or former spouse, that the applicant can demonstrate reflects the applicant's ability or willingness to repay. Additionally, on request by the applicant, the creditor must consider any information tending to indicate that the credit listing being considered by the creditor does not reflect the applicant's creditworthiness. For example, a creditor must consider information submitted by the applicant which is not reported through a credit bureau, which information is a pertinent element in the applicant's creditworthiness. A creditor may, however, restrict the types of credit history and credit

---

[115] *Id.*

[116] 12 CFR §202.6(b)(3).

[117] 12 CFR §202.6(b)(4).

[118] 12 CFR §202.6(b)(5) and Official Staff Commentary.

references that it will consider, provided that the restrictions are applied to all applicants without regard to any prohibited basis.[119]

Immigration Status

The immigration status of an applicant is a relevant element of the applicant's creditworthiness. In evaluating this element, the creditor may consider whether the applicant is a United States citizen, whether the applicant is a long-time resident, or just a temporary resident, and the applicant's type of visa.[120] This does not amount to discrimination based on national origin, as it legitimately reflects on the applicant's ability or willingness to repay.

Case History

An interesting case dealing with credit evaluation is *Markham v Colonial Mortgage Service Co Associates.*[121] In this case, the District of Columbia Circuit reversed the judgment of a district court granting the defendant's motion for summary judgment. The plaintiffs, who were engaged to be married, were seeking a loan in order to purchase a future home in Washington, D.C. The plaintiffs listed their separate incomes which, added together, satisfied the creditor's standard for creditworthiness. The creditor, however, refused to aggregate their incomes.

The district court's summary judgment in favor of the defendant was based on the conclusion that Illinois law grants creditors greater rights and remedies against married applicants than against unmarried applicants. The DC Circuit refused to see any relevance created by marriage with respect to the obligations of the plaintiffs to repay the debt as joint debtors. Defendant argued that to require it to aggregate the incomes of the plaintiffs would be far-reaching, because then it would be required to aggregate the incomes of all persons who apply for credit as a group. The court of appeals makes it clear that it simply requires the defendant to treat plaintiffs, a couple jointly applying for credit, the same as they would be treated as a married couple. In this case, the DC Circuit may have a strong point in the fact that the plaintiffs, having made a joint application, would have been jointly and severally liable on the debt in any case, married or not married.

§3.35 —Rules in Extending Credit

A creditor may not refuse to extend credit relying on a prohibited basis.[122] Additionally, the creditor may not condition the extension of credit upon certain factors which have no relationship to creditworthiness, but which have the result of discriminating on a prohibited basis.

---

[119] 12 CFR §202.6(b)(6) and Official Staff Commentary.
[120] 12 CFR §202.6(b)(7) and Official Staff Commentary.
[121] 605 F2d 566 (DC Cir 1979).
[122] 12 CFR §202.7.

Designation of Names

A creditor may not condition the extension of credit upon the applicant's use of a certain name on the applicant's account. The applicant is free to use the birth-given first name or surname, the spouse's surname, or a combined surname. The creditor, however, may require that joint applicants designate a single name for purposes of administering the account, not necessarily the husband's name.[123]

Open-End accounts

With respect to an existing open-end account, the creditor may not take any of the following actions on the basis of age, retirement, or a change in the applicant's name or status, unless there is evidence of the applicant's inability or unwillingness to pay due to the change:

1. Require reapplication
2. Change the terms of the account
3. Terminate the account[124]

Cosignatures

The purpose of the rule prohibiting cosignatures is to make sure that the persons protected under the ECOA will not be required to add a cosignature when they are creditworthy in their own right. This is particularly true with married women who, in the past, in order to obtain credit, had to depend on a spouse's willingness to cosign.

There are mitigations, however, to the rule prohibiting the requirement of cosigners. Requiring the cosignature of a spouse or of another person is justified in the following situations:

1. Unqualified applicants: the creditor may require a cosigner, but not necessarily the spouse, if the applicant does not meet the creditor's standard for creditworthiness. The additional party may be a cosigner, guarantor, surety, or the like[125]

2. Joint applicants: the creditor may require the signatures of all the applicants who apply for credit contemporaneously and who are jointly and severally liable on the debt[126]

3. Unsecured credit: When the applicant requests unsecured credit but relies on the property owned jointly with another person to establish creditworthiness, the creditor may require the signature of the other person if the creditor reasonably believes that the person's signature on the instrument is necessary, under state law, to permit the creditor to

---

[123] 12 CFR §202.7(b) and Official Staff Commentary.
[124] 12 CFR §202.7(c).
[125] 12 CFR §202.7(d)(5).
[126] 12 CFR §202.7(d)(1).

ʼreach that property in the event of the applicant's death or default. The creditor's reasonable belief must be supported by a thorough review of applicable state law[127]

4. Community property states: the bank may require that a spouse cosign the instrument if the married applicant resides in a community property state or the property on which the applicant is relying is located in such a state. Even then, the creditor can require the cosignature only if the applicable state law denies the applicant the power to manage or control enough community property to qualify for the credit requested, and the applicant does not have sufficient separate property to qualify for the credit requested, without regard to the community property[128]

5. Secured credit: when a loan is secured by a piece of property, the creditor may require the person, spouse or not, who owns an interest in that property to sign on the credit instrument if the creditor reasonably believes this to be necessary under state law to make that property available to satisfy the debt in the event of the applicant's default[129]

Note that the prohibition against requirement of the spouse's signature applies to business loans as well as consumer loans.[130]

§3.36 —Notification of Action Taken

The most important feature of the ECOA is the requirement that creditors, within a specified time period, must notify rejected applicants of the reasons for rejection. This requirement will force the creditor to act carefully and provide the applicant with the opportunity to correct the credit shortcomings or challenge the creditor's decision.

A creditor has the duty to notify the applicant of the action taken within 30 days after receiving a completed application, whether the action taken is favorable or adverse.[131] The application is considered completed when the creditor has obtained all the information needed to make the decision.[132]

If credit is approved, the decision may be communicated to the applicant in any manner, express or implied. For example, the creditor properly notifies the applicant when it gives the applicant the credit card, money, property, or services requested.[133] If the creditor makes a counteroffer, such as offering less credit or less favorable terms, the creditor must notify the applicant of the

---

[127] 12 CFR §202.7(d)(2).

[128] 12 CFR §202.7(d)(3).

[129] 12 CFR §202.7(d)(4).

[130] 12 CFR §202.3(d).

[131] 12 CFR §202.9(a)(1).

[132] 12 CFR §202.2(f).

[133] 12 CFR §202.9(a)(1) and Official Staff Commentary.

adverse action within 90 days after making the counteroffer, unless the applicant accepts or uses the credit offered during that time.[134]

The ECOA notice must be in writing and must communicate to the applicant the following:

1. A statement disclosing the ECOA's prohibited bases of discrimination in extending credit
2. The reasons for adverse action
3. A statement that the adverse action was based on the creditor's internal standards or policies and that the applicant failed to achieve the creditor's standards[135]

The Federal Reserve Board has extensively interpreted what would constitute an adequate statement of the reasons given for credit denial. Although the Board states that it does not mandate a specific number of reasons, it does, however, state that disclosure of more than four reasons is not likely to be helpful to the applicant.[136]

In *Fischl v General Motors Acceptance Corp*,[137] GMAC's notification of credit rejection stated: "credit references are insufficient." The Fifth Circuit, relying on the legislative history of the Act, states that the ECOA notice must achieve the purpose of not only protecting the consumer but also of educating the consumer. The consumer must know how and why the consumer's credit status is deficient in order to learn how to remedy it. The court therefore concluded that GMAC's statement, "credit references are insufficient," does not signal the nature of the applicant's deficiency and therefore fails to satisfy the informative purpose of the ECOA. A general statement that the adverse action was based on the internal standards or policies of the credit institution without specifying what these standards or policies are is clearly insufficient.[138]

Oral notifications may be used by small-volume creditors, defined as creditors who received no more than 150 credit applications in the previous year.[139] But the oral notice must disclose that the applicant has the right to written confirmation which, if requested by the applicant, must be given within 30 days of the request.[140]

In the case of multiple applicants, the creditor need provide only one notice to the primary applicant. When a single application is considered by more than one creditor, and the applicant expressly accepts or uses credit offered by one of the creditors, no notification of action taken by the other creditors is required. If no credit is extended, or if the applicant does not accept or use

---

[134] 12 CFR §202.9(a)(1)(iv).

[135] 12 CFR §202.9(a)(2) & (b).

[136] 12 CFR §202.9(b)(2) and Official Staff Commentary.

[137] 708 F2d 143 (5th Cir 1983).

[138] 12 CFR §202.9(b)(2).

[139] 12 CFR §202.9(d).

[140] 12 CFR §202.9(a)(2)(ii).

any credit offered, each creditor taking adverse action must send the ECOA notice to the rejected applicant.[141]

§3.37   —Adverse Action

What constitutes *adverse action* by a creditor is extensively defined by Regulation B.[142] *Adverse action* includes:

1. A refusal to grant credit in substantially the amount and terms requested. No adverse action takes place when the creditor makes a counteroffer and the applicant uses or accepts the new terms
2. A termination of the account or an unfavorable change in an existing account, unless the same action is taken on a substantial number of similar accounts
3. A refusal to approve an account transaction at a point of sale or loan, unless the refusal is a termination or an unfavorable change in the terms of the account that does affect a substantial number of similar accounts, or a refusal to increase the amount of credit available under the account
4. A denial of credit due to applicable law
5. A denial of credit because the creditor does not offer that type of credit[143]

In *O'Dowd v South Central Bell,*[144] the court held that a telephone company's requirement of a $100 deposit under threat of interruption of telephone services after 20 years of such services without deposit was an *adverse action* giving rise to the ECOA notice, since this is a change in the terms of an existing credit arrangement.

On the other hand, in *Sutliff v County Savings & Loan Co,*[145] a bank's interest rate increase charged to all mortgage loans of the same class was not an *adverse action* requiring notice. The court stated that *adverse action,* within the meaning of the ECOA and Regulation B, is action taken which is unique to the plaintiff or which affects only a small number of a class of accounts.

§3.38   —Special Purpose Credit Program

Regulation B contains an *affirmative action* provision that allows a creditor, in certain situations, to consider what the Act normally considers to be prohibited bases in evaluating a consumer's creditworthiness. A creditor is permitted to extend *special purpose credit* to applicants who are eligible under the following credit programs:

---

[141] 12 CFR §202.9(f) & (g).
[142] 12 CFR §202.2(c).
[143] *Id.*
[144] 729 F2d 347 (5th Cir 1984).
[145] 5 Consumer Cred Guide (CCH) ¶96,944 (ND Ohio 1982).

1. Any program expressly authorized by federal or state law to advantage an economically disadvantaged class

2. Any program offered by a not-for-profit organization for the benefit of its members or an economically disadvantaged class

3. Any program offered by a for-profit organization to meet special social needs if the program identifies the class of persons that it seeks to benefit and sets forth its procedures and standards for extending credit, and the class of persons that the program seeks to benefit probably would not receive such credit or would receive it on less favorable terms than are available to other applicants seeking similar credit from the organization[146]

A program will qualify as a *special purpose program* only if it does not discriminate against applicants on a prohibited basis (such as sex or race). However, the program may require its participants to share one or more common characteristics such as sex or race in order to be eligible for credit so long as the purpose of the program is not to exclude the protection afforded by the Act or Regulation B.[147] If the program is not set up in order to evade the Act or Regulation B, a creditor may request and consider information regarding the common characteristic(s) in order to determine the applicant's eligibility. This section, obviously, seeks to avoid penalizing creditors who wish to assist disadvantaged groups rather than discriminate against them by inquiring into the prohibited bases. Therefore, in any special purpose program, the creditor is permitted to request information from an applicant regarding marital status, alimony, child support, and the spouse's financial resources if financial need is one of the criteria under the program.[148]

§3.39 —Relation of ECOA to State Laws

The Act contemplates that the situation will arise where one of the Act's provisions will be inconsistent with state law. In anticipating this problem, Regulation B declares that the Act alters, affects, or preempts only those state laws that are inconsistent with the Act, and then only to the extent of the inconsistency. A state law will never be considered to be inconsistent if it provides *more* protection to the consumer than the Act.[149]

A state law is inconsistent with the Act and Regulation B to the extent that the law:

1. Requires or permits a practice prohibited by the Act and/or Regulation B

---

[146] 12 CFR §202.8(a).
[147] 12 CFR §202.8(b)(2).
[148] 12 CFR §202.8(d).
[149] 12 CFR §202.11.

2. Prohibits the individual extension of consumer credit to both parties to a marriage if each spouse individually and voluntarily applies for such credit

3. Prohibits inquiries or collection of data required to comply with the Act or Regulation B

4. Prohibits considering age or using age in a credit scoring system to favor an applicant

5. Prohibits inquiries necessary to establish special purpose credit programs[150]

Finally, neither the Act nor Regulation B alters any provisions of state property laws, laws relating to the disposition of decedent's estates, or federal or state banking regulations directed only toward insuring the solvency of financial institutions.[151]

§3.40 —Enforcement of the ECOA

The Act spells out specific methods for enforcing its provisions. It also defines the limits and remedies available to individuals who bring sufficient suits against creditors under the Act.

Administrative Enforcement

Numerous federal agencies are empowered to enforce the Act. Depending on the creditor to be regulated, agencies so empowered include the Comptroller of the Currency, Board of Governors of the Federal Reserve System Board, Directors of the Federal Deposit Insurance Corporation (FDIC), Federal Home Loan Bank Board, National Credit Union Administration, Interstate Commerce Commission, the Secretary of Agriculture, Farm Credit Administration, Securities and Exchange Commission, Small Business Administration, and the Secretary of Transportation. However, except to the extent that the administrative enforcement of the Act is specifically assigned to other agencies, the Act is enforced by the Federal Trade Commission (FTC).[152]

Enforcement by the Attorney General

Whenever any agency responsible for the administrative enforcement of the Act is unable to obtain compliance with the Act, the agency may refer the matter to the Attorney General, who may initiate a civil action.[153]

---

[150] 12 CFR §202.11(b).
[151] 12 CFR §202.11(d).
[152] 15 USC §1691c; 12 CFR §202.14(a).
[153] 12 CFR §202.14(b)(3).

Private Enforcement

The Act permits individuals who are injured or affected by a creditor who violates one of its provisions to sue for both actual and punitive damages.[154] In *Anderson v United Finance Co,*[155] the plaintiff sued a finance company after the company refused to allow the plaintiff to receive a loan without her husband's signature on the note. The district court ruled that the Act was not violated, and that, in any event, the plaintiff had not suffered any actual damages. The Court of Appeals for the Ninth Circuit reversed, holding that the defendant violated §202.7(d)(1) of Regulation B for requiring a cosignature when the plaintiff was creditworthy in her own right. Addressing the damages issue, the court ruled that actual damages include out-of-pocket expenses, injury to credit reputation, mental anguish, humiliation, and embarrassment suffered by the plaintiff. However, the court stressed that those damages will not be presumed once a violation is demonstrated. They must be specifically proven.

The Act also allows private plaintiffs to recover punitive damages, and limits these damages to $10,000 in individual suits. In determining the amount of punitive damages, the Act instructs the court to consider, among other factors, the amount of actual damages awarded, the frequency of failure of compliance by the defendant, the defendant's resources, the number of persons adversely affected, and the extent to which the defendant's actions were intentional.[156]

A recent court of appeals decision allowed punitive damages to be assessed against a defendant in the absence of actual damages. In *Fischl v General Motors Acceptance Corp,*[157] the Fifth Circuit stated that "[p]unitive damages may be awarded . . . regardless of proof of actual damages, if the creditor's conduct is adjudged wanton, malicious or oppressive, or if it is deemed to have acted in reckless disregard to the . . . law."[158]

Class Actions

The Act expressly permits class action suits. However, punitive damages are limited to the lesser of $500,000 or 1 per cent of the defendant's net worth.[159]

Attorney Fees and Court Costs

In the case of any successful suit brought by a private individual or a class of persons, attorneys' fees and court costs are added to any damages that the court awards.[160]

---

[154] 15 USC §1691e.
[155] 667 F2d 1274 (9th Cir 1982).
[156] 15 USC §1691e(b).
[157] 708 F2d 143 (5th Cir 1983).
[158] *Id* 148.
[159] 15 USC §1691e(b).
[160] 15 USC §1691e(d).

4

Credit Disclosures

§4.01   Introduction to the Truth in Lending Act

Congress has expressed the belief that consumers can contract meaningfully and in their best interests only if they have all the necessary information about the credit transaction disclosed to them. The Truth in Lending Act (TILA) was enacted with that purpose in mind.[1] TILA is essentially a disclosure statute. Section 101 of the Act provides: "It is the purpose of this subchapter to assure a meaningful disclosure of credit terms so that the consumer will be able to compare more readily the various credit terms available to him and avoid the uniformed use of credit."[2] A further purpose of such disclosure and informed use is to affect the market itself positively. The idea is that consumers' more informed choices will cause suppliers to lower their prices in order to remain competitive, thus benefiting the consumers. Credit itself is a commodity, like goods. Disclosure of the terms of credit should yield the same result as it would in any transaction for commodities. Similarly, hiding the terms of the deal in obfuscating language can give the seller or creditor an advantage. Before TILA was enacted, suppliers of credit used various methods to quote the amount and rate of the finance charge for the credit given.

Some credit suppliers showed only the amount and number of monthly payments that would be due, without giving a yearly percentage rate. Others used the "dollar add-on quotation," an expression of the dollar amount of the finance charge per annum in relation to the total initial loan, that is, a loan

---

[1] The Truth in Lending Act is the popular name for Title I of the Consumer Credit Protection Act of 1968, Pub L No 90-321, 82 Stat 146 (codified at 15 USC §1601 *et seq*). TILA is composed of five parts:

Part 1:   General Provisions
Part 2:   Credit Transactions
Part 3:   Credit Advertising
Part 4:   Credit Billing
Part 5:   Consumer Leases

[2] 15 USC §1601.

finance charge would be stated as "seven dollars per 100 dollars per year." Thus, a three-year loan of $2000 would be subject to a finance charge of $420, or $140 × 3. The annual percentage rate for such a loan, though it *sounds like* 7 per cent, is actually 12.83 per cent. Another method credit suppliers used was the "discount" method; the finance charge would be deducted from the principal of the loan in advance. Then, a charge of $7 per $100 of initial unpaid balance discounted for three years would actually give the consumer the use of only $1580 ($2000 − $420). The annual percentage rate equivalent given the "discounting" would be 16.01 per cent. Many credit grantors who offered revolving credit accounts simply stated a monthly rate of, for instance, 1 1/2 per cent, which, of course, amounts to 18 per cent over the course of a year. A fifth method of obfuscating the true finance charge was to fragment it so that it appeared partly as an add-on or discount rate and partly as a flat fee or extra charge for service or the like.

To see just how far such tactics could go, one may look to the example of a lender in Georgia who charged 8 per cent per year on the discount (to 18 months) taken from the principal, plus a flat fee of 10 per cent on the first $600 of initial unpaid balance. Under his system, a six-month loan of $500 carried a finance charge of $68.14, or an annual rate of 45.33 per cent.[3]

One wonders how consumers down on their luck can find their way through all the calculated smokescreens of all the nice people who want to lend them money! A meaningful comparison between lenders can be made only if all the credit grantors use the same basis for disclosing their finance charges and repayment terms. Thus, TILA requires a uniform quotation of the finance charge under the form of an annual percentage rate.

It would seem, however, that no matter what legislators do, there will always be a degree of naiveté among many consumers, except for the very sophisticated, with regard to the technical machinations. Even with the laws in effect, consumers are still unable to make the best possible choice, especially those consumers who need the most protection. Usually, the disclosure forms given to consumers are still so technical that the unsophisticated consumer is unable even to understand the language used, much less make a meaningful choice based on that language.

Nevertheless, it must be acknowledged that the requirements imposed on the credit business are useful, particularly in providing the consumer with leverage. When creditors sue debtors for default, the defendant debtor may use the Act as a shield, pointing out as a legal defense that the creditor has failed to comply with the disclosure requirements of the Act. The creditor's claim may thereby be reduced or even eliminated altogether under TILA. There is, in addition, a possible maximum $1000 civil penalty provided for in the Act against such a creditor.[4] Furthermore, state laws may subject the creditor to other penalties, including state Truth in Lending statutes incorporating federal law by

---

[3] National Commission on Consumer Finance, Consumer Credit in the United States 169-70 (1972); *see* P. Rasor, Consumer Finance Law 165-67 (1985).

[4] 15 USC §1640(a)(2)(A)(i).

reference. Finally, noncomplying creditors may face a class action suit that could culminate in a one-half million-dollar civil penalty.[5] Thus, TILA has become something of a nightmare for some creditors by making it difficult to sue debtors when the creditors have not complied with the Act. Thus, although consumers are no better at reading the technical language of credit agreements than they were before TILA, there is that element, perhaps even unknown to them, of being able to use TILA as a shield in times of trouble.

§4.02 The Truth in Lending Simplification and Reform Act

The leverage function of TILA lost much of its impact when Congress enacted the TILA Simplification and Reform Act (the Simplification Act). The new Act became fully effective on October 1, 1982.[6] The Simplification Act was more than an amendment; it changed TILA so drastically that many refer to it as the new TILA. Congress's version of TILA was strongly influenced by the Federal Reserve Board (FRB) and its staff. During the 12 years of TILA before Congress passed the Simplification Act, the Federal Reserve Board had enacted some 1,500 rulings to explain, interpret, and implement the old TILA. In the words of the Federal Reserve Board's own assessment, "the result of these multiple interpretations has been to complicate rather than facilitate compliance by laying one set of distinctions on top of another. Rather than resolving questions, this material, in the aggregate, has served to generate further questions."[7]

It seems, however, that the clamor for reforms came more from the leverage function of TILA disclosure requirements than from the complexity of the disclosures themselves.[8] The Simplification Act or "new TILA" changes four main areas of the old law:

1. It simplifies the disclosure requirements imposed upon creditors, especially in closed-end credit, by reducing the amount of information which the creditor must disclose to the consumer

2. Under the new Act, the creditor's liability arises only for noncompliance with substantial disclosure requirements and not for noncompliance with any requirement of the Act

3. The creditor may avoid civil liability altogether through the use of model disclosure forms promulgated by the Federal Reserve Board

4. Administrative enforcement is somewhat strengthened by the new Act

---

[5] 15 USC §1640(a)(2)(B); *see* J. Fonseca, Handling Consumer Credit Cases §8.1, at 296-301 (1986).

[6] Pub L No 96-221, tit 6, 94 Stat 132 (1980).

[7] 46 Fed Reg 28560 (May 27, 1981), §51, Supplemental Information (1981).

[8] J. Fonseca, Handling Consumer Credit Cases §8.1, at 299 (1986).

§4.03   Regulation Z

The legal practitioner who wants to work with TILA must become well acquainted with *Regulation Z*.[9] The Act empowers the Federal Reserve Board to interpret the Act by enacting rules and regulations in order to implement it. Under the old TILA, it was the Federal Reserve Board's practice to publish opinion letters, or official staff interpretations, one after another. These accumulated to create a morass of legal language and interpretation that caused more litigation than it avoided. Under the new TILA, there is only one opinion on Regulation Z, and the required procedures under the regulation are much simpler. It is necessary to be very familiar with Regulation Z, for the United States Supreme Court has shown great deference to the Federal Reserve Board in its interpretation of the Act.

An example of this deference is provided in the Supreme Court case of *Ford Motor Co v Milhollin*.[10] The case dealt with the old TILA, on the question of whether unearned interest charges accruing in the event of accelerated payment due to default must always be disclosed on the front page of a contract for extension of closed-end credit. While the lower courts decided that certain provisions of TILA mandated such disclosure, the Supreme Court disagreed, based on legislative history coupled with the FRB's interpretation in its staff commentary. The Court stated, "deference to the Federal Reserve is compelled by necessity; a court that tries to chart a true course to the Act's purpose embarks upon a voyage without a compass when it disregards the agency's views."[11] The standard to be applied was stated as follows: "[J]udges ought to refrain from substituting their own interstitial lawmaking for that of the Federal Reserve, so long as the latter's lawmaking is not irrational."[12] The concurring judges added, "We need not find that its construction is the only reasonable one, or even that it is the result we would have reached had the question arisen in the first instance in judicial proceedings."[13] A practitioner would do well to heed the voice of the Supreme Court in its deference to staff interpretations, past and present. Such interpretations will probably continue to govern the law in the area, unless "demonstrably irrational." This makes familiarity with Regulation Z and its current official staff commentary crucial to a proper understanding of the working of the Act.

§4.04   Scope of the Act: Consumer Credit Defined

TILA and Regulation Z operate to require certain disclosures whenever a consumer credit transaction is involved, and have no effect where the

---

[9] 12 CFR pt 226.

[10] 444 US 555 (1980).

[11] *Id* 568.

[12] *Id.*

[13] *Id* 571 (quoting Udall v Tallman, 380 US 1, 16 (1965), quoting Unemployment Commn v Aragon, 329 US 143, 153 (1946)).

transaction does not involve consumer credit. The Act defines consumer credit in terms of who a consumer is. Thus, a consumer credit transaction is one in which the one seeking the credit extension is a natural person, and the money, property, or services which form the subject of the transaction are to be used primarily for personal, family, or household purposes.[14] The term *credit* itself is the right granted by a creditor to a debtor to defer payment of a debt, or to incur debt and defer its payment.[15]

Regulation Z interprets the term *consumer credit* to mean credit offered or extended to a consumer primarily for private, family, or household purposes.[16] *Consumer* means a cardholder or natural person to whom consumer credit is offered or extended.[17] For rescission purposes only, a consumer includes a natural person in whose principal dwelling a security interest is or will be retained or acquired, if that person's ownership interest is or will be subject to the security interest.[18]

§4.05 Exempted Transactions

Extension of credit for purposes which are primarily business, commercial, or agricultural is outside the scope of the Act.[19] It is not always clear whether a credit extension is for a personal or business purpose. The case of *Thorns v Sundance Properties* [20] involved a loan obtained for the purpose of investing in a limited partnership formed to purchase an apartment building. The Thorns secured the loan with their personal residence, but the creditor, Sundance Properties, did not disclose to the Thorns a right to rescind, as TILA would require in a consumer credit transaction. The Thorns brought suit to rescind the loan transaction, but the district court granted summary judgment for Sundance on the ground that the transaction was outside the scope of TILA, not being a "loan for personal, family, or household purposes." Investment in a limited partnership to buy an apartment building was not, the court held, a personal, family, or household purpose, and, therefore, the loan was not consumer credit subject to TILA.

The Ninth Circuit, however, reversed the district court's holding, based on the Federal Reserve Board's official staff interpretation of the Regulation Z exemption rule. In determining whether credit to finance an acquisition such as securities, antiques, or art is primarily for a business or commercial purpose, as opposed to a consumer purpose, the staff suggests that the following factors be considered:

---

[14] 15 USC §1602(h).

[15] 15 USC §1602(e).

[16] 12 CFR §226.2(12).

[17] 12 CFR §226.2(11).

[18] *Id.*

[19] 12 CFR §226.3(a)(1).

[20] 726 F2d 1417 (9th Cir 1984).

1. The relationship of the borrower's primary occupation to the acquisition—the more closely related, the more likely it is to be a business purpose

2. The degree to which the borrower will personally manage the acquisition—the more personal involvement there is, the more likely it is to be a business purpose

3. The ratio of income from the acquisition to the total income of the borrower—the higher the ratio, the more likely it is to be a business purpose

4. The size of the transaction—the larger the transaction, the more likely it is to be a business purpose

5. The borrower's statement of the purpose of the loan[21]

Based on this interpretation, the Ninth Circuit reversed the decision of the district court and remanded. In the court's view, purchase of a limited partnership interest for investment purposes can be for a personal purpose under this interpretation. Conversely, a loan to expand a business, even though secured by the borrower's residence or personal property, or a loan to improve a principal residence to put in a business office, is a loan for a *business purpose* under the Act.

In a pre-Simplification case, *Sapenter v Drapero Inc,*[22] the debtor owned a six-unit apartment building which was mortgaged and about to be foreclosed. In order to avoid foreclosure, the debtor executed a mortgage on his own residence. The debtor later tried to set aside the mortgage on the residence, alleging that the defendant mortgagee had not complied with TILA disclosure requirements. The federal district court held that TILA did not apply because the loan was not primarily for personal, family, or household purposes. This outcome clearly conforms to the Official Staff Interpretation.

A credit transaction of over $25,000 will not qualify as a consumer credit transaction unless the extension of the credit is secured by real property or by personal property used or expected to be used as the consumer's principal dwelling.[23] A *dwelling* is defined as a residential structure that contains one to four units, whether or not the structure is attached to real property. The definition therefore includes, unlike the old TILA, mobile homes and trailers if they are used as residences.[24]

Public utility credit, such as gas, water, and electrical services, cable television services, and installation services on sewers, water lines, conduits, telephone poles, or the like is not considered consumer credit subject to TILA. This exception does not apply, however, to the extension of credit for the purchase of appliances, such as gas and electric ranges, telephones, or grills, nor does

---

[21] 12 CFR §226.3(a) and Official Staff Interpretation.

[22] 326 F Supp 871 (ED La 1971).

[23] 12 CFR §226(3)(b).

[24] 15 USC §1602(v); 12 CFR §226.2(19).

the exemption apply to the extension of credit for the financing of home improvement services such as heating or air conditioning systems.[25]

Securities or commodities accounts in which credit is extended by a broker-dealer registered with the Securities and Exchange Commission or the Commodity Futures Trading Commission are not subject to TILA. This exemption does not apply to a transaction with any other type of broker, such as one registered only with the state.[26]

Home fuel budget plans are also exempt. If no finance charge is imposed, TILA does not apply to an installment agreement for the purchase of home fuels where a set rate is charged each month and is adjusted at the end of the year to reflect actual consumption.[27]

Certain student loans are exempted from coverage under TILA. Prior to 1983, TILA applied to all student loans, but on October 15, 1982, Congress exempted federally insured student loans from the provisions of TILA. Thus, loans extended, insured, or guaranteed under the provision of Title IV of the Higher Education Act of 1968 (20 USC §1070) are exempted from TILA. Other student loans which are not federally insured do remain subject to TILA and other state disclosure laws.[28]

§4.06 *Creditor* Defined

A *creditor* subject to TILA is a person who regularly extends credit which is subject to a finance charge or is payable by written agreement in more than four installments whether or not a finance charge is imposed. Additionally, the *creditor* must be the person to whom the obligation is initially payable. A *creditor* may also be a person who honors a credit card or a person who issues the credit card.[29]

§4.07 —The Four-Installment Rule

Under the original TILA, there was no four-installment rule. The rule was issued by the Federal Reserve Board supplementing the Act's definition of creditor. The rule did not go unchallenged. It was attacked as an illegal exercise of Federal Reserve Board power. The Supreme Court resolved the issue in favor of the rule in *Mourning v Family Publications Service Inc*,[30] reasoning that to strike down the rule would be to give creditors the chance to avoid TILA by simply "burying" their finance charges in the quoted price of an item.

The Supreme Court upheld the rule as a reasonable way for the Federal Reserve Board to implement the purpose of the Act, for the rule could not be

---

[25] 12 CFR §226.3(c) and Official Staff Interpretation.

[26] 12 CFR §226.3(d) and Official Staff Interpretation.

[27] 12 CFR §226.3(e) and Official Staff Interpretation.

[28] 12 CFR §226.3(f) and Official Staff Interpretation.

[29] 15 USC §1602(f); 12 CFR §226.2(a)(17). *See* **ch 7.**

[30] 411 US 356 (1973).

seen as creating an unconstitutional irrebuttable presumption that all creditors that allow more than four installment payments actually charge for finance. Rather, it is a rule to discourage evasion by requiring disclosure by all members of the defined class.

In 1974, Congress added the rule to the statute itself and the Simplification Act has preserved it.[31] However, under the new Act, the four-installment rule applies only to credit transactions in which there is a written agreement.[32]

§4.08   —*Regularly* Extended Credit

One issue is how often a person must extend credit in order to qualify as a *creditor* under the Act. Regulation Z solves the problem by applying an objective test. A person *regularly* extends credit if that person extended credit more than 25 times in the preceding calendar year. In the case where the transaction is secured by a dwelling, the number is reduced from 25 to 5 times. If a person did not meet these standards in the preceding calendar year, the numerical standards will be applied to the current calendar year.[33] For example, if a person extended consumer credit 26 times in 1983, it is a creditor for the twenty-sixth extension of credit in 1983. Such a person is also a creditor for all extensions of credit in 1984. Conversely, if a person extended consumer credit 20 times in 1983, and extends consumer credit 75 times in 1984, the person is required to comply with the Act after the twenty-fifth credit extension in 1984 and for all extensions of credit in 1985.

Extensions of credit secured by a dwelling are counted toward the 25-extensions test. But, extensions of credit not secured by a dwelling are not counted toward the five extensions of credit secured by a dwelling test. For example, if, in 1985, a person extends consumer credit 23 times and consumer credit secured by a dwelling twice, that person becomes a creditor for the following extensions of credit. On the other hand, if the person extends consumer credit 10 times and consumer credit secured by a dwelling twice, the person is not a creditor under the five-time test.[34]

§4.09   —A Finance Charge Is Imposed

Except for the four-installment rule, a creditor, to be subject to TILA, must impose a *finance charge* which in itself has broader meaning than the term *interest*. *Finance charge* is defined as "the sum of all charges payable directly or indirectly

[31] 15 USC §1602(f).

[32] 12 CFR §226.2(17)(i).

[33] 12 CFR §226.2(17) note 3.

[34] 12 CFR §226.2(17) and Official Staff Interpretation.

by the person to whom the credit is extended, and imposed directly or indirectly by the creditor as an incident to the extension of credit."[35]

The criterion used to determine whether a charge is a finance charge under the Act is that it must be of a type not payable in a comparable cash transaction.[36] Thus, if the same charge is imposed in installment payments and cash transactions, then, the amount charged is not technically a finance charge.

If the charge in a credit transaction exceeds the charge imposed in a comparable cash transaction, only the difference between the two is a finance charge. Examples of a finance charge are:

1. Interest time-price differential
2. Service, transaction, activity, and carrying charges for maintaining an account, to the extent that they are not imposed for a similar account without a credit feature
3. A loan fee, finder's fee, or similar charge
4. Investigation appraisal or credit report fees
5. Insurance or other charge or premium protecting the creditor against the obligor's default or other credit loss

The following are examples of charges that are excluded from the finance charge:

1. Application fees charged to all applicants for credit, whether or not credit is actually extended
2. Late payment charges, if those late payments are unanticipated
3. Charges for unanticipated overdrafts
4. Fees charged for participation in a credit plan[37]

The following charges are equally excluded from the finance charge: certain fees incurred in a transaction secured by real property or in a residential mortgage transaction, if the fees are bona fide and reasonable in amount. Examples are fees for the examination, title insurance, fees for preparing deeds, mortgages, or similar documents, credit reports or notary fees, and escrow accounts for future payments of taxes and insurance.[38]

Premiums for credit life, accident, or health insurance may be excluded from consideration as finance charges if the lender specifically discloses to the borrower that they are not imposed as conditions for extending credit, and they are affirmatively accepted by the borrower in writing.[39] Discounts for prompt

---

35 15 USC §1605(a); 12 CFR §226.4(a).
36 15 USC §1605(a); 12 CFR §226.4(a).
37 12 CFR §226.4(c).
38 15 USC §1605(e); 12 CFR §226.4(c)(7).
39 12 CFR §226.4(d).
40 12 CFR §226.4(b)(9).

payment *are* finance charges.[40] Finally, security interest charges, if itemized and disclosed, may be excluded from the definition.[41]

To acquire a definite idea of which charges are finance charges subject to TILA disclosure requirements and which charges are not, it is advisable to consult Regulation Z (12 CFR §226.4) and the Official Staff Interpretations. This consultation is necessary because the distinction is not always clear, nor is it always a logical one.

§4.10 —The Person To Whom the Consumer Debt Is Initially Payable

The term *creditor* refers only to the person to whom the debt arising from the consumer credit transaction is initially payable on the face of the note or contract, or, lacking such evidence, by agreement.[42] The Simplification Act restricts the meaning of *creditor*. Under the old TILA, both the creditor and the creditor's assignee(s) were *creditors* required to comply with the disclosure requirements of the Act.[43] Under the Simplification Act and the new Regulation Z, the assignee is not a *creditor* if such assignee is not the person to whom the debt is initially payable. In other words, the obligation must be payable to the person in order for that person to be a *creditor* under the Act. Regulation Z further clarifies that if the instrument of indebtedness is made payable to *bearer*, the creditor is the person who initially accepts the obligation.[44]

§4.11 Credit Sales, Consumer Loans, and Consumer Leases

A credit sale is a sale in which the seller is also the creditor.[45] If the seller of the property or services has arranged for the financing by another party and is not itself a creditor, then the transaction is not a credit sale but a consumer loan, and only the financing party is deemed to be the creditor.

Finally, unless terminable by the consumer at any time without penalty, the term *credit sale* includes a bailment or lease if:

　　1. The consumer agrees to pay as compensation for the use of the property a sum substantially equivalent to or in excess of the total value of the property and services involved, and
　　2. The consumer will become the owner of the property or has such

---

[41] 12 CFR §226.4(e).
[42] 15 USC §1602(f); 12 CFR §226.2(17)(i).
[43] *See* Ford Motor Credit v Cenance, 452 US 155 (1981).
[44] 12 CFR §226.2(a)(17) and Official Staff Interpretation.
[45] 12 CFR §226.2(a)(16).

an option for no additional consideration or simply nominal consideration upon compliance with the agreement[46]

This definition adopts the distinction between a true lease and a conditional sale disguised as a lease found in the Uniform Commercial Code.[47] When the consumer transaction is a true lease, it is subject to a different set of provisions under TILA which apply solely to leases.[48] Regulation M, and not Regulation Z, implements and interprets the lease provisions of TILA.[49] Although Regulation M adopts the same policy and purpose as Regulation Z, it is separate from Regulation Z in order to "ease the regulatory burden and facititate compliance."[50]

§4.12 Open-End Credit

Once it is determined that a consumer credit transaction falls under the scope of the Act, it is important next to determine the type of credit involved, for the disclosure requirements and the applicable provisions of the Act vary according to the type of credit. Under the Act there are three types of credit: open-end credit; closed-end credit; and lease.

The Act defines open-end credit to mean a plan under which the creditor reasonably contemplates repeated transactions, has prescribed terms of such transactions, and has provided for a finance charge to be computed from time to time on the outstanding unpaid balance.[51] Thus, credit is open-end if it meets three criteria:

1. A plan must exist
2. Repeated transactions are contemplated
3. A finance charge may be imposed on an outstanding balance

Existence of a Plan

This first criterion connotes a contractual agreement between the creditor and the consumer. In an open-end credit plan, the total amount of credit that may be extended during the existence of the plan is actually unlimited, because

---

[46] *Id.*

[47] UCC §1-201(37) states: Whether a lease is intended as security is to be determined by the facts of each case; however, (a) the inclusion of an option to purchase does not of itself make the lease one intended for security, and (b) an agreement that upon compliance with the terms of the lease the lessee shall become or has the option to become the owner of the property for no additional consideration or for a nominal consideration does make the lease one intended for security.

[48] 15 USC §1667 *et seq.*

[49] Regulation M, 12 CFR §213.

[50] 46 Fed Reg 20949 (Apr 7, 1981).

[51] 15 USC §1602(i).

available credit is available as long as advances are repaid.[52] This unlimited credit during the duration of the plan distinguishes open-end credit from closed-end credit arrangements.

Repeated Transactions

This means that at the time the plan is agreed upon, the parties, or at least the creditor, must legitimately expect that there will be repeated business, rather than an isolated one-time-only extension of credit. This requirement is designed to proscribe those abuses commonly referred to as *spurious open-end credit*, wherein the creditor tries to avoid the closed-end credit disclosure requirements by calling the deal an open-end credit transaction when it is not. For example, this occurs in the case of the consumer who would like to purchase a consumer item from a dealer. The dealer-creditor, instead of admitting this to be a closed-end credit transaction and giving the consumer the required closed-end disclosures, requires the consumer to open a revolving charge account, even though both dealer and consumer know full well that this is their only transaction, with neither party contemplating further business between them. The key to determining *repeated transactions* is intent. Where such an intent exists, although the consumer does not ultimately take advantage of the open-end credit opportunity, the plan is still an open-end credit plan.[53] The type of business involved may indicate the type of credit plan. For example, it is not reasonable to expect an automobile dealer to sell a car under an open-end credit plan, or, for that matter, to expect an aluminum siding dealer to open such a plan to its customers.[54]

Finance Charge on an Outstanding Balance

There is no open-end credit if there is no possibility that a periodic finance charge will be imposed on the outstanding balance.[55] Nevertheless, there is still an open-end credit plan even though the consumer pays no finance charge during, for example, a *free ride* period, or even if the consumer opts to pay the whole balance and therefore incurs no finance charge.[56] Examples of common open-end credit plans are department stores' charge accounts, credit card purchases with bank cards, and certain revolving bank accounts.

It is not the name given to the credit by the creditor that will control the characterization of a given extension of credit. In a case that leaves the characterization unclear, several factors will be taken into account in order to determine the true nature of the plan.[57]

---

[52] 12 CFR §226.2(a)(20).

[53] 12 CFR §226.2(a)(20) and Official Staff Interpretation.

[54] *Id.*

[55] *Id.*

[56] *Id.*

[57] *See*, Mae's v Motivation for Tomorrow, Inc, 356 F Supp 47 (ND Cal 1973). *See generally*, D. Rothschild & D. Carrol, Consumer Protection Reporting Service pt II, ch 1, at 12 (1973).

§4.13 Closed-End Credit—Amount Financed

The term *closed-end credit* is defined by exclusion. Any credit arrangement that does not fall within the definition of open-end credit is closed-end credit.[58]

Closed-end credit plans are generally those which are extended only for a specific period of time, and the total amount and number of payments, as well as the due date, are agreed upon by the consumer and the creditor when the credit agreement is entered into. Examples of closed-end credit are: sales of large consumer items such as cars, furniture, appliances; real estate mortgages; home mortgages; bank or finance company loans.

The term *amount financed* is used in relation to closed-end credit. *Amount financed* is the amount of credit which the consumer can actually use.[59] Usually, the term is described as "the amount of credit provided to you, or on your behalf."[60] The amount financed is calculated by determining the principal loan amount or the cash price (subtracting any down payment), adding any other amounts that are financed by the creditor and are not part of the finance charge, and subtracting any prepaid finance charge.[61]

§4.14 Annual Percentage Rate

The two most important disclosures required by TILA relate to the finance charge and the annual percentage rate. Regulation Z requires that disclosures related to these two items "be more conspicuous than any other required disclosure."[62] The term *finance charge* is discussed in §4.09. Following is the meaning of the term *annual percentage rate* (*APR*).

Considered together with the finance charge, the annual percentage rate is the most important term under the Truth In Lending Act. It is the common denominator for measuring the finance charge itself. The annual percentage rate is simply the finance charge payable on the declining balance of the debt, stated on an annual percentage basis.

The means of calculating the annual percentage rate varies, depending on whether the credit is of the closed-end or open-end type. In calculating the annual percentage rate in open-end credit such as revolving charge accounts, several options are open to the creditor. The most popular method is to multiply each periodic rate by the number of periods in a year. If the monthly periodic rate is 1 1/2 per cent, then the annual percentage rate would be 1 1/2 × 12, or 18 per cent. Another method is the *quotient method*, which adopts a single average rate when more than one periodic rate is used. For example, a

---

[58] 12 CFR §226.2(a)(10).

[59] 15 USC §1638(a)(2)(A).

[60] 12 CFR §226.18(b).

[61] *Id.*

[62] 12 CFR §§226.5(a)(2), .17(a)(2).

creditor charging 18 per cent up to $500 and 12 per cent over $500 may disclose a single rate of 16 1/4 per cent with respect to a $700 balance.[63]

For closed-end credit transactions, Regulation Z provides annual percentage rate tables (Appendix J) which the creditor may adopt to determine the annual percentage rate. Any rate determined from those tables would satisfy the Act's requirements. Creditors, however, may use any other method, provided the rate so determined equals the rate determined in accordance with Appendix J.[64] The annual percentage rate is still considered accurate if it varies no more than 1/8 of 1 percentage point above or below the APR determined in accordance with Appendix J.[65]

§4.15   Disclosures in Credit Advertising

Under the Act, *advertising* is a commercial message in any medium that promotes directly or indirectly a credit transaction.[66] The act covers only commercial messages, whether in visual, oral, or print media. Thus, newspapers, announcements on radio and television, direct mail literature, and telephone solicitations are all covered. However, the term *advertising* does not include direct personal contacts, such as cost estimates for individual consumers, nor does the term include informational material distributed only to business entities.[67] The Act adopts an all-or-nothing approach with respect to the requirement of disclosures in credit advertising. Creditors are required to comply with the Act's disclosure provisions only if the creditor uses certain triggering terms in its advertising. The idea behind this all-or-nothing approach is that in order to complain of a problem of deception through advertising, a consumer must be confronted with specific terms that, without full disclosure, would be misleading to the consumer. Once such triggering terms are used by the advertiser, a consumer ought to be able to get a full picture of what the terms actually mean. Thus, Regulation Z provides that, whenever certain triggering terms appear in credit advertisements, certain required additional credit terms must also appear.[68]

§4.16   —Closed-End Credit Advertising

Under Regulation Z, the following are triggering terms requiring additional disclosures:

[63] *See* J. Fonseca, Handling Consumer Credit Cases §8:4, at 308-09 (3d ed 1986).
[64] 12 CFR §226.22(b)(2).
[65] 12 CFR §226.22(a)(2).
[66] 12 CFR §226.2(a)(2).
[67] *Id.* and Official Staff Interpretation.
[68] 12 CFR §226.24(c)(1).

1. Amount or percentage of any down payment if stated affirmatively, such as "only $500 down" or "10% down."[69] But "no down payment" requires no additional disclosure

2. Number of payments or period of repayment, such as "24 payments" or "2 years to pay"[70]

3. Amount of any payment, such as "payment as low as $100" or "$25 weekly."[71] More general language, such as "monthly payments to suit your needs" or "regular weekly payments" are not triggering terms

4. Amount of any finance charge, such as "only $500 interest," or "$500 total cost of credit."[72] But "no finance charge" or "no closing costs" are not triggering terms

Whenever the credit advertising contains any such triggering terms, the advertisement must show:

1. The total down payment as a dollar amount or percentage. As an example, "credit terms require minimum $100 trade-in" or "10% cash required" would be adequate disclosures[73]

2. The repayment terms, which may be expressed in a variety of ways in addition to an exact repayment schedule, such as "48 monthly payments of $27.83 per $1,000 borrowed"[74]

3. The *annual percentage rate*, using that term. If the rate may be increased after consummation, this fact must also be disclosed; but the advertisement need not describe the rate increase, its limits, or how it would affect the payment schedule[75]

§4.17 —Open-End Credit Advertising

Regulation Z requires additional disclosures if the open-end credit advertisement refers to any of the following:

1. Finance charge
2. Any charge other than finance charge
3. The fact that the creditor has or will acquire a security interest in the

---

[69] 12 CFR §226.24(c)(1)(i).

[70] 12 CFR §226.24(c)(1)(ii).

[71] 12 CFR §226.24(c)(1)(iii) and Official Staff Interpretation.

[72] 12 CFR §226.24(c)(1)(iv) and Official Staff Interpretation.

[73] 12 CFR §226.24(c)(2)(i) and Official Staff Interpretation.

[74] 12 CFR §226.24(c)(2)(ii) and Official Staff Interpretation.

[75] 12 CFR §226.24(c)(2)(iii) and Official Staff Interpretation. For further explanations of Regulation Z with respect to closed-end credit advertising, see FTC Bureau of Consumer Protection Memorandum and Consumer Fact Sheet, 5 Consumer Credit Guide (CCH) ¶96,752 (Mar 31, 1983).

property purchased under the plan, or in any other property identified by type of item
    4. Statement of billing rights[76]

The Federal Reserve Board staff gives the following examples of triggering terms requiring additional disclosures:

    1. Small monthly service charge on the remaining balance
    2. 12 per cent annual percentage rate
    3. A $15 annual membership fee buys you $2,000 in credit[77]

As a general rule, a given term in advertising would trigger further disclosure only if it is a positive term. Thus, for example, "no annual membership fee" is not a triggering term, because it makes no positive representation as to the substantive character of the credit arrangement offered.[78]

On the other hand, an advertising term may trigger other disclosures even if the positive representation is not explicit. The Staff gives as an example the statement, "the equity in your home becomes spendable with an XYZ line of credit." This statement includes implicitly the fact that the creditor will take a security interest in the consumer's home. Further disclosures are therefore required.[79]

§4.18 —Catalogues and Multi-Page Advertising

If the advertising is made through a catalogue or other multi-page advertising medium, then a single table or schedule will be sufficient for disclosure, if such table or schedule fulfills two conditions. The table or schedule must be in clear and conspicuous language, and the terms of the required disclosures must appear clearly in the catalogue and advertisement, with the page clearly stated in the advertisement. This is true for both open-end and closed-end credit advertising.[80]

§4.19 General Disclosure Requirements

Credit disclosures are different, depending on the type of credit involved, be it a closed-end credit, open-end credit, or lease. Besides the specific disclosure requirements for specific types of consumer credit transactions, there are general disclosure requirements that apply to all consumer credit transactions. The general requirements are the following:

---

[76] 12 CFR §226.16(b).
[77] *Id* and Official Staff Interpretation.
[78] 12 CFR §226(b)(1) and Official Staff Interpretation.
[79] 12 CFR §226(b)(2) and Official Staff Interpretation.
[80] 12 CFR §§226.16(c), .24(d).

1. The disclosure must be made clearly and conspicuously in writing, in a form that the consumer may keep[81]

2. The terms *required finance charge* and *annual percentage rate*, when required to be disclosed, shall be more conspicuous than any other term disclosed[82]

3. The creditor must meet the initial disclosure requirements before the first transaction is made, or before consumation of the transaction[83]

4. If the transaction involves more than one creditor, or more than one lessor, they must all be clearly identified, but only one creditor or lessor shall be required to make the disclosures. The creditors themselves will decide who is to make the disclosure[84]

5. If the transaction involves more than one consumer, the disclosures may be made to any consumer who is primarily liable on the account. However, if the right of rescission is applicable, then the initial disclosure statements and the right-of-rescission disclosure must be made to each consumer who has that right[85]

6. If a disclosure becomes inaccurate because of a subsequent event, new disclosures may be required if the changes result in an additional burden imposed upon the consumer through no fault of the consumer[86]

7. If the Board determines that a disclosure required by state law, other than a requirement relating to the finance charge or annual percentage rate, is substantially the same as the federal disclosure requirement, the creditor may choose to make only the state disclosure in lieu of the federal disclosure[87]

§4.20 Open-End Credit Disclosures

There are two sets of disclosures in open-end credit:

1. The initial disclosures made before the consumer opens any account with the creditor

2. The periodic disclosures which the creditor must furnish the consumer periodically, once the credit plan is established

The language in the periodic disclosures must be simple enough in meaning

---

[81] 12 CFR §§226.5(a), .17(a)(1), 213.4(a)(1).

[82] 12 CFR §§226.5(b), .17(a)(2).

[83] 12 CFR §§226.5(b), .17(b), §213(a)(2).

[84] 12 CFR §§226.5(d), .17(d), 213.4(c).

[85] *Id.*

[86] 12 CFR §§226.5(e), .17(e), 213.4(e).

[87] 12 CFR §§226.28(b), 213.7(a).

to enable the average consumer to relate the two sets of disclosures to one another. However, the language need not be identical.[88]

§4.21 —Initial Disclosure Statement

The Truth in Lending Act requires that the initial statement must be given "before opening any account under an open-end consumer credit plan."[89] This may be interpreted as requiring the initial disclosure statement as soon as the creditor approves the application for an account. Regulation Z, however, postpones initial disclosures to the time "before the first transaction is made under the plan."[90] In other words, it is not until the consumer is obligated on the plan by, for example, making the first purchase, receiving the first advance, or paying the fee under the plan that the initial disclosure statement must be furnished. Regulation Z postpones the time to take into consideration cases where the consumer did not himself or herself formally apply for the plan.[91]

On the initial disclosure statement, the following information must appear:

> 1. Finance charge: when finance charges begin to accrue and whether there is any "free-ride" period; each periodic rate used to compute the finance charge and the corresponding annual percentage rate, whether there are different periodic rates applicable to different types of transactions, and if a variable rate plan is offered, the way it is applied; the method used to determine the balance on which the finance charge is computed; and any other type of finance charge that may be imposed[92]
>
> 2. Charges related to the plan that are not finance charges, such as late payment charges, over-the-credit-limit charges, and taxes imposed on the credit transaction by a state or other governmental body[93]
>
> 3. The conditions under which the creditor may take a security interest in the consumer's property, and a description of the property so retained by type of item[94]
>
> 4. A statement of the consumer's rights with respect to billing disputes that is substantially similar to the form provided by Regulation Z (Appendix G)[95]

A security interest is a particular interest in property which is to secure compliance with a consumer credit contract. However, to be a security interest

---

[88] 12 CFR §226.6(1) and Official Staff Interpretation.

[89] 15 USC §1637(a).

[90] 12 CFR §226.5(b).

[91] D. Epstein & S. Nickles, Consumer Law 130 (2d ed 1981).

[92] 12 CFR §226.6(a).

[93] 12 CFR §226.6(b).

[94] 12 CFR §226.6(c).

[95] 12 CFR §226.6(d).

under TILA, the particular interest in property, whether personal or real, must be recognized as a security interest under applicable state or federal law. However, if a security interest is recognized under applicable law, TILA may exclude it from its disclosure requirements. The Act excludes three groups of security interests: incidental interests such as interests in proceeds, accessions, additions, fixtures, insurance proceeds, and premium rebates; interests in after-acquired property; and interests that arise solely by operation of law.[96]

§4.22 —Periodic Disclosure Statement

Since an open-end credit plan contemplates repeated transactions, the creditor must furnish the consumer periodic statements which contain detailed information with respect to the consumer's account. The following information must appear on the periodic statement:

1. The outstanding balance at the start of the billing period, using the term *previous balance*[97]

2. An identification of each credit transaction, unless an actual copy of the receipt or other credit document is enclosed[98]

3. Amounts credited to the consumer's account during the billing cycle[99]

4. Each *periodic rate*, using that term, the range of balances to which it is applicable, and the corresponding *annual percentage rate*, using that term[100]

5. The unpaid balance to which the periodic rate was applied, and an explanation of how that balance was determined[101]

6. An itemized statement of the amount of any finance charge debited to the account during the billing period, using the term *finance charge*[102]

7. The *annual percentage rate*, using that term[103]

8. An itemized statement of charges other than finance charge[104]

9. The closing date of the billing cycle and the account balance outstanding on that date[105]

---

[96] 12 CFR §226.2(a)(25).

[97] 12 CFR §226.7(a).

[98] 12 CFR §226.7(b).

[99] 12 CFR §226.7(c).

[100] 12 CFR §226.7(d).

[101] 12 CFR §226.7(c).

[102] 12 CFR §226.7(f).

[103] 12 CFR §226.7(g).

[104] 12 CFR §226.7(h).

[105] 12 CFR §226.7(i).

10. A statement of the period, if any, within which payment must be made to avoid finance charges[106]

11. The address to be used for notice of billing errors[107]

§4.23   Closed-End Credit Disclosures

The Simplification Act has drastically reduced the number of required disclosures in closed-end credit. Congress seemed to heed the United States Supreme Court's advice in *Ford Motor Credit Co v Milhollin*[108] that "meaningful disclosure does not mean more disclosure."[109] As the court stated, there is a need to avoid *information overload*.[110] *Information overload* will discourage the consumer from making a meaningful choice among the variety of credit offered. Although the Simplification Act has cut the number of required disclosures by half in closed-end consumer credit, the remaining half are still highly technical and thus require careful scrutiny to apply them correctly. Fortunately, Regulation Z has provided model disclosure forms. A creditor who adopts these forms in good faith is deemed to have complied with the Act's requirements, and, accordingly, will be relieved of any liability.[111]

§4.24   —Time Disclosures

Generally, the creditor in a closed-end credit transaction must make the disclosures before consummation.[112] Consummation is the time when a consumer becomes contractually obligated on a credit transaction.[113] State law determines that time, which is generally the time at which the creditor may sue the consumer for breach of contract if the consumer defaults on its terms. The disclosures need not be given at any particular time before consummation except in certain residential mortgage transactions.[114] However, it is not always clear when the disclosures should be made. In *Davis v Werne*,[115] the parties signed the contract, but later mutually rescinded it before any credit was actually extended. The consumer filed suit, alleging nondisclosure under TILA. The district court dismissed the claim on the ground that, because the defendant never did extend credit as agreed, no consumer credit transaction had been consummated within the meaning of the Act. The Fifth Circuit reversed. The court was of the opinion that "(t)he Truth-in-Lending Act is a

---

[106] 12 CFR §226.7(j).

[107] 12 CFR §226.7(k).

[108] 444 US 555 (1980).

[109] *Id* 568.

[110] *Id.*

[111] 15 USC §1640(f).

[112] 12 CFR §226.17(b).

[113] 12 CFR §226.2(a)(13).

[114] *See* §11.03.

[115] 673 F2d 866 (5th Cir 1982).

disclosure law. . . . It is the obligation to disclose, not *the duty of subsequent performance*, towards which the Act is directed"[116] (emphasis in original).

In *Dryden v Lou Budke's Arrow Finance Co*,[117] the plaintiff purchased an automobile with financing provided by the defendant. Upon finding out that the automobile was a "lemon," the plaintiff returned the car, and the defendant returned the plaintiff's down payment. The plaintiff nevertheless recovered statutory damages against the defendant for nondisclosure under TILA. The Eighth Circuit stated: "the statutory damages are explicitly a bonus to the successful TILA plaintiff, designed to encourage private enforcement of the Act, and a penalty against the defendant, designed to deter further violations."[118] *Waters v Weyerhauser Mortgage Co* [119] raises the issue of disclosure timeliness in a real estate transaction involving several events. The plaintiffs, is a class action, argued that the purchase was consummated on one or more of the following occasions: when they were advised in early June that their loans had been approved; when the defendant permitted them to occupy the house under a rental agreement prior to the final sale; when they purchased and installed improvements before July 27; when they incurred other expenses related to the purchase and occupancy of the house; when the lender sent escrow instructions to Lawyer's Title on June 6; and when they signed escrow instructions on April 19. The court, citing Nevada law, observed that a contract relating to land must be in writing. Accordingly, a contract for land is not consummated until reduced to writing and signed by the parties.[120] The court held that, before that event, no contractual relationship existed between the parties which required disclosure.[121]

§4.25 —Content of Closed-End Disclosures

The Act gives a long list of disclosures, but requires them only to the extent that they are relevant to a given transaction. For example, where no down payment is involved, the creditor may delete the down payment disclosure from the list. Appendix H of Regulation Z gives a number of model forms for various closed-end credit transactions.

Depending on the type of closed-end credit transaction, the creditor must give relevant information related to the following:

1. The identity of the creditor making the disclosure. Use of the

---

[116] *Id* 869. (The court, however, found that no violation of TILA disclosure requirements was present under the facts of the case).

[117] 630 F2d 641 (8th Cir 1980).

[118] *Id* 647.

[119] 582 F2d 503 (9th Cir 1978).

[120] *Id* 506.

[121] *Id.*

creditor's name is sufficient, but the creditor may also include an address and telephone number[122]

2. The net amount of the credit extended, using the term *amount financed,* and a description, such as "the amount of credit extended to you or on your behalf." The amount financed is calculated by: determining the principal loan amount or the cash price minus any down payment; adding fees or other charges financed by the creditor that are not part of the finance charge; and deducting any prepaid finance charge[123]

3. A written itemization of the amount financed, including funds disbursed to the consumer, to the consumer's account, or to a named third person, and the prepaid finance charge. However, the creditor need not disclose this information if the creditor provides a statement saying that the consumer has the right to receive such an itemization if desired, and the consumer does not request it[124]

4. The *finance charge,* using that term, and a description such as "the dollar amount the credit will cost you"[125]

5. The *annual percentage rate,* using that term, and a brief description such as "the cost of your credit as a yearly rate"[126]

6. A description of the variable rates, i.e., increases of APR after consummation, the circumstances, limitations, and effects of the increase[127]

7. The repayment schedule, including the number, amounts, and timing of the payments[128]

8. The *total of payments,* using that term, and a brief explanation such as "the amount you will have paid when you have made all scheduled payments."[129] In single payment transactions, the creditor may omit this disclosure[130]

9. Whether the consumer's obligation has a demand feature at the outset or can be converted into a demand obligation, i.e., the time of payment is left to the creditor's reasonable determination. This disclosure does not apply to transactions as a result of the debtor's default. These do not per se incorporate a demand feature[131]

10. The *total sale price,* using that term, if the transaction is a credit sale. The term *total sale price* must be followed by a descriptive explanation such as "the total price of your purchase on credit, including your down

---

[122] 12 CFR §226.18(a) and Official Staff Interpretation.

[123] 12 CFR §226.18(b).

[124] 12 CFR §226.18(c).

[125] 12 CFR §226.18(d).

[126] 12 CFR §226.18(e).

[127] 12 CFR §226.18(f).

[128] 12 CFR §226.18(g).

[129] 12 CFR §226.18(h).

[130] *Id* Note 44.

[131] 12 CFR §226.18(i) and Official Staff Interpretation.

payment of $___." The total sale price includes the cash price plus the finance charge and any other amounts, not part of the finance charge, that are financed by the creditor[132]

11. A statement indicating whether a penalty may be imposed or a rebate given if the consumer prepays in full[133]

12. A statement of late payment charges. The creditor needs to disclose this information only if charges are added to each late installment payment by a creditor who otherwise still continues the transaction on its original terms[134]

13. The fact that the creditor has or will take a security interest in any of the consumer's property identified by time or item[135]

14. A statement of the insurance premiums for credit life, accident, health, or loss of income that are not part of the finance charge as defined in the Act[136]

15. Certain security interest charges which are excluded from the finance charge such as taxes or fees paid to public officials for perfecting or releasing a security interest[137]

16. A contract reference advising the consumer to refer to the appropriate contract document for any information concerning the consumer's obligation[138]

17. Any assumption policy in a residential mortgage transaction, that is, whether the consumer's transferee may be permitted to assume the remaining obligation on its original terms[139]

18. If the consumer is required to maintain a deposit as a condition of the transaction, the creditor must disclose that the annual percentage rate does not reflect the effect of the required deposit. Certain deposits are not required deposits subject to this disclosure. For example, the requirement that the borrower be also a customer of the financing institution is not treated as a required deposit[140]

§4.26 The Consumer's Right of Rescission

The Truth in Lending Act gives the consumer a right to rescind any open-end or closed-end credit transaction in which the creditor takes a security interest in any property used or expected to be used as the principal dwelling of the

---

[132] 12 CFR §226.18(j).

[133] 12 CFR §226.18(k).

[134] 12 CFR §226.18(l) and Official Staff Interpretation.

[135] 12 CFR §226.18(m).

[136] 12 CFR §§226.18(n), .4(d).

[137] 12 CFR §§226.18(o), .4(e).

[138] 12 CFR §226.18(p).

[139] 12 CFR §226.18(q).

[140] 12 CFR §226.18(r) and Official Staff Interpretation.

consumer.[141] *Dwelling* means "a residential structure that contains one to four units whether or not that structure is attached to real property."[142] A houseboat or mobile home is a *dwelling* if it is used or to be used as the consumer's principal residence. Such a rescission right is similar to the *cooling-off period*, which exists in many states' home solicitation sales statutes, or in the federal door-to-door sales statute.[143]

When the right to rescind exists, the creditor must give notice of that right to the consumer. For that purpose, the creditor must deliver two copies of the notice to the consumer. The notice shall disclose the following in clear and conspicuous language:

1. The creditor's retention of a security interest in the consumer's principal dwelling
2. The consumer's right to rescind the transaction
3. How to exercise that right, giving the consumer the appropriate form and the address of the creditor's place of business
4. A description of the effects of rescission
5. The date the right to rescind expires[144]

A consumer who then wishes to exercise the right must notify the creditor in writing within a specified period of time. Specifically, the consumer must give written notification of rescission before midnight on the third business day following either consummation, delivery of the notice of consumer's right to rescind, or delivery of all material disclosures, whichever occurs last.

The term *material disclosures* means the required disclosures under TILA as to the annual percentage rate, the amount financed, the total of payments, and the payment schedule. If the creditor fails to deliver the required notice of the consumer's right to rescind, or fails to deliver the material disclosures, the right to rescind shall expire three years after the occurrence giving rise to the right of rescission or upon transfer of all the consumer's interest in the property, or upon sale of the property, whichever comes first.[145]

The Act and Regulation Z allow the consumer to modify or waive the right to rescind if the consumer determines that the extension of credit is needed to meet a bona fide personal financial emergency.[146] In order to make sure that this waiver is exercised freely by the consumer, Regulation Z prohibits the use of printed forms for waiver. To modify or waive the right to rescind, the consumer must give a written statement to the creditor describing the emergency and expressly and clearly waiving or modifying that right. The

---

[141] 12 CFR §§226.15, .23.
[142] 12 CFR §226.2(a)(19).
[143] *See* §§2.17-2.20.
[144] 12 CFR §§226.15(b) .23(b).
[145] 12 CFR §§226.15(a)(3), .23(a)(3).
[146] 12 CFR §§226.15(e), .23(e).

statement must bear the signature of the consumer or consumers waiving their right.[147]

§4.27 —Transactions Exempted from the Right of Rescission

In both closed-end and open-end credit transactions, the right to rescind does not apply to a residential mortgage transaction or a transaction in which a state agency is a creditor.[148] The Act defines a *residential mortgage transaction* to mean "a transaction in which a mortgage, deed of trust, purchase money security interest arising under an installment sales contract, or equivalent consensual interest is created or retained in the consumer's principal dwelling to finance the acquisition or initial construction of that dwelling."[149] In other words, a residential mortgage transaction involves financing that enables the consumer to acquire or build the consumer's principal dwelling, and the financing is secured by that dwelling. The consumer cannot rescind such a transaction.[150] For example, a loan to purchase a mobile home for use as a principal dwelling is not rescindable.

In the case of the exemption for state creditors, *only* state creditors are exempt. Transactions in which cities and other subdivisions of the state act as creditors are rescindable.[151]

Besides the above exemptions, three other exemptions are added to the list of nonrescindable transactions in closed-end credit:

> 1. Refinancing or consolidations by the original creditor which do not exceed the unpaid portion of the amount financed plus interest. For example, if the outstanding principal balance plus earned finance charge is $1,000 and the creditor refinances $1,000, the consumer has no right to rescind. However, if the new amount financed is $1,100, the consumer may rescind $100[152]

> 2. Multiple advances—The right of rescission does not arise with each subsequent advance if the multiple advances are treated as part of a single transaction. For example, if the creditor makes advances as construction progresses, disclosure and exercise of the right to rescind apply only to the beginning of the construction period and not to subsequent disbursements. However, if each new advance is treated as a separate transaction, they do apply[153]

---

[147] *Id.*

[148] 12 CFR §§226.15(f), .23(f).

[149] 12 CFR §226.2(a)(24).

[150] 12 CFR §§226.15(f)(1), .23(f)(1).

[151] 12 CFR §§226.15(f)(2), .23(f)(3) and Official Staff Interpretation.

[152] 12 CFR §226.23(f)(2) and Official Staff Interpretation.

[153] 12 CFR §226.23(f)(4) and Official Staff Interpretation.

3. A renewal of optional insurance premiums that is not considered a refinancing[154]

§4.28 —Effects of the Right of Rescission

The purpose of the right of rescission is to restore the parties as closely as possible to the status quo ante. Thus, when a consumer rescinds a transaction, the security interest giving rise to the right of rescission becomes void, and the consumer shall not be liable for any amount, including any finance charge. Within 20 calendar days of the notice of the consumer's exercise of the right of rescission, the creditor has the duty to return any money or property that has been given to anyone in connection with the transaction. Likewise, the creditor must take any action necessary to terminate the security interest which was taken on the consumer's dwelling. Once the creditor has met the above obligations, the consumer must return any money or property, or at least its reasonable value if return of the property would be impracticable or inequitable to the creditor, as in the case of lumber or bricks already incorporated into the consumer's home. If the creditor does not take possession within 20 calendar days after the consumer's tender, the consumer may keep it without further obligation.[155] These obligations may be modified by a court order.[156]

The issue of the consumer's obligation upon rescission arises in *Aquino v Public Finance Consumer Discount Co.*[157] In this case, the plaintiff, Aquino, purchased a used car from Sheehy Ford in October, 1981. The purchase price was financed with a $5,000 loan from Public Finance Consumer Discount Co (Public). The loan was secured by a mortgage on Aquino's home, a lien on her car, and a security interest in Aquino's household goods. In January, 1983, Public repossessed the plaintiff's car. In February, 1983, the plaintiff sent out a notice demanding rescission of the loan.

Although Public had provided the plaintiff Aquino with the proper form as to the plaintiff's right to rescind, Public failed to specify the date upon which the three-day period was to expire. Because of this omission, Aquino preserved the right to rescind the transaction almost two years after she obtained the loan. Public acknowledged Aquino's right of rescission, but argued that Aquino had to return the $5,000 loan to Public. Aquino stated that her sole obligation under the law was to return the car she had received in the underlying transaction. Since Public had already repossessed the car, her obligation was satisfied. The court recognized that Aquino's position might be valid in a credit sale where the seller is also the creditor. Allowing the buyer to return the property purchased to the seller would return the parties to the status quo.

The transaction between Aquino and Public, however, was not a credit sale,

---

[154] 12 CFR §226.23(f)(5).

[155] 12 CFR §§226.15(d), .23(d).

[156] 15 USC §1635(e).

[157] 606 F Supp 504 (ED Pa 1983).

but a consumer loan. There was no evidence that Public and the car dealer, Sheehy, were so closely connected as to make Public the alter ego of Sheehy. To allow Aquino to simply return the property, and not the monetary equivalent of the credit extended, would not return the parties to the status quo ante. Following this reasoning, the court ordered Aquino to return to Public $681.97, representing the difference between the total amount of the loan ($5,000) and what Aquino had already paid Public ($1,768.03) plus the amount for which Public sold Aquino's repossessed car ($2,550.00).

If it is determined that a creditor has violated the section on the consumer's right to rescind, the court may, in addition to rescission, hold the creditor civilly liable for violation of the Act.[158] The one-year statute of limitations in TILA[159] does not apply to the right of rescission. Therefore, a consumer may still rescind the transaction more than one year after the date of consummation if the creditor has failed to provide the required disclosures.[160]

§4.29 —Who May Exercise the Right of Rescission

Rescission rights apply to consumer credit transactions in which a lien or security interest is placed on the consumer's principal dwelling. Consequently, if the lien is placed on a person's house, but the credit extended is for a business purpose, then the TILA right of rescission cannot be available to the borrower. Any consumer whose ownership interest is or will be affected by the security interest has the right to rescind the transaction and receive the disclosures. Therefore, a person who is not an obligor on the transaction is still entitled to receive the disclosures and rescind the transaction. For example, a wife who owns a house jointly with her husband will be able to exercise the right, even though she has not signed the note. She is also entitled to receive two copies of the rescission notice and one copy of the disclosures.[161] Survivors who, under state law, inherit an ownership interest in the debtor's principal dwelling do have the right to rescind.[162]

Since the right of rescission is based on the consumer's ownership interest in the dwelling, it would seem that a non-owner cohabiter has no right to rescind. However, in *Pearson v Colonial Financial Services Inc,*[163] the court held that a cohabiter could rescind. The trustee in bankruptcy also has that right on behalf of the bankrupt's estate, but the bankrupt does not.[164]

---

[158] 15 USC §1635(g).

[159] 15 USC §1640(e).

[160] See the 3-year time limit described in **§3.18.**

[161] 12 CFR §§226.15(a)(4), .23(a)(4).

[162] James v Home Constr Co, 621 F2d 727 (5th Cir 1980); Smith v Number 2 Galesburg Crown Fin Corp, 615 F2d 407 (7th Cir 1980).

[163] 526 F Supp 470 (MD Ala 1981).

[164] *In re* Gassaway v Federal Land Bank, 28 BR 842 (Bankr Ct Miss 1983).

§4.30 —Remedies for Violations of Rescission Rights

A creditor who fails to take the appropriate steps to rescind after the consumer has given notice of the consumer's intention may be ordered to pay the statutory damages for violation of the provisions of the Act, even though other remedies, including rescission, are available. The consumer is not required to choose between remedies.[165] In the *Aquino* case cited above,[166] the defendant was ordered to pay the plaintiff the maximum statutory damages of $1,000 and attorneys' fees for failure to honor the plaintiff's right to rescind, even though, in a prior action which was later settled out of court, the plaintiff had recovered from the defendant damages for rescission disclosure violation. The court pointed out that this double recovery was intended by Congress, because not to permit additional recovery of statutory damages for failure to honor a rescission notice would surely undermine a creditor's incentive to honor valid rescission demands.[167]

§4.31 Consumer Leases

Consumer leases are also subject to TILA disclosure requirements. Originally, Regulation Z also implemented the Act's provisions on consumer leases. However, for the sake of clarity, the regulations on consumer leases were taken out of Regulation Z and incorporated in Regulation M.[168] The Act's sections on consumer leases are 15 USC §1667(a)-(e).

Section 15 USC §1667 defines *consumer lease* to mean a contract in the form of a lease or bailment:

1. For the use of personal property
2. By a natural person
3. For a period of time exceeding four months
4. For a total contractual obligation not exceeding $25,000
5. Primarily for personal, family, or household purposes

Whether or not the lessee has the option to purchase or otherwise become the owner of the property at the expiration of the lease is irrelevant. Whether a contractual relationship is created between the lessor and the lessee is determined under state or other applicable law. The Regulation does not make this determination.[169]

Nevertheless, §1667 and Regulation M do not apply to:

---

[165] 15 USC §1635(g). *See* Burley v Vostrop Loan Co, 407 F Supp 773 (DC La 1976).

[166] Aquino v Public Fin Consumer Discount Co, 606 F Supp 504 (ED Pa 1985).

[167] *Id* 511.

[168] 12 CFR pt 213.

[169] 12 CFR §213.2(b) and Official Staff Interpretation.

1. Credit sales.[170] A credit sale is a bailment or lease (unless terminable without penalty at any time by the consumer) under which the consumer agrees to pay as compensation for use, a sum substantially equivalent to or in excess of the total value of the property and services involved and will become, or has the option to become, for no consideration or for nominal consideration, the owner of the property upon compliance with the agreement.[171] This provision conforms with the Uniform Commercial Code's definition of security interests disguised as leases which are really conditional sales.[172] Regulation M therefore applies only to true leases, even where the lessee has the option to purchase the property, but apparently not for nominal or no consideration at the end of the lease, unless the leased property has no salvage value

2. Leases for agricultural, business, or commercial purposes[173]

3. Leases made to an organization[174]

4. Leases of safe deposit boxes[175]

5. Leases of personal property incidental to a service[176]

6. Lease transactions involving personal property which are incident to the lease of real property, and which provide that the lessee has no liability for the value of the property at the end of the lease term except for abnormal wear and tear, and the lessee has no option to purchase the leased property.[177] This exemption obviously applies to leases of furnished apartments and the like.

§4.32 Lease Disclosure Requirements—Generally

The purpose of lease disclosure requirements is to insure the lessees of personal property be given meaningful disclosure of lease terms and to delimit their ultimate liability. The disclosures that TILA and Regulation M require must be made to the lessee at every stage of the transaction: advertising; before consummation; and at renegotiation or extension.

The disclosures must be made either together with the contract evidencing the lease, on the same page as and above the place for the lessee's signature, or in a separate statement identifying the lease transaction.[178] The disclosures must be made clearly, conspicuously, and in a meaningful sequence. In particular, Regulation M specifies that all numerical amounts and percentages

---

[170] 12 CFR §213.2(6).

[171] 12 CFR §226.2(a)(16).

[172] UCC §1-201(37).

[173] 12 CFR §213.2(6).

[174] *Id.*

[175] 12 CFR §213.2(a)(6) and Official Staff Interpretation.

[176] *Id.*

[177] 12 CFR §213.3.

[178] 12 CFR §213.4(a)(2).

must be stated in figures, and must be printed in no less than the equivalent of 10-point type or .075-inch computer type, or elite-size typewriter numerals, or shall be legibly handwritten. All these requirements are designed to make the figures conspicuous.

§4.33 —Lease Advertising Disclosures

Advertisement for leases is provided for at 15 USC §1667(c) and Regulation M, 12 CFR §213.5(a). No advertising may state the availability of a lease of property on certain terms or amounts unless the lessor usually and customarily leases property, or will lease such property, at those precise terms and amounts.[179] This requirement is aimed at deceptive or bait advertising.

All persons who ever advertise consumer lease transactions must comply with the lease advertising provisions, not just those defined as lessors under the Regulation.[180] Thus, the law applies to merchants, automobile dealers, and the like, even though they are not lessors, but advertise consumer lease transactions.[181] However, disclosures are required only if certain triggering terms are used. These relate to:

1. The amount of any payment
2. The number of required payments
3. A statement that a down payment or other payment is required at the lease's consummation

If any one of these triggering terms appears on the advertisement, then the lessor, or anyone subject to the regulation, must clearly and conspicuously disclose the following:

1. That the transaction advertised is a lease
2. The total amount of any payment, such as a security deposit, required at the consummation
3. The number, amounts, due dates, or periods of scheduled payments, and the total of such payments under the lease
4. A statement as to whether the lessee has the option to purchase the leased property, and then at what price and time
5. A statement as to the amount, or method of determining the amount, of any liabilities the lease imposes upon the lessee at the end of the term, and a statement that the lessee shall be liable for the difference, if any, between the estimated value of the leased property and its realized value at the end of the lease term, if the lessee has such liability

The rule dealing with catalogues and multi-page advertising applicable to

---

[179] 12 CFR §213.5(a).
[180] 12 CFR §213.5(a) and Official Staff Interpretation.
[181] *Id.*

both open-end and closed-end credit also applies to leases. The lessor need not make the required disclosures on all the merchandise tags, provided these conspicuously refer to a sign or display with the required disclosures prominently posted in the lessor's showroom.

§4.34 —Consumer Lease Disclosures

Any lessor must make the required disclosures prior to the consummation of the lease. The date of consummation is determined by state or other applicable law, but not by the Act or Regulation M. When a transaction involves more than one lessor, only one lessor, chosen by the lessors, need make the disclosures. Similarly, if more than one lessee is involved, the disclosures need be made only to the lessee who is primarily liable on the lease.[182] A lessor may choose to provide additional information or disclosure not required by law, but such an option may not be used to mislead or confuse the lessee or to contradict or detract from the information required to be disclosed.[183]

Under 15 USC §1667 and Regulation M (12 CFR §213.4), the lessor must disclose the following:

1. A brief description of the leased property, sufficient to identify the property to the lessee and lessor[184]

2. The total amount of any payment, security deposit, trade-in allowance, or any advance payment to be paid by the lessee at the inception of the lease[185]

3. The number, amounts, due dates, or periods of payments and the total amount of such periodic payments[186]

4. The total amount paid or payable for official fees, registration, certificate of title, license fees, or taxes[187]

5. The total amount of all other charges, individually itemized, which are not included in the periodic payments[188]

6. A brief identification of insurance in connection with the lease, paid or not paid by the lessee[189]

7. A statement identifying any express warranties or guarantees available to the lessee, made by the lessor or manufacturer, with respect to the leased property[190]

---

[182] 12 CFR §213.4(c).

[183] 12 CFR §213.4(f).

[184] 15 USC §1667a(1); 12 CFR §213.4(g)(1).

[185] 15 USC §1667a(2); 12 CFR §213.4(g)(2).

[186] 12 CFR §213.4(g)(3).

[187] 15 USC §1667a(3); 12 CFR §213.4(g)(4).

[188] 15 USC §1667a(4); 12 CFR §213.4(g)(5).

[189] 15 USC §1667a(7); 12 CFR §213.4(g)(6).

[190] 15 USC §1667a(6); 12 CFR §213.4(g)(7).

8. An identification of the party responsible for maintaining or servicing the leased property, together with a brief description of the lessor's standards for wear and use, if the lessor sets such standards[191]

9. A description of any security interest held or to be retained by the lessor, and a clear identification of the property to which the security interest relates[192]

10. The amount, or method of determining the amount, of any penalty or other charge for delinquency, default, or late payments[193]

11. A statement of whether the lessee has the option to purchase the leased item at what price, and if prior to the end of the lease term, at what time, and the price or the method of determining the price[194]

12. A statement of the conditions under which the lessee or lessor may terminate the lease prior to the end of the lease term, and the amount, or method of determining the amount, of any penalty or other charge for early termination[195]

13. A statement that the lessee shall be liable for the difference between the estimated value of the property and its realized value at early termination, or at the end of the lease term, if such liability exists[196]

14. If the lessee's liability is based on the estimated value of the leased property, a statement indicating that the lessee may obtain, at lessee's expense, a professional appraisal by a third party of the value of the property, and which third party is agreed upon by the lessee and the lessor, and which appraisal shall be final and binding on the parties[197]

If, at the time of disclosure, certain information or amounts are unknown to the lessor, the lessor may use estimates, but must clearly identify them as such.[198]

§4.35 —Disclosures at Renegotiation or Extension of Lease

Leases that are renegotiated or extended are considered new leases, and thus subject to the disclosure requirements of Regulation M.[199] However, there are exceptions, namely:

---

[191] 12 CFR §213.4(g)(8).

[192] 15 USC §1667a(8); 12 CFR §213.4(g)(9).

[193] 12 CFR §213.4(g)(10).

[194] 15 USC §1667a(5); 12 CFR §213.4(g)(11).

[195] 15 USC §1667a(11); 12 CFR §213.4(g)(12).

[196] 15 USC §1667a(4); 12 CFR §213.4(g)(3).

[197] 15 USC §1667a(10); 12 CFR §213.4(g)(14).

[198] 12 CFR §213.4(d).

[199] 12 CFR §213.4(h).

1. Leases of multiple items when a new item is provided or a previously leased item is returned, and the average payment allocable to a monthly period is not changed by more than 25%

2. Leases which are extended for not more than six months on a month-to-month basis[200]

Lessors who fail to comply with the disclosure requirements at advertising, consummation and renegotiation, or extension of the consumer lease are subject to all the liability provisions of TILA.[201]

§4.36 Administrative Enforcement of the Truth in Lending Act

TILA provides for three types of enforcement; administrative, criminal, and private. No fewer than nine federal agencies are authorized to enforce the provisions of TILA, but the primary burden of enforcement is on the Federal Trade Commission. The FTC is responsible for the largest area in which the Act must be enforced: retail and department stores, finance companies, nonbank credit card issuers, and all other creditors. Each of the federal agencies has the authority to set up its own procedures for enforcement of the Act,[202] and so, in order to ensure uniformity of implementation, the Board of Governors of the Federal Reserve System is authorized to issue authoritative regulations and interpretations.[203]

Other agencies responsible for enforcing the Act are the Controller of the Currency, for national banks, the Federal Reserve Board, for member banks that are not national banks, the Federal Deposit Insurance Corporation, for insured banks not members of the federal reserve system, the Federal Home Loan Bank Board, for savings institutions not insured by the Federal Deposit Insurance Corporation (FTIC), the National Credit Union Administration, for federal credit unions, the Farm Credit Administration, for federal farm credit, and the Secretary of Agriculture, for creditors subject to the Bankers and Stockyards Act.[204] All the TILA activities not regulated by one of the above eight agencies are under the administration of the Federal Trade Commission.[205]

Although the agencies have the authority to enforce all of the provisions of the Act, enforcement focuses mainly on violations with respect to the annual percentage rate and the finance charge disclosure provisions.[206] Where an

---

200 *Id.*

201 15 USC §1667(d); 12 CFR §213.8(c).

202 15 USC §1607(d).

203 15 USC §1604(a).

204 15 USC §1607(a).

205 15 USC §1607(c).

206 15 USC §1607(e).

annual percentage rate or finance charge is inaccurately disclosed, the relevant agency will notify the creditor of the error, and may require the creditor to make an adjustment of the account of the debtor, to make sure that the debtor is not required to pay more than the properly computed and disclosed annual percentage rate, or finance charge, whichever is lower.[207]

Except where the disclosure error resulted from a willful violation with intent to mislead, no adjustment of the debtor's account may be ordered in the following cases:

1. Where the error is less than 1/4 of 1 per cent in the annual percentage rate

2. Where the adjustment would have a significantly adverse impact on the safety or soundness of the creditor; the agency may in such a case require a partial adjustment in an amount which does not have such an impact

3. Where the amount of the adjustment would be less than one dollar

4. Where more than two years have passed after the violation, in an open-end credit plan. In the case of closed-end credit, no adjustment can be ordered more than two years after the consummation of the agreement to extend credit, or after the expiration of the life of the credit plan, whichever is later[208]

5. Finally, no adjustment can be ordered if the creditor, within 60 days after discovering the disclosure error, notifies the debtor and makes the necessary adjustment in the debtor's account[209]

It must be remembered that none of these mitigations of federal agencies' enforcement powers apply where there is a finding of a clear and consistent pattern or practice of violations, gross negligence, or willful conduct. Most violations of TILA are corrected through informal agency exchanges, and correspondence with the violator. However, since any violation of the Act is also a violation of the agency's enabling statute, the agency may still exercise any other enforcement authority conferred upon the agency by law, independently of TILA. Thus, for instance, the FTC may have the power to issue cease-and-desist orders against deception and unfair trade practices under §5 of the FTC Act.[210] Except where there is a willful violation, Congress has given the enforcement agencies discretionary power to enforce or not in certain specific circumstances deemed to be of minor importance.[211]

---

[207]

[208] 15 USC §1607(e)(3).

[209] 15 USC §1607(d)(5).

[210] 15 USC §45(a).

[211] 15 USC §1607(e)(2).

§4.37   Criminal Enforcement

The United States Attorney General's office prosecutes violations of the Act. Criminal liability applies to whether, willfully and knowingly, a creditor gives false or inaccurate information, or fails to provide information which is required to be disclosed under the Act, uses any charge or table authorized by the board in such a manner so as to consistently understate the annual percentage rate, or otherwise fails to comply with any requirement under the Act. Such a person shall be fined not more than $5,000, or imprisoned not more than one year, or both.[212]

A creditor participating in credit programs administered, insured, or guaranteed by a department or agency of the United States may not be held criminally liable for violations resulting from the use of instruments that are required by the department or agency.[213] Similarly, no criminal liability can be imposed for any act committed in good faith, and in conformity with any interpretation or approval by an official or employee of the Federal Reserve Board authorized to issue such interpretation or approval.[214]

§4.38   Private Enforcement

In addition to administrative and criminal enforcement of TILA, the Act provides an important third method: private enforcement. Although the 1980 Simplification Act has substantially restricted private enforcement, private suits still constitute a meaningful weapon in the hands of the consumer against a creditor who ignores the requirements of the Act. Private enforcement may take the form of an individual action or a class action.[215]

Individual Action

The consumer wishing to take advantage of private enforcement under the Act may bring action in a federal district court or state court of competent jurisdiction within one year of the violation. In the case of a credit transaction, the plaintiff may recover the statutory penalty of twice the finance charge. However, the maximum statutory recovery cannot be greater than $1,000 and the minimum can be no less than $100. In the case of a consumer lease, the statutory penalty is fixed at 25 per cent of the total amount of monthly payments under the lease. If successful, the plaintiff may also recover any actual damages, court costs, and reasonable attorneys' fees.[216]

---

[212] 15 USC §1611.

[213] 15 USC §1612(c)(d).

[214] 15 USC §1640(f).

[215] 15 USC §1640(a)-(h).

[216] 15 USC §1640(a).

Class Action

The grounds on which a class action may be brought are the same as for individual actions. The minimum recovery provisions for individual actions, however, do not apply here. TILA was amended in 1976 to put a ceiling on the amount recoverable in such an action. Thus, currently, the total recovery by any class or series of classes in an action against the same creditor for the same violation is limited to the lesser of $500,000 or 1 per cent of the creditor's net worth.[217]

The law also provides that, in determining the amount of award in any class action, the court shall consider the amount of any actual damages awarded, the frequency and persistence of failures of compliance by the creditor, the creditor's resources, the number of people in the class adversely affected, and the extent to which the creditor's failure of compliance was intentional. This list of considerations is not exhaustive.[218]

§4.39   Limitations on Liability

The Simplification Act has considerably limited the number of instances which could give rise to the creditor's civil liability. Generally, civil liability is eliminated for disclosure violations which are deemed to be insignificant. The law specifies a number of significant violations.

In open-end credit, only the failure to make the following disclosures can give rise to civil liability:

1. Failure to comply with the rescission requirements of the Act
2. Failure to make the disclosures required upon the opening of an account
3. Failure to disclose certain specific items during the billing cycle which are deemed to be of material importance. These items are exhaustively enumerated at 15 USC §1640(a)(3)
4. Failure to comply with state disclosure requirements, if the board deems these requirements to be substantially the same as those of the Act

These limitations on the circumstances giving rise to liability also apply to closed-end credit violations. The creditor is civilly liable only for failure to comply with the rescission requirements and failure to make the following disclosures: amount financed; itemized finance charge; annual percentage rate; total of payments; number, amount, due dates, or periods of payments; and the fact that a security interest has been taken.[219]

The Simplification Act is very specific about whether the Act's list of violations that may give rise to liability is exhaustive. Section 1640(a)(3) states

---

[217] 15 USC §1640(a)(1)(B).
[218] 15 USC §1640(a)(1)(2).
[219] 15 USC §1640(a)(3).

that the creditor "shall have liability *only* for failing to comply with the requirements" specifically cited in the Act (emphasis added).

Furthermore, the creditor's civil liability is altogether eliminated in the following situations:

1. Correction of error within 60 days of its discovery and prior to suit or to written notice by a consumer[220]

2. Unintentional or bona fide errors, notwithstanding the maintenance of procedures reasonably adopted to avoid any such error. Examples of acceptable errors under this rule are clerical calculation errors and computer malfunctions[221]

3. Application of rules, regulations, or interpretations by the Board, or conformation to the interpretations of an authorized official of the Board[222]

In view of all the new limitations on the creditor's liability, the consumer's use of TILA as a shield against the creditor's action for payment may no longer be as effective as under the old Act.

§4.40   Truth in Lending and State Laws

Most states had enacted credit disclosure statutes patterned after the Truth in Lending Act prior to the Act's Simplification and Reform. Some of the states merely reproduced the old TILA in their own statutes. Other states simply declared that compliance with the federal TILA was compliance with the state credit disclosure requirements.

With the passage of the Simplification Act, creditors face new compliance problems because of the divergence of state and federal disclosure requirements created by the new Act. Except where the state requirements are deemed inconsistent with federal requirements, TILA does not prevent, annul, or alter state disclosure requirements.[223]

A state law is inconsistent with the federal TILA if it requires a creditor to make disclosures or take actions which contradict the requirements of federal law. For example, a state law contradicts TILA if it requires the use of the same term to represent a different meaning or amount than the federal law, or if it requires the use of a different term than federal law to describe the same item.[224]

A creditor, state, or other interested party may request that the Federal

---

[220] 15 USC §1640(b).

[221] 15 USC §1640(c).

[222] 15 USC §1640(f).

[223] 15 USC §1610(a)(1).

[224] 12 CFR §226.28(a)(1).

Reserve Board determine whether a state law is consistent with TILA.[225] If the Board determines that a state law is inconsistent, then the lenders in that state may not make the inconsistent disclosures, and no state liability may attach due to the creditor's failure to use the state's inconsistent term or form.[226]

Since 1983, the Federal Reserve Board has determined that required disclosures in five states have been preempted by the federal TILA. These five states are Arizona, Florida, Missouri, Mississippi, and South Carolina.[227]

The Federal Reserve Board has the authority to exempt from TILA any class of credit within any state, if the Board determines that under the law of that state, the requirements are substantially similar to those imposed by the Act and Regulations Z and M, and that there is adequate provision for enforcement.[228] Thus, if the FRB approves the state exemption, the creditors in that state may make the state-required disclosures in lieu of those required under the federal TILA. None of the state exemptions, however, extends to the civil liability provisions of TILA.[229] This is to allow consumers in exempted states to continue to bring TILA damages actions in either state or federal courts. By the same token, creditors retain the defenses provided for under the federal TILA.[230] Regulations Z and M, together with the official staff interpretations, have given the criteria for the determination of preemption or exemption.[231] Effective October 1, 1982, the Federal Reserve Board has granted exemption to five states: Maine, Connecticut, Massachusetts, Oklahoma, and Wyoming.[232]

---

[225] 15 USC §1610(a)(1); 12 CFR §226.28(a)(1).

[226] 15 USC §1610(a)(1); 12 CFR §226.28(a)(1).

[227] Az: Ariz Rev Stat Ann §§44-287B.5, 44-287B.6, 44-287B.7 (1967); Fla: Fla Stat Ann §§520.07(2)(f), 520.34(2)(f); 520.07(2)(g), 520.34(2)(g), 520.07(2)(h), 520.34(2)(h), 520.07(2)(i), 520.34(2)(i) (West 1979); Mo: Mo Rev Stat §§365.070-6(9), 408.260-5(6), 365.070-6(10), 408.260-5(7), 365.070-2, 408.260-2, 365.070-6(ii), 408.260-5(8), 365.070-6(12), 408.260-5(9)(1979); Miss: Miss Code Ann §§63-19-31(2)(g) (Harrison 1972); SC: SC Code Ann §37-10-102(c) (in part) (Law Co-op 1976); 12 CFR §226.28(a)(8)-(12) and Official Staff Interpretations.

[228] 15 USC §1610(a)(2); 12 CFR §226.29(a).

[229] 12 CFR §226.29(b).

[230] *Id* and Official Staff Interpretation.

[231] *See* 12 CFR §§226.28, .29 and Official Staff Interpretations.

[232] 12 CFR §226.29(a)(4) and Official Staff Interpretations. Consumer Credit Code. Connecticut: Credit transactions subject to the Connecticut Truth-in-Lending Act. Maine: Credit or lease transactions subject to the Maine Consumer Credit Code. Massachusetts: Credit transactions subject to the Massachusetts Truth-in Lending Act. Oklahoma: Credit or lease transactions subject to the Oklahoma Consumer Credit Code. Wyoming: Credit transactions subject to the Wyoming Consumer Credit Code.
In all the five states, the exemption does not apply to transactions in which a federally chartered institution is a creditor or lessor.

5

Charge and Rate Regulation

§5.01   Historical Background

The aim of charge and rate regulation is to provide credit to the consumer at reasonable rates. Most states have usury laws to curb imposition of interest above a statutory limit. The term *usury* itself has changed in meaning with the passage of time. Originally, usury meant a payment for the use of money. It did not mean, as it does today, the taking of an interest higher than that permitted by law. Very ancient societies recognized the legitimacy of imposing a charge upon the lending of money. These early societies simply sought to limit the maximum charge for such lending. For instance, the Code of Hammurabi of the Babylonian period (1900-732 BC) set a maximum annual rate of 33 1/3 per cent for loans of grain, and 20 per cent for loans of silver.[1] Thus, interest at that time was not illegal per se; only those rates above the legal ceiling were prohibited. With the advent of the Christian era, the taking of any interest was considered sinful. The bibical injunction against usury was expressed in these terms:

> And if thy brother be waxen poor, and fallen in decay with thee, then thou shall relieve him: yea, though he be Stranger, or a sojourner; that he may live with thee.
> Take thou no usury of him, or increase: fear thy God, that thy brother may live with thee.[2]

The injunction against usury was based partly on the belief that it is sinful to exploit the poor one, or a brother, or a person in need, for mostly people in need borrowed money in those times. Prohibition against usury was the same as prohibition against theft, since usury was seen as getting something for nothing. Both church and state forbade usury except when used against the "foes of God's people." The Second Lateran Council codified this prohibition in 1139.[3]

An examination of how this commandment has fared through the centuries even provides a remarkable window into the ethical evolution of our society.

---

[1] Report of the National Commission on Consumer Finance, Consumer Credit in the United States 91 (1972) [hereinafter National Report].

[2] *Id* 92 (citing *Leviticus* 25:35-37).

[3] National Report, *supra* note 1, at 92.

Benjamin Nelson has explored this "tangled history of the 'transvaluation of values' which culminated in the spirit of capitalism." He states,

> To follow its meanderings from the Jerusalem of the Prophets and Priests to mid-nineteenth century Europe is to survey the major phases of the ethical evolution of the West: first the kinship morality of the tribal society; then the universal brotherhood of Medieval Christianity; and finally the utilitarian liberalism of modern times. . . .[4]

In the consumer era, consumer credit has become a fact of life—and it is not only the poor who borrow. However, the taint or opprobrium attached to taking excessive interest from the lending of money remains. This historical reluctance to give creditors free rein can be seen in the enactment of many statutes that limit charges on consumer credit. The usury statutes usually fix the maximum rates at 6 or 8 per cent. However, there are now so many exceptions to the rule that the question of rate regulations has become a maze of different rates, applying to different types of lending institutions.

As the Report of the National Commission on Consumer Finance has pointed out, a compilation of consumer credit legislation reveals "the present hodgepodge of legislation characteristic of most states."[5] For example, New York has separate statutes regulating installment loans by commercial banks, loans by industrial banks, bank check credit plans, revolving charge accounts, motor vehicle installment sales financing, installment financing of other goods and services, insurance premium financing, loans by consumer finance companies, and loans by credit unions. All this results in a market segmentation which is rendered even more fragmentary by other regulations on the types of credit granted, the amount of credit, and the classes of credit grantors.

§5.02   Regulation or No Regulation?

There has always been a debate as to whether interest rates on consumer credit should be regulated. One school of thought, led by economist Milton Friedman, supports free rates: prices for credit should be determined by free market competition without being hindered by government interference. The other school of thought supports the view that there should be a decreed ceiling on the price of consumer credit. Proponents advance the following purposes for this view: to redress unequal bargaining power; to avoid overburdening consumers with excessive debts; to administer credit grantors as though they were public utilities; and to assure that consumers pay fair rates of credit.[6]

Despite these purposes, the National Commission On Consumer Finance, after a survey of lenders' practices, came to the conclusion that "on balance,

---

[4] B. Nelson, The Idea of Usury 19 (1960).

[5] National Report, *supra* note 1, at 94.

[6] Report of the National Commission on Consumer Finance, Consumer Credit in the United States 95 (1972).

rate ceilings are undesirable. When markets are reasonably competitive, imposition of rate ceilings on consumer credit transactions neither assures that most consumers will pay a fair price for the use of credit nor prevents overburdening them with excesive debt."[7] In spite of the conclusion of the Report, however, usury laws still exist on the books for almost all the states. The maximum rates in these laws vary between 5 per cent and 18 per cent. The laws appear to be a result of the fact that moral and religious compunctions are hard to leave behind, despite changes in the realities of economic life. However, modern realities dictate that the states carve out important areas where a higher rate of interest is allowed, such as in the following areas.

Uniform Small Loan Laws

A low usury rate, and any penalty attached to one who exceeds that rate, may well result in the denial of a loan to a needy consumer. Prior to the enactment of small loan laws, the need of the consumer could not be satisfied within the bounds of legality, and so, not surprisingly, it was satisfied outside the law. Lending at illegal rates flourished in many cities in states which had tight usury statutes, even in those states with severe penalties. The illegal interest rate could reach 33 per cent or more per month.

In the first decade of this century, the Russel Sage Foundation became interested in this problem of small loans and high usury rates. The foundation sponsored the development of uniform small loan laws which attempted to curb the excesses of the small consumer loan by regulating the small loan financing industry, requiring lenders to be licensed and to obey the law, fixing more realistic legal rates by raising the rates considered usurious, fixing them originally at 3 1/2 per cent per month, and subjecting lenders that violated the small loan laws to strict criminal penalties. The original maximum loan amount governed by these laws was $300.

The Uniform Small Loan Laws were soon adopted in all states, except Arkansas. Some states allowed different rates, or allowed a higher loan amount, but all adopted the main tenets of the uniform laws.

Industrial and Installment Loan Laws

The industrial loan laws are applications of the Morris Bank Plan, developed around 1910 by Arthur Morris, a clever lawyer. The plan seeks to secure an interest rate higher than that permitted under the usury laws. Under this plan, the borrower pays interest at the legal rate for the full term of the loan, and in a "separate" transaction, agrees to make monthly deposits with the lender. The deposits are enough under this plan to repay the loan at its maturity date. This mechanism succeeded in increasing the amount of interest charged without conflicting with the usury laws. Thus, the actual interest rate on a loan, discounted at 8 per cent and payable in 50 equal weekly installments, would amount to 17.7 per cent if the contract was met promptly. The rate can be even

---

[7] *Id* 108.

higher if the borrower defaults on payments.[8] Most of the states adopt the Morris scheme in their industrial and installment loan laws, which then allow an interest rate higher than that permitted by the state usury statutes. No dollar limit is imposed upon these loans.

Besides these two types of loans, most states have adopted special statutes for credit unions, pawnbrokers, home improvement loans, small loans, industrial and installment loans, check loans, and others allowing a higher interest rate than the legal usury limit. From the consumer standpoint, the usury statutes rarely apply.

§5.03   The Time-Price Doctrine

The time-price doctrine is perhaps the most important exception to the legal usury ceiling. It is based on the distinction between lender credit and seller credit. This distinction allows a seller of goods to fix one price for a sale in cash, and another price for a sale on credit. The difference between the two prices is not considered to be a finance or interest charge, and, therefore, is not subject to the usury law.

The doctrine was first enunciated in an 1827 English case, *Beete v Bidgood*,[9] and recognized in the United States in *Mitchell v Griffith*.[10] The doctrine is best stated in the leading American case recognizing the doctrine, *Hogg v Ruffner*:

> [I]t is manifest that if A proposed to sell to B a tract of land for $10,000 in cash or for $20,000 payable in 10 annual installments, and if B prefers to pay the larger sum to gain time, the contract may not be called usurious. A vendor may prefer $100 in hand to double the sum in expectancy, and a purchaser may prefer the greatest price with the longer credit; and one who will not distinguish between things that differ, may say, with apparent truth, that B pays 100% for forbearance and may assert that such a contract is usurious; but whatever truth there may be in the premise, the conclusion is manifestly erroneous. Such a contract has none of the characteristics of usury; it is not for the loan of money or the forbearance of the debt.[11]

Another court gives an additional justification to the time-price doctrine. "A purchaser is not like the needy borrower, a victim of a rapacious lender since he can refrain from the purchase if he does not choose to pay the price asked by the seller."[12]

---

[8] *See* Benfield, *Money, Mortgages, and Migraine—The Usury Headache,* 19 Case W Res 819, at 841-42 (1967-68).

[9] 108 Eng Rep 792 (1827).

[10] 22 Mo 515 (1856).

[11] 66 US (1 Black) 115, 118-19 (1861).

[12] General Motors Acceptance Corp v Weinrich, 218 Mo App 68, 77-78, 262 SW 425, 428 (1924).

Theoretically, there is no difference between a seller extending credit and a lender extending credit. Consider a seller who, after extending credit to the borrower, assigns the claim against the borrower to a finance company. The time-price doctrine would allow the latter to evade the usury laws. Likewise, consider a lender who advances the fund to the seller, who in turn extends credit to the buyer. This will have the same result, allowing the lender to evade the usury laws. From the borrower's point of view, there is no difference. However, the courts invented this doctrine through the necessity of saving the large installment credit sales system from the unrealistic low interest ceilings imposed by the state usury laws, in the absence of any installment sales legislation similar to small loan laws. The courts continue to maintain this doctrine throughout the United States, except in Arkansas and Nebraska. As an Arizona court concluded in *Howell v Mid-State Homes, Inc*,[13] any change in the time-price doctrine should be initiated by the legislature and not by the courts.

Today, most states have retail installment sales statutes which fix the maximum interest or finance charge that may be imposed in credit sales. Although the statutes vary in scope, some covering only sales of motor vehicles, some covering sales of other goods, some for business purposes, and some only for nonbusiness purposes, they all have a common feature, to allow a maximum finance charge which is higher than the state legal usury rate.

§5.04   What Is Usury?

Usury can be defined as the illegal overcharging of interest on a current loan or forbearance of money. Usury consists of four elements:

1. A loan or forbearance of money
2. An overcharge of the legal rate of interest
3. An understanding between the parties that the principal shall be payable absolutely
4. An intent to violate the usury limit

§5.05   —Loan or Forbearance of Money

Forbearance means to withhold a demand for money currently due. As stated above, usury statutes usually apply only to lender credit. Seller credit is protected under the time-price doctrine, being considered not to be a loan or forbearance of money in the traditional usury sense.

Wisconsin v JC Penney Co[14] is one of the leading cases that refused to apply the time-price doctrine to an installment sale involving revolving charge accounts. The Wisconsin Supreme Court found that the retail store's imposi-

---

[13] 13 Ariz App 371, 476 P2d 892 (1970).
[14] 48 Wis 2d 125, 179 NW2d 641 (1970).

tion of the 1 1/2 per cent per month charge upon the consumer's declining balance of the account violated the state's 12 per cent usury limit. The court reasoned that there was a forbearance in the traditional definitional sense, i.e., an agreement to refrain from collecting an existing debt. The debt did arise at the time the purchase was made, and the actual forbearance occurred at that time.

The defendant, J.C. Penney Co., argued that the monthly charge was a time-price differential and therefore not subject to the usury statutes, because when it sold merchandise under its revolving charge account plan, it charged a higher sale price than the price at which it sells the merchandise for cash. In other words, J.C. Penney argued, there was no forbearance.

The court determined that the transaction involved did not quote a cash price and a credit price. It was no more than an agreement by the creditor not to attempt to collect the debt for an agreed length of time. The court noted that the agreement did not expressly provide for such forbearance on the part of the defendant, J.C. Penney. However, a promise to forbear may be implied.[15] The court repeated several times that it would look beyond the form of the transaction to its substance, and concluded that there was a forbearance in this case.

More states rejected the Wisconsin decision than adopted it. The question became moot, however, when the states enacted the retail installment sales statutes, and the statutes governing sales on open-end credit. These statutes regulate interest, finance charges, and other issues involved with these types of transactions. The time-price doctrine can no longer be invoked to justify a violation of those specific statutes.

In *GTT Leisure Products, Inc v Camella*,[16] the time-price doctrine still applied. The case involved the sale of stereo equipment by a wholesale distributor to a retailer for purposes of resale. The court held that the charges imposed on past due accounts were not interest charges, but charges for the privilege of purchasing on credit. Prohibitions against usury were inapplicable to a sale of property on credit. In this case, the state retail installment sales statute was inapplicable because the sale by a wholesaler to a retailer for resale was not within the scope of the statute.

§5.06 —Imposition of a Rate That Exceeds the Legal Maximum

To constitute usury, there must be exaction of a rate which exceeds the rate set by usury law or the specific statute. The existence of usury is not dependent on the actual receipt of the unlawful interest. The test of usury is whether the contract, if performed, would result in obtaining an interest rate higher than the legal maximum and whether such result was intended.

---

[15] 179 NW2d at 645.
[16] 58 AD2d 1040, 397 NYS2d 292 (1977).

Some states have in their statutes provisions allowing higher interest than the ordinary legal interest, but not exceeding a given ceiling, if it is agreed upon beforehand by contract. For instance, in North Carolina, the legal rate is 8 per cent. However, as of February, 1987, parties may contract for 16 per cent for a loan of $25,000 or less. Over the $25,000, there is no rate limit.[17]

In *Triton Oil & Gas Corp v Marine Contractors & Supply Inc,*[18] the existence of such an agreement is at issue. There was no written agreement between the debtor and creditor concerning the interest to be charged on any outstanding balance. Therefore, the legal 6 per cent rate of interest was read into the agreement. However, in that case, the creditor in fact charged 10 per cent interest by unilaterally deducting this interest from the debtor's share of the proceeds. Even though the debtor never complained of the charges, the debtor never paid them either, and the court held there was no evidence of an agreement between the parties as to the 10 per cent interest charge. Had such an agreement existed, the 10 per cent charge would not have been usurious under Texas law.

Note that there is no requirement that the loan or interest be payable only in money. There might be usury when the repayment of principal and interest is in kind under the form of property or services, the value of which is not speculative, and which is so obviously in excess of the legal interest as to imply an intent to evade the usury laws.[19]

§5.07 —The Amount Must Be Due Absolutely

To constitute usury, it is required that the sum of the loan be repayable absolutely. If it is payable only upon some contingency, then there can be no usury. However, if the contingency selected is so far-fetched as to be utterly improbable, and therefore chosen with a view toward escaping the statutory requirement, then the obligation is usurious.[20] In other words, if the lender incurs no real hazard or risk, then there is no justification for a higher interest rate, and an excessive charge will be treated as usurious. For example, where the debtor is the beneficiary of a trust, and the repayment of the loan is contingent upon the debtor's surviving his mother, and the lender takes a life insurance policy on the debtor's life, the court held that the lender did not incur any real hazard, and so the loan was usurious.[21] Conversely, if the loan is for

---

[17] *See* 1 Consumer Credit Guide (CCH), pt 510 for a Table of State Usury Laws.

[18] 644 SW2d 443 (Tex 1982).

[19] 45 Am Jur 2d *Interest and Usury* §168 (1969).

[20] *See* Annotation, *Contingency as to Borrower's Receipt of Money or Other Property from which Loan is to be Repaid as Rendering Loan Usurious,* 92 ALR3d 623 (1979), for examples of such contingencies.

[21] De Korwin v First Natl Bank, 170 F Supp 112 (ND Ill 1958), *affd,* 275 F2d 755 (7th Cir), *cert denied,* 364 US 824 (1960).

a risky investment, an imposition of interest which exceeds the legal maximum rate is not usurious.[22]

The risk must be a substantial one. The standard is whether a prudent man would take such a risk for the legal interest only. It must not be intended as a mere cover for exacting more than the legal maximum interest rate. In all these transactions, the court will look to the substance rather than the form of the transaction.[23]

§5.08   —Intent to Violate the Usury Limit

To constitute usury, there must be an intent to take more than what is allowed by law. The actual intent refers not to the illegality but to a rate of interest which is proscribed as illegal. The courts presume intent to violate the law when the contract on its face provides for an interest rate which in fact exceeds the legal limit. The only way the lender can rebut this presumption of intent is to prove that there was a bona fide error in the preparation of the document. The bona fide error is generally limited to one which is nonrecurring. Repeated errors caused by the use of an erroneous or improper method of computation of the interest or by errors in the computer programming are not considered bona fide errors.[24]

It has been held generally that a mistake in the amount or calculation of interest committed by an attorney, bookkeeper or clerk, or similar subordinate will not render a loan usurious absent a showing of usurious intent on the part of the creditor. On the other hand, a mistake by an employee may denote usury, where one can prove that the lender intended to receive the excess amount.[25] A mistake of law is not a defense.

Sometimes the usury is not apparent on the face of the document. Some courts can still find usury if it can be shown that the lender did intend to evade usury laws by structuring the contract as it did. For example, in *Handi Investment Co v Mobil Oil Corp*,[26] the court held that whether intent exists is a question of fact which can be determined from all the circumstances of the case. The court found that the fact that when a distributor of oil, renewing a loan to a gas station, reduced a discount previously granted to the gas station owner, a prima facie case of usury resulted. Although the price even after the discount was the normal price customarily charged to Mobil Oil retail dealers, the court held that this fact per se did not bar the usury issue.

---

[22] *See* Whitemore Homes, Inc v Fleishman, 190 Cal App 2d 554, 12 Cal Rptr 235 (1961).

[23] *See* 45 Am Jur 2d *Interest and Usury* §§154-159 (1969).

[24] *See* Southland Mobile Home Corp v Webster, 263 Ark 100, 563 SW2d 430 (1978). But in Libowsky v Lakeshore Commercial Fin Corp, 110 Wis 2d 742, 330 NW2d 248 (Ct App 1982), *review denied*, 110 Wis 2d 748, 331 NW2d 391 (1983), the court held there was no intent because of programming error.

[25] Ford Motor Credit Co v Hutcherson, 277 Ark 102, 640 SW2d 96 (1982).

[26] 550 F2d 543 (9th Cir 1977).

In *Lockhart Co v Naef*,[27] the parties designated a loan as a *consumer loan* in order to benefit from a higher rate. But this fact itself was not enough for a finding of usury. One must find that the lender "knowingly, and with corrupt intent," charged a usurious rate.[28]

§5.09   Usury and the Uniform Consumer Credit Code

As we have seen, state usury legislation is a crazy quilt. The legal usury limit is usually subject to a multitude of exceptions, provided by numerous specific statutes.

The most innovative feature of the Uniform Consumer Credit Code (U3C) is its treatment of rate regulation, a treatment which aims at eliminating the fragmented approach existing under state law. The U3C is based on the assumption that competition is the best method of determining prices of nonmonopoly commodities and services. On the other hand, the protection of unsophisticated credit recipients calls for the setting of a ceiling on the price of credit.[29]

In view of these findings, the drafters of the U3C proposed to simplify and unify the law on credit and finance charges. The U3C also, instead of fixing rates, provides for graduated rate ceilings. The basic assumption and policies adopted in the first 1968 U3C are basically undisturbed by the 1974 versions, except for some minor adjustments.

By setting high ceilings but not fixing rates, the U3C drafters intended to preserve competition within the law. The rate ceilings are graduated according to the amount of the loan granted. Under U3C §2-201 (1968), the credit service charge may not exceed

> (a) the total of:
> (i) 36 percent per year on that part of the unpaid balances of the amount financed which is $300 or less;
> (ii) 21 percent per year on that part of the unpaid balances of the amount financed which is more than $300 but does not exceed $1,000; and
> (iii) 15 per cent per year on that part of the unpaid balances of the amount financed which is more than $1,000; OR
> (b) 18 percent per year on the unpaid balance of the amount financed.

The 1974 U3C adopts the same policy of setting ceilings and not fixing

---

[27] 107 Idaho 888, 693 P2d 1090 (Ct App 1984).
[28] 693 P2d at 1092.
[29] U3C Prefatory Note, 7 ULA 583.

rates.[30] The drafters believe this policy will provide more effective competition than fixing rates.[31]

The policy adopted by the U3C, setting ceilings but not fixing rates, was approved by the National Commission on Consumer Finance in its 1972 Report:

> [The Commission recommends] that policies designed to promote competition should be given the first priority, with adjustment of rate-ceilings used as a complement, to expand the availability of credit. As the development of workable competitive markets decreases the need for rate-ceilings to combat market power in concentrated markets, such ceilings may be raised or removed.[32]

The U3C deals separately with open-end credit. For open-end credit, a 1 1/2 per cent per month rate ceiling on the first $500 balance and a 2 per cent per month ceiling for a balance of more than $500 are established.[33]

§5.10 Supervised Lenders and Supervised Loans

Those making consumer loans at interest rates in excess of 18 per cent must obtain a license. Such lenders are called *supervised lenders.* "Supervised lender means a person authorized to take, or take assignments of, supervised loans, under a license issued by the Administrator or as a supervised financial organization."[34] Supervised financial organizations are not required to obtain a license because they are always subject to supervision by a state or federal agency. "Supervised loan means a consumer loan, including a loan pursuant to open-end credit, in which the rate of the finance charge exceeds 18 per cent per year."[35] A licensee may not conduct the business of making supervised loans at a place other than the place of business for which the license is granted.[36] Some states, adopting the 1968 U3C (such as Colorado, Idaho, and Oklahoma), adopted the *Brick Wall Amendment,* which prohibits a supervised lender from selling or leasing goods at the place of business where supervised loans are made. This amendment expressed the concern of banks and consumer finance companies with the possibility of major retailers making supervised loans while also selling goods.

The 1974 U3C does not include such a provision specifically. Instead, it merely provides that a supervised lender may not carry on other business for the purpose of evasion or violation of the statute at the location where

---

[30] U3C §2.201, .401 (1974).

[31] U3C §2.201 comment (1974).

[32] Report of the National Commission on Consumer Finance, Consumer Credit in the United States 27 (1972).

[33] U3C §2.202 (1974).

[34] U3C §1.301(42) (1974).

[35] U3C §1.301(43) (1974).

[36] U3C §2.302(6) (1974).

supervised loans are made.[37] In other words, supervised lenders may engage in transactions on their premises other than loaning money, if such transactions are legitimate. As an example, commercial banks, besides lending money, typically provide other services to customers with no purpose of violating provisions on maximum charges. However, tie-in sales of goods or services in connection with loans are a violation of the statute, because they are carried on to evade the rate ceilings applicable to such sales of goods or services.[38]

§5.11   Usury Remedies under the Uniform Consumer Credit Code

Generally, if a person is charged an interest rate in excess of that allowed by the statute, that person has a right to a refund of the excess payment.[39] Under the 1968 U3C, if a person makes a *supervised loan* without authority, the loan is void, and the debtor is not obligated to pay either the principal or the finance charge.[40] The 1974 U3C no longer provides for avoidance of the loan in these circumstances. The consumer has only the right to a refund of any excess charge paid.[41]

In dealing with interest and usury, one should not lose sight of the U3C's extensive provisions on unconscionability which give the court the right to refuse to enforce an agreement in which an unconscionable clause or agreement is present.[42] These provisions on unconscionability are derived from the Uniform Commercial Code.[43] The difference is that under the U3C, the standard of unconscionability is judged with a consumer transaction in mind, and not in the context of knowledgeable merchants. As Comment 2 of §5-108 of the U3C states, the basic test for unconscionability is whether, in the totality of circumstances surrounding the case, the contract or clause in question is so one-sided at the time of the making of the contract as to be unconscionable.[44]

§5.12   Federal Usury Law: The Most Favored Lender Status

Federal law has an important impact on state usury laws. As we have seen, lending institutions are of two main types: depository institutions and

---

[37] U3C §2.309 (1974).

[38] U3C §2.309 comment (1974).

[39] U3C §§5.202(3) (1968), .201(2) (1974).

[40] U3C §5.202(2) (1968).

[41] U3C §5.201(2) (1974).

[42] U3C §5.108 (1974).

[43] UCC §2-302.

[44] Miller & Warren, *The 1974 Uniform Consumer Credit Code*, 23 Kan L Rev, 619 639-42 (1975).

non-depository institutions.[45] Commercial banks are the best known type of depository institutions. They can be chartered federally or by the state. The National Bank Act of 1863 authorizes the federal chartering of commercial banks. In spite of the label *commercial*, these banks account for over 40 per cent of the outstanding consumer credit in the United States.

Section 85 of Title 12 of the United States Code authorizes federally chartered national banks to charge either 1 per cent above the federal reserve discount rate for 90-day commercial paper or the rate allowed by the laws of the state, whichever may be greater. This means that federal law authorizes a national bank to charge interest at the highest rate permitted to lenders by the laws of the state in which the bank is located, making it the most favored lender.

Tiffany v National Bank,[46] was the first case to interpret the most favored lender doctrine under §85. In that case, the court held that a national bank could lawfully charge 9 per cent on a loan, since the Missouri law allowed a rate of 10 per cent to lenders generally, even though Missouri state banks were limited to a rate of 8 per cent. Thus, national banks are granted the most favored lender status, allowing them to charge the highest rate available under state law if state law permits some lenders to charge more than others.

The Office of the Comptroller of the Currency, interpreting §85, adopted Tiffany's basic holding.[47] A national bank may charge interest at the maximum rate that state law permits to any competing state-chartered or state-licensed lending institution, not necessarily a state bank. For example, a national bank, without being licensed by state law, may lawfully charge the highest rate permitted to be charged by a state-licensed small loan company.

In a more recent case, *Marquette National Bank v First Service Corp*,[48] the Supreme Court held that a bank may export a high interest rate allowed by the law of the state where the national bank is located to other states which have lower lending rates. In *Marquette*, the First National Bank of Omaha (Omaha Bank) had its chartered address in Omaha, Nebraska, and was a card-issuing member in the BankAmericard plan. Omaha Bank had sought to enroll in its plan residents, merchants, and banks of the state of Minnesota. Nebraska law allowed Omaha Bank to charge interest on the unpaid balances of revolving charge accounts at an annual rate of 18 per cent for amounts under $1000 and 12 per cent on amounts of $1000 and over. Minnesota law, however, permitted only a maximum of 12 per cent annual interest on such accounts. To compensate for the reduced interest, Minnesota law permitted banks to charge annual fees up to $15 for use of bank credit cards. Marquette National Bank of Minnesota (Marquette), also an issuer of BankAmericards, sought to enjoin Omaha Bank from soliciting customers in Minnesota unless it complied with Minnesota law. Marquette claimed that it was losing customers to Omaha Bank because it was forced to charge a $10 annual fee. Omaha Bank argued that the

---

[45] See §§3.02-3.09.

[46] 85 US 409 (1874).

[47] 12 CFR §7.7310.

[48] 439 US 299 (1978).

National Bank Act preempted Minnesota law. The Supreme Court, citing *Tiffany*, reiterated that national banks have long been national favorites, and that the legislative history of the Act shows Congress's intent to facilitate a national bank system. Accordingly, the Act allows exportation of interest rates available to a national bank in one state with a higher interest ceiling to other states with lower interest ceilings. If such an exportation impairs the ability of states to enact effective usury laws, the impairment, stated the Supreme Court, has always been implicit in the structure of the National Bank Act, since the citizens of one state were free to visit a neighboring state to receive credit at foreign interest rates.

Under the most favored lender doctrine, the national bank cannot choose the highest rate allowed to any state lender on any type of loan, but can only charge the highest rate which a state lender could charge for the type of loan which the national bank is actually making.[49] Thus, a national bank may not use the rate charged by a state finance company in making a type of loan that the state finance company is not authorized to make. The purpose of the National Bank Act is to allow national banks to compete with state banks. In our example, if the finance company is not authorized to make that type of loan, then there is no competition with the national bank for that type of loan. On the other hand, a national bank may adopt the highest rate allowed a state lender for the type of loan that the state lender has legal authority to make, although it has not actually made such a loan.

As stated, the purpose of the most favored lender doctrine is to allow national banks to compete with *state* lenders. Therefore, a national bank may not adopt the rates of other federal lenders with whom they compete in a state.[50] For example, since 1980, under the National Credit Union Act, federal credit unions have been allowed to charge 21 per cent interest. A national bank cannot invoke this rate under the most favored lender doctrine. However, the national bank may achieve the same result through state parity laws, which we shall examine below.

§5.13   State Parity Laws

State parity laws are based on the same principle as the most favored lender doctrine of the National Bank Act. Parity statutes enacted in the early 1980s allow one type of state lender the same rate ceiling permitted another type of lender located in the state. For instance, a state savings and loan may charge the same rate as a federal savings and loan located in the state. The legislative purpose of state parity laws is said to be to promote competitive equality among different types of lenders. This is not exactly true, because what state parity

---

[49] *See* Attorney Gen v Equitable Trust Co, 294 Md 385, 450 A2d 1273 (1982).

[50] Comptroller of the Currency Op, 5 Consumer Credit Guide (CCH) ¶96,744 (Jan 19, 1983).

laws actually do is to change only the rate, and leave the other restrictions and powers applicable to each different type of lender unchanged.

A recent decision in Utah has raised the problem of the constitutionality of parity statutes. In *Utah League of Insured Savings Associations v State*,[51] the court declared that a provision in the Utah Savings and Loan Association Act allowing state associations to exercise and acquire any right or privilege that federal savings and loan associations acquired was an unconstitutional delegation of legislative authority. The Utah legislature cannot delegate to the federal government the constitutional duty to make laws for the state of Utah.

More importantly, state parity statutes would indirectly allow a national bank to adopt the higher rate adopted by other federal lenders within the state. In the above example of the federal credit union, if a state parity statute allows a state lender to adopt the same rate as the federal credit union, then the national bank can apply that higher interest rate to the type of loan that both the federal lender and the state lender are authorized to make.[52] This result seems to go beyond what Congress had in mind.

§5.14   The Depository Institutions Deregulation and Monetary Control Act of 1980

The purpose of Congress in enacting the Depository Institutions Deregulation and Monetary Control Act[53] (DIDMCA) was to provide other lenders with the same interest rate advantage as national banks. The provisions of DIDMCA extend the most favored lender doctrine to federally insured depository institutions that are not national banks.[54] Thus, the following lending institutions can take advantage of the most favored lender status:

1. State-chartered commercial banks using federal deposit insurance[55]
2. Federally insured or chartered savings and loan associations[56]
3. State mutual savings banks and savings and loan associations if they are federally insured[57]
4. Federally insured credit unions[58]

As a result, these lending institutions may charge the higher of the following rates: the rate allowed them under state law; the federal alternate rate; or the

---

[51] 555 F Supp 664 (D Utah 1983).

[52] *See* Tenn Atty Gen Op No 620, 5 Consumer Credit Guide (CCH) ¶96,966 (Dec 7, 1981).

[53] Pub L No 96-221, 94 Stat 161 (codified in scattered sections of 12 USC).

[54] 12 USC §521.

[55] 12 USC §1831(a).

[56] 12 USC §1730(g).

[57] *Id.*

[58] 12 USC §1785(g).

highest rate allowed any lender making similar loans in the state, especially finance companies.

The giving of the most favored lender status to these federally insured lending institutions was challenged in some quarters. The challenge was based on the following arguments:

>   1. Language differences exist between statutory provisions for national banks and other depository institutions
>   2. The lack of legislative history justifying that expansion
>   3. The danger of overlooking the local character of these institutions[59]

Under DIDMCA, the nature of federal preemption varies according to the type of loan. There are four main areas:

>   1. Residential real property loans
>   2. Obligations issued by depository institutions
>   3. Business and agricultural loans of $25,000 and more
>   4. Other loans

The maximum interest rates vary according to the type of loan, and the role of state law also varies according to the above categories.

§5.15 —Residential Real Property Loans

Effective April 1, 1980, the provisions of state laws or constitutions that limit the rate or amount of interest, discount points, finance charges, or other charges are not to apply to any loan, mortgage, credit sale, or advance which is

>   1. Secured by a first lien on residential real property
>   2. Is made after March 31, 1980
>   3. Is either insured under the National Housing Act or made by a lender that is a federally insured or regulated institution[60]

However, a state may opt out or override this provision by adopting a law which states explicitly and by its terms that the state does not want the preemption to apply to loans in the state.[61] This option must have been adopted before April 1, 1983, to be effective.

Federal preemption of state usury laws also applies to mobile home loans that are secured by a first lien. However, different requirements must be met for the loan to qualify for federal preemption. Federal preemption could be

---

[59] *See* Arnold & Rohner, *The Most Favored Lender Doctrine for Federally Insured Financial Institutions—What Are Its Boundaries?*, 31 Cath UL Rev 1, at 9-12 (1981).

[60] 12 USC §1735f-7 note (a)(1); Pub L No 96-221, §501(a)(1), 94 Stat 161.

[61] 12 USC §1735f-7 note (b)(2).

obtained only if the lender complies with the consumer protection provisions specified in regulations supplied by the Federal Home Loan Bank Board. These regulations pertain to balloon payments, prepayment penalties, late charges, deferral fees, notice before repossession or foreclosure, and interest rebates upon prepayment.[62]

§5.16   —Obligations of Depository Institutions

Effective April 1, 1980, the provisions of state law or constitutions that expressly limit interest which may be charged on any deposit or account, or other obligation of federally insured depository institutions under the Federal Deposit Insurance Act (FDIC), the Federal Credit Union Act (FCUA), The Federal Home Loan Bank Act, or the National Housing Act are preempted.[63]

Thus, state usury laws cannot apply to obligations, bonds, and notes issued by those lending institutions, nor to the interest paid on deposits and accounts. State law cannot override this preemption.

§5.17   —Business and Agricultural Loans of $1,000 or More

The federal preemption of state laws governing rates on business and agricultural loans under the DIDMCA expired on April 1, 1983; however, a discussion of its provisions here is useful for information.

For business and agricultural loans of $1,000 or more, notwithstanding any state constitution or statute, a lender could charge an interest rate no more than 5 per cent in excess of the discount rate including surcharge on 90-day commercial paper in effect at the federal reserve bank in the federal reserve district where the lender was located.[64] What constituted a business or agricultural loan was not defined by the federal statute. Business and agricultural loans could take various forms. They could take the form of a credit sale, as well as any other forbearance, advance, renewal, or extension of credit.

The Federal Reserve Bulletin published monthly by the Board of Governors of the Federal Reserve System provides the discount rate on 90-day commercial paper. The federal discount rate is not really a result of the market rate, but is set by the Federal Reserve Board. The federal statute allowed the creditor to charge up to 5 per cent in excess of the discount rate, including any surcharge on 90-day commercial paper, but did not specify the date on which the federal discount rate should be determined.

It was generally understood that the rate should be determined at the time the loan was made; the question became more complex when the lender made a variable-rate loan. Should the maximum rate then be set at the time the loan

---

[62] 12 USC §1735f-7 note (c).

[63] 12 USC §1735f-7 note (a)(2)(A).

[64] 12 USC §86a(a).

was made, or should it be recomputed with each change in the federal discount rate? To these questions, there was no answer in the statute.[65]

§5.18   —Other Loans

Federal law prohibits the taking of an interest higher than that provided by law.[66] Generally, federally insured depository institutions are authorized to charge a rate for loans no greater than 1 per cent above the 90-day commercial paper discount established by the Federal Reserve, or at such higher rate as permitted under state law.[67]

State laws that limit the rate to less than 1 per cent over the 90-day commercial paper discount rate are preempted. However, a state may override the federal preemption by adopting a measure that indicates that it does not want the preemption to apply.[68] There is no *sunset* provision, i.e., there is no deadline for the state to act in order to override a federal preemption. A number of states have overridden the federal preemption of state usury laws.[69]

§5.19   The Strange Case of Arkansas

For decades, the Constitution of Arkansas dictated a 10 per cent rate ceiling for all credit transactions. There is no statutory or judicial exemption to that unique rate. The effects of this low ceiling have been the subject of several studies.[70] The studies indicate that many Arkansas consumers were denied loans or were unable to obtain credit. Small loan companies and retailers left the state for greener pastures, and the far more nefarious loan sharking operations flourished in their place. High-risk borrowers were forced to seek credit in the illegal market, operated by syndicates and organized crime.[71] With the federal preemption, Arkansas has been rescued from its self-inflicted wound. Still, however, the people of Arkansas in 1980 resoundingly defeated a proposed constitutional amendment which would have removed the 10 per cent ceiling. Not until the 1982 general elections did Arkansas amend its

---

[65] *See* Burke, *Federal Preemptions of State Usury Laws,* 37 Bus Law 747, 760 (1983).

[66] 12 USC §86.

[67] 12 USC §1730(g) applicable to state and federally insured saving and loan associations; 12 USC §1831(d) applicable to state-chartered banks and foreign banks insured by the FDIC; 12 USC §1785(g) applicable to credit unions insured by the NCU Shared Insurance Funds.

[68] 12 USC §1730(g).

[69] *See* Beutel & Schroeder, Bank Officer's Handbook of Commercial Banking Law §268 n24 (50th ed 1986 Supp), for a list of preemptions.

[70] *See, e.g.,* Note, *Usury Legislation—Its Effect on the Economy, and a Proposal for Reform,* 33 Vand L Rev 199, 212-18 (1980).

[71] Special Project, *An Empirical Study of the Arkansas Usury Law: With Friends Like That . . .,* 1968 U Ill L Rev 54.

constitution to provide for higher than a 10 per cent ceiling. The ceiling, effective December 2, 1982, is set at 17 per cent for consumer loans and sales and 5 per cent above the Federal Reserve discount rate for 90-day commercial paper for other types of loans.[72]

§5.20   Rebates and Usury

Generally, loans are paid on the due date. A lender may refuse to accept a payment before it is due, or it can accept prepayment, but impose a prepayment penalty or retain the unearned prepaid interest. This general rule may be modified by agreement between the parties or by law. The parties may agree that prepayment will not be subject to any penalty, or that prepaid interest will be refunded. More often, it is the consumer credit legislation that prohibits prepayment penalty and imposes on the lender the duty to refund the unearned interest. The Uniform Consumer Credit Code is an example of such legislation.[73] Other state laws such as small loan acts and installment loan acts also prohibit prepayment penalties or require refunds of unearned interest.[74]

Usually, the lender pre-computes the interest for the duration of the loan and adds the total finance charge to the principal amount financed. The result is a sum which represents the total amount of the debt which is then divided into equal periodic payments. This type of transaction is referred to as a pre-computed or add-on credit transaction which applies either to a loan or a credit sale.

In case of prepayment or default, the failure to compute the unearned interest on a loan could give rise to a usury problem. The issue then is to select an adequate method of computing unearned interest, since there is no allocation of principal and interest in a periodic installment payment.

There are three common methods of calculating the rebate on unearned interest:

1.   The pro rata method
2.   The rule of 78
3.   The actuarial method[75]

These methods do not yield exactly the same results, and are sometimes in favor of the debtor, sometimes in favor of the creditor, depending on the method in use.

---

[72] Ark Stat Ann §67-1004 (1980).

[73] U3C §§2.509, 2.510 (1974).

[74] I Consumer Credit Guide (CCH) for small loan laws and for installment loan laws.

[75] Most of the materials used to explain these methods are from Perna, *Computing Interest Rebates Under the Rule of 78ths: A Formula for Usury Upon Default in Maximum-Interest Precomputes Credit Transactions,* 10 St Mary's LJ 94 (1978).

§5.21   —The Pro Rata Method

This is the simplest method of calculating unearned interest. The calculation is based on the assumption that the interest is earned in direct proportion to the ratio of the time before prepayment or default and the length of the loan obligation. To illustrate, suppose the loan is $1,200 and the interest charged is 10 per cent per year, resulting in a precomputed interest of $120. Suppose the debtor defaults after the sixth monthly payment. The debtor will have paid $660 ($600 of the principal and $60 in interest). The debtor will have to pay no further interest, nor will a rebate be in order, as the finance charge has already been prorated. In other words, interest is computed as if the loan had been originally scheduled for a period equal to the number of installments paid prior to the default.[76]

This method favors the debtor because it ignores the fact that the debtor has use of a greater cash amount at the beginning of the loan contract than later and, therefore, the interest must be greater during that period. In view of this, some jurisdictions require creditors to use only the pro rata method for calculating the interest rebates when the debtor is in default and the creditor accelerates payment.[77]

§5.22   —The Rule of 78

The Rule of 78, also called the *sum-of-the-digits method,* is usually invoked to compute the rebate of unearned interest for prepayment, default, or consolidation of pre-computed credit transactions. Contrary to the pro rata method, the Rule of 78 takes into account the declining principal balances at the end of each periodic installment.

On our example above ($1,200 principal and $120 interest), the debtor will have the use of the following amounts of the loan proceeds.

Month	Use of the Amounts of the Loan Proceeds
1	12 × $100 = $1200
2	11 × $100 = $1100
3	10 × $100 = $1000
4	9 × $100 = $ 900
5	8 × $100 = $ 800
6	7 × $100 = $ 700
7	6 × $100 = $ 600
8	5 × $100 = $ 500
9	4 × $100 = $ 400
10	3 × $100 = $ 300

[76] *Id* 108.

[77] Garrett v GAC Fin Corp, 129 Ga App 96, 198 SE2d 717 (1973).

$$
\begin{array}{rl}
11 & 2 \times \$100 = \$\ 200 \\
\underline{12} & \underline{1 \times \$100 = \$\ 100} \\
78 & 78 \times \$100 = \$7800
\end{array}
$$

The sum of the digits in the first column, 1-12, equals 78. In the second column, the figures indicate the amount of the loan at the debtor's disposal after each month. Since the amount of the loan at the debtor's disposal is greater in each month than it is in the following month, the finance charge earned by the creditor during each month is at the same time greater than the finance charge earned in the following month. Thus, if the debtor defaulted at the end of the sixth installment, the interest allocated to the first six months must be greater than that of the following months, because the debtor had the use of a greater amount of the loan.

The amount of interest actually earned during the first six months period is computed as follows:

$$
\frac{(1200 + 1100 + 1000 + 900 + 800 + 700)}{(1200 + 1000 + 1000 + \ldots + 200 + 100)} = \frac{5700}{7800} = \frac{57}{78}
$$

By applying this ratio to the total interest charged for the year ($120), the creditor has the right to earned interest of $87.69 which is the result of $120 $\times$ 57/78. On the other hand, the debtor has the right to an interest rebate of $32.31 ($120 − $87.69).

Given default or prepayment at any month, the allocation of earned and unearned interest can be computed according to the following table.

Month of Loan	Allocation Fraction	×	Total Finance Charge	=	Monthly Allocation of Interest	
1st mo.	1200/7800 × $120 =		12/78 × $120 =		$ 18.46	
2nd mo.	1100/7800 × $120 =		11/78 × $120 =		$ 16.92	
3rd mo.	1000/7800 × $120 =		10/78 × $120 =		$ 15.38	
4th mo.	900/7800 × $120 =		9/78 × $120 =		$ 13.85	
5th mo.	800/7800 × $120 =		8/78 × $120 =		$ 12.31	
6th mo.	700/7800 × $120 =		7/78 × $120 =		$ 10.77	$87.69
7th mo.	600/7800 × $120 =		6/78 × $120 =		$ 9.23	
8th mo.	500/7800 × $120 =		5/78 × $120 =		$ 7.69	
9th mo.	400/7800 × $120 =		4/78 × $120 =		$ 6.15	
10th mo.	300/7800 × $120 =		3/78 × $120 =		$ 4.62	
11th mo.	200/7800 × $120 =		2/78 × $120 =		$ 3.08	
12th mo.	100/7800 × $120 =		1/78 × $120 =		$ 1.54	$32.31
Totals	7800/7800 × $120 =		78/78 × $120 =		$120.00	

We can arrive at the same result by using the so-called refund factor formula as follows:

$$\frac{p\,(p\,+\,1)}{n\,(n\,+\,1)}$$

In the formula, p represents the number of installments remaining after default and n represents the total number of installments originally agreed upon. Applying this to our formula, $p = 6$ and $n = 12$. So,

$$\frac{6 \times (6 + 1)}{12 \times (12 + 1)} \;=\; \frac{6 \times 7}{12 \times 13} \;=\; \frac{42}{156} \;=\; 0.26923$$

This figure multiplied by $120 (the total finance charge) gives us the amount of total unearned interest rebate, $32.31.

There are ready made tables which set forth this refund factor. All one needs is to know the total finance charge for the period of the loan and multiply it by the figure conveniently provided in the Unearned Rebate column:

12-Month Loan

Months	Earned This Month	Cumulative Earned	Unearned (Rebate)
1	.15385	.15285	.84615
2	.14103	.29487	.70513
3	.12821	.42308	.57692
4	.11538	.53846	.46154
5	.10256	.64103	.35897
6	.08975	.73077	.26923
7	.07692	.80769	.19231
8	.06410	.87179	.12821
9	.05128	.92308	.07692
10	.03846	.96154	.03846
11	.02564	.98718	.01282
12	.01282	1.00000	.00000

In our example, the borrower is entitled to a rebate of $120 × .2693, or $32.3076.

The Rule of 78 has been popular with creditors because it is simple and gives creditors an edge.[78]

§5.23   —The Actuarial Method

Some states require the use of the actuarial method, because, while the Rule of 78 is useful and simple over the short term, long-term loan repayment under

---

[78] D. Epstein & S. Nickles, Consumer Law 364 (Nutshell Series 1980).

that method breaks down to the advantage of the creditor, and to the detriment of the consumer. The 1974 U3C, therefore, required use of the actuarial method for loans payable in more than 48 installments.[79]

The actuarial method is defined in U3C §1-301(1):

> Actuarial method means the method of allocating payments made on a debt between the amount financed and the finance charge, pursuant to which a payment is applied first to the accumulated finance charge, and any remainder is substracted from, or any deficiency is added to, the unpaid balance of the amount financed.

The assumption underlying the method defined here is that a periodic payment is applied first to the accumulated unpaid finance charge. If the payment exceeds the unpaid accumulated finance charge, the remainder of the payment is applied to reduce the unpaid balance of the amount financed.[80]

The U3C gives this example to illustrate the actuarial method:

Suppose the amount financed on a four-month contract is $500, and that the finance charge is $12.56 (1 per cent per month or 12 per cent annual rate). The monthly payment for the four-month period, including principal and interest, would be $128.14. The first month of payment is usually one month from the date of the contract. The following table will illustrate the actuarial method.

(A) Unpaid Balance of Amount Financed		(B) Monthly Rate		(C) Finance Charge	(D) Amount Financed	Total Monthly Payment (C) + (D)
500.00	×	1%	=	5.00	123.14	128.14
376.86	×	1%	=	3.77	124.37	128.14
252.49	×	1%	=	2.57	125.62	128.14
126.87	×	1%	=	1.27	126.87	128.14
				12.56 +	500.00 =	512.56

Note that in the first month, the finance charge of $5 (1% × 500) of the monthly payment of $128.14 is applied first to the finance charge, leaving a balance of $123.14. This last amount is then applied to reduce the unpaid balance of the loan from $500 to $376.86. The same process is repeated in the following months.

Use of the actuarial method requires reference to computer tables which translate add-on rates to actuarial rates. The actuarial method operates more in favor of the debtor than the Rule of 78. The latter is based on the inaccurate assumption that the successive *amounts used* decrease equally each month. In fact, the balance of the principal financed declines each month in varying amounts. As a consequence of this inaccuracy, the finance charge allocable to

---

[79] U3C §2.510(5) (1974).

[80] U3C §1.301(1) comment (1974).

the creditor is inflated, especially in the first months of the payment schedule. Thus, the actuarial method is the *true method* against which the results of the Rule of 78 method can be measured.[81]

With the notable exception of the U3C, most usury statutes do not provide a statutory formula for calculating rebates. In the states that do not enact the U3C, would the adoption of the Rule of 78, which favors the creditor in long-term loans, be considered a usurious practice? The answer seems to be no.[82] Usually the courts, even though acknowledging that the Rule of 78 favors the creditor more than the actuarial method, refuse to consider the difference as a prepayment penalty, or as a usurious practice prohibited by law.[83]

Under the Truth-in-Lending Act, there is no specific requirement for disclosure by the creditor of the method to be used in computing rebate of unearned portions of the finance charge, nor is the creditor required to adopt any specific method to compute earned or unearned finance charges.[84]

§5.24   Flipping

Loan flipping occurs when, before maturity, the debtor is enticed to contract a new loan in order to repay the old loan and usually to obtain an additional amount of cash as well. The debtor is left with the impression that this is merely a small new loan to cover the balance of the old amount, but in reality, the debtor is incurring a heavier burden than the debtor was counting upon.

Flipping is a form of refinancing a loan, but the term is derogatory and connotes the evils of the practice. Borrowers generally do not realize that, instead of being a simple refinancing of the old debt, flipping considerably increases the borrower's obligations because the earlier debt is combined with the new one. All this raises the cost of credit to the consumer because of the aggregation of precomputed finance charges, insurance, and other costs, and the absence of rebates for unearned interest on the old loan.

In re Branch [85] is a classic flipping case. The case involved a debtor, employed as a porter at a Tennessee hospital, whose monthly earnings were $200. The debtor got a loan on December 22, 1964, from a finance company, and executed a note in the sum of $72 payable in 12 monthly installments of $6 each. The total included:

Cash received by debtor $59.04
Precomputed interest charges 4.32

---

[81] *See* Hunt, *The Rule of 78: Hidden Penalty for Prepayment in Consumer Credit Transactions,* 55 BU L Rev 331 (1975).

[82] Winkle v Grand Natl Bank, 267 Ark 123, 601 SW2d 559 (1980). Also *In re* Box, 41 BR 27 (Bankr ND Tex 1984).

[83] Boine v Hibernia, 493 F2d 135 (9th Cir 1974); *contra* Scott v Liberty Fin Co, 380 F Supp 475 (DC Neb 1974).

[84] 12 CFR §226.18(k) & (z) and Official Staff Interpretation.

[85] Bankr L Rep (CCH) ¶61,943 (Bankr ED Tenn 1966).

Investigation charges 2.88
Life insurance premium 1.44
Accident & Health premium 4.32

Total $72.00

Within a period of 11 months, the loan was flipped four times. Each time, the lender retained the precomputed interest charge on the old loan and imposed new interest charges on the new amount of the loan. Each time, the lender imposed higher and higher investigation charges, life insurance premiums, and recording fees. After the fourth flipping on a total cash amount of $1,548.02 actually received by the debtor, or paid to others for the benefit of the debtor, the lender charged $716.58 in interest, $185.04 for investigation fees, $678.41 for insurance premiums, and $9.50 for recording charges. Considering that any interest charge over 6 per cent was usurious in Tennessee at that time, the result should be obvious. If one includes all the charges imposed, the computation shows a return of $102.00 per $100 actually loaned, or 53.25 per cent interest over a three-year period.

As the court noted, "these transactions indicate interest on interest on interest on interest on interest." Furthermore, upon the fifth flipping, the creditor took a second mortgage on the debtor's home and a security interest in the debtor's household goods and automobile.

Thus, flipping, besides involving usurious rates, also increases the debtor's liabilities, and is often accompanied by illegal and unscrupulous practices. Usury law may be used to combat flipping, but, unfortunately, these laws are not very effective in many states because of the mild penalties imposed. The U3C provides a more direct approach.

The U3C requires that in the refinancing of a precomputed transaction, the balance owing be treated as though it is prepaid, and that the consumer be credited with all the refunds computed. The creditor is not allowed to collect any new charges on the refinancing except a small minimum charge allowed by the law.[86] All this is to take away the incentive to flip loans. Besides using these specific U3C provisions, one who is confronted with an unscrupulous creditor might well use in such a case the unconscionability doctrines found in §2-302 of the Uniform Commercial Code or §5.108 of the U3C.

Also, flipping may constitute an unfair and deceptive act or practice which is prohibited by state and federal laws. Under the Truth-in-Lending Act, except for some adjustments of the loan which do not result in any heavier obligation imposed upon the debtor, refinancing is treated as a new loan, and as such, is subject to all the required disclosures that the creditor must give.[87]

---

[86] U3C §2.504 and comment (1974).
[87] Regulation Z, 12 CFR §226.20(a).

§5.25   Consolidation

Consolidation groups a number of short-term, low-interest loans into a single long-term transaction, generally at a higher interest rate. Consolidation may involve multiple flippings or refinancings. Consolidation would allow a creditor to acquire an interest in the debtor's property, including the debtor's home, that usually is not available as collateral in small debt transactions, thus allowing the creditor to reach into the debtor's property, especially non-purchase money residential property. Lenders' speculation in real estate is a reason behind the growth of consolidation practices.[88]

The abuses involved in consolidation are similar to those of flipping. They may be curtailed by the usury statutes, or statutes limiting second mortgage lending, or statutes prohibiting the use of certain types of property as collateral.[89]

The U3C closely regulates finance charges on consolidations of consumer loans and consumer credit sales. Sections 2, 3, and 4 under subsection 1 of §2.505 (1974) provides:

> (2) If a consumer owes an unpaid balance to a creditor with respect to a consumer credit transaction and becomes obligated on another consumer credit transaction with the same creditor, the parties may agree to a consolidation resulting in a single schedule of payments. If the previous consumer credit transaction was not precomputed, the parties may agree to add the unpaid amount of the amount financed and accrued charges on the date of consolidation to the amount financed with respect to the subsequent consumer credit transaction. If the previous consumer credit transaction was precomputed, the parties may agree to refinance the unpaid balance pursuant to the provisions on refinancing (Section 2.504) and to consolidate the amount financed resulting from the refinancing by adding it to the amount financed with respect to the subsequent consumer credit transaction. In either case the creditor may contract for and receive a finance charge as provided in subsection (3) based on the aggregate amount financed resulting from the consolidation.

> (3) If the debts consolidated arise exclusively from the consumer credit sales the transaction is a consolidation with respect to a consumer credit sale and the creditor may make a finance charge not exceeding that permitted by the provisions on finance charge for consumer credit sales other than open-end credit (Section 2.201). If the debts consolidated include a debt arising from a prior or contemporaneous consumer loan, the transaction is a consolidation with respect to a consumer loan and the creditor may make a finance charge not exceeding that permitted by the

---

[88] National Consumer Law Center, M. Leymaster, Consumer Usury and Credit Overcharges §6.8.3 (1982) (The Consumer Credit and Sales Legal Practices Series).
[89] *Id.*

provisions on finance charge for consumer loans by lenders not super-vised lenders (subsection (a) of Section 2.401) or for consumer loans by supervised lenders (subsection (2) of Section 2.401), whichever is appropriate.

(4) If a consumer owes an unpaid balance to a creditor with respect to a consumer credit transaction arising out of a consumer credit sale, and becomes obligated on another consumer credit transaction arising out of another consumer credit sale by the home seller, the parties may agree to a consolidation resulting in a single schedule of payments either pursuant to subsection (2) or by adding together the unpaid balances with respect to the two sales.

In other words, the U3C permits two methods of consolidating the balances of separate loans. The first method is the rewrite method or refinancing: the finance charge is based on the new amount, and the debtor has the right to a refund of unearned finance and other charges as in the case of refinancing. The second method is a true consolidation: the balances owing are added together and made payable in one single payment, and, therefore, no refund of finance charge is involved. In all cases, the creditors must comply with the provisions on finance charges for consumer loans and consumer credit sales. Again, all the statutes and theories of laws applicable to refinancings are also applicable to consolidations.

§5.26 Refinancing, Consolidation, and Purchase Money Security Interests

Often in a consumer credit sale, the extender of credit, either the seller or lender, takes a security interest in the goods sold as security for the loan. This is called a purchase money security interest.

Purchase money secured lenders are the favorites of the law. They usually have priority over all other creditors, unsecured and secured.[90] The question is, when the loan is refinanced or consolidated, will the creditor retain its status of purchase money secured lender? In other words, does the refinancing or consolidation result in a new loan which destroys the purchase money nature of the creditor's claim?

In re Matthews [91] illustrates this issue. In that case, the Matthewses borrowed $4,064.20 from Transamerica Financial Services by a September, 1978, agreement calling for 36 monthly payments of $165. The proceeds of the loan were to pay for the purchase of a piano and a stereo. The latter, and other household goods and personal property, were collateral for the loan. On October 31, 1979, Transamerica refinanced the loan by issuing a new loan of $4,245.01. From that amount, Matthews paid off the balance of the old loan,

---

[90] *See* Bankr Code, 11 USC §552(f); UCC §§9-301(2), 9-312(3)(4).
[91] 724 F2d 798 (9th Cir 1984).

$3,902.64, and $279.23 in insurance charges, and received $63.14 in cash. The Matthewses filed for bankruptcy in November, 1980. Transamerica filed a petition in the bankruptcy court for relief from the automatic stay against repossession of the collateral. Under Bankruptcy Code §522(f), the bankrupt may invalidate a nonpossessory, non-purchase money security interest in exempt household goods and furnishings. Pursuant to this provision, the Matthewses opposed Transamerica's action, contending that, upon refinancing, Transamerica lost the purchase money security interest. The bankruptcy court held for the Matthewses. The Bankruptcy Appellate Panel of the Ninth Circuit reversed. The Ninth Circuit reviewed the panel's interpretation and reversed the panel's decision.

The court held that when Transamerica made the decision to issue a new loan, it sacrificed its purchase money security interest. The Court looked to the definition of UCC §9-107(b), defining a purchase money security interest as a security interest "taken by a person who . . . gives value to enable the debtor to acquire rights in or the use of collateral. . . ."

The court reasoned that the Matthewses did not use the new loan proceeds "to acquire rights in or the use of" the piano or stereo. They already owned them. The court also took the creditor's own words, that the new loan was to "pay the net balance due on the old loan."

When confronted with the same issue, the Third Circuit had a somewhat different view. The Third Circuit agreed with a lower court that the purchase money security interest was not extinguished upon consolidation of the debt. The issue should be simply a question of allocating the payments to the respective debts. In *Pristas v Landaus, Inc* [92] the court relied on Pennsylvania's Goods and Services Installment Sales Act for a specific method for allocating payments.

§5.27   Delinquency Charges

A distinction must be made between default and delinquency. Default occurs when a borrower fails to pay or breaches any obligation defined by the contract as constituting default.[93] Upon default, the creditor can pursue the legal remedies accorded by the contract and by law, such as acceleration of payment, repossession of the collateral, or other means of judicial enforcement for the collection of the debt. Delinquency, on the other hand, occurs when the debtor simply misses a single scheduled repayment, and the debtor may cure the contract violation by paying the missed installment. Often the contract provides for additional charges.

Thus, the basic difference between default and deficiency is that, in default, the borrower usually does not have the right to cure, even by paying a late charge; but in delinquency, the contract remains intact and the borrower has

---

[92] 742 F2d 797 (3d Cir 1984).

[93] *See* **ch 10.**

the right to cure. This distinction is blurred, however, in practice. Delinquency may give rise to a default remedy, such as acceleration at will, if, due to the delinquency, the creditor, in good faith, deems itself to be insecure. Some contracts may stipulate a number of delinquencies which would constitute default. On the other hand, some consumer statutes, such as the U3C, provide that, even upon default, the debtor must be given the right to cure before the creditor may pursue its legal remedies.[94]

Charges for tardy payment *may* be usurious. Most usury statutes seek to limit the amount and regulate the timing of such charges. For instance, the U3C allows late charges of no more than five dollars or 5 per cent of the unpaid amount due, whichever is lower.[95] Moreover, such charges can be levied only after a grace period of 10 days has elapsed.

As an example, if the unpaid amount due is $500, the late charge would be a maximum charge of $2.50; but if the unpaid amount is $15,000, the maximum charge is limited to $5. There are consumer advocates who would reject any delinquency charges at all; but the U3C did not adopt this view, because it would result in delinquent consumers paying a lower finance charge than diligent consumers. In open-end credit, no delinquency charge may be imposed, because, under such a plan, the finance charge continues to accumulate, thus compensating the creditor for any delinquency.[96]

Delinquency charges may give rise to abuses. A creditor may collect multiple delinquency charges stemming from a single delayed payment. This is *pyramiding*. As an example, suppose the installment payment is due on the first of the month. Suppose the consumer fails to pay the $100 monthly installment on January 1, and the creditor assesses a late charge of $2.50. Suppose, then, that the consumer makes a timely payment on February 1. The creditor may allocate the late charge payment of $2.50 to the $100 February payment, and conclude that the consumer is again delinquent in February. If this is repeated throughout the remaining period of the loan obligation, there is an accumulation of late charges each month, based on only one single delinquency.

In order to avoid this problem of multiple delinquencies, the U3C provides that payments are applied first to current installments and then to delinquent installments. Furthermore, no delinquency charge may be collected on an installment which is paid in full within the 10-day grace period, even though an earlier maturing installment, or a delinquency or deferral charge on an earlier installment, has not been paid in full. In other words, in our example, the creditor could collect only the $2.50 delinquency charge for January if the consumer makes all the other payments on time.[97]

---

[94] U3C §§5.110, .111 (1974).

[95] U3C §1.502(1) (1974).

[96] U3C §2.501 comment 2 (1974).

[97] U3C §2.502(3)(1974).

§5.28   The United States Rule

The compounding of interest, which is the charging of interest on interest as well as on principal, is prohibited by the United States Rule. This rule stems from the common law rule requiring segregation of earned interest arrearages. In other words, interest is allowed only on principal. Unpaid finance charges, including delinquency charges, must be kept separate from the unpaid principal, preventing unpaid credit charges from accruing or earning interest. We have seen that compounding in refinancings results in flippings, and, as such, would give rise to a practice illegal under the usury statutes, or other specific statutes.[98]

§5.29   Deferral Charges

Deferral may be provided by agreement between the lender and the borrower before or after default. The borrower is allowed to postpone a payment in return for a fee or charge. This extra payment would compensate the lender for the interest lost because of the extension of the repayment schedule. The deferral fee is identical to late charges for delinquencies in precomputed loans. Lenders usually prefer refinancings to deferrals because the refinancing of a loan is more lucrative.

Deferral charges are considered interest, and, as such, are subject to the statutes governing rate of interest for credit extension. Any interest stemming from deferral, then, must reflect the corresponding amount of principal due and the length of the additional time period. The parties must agree to the deferral. Absent the borrower's agreement, deferrals would be illegal and unenforceable. Under the U3C, however, the creditor has a unilateral right to convert a precomputed consumer loan to one in which the finance charge is based on the unpaid balance. If the borrower defaults on two installments on a precomputed loan for 10 days or more, such a conversion is still legal, but the rate of the finance charge based on the unpaid balance must not exceed the rate disclosed to the consumer when the loan was precomputed.

Furthermore, the U3C requires that an appropriate rebate be made. In other words, while the law allows a creditor to be compensated in case of delinquency and deferral, the creditor may not use these situations to unilaterally increase the rate of the finance charge or to impose a finance charge higher than that disclosed to the consumer at the time the loan was precomputed.[99] The U3C also requires use of the Rule of 78 in the computation of the deferral charge.[100]

---

[98] *See* Dixon v Brooks, 678 SW2d 728 (Tex Ct App 1984) compounding interest on late charges may constitute usury. *See* National Consumer Law Center, M. Leymaster, Consumer Usury and Credit Overcharges §6.3.2 (The Consumer Credit and Sales Legal Practices Series (1982)).

[99] U3C §2.502(4)(1974).

[100] U3C §2.503 (1974).

§5.30   Balloon Payments

Balloon payments are a form of unequal payment with, usually, a very large payment at the end of the loan. Balloon payments may be legitimate when the consumer has an irregular income, or reasonably expects to have greater income at the end of the loan period. But it can be a deceptive practice when it is used to lure consumers into incurring debts. Consumers may be enticed into a credit transaction made attractive by little or no down payment coupled with very low first installments. Sometimes the small payments at the beginning do not even pay the interest as it comes due. The unpaid principal and interest thus accumulate, resulting in balloon payments that could be prohibitive. This is the phenomenon known as negative amortization. If the interest is compounded, the problem is even worse.

Balloon payments by themselves are not prohibited. For example, the Truth-in-Lending Act (TILA) allows them, but requires disclosure of the payment schedule, which includes the numbers, amounts, and timing of payments scheduled to satisfy the loan.[101] The U3C allows a borrower to refinance without penalty any scheduled payment that is more than twice as large as the average ordinary scheduled payment. The terms of refinancing a balloon payment must be no less favorable to the borrower than the terms of the original transaction.[102] This requirement seeks to avoid the abusive practice in which the debtor, unable to pay the large balloon payment, is forced to refinance the loan at a much higher rate of interest. Legitimate balloon payments, i.e., payments scheduled to adjust to the seasonal or irregular income of the borrower, are not subject to this requirement.

The U3C also requires supervised loans, defined as loans that exceed the legal interest rate, to be arranged according to a regular schedule of payments at substantially equal intervals and amounts.[103] When the debtor refinances the loan, no penalty may be imposed, and, under the refinancing schedule, balloon payments are not allowed.[104]

One must be alert to the presence of usury in any balloon payment arrangement. Illegitimate balloon payments may be covered by the appropriate usury statutes and may constitute an unfair or deceptive act or practice under state and federal law. Additionally, the doctrine of unconscionability may also be used successfully in appropriate circumstances.

§5.31   Usury and Conflict of Laws

As usury rates vary from state to state, problems of conflict of laws sometimes arise. Conflict of laws issues arise naturally when a transaction has contact with

---

[101] Regulation Z, 12 CFR §226(g).

[102] U3C §3.308(1)(1974).

[103] U3C §2.308(1)(1974).

[104] U3C §3.308 comment 1 (1974).

more than one state. Suppose a buyer resides in State A and purchases an automobile from a seller in State B or borrows money from a lender located in State B. Suppose State A's maximum interest rate is 10 per cent and State B's maximum interest rate is 12 per cent. Can the seller or lender in State B be allowed to charge the resident of State A State B's maximum rate of 12 per cent, or is such a creditor limited to the 10 per cent ceiling of State A? The Restatement of Conflict of Laws takes the position that a contract is not usurious "if it provides for a rate of interest that is permissible in a state to which the contract has a substantial relationship and is not greatly in excess of the rate permitted by the general usury statute of the state whose contract law would normally control."[105]

The conflict of laws issue had been unsettled for a long time before the Supreme Court handed down its decision in *Marquette National Bank v First Service Corp.*[106] One of the first cases that dealt with the issue was a Montana case, *Colorado National Bank v Coder.*[107]

In this case, Colorado had no rate ceiling and Montana had a 10 per cent rate ceiling. A national bank domiciled in Colorado issued a BankAmericard to a cardholder who was at all times a Montana resident. The bank charged 18 per cent, which was not usurious in Colorado. The Montana court held that the rate was usurious under the Montana usury statute and subjected the bank to a usury penalty. The bank argued vainly that federal law[108] would authorize it to charge Montana cardholders the same rate it charged Colorado residents. The court held otherwise, interpreting the federal statute to allow national banks to charge only what state banks could charge in the state where the cardholder resides. The decision of the court seems to be against the Restatement's *substantial relationship* test.

In *State ex rel Meir Henry v Spiegel Inc,*[109] the court held that the usury law of the consumer's state governs the transaction, not the law of the seller's state, even in the face of an agreement by the parties to be bound by the law of the seller's state. In this case, the defendant, Spiegel, is a Delaware corporation with its principal place of business in Oakbrook, Illinois. It sells merchandise through catalogs to residents of South Dakota. The catalogs contain credit application forms for ordering merchandise. The forms, as signed by the consumers, provide for an annual interest rate of 19.8 per cent, which is below the usury ceiling in Illinois. South Dakota limits the annual rate on a retail revolving charge account to 12 per cent per year. Thus, the transaction is unlawful in South Dakota but lawful in Illinois. Which law would apply? Spiegel argued that South Dakota's regulation of the interest rate would constitute a

---

[105] Restatement (Second) of Conflict of Laws §203 (1964).

[106] 439 US 299 (1978).

[107] [1969-1973 Transfer Binder] Consumer Credit Guide (CCH) ¶99,018 (Dec 29, 1972). *See* B. Clark, The Law of Bank Deposits, Collections and Credit Cards §9.9[2] (rev ed 1981).

[108] 12 USC §85.

[109] 277 NW2d 298 (SD), *appeal dismissed*, 444 US 804 (1979).

restriction of Spiegel's interstate commerce, and, as such, is a violation of the Commerce Clause of the United States Constitution.

The court cited decisions from three United States courts of appeals to conclude that the South Dakota usury law involves a legitimate local interest based on public policy. This limitation does not place a burden on interstate commerce that is clearly excessive in relation to the local benefits, and, therefore, is not unconstitutional.

But, as we have seen,[110] these restrictive interpretations were soon rejected with respect to bank credit card issuers. In *Fisher v First National Bank,*[111] a national bank card issuer headquartered in Omaha issued a credit card to an Iowa resident. The latter sued the bank for usury because the interest charged was higher than that allowable under Iowa law. The lower court based its decision, upholding the higher interest rate, on the location of the contract, deemed to have taken place in Nebraska. The Eighth Circuit agreed with the lower court's conclusion, but arrived at the conclusion through different reasoning. The Eighth Circuit simply applied 12 USC §85, the controlling federal law, in deciding that the locale of the transaction was not important. The United States Supreme Court, in *Marquette National Bank v First Service Corp,*[112] has settled the issue definitively by a unanimous decision.

While the conflict of laws issue has been settled with respect to revolving charge accounts (open-end credits), the issue of usury in closed-end credit in interstate transactions is yet to be settled.

§5.32 Usury Remedies under State Law

Remedies for most impositions of usurious interest rates or unearned finance charges are provided for in the state usury statutes. One should also look to the remedies provided by specific statutes, such as the retail installment sales or small loan statutes, that govern the given transaction.

Remedies under state usury laws vary greatly from state to state. In some states, a usurious contract becomes null and void. In some other states, the lender has to pay an amount equal to twice the interest rate charged. In other states, the remedy is even less severe: the usurer must forfeit only the excess amount charged.

Some states do not have usury ceilings for certain types of transactions. For instance, under Idaho's usury statute, commercial notes are exempt from the 10 per cent state usury ceiling if the parties "agree in writing, which clearly sets forth the rate of interest charged, to pay any rate of interest."[113]

---

[110] *See* **§5.12.**

[111] 548 F2d 255 (8th Cir 1977).

[112] 439 US 299 (1978); *see* **§5.12.**

[113] Idaho Code §28.22.105 (1977).

In *Howes v Curtis*,[114] an Idaho case decided under the statute, the Idaho Supreme Court found usury because the lender did not disclose the real interest charged. A broker's fee was imposed on the plaintiff even though there was no broker involved in the transaction.

Some states, such as New York and New Jersey, have no civil usury statutes, only criminal usury statutes. Criminal rate ceilings are much higher than rate ceilings in civil statutes. For instance, in New York, the criminal usury ceiling is 25 per cent, and in New Jersey, 30 per cent.

Criminal statutes do not provide for civil remedies, but a contract that violates the statutes will be illegal, and, as such, will be unenforceable. It can then be raised as a defense against any action to collect. An action for usury may be based on tort or contract theories. Illegality defeats even the rights of a holder in due course. Additionally, a violation of the usury limit may constitute an unfair and deceptive act or practice punishable under the relevant statute or common law doctrine.

If the borrower seeks to rescind the contract, alleging usury, must the borrower return the borrowed amount under the equitable doctrine of *restitutio in integrum*? The borrower may not be in a position at that point to return the funds. How might this be overcome? A court may apply the common law theories of laches or estoppel to deny the creditor's claim to a refund. On the other hand, in order to prevent unjust enrichment of the borrower, the court may set forth a program of installment payments for the return of the principal.

§5.33   Usury Remedies under Federal Law

Disclosure Acts

The Truth-in-Lending Act and other federal disclosure statutes may provide remedies for nondisclosure. Usurious lenders usually hide the true credit terms through various obfuscation schemes, and, thus, would violate the Truth-in-Lending and similar disclosure acts.

Federal Trade Commission Act

Usurious transactions may also be deemed to be unfair and deceptive acts or practices. These are prohibited by §5 of the Federal Trade Commission Act.[115]

The National Bank Act

The National Bank Act[116] also gives borrowers a cause of action against national banks for the overcharge of interest rates. As we know, §85 allows a national bank to charge interest at the rate allowed by the laws of the state in

---

[114] 104 Idaho 562, 661 P2d 729 (1983).

[115] *See* §§2.05-2.10.

[116] 12 USC §85.

which it is located, or at a rate of 1 per cent in excess of the discount rate on 90-day commercial paper in effect at the Federal Reserve Bank in the district in which the bank is located, whichever is greater. The taking or charging of an interest rate greater than that allowed, when knowingly done, is deemed a forfeiture of the entire interest.[117] In addition, a borrower who has already paid the unlawful rate may recover twice the amount of interest extended.[118] The plaintiff must prove that the defendant lender knowingly exceeded the interest allowed.[119]

Plaintiff may bring an action in a federal district court or in an appropriate state court. The statute of limitations is two years from the time the usurious transactions occurred.[120]

RICO

A weapon recently entering the consumer's hands has been provided by the Racketeering Influenced and Corrupt Organizations Act (RICO) of the Organized Crime Control Act of 1970.[121] It is not the purpose of this book, nor is it within the author's ability, to deal with all the intricacies and complexities of RICO. We rather deal summarily with the aspect of this Act which can give the consumer a cause of action against the collection of an unlawful debt.

The original intent of Congress in enacting RICO was to deal with organized crime. However, the interpretation of RICO's broad provisions in recent years gives consumers a powerful civil remedy against legitimate business not related to gangsterism.[122]

Under RICO, it is unlawful to:

1. Receive or use income derived from a pattern of racketeering activity or through collection of an unlawful debt, and to use such income in order to acquire an interest in an enterprise engaged in interstate commerce
2. Acquire or maintain an interest in an enterprise through a pattern of racketeering activity, or through collection of an unlawful debt
3. Conduct or participate in the conduct of an enterprise through a pattern of racketeering activity or collection of unlawful debt
4. Conspire to commit any offenses described above[123]

---

[117] 12 USC §86.

[118] *Id.*

[119] *See* McAdon v Union Natl Bank, 535 F2d 1050 (8th Cir 1976) on how to establish such evidence.

[120] 12 USC §86.

[121] 18 USC §§1961-1968.

[122] *See* Blakcy, *The Rico Civil Fraud Action in Context: Reflections on Bennett v Berg*, 58 Notre Dame L Rev 237 (1982).

[123] 18 USC §1691(a)(d). A *racketeering activity* involves murder or threat of murder, any act or threat involving murder, kidnapping, gambling, arson, robbery, bribery, extortion, or dealing in narcotic or other dangerous drugs, which is chargeable under

Thus, an action under RICO is triggered by a pattern of unlawful activity, or collection of an unlawful debt.

Collection of an unlawful debt does not require a *pattern or practice*. Thus, a single collection could qualify. The Act defines an unlawful debt as a gambling debt or a debt incurred in connection with "the business of lending money or a thing of value at a rate usurious under State or Federal Law, where the usurious rate is at least twice the enforceable rate."[124]

RICO was not popular with lower courts, which were reluctant to apply the provisions of the Act to legitimate businesses. The courts either required an organized crime nexus or a criminal conviction in order to proceed on the civil suit. The garden variety of business or consumer fraud was held to be outside the scope of the Act. However, the Supreme Court rejected these restrictions soundly.

In *Sedima SPRL v Imrex Co*,[125] the plaintiff claimed that the defendant was presenting inflated bills, cheating the plaintiff out of a portion of its proceeds by collecting for nonexistent expenses. In addition to the common law claims of unjust enrichment, conversion, breach of contract, and breach of fiduciary duty, the plaintiff also asserted claims under RICO, based on mail and wire fraud. The district court held that the complaint must allege a RICO-type injury, either some sort of racketeering injury or a competitive injury. Accordingly, the district court dismissed the RICO allegations for failure to state a claim. The Court of Appeals for the Second Circuit affirmed, reasoning that Congress's intent in RICO was to compensate the victims of "certain specific kinds of organized criminality."[126] The Court of Appeals found the complaint defective for not alleging that the defendants had already been criminally convicted.

The Supreme Court rejected all the restrictions on which such lower courts had based their decisions. The court conceded that, in the civil remedy aspect, "RICO is evolving into something quite different from the original conception of its enactors."[127] But this extraordinary use, according to the court, was primarily the result of the breadth of the predicate offenses. Any restriction of that use would constitute "a form of statutory amendment,"[128] that would be inappropriate for the court to undertake.

The same reasoning can be found in *United States v Turkette*,[129] where the court noted that unambiguous language must be interpreted according to its clear

---

state law or federal law. A *pattern of racketeering activity* requires at least two acts within a time period of 10 years, excluding any period of imprisonment. 18 USC §1691(5).

[124] 18 USC §1961(6).

[125] 473 US 479 (1985). *See also* American National Bank & Trust Co v Haroco, Inc, 473 US 606 (1985).

[126] 741 F2d 482, 494 (2d Cir 1984).

[127] 473 US at 500.

[128] *Id.*

[129] 452 US 576 (1981).

meaning "absent a clearly expressed legislative intent to the contrary." The Court was thus "compelled by the statutory language to construe RICO to reach garden-variety fraud and breach of contract cases."[130] As a result of those decisions, RICO has become a powerful weapon in the hands of the consumer, because it provides potent civil remedies including attorneys' fees and treble damages.[131] Such a weapon is generally not provided in federal or state usury statutes. The Act, being a criminal statute, subjects the defendant to fines of up to $20,000, imprisonment up to 20 years, or both, and forfeits to the United States any property acquired in violation of the Act.[132]

RICO has served as a model for similar state legislation in about half the states. Among them, California,[133] Illinois,[134] and Pennsylvania[135] do not provide a civil cause of action for damages under their RICO statute.[136]

---

[130] *Id* 580.

[131] 18 USC §1964(c).

[132] 18 USC §1963.

[133] Cal Pen Code §§186-186-8.9 (West Supp 1987).

[134] Ill Stat Ann ch 56 1/2, §§1651-1660 (Smith-Hurd 1985).

[135] 18 Pa Cons Stat §911 (1983).

[136] For a good review of the cases decided under RICO, *see* National Consumer Law Center, Consumer Usury and Credit Overcharges §2.44 (Consumer Credit and Sales Legal Practices Series 1986 Supp).

6

Credit Insurance

§6.01 Introduction

Credit insurance refers to insurance sold in connection with a credit transaction. The two most common types of credit insurance are life insurance and accident and health insurance. Life insurance pays off the loan if the consumer dies. Accident and health insurance protects the creditor against loss if the debtor is unable to pay the debt through illness or disability. The term credit insurance as used here is distinct from property insurance which protects the creditor's equity in big item collaterals such as automobiles or household goods against casualty risks such as fire, theft, vandalism, or collision.

Although credit insurance protects creditors principally, debtors also welcome it. A survey made by an Ohio University research group showed that 90 per cent of the people surveyed accepted the credit insurance idea.[1] This

---

[1] Report of the National Commn on Consumer Finance, Consumer Credit in the United States 83 (1972).

popularity may be explained by the debtor's natural desire not to leave debts to their loved ones in the event of death or disability.

§6.02 Credit Life Insurance

Credit life insurance first appeared in 1917, but did not gain momentum until the end of World War II. At that time, only 7 per cent of the outstanding consumer credit transactions had credit insurance. In the years after the war, the credit insurance industry boomed, and in 1970, the amount of credit insurance in force covered nearly 70 per cent of consumer credit transactions. That percentage continued to increase as the volume of consumer credit itself increased. By 1980, credit insurance alone reached $165 billion, and 90 per cent of consumer credit transactions were covered by credit life insurance.[2]

Credit life insurance may be sold on an individual or group basis. On an individual basis, the debtor will approach an insurance company and negotiate the terms, and then purchase from the insurance company a policy to cover the amount of the outstanding debt. The policy is usually in the form of decreasing term insurance with the face amount of the policy declining as time passes and the debt matures. Individual policies are rarely sold, because a typical consumer debt is small in amount and has a short maturity (usually less than three years), making such a policy uneconomical and unattractive for the insurer. As a result, the debtor must pay a higher premium. Therefore, most credit insurance policies are established on a group basis.

The mechanics of group credit life insurance are different from those of individual credit life policies. The insurance company issues the policy directly to the creditor, who is the beneficiary. The insured group is a designated class of debtors/buyers/borrowers. Upon the death of the insured debtor, the insurance company will pay the unpaid balance of the obligation to the creditor. The policies typically provide decreasing term insurance for each member of the group. Group credit life insurance policies usually provide for a limit on the amount of credit that may be written on one insured debtor. If the creditor extends credit above that stipulated amount, the amount of insurance remains the same and covers only that part of the debt which does not exceed the stipulated amount, until the amount of the debt, through periodic payments, reaches the stipulated level. Thereafter, the debt and the insurance decrease at the same rate.

The premiums paid for credit life insurance are usually at flat rates. Premiums do not vary with the age of the insured debtor, although the insurance company may set a maximum age limit. However, within that limit, age is irrelevant.

The creditor, who is both the policyholder and the beneficiary of the insurance, pays the insurance company and passes on the premium cost to the debtor. Sometimes these costs may be included in the finance charge, or in the

---

[2] P. Rasor, Consumer Finance Law 451 (1985).

price of goods and services, in such a way that the debtor is not even aware of the insurance. Credit unions are known to do this often. However, in most instances, the debtor pays a specific insurance premium charge, which is clearly designated.

The creditor may assess the premium charge through two methods. Under the first method, the creditor each month computes an initial, single premium for each new debt and pays the aggregate of all these single premiums to the insurance company. In other words, the initial single premiums pay once and for all for the full term of coverage. Under the second method, a premium is calculated on the outstanding insured indebtedness for each month and passed on to the debtor periodically.

The first method is more often used, because then the premium cost is assessed at once and passed on to the debtor right away, as a specific identifiable charge. The second method is rarely used because of the problems the creditor has with delinquent accounts. The creditor is unable to collect from the debtor and yet still has to pay insurance premiums on the debtor's life.[3]

§6.03   Credit Accident and Health Insurance

While less common than the credit life insurance, this type of insurance is also growing. Like credit life insurance, this type of insurance is usually written on a group basis and is assessed at a flat rate regardless of age. Like credit life insurance, the creditor is the policyholder and beneficiary of the insurance.

Credit accident and health insurance differs from credit life insurance in two aspects. First, it has a wider variety of possible plans than credit life insurance. For example, the length of time one must be disabled to get the benefit of the insurance may vary. Most policies provide that the insured must be disabled for a period of 14 to 30 days, and the benefits occur only after the expiration of this qualification period. Second, the method of determining the benefits may also vary. Unlike credit life insurance, where full benefits are payable on the insured's death, credit accident and health insurance may be payable either on a pro rata basis or as a full monthly payment. The pro rata method, the most commonly used, provides for a payment of one-thirtieth of a monthly installment for each day of disability. The full payment method provides for payment of the full monthly installment if the debtor is disabled at the monthly due date.[4]

---

[3] Report of the National Commn on Consumer Finance, Consumer Credit in the United States 84 (1972).

[4] Report of the National Commn on Consumer Finance, Consumer Credit in the United States 84-85 (1972).

§6.04 Credit Insurance Abuses

Creditors' abuses in the area of credit insurance has made legislation necessary to help regulate the field. An example of such abuses is a story printed in the February 26, 1985, *Wall Street Journal*.[5]

One month before Christmas, Katherine Snow, an unmarried mother having a monthly income of $423.00, borrowed $126.32 from Thorp, a finance company. In addition to the credit, the lender induced her to borrow an additional $14.74 for credit life insurance, $73.44 for property insurance, and $202.00 for term life insurance. Finally, for an additional $24.50, she became a member of the ITT consumer thrift club, allowing her to receive discounts on various consumer products. The rate of interest at this time was 22 per cent. Ms. Snow ended up borrowing or paying $441.40 (plus interest) in order to make her $126.32 Christmas purchases.

This sort of credit abuse is known as *packing:* adding other payments for so-called "optional" insurance and other features to the original amount of the loan. This usually occurs without the consumer's full awareness of what is going on. Often unsophisticated consumers are so happy to get the loan that they will sign all the papers placed before them. As Ms. Snow testified later, she did not know she had purchased all this insurance: "I bought more insurance than I borrowed money, if that makes any sense."

There is more than one reason why creditors encourage borrowers to buy credit insurance. Apart from the creditors' legitimate concerns to protect their loans against the debtor's risk of death or disability, the practice of encouraging such insurance can be quite profitable.

State laws generally prohibit creditors from taking a mark-up on the premium. Creditors cannot charge the debtor more than the actual premium paid by the creditor to the insurance company. Creditors cannot receive commissions for buying policies from insurance companies. Creditors, however, receive compensation in the form of "dividends and/or rate credits when earned, based on the experience of the group."[6] The amount of that compensation depends upon the claims experience of the insurance company with the creditor's particular group of debtors and the size of premiums charged. If the insurance company has a large margin of underwriting profit, i.e., the claims it pays are much less than the premiums it collects, then the dividends and rating credits it pays the creditor are large, and vice versa. This method of computing compensation results in encouraging creditors to select those insurance companies that charge high insurance premiums in order to get higher yields. This is the phenomenon of reverse competition; there is no incentive to make the prospect more palatable to the consumer. The conflict of interest which is built into this relationship between creditor and insurance

---

[5] Wall Street J, Feb 26, 1985, at 1, col 6.

[6] Report of the National Commn on Consumer Finance, Consumer Credit in the United States 85 (1972).

company on the one hand, and the creditor and the consumer on the other hand, is the focus of the consumer protection laws in this area.

Coupled with the reverse competition phenomenon is the fact that the consumer really has no alternative in choosing insurance companies, because the cost of an individual policy would be prohibitive. Moreover, the consumer has no say in the creditor's selection of an insurance company which will charge lower premiums. Unless legislation intervenes to redress the imbalance, there would be little consumers could do to protect themselves. In effect, consumers have no bargaining power to bring to bear upon the transaction. As banks and other lenders become more and more involved in the insurance business, the potential for tying loan extensions to the purchase of insurance has increased.

In spite of all the legislation in this area, the abuses still abound. Reforms are still waiting to happen in some states because of the combined lobbying power of banks, finance companies, and car dealers. Tennessee Commissioner of Commerce and Insurance John L. Neff was quoted as saying: "The problem of credit life insurance in the United States is a national scandal. I know of no other product where the public is so blatantly abused by what are supposed to be responsible financial institutions."[7]

§6.05 Legislation Concerning Credit Insurance

The provisions regulating consumer credit insurance have several sources. The National Association of Insurance Commissioners (NAIC) has drafted a model statute called the NAIC Model Act to provide for the regulation of credit life insurance and credit accident and health insurance. More than 30 states have adopted legislation patterned after the Act.[8]

The Model Act regulates:

1. Individual and group credit life, accident, and health insurance involving transactions of less than 10 years' duration
2. The limits of the amount of insurance in relation to the amount of indebtedness
3. The debtor's rights

Specific approval of rates and forms, as well as the supervision of the insurance, is delegated to the State Insurance Commissioner or a corresponding state official.

Another source of law in this area is the Uniform Consumer Credit Code.[9] The U3C regulates insurance related to a consumer credit transaction in which the payment schedule is less than 10 years.[10]

---

[7] Wall Street J, Feb 26, 1985, at 1, col 6.

[8] See I Consumer Credit Guide (CCH) ¶580 for a summary of the state statutes.

[9] U3C §4.102(1) (1974).

[10] U3C §4.103(1)(a) (1974).

The term *consumer credit insurance* under the U3C does not cover insurance procured by a creditor to guard against loss due to the consumer's default except by reason of death or disability of the consumer.[11] If the state adopting the U3C also adopts the NAIC Model Act, the NAIC Act deals with administrative controls, liabilities, and penalties imposed upon persons acting as insurers, while the U3C deals with creditors and debtors. In case of contradiction or inconsistency between the NAIC Act and the U3C, however, the provisions of the U3C are controlling.[12]

State retail installment sales laws also pertain to some aspects of consumer credit insurance. Such laws govern the insurance premiums and the duty of the creditor-seller to deliver a notice of the insurance or a copy of the policy to the debtor-buyer. These acts also require disclosure of the insurance coverage and costs.

Another source of relevant law are the federal and state Truth in Lending Acts, which require disclosures of the credit terms, including insurance costs, to the consumer.

§6.06 The Truth in Lending Act Disclosures

It is rare that the consumer declines an insurance suggested or proposed by the creditor. As explained above, especially in the case of loans, the borrower does not have alternatives, and the premiums are comparatively low. Credit insurance premiums are therefore usually a part of the consumer cost in credit transactions. The TILA requires the disclosure of the insurance premiums under certain conditions. The TILA disclosure requirement concerning credit insurance gives rise to some controversial issues of interpretation.

Regulation Z provides that premiums for credit life, accident, health, or loss of income insurance may be excluded from the finance charge if the following conditions are met:

1. The insurance coverage is not required by the creditor, and this fact is disclosed

2. The premium for the initial term of insurance coverage is disclosed. If the term of insurance is less than the term of the transaction, the term of insurance shall also be disclosed

3. The consumer signs or initials an affirmative written request for the insurance after receiving the disclosures above specified[13]

The requirement that the insurance premium be included in the finance charge and disclosed as such is dictated by the fact that the lender may bury

---

[11] *Id.*

[12] U3C §4.102(2) (1974).

[13] 12 CFR §226.4(d) (1986).

additional finance charges in the insurance premium. Creditors who get a profit from the sale of credit life and disability insurance may artificially advertise a low finance charge. The intent of Congress in requiring the premiums to be included in the finance charge is to defeat this deceptive and misleading practice.

The TILA however, requires this disclosure only if the insurance policy is itself required by the creditor. If it is voluntary, no disclosure is required. The question of whether the insurance is required or voluntary is not always clear. It is itself a factual question.[14]

In *Fisher v Beneficial Finance Co*,[15] the plaintiff borrower contended that by indicating the cost of the insurance in the disclosure form when it was first presented to her, the lender had implicitly represented that the insurance was required. As a result, the lender's failure to include the insurance premium in the finance charge violated the Truth in Lending Act. Although the court denied the plaintiff summary judgment, it sent the case to trial, thus accepting as a legitimate claim the allegation that, by its conduct, the lender may have in fact required the insurance.

Similarly, in *Marine Midland Bank v Burley*,[16] the consumer credit contract stated explicitly that the insurance was voluntary and not required for the credit, and the consumer did sign the contract. Yet the court allowed the consumer to prove that his purchase of the insurance was required as a condition of his obtaining a loan. In other words, the court did not bar this kind of proof, even though the creditor had complied with the Act in a literal way. Thus, before these courts, a literal compliance with the Act does not seem to be enough.

Other courts are less sympathetic to the consumer. For instance, in *Mims v Dixie Finance Corp*,[17] the plaintiff contended that the creditor's disclosure that insurance was not required was not true, and, therefore, the premium should have been included in, and disclosed as, the finance charge. The plaintiff alleged that after she had applied for the loan, she was presented with the entire contract, including the insurance authorization, already filled out. She was never asked whether she wanted the insurance, and she did not request it. When she was presented with the contract, all filled out already, she had assumed the insurance was required. Although sympathetic to the plaintiff's situation, the court did not accept her argument. The court stated: "A plaintiff must prove that the creditor specifically and unequivocally informed her that

---

[14] *Id* and Official Staff Interpretation. *See* Sheffey, *Credit Life and Disability Insurance Disclosures Under Truth in Lending: The Triumph of Form over Substance,* 8 Fla St UL Rev 463 (1980).

[15] 383 F Supp 895 (DRI 1974).

[16] 73 AD2d 1041, 425 NYS2d 429 (1980).

[17] 426 F Supp 627 (ND Ga 1976).

insurance was required, in order to contradict a recital to the contrary. . . ."[18] Similarly, in *Anthony v Community Loan & Investment Corp*,[19] the court said,

> Although plaintiff asserts that she never requested or desired insurance coverage but merely signed the documents when told to do so, this assertion is insufficient to vary the terms of the contract. . . . The defendant correctly contends that absent a claim of illiteracy, fraud or duress, no extraneous oral evidence can be presented by plaintiff to prove that the defendant gave her the impression that the insurance was required.[20]

The *Anthony* holding was again invoked by the Fifth Circuit Court of Appeals to vacate an FTC order in *In re USLIFE Credit Corp v FTC*.[21] In this case, the FTC, through an enforcement action, found that the lender had engaged in a number of practices which amounted in fact to requiring insurance. These practices included:

1. Quoting monthly repayment figures which included insurance
2. Automatically including insurance charges on the loan agreement and disclosure papers presented to consumers for signature
3. Marking an "X" by the signature line reserved for authorization of insurance without permission of the borrower
4. Presenting typed loan agreements to consumers for signing without disclosing the purpose of the signatures

The FTC found that these practices in fact undermined the borrower's insurance election, or at least confused borrowers concerning their right to refuse insurance. The Fifth Circuit vacated the FTC order, finding that the FTC "missed the point" of *Anthony*.

The cases we have cited really go to the issue of coercion: to what extent the consumer was coerced into subscribing to the creditor's insurance policies.

§6.07 Coercion

Coercion is the key issue in what constitutes a credit insurance abusive practice. The question here is, to what extent is the consumer free to acquire or decline credit insurance? Although the borrower may perceive the benefits of the insurance, and may want it, a good number of purchasers of life and credit disability insurance believe that they are *required* to buy insurance as a condition for receiving the loan.

Even within the lending companies, there is pressure on employees to induce consumers to buy all types of credit insurance. There is an expected percentage

---

[18] *Id* 631.

[19] 559 F2d 1363 (5th Cir 1977).

[20] *Id* 1369.

[21] 599 F2d 1387 (5th Cir 1979).

of purchases of insurance related to the number of loans made, known as the *penetration rate*. The performance of the lender's employees is judged partly on the basis of this rate.

One survey revealed that 20 per cent of borrowers believed that the insurance was a condition for loan extension.[22] The high penetration rate percentage, sometimes approaching 100 per cent, which involves so many consumers in need of money in very small loans, indicates that the purchase of this insurance is often not voluntary. All the papers are prepared ahead of time, and the borrower, happy to have the loan approved, is relieved to be signing them. Thus, the issue of coercion is a very subtle one, and the extent of disclosure of the consumer's options becomes an important factual question, not only of form, but of substance.

Some state statutes prohibit the creditor from requiring the consumer to purchase credit insurance. Usually this prohibition appears in small loan statutes.[23] But then the prohibition has no effect upon larger operators, such as banks, sellers, retailers, and dealers who are not subject to these statutes.

The NAIC Model Act and the U3C do *not prohibit* the creditor from requiring the consumer to purchase credit insurance.

Section 11 of the NAIC provides:

> When credit life insurance or credit accident and health insurance is required as additional security for any indebtedness, the debtor shall, upon request of the creditor, have the option of furnishing the required amount of insurance through existing policies of insurance owned or controlled by him or of procuring and furnishing the required coverage through any insurer authorized to transact an insurance business within this state.

Likewise, §4.109 of the U3C reads:

> If a creditor requires insurance, upon notice to him the consumer has the option of providing the required insurance through an existing policy of insurance owned or controlled by the consumer, or through a policy to be obtained and paid for by the consumer, but the creditor for reasonable cause may decline the insurance provided by the consumer.

Thus, these statutes merely require the creditor to give the debtor the option to buy the insurance through the creditor or procure the insurance from another source. What protection does this afford? Very little. Individual insurance, as already discussed, is very expensive. As a matter of fact, few creditors "require" insurance through themselves because then they would

---

[22] Consumer Credit Life and Disability Insurance, A Study by the College of Business Administration of Ohio University 73-74 (C Hubbard ed 1973).

[23] *See* 1 Consumer Credit Guide (CCH) ¶540 for Summary of Small Loan Statutes.

have to make the disclosures set forth in the Truth in Lending Act, these disclosures being contingent on the voluntariness of the insurance purchase.

In 1972, The National Commission of Consumer Finance made the following report:

> The creditor is in an unusually powerful position to "persuade" or "sell" credit insurance to debtors. This is probably more likely in the cash credit (loan) segment of the market than in the sales segment because the typical cash borrower normally has fewer alternative sources of credit available than the credit purchaser.
>
> The debtor is usually in an inferior bargaining position with the creditor. The creditor or lender usually will not openly and directly state that the purchase of credit insurance is required for a loan or credit purchase. This is particularly true since the Truth in Lending Act (TILA) became effective, because under TILA, if credit insurance is required, the premium must be included in the finance charge, and therefore, in the annual percentage rate. However, it seems probable that subtle pressure is used in the sale of the insurance to debtors, evidenced by the unusually high percentage of debtors who purchase insurance. It is not unusual for cash lenders to have an "insurance penetration" of 95 to 98 percent. Even in light of the indicated preference of borrowers for these coverages, these high percentages of acceptance of insurance indicate that some coercion is probably used.[24]

§6.08 Excessive Coverage

Although group credit insurance is much less expensive than individual insurance, group credit insurance is nevertheless more costly than other types of group life insurance.

First, there is the technique of maintaining the same rate of insurance for the total amount of the loan throughout the loan period in spite of the fact that the amount of loan outstanding decreases each month as it is paid. This is the level term insurance policy, as opposed to the declining term policy. In other words, a level term of insurance is maintained which does not take into account the declining amount of the outstanding loan.

The NAIC Model Act, as well as the U3C, prohibit level term type policies. The NAIC Model Act, §4, states:

> A. Credit Life Insurance
> (1) The initial amount of credit life insurance shall not exceed the total amount repayable under the contract of indebtedness and, where an indebtedness is repayable in substantially equal installments, the amount

---

[24] Report of the National Commn on Consumer Finance, Consumer Credit in the United States 85 (1972).

of insurance shall at no time exceed the scheduled or actual amount of unpaid indebtedness, whichever is greater.

B. Credit Accident and Health Insurance

The total amount of periodic indemnity payable by credit accident and health insurance in the event of disability, as defined in the policy, shall not exceed the aggregate of the periodic scheduled unpaid installments of the indebtedness; and the amount of each periodic indemnity payment shall not exceed the original indebtedness divided by the number of periodic installments.

Similarly, §4.202 of the U3C provides:

(1) Except as provided in subsection (2):

(a) in the case of consumer credit insurance providing life coverage, the amount of insurance may not initially exceed the debt and, if the debt is payable in installments, may not exceed at any time the greater of the scheduled or actual amount of the debt; or

(b) in the case of any other consumer credit insurance, the total amount of periodic benefits payable may not exceed the total of scheduled unpaid installments of the debt, and the amount of any periodic benefit may not exceed the original amount of debt divided by the number of periodic installments in which it is payable.

(2) If consumer credit insurance is provided in connection with the open-end credit account, the amounts payable as insurance benefits may be reasonably commensurate with the amount of debt as it exists from time to time. If consumer credit insurance is provided in connection with a commitment to grant credit in the future, the amounts payable as insurance benefits may be reasonably commensurate with the total from time to time of the amount of debt and the amount of the commitment. If the debt or the commitment is primarily for an agricultural purpose and there is no regular schedule of payments, the amount payable as insurance benefits may equal the total of the initial amount of debt and the amount of the commitment.

Another problem of excessive coverage is known as *pyramiding*. When a loan is refinanced, the creditor may sell insurance to cover the new obligation. Instead of cancelling the insurance on the previous loan and refunding the premium to the borrower, the lender charges a new premium, and may also retain the refund on the previous insurance.

Section 5 of the NAIC Model Act prohibits this type of abuse: "If the indebtedness is discharged due to renewal or refinancing prior to the scheduled maturity date, the insurance in force shall be terminated before any new insurance may be issued in connection with the renewed or refinanced indebtedness."

The U3C, §4.110, has a similar provision

(1) A creditor may not contract for or receive a separate charge for

insurance in connection with a deferral (Section 2.503), a refinancing (Section 2.504), or a consolidation (Section 2.505), unless:

(a) the consumer agrees at or before the time of the deferral, refinancing, or consolidation that the charge may be made;

(b) the consumer is to be provided with insurance for an amount or a term, or insurance of any kind, in addition to that to which he would have been entitled had there been no deferral, refinancing, or consolidation;

(c) the consumer receives a refund or credit on account of any unexpired term of existing insurance in the amount required if the insurance were terminated (Section 4.108); and

(d) the charge does not exceed the amount permitted by this Article (Section 4.107).

(2) A creditor may not contract for or receive a separate charge for insurance which duplicates insurance with respect to which the creditor has previously contracted for or received a separate charge.

Another problem with excessive coverage is that, in some cases, the consumer already has sufficient life insurance coverage to cover the indebtedness and can provide the creditor protection by simply naming the creditor as a beneficiary under the existing life insurance policy. The creditor, however, still urges the consumer to purchase new credit life insurance. Section 11 of the NAIC Model Act prohibits this practice.

> When credit life insurance or credit accident and health insurance is required as additional security for any indebtedness, the debtor shall, upon request to the creditor, have the option of furnishing the required amount of insurance through existing policies of insurance owned or controlled by him or of procuring and furnishing the required coverage through any insurer authorized to transact an insurance business within this state.

In 80 per cent of the cases wherein the debtor dies, the estate of the debtor will pay the creditor anyway, with or without credit life insurance. Further, more often than not, the debtor's estate does not get the refund that the debtor had contracted for, and thus gets no benefit from the insurance. Worse still, dishonest creditors do not hesitate to receive double payment: one from the debtor's estate, and one from the insurance policy.[25] The Model Act therefore requires disclosure of the policy and that a certificate of insurance be sent to the borrower.[26] Often, it happens that, even when the deceased debtor's family is aware of the insurance, and when the insurance is written for an amount

---

[25] *Hearings on Consumer Credit Insurance Act of 1969*, 91st Cong, 1st Sess 186 (testimony of Ronald Roberts).

[26] National Association for Insurance Commissioners Model Act, §6 (1977).

greater than the actual claim, the difference, which is supposed to be paid to the estate, is not so paid, but is retained by the creditor.

Another problem is that of ineligibility. Borrowers are made to purchase credit insurance for which they may not be eligible. Some policies have age limits, and borrowers may be beyond those limits, or, in the case of disability insurance, a past illness may make a borrower ineligible, but the creditor has him or her pay anyway. This certainly constitutes a prohibited unfair and deceptive act or practice.

§6.09   Overpricing

With the decrease in the mortality rate, and because credit life insurance in consumer transactions covers a very short period of time, recent studies have shown that insurers in fact pay benefits pursuant to credit life insurance at the low rate of 20¢ per $100.[27]

In 1977, the premiums were $1,450,000,000, and death benefits were $508,000,000, for a loss ratio of just over 1/3.[28] Thus, there is an annual cumulative overcharge of almost $900 million, after overhead and other administrative expenses are paid.[29] Credit life insurance costs much more than ordinary life insurance because of the short timespan involved in consumer credit transactions.

Twenty years ago, the NAIC recommended a minimum loss ratio of 50 per cent. This means that for every $100 collected in premiums, insurers are required to return 50 per cent of their premium income in the form of insurance benefits to the beneficiaries. Many experts feel that an even higher ratio (75 to 80 per cent) would be more realistic, allowing insurers to keep only 20 to 25 per cent of the premiums. Recently, the NAIC suggested that the minimum loss ratio should be 60 per cent. According to many experts, the overcharge per year in the United States approaches $1 billion.[30]

In order to prevent abuses, a number of states, acting upon the recommendations of NAIC, subject credit life insurance to premium rates which produce a loss ratio of at least 50 to 60 per cent. Other states have simply set a maximum rate without any reference to loss ratio. The state requirements, however, did not correct all the abuses and did not solve all the problems.

Not the least of the law's problems is enforceability. As for the maximum rate limit, the law will have the effect of encouraging insurers that charge a lower rate than the maximum to increase their rates upwards to the legal maximum and creditors would probably urge the insurers to do so, in order to collect the

---

[27] M. Greenfield, Consumer Transactions, Guide for Teachers 138 (1983).

[28] American Council of Life Insurance Fact Book 57 (1978).

[29] *Credit Life Insurance Hearing before the Subcomm on Authority Monopoly and Business Rights, on the Committee for the Judiciary,* 96th Cong, 1st Sess Serial 36-44, at 1 (1979) (Senator Howard Metzenbaum of the United States Senate).

[30] *Id* 3.

benefits. Because of the complexity of the issue, some experts, such as the Executive Director of the National Consumer Law Center, have proposed prohibiting altogether any separate charge for credit insurance.[31] Some credit unions now do provide free credit insurance.

§6.10 Claims Abuses

According to one study, in 61 per cent of the cases, insurers took too long to settle, and in 40 per cent of the cases, insurers did not pay as expected.[32] The problem was especially serious in the case of disability insurance, in which many claims are denied on the ground of ineligibility. This is a result of the usual practice of not conducting any examination of the insured at the time the policy is contracted for. Without examination, of course, there is no preliminary finding of ineligibility, and so, the contract is often entered into, and premiums are often paid, whether or not the insured is eligible for coverage.

In *Southards v Central Plains Insurance Co*,[33] the consumer's claim was denied, because, when he purchased the insurance, he had a kidney condition of which he was ignorant. In another case, *Lucas v Continental Casualty Co*,[34] the plaintiff had bought a car from Smith Motors. When credit insurance was discussed, the plaintiff told the salesman that he had a heart condition. The salesman, however, assured the plaintiff that he would be covered anyway. When the plaintiff suffered a heart attack, the insurers refused to pay. Relying on the *pre-existing condition* provision of the policy, the trial court rendered summary judgment for the insurer. The appellate court remanded the case for the plaintiff to prove that the salesman was an agent of the insurer, who would therefore have power to waive the *pre-existing condition* provision. Here, the plaintiff was more fortunate than in *Southards*, but only after many reversals.

§6.11 Property Insurance

Property insurance is the most lucrative type of insurance. Unlike the other types, it is hardly regulated by any law. This type of insurance covers the collateral used as security for the loan. Creditors seek to protect themselves against the risks that the property used as collateral may be destroyed, stolen, or damaged. Property credit insurance normally covers only the vender's single interest (VSI), not the replacement value of the property. Typically, VSI pays the lesser of the actual loss suffered on the insured property and the unpaid balance on the loan. For example, if the property is worth $5,000 and the buyer still owes $2,000, if the car is destroyed or stolen, the policy would pay only $2,000 to the creditor. The consumer gets nothing from this type of insurance

---

[31] *Id* 57 (statement of Robert A. Sable).

[32] M. Greenfield, Consumer Transactions, Guide for Teachers 139 (1983).

[33] 201 Kan 499, 441 P2d 808 (1968).

[34] 120 Ga App 457, 170 SE2d 856 (1969).

upon such loss of the property. Consumers generally do not realize the limited character of this insurance. Often they assume that it is like ordinary auto insurance, and are therefore surprised at the low premiums. If the property has a fair market value which is less than the owed amount, then the borrower could be liable for the difference. For instance, if the car is now worth $2,000 and the borrower still owes $3,000, the insurer will pay $2,000, and the borrower must pay the difference of $1000. Lenders and insurers usually tend to ignore the salvage value of the property, or simply set a low fair market, and thus increase the liability of the borrower.

Property insurance gives creditors and insurers huge profits. The loss ratio may be as low as 7 to 25 per cent, and the commission to creditors as high as 60 per cent.[35] As an example, between 1957 and 1966, GMAC's income from the sale of property insurance amounted to $4 million dollars per year, almost six times GMAC's income from credit life and disability insurance.[36]

As stated above, except for some disclosure requirements imposed by the Truth in Lending Act, there is no legislation dealing specifically with property insurance to prevent its abuses. Fortunately, some courts, by using the common law theories of fraud and deception, have sought to redress some of these abuses. *Jim Short Ford Sales v Washington*,[37] followed by *Ford Motor Credit Co v Washington*,[38] are good illustrations of this approach.

The plaintiff in these cases purchased an automobile from a dealership with financing from Ford Motor Credit Company (FMCC). As a condition of the loan, FMCC required collision insurance on the automobile. The dealer informed plaintiff that the insurance would be placed through a "reputable" insurance broker, Norman Smoake. Smoake, whose license was not renewed by the Department of Insurances, allegedly applied for insurance with an insurance company, but no insurance was ever issued to plaintiff.

Despite this, FMCC still required a new insurance coverage from plaintiff, although it declined to reimburse him for the premium already paid. Subsequently, plaintiff had to purchase a policy with plaintiff's own funds. Evidence at the trial showed that the dealership and its agent insurance representative got a sizable kickback from Smoake for every insurance transaction which was substantially overcharged.

The trial court found the existence of a conspiracy between the dealership, its agent, and the insurance broker to conceal the truth and defraud plaintiff. Plaintiff received a jury verdict of $5,000 compensatory damages (subsequently remitted to $750) and $150,000 in punitive damages against the above defendants. The trial court, however, directed a verdict in favor of the financing company, FMCC.

On appeal, the Supreme Court of Alabama reversed the judgment of the trial court and remanded for a new trial as to FMCC. The court reasoned that FMCC

---

[35] M. Greenfield, Consumer Transactions, Guide for Teachers 468 (1983).

[36] *Id.*

[37] 384 So 2d 83 (Ala 1980).

[38] 420 So 2d 14 (Ala 1982).

was closely connected with the dealer by providing the loan forms and approving the terms of the transactions.[39]

The court concluded that FMCC should have known all the facts surrounding the insurance transactions between the dealer and the broker and should have disclosed these facts to the consumers. In failing to do so, FMCC was guilty of fraud. On rehearing, the Supreme Court confirmed the jury verdict of $75,000 in punitive damages imposed on FMCC.

Cases like this are rare. Many insurance abuses remain undetected and are seldom brought to the attention of the public and the courts. Tighter legislative control is very much needed in this area.

[39] 384 So 2d at 85.

7 Credit Cards

§7.01   Introduction

The credit card is a phenomenon of our consumer-oriented society. Issued first in the early 1950s, bank cards originally were restricted to regional use.

The precursor of the present-day credit card actually appeared before 1920 in the form of the *credit coin*. This was a small piece of metal which displayed the merchant's name, together with the customer's account number. The coins were issued by retail department stores to stimulate sales by encouraging credit purchases.[1]

The true plastic revolution began, however, with the issuance of national bank cards. In 1966, Bank America issued its BankAmericard, the first bank card to operate on a national, and later international, level. Later, other interbank card systems entered the field, such as Interbankcard, Midwest Bank Card, and Mastercharge. Currently, the two most conspicuous bank card systems are VISA (formerly BankAmericard) and MasterCard (formerly Mastercharge).

Customers were actively using over six million credit cards issued by federally insured banks by the end of 1969. By 1971, bank card billings amounted to $4 billion.[2] The total revolving bank credit, most of which is represented by bank credit cards, has now exceeded $27 billion and shows no sign of declining in the near future.[3]

MasterCard and VISA share equally the bank credit field. The new trend is to develop credit cards which will double as debit cards, thereby allowing the user to effect electronic fund transfers (EFTs) at Automated Teller Machines (ATM) or Point of Sale (POS) terminals in retail establishments.[4]

§7.02 Legislation Governing Bank Credit Cards

Prior to 1970, there was practically no legislation governing credit card transactions. Likewise, little case law existed on the topic. Although credit cards were subject to great abuse, the law regarding the liabilities of the credit card issuer, the credit cardholder, and the merchant honoring the credit card remained vague. As one author commented, "There is virtually no authority, judicial or statutory, that directly controls the legal problems which may be expected to arise from the tripartite credit card transaction."[5]

The flurry of 1970s legislation aimed at consumer credit protection contributed to resolving many of these legal problems. The Consumer Credit Protection Act (CCPA)[6] is an example of this legislation. The CCPA is a federal statute governing consumer credit cost disclosures, garnishment, and credit reporting agencies. Its subchapter dealing with consumer credit cost disclosure

---

[1] *See* Comment, *The Tripartite Credit Card Transaction: A Legal Infant?*, 48 Calif L Rev 459, 460 (1960).

[2] 118 Cong Rec S6894 (daily ed Apr 27, 1972), *cited in* Comment, *The Bank Credit Card and the Consumer: Programming Justice into the Cashless Society*, 7 Val UL Rev 503 (1973).

[3] Fed Res Bull A42 (July 1980).

[4] *See* **ch 8** on Electronic Fund Transfers.

[5] Comment, *The Tripartite Credit Card Transaction: A Legal Infant?*, 48 Calif L Rev 459 (1960).

[6] 15 USC §1601 *et seq.*

is best known as the Truth in Lending Act (TILA), which requires the creditor to clearly and conspicuously disclose the terms and conditions of the credit contract.

TILA's stated purpose is the promotion of free competition in the marketplace through the dissemination of information to consumers.[7] Since 1968, TILA has been amended to deal with the problems of unsolicited cards and liability for unauthorized use.[8] In 1980, TILA was revised and became the Truth in Lending Simplification and Reform Act.[9] The revisions were so substantial that the Federal Reserve Board characterized the legislation as the "new Truth in Lending Act."[10] The Fair Credit Billing Act[11] has also been enacted to deal with the consumer's defenses against the card issuer.

Prior to the federal enactments of the 1970s, a number of states passed legislation dealing with the problem of the cardholder's liability for unauthorized use. A prime example is the California Song-Beverly Credit Card Act of 1971.[12] The National Conference of Commissioners on Uniform State Law codified this type of legislation in §3.403 of the 1974 version of the Uniform Consumer Credit Code (U3C).

A number of states have adopted various versions of the U3C to deal with the problems created by the use of credit cards. They have done so either indirectly, through their general treatment of claims assignment, as discussed in more detail in Chapter 9, or directly, through provisions aimed at the specific topic of credit card use. Most of the state legislation, however, is of little importance in view of the federal legislation on the matter.

§7.03   Description of the Credit Card Transaction

There are three types of credit cards. The first, referred to as *merchant credit cards*, are issued by large retailers, such as Sears, to enable the consumer to make credit purchases from them. This type of credit transaction was created primarily to stimulate sales. The purpose of the card is to simplify the credit transaction and to identify the customer. Merchant credit cards generally do not raise complex legal problems. Those that do arise are generally limited to disclosure and billing issues.

The second type of credit card is the *travel and entertainment card*. This type is exemplified by American Express, Diners Club, and Carte Blanche. Credit cards issued by oil companies are also included in this category.

The third type of credit card is the kind used for paying third parties, and

---

[7] 15 USC §1601.

[8] Pub L No 91-508, §502, 84 Stat 1114 (1970).

[9] Pub L No 96-221, 94 Stat 125 (1980).

[10] Regulatory Analysis of Revised Regulation Z, 46 Fed Reg 20941, 20949 (Apr 7, 1981).

[11] 15 USC §1681 *et seq.*

[12] Cal Civ Code §1747.90 (West 1985).

as credit devices. These are referred to as *bank credit cards* or *lender credit cards.* The two giants in this field again are MasterCard and VISA. Except for transactions involving merchant credit cards, credit card transactions involve a tripartite arrangement.

The Tripartite Arrangement

Much has been written on the nature of the tripartite credit card arrangement.[13] Basically, the transaction involves three parties: the card issuer (generally a bank), the cardholder, and the merchant-supplier who has agreed to honor the card. The issuer allows the cardholder to use the credit card up to an agreed limit for the acquisition of goods or services from the supplier. Thus, three contracts are involved in the tripartite arrangement.

The first contract exists between the issuer and the cardholder. This contract spells out the credit terms, such as the amount of credit available, the interest to be charged, and the method of payment. The consumer is entitled to use the card to purchase goods and services at establishments that have agreed to honor the card. At the time of monthly billing, the consumer is given the option of either paying the account in full or simply paying a portion. If the customer pays in full, the issuer charges no interest. If, however, the customer elects to pay only a portion, interest will be charged and calculated in the monthly payment. The card thus serves both as a means of payment and as a credit device.

The second contract exists between the issuer and the merchant who honors the card. This contract establishes the procedure for honoring the card. For example, the transaction must be evidenced by a sales slip which has been signed by the cardholder. The merchant must check the "hot card" list, the expiration date of the card, and whether any given purchase exceeds the credit limit. The contract also establishes the terms and conditions under which the issuer will purchase from the merchant the sales slips derived from the credit card transaction.

The third contract is between the merchant and the cardholder. This contract is typically a contract for the sale of goods or services, with the purchase price being collected by the card issuer. The merchant gives express or implied warranties to the cardholder, who has all the legal remedies under applicable laws and statutes.[14] It is this contract which gives rise to the entire credit card transaction.

This description of the tripartite system has been greatly simplified. Most credit card transactions actually involve more than three parties. Instead of a single issuing bank with whom the cardholder transacts, most credit card

---

[13] *See, e.g.,* Comment, *The Tripartite Credit Card Transaction: A Legal Infant?,* 48 Calif L Rev 459 (1960); Comment, *Development of Consumer Defenses Under a Tripartite Credit Card System,* 29 Syracuse L Rev 1279 (1979); B. Clark, The Law of Bank Deposits, Collections and Credit Cards §9.2 (1981).

[14] If the sales contract involves goods, it is subject to Article 2 of the UCC. Article 2 may apply to furnishing of services by analogy. *See* UCC §§2-312 to 2-318.

systems include a second depository bank, (the merchant bank) from which the merchant receives payment. Thus, it is technically incorrect to qualify a bank credit card transaction as a purely tripartite arrangement.

Described simply, the merchant bank solicits the merchant for the program and serves as the primary contact. It is this bank that finances the merchant's account receivable by discounting the sales slip signed by the consumer and crediting the merchant's account for the amount of the proceeds. The merchant bank will then collect the sales slips from the issuing bank through a national bank card clearing system. The issuing bank remits the amount of the purchase slips to the merchant bank, and then charges them to the cardholder's account.

§7.04   Legal Nature of the Credit Card Transaction

The legal nature of this transaction has been the source of much commentary. Two principal theories have emerged. One theory analogizes the credit card to a letter of credit. The second theory likens the transaction to the assignment of accounts receivable.

According to the letter of credit theory, the merchant who supplies goods and services to the cardholder seeks, through the credit card system, to substitute the credit of a solvent institution, i.e., the issuing bank, for that of the cardholder. This is analogous to the letter of credit arrangement wherein the buyer, at the seller's request, instructs a bank to issue a letter of credit which will make the seller's transaction secure. Through this letter, the bank promises to honor the seller's request for payment upon the seller's compliance with the conditions specified in the letter of credit. Thus, the bank's duty to pay the seller exists independently of the underlying transaction between the seller and buyer.

According to the assignment theory, on the other hand, the issuing bank is but a factor who purchases chattel paper from the merchant. The merchant assigns the chattel paper, to which the cardholder has subscribed, to the merchant bank, which in turn assigns the paper to the issuing bank.

Neither of these theories, however, adequately describes the nature of the credit card transaction. First, there is a difference between bank credit cards and letters of credit. Letters of credit are essentially contracts between the issuer and the beneficiary, i.e., the merchant-supplier. Bank credit cards, on the other hand, are essentially contracts between the issuer and the cardholder. In letters of credit, the issuer generally has no recourse against the seller-beneficiary who complies with the terms of the letter if the buyer-customer fails to reimburse the issuer. This is not so in a credit card transaction. Many bank credit card agreements give the issuer recourse against the merchant if the cardholder refuses to pay because of a dispute with the merchant.

The second theory, which treats credit card transactions as an assignment of accounts receivable, is not generally accepted. In practice, such treatment would have a devastating impact on the assignees of the sales slips. The most obvious effect would be the subjection of these transactions to Article 9 of the

Uniform Commercial Code, which governs the assignment of chattel paper and accounts receivable.

At the heart of the problem lies the question of whether the cardholder's obligation to pay is initially owed to the supplier or to the card issuer. This problem is important to the question of the issuer's liability for the supplier's breaches of contract.

Financial institutions prefer the letter of credit analogy, which stresses the independence of the contracts between the parties involved in the transaction. This independence would insulate the financial institution from the cardholder's claims and defenses against the supplier. On the other hand, consumer groups argue for the assignment theory, which would subject the card issuer to the cardholder's claims and defenses against the supplier.

The rise of federal legislation in the last two decades designed to preserve the consumer's claims and defenses against the seller, even in a "direct loan" situation, has rendered this theoretical discussion moot, at least as far as the consumer is concerned.[15] In the consumer field, credit card transactions should be regarded as sui generis transactions subject to their own laws and regulations.

§7.05 Cardholder Liability for Unauthorized Use

In a credit card transaction, the two most important issues are the liability of the cardholder for unauthorized use of the credit card, and the preservation of the consumer's claims and defenses in a credit card transaction.

Unauthorized use generally includes cases of loss and theft. The manner in which credit cards are used gives rise to such abuse, since the merchant honoring the credit card usually does not ask for any identification other than a signature, which may be easily falsified. Prior to the volley of federal regulations in this area, card issuers usually dealt with fraudulent use through contractual agreements with the cardholder. The extent to which the courts upheld those contractual agreements, especially when they involved consumers, was an area of great interest.

One of the early cases dealing with the liability of credit card holders was *Union Oil Co v Lull.*[16] In this case, the Supreme Court of Oregon ordered a retrial because the trial court had misdirected the jury on the question of the cardholder's liability. The defendant's credit card had been fraudulently used to make 55 separate, unauthorized purchases of gas totaling $1,454.25. The thief made the purchases during the course of a road trip which began in Oregon, wound down through the Southwestern states, zigzagged up through the Midwest, and finally ended in Chicago, Illinois. The defendant remained unaware of the charges until he received the bill and copies of the credit tickets

---

[15] See **ch 9** on Assignment of Claims and Preservation of Consumer's Claims and Defense.

[16] 220 Or 412, 349 P2d 243 (1980).

which evidenced the sales. He testified that he did not notice that his card was missing during that period because he had not needed any gas.

The Oregon Supreme Court began its opinion by stating that the cardholder was bound by the notice clause in the credit card `agreement, regardless of whether the cardholder had read the fine print. Here, the clause stated that the customer "guarantees" payment for products or services rendered "to anyone presenting this card." This guarantee would continue "until the card is rendered or written notice is received by the company that it is lost or stolen."[17] In interpreting this language, the court held that the cardholder remained liable, even if the jury should find that he had not been negligent in handling the card, or in giving prompt notice of the theft as soon as he was reasonably able to do so.

The court also ruled, however, that the issuer, as the entity benefiting from the guarantee, held an implicit duty of care to identify an imposter so that the defendant would be protected from the card's unauthorized use. The issuer had the burden of proving that the gas station attendant, "as the issuer's agent," had properly discharged this duty. Whether the gas station had been negligent in honoring the card, which indicated a different state of residence than that shown on the license plate of the car driven by the wrongdoer, was a question of fact for the jury.

The court concluded that the indemnity agreement should be interpreted as subjecting the cardholder to liability for unauthorized sales only if due care has been exercised by the merchant-supplier in ascertaining the identity of the person presenting the card. Furthermore, Union Oil's right to recover upon presentation of a Union Oil card at a service station of an associated company with whom Union Oil had contracted for reimbursement would be no greater than the right of the dealer making the sale. The court recognized that in such a case Union Oil would be regarded as the assignee of the dealer's claim against the cardholder. If so, then Union Oil would take the assignment of the claim subject to its incumbent infirmities.[18] It is generally impossible, however, to prove that a gas station has exercised this duty of care. Thus, the test becomes whether the presentation of the card would prompt a reasonable man to inquire as to the customer's right to use the card. As the court said, this must be a jury question. Therefore, although the court upheld the fine-print clause, the court gave it an interpretation that actually protected the consumer.

Although the card in *Lull* involved a two-party credit arrangement, the court's reasoning, using the assignment theory, also applies to a three-party credit card arrangement. When applying this theory, other courts have held that the cardholder is freed of liability for unauthorized use when the supplier is negligent or acts in bad faith.

An example of such a case is *Gulf Refining v Williams Roofing.*[19] In this Arkansas case, an employee of the oil company's retail outlets retained a Gulf gas card

---

[17] *Id.*

[18] 349 P2d at 252.

[19] 208 Ark 362, 186 SW2d 790 (1945).

after the rightful owner failed to collect it. The employee then went on a "90 day orgy of buying." The suppliers who honored the card acted negligently. Some, in fact, acted in collusion by providing the thief with fictitious purchase slips. The Arkansas Supreme Court relied on the assignment theory and dismissed the oil company's claim for reimbursement. The Arkansas Supreme Court followed *Lull*. The court read into the agreement between the issuer and the cardholder, which had required the cardholder to indemnify the merchant-supplier for unauthorized use, an implicit stipulation that such an agreement would operate only where the merchant-supplier had acted neither fraudulently nor negligently.[20]

Other courts focused not on the supplier's conduct, but on the consumer's conduct, to determine liability for unauthorized use. In *Sears Roebuck v Duke*,[21] the court held that the cardholder should be liable only if he was negligent or at fault, either regarding the loss of the card or in failing to report the loss to the issuer.

Decisions along these lines imply that card issuers are better able to absorb the loss than the individual consumer. It was this realization that prompted the onslaught of federal legislation.

§7.06 —Federal Protection of Credit Card Users

In 1970, Congress amended the Federal Consumer Credit Protection Act (CCPA) to include three new sections. These deal with credit card disclosures, billing error resolutions, and consumer liability for lost or stolen credit cards.[22] A cardholder is liable for the unauthorized use of a credit card only if the following six conditions are met:

1. The card is an accepted credit card
2. The liability is not in excess of $50
3. The card issuer gives adequate notice to the cardholder of the potential liability
4. The card issuer has provided the cardholder with a description of a means by which the card issuer may be notified of loss or theft of the card
5. The unauthorized use occurs before the card issuer has been notified that an unauthorized use of the credit card has occurred or may occur as the result of loss, theft, or otherwise
6. The card issuer has provided a method whereby the user of such card

---

[20] Some courts enforce the notice clause to hold the cardholder liable for unauthorized use. *See, e.g.*, Uni-Serv Corp v Vitiello, 53 Misc 2d 396, 278 NYS2d 969 (Civ Ct 1967); Texaco Inc v Goldstein, 34 Misc 2d 751, 229 NYS2d 51 (Mun Ct 1962), *affd mem*, 39 Misc 2d 552, 241 NYS2d 495 (Sup Ct 1963); *see* B. Clark, *The Law of Bank Deposits, Collections and Credit Cards* §9.3(1) (1981).

[21] 441 SW2d 521 (Tex 1969).

[22] 15 USC §1643.

can be identified as the person authorized to use it, such as a signature, photograph, fingerprint, or some electronic or mechanical device.[23]

The burden is on the issuer to prove that the above conditions are met.

The term *accepted credit card* means any "credit card which the card-holder has requested and received, or has signed or has used, or authorized another to use, for the purpose of obtaining money, property, labor, or services on credit."[24] The issuance of unsolicited credit cards is prohibited. It is unlawful to issue a credit card except in response to a request or application for a new card, or as a renewal or substitution for an accepted card.[25]

The cardholder must be given adequate notice of the cardholder's potential liability. *Adequate notice* is notice which is in writing and has set forth the pertinent facts clearly and conspicuously.[26] The reason for this requirement is to insure that the cardholder can reasonably perceive the notice and understand its meaning. This excludes the fine print which the common law had accepted. The notice may be printed on the credit card itself, on the periodic statement of the account, or by any other means which would reasonably assure its receipt by the cardholder.[27] Regulation Z further specifies that to be adequate, the notice must state that the cardholder's liability should not exceed $50.[28] It must also state the means by which the cardholder may provide oral or written notice to the card issuer of the card's loss or theft. In other words, the card issuer must provide the holder with the address and phone number by which to notify the issuer of loss or theft. Regulation Z allows notification to be made in any manner at the option of the cardholder: in person, by telephone, or in writing.[29]

The practical difficulty for card issuers in meeting all the required conditions imposed by the statute and regulations may eventually result in the complete elimination of the $50 liability limit for unauthorized use. Since the $50 limit does not apply if the use is authorized, it is vital to determine whether use was indeed authorized or unauthorized.

§7.07   —Unauthorized Use Defined

The term *unauthorized use* in connection with the liability of the cardholder means "a use of a credit card by a person other than the cardholder who does not have actual, implied, or apparent authority for such use and from which the cardholder received no benefit."[30]

---

[23] *Id.*

[24] 15 USC §1602(1).

[25] 15 USC §1642.

[26] 15 USC §1602(j).

[27] *Id.*

[28] 12 CFR §226.12(b)(ii).

[29] 12 CFR §226.12(3).

[30] 15 USC §1602(o).

In *Young v Bank of America National Trust & Savings*,[31] the plaintiff-cardholder sued the card issuer for hounding her for payments even though she had already reported her card's theft. The plaintiff sought punitive damages and recovery for emotional distress. The trial court granted her $100,000 in compensation and treble damages. The court of appeals affirmed the decision. The facts are as follows:

On May 24, 1979, the plaintiff permitted a friend, Wooden, to use her Bank America VISA for the sole purpose of purchasing a one-way air ticket to Hawaii. She limited the amount he could charge to approximately $150, and stipulated that he must phone her from Hawaii every day. She also requested that he return the card to her when he got back. Wooden never called the plaintiff, nor did he ever return.

On May 26, the plaintiff phoned the bank and reported that the card had been stolen. She requested an immediate cancellation of the card. On September 3, 1979, the bank recovered the credit card. By then, $2,198.32 had been charged. The bank refused to adjust the plaintiff's balance and continued to bill her for the charges.

The issue in the case was whether Wooden's use was authorized. The bank contended that since Wooden had apparent authority to use the card, the card could not really be considered lost or stolen. The court disagreed, however, finding that the card was indeed stolen and its use unauthorized. Wooden had retained the credit card beyond any permission given, with intent permanently to deprive the plaintiff of ownership. Therefore, the card was stolen within the meaning of the statute. By properly informing the bank that the card was stolen and that any subsequent use was unauthorized, the plaintiff had fulfilled her duties under the statute, and her liability was limited to $50. The court further concluded that this was an action based not in contract, but in tort, and thus permitted compensation including damages for emotional distress. In justifying the award of treble damages to the plaintiff, the court stated, "given the severe mental and emotional pain suffered by the [the plaintiff] over several months, and the [b]ank's computer-hearted insensitivity toward its customer, the award was not excessive."[32]

An Alabama court restricted its interpretation of the term *unauthorized use* in *Martin v American Express, Inc.*[33] In this case, the cardholder, Martin, gave his card to a business associate, McBride, to enable the latter to use the card for the purpose of a joint business venture. Martin orally told McBride that he could charge up to $500 on the credit card. Martin had asked American Express, prior to giving his card to McBride, not to permit the total charges to exceed $1000. McBride however, exceeded the authorized limit and shortly thereafter disappeared.

---

[31] 141 Cal App 3d 108, 190 Cal Rptr 122 (1983).
[32] *Id* at 115, 190 Cal Rptr at 127.
[33] 361 So 2d 597 (Ala Civ App 1978).

The court held that where a cardholder, absent the presence of fraud, duress, or the like, voluntarily permits the use of his or her credit card by another, the cardholder has authorized the use of that card and is thereby responsible for any charges. The court did not accept Martin's argument that the law of agency should apply, whereby a principal may not be held liable for an agent who acts outside the scope of the given authority.

Instead, the court ruled that one should not look to the common law for interpretation when the plain language of the statute is clear. Concerning Martin's notification to American Express asking the company to permit no more than $1000 to be charged, the court said that adherence to such notification would impose a "difficult and potentially disastrous burden" on the card issuer.[34] In short, the court interpreted the term *unauthorized use* to exclude situations in which a cardholder voluntarily allows another to use the card, even though that third person subsequently misuses the card. The court reasoned that to allow otherwise would encourage claims by dishonest cardholders.[35]

§7.08   —Unauthorized Use by Family Members

A situation which often arises is the misuse of a credit card by a member of the cardholder's family. In *Society National Bank v Kienzle*,[36] the court invoked Ohio law to exonerate the cardholder-husband from any liability to the issuer for charges on the card made by the cardholder's wife. In Ohio, a husband is not answerable for his wife's acts unless she acts as his agent and he subsequently ratifies those acts. The court held that the issuer had not met the burden of proof to show that the use was authorized, that the wife acted as the cardholder's agent, or that he ratified her conduct.

The same approach was taken by the court in *Fifth Third Bank/VISA v Gilbert*,[37] In this case, the cardholder's minor daughter inexplicably obtained access to the charge account and went on a $1,100 shopping spree. The card had been in the exclusive possession of the cardholder, who resided some distance from the daughter. After placing the burden of proof on the issuer to show that the use was authorized, the court ruled that VISA had not met that burden.

In both *Kienzle* and *Fifth Third Bank*, the method by which the family member obtained access to the account was unexplained. Both courts ruled that the $50 liability limit applied. However, in the cases where the cardholder has voluntarily permitted another to use a card, and that person has exceeded the permitted amount, the $50 limit does not apply.

---

[34] *Id* 700.
[35] *Id* 601.
[36] 11 Ohio App 3d 178, 463 NE2d 1261 (1983).
[37] 478 NE2d 1324 (Ohio Mun Ct 1984).

In *Walker Bank & Trust Co v Jones*,[38] the court had another view of when an *unauthorized* use by a family member occurred. *Walker* represents two cases, one involving Jones and another involving one Harlan, which were consolidated on appeal because of similar facts. In both cases, the wives originally requested the cards. In the Jones case, credit cards were issued to the wife and her husband in each of their names. In the Harlan case, the wife requested that her husband be added to the account as an authorized user. Upon marital separation, the wives informed the bank that they would no longer honor charges made by their husbands on the accounts. In both cases, the bank demanded return of the credit cards, and closed the accounts. Defendant Jones and her husband continued to use the cards. She finally relinquished her card to the bank, but not until $2,685.70 were charged to the account. Defendant Harlan returned the card three months after her notice to the bank. In the interim, charges were made to her account by her husband. Defendants argued that their liability was limited to $50 for their husbands' unauthorized use of the cards.

The bank, on the other hand, argued that the husbands' use of the credit cards was at no time unauthorized because they had "actual, implied or apparent authority" to use them. Their signatures were the same as the signatures on the cards, and their names the same as those imprinted on the cards. The bank further contended that the wives' notification to the card issuer had no bearing whatsoever on whether the use was unauthorized, so as to entitle them to the $50 statutory limit. The court agreed. Deciding that the husbands had *apparent authority* because the wives had requested that the cards be issued in their names, the court held that the wives' liability was governed by their contracts with the bank and not by the Truth in Lending Act's statutory limitation. The defendants' failure to promptly return the cards to the bank justified the bank's disregard of the notifications. The court concluded that "justice is better served by placing the responsibility for the credit escapades of an errant spouse . . . on the cardholder rather than the Bank."[39]

The case was strongly criticized for several reasons:

1. The Utah court's holding runs counter to the purpose of Congress through TILA which is to place the burden of card loss on the party which is in a better position to control credit card losses and bear the costs

2. The court placed an impossible burden on the cardholders by requiring the wives to return their runaway husbands' cards. Here, the wives could not even find their husbands

3. The Court failed to address any obligation which the card issuer might have to exercise reasonable care to avoid credit card abuses[40]

---

[38] 672 P2d 73 (Utah 1983).

[39] *Id* 76.

[40] National Consumer Law Center, The Consumer Credit and Sales Legal Practices Series, Truth in Lending in Transition §1.9.4, at 70-71 (1985 Supp). The dissenting opinion in *Walker* adopted the same arguments.

§7.09 —Unauthorized Use by Employees of Corporate Entities

Another situation which frequently arises is the misuse of corporate credit cards by employees. Again, the question arises as to whether the $50 liability limit applies. Prior to 1974, applicability of the $50 liability limit to corporate credit cards was already being questioned, since TILA excluded from its coverage "credit transactions involving extensions of credit for business or commercial purposes . . . or to organizations."[41] The liability limit thus appeared not to apply when credit cards were used by individuals for business purposes or when a company used a card for any purpose. However, §1643 of TILA, dealing with cardholder liability, does not specifically require that the cardholder be a consumer. The court faced this problem in *American Airlines Inc v Remis Industries, Inc.*[42] Remis contracted with American Airlines for Air Travel Cards, which permitted Remis's employees to purchase air tickets on credit. Lerner, Remis's Vice-President and General Manager, was informed of a billing error which alerted him to the fact that six round-trip tickets from Miami to Curacao had been fraudulently charged to his card, which had been either lost or stolen. The tickets totalled $14,000. Lerner promptly informed American Airlines, who nevertheless requested payment. Upon Remis's refusal to pay, American Airlines filed a complaint. Remis argued in its answer that the amount stemmed from an unauthorized use of the card; that American Airlines was negligent in permitting the unauthorized use; and that Remis's liability was limited to $50. American Airlines argued in its motion for summary judgment that the contract obligated the company to pay for all tickets prior to American Airlines' notification of loss.

Interpreting TILA's legislative history, the court pointed out that its original provisions were enacted in 1968 with no reference to credit card transactions. The purpose of the Act was simply to assure a meaningful disclosure of credit terms. The Act was amended in 1970 to include credit card provisions. The court stated that applying §1603 on transactions exempted from TILA to limit the scope of the credit card provisions would produce "such a statutory obfuscation that it would surely thwart the intent of Congress."[43] Further, confusion would result when trying to determine whether a card is used for business purposes, or a personal purpose, given that the two uses often overlap.[44] In holding for Remis, the court stated that Congress intended to protect all credit cardholders, corporate or individual, without exception. The court also noted that, subsequent to the transaction in this case, the Federal Reserve Board has amended Regulation Z to bring corporate cardholders as

---

[41] 15 USC §1603(1).

[42] 494 F2d 196 (2d Cir 1974).

[43] *Id* 201.

[44] *Id.*

well as individuals expressly into TILA's scope.[45] In 1974, Congress amended TILA to include business credit cards under the scope of the $50 liability limitation.[46] However, the card issuer may contract with an organization that provides cards to 10 or more of its employees for a liability limit beyond TILA's statutory limit, as long as this does not expand the liability limit for the employees themselves. Thus, if an employee loses a company card, and an unauthorized person uses it, the employee may not be liable for more than $50, but the company might.

In practice, many card issuers do not even impose a $50 limit on the cardholder. First, the conditions required by federal law are so stringent that it is not always possible for the card issuer to meet them all, and secondly, the issuer wants to keep the goodwill of the customers in a competitive market. The annual fees which card issuers now impose upon cardholders may cover these potential losses incurred from unauthorized use. Note that the statutory limit applies regardless of whether the cardholder is negligent. Federal law on this point defers to state law if state law offers more protection to the consumer.[47]

§7.10 Preservation of the Cardholder's Claims and Defenses against the Card Issuer under State Law

Suppose the goods purchased from a merchant through a credit card prove to be defective. May the cardholder refuse to pay the card issuer after the cardholder has received the bill?[48] Before the enactment of federal laws and state statutes which dealt specifically with this problem, how the tripartite credit transaction was characterized bore heavily on the answer to this question.

Impact of the Assignment Theory and the Direct Loan Concept

If the transaction between the cardholder and the issuer is considered a *direct loan*, completely independent from the transaction between the merchant and cardholder which gives rise to the use of the credit card, then the consumer must continue to pay the card issuer for the defective goods. But, if the obligation of the cardholder is considered to be owed initially to the merchant, with the issuer simply acting as the assignee of the merchant's claim against

---

[45] 12 CFR §226.12(5). In Koerner v American Express, 444 F Supp 334 (ED La 1977), *revd*, 452 US 233, dealing with billing errors, the court excluded corporate cardholders from the protection afforded the consumer. The court in this case noted that the Fair Credit Billing Act, a 1979 amendment to TILA (15 USC §1666) "provided its own internal qualifications" and therefore did not cover business entities.

[46] 15 USC §1645.

[47] 15 USC §1643(c).

[48] See **ch 9** on Assignment of Claims and Preservation of Consumer's Claims and Defenses.

the cardholder, then the consumer should be permitted to refuse to pay the issuer. Likewise, any defense or claim that the cardholder has against the merchant should be good against the card issuer.

Until recently, statutes which preserved the consumer's claims and defenses against the assignees usually applied to installment sales contracts. They generally did not apply to bank credit card transactions, because these transactions were defined as consumer loans rather than consumer credit sales. In fact, the 1968 version of the Uniform Consumer Credit Code (U3C) ignored bank credit card transactions altogether.[49]

The inequities suffered by consumers as a result of this distinction may be seen in *Payne v Filter Queen, Inc.*[50] In this case, defrauded consumers brought a class action suit against Filter Queen of Haywood, Inc. (Filter Queen), seeking contract rescission and damages against the company, as well as against the finance company which had financed the sale. Some of the consumers had entered into sales contracts with Filter Queen, but their contracts were subsequently assigned to the finance company. Other consumers used bank credit cards following an arrangement between Filter Queen and the bank card issuer. Waiver of defense clauses were written into both installment sales contracts and in the credit card arrangements signed by the consumers.

Filter Queen's salesmen used techniques "which read like a handbook on consumer fraud."[51] Under the existing California law, waiver of defense clauses were illegal in installment sales contracts, but not in credit card contracts. The critical issue was whether the consumers who used bank credit cards were still required to pay the bank issuer, despite Filter Queen's fraud.[52]

Payne illuminates the potential for injustice if the law treats consumers differently based on the method by which the consumer chooses to pay for the goods. One of the first states to deal with this problem was California.

The California Song-Beverly Act

The Song-Beverly Act[53] was an attempt to subject card issuers to the cardholder's claims and defenses, with certain limitations. These limitations aimed at striking a compromise between the concerns of the consumer advocates and the interests of the banking community.

Under Song-Beverly, consumers could assert their claims and defenses

---

[49] The 1972 U3C still excludes a credit card transaction from the definition of *consumer credit sale* (§1.301(12)(b)(i)) and includes it in the term *loan.* (§1.301(25)(a)(11)).

[50] Civ No 384418 (Alameda County Super Ct Cal June 16, 1969), *affd subnom* Payne v United Cal Bank, 23 Cal App 3d 850, 100 Cal Rptr 672 (1972), *cited in* Note, *Preserving Consumer Defenses in Credit Card Transactions,* 81 Yale LJ 287, 293 (1971).

[51] *Id.*

[52] At the time the case was cited in the above article, it was on appeal from a decision granting the bank's motion to dismiss the complaint without leave to amend, because of failure to establish a proper class. The result went unreported. *Id* 292, n24.

[53] Cal Civ Code §1747.90(g) (West Supp 1975) This law was repealed in 1982. California has now adopted the Fair Credit Billing Act provisions.

against the card issuer, but only when sued by the card issuer for nonpayment.[54] The cardholder did not possess an affirmative right to sue the card issuer for any claim or loss resulting from the supplier's conduct.[55] Under the Act, the consumer is deemed to have waived the defenses if the consumer, after notifying the card issuer of the supplier's defects as required by law, pays off the disputed amount.[56]

Due to all these limitations, Song-Beverly was an ineffective consumer weapon and did not "cause much of a stir."[57]

The Uniform Consumer Credit Code (U3C) and Other State Laws

The revised Uniform Consumer Credit Code (U3C), in 1974, followed the California Song-Beverly Act, except that both the residence of the cardholder and the place where the sale occurred must be in the same state or within 100 miles of each other. Section 3.403(3) states:

> Except as otherwise provided in this section, a card issuer, including a lender credit card issuer, is subject to all claims and defenses of a cardholder against the seller or lessor arising from the sale or lease of property or services pursuant to the credit card:
>
> (a) if the original amount to the card issuer with respect to the sale or lease of the property or services as to which the claim or defense arose exceeds $50;
>
> (b) if the residence of the cardholder and the place where the sale or lease occurred are [in the same state or] within 100 miles of each other;
>
> (c) if the cardholder has made a good faith attempt to obtain satisfaction from the seller or lessor with respect to the claim or defense; and
>
> (d) to the extent of the amount owing to the card issuer with respect to the sale or lease of the property or services as to which the claim or defense arose at the time the card issuer has notice of the claim or defense. Notice of the claim or defense may be given before the attempt specified in paragraph (c). Oral notice is effective unless the card issuer requests written confirmation when or promptly after oral notice is given and the cardholder fails to give the card issuer written confirmation within the period of time, not less than 14 days, stated to the cardholder when written confirmation is requested.

Section 3.403 adopts a compromise solution. The $50 limit is justified on the ground that transactions of $50 or less should have the finality of cash transactions. The rationale for the geographic limitation is that the normal area

---

[54] Cal Civ Code §1747.90(a) (West Supp 1973).

[55] Cal Civ Code §1747.90(d) (West Supp 1973).

[56] Cal Civ Code §1747.90(b), (d) (West Supp 1973).

[57] Max Factor III, *The Credit Cardholder's Rights to Assert Claims and Preserve Defenses Under the Fair Credit Billing Act*, 4 San Fern VL Rev 215, 222 (1975).

for credit card use is usually close to the cardholder's residence. Further, issuers could not reasonably be expected to police distant merchants.[58]

Other state statutes which adopt the Model Consumer Credit Act promulgated in 1973 by the National Consumer Law Center impose no dollar limit or geographical limitation on the consumer's right to assert claims and defenses against card issuers.[59] Other states have adopted variations. Wisconsin, for example, imposes a $100 limit.[60]

§7.11   Preservation of the Cardholder's Claims and Defenses against the Card Issuer under Federal Law: The Fair Credit Billing Act

The diversity in the state statutes in an area where interstate transactions are so numerous calls for federal legislation. A 1972 Report of the National Commission on Consumer Finance (NCCF) recommended that all consumers be able to assert defenses if purchases exceeded $50. As a result of the recommendation, Congress enacted the Fair Credit Billing amendments to the Consumer Credit Protection Act.[61]

Under federal law, a card issuer is subjected to all claims other than tort claims and defenses arising out of any transaction in which the credit card is used as a method of payment or extension of credit. The prerequisites for the cardholder's assertion of claims and defenses are:

> 1. A preliminary good faith attempt must be made to resolve the disagreement with the merchant
> 2. The amount involved must exceed $50
> 3. The transaction which gives rise to the use of the credit card must be in the same state as the cardholder's mailing address, or within 100 miles of such address[62]

The dollar amount and geographical limitations do not apply to merchant credit cards or to credit cards issued by an entity which is closely connected with the supplier.[63]

The right of the cardholder to assert claims and defenses against the card issuer operates only as a shield, but not as a sword. The amount asserted by the cardholder may not exceed the amount of outstanding credit in the

---

[58] U3C Prefatory Note (West 1985), at 899.

[59] Model Consumer Credit Act §2.603 (1973).

[60] Wis Stat §422.408 (1979).

[61] 15 USC §1666.

[62] 15 USC §1666(i).

[63] 15 USC §1666i(a).

disputed transaction at the time the cardholder first notifies the card issuer or the merchant-supplier of the claim or defense.[64]

Questions of interpretation may arise regarding what constitutes a good faith attempt to resolve the dispute, where a transaction is deemed to occur, for applying the geographic limitation, and what transactions are deemed to be *purchases* with the credit card.

Good Faith Attempts at Dispute Resolution

As the Federal Reserve Board explains, the resolution of a dispute with a merchant does not require any specific procedures or correspondence between the consumer and the supplier. When the merchant is in bankruptcy proceedings, for example, the consumer is not required to file a claim. Whether there was a good faith attempt is a matter of factual determination in each case.[65]

Geographical Limitation

Where a transaction is deemed to occur for applying the geographic limitation raises problems regarding mail or phone orders. In a phone order, one would think that, in view of the goal of consumer protection, the order would be deemed to be at the consumer's location. However, the Federal Reserve Board has decided that this must be determined under state or other applicable law.[66]

Transactions Which are Purchases with the Credit Card

A credit card is defined by the Truth in Lending Act as "any card, plate, coupon book, or other credit device existing for the purpose of obtaining money, property, labor or services on credit."[67] This definition excludes situations in which the consumer uses a credit card to obtain a cash advance, even if the consumer then uses the money to purchase goods or services, because the property or services are not purchased directly with the credit card. Purchases made with a check guarantee card in conjunction with a cash advance check are also excluded, because a check which triggers an overdraft is not considered "a purchase with a credit card." In other words, only transactions in which the card is used as a credit device for purchase are subject to the rule.

§7.12   Prohibition of Unauthorized Offsets

If the consumer also has an account other than the credit card account with the issuer, the card issuer may not, in order to offset the consumer's debts arising through the use of the credit card, take any action against the funds

---

[64] 15 USC §1666i(b).

[65] 12 CFR §226.12 Official Staff Interpretations 12(c)(3)(i), (1985) at 703.

[66] *Id* 12(c)(3)(ii).

[67] 15 USC §1602(k).

which the consumer has deposited with the card issuer. The card issuer may not apply the funds in a consumer's checking account to offset the debts which the consumer has incurred by use of the credit card, freeze the account, or place a hold on the cardholder's funds, unless such action is authorized by the cardholder through a contract or occurs pursuant to a court order or judgment.[68] If the consumer agrees to the issuer's use of the deposit account as a security interest for transactions, or for debts incurred under the credit card plan, such a security interest must be disclosed to the consumer in the issuer's initial disclosures.[69] Automatic payment plans which allow the card issuer to periodically offset credit card indebtedness against funds held on deposit are not prohibited if the cardholder authorizes such a plan in writing and signs or initials the agreement.[70]

§7.13   Credit Card Disclosures

The disclosure requirements of the Truth in Lending Act (TILA) apply to credit cards.[71] Under the original TILA enacted in 1968, the disclosure requirements were severe and often obtuse in their complexity. As a result, TILA and Regulation Z, which implemented the Act, generated a great deal of paperwork between 1968 and early 1980. More than 1,500 interpretations and letters were published by the Federal Reserve Board (FRB) and its staff. As the FRB remarked, "the cumulative effect of the interpretations has been to complicate, rather than facilitate compliance by layering one set of distinctions on top of the other. Rather than resolving questions, this material in the aggregate has served to generate further questions."[72]

In 1978, a movement was initiated to amend TILA. This legislative process culminated in President Jimmy Carter's signing, on March 31, 1980, the Depository Institutions Deregulation and Money Trade Control Act of 1980.[73] The Act included the Truth in Lending Simplification and Reform Act (the Simplification Act).[74] The changes were so drastic that the Federal Reserve Board characterized the legislation as a new TILA.[75]

The Simplification Act took effect in April, 1982. It did precisely what its name promised. The Act simplified the disclosure requirements by retaining only the information deemed to be useful for the consumer's credit decision.

---

[68] 15 USC §1666h; 12 CFR §226.12(d).

[69] 12 CFR §226.12(d)(2).

[70] 12 CFR §226.12(d)(3).

[71] 15 USC §1602(k).

[72] National Consumers Law Center, The Consumer Credit and Sales Legal Practice Series, Truth in Lending in Transition 2 (1982).

[73] Pub L No 96-221, 94 Stat 125 (1980).

[74] 15 USC §1601 *et seq.*

[75] 46 Fed Reg 10949 (Feb 5, 1981).

For example, information not related to the financial cost of credit was eliminated from the disclosure requirement.

Despite the presence of the new Act, a familiarity with the former requirements is useful for several reasons. A good number of states retain vestiges of the old TILA drafted into their statutes. This retention is based on the principle that federal law does not preempt state law if the latter offers more protection to the consumer. Also, it is thought that the old Act still applies to contracts formed prior to April 1, 1982.

Disclosure requirements for credit cards are generally explained in §§4.09 and 4.13 dealing with open-end credit disclosures. We simply reiterate here some of the most salient features of those disclosure requirements.

§7.14 —Initial Disclosures

Bank credit cards are open-end credit arrangements. An open-end credit plan under TILA means an arrangement "under which the creditor reasonably contemplates repeated transactions, which prescribes the terms of such transactions, and which provides for a finance charge which may be computed from time to time on the outstanding unpaid balance."[76] The amount of credit that may be extended to the consumer during the term of the plan (up to any limit set by the creditor) is generally made available to the extent that any outstanding balance is paid.[77]

TILA requires banks to make disclosures initially when a consumer applies for credit, and then periodically at the time of billing (i.e., monthly). These rules are incorporated in the original TILA and were subsequently amended in the Simplification Act.[78] Regulation Z also has been amended to reflect the new requirements.

The initial disclosure is usually attached to or incorporated in the application for credit. There are four basic initial disclosures.

1. The finance charge and its computation
2. Other charges
3. Security interest
4. Disclosure of the consumer's billing rights[79]

The disclosures must state when finance charges begin to accrue, whether a free ride exists, the periodic rate which may be used to compute the finance charge (if more than one periodic rate is used, each must be disclosed along with its applicable range of balance), and the method used to compute the finance charges.

---

[76] 15 USC §1602(i).

[77] 12 CFR §225.2(20).

[78] Pub L No 96-221, tit 6, §127, 94 Stat 125 (1980).

[79] 15 USC §1637(a); 12 CFR §226.6.

If there are any charges other than the finance charges, these must be explained also. Examples of *other charges* are late payment and over-the-credit-limit charges, fees for documentary evidence of transactions requested by the cardholder, and taxes imposed by a state or other governmental body. As such, *other charges* are charges related to the credit card plan that are not finance charges per se.[80]

If a creditor intends to acquire a security interest in property purchased under an open-end credit plan, or in other property, this security interest must be identified by item or type. Usually, for bank cards, card issuers do not receive collateral for extended credit. However, if such a security interest should arise, (for example, pursuant to a judgment for nonpayment or when advances reach a certain amount) this also must be disclosed. In particular, the bank card issuer must disclose the cardholder's right to assert claims or defenses against the issuer, as well as the time and procedure for resolution.[81] No new initial disclosures need to be provided when a consumer's account is closed and reopened with a new account number, as when a credit card is reported lost or stolen and a new account number is assigned for security reasons.[82]

§7.15 —Periodic Disclosures

Once the credit plan is established, the card issuer must periodically furnish to the consumer a statement of account, or a billing statement, to allow the consumer to compare the monthly, periodic, or annual rates to those of other lenders. Periodic statements also apprise the consumer of the consumer's financial status with respect to the issuer.

To the extent applicable, the periodic statement must disclose:

1. The previous balance, i.e., the account balance outstanding at the beginning of the billing cycle
2. Identification of each credit transaction, the amount, and the date of the purchase or the date of debiting the transaction to the consumer's account
3. The total amount credited to the account during the billing period
4. Each periodic rate that may be used to compute the finance charge, the range of balance to which it is applicable, and the corresponding annual percentage rate. If different periodic rates apply to different types of transactions, the types of transactions to which the periodic rates apply shall also be disclosed
5. The balance on which the finance charge is computed, and an explanation of how that balance was determined
6. Unless the monthly charge is 50 cents or less, the amount of any finance

---

[80] 12 CFR §226.6(b)(1) and Official Staff Interpretations.
[81] 12 CFR §226.6(d).
[82] 12 CFR §226.5(b)(2)(3) and Official Staff Interpretation.

charge debited or added to the account during the billing cycle, using the term *finance charge*. The components of the finance charge shall be individually itemized and identified to show the amount(s) due to the application of any periodic rates and the amount(s) of any other type of finance charge. If there is more than one periodic rate, the amount of the finance charge attributable to each rate need not be separately itemized and identified

7. The annual percentage rate when a finance charge is imposed during the billing cycle

8. The amounts, itemized and identified by type, of any charges other than finance charges debited to the account during the billing cycle

9. The closing date of the billing cycle and the account balance outstanding on that date

10. The free-ride period, i.e., the date by which the new balance or any portion of the new balance must be paid to avoid additional finance charges

11. Address to be used for notice of billing errors[83]

§7.16 —Additional Disclosures

In addition to the initial and periodic disclosures, the creditor is required to make other disclosures regarding notice of billing rights, term modification, or new features added to the existing credit plan. A creditor must deliver to the consumer a statement of billing rights similar to the one provided in the initial disclosure. This must be delivered at least once a year, at intervals of not less than six and no more than eighteen months.[84] As an alternative, the creditor may mail or deliver to the consumer a summary of the initial billing rights notice with each periodic statement.[85]

When a term which was disclosed in the initial statement is changed, or when the required minimum periodic payment statement is increased, the creditor must give written notice of the change to the consumer who may be affected by the change. Notice must be mailed or delivered at least 15 days prior to the effective date of the change. This 15-day limit may be shortened when the consumer has agreed to the change, or when the change increase is due to the consumer's delinquency or default.[86]

When the change is other than an increase in the periodic rate or other finance charge, no notice is required if the change is due to the consumer's default or delinquency. Accordingly, the creditor is completely excused for lack

---

[83] 15 USC §1637(b); 12 CFR §§226.7, .8.

[84] 12 CFR §226.9(a)(1).

[85] 12 CFR §226.9(a)(2).

[86] 12 CFR §226.9(c)(1).

of notice if the change involves late payment charges, default, or delinquency charges other than those included in the finance charge.[87]

A creditor who adds a new feature to a consumer's existing credit plan is also required to inform the consumer before the consumer uses the new feature. If the terms differ from those in the initial disclosure statement, the creditor must deliver to the consumer another initial disclosure statement describing the feature.[88]

§7.17   —Penalties for Violation of Disclosure Requirements

Private Action

Any creditor who fails to comply with the disclosure requirements can be liable for: an amount equal to the sum of any actual damage sustained by the consumer; and an amount equal to twice the finance charge, which shall be not less than $100 nor more than $1000.[89] The consumer may also recover court costs as well as reasonable attorneys' fees.[90]

The provision for the recovery of both actual damages and statutory damages reflects the intent of Congress to enforce the statute by encouraging individual actions. Thus, the consumer may recover statutory damages even though the consumer did not suffer any actual damage as a result of the creditor's failure to disclose.

For example, in *White v Arlin Realty Development Corp*,[91] the creditor did not sufficiently identify the transaction on the periodic statement. The cardholder did not pay any finance charges on the unidentified transaction and still recovered the statutory penalty. The court stated that Congress intended to define *injury in fact* as a failure to disclose the required information.

In view of the flood of litigation which occurred as a result of the statutory penalty for what were essentially technical violations, the Simplification Act of 1980 limited the number of disclosure violations which give rise to the statutory penalty. Currently, only a failure to comply with initial disclosures and a failure to disclose in the periodic statements requirements deemed to be *substantial* are punishable under TILA.

Class Action

The most famous class action case to date regarding credit cards is *Ratner v Chemical Bank New York Trust Co.*[92] In this case, Chemical Bank failed to disclose an 18 per cent annual rate in monthly billing statements mailed to MasterCard

---

[87] 12 CFR §226.9(c)(2).

[88] 12 CFR §226.9(b)(1)-(2).

[89] 15 USC §1640(a)(1)(2)(A)(i).

[90] 15 USC §1640(a)(3).

[91] 540 F2d 645 (4th Cir 1975).

[92] 329 F Supp 270 (SDNY 1971).

customers who had outstanding balances but had incurred no finance charges. Although the court ruled that the cardholders suffered no actual damages as a result of the omission, Chemical Bank was still subject to the minimum statutory penalty. Since Chemical Bank had issued the card to 130,000 people, at $100 each, the bank could have been liable for $13 million.

The banking community was outraged by this decision. In the retrial, the court held that the class action had been inappropriate because each cardholder could enforce the law as a "private attorney general" and also recover a $100 minimum civil penalty plus court costs, and because the punishment was out of proportion to the damages.[93]

As a result of the *Ratner* decision, Congress amended the Fair Credit Billing Act dealing with class actions. Under the new provision, there is no minimum recovery for each member of the class, except recovery for actual damage. Furthermore, the total recovery for any class action, or series of class actions, out of the same violation is limited to an amount not exceeding the lesser of $500,000 or 1 per cent of the net worth of the creditor.[94]

In determining the amount of award in any class action, the court shall not limit itself to the technical violation, but shall consider all the relevant factors including, but not limited to, the amount of actual damages awarded, the frequency and persistence of the violations, the creditor's resources, the number of persons adversely affected, and the extent to which the creditor's failure was intentional. Thus, the amendment provides for a flexible examination of the problem.[95]

Further Restrictions on the Scope of Civil Penalty

The Simplification Act further restricts the scope of civil penalty by exonerating the card issuer for violations found to be unintentional or the result of bona fide error.[96] Examples of bona fide errors include clerical error, computer malfunction, and printing errors. An error of legal judgment is not a bona fide error.[97] Creditors are not subject to the penalty for violations which are the result of good faith compliance with the rules, Regulation Z, or interpretation by the Board, or by an authorized official of the Federal Reserve Board.[98]

Civil penalty is further restricted to the extent that multiple failures to disclose to any person give rise only to a single recovery. A continued failure to disclose, however, after a recovery has been granted, shall give rise to multiple recoveries.[99] Furthermore, the cardholder may not offset any amount

---

[93] Ratner v Chemical Bank NY Trust Co, 54 FRD 412, 416 (SDNY 1972).

[94] 15 USC §1604(a)(2)(B).

[95] 15 USC §1604(a)(3).

[96] 15 USC §1640(c).

[97] *Id.*

[98] 15 USC §1640(f).

[99] 15 USC §1640(g).

for which a creditor is potentially liable to the cardholder for failure to disclose until the creditor's liability has been determined by a court's judgment.[100] This means that the consumer cannot withhold a billing charge of $100, for example, alleging a disclosure violation, in order to offset a potential minimum civil penalty of $100. The consumer may, however, assert such a violation in an original action or as a defense or counterclaim to an action by the creditor for payment.

Persons Subject to the Penalty

Any creditor is liable for failure to make the required disclosures. The term *creditor* generally means the card issuer, when dealing with bank credit cards. *Creditor* may also denote the person honoring the credit card, i.e., the supplier of the goods or services.[101] When the latter is required to disclose certain information, failure to comply with the law will subject the person to the same penalty imposed on the card issuer. Thus, failing to disclose, prior to its imposition, that the additional charge on a credit sale is a finance charge will subject a merchant to the dual liabilities of actual and statutory damages.[102]

§7.18   Billing Error Resolution

Any consumer who has experienced a billing error knows the embarrassment of computer hot lists and hounding by the credit departments of financial institutions. In an effort to mitigate these problems, the Fair Credit Billing Act[103] was enacted as an amendment to the Truth in Lending Act to outline procedures for resolving billing errors incurred on open-end credit and credit card accounts. Regulation Z interprets and implements the Act.

The billing error resolution procedures under the Fair Credit Billing Act and Regulation Z apply to all *consumer* credit card plans, regardless of whether the credit card is issued for open-end or closed-end credit. Credit for business purposes is not covered.

The term *consumer,* used with reference to a credit transaction, describes a transaction "in which the party to whom credit is offered or extended is a natural person, and the money, property, or services which are the subject of the transaction are primarily for personal, family, or household purposes."[104]

What happens if a credit card is issued both for consumer and business purposes? Should the required procedures apply to billing errors? *American Express Co v Koerner,*[105] is an illustration on point. In this case, John E. Koerner & Co applied to American Express for a *company account* designed for business

---

[100] 15 USC §1640(h).

[101] 15 USC §1602(1).

[102] 12 CFR §226.9(d).

[103] Pub L No 90-321, tit I, 82 Stat 146 (1968) (codified at 15 USC §1666).

[104] 15 USC §102(h).

[105] 452 US 233 (1981).

customers. The Koerner Company asked American Express to issue cards bearing the company name to Louis R. Koerner, Sr., and four other officers of the corporation. Louis R. Koerner signed a *company account* form and agreed to be jointly and severally liable with the company for the expenses incurred through the use of the company card issued to him. Koerner used his card mostly for business, although occasionally for personal expenses. He sent a personal check to American Express for personal expenses, while the company paid his business expenses.

A dispute arose between the Koerner Company and American Express concerning the charges appearing on the account. The total amount of the dispute for which the company refused to pay was $55.

When Koerner attempted to use his card for a business trip, he was informed that the account had been cancelled. Action in court followed. Koerner charged that American Express had failed to comply with the required procedures in resolving the billing dispute.

The district court granted American Express's motion for summary judgment on the ground that TILA exempts credit transactions for business and commercial purposes, which was the case here. The Fifth Circuit Court of Appeals reversed, based on the fact that American Express could recover from Koerner personally and, therefore, should abide by the procedure for resolution of billing errors in a consumer's credit card statement.

The Supreme Court reversed. The court found that the threshold requirement of *extension of consumer credit* was not satisfied. The company's account was opened primarily for business purposes and not "primarily for personal, family, household, or agricultural purposes." In particular, the transactions giving rise to the billing dispute were business transactions and not consumer credit transactions.[106]

§7.19 —Billing Error Defined

According to the Fair Credit Billing Act and Regulation Z, the term *billing error* includes any of the following seven situations:

> 1. Statement of an extension of credit that is unauthorized by the cardholder. The user of the card has no actual, implied, or apparent authority to use the consumer's credit card or open-end credit plan
> 2. Statement of an extension of credit that is not sufficiently identified
> 3. Statement of an extension of credit for property or services not accepted by the consumer or not delivered to the consumer as agreed
> 4. The creditor's failure properly to credit a payment or other credit issued to the consumer's account
> 5. A reflection on a periodic statement of a computational or similar error of an accounting nature that is made by the creditor

---

[106] *Id* 240-46.

6. A statement of an extension of credit for which the consumer requests additional clarification, including documentary evidence. Note that the request is treated as a billing error only if it is accompanied by an allegation of error or a request for clarification. A request for documentation alone is not a billing error

7. The creditor's failure to mail or deliver a periodic statement to the consumer's last known address if that address was received by the creditor, in writing, at least 20 days before the end of the billing cycle for which the statement was required[107]

A consumer who believes that a billing error has been made on the periodic statement must send a written notice to the creditor within 60 days from the date of receipt of the first periodic statement that reflects the alleged billing error. This notice must be clear enough to enable the creditor to identify the consumer's name and account number, as well as the type, date, and amount of the error.[108]

§7.20 —Error Resolution Procedures

If the creditor believes that a billing error has occurred as asserted, the creditor must correct the error and credit the consumer's account to the extent of the error, as well as for finance charges that may have accrued. This must occur within 90 days of the creditor's receipt of the notice. If, however, an investigation leads the creditor to believe that no error has been made, the creditor must send to the consumer, within the 90-day time period, a written explanation of the reasons for this belief. The creditor must also furnish evidentiary documentation of the consumer's indebtedness, if the consumer so requests. If a billing error occurs other than one alleged by the consumer, the creditor must correct the billing error and credit the consumer's account with the erroneous amount as well as any related finance charges which have accrued.[109]

The Fair Credit Billing Act imposes a number of restrictions on the creditor while the billing error is being investigated. The restrictions include:

1. The consumer's right not to pay the disputed amount, including the finance and other charges. In the case in which the cardholder maintains a deposit account with the card issuer, and has preauthorized automatic periodic deductions, the card issuer is prohibited from deducting any part of the disputed amount from the cardholder's deposit account. This

---

[107] 15 USC §1666(b); 12 CFR §226.13(a).

[108] 12 CFR §226.13(b).

[109] 12 CFR §226.13(e).

applies only if the billing error notice is received more than three business days before the scheduled payment date[110]

2. The creditor is prohibited from making, or threatening to make, an adverse report to third parties about the consumer's credit standing, and from stating that the account is delinquent. This prohibition applies to the creditor's agents as well as to the creditor[111]

3. As a general rule, pending resolution, the creditor cannot accelerate, restrict, or close a consumer's account. The creditor can, however, collect any other undisputed amount. Likewise, the creditor is allowed to apply the disputed amount against the credit limit on the consumer's account[112]

The consumer may still insist that a billing error did exist despite the card issuer's finding after investigation that there was no error. The card issuer who has fully complied with the billing error resolution requirements has no further responsibilities.[113] However, if the consumer notifies the creditor that the consumer still disputes the bill, the card issuer is subject to certain limitations:

1. The card issuer is prohibited from reporting that an amount is delinquent, although the card issuer is permitted to report that the amount is in dispute

2. The card issuer must mail or deliver to the consumer, at the time the report is made, a written notice of the name and address of each person to whom the creditor makes a report

Upon subsequent resolution of the delinquency, the card issuer must promptly report such to all persons to whom the creditor has made a report.[114] Since the Fair Credit Billing Act does not require any further investigation from the card issuer, the parties must resolve their dispute under applicable state law.[115]

§7.21 Relationship between Federal Law and State Law

In general, state laws are preserved as long as they are not inconsistent with federal law.[116] Inconsistencies may pertain to disclosure requirements, correction of billing errors or regulation of credit reports, and credit billing.

---

[110] 12 CFR §226.13(d)(1).

[111] 12 CFR §226.13(d)(2).

[112] 15 USC §1666(d); 12 CFR §226.13(d)(1).

[113] 12 CFR §226.13(h).

[114] 12 CFR §226.13(g)(4).

[115] See D. Rothchild & D. Carroll, Consumer Protection Reporting Service 11:4.04 (1973).

[116] 15 USC §1666j; 12 CFR §226.28.

Generally, the state law is inconsistent if it requires the creditor to take action that contradicts federal law.

With respect to disclosure requirements, Regulation Z provides that a state law is contradictory if it uses the same term to represent a different amount, or a different meaning, than that expressed by the same term in federal law. A state law is also contradictory if it requires the use of a term different from that required in the federal law to describe the same item.[117] For example, the state law is preempted if it requires the term *finance charge* to include fees that federal law excludes or to exclude fees that federal law includes.

Concerning correction of billing errors and regulation of credit reports, a state law is preempted if it provides rights, responsibilities, or procedures for consumers or creditors that are different from those required by the federal law. However, an exception is made for a state law that allows a consumer to inquire about an account, and requires the creditor to respond to such inquiries, beyond the time limits that federal law imposes for the consumer's submission of written notice of a billing error. Such a state law is not preempted with respect to the extra time period. For example, Regulation Z requires the consumer to give written notice of a billing error within 60 days after transmission of the periodic statement showing the alleged error. A state law that allows the consumer 90 days to submit the notice remains effective with respect to the extra 30 days.[118]

The Federal Reserve Board staff gives the following examples of state laws that would be preempted.

> 1. A state law that provides different time limits for error resolution subject to the exception discussed above
> 2. A state law that requires the creditor to take different steps to resolve errors
> 3. A state law that has a narrower or broader definition of *billing error*[119]

Concerning credit billing, the test of inconsistency is whether the creditor can comply with state law without violating federal law. For example, a state law is preempted if it allows the card issuer to offset the consumer's credit card indebtedness against the funds held by the card issuer, since federal law prohibits such action. On the other hand, a state law that allows the consumer to assert claims and defenses against the card issuer without the limitations of $50 and 100 miles is not inconsistent with federal law. The focus is on whether state law is more protective of the consumer than federal law.

A state may request the Board to determine whether its law is consistent with TILA and Regulation Z. Furthermore, a state may apply to the Federal Reserve Board for exemption from the requirements of the Act and Regulation Z

---

[117] 12 CFR §226.28(a).

[118] 12 CFR §226.28(b).

[119] 12 CFR §226.28 and Official Staff Interpretations.

dealing with credit transactions and credit billing. The Board will grant such an exemption if it determines that the state law is substantially similar to federal law or affords the consumer greater protection than federal law, and if there is adequate provision for enforcement.[120]

---

[120] 12 CFR §226.29(a).

8

Electronic Fund Transfers

§8.01 Introduction

The goal of the banking system in the last decades has been to depend less on the traditional payment method of checks and currency and to create a "cashless" or at least "less cash" society. The broad technological changes brought on by electronics and computers offer the banking system that opportunity. Electronic fund transfers (EFTs) are the product of the electronic and computer age. An *electronic fund transfer* is "a payment system in which the processing and communications necessary to effect economic exchange, and the processing and communications necessary for the production and distribution of services incidental or related to economic exchange, are dependent wholly or in part on the use of electronics."[1]

Since their inception in the 1970s, the uses of EFT systems have grown rapidly. Initially reserved for use in their behind-the-scenes operations, banks are now falling over themselves and each other in the rush to provide EFT services to individual consumers.

Following are some typical services the EFT system offers:

1. Shoppers may pay for goods at retail stores by using a card inserted in an electronic terminal. Their accounts are charged electronically and they carry less cash

2. Bank customers may deposit or withdraw cash at any time of the day or night by using their cards in an unattended machine

3. Employees may have their pay deposited directly into their checking or savings accounts without ever receiving a paycheck. The employer makes the deposits by delivering a magnetic tape to the depository institution

4. Families may pay monthly installments on mortgages or loans or pay regular premiums on insurance by preauthorized charges to their checking or savings accounts

5. Families may pay regular bills, such as those for utility services, by a telephone call to their bank or thrift institution authorizing the debit to their deposit account[2]

Many states have enacted legislation to clarify users' rights and responsibilities in this new form of payment system. However, states vary widely in the

---

[1] EFT and the Public Interest, a Report of the National Commission on Electronic Fund Transfers 1 n1 (1977).

[2] *Id* 1, 2.

degree of protection they afford the consumer. Many simply provide for the general use of the system and neglect to address the unique problems of the consumer.[3]

In 1973, Congress stepped into the picture. It set up the National Commission on Electronic Fund Transfers (NCEFT) to study the impact this new technology was having on American society. Bureaucratic tussles delayed the study's actual starting date until 1976. That year the Commission embarked on a comprehensive review of the EFT system and announced its goal of providing "explicit recommendations so that the government might develop a national policy for the orderly development of EFT systems in the United States."[4]

Consumer protection was not Congress's first priority when it established the Commission. Rather, consumer protection fell at the bottom of a list of nine enumerated goals headed by "the need to preserve competition among the

---

[3] Thirty-two states have enacted laws that expressly regulate the establishment and use of EFT systems: Arkansas, Ark Stat Ann §§67-367 to 67-367.10 (1980); California, Cal Fin Code §§550-561 (West Supp 1984); Colorado, Colo Rev Stat §§11-6.5-101 to -111 (Supp 1983); Connecticut, Conn Gen Stat §§36-193(a)-(h) (Supp 1983); Delaware, Del Code Ann tit 5, §770 (Supp 1982); Florida, Fla Stat Ann §658.65 (West Supp 1984); Illinois, Electronic Fund Transfer Transmission Facility Act Ill Ann Stat ch 17, §§1301-1343 (Smith-Hurd Supp 1983-84); Iowa, Iowa Code Ann §§524.803(1), .821, 527.1-.12 (West Supp 1983-84); Kansas, Kan Stat Ann §9-1111 (1982); Maine, Me Rev Stat Ann tit 9-B, §§131, 334 (1975 & Supp 1982); Maryland, Md Fin Inst Code Ann §5-502 (1980 & Supp 1983); Massachusetts, Mass Gen Laws Ann ch 1147, §64 (West 1983); Michigan, Mich Comp Laws Ann §§488.1-.31 (West Supp 1984-85); Minnesota, Minn Stat Ann §§47.61-47.65 (West Supp 1984); Missouri, Mo Ann Stat §362.108 (Vernon Supp 1984); Montana, Mont Code Ann §§32-6-101 to -402 (1983); Nebraska, Neb Rev Stat §8-157 (1977); New Jersey, NJ Stat Ann §17:9A-19 (West Supp 1983); New Mexico, NM Stat Ann §§58-16-1 to -17 (Supp 1983); New York, NY Banking Law §105-a (McKinney Supp 1983-84); North Carolina, NC Gen Stat §§53-62 (1983); North Dakota, ND Cent Code §6-03-02 (Supp 1983); Oklahoma, Okla Stat Ann tit 6, §442 (West Supp 1983); Oregon, Or Rev Stat §§706.005, 714.200-270, 716.645 (1981); Rhode Island, RI Gen Laws §19.29-1 (1982); South Dakota, SD Codified Laws Ann §51-20A-2 (1979); Tennessee, Tenn Code Ann §§45-2-601, 45-3-104, -301, -308 (1980); Texas, 1983 Tex Sess Law Serv ch 391 (Vernon); Utah, Utah Code Ann §§7-16-1 to -18 (1982); Virginia, Va Code §§6.1-39.1, -39.2 (1983); Washington, Wash Rev Code §§30.43.010 -.050 (1983).

Eleven states include consumer protection provisions in their EFT statutes: Colorado, Colo Rev Stat §11-6.5-109 (Supp 1983); Florida, Fla Stat Ann §658.65(10), (12) (West Supp 1984); Iowa, Iowa Code Ann §§537.6-.10 (West Supp 1983-84); Kansas, Kan Stat Ann §9.1111(d) (1982); Michigan, Mich Stat Ann §488.1-.31 (Callaghan 1983); Minnesota, Minn Stat Ann §47.69 (West Supp 1984); Montana, Mont Code Ann §§32-6-104 to -106, 32-6-301 to -303 (1983); New Mexico, NM Stat Ann §§58-16-12 to -16 (Supp 1983); Texas, 1983 Tex Sess Law Serv ch 391 (Vernon); Virginia, Va Electronic Funds Transfer (EFT) Reg (Apr 26, 1977); Wisconsin, Wis Stat Ann §943.41 (West 1982). *See* Vergari, *Latent Legal Repercussions in Electronic Financial Services and Transactions,* 34 Def LJ 539, 549-50 (1985).

[4] EFT and the Public Interest, a Report of the National Commission on Electronic Fund Transfers 3 (1977).

financial institutions and other business enterprises using such a system."[5] The interim report was criticized as dealing inadequately with consumer issues. By the time the second phase of the study had gotten under way, the Commission was facing the fact that consumer protection must become its primary goal. For, without the assurance that their rights would be protected, consumers would simply refuse to use the ETF system—and consumer use had become the system's linchpin.[6]

The Commission identified several major problem areas for consumers who use the ETF system. These include:

1. The consumers' privacy
2. The consumers' inability to control the accuracy of the transaction
3. The consumers' freedom of choice whether or not to use the EFT system. This should be guaranteed. Employers should not be permitted to require as a condition of employment that an employee do business with a particular financial institution
4. Full disclosure by the financial institution of the terms and conditions of the EFT service, and the consumer's respective rights and duties
5. The impact of unsolicited cards on the consumer and the competition among depository institutions
6. The problem of unauthorized transfers through card theft, error, and malfunction in the system demands immediate attention. The press abounds with horror stories of consumers losing hundreds of dollars only to discover they have no legal recourse

Thus, consumer rights are moving into the EFT spotlight. It merits repeating that if consumers are to be persuaded to use the system, they first must be assured that their rights will be protected.[7] On the other hand, the Commission

---

[5] EFT in the United States, Policy Recommendations and the Public Interest, The Final Report of the National Commission on Electronic Fund Transfers 3 (1977) [hereinafter NCEFT Final Report]

The other goals are, among other things . . . :

2. The need to promote competition among financial institutions and to assure Government regulation and involvement or participation in a system competitive with the private sector be kept to a minimum.
3. The need to prevent unfair or discriminatory practices by any financial institution or business enterprise using or desiring to use such a system.
4. The need to afford maximum user and consumer convenience.
5. The need to afford maximum user and consumer rights to privacy and confidentiality.
6. The impact of such a system on economic and monetary policy.
7. The implications of such a system on the availability of credit.
8. The implications of such a system expanding internationally and into other forms of electronic communications.
9. The need to protect the legal rights of users and consumers.

[6] *Id* 5.
[7] *Id* 7-10.

believed that burdensome regulation of EFT providers would hamper the development of the system.[8]

Interest in electric fund transfers increased concomitantly with the Commission's work. Independent bills were introduced in the Senate and the House of Representatives to provide for consumer protection in the use of EFTs.[9] As a result of a last-minute compromise, both the House of Representatives and the Senate adopted a modified version of the Senate bill.[10]

On November 10, 1978, President Carter signed EFTA into law. The Act became effective on May 10, 1980. However, two sections, one dealing with consumer liability for unauthorized transfers and the other dealing with the issuance of access devices to EFTs, were considered so important that they became effective 15 months earlier, on February 8, 1979.[11]

The Federal Reserve Board was given the authority to prescribe regulations with which to implement the Act.[12] However, Congress required the Board to adhere to a number of guidelines in formulating the rules. These included:

> 1. Consultation with other agencies to allow for the continuing evolution of electronic banking services and the technology utilized in such services
>
> 2. Consideration of the cost/benefit of the rules, their impact on competition among EFT providers, and their ultimate cost to the consumer. To the extent practicable, the Board had to demonstrate that the protection the proposed regulations would provide for consumers outweighed the compliance costs imposed on consumers and financial institutions. Furthermore, the Board had to promptly send any proposed regulations and accompanying analyses to Congress.[13]

---

[8] *Id* 4.

[9] The Senate Committee on Banking, Housing, and Urban Affairs reported S 3156, the Fair Fund Transfer Act, on May 26, 1978. 124 Cong Rec 78449 (daily ed May 26, 1978). The House Committee on Banking, Finance, and Urban Affairs reported HR 13007, the Electronic Fund Transfer Act, on June 21, 1978. 124 Cong Rec H5912 (daily ed June 21, 1978).

On August 11, 1978, the House of Representatives passed HR 130076, the Electronic Fund Transfer Act, by a vote of 314 to 2. 124 Cong Rec H8489-8490 (daily ed Aug 11, 1978). On October 12, 1978, the Senate considered a modified version of S 3156 and adopted it as title XI of HR 14279, the Financial Institutions Supervisory Act Amendments of 1977 [sic], by voice vote. 124 Cong Rec S18476 (daily ed Oct 12, 1978). After changing its title and making minor technical changes, the Senate version of the bill was adopted by both the House of Representatives and the Senate on Oct 14, 1978. *See* Schellie, *Electronic Fund Transfer Act,* 34 Bus Law 1441, 1443 (1979).

[10] 124 Cong Rec H13071 (daily ed Oct 14, 1978). 124 Cong Rec S19146 (daily ed Oct 14, 1978).

[11] Financial Institution Regulatory and Interest Rate Control Act of 1978, Pub L No 95-630, tit xx, 92 Stat 3641, 3728 (codified at 15 USC §§1693-93r). This legislation added a new title, Title IX, to the Consumer Credit Protection Act.

[12] EFTA §904, 15 USC §1693b.

[13] EFTA §904(a), 15 USC §1693b(a)(4).

3. Congress also directed the Federal Reserve Board to issue model clauses for optional use by financial institutions to facilitate compliance with the Act. The guidelines specifically required that the clauses be drafted in "readily understandable language" to assist consumers in understanding their rights and responsibilities[14]

4. Finally, the guidelines authorized the Board to modify the requirements which the Act imposed on small financial institutions. This alleviated undue burdens these institutions faced in complying with EFTA. Based on this authorization, the Board exempted institutions whose assets total $25 million or less from complying with certain provisions of the Act

Of the four guidelines issued by Congress to the Board, the most significant was the requirement that the Board analyze the costs and benefits of the proposed regulations. This stipulation was unique in the area of consumer credit regulations. It indicated the extreme care taken by Congress not to impose undue burdens on the providers of EFTs. We may contrast this to the free rein Congress gives to the Board in implementing the Truth in Lending Act.

Pursuant to Congress's directives, the Federal Reserve Board issued Regulation E on March 28, 1979.[15] Any practitioner dealing with EFTA must consult Regulation E carefully, keeping in mind that while E clarifies and implements the Act, it does not necessarily reflect the congressional intent, and, therefore, may be challenged.

For example, with regard to consumer liability for unauthorized transfers, Rep Annunzio (D-Ill), Chairman of the House Banking Subcommittee on Consumer Affairs and initial promoter of the Act in the House of Representatives, charged that Regulation E, as originally issued, "distorted the intent of Congress" with regard to consumer liability for unauthorized transfers.[16] In response to the criticism, the Board later had to amend the controversial interpretation.

§8.02 Purpose and Scope of the Electronic Fund Transfer Act

The purpose of EFTA is "to provide a basic framework establishing the rights, liabilities, and responsibilities of participants in electronic fund transfer systems. The primary objective of this title is the provision of individual consumer rights."[17] The Senate Committee pointed out that legislation

---

[14] EFTA §904(b), 15 USC §1693b(b).

[15] 44 Fed Reg 18480 (Mar 28, 1979); 12 CFR §205.

[16] News Release from Congressman Frank Annunzio (Apr 10, 1979), *cited in* Einhorn, *A Banker's Guide to the Electronic Fund Transfer Act*, 96 Banking LJ 772, 774 (1979).

[17] EFTA §902(b), 15 USC §1693(b).

protecting consumer rights increases public confidence in the system, and described EFTA as an "EFT Bill of Rights" for consumers.[18] The Act focuses on those electronic and computerized banking services which consumers utilize most frequently. This explains the limited scope of the Act and the restrictive definition of what constitutes an electronic fund transfer to which the Act applies. It is important to be familiar with key definitions of the Act.

Financial Institution

This term refers to a state or national bank, a state or federal savings and loan association, a mutual savings bank, a state or federal credit union, or any other entity that *directly or indirectly holds an account belonging to the consumer.*[19] The intent of Congress here is to subject to the Act not only banks, but all other entities that are likely to offer EFT services to consumers. The Act could apply, for example, to issuers of travel and entertainment cards which gain access to EFT networks and provide EFT services to consumers. These may allow consumers to use a card such as American Express not only as a credit card to pay for goods and services, but also as a debit card allowing withdrawal of funds directly from the consumer's bank account.

Regulation E clarifies this intent of Congress. According to the Regulation, the term *financial institution* includes "any person who issues an access device and agrees with the consumer to provide EFT services."[20] The definition thus includes not only EFT systems that access a consumer's bank account, but also those systems which access other types of consumer accounts, such as mutual fund shares or accounts at a stock brokerage. A consumer's *account* is defined as a demand deposit, savings deposit, or any other asset account "established primarily for personal, family, or household purposes."[21] Under the Act, *account* does not include a trust account or an occasional or incidental credit balance in a credit plan.[22]

Consumer

A consumer is a natural person who uses EFT services.[23] Under this definition, a non-natural person, such as a corporate entity, is not protected under the Act.

Electronic Fund Transfer

What constitutes an EFT is most important, because this definition also

---

[18] S Rep No 915, 95th Cong, 2d Sess, *reprinted in* 1978 US Code Cong & Admin News 9273, 9405

[19] EFTA §903(8), 15 USC §1693a(8).

[20] 12 CFR §205.2(i).

[21] EFTA §903(2), 15 USC §1693a(2).

[22] *Id.*

[23] EFTA §903(5), 15 USC §1693a(5).

defines the scope of the Act. The Act's definition focuses on four types of EFT services which consumers utilize most frequently:

1. Automated Teller Machines (ATMs)—these allow a consumer to perform various bank operations 24 hours a day

2. Pay-by-phone systems—this service permits a consumer to give payment orders to the bank by telephone

3. Direct Deposit and Automatic Payments—these systems allow wages or social security benefits to be automatically deposited in the consumer's bank account. They also permit automatic payments of regularly recurring payments, such as utility bills, rents, or insurance premiums

4. Point-of-Sale Transfers—this enables a consumer, by using the computer terminal at a retail establishment, to transfer money instantaneously from the consumer's account into that of the merchant[24]

The definition emphasizes that EFTs, as governed by the Act, are not limited to these four examples. Generally, EFTs under the Act include any transfer of funds, other than a transaction originated by check, draft, or similar paper instrument, which is initiated through an electronic terminal, telephone, computer, or magnetic tape, so as to authorize a financial institution to debit or credit a consumer's account. The term *EFT* also includes all transfers resulting from debit card transactions, including those that do not involve an electronic terminal at the time of the transaction.[25] However, not all payments or banking services which utilize computer and electronic technology, and which do not originate with a check or other paper item, are subject to the Act. The Act excludes from its scope a number of electronic transfers as described in §8.03.

Electronic Terminal

This term simply indicates an electronic device other than a telephone, through which a consumer may initiate an EFT. The term includes, but is not limited to, point-of-sale transfers, ATMs, and cash dispensing machines.[26]

§8.03   Excluded Transactions

The Act does not apply to:

1. Check guarantee or authorization services which accept or certify checks, drafts, or similar paper instruments not directly debiting or crediting a consumer's account

2. Transactions through the Federal Reserve Communications System,

---

[24] EFTA §903(6), 15 USC §1693a(6).

[25] 12 CFR §205.2(g).

[26] EFTA §903(7), 15 USC §1693a(7); 12 CFR §205.2(h).

such as Fedwire or Bankwire or other similar networks, which service financial institutions and businesses

3. Securities and commodities transfers, whose primary purpose is the purchase or sale of securities and commodities regulated by the Securities and Exchange Commission or the Commodity Futures Trading Commission

4. Certain automatic transfers, such as transfers from a savings account to a demand deposit account, pursuant to an agreement between a consumer and a financial institution for the purpose of covering an overdraft or maintaining a required minimum balance in the consumer's demand deposit account. Regulation E broadens the scope of this exemption to include individual transfers, made under a general agreement between a consumer and a financial institution, and absent a specific request from the consumer. These include: a transfer of funds from a checking to a savings account; the crediting of interest to a savings account; any transfer from a consumer's account to that of a financial institution, such as a loan payment; and a transfer from a consumer's account to an account of another consumer within the financial institution, who is a member of the transferor's family

5. Certain telephone-initiated transfers—these include fund transfers which are initiated by a telephone conversation between a consumer and an officer or employee of the financial institution and which are nonrecurring or not pursuant to a prearranged plan.[27] However, orders to make bill payments are examples of regular telephone orders to the bank which the Act covers

A Texas court recently had the opportunity to determine whether a particular transaction was governed by the Act. In *Kashanchi v Texas Commerce Medical Bank*,[28] the plaintiff and her sister held a joint savings account in the defendant's bank. Through a telephone conversation with a bank employee, someone other than the plaintiff or her sister withdrew $4900 from the account. After receiving the bank statement, the alarmed plaintiff promptly notified the bank that the transfer had been unauthorized and demanded that the bank recredit her account in accordance with the Act. The bank refused, and the plaintiff filed suit. The district court dismissed the action, holding that the Act did not apply to the case.

The issue on appeal centered on the term *consumer*, as used in EFTA and Regulation E. Regulation E states that the exception applies to "any transfer of funds which is initiated by a telephone conversation between a consumer and an officer or employee of the financial institution which is nonrecurring and not pursuant to a prearranged plan."[29] The plaintiff argued that, in her case, the exception did not apply, because the term *consumer* should be

---

[27] 12 CFR §205.3(d).

[28] 703 F2d 936 (5th Cir 1983).

[29] 12 CFR §205.3(e).

understood as *account holder*. Since the telephone conversation was not initiated by either account holder, the exemption was therefore inapplicable.

The Fifth Circuit Court of Appeals did not agree. The court stated that *consumer* meant any *natural person*, not simply the account holder. The court said that if Congress intended the term to apply only to account holders, then it would have clearly stated as much.

The court justified its interpretation by the Act's overall policy. EFTA is a special design to deal with a banking and payment service which depends on computers and involves no human contact between the service providers and the consumer. Congress excluded occasional consumer-initiated transfers from the Act because these are handled personally and, therefore, are not prone to computer error or institutional abuse.

The court argued that EFTA was created in an effort to fill the gaps left by existing laws which inadequately covered this type of service. The court pointed out that the plaintiff might have an action under state law for conversion or breach of contract. In conclusion, the court held that the Act does not cover fund transfers initiated between any natural person and an officer or employee of a financial institution not occurring regularly or according to a prearranged plan.[30]

Regulation E has added two more exemptions from the Act. These are:

1. Transfers to and from trust accounts[31]
2. Preauthorized transfers to financial institutions which have assets of $25 million or less[32]

In spite of Regulation E, the parameters of the Act are not always readily discernible. For instance, the Act exempts from EFTA automatic transfers within the same financial institution. These transfers affect consumers' individual accounts, yet they occur without a specific request from the consumer.

A question arises as to whether this exemption applies to the *paired banking system* which exists in Rhode Island. Under this system, a thrift institution shares quarters, statistics, and personnel with a commercial bank. Customers receive a single unified statement issued by one institution, although the institutions' respective accounts are distinguished by number and type. The question becomes whether transfers within the paired institutions qualify as intra-institutional transfers outside the scope of EFTA. The Board has answered this question affirmatively, but only "under the unique circumstances that exist in Rhode Island."[33]

On the other hand, transfers to and from a consumer's account at affiliated institutions, such as a subsidiary institution or institutions within the same

---

[30] 703 F2d at 942.

[31] 12 CFR §205.3(f).

[32] 12 CFR §205.3(g).

[33] 12 CFR §205.3 and Official Staff Interpretation.

holding company, do not qualify as intra-institutional transfers and thus are not exempted from the Act.[34] Therefore, it is not always easy to discern which transactions are covered. The same ambiguity applies to transactions initiated with a paper instrument and subsequently converted into electronic form. Does the Act apply?

It appears that Congress originally intended to regulate only the familiar EFT services, thereby giving the Act an extremely narrow scope. By focusing only on transfers which are initiated electronically, the Act excludes transactions initiated by check, draft, or other paper instruments. Apparently, EFTA does not cover transactions initiated with a paper instrument and subsequently converted into electronic form.

One problem causing particular concern is that of *check truncation*, a single transaction initiated by a check but subsequently converted to an electronic form. The depositor bank retains the check or draft, taking the essential information from the item and transmitting it electronically to the payor bank. The depositor bank does not return the actual check to the payor bank or to the consumer.

The Federal Reserve Board's staff argued that the consumer does not receive adequate protection, because the consumer must rely on the bank's periodic statements in order to prove payment. Furthermore, the information provided on this statement does not include all the basic information EFTA requires for electronic fund transfers.[35] In spite of these arguments, check truncation systems continue to be omitted from EFTA's scope, because the transfers are initiated by a paper instrument rather than electronically. It is possible that technological advances in this area will force a broader reading of the Act's scope in the future.

§8.04   Disclosure Requirements—Generally

It is essential that consumers using EFT services be informed of their rights and responsibilities, and of the terms and conditions governing such services. Consumers need to know how the services will affect their accounts with the financial institutions. Recognizing this, the Act requires EFT providers to disclose the terms and conditions of the services before and after the consumer uses them. The disclosures must be expressed "in readily understandable language" at the time the consumer contracts for the EFT service.[36] Generally, the requirement for disclosure is patterned after the Truth in Lending Act provisions dealing with credit cards.[37] However, EFTA exceeds the scope of these provisions by requiring additional disclosures, especially those concern-

---

[34] *Id.*

[35] *See* Brandel & Olliff, III, *The Electronic Fund Transfer Act: A Primer*, 40 Ohio St LJ 531, 545-47 (1979).

[36] 15 USC §1693c(a).

[37] Truth in Lending Act §127, 15 USC §1637 (1976).

ing the consumer's rights and responsibilities in error resolution.[38] Regulation E further provides that the financial institutions may opt to combine further terms and conditions required by other laws with the disclosures required by EFTA.[39]

Failure to comply with the Act's disclosure requirements will preclude a financial institution from holding a consumer liable for any unauthorized transfer from the consumer's account.[40] Furthermore, such a failure may subject the financial institution to civil and criminal liability.[41] The Federal Reserve Board has issued model disclosure forms to facilitate compliance with the law.[42] Although financial institutions are not required to use these forms, those institutions that choose to use them will not be subject to civil or criminal liability for a failure to comply with the Act's disclosure requirements.[43]

§8.05 —Initial Disclosure of Terms and Conditions

The financial institution must disclose the terms and conditions of the consumer's use of an EFT at the time the consumer contracts for the service. The disclosure must be expressed in language which will be easily understood, and must include:

1. The consumer's liability for unauthorized transfers and, at the financial institution's option, notice of the advisability of promptly reporting loss or theft of the access device or unauthorized transfers

2. The telephone number and address of the person or office to be notified when the consumer believes an unauthorized transfer has been or may be made

3. The financial institution's business days. Business days are defined as any day on which the institution's offices are open to the public for the purpose of conducting business

4. The type and nature of the electronic fund transfer that the consumer may make, as well as any limitations on the frequency and dollar amount of the transfers. However, the details of such limitation may not be disclosed if the loss of such confidentiality would damage the system's security

5. Any charge for electronic fund transfers

6. A summary of the consumer's right to receive documentation of transfers, such as receipts and periodic statements

---

[38] 15 USC §1693c(a)(7).

[39] 12 CFR §205.4(c).

[40] 15 USC §1693g(a).

[41] 15 USC §§1693m, §1693n.

[42] 15 USC §1693b(b).

[43] 15 USC §1693m(d)(2).

7. The consumer's right to stop payment of a preauthorized electronic fund transfer, and the procedure for initiating such an order. A *preauthorized transfer* is defined as a transfer authorized in advance to recur at substantially regular intervals

8. A summary of the financial institution's liability to the consumer for failing to make or stop certain transfers

9. The circumstances under which the financial institution, in the ordinary course of business, will disclose information regarding the consumer's account to third parties

10. A notice concerning error resolution procedures and the consumer's rights under those procedures[44]

§8.06   —Change-in-Terms Disclosure and Error Resolution Notice

The financial institution must notify the consumer of any change in any term or condition of the consumer's account which is subject to initial disclosure. This requirement applies only if such changes would result in the consumer's greater cost or liability, or if it decreases access to the consumer's account.[45] Examples include a decision by the financial institution to increase the fees or charge or to reduce the amount of the dollar transfer.

The notification to the consumer must be in writing and made at least 21 days before the effective date of the change. However, the financial institution may make an immediate change without prior notice, if such change is immediately necessary to maintain or restore the security of the transfer or the account.[46]

Regulation E further requires that, unless disclosure would jeopardize the security of the accounts system, the financial system must disclose a permanent change to the consumer in the next regular periodic statement, or within 30 days.[47] An example of a disclosure that may jeopardize the security of the system is that of the dollar amount limit that the consumer can withdraw daily from the ATMs. Since the secrecy of the limits is essential to the security of the account or system against theft, the financial institution need disclose only that certain limits exist, but it is not required to state exactly what those limits are. If the limits are made stricter after the initial disclosure, no new disclosure is required. However, if no limits are imposed initially, but limits are then adopted, the financial institution must disclose this change, although again, no details of the limits need to be disclosed.[48]

Besides the error resolution notice which is part of the initial disclosure,

---

[44] 15 USC §1693c(a); 12 CFR §205.7.

[45] 15 USC §1693c(b).

[46] *Id.*

[47] 12 CFR §205.8(a).

[48] 12 CFR §205.8(a) and Official Staff Interpretation.

Regulation E requires also periodic notice of error resolution, either at least once for each calendar year or with each periodic statement. The Board suggests that the following model notice be sent on or with the periodic statement:

IN CASE OF ERRORS OR QUESTIONS ABOUT
YOUR ELECTRONIC TRANSFERS

Telephone us at [insert telephone number]

or

Write us at [insert address] as soon as you can, if you think our statement or receipt is wrong, or if you need more information about a transfer on the statement or receipt. We must hear from you no later than 60 days after we sent you the FIRST statement on which the error or problem appeared.

1. Tell us your name, address, and telephone number (if any).

2. Describe the error or the transfer you are unsure about, and explain as clearly as you can why you believe there is an error or why you need more information.

3. Tell us the dollar amount of the suspected error. We will investigate your complaint and will correct any error promptly.

If we take more than 10 business days to do this, we will recredit your account for the amount you think is in error, so that you will have use of the money during the time it takes us to complete your investigation.

(44 FR 59471, Oct. 15, 1979, as amended at 45 FR 8264, Feb. 6, 1980)

The Board emphasizes that if a financial institution does not send periodic statements to certain EFT consumers, it must send the the error resolution notice annually.[49]

§8.07 Documentation of Transactions

When a transaction is initiated by check or by draft, consumers generally use the cancelled item to record the transaction. Consumers want to keep written records of their account activity for legitimate purposes. They want to know which funds are available, detect error, be able to furnish proof of payment of debts, and have the records on hand for tax purposes. Written records of consumers' account activity are thus vital. Electronic fund transfers by their nature preclude paper use. Therefore, an alternative method of documenting account activity must be provided to the consumer. In its final report, the NCEFT emphasized the importance of this documentation. The report stated: "Consumers should be provided with frequent, accurate, and comprehensive statements of account activity. Although account statements are important in

---

[49] *Id.*

a non-EFT environment they become crucial in a EFT system. . . ."[50] Documentation of EFT transactions would include written receipts to users for every EFT transaction which occurs at the ATMs and periodic statements of account activity.

At the same time, the Commission suggested that the stringent requirements on documentation should not burden financial institutions if there is no practical need to do so, and if the consumer already has adequate protection.[51] The Federal Reserve Board, through Regulation E, further refines and explains these provisions.

§8.08   —Receipts at Electronic Terminals

The Act requires that for each electronic fund transfer initiated by a consumer from an electronic terminal, the financial institution holding such consumer's account shall, directly or indirectly, at the time the transfer is initiated, make available to the consumer written documentation of such transfer. The documentation shall clearly set forth, to the extent applicable:

1. The amount involved and date the transfer is initiated
2. The type of transfer
3. The identity of the consumer's account with the financial institution from which or to which funds are transferred
4. The identity of any third party to whom or from whom funds are transferred
5. The location or identification of the electronic terminal involved[52]

This law does not require the financial institution to always make available to the consumer a written receipt of the transfer. Thus, an ATM may be programmed to provide a receipt only if the consumer wants one.[53]

Regulation E specifies that a financial institution may request that a third party, such as a merchant who operates a terminal, provide a receipt to a consumer.[54] The financial institution that holds the consumer's account and provides the EFT service remains responsible for the availability and content of the receipt.

In order to preserve the privacy and security of the consumer's account, that consumer's receipt must indicate, not the consumer's account number, but the type of account and the nature of the transfer, such as *withdrawal from checking*, or *transfer from savings to checking*. Codes may be used on the receipt if a full explanation of the code is printed on the receipt. The location of the terminal

---

[50] EFT in the United States, Final Report of the National Commission on Electronic Fund Transfers 46-47 (1977).

[51] *Id.*

[52] 15 USC §1693d(a).

[53] 12 CFR §205.9 and Official Staff Interpretation.

[54] 12 CFR §205.9(a) note 2.

where the transaction is conducted may be indicated by description, identification number, or code. Finally, a code may be used to identify the third party to or from whom funds are transferred if it is explained elsewhere on the receipt.[55]

§8.09 —Periodic Statements

The Act requires that the financial institution provide each customer with a periodic statement recording each electronic fund transfer made. This statement must be delivered at least monthly. If no transfer has occurred, then the statement must be delivered at least quarterly.[56] Each periodic statement must include:

1. Each electronic fund transfer occurring during the period. This information may be provided on accompanying documents, such as copies of formal receipts, posting memos, deposit slips, and the documents that, together with the statement, disclose all the required information[57]

2. The amount of the transfer, together with any charge

3. The date the transfer was debited or credited to the account

4. The title of the transfer and the type of account which it affected

5. The location where each transfer occurred

6. The address and telephone number to be used for inquiry or notice of errors, indicated by such language as *Direct Inquiries To*

7. The balance of the consumer's account at the beginning and the close of the period[58]

The Act makes two exceptions to these requirements:

1. The financial institution may update a passbook account by simply entering the amount and date of recent EFTs in the passbook or other document when presented by the consumer. (Passbook accounts generally may be accessed by EFT only for preauthorized credits, such as social security benefits)

2. For accounts other than passbook accounts which cannot be accessed by EFTs other than for preauthorized credits, the financial institution need only provide a quarterly, rather than a monthly, statement for the period in which a transfer occurs[59]

---

[55] 12 CFR §205.9a.

[56] 15 USC §1693d(c).

[57] 12 CFR §205.9 and Official Staff Interpretations.

[58] *Id.*

[59] 15 USC §1693d(d)(e).

Furthermore, financial institutions are required to provide receipts for EFTs which occur at an electronic terminal which:

1. Only permits cash withdrawals by the consumer
2. Cannot make a receipt available to the consumer at the time the transfer is initiated (for example, a terminal which has run out of paper)
3. Cannot be modified to provide a receipt at the time
4. Was purchased or ordered by the financial institution prior to February 6, 1980

In all these cases, the financial institution must deliver to the consumer a written receipt which properly describes the transaction on the next business day following the transfer.[60]

Regulation E also exempts periodic statements for certain intra-institutional transfers. If a consumer has more than one account at the same institution, a statement needs to be delivered only for the account in which the EFT activity occurs.[61]

Because some foreign-based terminals do not have all of the information required by the Regulation, the financial institution is expected only to make a good faith attempt to provide EFT information in the periodic statement for transfers initiated outside the United States. The financial institution should identify, if possible, the country and city, but not necessarily the specific terminal.[62]

§8.10   —Documentation of Transactions and Problem of Proof

Under the Act, any documentation received by the consumer, including a receipt at the terminal or a periodic statement recording an electronic fund transfer made to another person, shall constitute prima facie evidence that such transfer was made.[63] The legislative history indicates that the term *to another person* must be understood as meaning to any third party other than the depository institution. The goal of this section is to provide the consumer with the same evidence of payment, for income tax or other purposes, as a cancelled check.[64]

The problem of proof arises particularly when a receipt is given for cash deposits which a consumer makes at an automated teller machine. The consumer places cash or checks in an envelope, inserts it in the ATM, and receives a receipt for the amount that the consumer has keyed into the ATM.

---

[60] 12 CFR §205(f).

[61] 12 CFR §205.9 and Official Staff Interpretation.

[62] 12 CFR §205.9(i) and Official Staff Interpretation.

[63] 15 USC §1693d(f).

[64] S Rep No 915, 95th Cong, 2d Sess, *reprinted in* 1978 US Code Cong & Admin News 9273, 9415.

If the law is interpreted to mean that the receipt constitutes prima facie evidence of the transfer to the financial institution, then the consumer may rely on this receipt in a dispute with the financial institution. The financial institution, however, cannot verify the amount actually deposited in the ATM until it has actually counted the cash or substantiated the checks. Because of this, the NCEFT recommended that the ATM should serve only as a night depository, and any receipt delivered to the consumer for the alleged amount deposited should not be given undue consideration by courts and juries.[65]

The NCEFT argues that if any debit or credit memorandum regarding electronic fund transfers were to constitute proof of payment, the potential for fraudulent abuse would be substantial. The Commission therefore suggests that a broad mandate would be unwise.

The Act was not entirely clear on this point. Some commentators have argued that such deposits might be outside the scope of EFTA because they are originated by a paper instrument in the form of checks, deposit slips, or other paper items in the envelope. Furthermore, the ATM deposit by the consumer to the consumer's own account would not constitute a transfer "made to another person" within the definition in §906(f) of the Act.[66] The Federal Reserve Board has adopted this interpretation and is of the opinion that deposit receipts do not constitute prima facie proof of payment because there is no payment to another person.[67]

However, the spirit of consumer protection seems to demand that, once a receipt is delivered to the consumer, the burden should be placed on the financial institution to prove that the receipt fails to reflect the actual transfer. Thus, there should be a presumption that the receipt reflects a deposit made, obliging the financial institution to come forward with evidence to rebut that presumption. The court adopted this position in *A McEvans v Citibank, NA* [68] a pre-EFTA case.

The consumer here, Ms. McEvans, used a Citibank ATM, at the LaGuardia Place branch, to deposit $600 in her account. The deposit consisted of one $100 bill and ten $50 bills. Ms. McEvans placed the cash in a letter-sized envelope provided by the bank. However, she forgot to include a deposit slip in the envelope. Ms. McEvans inserted her access card into the ATM and punched the appropriate code in order to request a receipt. The machine accepted the deposit but, due to a malfunction, failed to return the requested receipt.

The plaintiff phoned the LaGuardia Place branch four days later and informed them of her deposit and the machine's malfunction. The next day, however, when she attempted to make a cash withdrawal, the ATM informed

---

[65] EFT in the United States, Policy Recommendations and the Public Interest, The Final Report of the National Commission on Electronic Fund Transfers 48-49 (1977).

[66] *See* Brandel & Olliff, III, *The Electronic Fund Transfer Act: A Primer*, 40 Ohio St LJ 531, 551, n108 (1979).

[67] 12 CFR §205.9 and Official Staff Interpretation.

[68] 96 Misc 2d 142, 408 NYS2d 870 (NY City Civ Ct 1978).

her that her account was overdrawn. Ms. McEvans again contacted the bank. The bank stated that her $600 deposit had not been received. An investigation was conducted which revealed that the only cash deposit received that month without a deposit slip was for $350, not $600. The bank also discovered that the machine had failed to print the plaintiff's account number on the envelope. Therefore, there was no way of determining whether the $350 belonged to her.

The branch manager testified that envelopes received at the terminal enter a safe opened by two dials. A different employee controlled each dial, and two people were required to open the safe. Once the safe was opened, only a management officer could open the inner box which contained the envelopes. The opening of the envelopes also required two persons, one who actually opened the envelopes and counted the contents, and the other who witnessed the procedure. The defendant bank pointed to the contract agreement between the consumer and the bank which conspicuously appeared on the deposit envelopes and initial deposit agreement. The contract specified that final credit for currency deposits was subject to the bank's count.

The court drew a parallel between the ATM deposit and the traditional night deposit. Until final credit was given by the bank, the relationship between the night depositor and the bank is that of a mutually benefited bailor and bailee. Bailment law imposes a duty of reasonable care in keeping and safeguarding the bailor's property.

The court recognized there had been no ATM deposit case precedents in New York, only cases dealing with night depositories. While the court did not hold that all cash deposits claimed to be placed in an ATM are presumed accurate until the presumption is satisfactorily rebutted by the bank, the court did go as far as possible to protect the consumer. In reaching its decision, the court relied on a minor variation in the bank's usual procedure. Instead of one person standing by passively as a witness, the envelopes were opened by a teller and a head teller, thereby technically violating the bank's internal procedure.

The plaintiff admittedly was helped in the case by a witness who testified that she observed Ms. McEvans insert the $600 in the envelope. The court accepted this as sufficient to support the plaintiff's cause of action in negligence against the bank. The court concluded that the plaintiff had sustained her burden of proof.

§8.11 Preauthorized Transfers

A *preauthorized transfer* is defined as an electronic fund transfer authorized in advance to recur at substantially regular intervals. Special provisions of EFTA that apply to preauthorized transfers provide for an avoidance of unnecessary costs for EFT providers without comparable benefit to the consumer. Preauthorized transfers apply to both credits and debits. Concerning credits, the consumer may authorize the deposit of wages, dividends, and social security benefits to the consumer's account through EFTs. Preauthorized debits may be in fixed amounts, such as rent or mortgage payments, or variable amounts, such as utility bills or credit card payments.

A preauthorized transfer exists when the three following conditions are met:

1. The debit or credit is automatic, i.e., made without the consumer's instruction, once the consumer has initially authorized the service
2. It must be an EFT as defined by the Act
3. The debits or credits must recur at substantially regular intervals[69]

Once these elements exist, *preauthorized transfer* may cover transfers between the consumer's account and the financial institution, third parties, and between two or more accounts of the consumer in the same financial institution.

In general, the consumer gets less documentation from the financial institution in preauthorized transfers than in non-preauthorized transfers. The financial institution may choose to give the consumer positive notice or negative notice of the credit. Positive notice means that the financial institution notifies the consumer when the credit is received. Negative notice means that the financial institution is required to give notice only if the credit is not received on schedule. Either notice must be given promptly.

In the case of positive notice, the Federal Reserve Board has interpreted *promptly* to mean two business days after the transfer occurred.[70] Positive notice of the credit is not required if the payor already has notified the consumer that the transfer has been made. In the case of negative notice, *promptly* means two business days after the date on which the transfer was scheduled to occur.[71] Whether positive or negative notice is used is left completely to the option of the financial institution, but the means of notice elected must be disclosed to the consumer at the time the consumer contracts for the service.[72]

Preauthorized debits must be authorized by the consumer in writing, and a copy of the authorization must be given to the consumer by the party that obtains the authorization from the consumer.[73] For example, if a consumer is to authorize a landlord to initiate preauthorized electronic fund transfers from the consumer's account for rent payments, the consumer must consent to it in writing, and the landlord must provide a copy of the authorization to the consumer. If the preauthorized transfer from the consumer's account varies in amount from the previous transfer relating to the same authorization, the financial institution or the designated payee must, in at most 10 days before the scheduled transfer payment date, send a written notice of the difference to the consumer.[74] At the consumer's option, the consumer may consent to receive notice only in specified circumstances, as, for example, when the difference in amount exceeds that agreed upon or does not fall within a certain difference in amount exceeds that agreed upon or does not fall within a certain range.[75]

---

[69] 12 CFR §205.2(j). *See* Broadman, *Electronic Fund Transfer Act: Is the Consumer Protected?*, 13 USF L Rev 245, 274-75 (1979).

[70] 12 CFR §205.10(a)(i).

[71] 12 CFR §205.10(a)(ii).

[72] 15 USC §1693d(b).

[73] 15 USC §1693e(a); 12 CFR §205.10(b).

[74] 15 USC §1693e(b); 12 CFR §205.10(d).

[75] 15 USC §1693e(b); 12 CFR §205.10(d).

The Act gives the consumer the right to stop payment on a preauthorized transfer by notifying the financial institution orally or in writing at any time, up to three business days preceding the scheduled date of the transfer.[76] The financial institution may not be satisfied with an oral notification and may require the consumer to give written confirmation within 14 days of oral notification.[77] The financial institution must, however, disclose to the consumer the requirement of the written confirmation at the time the oral notification is made. The financial institution must also disclose the address to which the written confirmation should be sent. Once these disclosure conditions are met, the oral stop payment order ceases to be effective 14 days after it has been communicated to the financial institution, unless confirmed in writing.[78]

§8.12　Liability for Unauthorized Transfers

The issue of the consumer's liability for transfers initiated by a third party not authorized by the consumer is deemed by Congress to be so crucial to public confidence in the EFT system that the effective date of the provisions of the Electronic Fund Transfer Act dealing with this issue was established 15 months earlier than most of the other provisions of the Act.[79] In allocating the risk of loss for unauthorized transfers between the financial institution and the consumer, Congress assigned the main responsibility to the financial institution, but also held the consumer liable according to a scale based upon the degree of the consumer's negligence. Congress did not adopt the $50 flat liability applicable to the unauthorized use of credit cards under the Truth in Lending Act.[80] The difference may be justified on the ground that in credit cards, the financial institution generally imposes a ceiling on the credit allowed the consumer ($1,000 to $2,000), and, therefore, the risk of loss which could occur is limited. Such a limit does not exist in EFTs. Accordingly, another system of liability must be devised. The Act provides for a complex three-tier liability system which is not a model of statutory drafting. Fortunately, the Federal Reserve Board has since clarified the language of the Act.

§8.13　—Unauthorized Transfer Defined

The Act and Regulation E define an *unauthorized electronic fund transfer* to mean an electronic fund transfer from a consumer's account which is initiated by a

---

[76] 15 USC §1693e(a); 12 CFR §205.10(e).

[77] 15 USC §1693e(a); 12 CFR §205.10(e).

[78] 12 CFR §205.10(c).

[79] §921 of Pub L No 90-321 (as added Pub L No 95-630, tit XX, §2001, 92 Stat 3741 (Nov 10, 1978).

[80] TILA 15 USC §1643(a)(1).

person, other than the consumer, who lacks actual authority to initiate the transfer, and from which the consumer receives no benefit.[81] The transfer, although initiated by a person other than the consumer, is nevertheless still authorized if:

1. The consumer furnishes such a person with the access device, unless the consumer has notified the financial institution that transfers by that person are no longer authorized

2. The consumer, with fraudulent intent, acts in concert with the person who initiates the transfer[82]

Questions have been raised regarding the meaning of the term *furnish*. The Board has now settled the issue. According to the Board, the term *furnished* assumes that the consumer has authorized the person to use the access device to make transfers other than via fraud or duress.[83] Thus, only clearly involuntary acts are considered to be unauthorized. If the consumer furnishes the access device or authorizes its use to another person who exceeds the authority, then the consumer remains liable unless the financial institution has been notified that the transfers are unauthorized. *Ognibene v Citibank*[84] illustrates the meaning of the term *unauthorized transfers*.

On August 16, 1981, plaintiff-consumer went to one of defendant bank's ATM machines to withdraw $20 from his account. Two machines were situated next to each other at this particular transaction center, with a telephone placed in between. As plaintiff approached the machines, a man was talking on the telephone, apparently to the bank's customer service, regarding the malfunctioning of one of the machines. As plaintiff activated his machine, the man turned to him and asked if he could insert plaintiff's ATM card into the "malfunctioning" machine to see if it would work. The man appeared to be following instructions given by the person on the other end of the phone. Plaintiff handed the man his card, who inserted it into the machine twice. The man said into the phone, "Yes, it seems to be working."

Computer records showed that two withdrawals of $200 each were made that day from plaintiff's account within one minute of each other. They came immediately after a $20 withdrawal. Plaintiff brought action against the bank, arguing that since he had only authorized the $20 withdrawal, and had neither initiated nor benefited from the two $200 withdrawals, he should not be held liable for $400 in withdrawals from his account.

The court interpreted EFTA and concluded that, under EFTA, the withdrawals were unauthorized because:

1. They were initiated by a person other than the customer

---

[81] 15 USC §1693a(11); 12 CFR §205.2(1)

[82] *Id.*

[83] Regulation E 12 CFR §205.2 and Official Staff Interpretation.

[84] 112 Misc 2d 219, 446 NYS2d 845, (NY City Civ Ct 1981).

2. The customer received no benefit from them

3. The customer did not furnish such person with access to the account

The court defined *access* to mean furnishing *both* the card and code, since one was useless without the other.[85]

The court found that the unauthorized person had obtained access due to the defendant's own negligence in failing to inform the plaintiff of a scam to defraud ATM users of cash. The plaintiff, the court found, was a victim of this scam.

The burden of going forward to show that a transfer was unauthorized is on the consumer. The bank then has the burden of proof of consumer liability, and to meet that burden, it must show that the transfer was authorized.

The term *unauthorized transfers* excludes transfers initiated by the financial institution or its employees, such as the case in which the bank's employee fraudulently takes the money from a consumer's account by electronic means. Although these transfers are in fact *unauthorized,* they are not technically an *unauthorized transfer* under the Act or Regulation E. The liability provisions for *unauthorized transfers* do not apply to them.[86]

§8.14   —Consumer's Liability for Unauthorized Transfers

There are three conditions which must be met before a financial institution may hold a consumer liable for unauthorized transfers:

1. The access device used for the unauthorized transfer must be an *accepted* access device. An *access device* means a card, code, or other means of access to a consumer's account which the consumer may use to initiate an electronic fund transfer. A personal identification number (PIN) is an example of an access device. An access device becomes an *accepted access device* when the consumer to whom the access device is issued: requests and receives it, or signs or uses or authorizes another to use it; or requests validation of an access device issued on an unsolicited basis; or receives an access device in renewal of, or substitution for, an accepted access device[87]

2. The financial institution must have provided a means of identifying the consumer to whom the access device was issued. The identification may be done by a signature, photo, fingerprint, or electronic or mechanical confirmation, such as through the use of a code, i.e., the PIN[88]

3. The financial institution must have disclosed the amount for which

---

[85] *Id* at 222-23, 446 NYS2d at 847.

[86] 12 CFR §205 and Official Staff Interpretation.

[87] 15 USC §1693(a)(1); 12 CFR §205.2(a)(1).

[88] 15 USC §1693g(a); 12 CFR §205.6(a).

the consumer may be held liable, the telephone number, the address of the office to be notified of the unauthorized transfers, and the financial institution's business days. These disclosures must all be in writing[89]

§8.15 —Amount of Consumer's Liability

Basically, the Act provides for a three-tiered level of consumer liability. A consumer may be held liable up to $50, $500, or an unlimited amount.

The $50 Liability

Once the financial institution has met the conditions for imposing liability upon the consumer, the consumer may be held liable for the amount withdrawn before the consumer notifies the financial institution that the transfer was unauthorized. However, the consumer may not be held liable for more than $50.

This $50 limit has been the subject of a hot debate. The NCEFT recommended that the consumer should have no liability for unauthorized transfers unless the financial institution could prove that the consumer's negligence contributed substantially to the occurrence, and that the financial institution exercised reasonable care to prevent the loss. The NCEFT recommended conversely, that if the consumer's negligence was proved, then the consumer's liability should be unlimited.

The NCEFT provided strict objective standards by which to define negligence. Negligence was limited to: writing the PIN on the card; keeping the PIN with the card; voluntarily permitting the access device to come into the possession of another person who makes or causes unauthorized transfers to be made; and failing to notify the financial institution of the unauthorized use within a certain time period.[90]

Consumer advocates objected to the potential for the consumer to be held liable for an unlimited amount, even if this liability was based on negligence. They argued that the array of legal resources available to financial institutions ultimately enabled them to shift the loss to the consumer anyway.[91] Except for the consumer's failure to report the loss or theft or unauthorized use, Congress refused to adopt the negligence standard, because it feared the potential for widespread litigation. Under the EFTA, if an authorized transfer occurs before

---

[89] 12 CFR §205.6(a)(3).

[90] EFT in the United States, Policy Recommendations and the Public Interest, The Final Report of the National Commission on Electronic Fund Transfers 58.

[91] *Electronic Fund Transfer Consumer Protection Act: Hearings on §2065 Before the Subcomm on Consumer Affairs of the Senate Comm on Banking, Housing and Urban Affairs*, 95th Cong, 1st Sess 74, 178 (1977); Brandel & Olliff, III, *The Electronic Fund Transfer Act: A Primer*, 40 Ohio St LJ 531, 556 (1979).

the consumer is aware of the loss or theft, the consumer's maximum liability is $50, or the actual amount withdrawn, whichever is less.[92]

The $500 Liability

This liability applies if the consumer fails to notify the financial institution within two business days after learning of the loss or theft of the access device. This $500 liability includes the $50 limit of the first tier of liability for unauthorized transfers that occur before the close of the two business days.[93]

To clarify the $500 limit rule, the Board gives the following example:

Date and Event

June 1 — C's card is stolen

June 2 — $100 unauthorized transfer

June 3 — C learns of theft

June 4 — $25 unauthorized transfer

June 5 — Close of two business days

June 7-8 — $600 in unauthorized transfers that could have been prevented had notice been given by June 5

June 9 — C notifies bank

C's liability will be computed as follows:

1. Before the close of the two business days, even though the amount of the unauthorized transfers was $125, C's liability is limited to $50

2. After the close of the two business days, although the unauthorized transfers amounted to $600, C is liable for only $450, because the maximum liability which could be imposed upon the consumer for failing to report the loss or theft of the access device within two business days after the consumer learns of the loss or theft cannot exceed $500[94]

Unlimited Liability

There is no limit to the consumer's liability for unauthorized transfers if the consumer fails to report unauthorized EFTs within 60 days of transmittal of a periodic statement reflecting an authorized transfer.[95]

Regulation E interprets this EFTA rule as follows:

If the consumer fails to report within 60 days of transmittal of the periodic statement any unauthorized electronic fund transfer that appears on the statement, the consumer's liability shall not exceed the sum of
(i) the lesser of $50 or the amount of unauthorized electronic fund transfers that appear on the periodic statement or that occur during the 60-day period, and
(ii) the amount of unauthorized electronic fund transfers that occur

---

[92] 15 USC §1693g(a)(1).

[93] 15 USC §1693g(a)(2).

[94] 12 CFR §205.6 and Official Staff Interpretation

[95] 15 USC §1693g(2); 12 CFR §205.6(2) (1985).

after the close of the 60 days and before notice to the financial institution and that the institution establishes would not have occurred but for the failure of the consumer to notify within that time.[96]

This rule is similar to the Uniform Commercial Code rule governing the consumer's negligence regarding checks. Failure to notify the financial institution of the unauthorized withdrawals within 60 days of transmittal of the periodic statement is considered prima facie evidence of negligence. Note, however, that under §4-406(4) of the UCC, the 60-day period starts from the time the statement and other documentations "are made available to the customer." It appears that the term *transmittal* under EFTA and Regulation E indicates that the mailbox rule applies. Requiring the notification period to begin with *transmittal* of the periodic statement results in the possibility of the consumer's incurring liability before receiving notification of the transfer. This seems unreasonable. The consumer should be held liable only after the documentation is made available to him or her.

The following examples, given by the Federal Reserve Board staff, show that the consumer may incur more than one liability in the same case.

Example 1—In which both $500 and unlimited liability apply[97]

June 1 — Consumer's (C) card is stolen

June 3 — C learns of theft

June 5 — Close of two business days

June 7 — $200 unauthorized transfer that could have been prevented had notice been given by June 5

June 10 — Periodic statement is transmitted to C (for period from 5/10 to 6/9)

June 15 — $200 unauthorized transfer that could have been prevented had notice been given by June 5

July 10 — Periodic statement of C's account is transmitted to C (for period from 6/10 to 7/9)

Aug. 4 — $300 unauthorized transfer that could have been prevented had notice been given by June 5

Aug. 9 — Close of 60 days after transmittal of statement showing unauthorized transfer

Aug. 10 — Periodic statement of C's account is transmitted to C (for period 7/10 to 8/9)

Aug. 15 — $100 unauthorized transfer that could have been prevented had notice been given by August 9

Aug. 20 — C notifies bank

C's liability is computed as follows:

---

[96] 12 CFR §205.6(b)(2).

[97] 12 CFR §205.6 and Official Staff Interpretation.

	Unauthorized Transfers	C's liability
Amount of transfers before close of two business days: $0		$ 0
Amount of transfers, after close of two business days and before close of 60-day period, that would not have occurred but for C's failure to notify within two business days: $700		$500
Amount of transfers, after close of 60 days and before C's notice to bank, that would not have occurred but for C's failure to notify within 60 days: $100		$100
C's total liability		$600

Example 2—in which both $50 and unlimited liability apply[98]

Facts same as in Example 1, except that C does not learn of the card theft, but questions the account balance, and notifies bank on August 20 of possible unauthorized transfers.

C's liability is computed as follows:

	Unauthorized Transfers	C's liability
Amount of transfers appearing on the periodic statement or occurring during the 60-day period: $700		$ 50
Amount of transfers, after the close of 60-day period and before notice, that would not have occurred but for C's failure to notify within 60 days: $100		$100
C's total liability		$150

Problems of Definition

The Board had difficulty in defining the terms *notice of loss* and *business day*. Originally, the Board adopted the definition of notice provided by Regulation Z in the Truth in Lending Act. Regulation Z states that notice of theft or loss of a credit card is effective when received by the issuer or, whether or not received, at the expiration of the time generally required for transmittal, whichever is earlier.[99]

Consumer groups spearheaded by Representative Frank Annunzio criticized this definition of notice as contrary to consumer interests, as well as to congressional intent.[100] Consequently, Regulation E now adopts the mailbox rule, under which notice to a financial institution is deemed given "when a consumer takes such steps that are reasonably necessary to provide the

---

[98] *Id.*

[99] 12 CFR §226.13(e).

[100] *See* Battey, *Annunzio Hits Fed Card Loss Rules*, Am Banker, Apr 10, 1979, at 2.

financial institution with the pertinent information."[101] It is not necessary that a particular officer, employee, or agent of the financial institution actually receives the information.

Business day is defined in the Act as any day on which the offices of the consumer's financial institution are open to carry on "substantially all business functions."[102] The Board interprets this term to include processing claims of account errors. Thus, Saturday may not be a business day, even if the financial institution's offices are open to the public that day, because claims of account errors are not processed on Saturday.[103]

Problems of Proof

In spite of the Board's effort to clarify the issues left unclear by EFTA, serious proof problems may still arise with unauthorized transfers. The consumer's liability for more than $50 hinges on the consumer's lack of notice, or on the consumer's failure to notify the financial institution after becoming aware of the loss or theft. Here, it may be difficult to prove when the consumer has learned of the loss or theft.

The requirement to report the loss or theft within two business days is extended to a longer period in extenuating circumstances.[104] Examples include extended travel or hospitalization. The reporting period is extended to a reasonable time under the circumstances. Here, evidentiary problems may arise in determining which circumstances are *extenuating* and how much time is *reasonable*. At any rate, the burden of proof remains on the financial institution to establish that the conditions of liability have been met.[105]

Another difficulty arises when an unauthorized transfer does not involve an access device. Under EFTA and Regulation E, a consumer's liability for an unauthorized transfer is conditioned upon the use of an accepted access device. Therefore, if no access device is used, no liability should be imposed upon the consumer. The Federal Reserve Board's official staff interpretation, however, states instead, that failure of the consumer to report an unauthorized EFT made without an access device may still subject the consumer to full liability. This will occur if the consumer fails to report the unauthorized EFT, made with or without an access device, within 60 days of transmittal of the periodic statement reflecting the transfer.[106] On the other hand, the staff specifically states that a consumer is not liable for unauthorized EFTs initiated by the financial institution or its employees.[107] It seems, therefore, that the unlimited liability of the consumer for failing to report an unauthorized EFT within the

---

[101] 12 CFR §205.6(c).

[102] 15 USC §1693a(4).

[103] 44 Fed Reg 18470 (Mar 28, 1979).

[104] 15 USC §1693g(a)(2).

[105] 15 USC §1693g(b).

[106] 12 CFR §205.6 and Official Staff Interpretation.

[107] *Id.*

60-day period rests in part on the identity of the third person who makes the unauthorized transfer. It is not based purely on the consumer's negligence in failure to make the report. Perhaps the difference may be justified by the legislature's intent to free the consumer of liability when there is contributing negligence on the part of the financial institution.

§8.16 —Correlation between EFTA and the Truth In Lending Act Regarding Limitation on Consumer's Liability for Unauthorized Transfers

The Truth in Lending Act (TILA) limits to $50 consumer liability for loss resulting from the unauthorized use of a credit card.[108] The Electronic Fund Transfer Act (EFTA), on the other hand, provides for a three-tiered range of liability for the unauthorized use of an access device.

If the access device is a card which serves both as a credit card and a debit card, a conflict may arise between the provisions of TILA and EFTA. Furthermore, a single transaction may involve both an EFT debit and an extension of credit. EFTA has no provision to deal with this potential conflict.

The Board solved this problem in Regulation E. The Regulation provides that TILA governs the liability for unauthorized use of a single debit-credit card where the card is used solely as a credit card, and the transaction does not involve an EFT. On the other hand, EFTA governs the limitations on consumer liability when an EFT debit transaction is involved or the unauthorized transaction involves an extension of credit under an agreement between a consumer and a financial institution to cover overdrafts, or to maintain a specified minimum balance in the consumer's account. Third, both TILA and Regulation Z govern the consumer's liability for unauthorized use of a credit card which is also an access device, but which does not involve an electronic fund transfer.[109]

To illustrate, suppose the consumer's credit card-access device is used to make unauthorized withdrawals from the checking account and, separately, to obtain cash advances from the line of credit. Regulation E would apply to an unauthorized transfer from the consumer's checking account. Regulation Z would apply to the cash advance from the credit line. As a result, the consumer's liability, limited to $50 under Regulation Z, may extend to $50, $500, or an unlimited amount under Regulation E.[110] Thus, the respective application of TILA and EFTA depends upon the nature of the unauthorized transaction.

---

[108] 15 USC §1643(a)(1).

[109] 12 CFR §205.6(d).

[110] 12 CFR §205.6, -.11.

§8.17 Error Resolution

"To err is human," as the saying goes, but when a machine not only errs, but continues to make the same error, serious problems can arise. Examples include computational mistakes, the incorrect entering of a debit, or the failure to enter a legitimate credit.

For traditional paper instrument transactions, the Uniform Commercial Code does not provide for formal error resolution. The Fair Credit Billing Act does, however, explicitly provide for steps to resolve credit card billing disputes. When the consumer brings the error to the attention of the credit card issuer, the issuer must investigate the claim. Typically, the card issuer has up to 90 days to investigate and correct a credit card billing error.[111]

In EFT transactions, errors can have dire consequences, because they may completely deplete the consumer's account, and the consumer may be left without funds to pay for such essentials as rent, utilities, and food. Therefore, EFTA provides for an elaborate error resolution procedure, which Regulation E has clarified and supplemented.

§8.18 —Error Defined

The Electronic Fund Transfer Act provides a broad definition of the term *error*. An *error* consists of:

1. An unauthorized electronic fund transfer
2. An incorrect electronic fund transfer from the consumer's account
3. The omission from a periodic statement of an electronic fund transfer to or from the consumer's account that should have been included
4. A computational error by the financial institution
5. The consumer's receipt of an incorrect amount of money from an electronic terminal
6. A consumer's request for additional information or clarification concerning an electronic fund transfer or any documentation required by the Act
7. Any other error described in regulations of the Board[112]

Regulation E has a similar definition, but it specifically excludes both routine account balance inquiries and requests for documentation for purposes of tax or record-keeping.[113]

Congress attaches great importance to the error resolution procedure. Treble damages may be imposed on the financial institution that fails to comply

---

[111] *See* §7.18.

[112] 15 USC §1693f(f).

[113] 12 CFR §205.11(7).

with the Act in bad faith, fails to correct an error, or does not have a reasonable basis for denying that an error is made.[114]

§8.19   —Error Resolution Procedure

The consumer must give oral or written notice of the alleged error within 60 days of transmittal of records, such as periodic statements, documenting the error. The financial institution may require written confirmation within 10 business days of an oral notice, but only if it advises the consumer of the requirement and gives the consumer the address to which confirmation must be sent. If the consumer fails to provide the written confirmation within the 10-day period, the financial institution need not provisionally recredit the consumer's account, and is not liable for treble damages.

The consumer must give enough information in the oral or written notice to enable the financial institution to identify the name and account number of the consumer and to identify the documentation on which the error is found. The consumer must also describe the error and state the reason for the consumer's belief that an error has occurred.[115]

Under the Fair Credit Billing Act, the financial institution has up to 90 days to investigate a claim regarding credit cards.[116] Congress deemed this too lengthy for EFT errors, because the consumer may be deprived of essential funds. Therefore, the committee allows only 10 business days for the financial institution to investigate an alleged EFT error. The investigation period may be extended to 45 calendar days after the financial institution has received notice of the error if the financial institution provisionally recredits the consumer's account for the amount alleged to be in error and allows the consumer full use of these funds. The financial institution must provide this provisional credit within 10 days of receiving notice of the error.[117]

If the financial institution is at fault, it must correct the error, including the crediting of interest where applicable, within one business day after such determination.[118] If the financial institution determines, after its investigation, that an error did not occur, then it must deliver or mail to the consumer an explanation of its findings within three business days after the conclusion of its investigation. If the consumer so requests, the financial institution must make available a reproduction of all the documents on which it relied in its determination that an error did not occur.[119]

Regulation E adds a provision extending the time period in which the financial institution must complete its investigation. If the notice of an error involves an EFT outside of the United States or an EFT from a point-of-sale

---

[114] 15 USC §1693f(e).

[115] 15 USC §1693f(a).

[116] 15 USC §1666(a)(1)(B).

[117] 15 USC §1693f(c).

[118] 15 USC §1693f(b).

[119] 15 USC §1693f(d).

debit card transaction, the financial institution has 20 business days to investigate, rather than 10, if it does not give the consumer provisional credit. If it does provide provisional credit, then it has 90, rather than 45, calendar days to investigate.[120]

If the consumer alleges that the error consists of an unauthorized transfer, the burden of proof is on the financial institution to show that the transfer was authorized and to prove the extent of the consumer's liability.[121] Conversely, in disputes involving errors other than unauthorized transfers, the burden of proof is on the consumer to show that an error has occurred.[122]

§8.20   —Liability of the Financial Institution

The financial institution may be subject to treble damages in two situations:

> 1. The financial institution's failing to conclude the investigation within 10 days and not provisionally recrediting a consumer's account within the 10-day period after receiving notice of error, and either not making a good faith attempt to investigate the alleged error or not having a reasonable basis for believing that the consumer's account was not in error[123]
>
> 2. The financial institution's knowingly and willfully concluding that the consumer's account is not in error, when such conclusion could not reasonably have been drawn from the evidence available to the financial institution at the time of its investigation[124]

If an error is found, the financial institution is required to refund those fees or charges that were imposed on the consumer's account, with the exception of those that would have been imposed even if the error had not occurred.[125] If the financial institution decides that no error occurred, or an error did occur, but in a different manner or amount from that described by the consumer, it must mail or deliver to the consumer an explanation of its findings within three business days after concluding its investigation. In no event should this occur later than 10 business days after receipt of the consumer's error notice if provisional recrediting did not occur. The financial institution must also include, in its explanation, notice of the consumer's right to request the documents which the institution relied on in making its determination.[126]

In reversing a provisional credit, the financial institution must notify the

---

[120] 12 CFR §205.11(c)(4).

[121] 15 USC §1693g(b).

[122] 12 CFR §205.11(b)(iii).

[123] 15 USC §1693f(e)(1).

[124] 15 USC §1693f(e)(2).

[125] 12 CFR §205.11(e)(1)-(2).

[126] 15 USC §1693f(d); 12 CFR §205.11(f)(1).

consumer orally or in writing of the date and amount of the debit. It must also state that it will honor for five business days after transmittal of the notice the consumer's orders to pay third parties. The institution need only honor the items that it would have paid had the provisionally recredited funds not been debited.[127]

The Board gives an example which illustrates how the above requirement should be interpreted. Assume that, after an investigation, no error was found to have taken place, and an account with a balance of $155 is debited in an amount of $100 for provisionally recredited funds, leaving a balance of $55. Assume further that two checks for $150 and $200 are then presented by third parties. The financial institution need honor only the $150 item. Moreover, the institution need honor only those items which include preauthorized transfers payable to third parties. The consumer is not allowed ATM or other cash withdrawals.[128]

§8.21   —EFTA Error Resolution and Relation to the Truth in Lending Act

A problem arises when a consumer uses a combined credit card-access device to withdraw funds at an ATM and later alleges that an error has occurred. The issue is which error resolution procedures apply, those of Regulation E or Regulation Z? The error resolution procedures under EFTA are more stringent than those applicable to open-end credit accounts under the Fair Credit Billing Act and Regulation Z. The latter gives a much longer period for the card issuer to investigate and respond and imposes less severe sanctions for noncompliance.[129] The two acts would conflict in a case in which the consumer alleges an error in a transaction involving both a withdrawal of funds or a deposit and access to a preauthorized, open-end line of credit.

Although EFTA does not address this potential conflict, Regulation E does. If an EFT also includes an extension of credit under an agreement between a consumer and a financial institution to extend credit when the consumer's account is overdrawn or to maintain a specified minimum balance in the consumer's account, then Regulation E applies instead of Regulation Z. However, if a consumer uses a combined credit card and access device to withdraw funds at an ATM directly from a no-overdraft credit line, and later alleges an error, then Regulation Z applies. This is because the transaction does not involve an EFT as defined by EFTA. EFTA does not deem the credit line to be a consumer asset account.[130]

---

127 12 CFR §205.11(f)(2)(ii).
128 12 CFR §205.11 and Official Staff Interpretation.
129 15 USC §§1666-66j; 12 CFR §226.13.
130 12 CFR §205.11 and Official Staff Interpretation.

§8.22 Issuance of Access Devices

Prior to the enactment of EFTA, there was widespread abuse of unsolicited credit cards forced upon consumers. Hundreds of thousands of unsolicited cards were stolen each year which resulted in considerable hardship for the consumers. On the other hand, to prohibit unsolicited cards completely would stifle competition by preventing potential EFT providers from entering the field. Congress, therefore, adopted a compromise solution between the need to prevent harassment of consumers through the issuance of unsolicited cards and the need to preserve competition in the marketplace.

Under EFTA, financial institutions may distribute unsolicited devices, EFT cards, codes, or other means of access, on the condition that these devices are incapable of being used to access a consumer's account. Validation of the devices, so that they are capable of accessing an account, may occur only in response to a request or application from the consumer. Cards issued as a renewal or replacement of an accepted card, code, or other access device may be sent on an unsolicited basis.[131] The financial institution must fully disclose the consumer's rights and liabilities if the access device is validated. The financial institution must also disclose and explain that the unsolicited device is not validated and tell the consumer how the consumer may dispose of it if validation is not desired.[132]

A personal identification number (PIN) issued at the consumer's request constitutes both a way of validating the debit card and a means of identifying the consumer. The financial institution has not met the requirement that an unsolicited access device be nonvalidated when issued when it issues an unsolicited debit card and PIN to a consumer with the instruction that the consumer not use the card and PIN until the consumer has come to the financial institution for verification of the consumer's identity. There is no compliance because the consumer could still initiate EFTs.[133] The consumer is not liable if an unsolicited card is intercepted and used by a thief, since the consumer is liable for unauthorized transfers only if the means used to make these withdrawals was an *accepted* device, which it would not be here.

Since a credit card may be used as an access device and vice versa, the question arises as to the respective application of the Truth in Lending Act and the Electronic Fund Transfer Act to a particular issuance. The rules under Regulation E indicate that the primary function of the card determines the applicable law. If the card is primarily used as a credit device, then TILA and Regulation Z apply. If the main function of the card is to operate an EFT, then EFTA and Regulation E would apply.[134]

---

[131] 15 USC §1693i(a)(b).

[132] *Id.*

[133] 12 CFR §205.5 and Official Staff Interpretation.

[134] 12 CFR §205.5(c).

§8.23 Compulsory Use of Electronic Fund Transfers

The consumer should retain the freedom to choose whether to use EFTs. As the National Commission on Electronic Fund Transfers pointed out, "EFT should be a means to preserve consumer choice, not to narrow it."[135] In view of this policy, the Act provides that no person may:

1. Condition the extension of credit to a consumer on such consumer's repayment by means of preauthorized electronic fund transfers
2. Require a consumer to establish an account for receipt of electronic fund transfers with a particular financial institution as a condition of employment or receipt of a government benefit.[136]

EFTA authorizes employers, creditors, and the government, however, to demand that consumers use EFT systems by requiring that the consumer receive wages or other benefits by direct deposits in the consumer's account. The Act merely prevents employers, creditors, or the government from requiring the consumer to establish an account with a particular institution. As long as the consumer is free to choose the depository institution with which to establish an account, the consumer's freedom is deemed to be preserved under the Act. Creditors can require that consumers' payments be made by EFT systems, employers can pay through direct deposit accounts, and government may directly deposit social security or welfare checks into consumers' accounts.

The Act prohibits a person from requiring a consumer to repay a loan by means of preauthorized EFTs as a condition of extending credit to the consumer. In one case, the court interpreted this provision to mean that as long as no extension of credit is involved, sellers, landlords, or other creditors are allowed to require repayment by EFT.[137]

§8.24 Civil Liability of Financial Institutions

The Electronic Fund Transfer Act has two provisions regarding civil liability of financial institutions. One governs the financial institution's liability for failing to make or stop an EFT according to the consumer's order.[138] The other deals with the financial institution's liability for failing to comply with the provisions of the Act in general.[139] Determining the damages resulting from

---

[135] EFT in the United States, Policy Recommendations and the Public Interest, The Final Report of the National Commission on Electronic Fund Transfers 41 (1977).

[136] 15 USC §1693k.

[137] *In re* Park Knoll Assoc v New York State Div of Hous & Community Renewal, Index No 11918/78 (NY Sup Ct Sept 26, 1978).

[138] 15 USC §1693h.

[139] 15 USC §1693m.

these two types of violations is not an easy task, due to the lack of specificity of the Act's relevant provisions.[140]

§8.25 —Liability for Failure to Make or Stop EFT

A financial institution shall be liable to a consumer for all damages proximately caused by its failure to make an EFT, in accordance with the terms and conditions of the account, in the proper amount, or in a timely manner, when properly instructed to do so by the consumer.[141] The financial institution, however, is not liable when:

1. The consumer's account has insufficient funds and the insufficiency does not result from any error of the financial institution
2. The funds are subject to legal process or other encumbrances which prevent the transfer
3. The transfer exceeds an established credit limit
4. An ATM has insufficient cash to complete the transaction, unless the insufficiency is due to the financial institution's failure to credit a deposit of funds to the consumer's account which would have provided sufficient funds to make the transfer[142]
5. As otherwise provided by the Board[143]

So far, the Board has not provided any regulation concerning this matter. The Board has indicated only that the financial institution can limit its liability by including exculpatory language in the account agreement since, under the Act, the financial institution's liability is based on its failure to make an EFT, *in accordance* with the terms and conditions of an account.[144] This option given the financial institution must be read in conjunction with the Act's prohibition of agreement between a consumer and any other person which may constitute a waiver of any right conferred or cause of action created by the Act.[145]

Section 1-102(3) of the Uniform Commercial Code may give an answer to this seeming contradiction. UCC §1-102(3) provides that "the obligations of good faith, diligence, reasonableness and care . . . may not be disclaimed by agreement but the parties may by agreement determine the standards by which the performance of such obligations is to be measured if such standards are not manifestly unreasonable."

---

[140] *See* Down, *Damages Under the Federal Electronic Fund Transfer Act: A Proposed Construction of Sections 910 and 915*, 23 Am Bus LJ 1 (1985); *See also,* Hewes, III & Preston, *Is There a Time Bomb in the Electronic Fund Transfer Act*, 100 Banking LJ 274 (1983).

[141] 15 USC §1693h(a)(1).

[142] 15 USC §1693h(a)(2).

[143] 15 USC §1693h(a)(1).

[144] 44 Fed Reg 59,464 (1979). *See* Brandel & Oliff, *The Electronic Fund Transfer Act: A Primer*, 40 Ohio St LJ 531, 562 n 164 (1979).

[145] 15 USC §1693l.

A financial institution shall also be liable to the consumer for failing to carry out the consumer's stop payment order of a preauthorized transfer from the consumer's account.[146] A financial institution, however, shall not be liable for failure to make or stop an EFT where the financial institution can show that its failure to act resulted from:

1. An act of God or other circumstances beyond its control, that it exercised reasonable care to prevent the occurrence, and that it exercised the required diligence

2. A technical malfunction which was known to the consumer at the time the consumer attempted to initiate an EFT or, if the transfer was preauthorized, at the time such transfer should have occurred[147]

If the failure to make an EFT was not intentional and resulted from a bona fide error, notwithstanding the maintenance of procedures reasonably adopted to avoid any such error, the financial institution shall be liable only for actual damages proved to be a result of,[148] as opposed to "all damages proximately caused" by, the financial institution's failure.

§8.26 —Liability for Noncompliance with EFTA Provisions

Section 915 of the Act,[149] entitled *civil liability*, is a more general liability provision for noncompliance with the provisions of the Act. Under this general liability provision, any person who violates any provision of the EFTA, other than violations for failing to make or stop an EFT according to the terms and conditions of the consumer's account contract, is liable for any actual damages that result from such violation.[150] In addition, if the consumer brings an individual action, the consumer may recover a penalty of not less than $100, but not more than $1,000.[151] This statutory penalty is available even in the absence of any actual damages. The consumer is not entitled to the minimum penalty, however, if a class action is instituted. The total penalty recoverable in a class action or series of class actions arising out of the same violation may not exceed the lesser of $500,000 or 1 per cent of the net worth of the defendant plus the actual damages of each class member.[152] The successful

---

[146] 15 USC §1693h(a)(3).
[147] 15 USC §1693h(b).
[148] 15 USC §1693h(c).
[149] 15 USC §1693m(a)(2)(B).
[150] 15 USC §1693m.
[151] 15 USC §1693m(a)(1)-(2).
[152] 15 USC §1693m(a)(2)(B).

plaintiff shall recover the costs of the action and reasonable attorneys' fees as determined by the court.[153]

In determining what may be recovered, the court must consider, among other factors, the frequency and persistence of the violation, the nature of the violation, and whether the violation is intentional. Additionally, the resources of the defendant, as well as the number of persons adversely affected by the noncompliance, must be considered in a class action.[154]

There are qualifications to the financial institution's general civil liability, however. The financial institution shall not be held liable if it can show by a preponderance of the evidence that the violation was not intentional and resulted from a bona fide error, notwithstanding the use of procedures reasonably designed to avoid the error.[155] The Act further specifies that the financial institution will not be liable for any act or failure to act in good faith in conformity with a rule, regulation, or interpretation or approval by the Board or its official, or use of a model clause offered by the Board, even if such is later rescinded by judicial or other authority.[156]

The financial institution may preempt a lawsuit by notifying the consumer concerned of the failure, making an appropriate adjustment to the consumer's account, and paying actual damages, if any. In the case of failure to make or stop an EFT, the financial institution must pay all damages proximately caused by the failure.[157]

This action must be brought within one year of the alleged violation. Regardless of the amount in controversy, the suit may be brought in a federal district court or in a state court of competent jurisdiction.[158]

If the court finds that a suit was brought in bad faith or for purposes of harassment, it may order the plaintiff to pay the defendant's reasonable attorneys' fees.[159] The legislative history makes it clear that this provision was intended to apply only when an action was "clearly vexatious and without merit."[160]

§8.27 —Computation of Damages

If a financial institution fails to make or stop an EFT, it is liable for *all damages proximately caused* by such a failure. However, only *actual damages* are imposed if the failure is unintentional, or results from a bona fide error, despite the fact that care has been taken to avoid such an error. For any other violation of the

---

[153] 15 USC §1693m(a)(3).

[154] 15 USC §1693m(b).

[155] 15 USC §1693m(c).

[156] 15 USC §1693m(d).

[157] 15 USC §1693m(e).

[158] 15 USC §1693m(g).

[159] 15 USC §1693m(f).

[160] *See* Senate Committee on Banking, Housing & Urban Affairs, Record to accompany S3156, S Rep No 915, 95th Cong, 2d Sess 17 (1978).

provisions of the Act, the financial institution is liable for, in addition to the statutory penalty, only the actual damages sustained by the consumer as a result of the violation. The definitions of *all damages proximately caused* and *actual damages* do not appear anywhere in the Act, nor are they interpreted by Regulation E.

Concerning the financial institution's liability for failing to make or stop an EFT, the drafters' intent was to set the same standards of liability for financial institutions in EFTs that now apply to checking under the Uniform Commercial Code.[161] Regardless of this intent, the Act does not faithfully reflect the UCC approach to this problem. While the Act imposes the same liability for both failure to make an EFT and failure to stop payment, the UCC treats them separately and provides different standards of liability. A failure to make payment is wrongful dishonor under §4-402 of the Uniform Commercial Code, and the failure to make a stop payment is separately dealt with in §4-403.

With respect to wrongful dishonor, UCC §4-402 provides:

> A payor bank is liable to its customer for damages proximately caused by the wrongful dishonor of an item. When the dishonor occurs through mistake liability is limited to actual damages proved, damages may include damages for an arrest or prosecution of the customer or other consequential damages. Whether any consequential damages are proximately caused by the wrongful dishonor is a question of fact to be determined in each case.

Mistake usually has been interpreted as unintentional error. Some courts include in the concept negligent acts such as the bank's mistakenly debiting the customer's account[162] or crediting the deposit to the wrong account.[163] Mistake in wrongful dishonor, however, must be distinguished from the bank's negligence in general defined by the UCC as "failure to exercise ordinary care in handling an item,"[164] for which the measure of damages is simply "the amount of the item reduced by an amount which could not have been realized by the use of ordinary care."[165] The term *mistake* in §4-402 of the UCC was to make clear the drafters' intent not to embrace either tort or contract theory as a basis of the bank's liability.[166]

Mistake or unintentional error is contrasted with intentional or bad faith dishonor. Intentional errors give rise to a claim for proximately caused

---

[161] S Rep No 915, 95th Cong, 2d Sess, *reprinted in* 1978 US Code Cong & Admin News 9403, 9417.

[162] *See* Domayer v Columbus Bank & Trust Co, 151 Ga App 38, 258 SE2d 725 (1979).

[163] Harvey v Michigan Natl Bank, 19 UCC Rep Serv (Callaghan) 906 (Mich Ct Common Pleas 1974). *See* Hewes, III & Preston, *Is There a Time Bomb in the Electronic Fund Transfer Act,* 100 Banking LJ 274, 280-81 (1983).

[164] UCC §4-103(5).

[165] *Id.*

[166] UCC §4-402 comment 2.

damages, while unintentional errors give rise only to actual damages proved. The requirement of actual damages proved in the Uniform Commercial Code was to change the common law rule, which provided that, when a merchant was a customer of a bank, a wrongful dishonor by the bank of an item issued by the merchant was considered defamation per se. The merchant would then recover damages automatically without having to prove that damages had in fact occurred.[167]

Since the intent of Congress in EFTA is to adopt an approach similar to that of the Uniform Commercial Code, the cases decided under the UCC become guidelines for interpretation of the damages provisions of EFTA. Some courts take a narrow view of the term *actual damages*. For example, in *Bank of Louisville Royal v Sims,*[168] the Kentucky Court of Appeals, applying §4-402 of the Uniform Commercial Code on wrongful dishonor, struck down the decision of the lower court granting the consumer damages for two weeks of lost wages and for "illness, harassment, embarrassment and inconvenience." The Kentucky Supreme Court allowed the plaintiff to recover only $1.50 for a telephone call. Professors White and Summers believe the court decided the case erroneously and that the Code drafters intended to allow recovery for mental distress and other intangible property as part of the *actual damages proved.*[169] The authors based their opinion on the third sentence of UCC §4-402, which reads: "If so proximately caused and proved, damages may include damages for an arrest or prosecution of the customer or other consequential damages."

The court in *Kendall Yacht Corp v United California Bank*[170] adopted a more expansive view of the term *actual damages proved.* The court upheld the trial court's finding that, as a result of a mistaken wrongful dishonor, the plaintiff suffered, among other consequences to the plaintiff's reputation and credit, severe mental and emotional distress and marital problems.

The court equated the term *actual damages* with *compensatory damages,* which includes mental and emotional distress as well as injury to reputation. The court reasoned that, since UCC §4-402 explicitly allowed recovery for damages for an arrest or prosecution, and certainly mental and emotional injuries are caused by arrest and prosecution, there was no reason to disallow damages for mental and emotional distress experienced by the plaintiff as a result of the bank's wrongful dishonor.[171] This expansive view, which equates *actual damages* with *damages proximately caused,* or considers compensatory and consequential damages to include even recovery for mental and emotional distress, is generally supported by commentators and courts.[172] If the interpretation of UCC §4-402 is applied to measure the financial institution's civil liability under

---

[167] UCC §4-402 comment 3.

[168] 435 SW2d 57, 7 UCC Rep Serv (Callaghan) 234 (Ky 1968).

[169] White & Summers, Uniform Commercial Code §17-4, at 675 (1980).

[170] 50 Cal App 3d 951, 123 Cal Rptr 848 (1975).

[171] *Id* at 957, 123 Cal Rptr at 854.

[172] *See* Dow, *Damages Under the Electronic Fund Transfer Act: A Proposed Construction of Section 910 and 915,* 23 Am Bus LJ 1, 57 (1985).

EFTA for failure to make a payment, there is no difference in the recovery for intentional and bona fide errors, except for punitive damages.

Concerning stop payment orders, however, there is a difference between the financial institution's liability under the Uniform Commercial Code and the Electronic Fund Transfer Act. Under §4-403(3) of the Uniform Commercial Code, a consumer who seeks to recover from the bank must prove the amount of loss resulting from the bank's payment contrary to the consumer's stop payment order. Thus, if the stop payment order is unjustified, as when a buyer orders the bank not to honor a check issued to the seller in payment for goods even though they conform to the contract, the buyer cannot hold the bank liable if it pays. Here, the consumer cannot prove that the consumer has incurred a loss, since the seller has the right to payment anyway. Furthermore, even if the buyer can prove the loss, as when the goods are defective and the buyer has no obligation to pay, the bank can still recover the amount it must recredit to the consumer's account by subrogating to the rights of the consumer or of a holder in due course against the seller who would be unjustly enriched by the bank's payment.[173]

EFTA does not adopt the UCC distinction. The financial institution will be equally liable for the failure to carry out the consumer's order either to execute an EFT or stop an EFT transaction. Regarding the failure to stop an EFT order, the financial institution will always be liable regardless of whether the consumer is or is not unjustly enriched as a result of the bank's failure. Many banks deplore this legal arrangement.[174]

The EFTA position may be justified because, unlike the UCC, whose purpose is to govern the professional commercial world, EFTA is a consumer-oriented statute. Congress has rightly decided that financial institutions are in a better position to protect themselves than consumers.

§8.28   Criminal Liability

In addition to civil liability, a provider of EFT services may be criminally liable for knowingly and willfully:

---

[173] This bank's right of subrogation, a marvel of the banks' lobbying, is provided in UCC §4-407 as follows:

> If a payor bank has paid an item over the stop payment order of the drawer or maker or otherwise under circumstances giving a basis for objection by the drawer or maker, to prevent unjust enrichment and only to the extent necessary to prevent loss to the bank by reason of its payment of the item, the payor bank shall be subrogated to the rights
> (a) of any holder in due course on the items against the drawer or maker, and
> (b) of the payee or any other holder of the item against the drawer or maker either on the item or under the transaction out of which the item arose; and
> (c) of the drawer or maker against the payee or any other holder of the item with respect to the transaction out of which the item arose.

[174] *See* Hewes & Preston, *Is There a Time Bomb in the Electronic Fund Transfer Act,* 100 Banking LJ 274, 280 (1983).

1. Giving false or inaccurate information
2. Failing to provide information required to be disclosed by the Act or Regulation
3. Otherwise failing to comply with any provision of the Act[175]

The Act also imposes criminal liability for violations of the Act which affect interstate or foreign commerce. Among these violations are the fraudulent use or transportation of lost, stolen, forged, or counterfeited debit instruments to obtain $1,000 or more worth of money, goods, or services.[176] A *debit instrument* means a card, code, or any device which allows a person to initiate an electronic fund transfer and which is not a check, a draft, or similar paper instrument.[177] A person who is criminally liable may be fined up to $5,000 and imprisoned for up to one year, or both.[178]

§8.29   Relationship of EFTA to State Law

Prior to the enactment of EFTA, a majority of the states had laws regulating electronic fund transfers. However, only a small minority of states had on their books provisions aimed at the protection of the consumer using them

EFTA does not preempt such state laws automatically. EFTA preempts state laws only when those laws are inconsistent with the provisions of EFTA, and then only to the extent of the inconsistency. As a rule, a state law is not inconsistent if it affords greater consumer protection than that afforded by the Act.[179]

Congress gives the Board the power to determine when a state law is inconsistent with the Act. In using this power, the Board sets forth standards for preemption of state law. An inconsistency causing preemption may exist when state law:

1. Requires or permits a practice or act which is prohibited by EFTA or Regulation E
2. Provides for consumer liability for unauthorized withdrawals which exceeds the liability imposed by the Act and Regulation E
3. Provides for longer time periods than the Act and Regulation E for error correction, or fails to require the recrediting of the consumer's account during the institution's extended period for investigating errors
4. Provides for disclosures of documents that are different in content

---

[175] 15 USC §1693n(a).
[176] 15 USC §1693n(b).
[177] 15 USC §1693n(c).
[178] 15 USC §1693n(a)-(b).
[179] 15 USC §1693q.

from those required by the Act and Regulation E, except when the disclosures related to rights are greater under the state law.[180]

Regulation E provides procedures for a determination of a preemption. In essence, any request for the determination must give the Board sufficient information concerning the state law in question to provide for the full comparison of the relevant state law and the provisions of the Act. It must also provide for a comparison of the civil and criminal liability between state law and the Act.[181]

In spite of these guidelines, it is not always easy to deal with the interplay of state and federal law. Since federal law preempts state law only to the extent of inconsistency, one may have to deal with both. Federal law may apply to certain aspects of the case, while state law controls other aspects of the case. To what extent one would be able to select aspects of the federal and state laws is yet to be seen. But the language of EFTA stating that state law is preempted *to the extent that it is inconsistent* seems to indicate that such a choice is possible. Furthermore, in an Official Staff Interpretation of the Michigan statute, a dual application of state and federal law is accepted. The Staff's opinion states:

> The scope of the Michigan statute appears to be narrower than that of the Federal EFT Act and seems to cover only terminal-based transfers. To the extent that this is the case, the Federal provisions will continue to govern all electronic fund transfers that are outside the scope of the State statute.[182]

As an example, let us compare Michigan law and the federal EFT Act dealing with the issue of consumers' liability for unauthorized transfers.

Michigan adopts the solution recommended by the National Commission on Electronic Fund Transfers which absolves the consumer from any liability if the consumer is not negligent. The consumer's negligence is defined objectively. It includes:

1. Writing the PIN on the card or other access device
2. Keeping the PIN with the card or other access device
3. Voluntarily permitting the access device (PIN and card) to come into the possession of one who makes, or causes to be done, unauthorized use

Absent negligence so defined, the consumer will not be liable for *any* amount. However, the consumer shall be liable for the full amount of any subsequent unauthorized use if the consumer fails to notify the financial institution of an unauthorized use within 30 days after the receipt of the statement containing an unauthorized use.[183]

---

[180] 12 CFR §205.12(b).

[181] 12 CFR §205.12(c).

[182] 46 Fed Reg 19217 (Mar 30, 1981).

[183] Mich Comp Laws Ann (West 1987) §488.14 Mich Stats Ann §23.1137 (Callaghan 1983).

Comparing Michigan EFT law with the three-tiered liability of the EFT Act, it is not clear which law is more protective of the consumer. Under federal law, the consumer's negligence is not considered in computing the consumer's liability, except to the extent that the consumer fails to give notice of the loss or theft of the card and of the unauthorized transfer appearing on the consumer's account statement. As a result, any consumer who is reasonably diligent in reporting the loss or theft of the card or its unauthorized use is liable for no more than $50, or the amount of actual withdrawal, whichever is less. However, such a consumer would have no liability at all under Michigan law.

On the other hand, if the consumer writes the consumer's PIN on the access device, one of the three acts defined as negligence under Michigan law, such a consumer would be fully liable under Michigan law but would, if proper notice is given, have a maximum liability of $50 or $500 only under federal law. In addition, if the consumer can prove that the financial institution did not exercise reasonable care to prevent the loss, the consumer may be freed of any liability under Michigan law by claiming contributory negligence. Under the circumstances, is Michigan law or federal law more protective?[184] Following is the ruling of the Board on the issue:

> Section 14 of the State statute, which governs the consumer's liability for unauthorized use of an account, is inconsistent with §205.6 of Regulation E. The State provision is not more protective of the consumer and is preempted. The negligence standard contained in the State statute could result in the consumer's increased exposure to liability. Under the State statute, negligent consumers appear to be liable for all unauthorized transfer, and nonnegligent consumers may be liable for such transfer if they fail to notify a financial institution within 30 days of an unauthorized transfer. Regulation E limits liability based on the promptness of a consumer's notice to the financial institution, and imposes unlimited liability for subsequent transfer after 60 days have elapsed, rather than after 30 days as the State statute provides. Preemption of a negligence standard is also supported by the EFT Act's legislative history which shows that the Congress rejected a negligence standard in the Federal law in favor of liability based on promptness of notification.[185]

As the Michigan example shows, it is not always clear whether state law or federal law is more protective of the consumer.

---

[184] See White & Summers, Uniform Commercial Code §16-9, at 640-45 (1980).
[185] 12 CFR §205.12 and Official Staff Interpretation.

9

Assignment of Claims and Preservation of Consumers' Claims and Defenses

§9.01 Introduction

A consumer buys goods from a seller. Although short of cash, the consumer may still obtain the goods by using one of several methods.

First, the consumer can obtain credit directly from the seller, with or without a down payment, in return for an oral promise to pay the balance in the future. This gives the seller a right to payment against the consumer for the goods sold. This right is described as an *account,* or an *account receivable.*[1]

Second, if the seller is not satisfied with a simple promise, the seller may demand from the consumer a writing or writings. The writing may consist of a single promissory note. If it is executed alone, it is called an *instrument.*[2] The instrument may be negotiable or nonnegotiable. The Uniform Commercial Code (UCC) defines a *negotiable instrument* as any writing payable to order or to bearer, which contains an unconditional promise or order to pay a sum certain in money on demand or at a definite time.[3] Any instrument not fitting this description is considered *nonnegotiable.*

The promissory note also may be executed with a security agreement which gives the seller a security interest in the goods sold. In this case, the writings are called *chattel paper,* which is defined by the UCC as "a writing or writings which evidence both a monetary obligation and a security in, or a lease of, specific goods."[4] The promissory note and the security agreement may be executed in a single document or in separate documents.

Third, rather than extending credit itself to the buyer, the seller may refer the buyer to a financing institution which may or may not be connected with the seller. The financing institution will then extend a direct loan to the buyer, enabling the buyer to use the cash to obtain the goods from the seller.

---

[1] UCC §9-106 defines an *account* to mean "any right to payment for goods sold or leased or for services rendered which is not evidenced by an instrument or chattel paper, whether or not it has been earned by performance."

[2] UCC §9-105(1)(i) defines *instrument* as "a negotiable instrument (defined in Section 3-104), or a certificated security (defined in Section 8-102) or any other writing which evidences a right to the payment of money and is not itself a security agreement or lease and is of a type which is in ordinary course of business transferred by delivery with any necessary indorsement or assignment."

[3] UCC §3-104 provides:

    (1) Any writing to be a negotiable instrument within this Article must:

    (a) be signed by the maker or drawer; and

    (b) contain an unconditional promise or order to pay a sum certain in money and no other promise, order, obligation or power given by the maker or drawer except as authorized by this Article; and

    (c) be payable on demand or at a definite time; and

    (d) be payable to order or to bearer.

[4] UCC §9-105(1)(b).

§9.02   Discounting

Except in the case of a direct loan, the seller may discover, after extending credit to the buyer, that cash is needed before the buyer's obligation to pay has matured. The seller may need this cash, for example, to replenish inventory, purchase raw materials, or pay overhead expenses. In this case, the seller may assign the claim against the buyer to a financial institution, generally at a discount representing the time value of the money. Either the seller (the *assignor*) may collect the claim directly from the buyer (the *account debtor*) on behalf of the financial institution, or the financial institution (the *assignee*) may assume that burden itself. In the latter case, the assignee will notify the account debtor of the assignment and request that the payment be made directly to it.

Assignments fall into two categories: assignments *with recourse* and assignments *without recourse.* In an assignment with recourse, the assignor retains responsibility to the financial institution in case the account debtor defaults. This assignment may be construed as credit given by the financial institution to the seller in return for a security interest in the seller's chattel paper or account.

In an assignment without recourse, the assignee bears the risk of the consumer's default. This type of assignment may be construed simply as the sale of the account or chattel paper by the seller to the financial institution, with the risk of loss upon the latter. While the nature of the business involved generally determines the type of assignment chosen,[5] the consumer's duty to pay remains the same.

§9.03   Consumer's Duty to Pay and Seller's Duty to Perform

Suppose the goods which the consumer obtains on credit are defective. Must the consumer still pay? If the transaction involves only the buyer and the seller, the seller's failure of consideration will abrogate the buyer's duty to pay. The buyer may use one of several theories here in defense, including failure of consideration or breach of warranty in contract law, and fraud or misrepresentation in tort.

Under the law of assignment, the assignee simply *steps into the shoes* of the assignor. This rule prevents the assignee from acquiring additional rights. Therefore, if the consumer can show that he or she has no duty to pay the seller-assignor, then the consumer will also avoid the duty to pay the financier-assignee. The latter may defeat this rule by using several methods, all with the same goal of isolating the consumer's duty to pay from the seller's duty to perform. These methods include:

---

[5] UCC §9-502 comment 4 states that the determination of whether a particular assignment constitutes a sale or a transfer for security is left to the courts.

1. The use of a waiver of defense clause in the contract between the seller and the consumer
2. The use of the holder in due course doctrine
3. The use of the direct loan concept

§9.04 —Waiver of Defense Clauses

A typical waiver of defense clause reads as follows:

> The buyer hereby acknowledges notice that the contract may be assigned and that the assignees will rely upon the agreement contained in this paragraph, and agrees that the liability of the buyer to any assignee shall be immediate and absolute and not affected by any default whatsoever of the seller assigning this contract; and in order to induce assignees to purchase this contract the buyer further agrees not to set up any claim against such seller as a defense, counterclaim or offset to any action by any assignee for the unpaid balance of the purchase price or for possession of the property.[6]

The waiver of defense clause usually appears in small print in the sale or lease agreement or in the instrument evidencing the seller's right to payment. As stated, the main purpose of this clause is the isolation of the assignee's right to payment from the seller's duty to perform. Such a waiver requires the consumer to pay, even though the consumer has purchased defective goods or has been defrauded by the seller.

§9.05 —The Holder in Due Course Doctrine

Engendered by the negotiable instruments law, the holder in due course doctrine applies each time the instrument executed by a debtor qualifies as negotiable. Lord Mansfield first expounded the doctrine in 1758 in the case of *Miller v Race*.[7] In this case, negotiable instruments drawn on the Bank of England, called bills of exchange, were stolen and subsequently sold to an innocent purchaser. Lord Mansfield held that the law should regard such instruments as money. As a consequence, a good faith purchaser of the instruments, having no notice of any claim or defense pertaining to them, should prevail over all other parties, especially over the owner or the person obliged to pay the instruments.

The *holder in due course* term appeared in the English Bills of Exchange Act of 1882. American courts immediately seized the concept, and the Negotiable Instruments Law of 1896 incorporated it. The Uniform Commercial Code reaffirmed the doctrine. The UCC states that to become a holder in due course,

---

[6] Unico v Owen, 50 NJ 101,232 A2d 405 (1967).

[7] 97 Eng Rep 398 (1758).

a person must take the instrument "for value; and in good faith; and without notice that it is overdue, or has been dishonored, or of any defense against or claim to it on the part of any person."[8] Once a person qualifies as a holder in due course, such a person will cut off most claims and defenses of the obligor on the instrument.[9]

The effects of the holder in due course doctrine may be seen in *Universal CIT Credit Corp v Ingel*.[10] In this case, the defendant-consumer purchased goods from Allied Aluminum, agreeing to pay for them in installments. When the goods proved to be defective, the defendant stopped the payments. The plaintiff, to whom Allied had assigned the note and the contract, brought the action to force the consumer to pay the remainder.

In upholding a directed verdict for the plaintiff, the court stated that evidence failed to show that the note and the contract were "part of the same instrument,"[11] and any variance between the note and the contract was not the court's concern.[12] The consumer's duty to pay the assignee, who qualified as a holder in due course, existed independently of the seller's duty to perform. The court brushed aside the defendant's argument that the plaintiff had *reason to know* of Allied's fraud. The court refused to admit evidence that would have shown Allied's widely known history of fraudulent business practices. The court also refused to admit testimony indicating the possibility of fraud and breach of warranty in the particular transaction involving the defendant. In justifying the exclusion of a letter urging payment, which the plaintiff had mailed to the defendant, acknowledging Allied's deficient performance, the court stated, "it is immaterial that the plaintiff may have found out about Allied's allegedly fraudulent representations after the note was purchased."[13]

As this case shows, the holder in due course doctrine cuts off *personal* defenses which are otherwise available to the defendant against the seller, including failure of consideration, fraud, and misrepresentation. Only *real* defenses, such as infancy, illegality, duress, and fraud in the factum are preserved.[14] Real

---

8 UCC §3-302(1).

9 UCC §3-305.

10 347 Mass 119, 196 NE2d 847 (1964).

11 *Id* at 123, 196 NE2d at 850.

12 *Id* at 124, 196 NE2d at 857

13 *Id* at 125, 196 NE2d at 852.

14 UCC §3-305, defining the rights of a holder in due course, states:

    To the extent that a holder is a holder in due course he takes the instrument free from (1) all claims to it on the part of any person; and
    (2) all defenses of any party to the instrument with whom the holder has not dealt except

        (a)   infancy, to the extent that it is a defense to a simple contract, and
        (b)   such other incapacity, or duress, or illegality of the transaction, as renders the obligation of the party a nullity; and
        (c)   such misrepresentation as has induced the party to sign the instrument with neither knowledge nor reasonable opportunity to obtain knowledge of its character or its essential terms; and

defenses offer little protection to the consumer, because situations giving rise to them occur much less frequently than those yielding personal defenses. Furthermore, state laws vary widely in their recognition and acceptance of real defenses.

The law further strengthens the position of the holder in due course by applying the subjective test in determining whether a holder acts in good faith.[15] This test is often referred to as the *pure heart, empty head* test. It deems that a person acts in good faith if the person lacks knowledge of the defense or claim, even though this appears unreasonable or negligent. Under this test, the court will grant holder in due course status unless the consumer can show that the holder possessed actual knowledge of the facts giving rise to the consumer's defense or claim.

The drafters of the Uniform Commercial Code originally included an objective commercial standard in the good faith provision of §3-302(1)(b), which defines a holder in due course. According to this provision, good faith required the purchaser to observe the *reasonable commercial standards* of the business or trade in which the purchaser was engaged.[16] The drafters explained that this requirement made explicit that which had long been implicit in the case law treatment of the good faith concept.

Attorneys representing New York banking interests sprang to the energetic defense of the subjective test. They successfully argued that it, not the objective test, had long been the law in New York. The drafters withdrew the offending clause and as a result, the pure heart, empty head standard determines good faith. If the financier does not have actual knowledge of the facts giving rise to the customer's defense or claim against the seller, then the financier qualifies as a holder in due course, regardless of the circumstances.

The case of *Graham v White-Phillips Co*[17] illustrates the extent to which courts will go in applying the subjective test. In this case, a thief had stolen a number of negotiable bonds from the plaintiff. Notice of the theft had been given to dealers throughout the country, describing the stolen bonds. The Supreme Court assumed, as did the lower court, that the defendant, the White-Phillips Company, had received the notice. The defendant testified, however, that when it purchased the bonds it had forgotten the notice and, therefore, took them without actual knowledge of the theft. The trial court held that as a matter of law, the defendant was not a holder in due course.

The Seventh Circuit Court of Appeals and the Supreme Court agreed that the lower court had erred. The Court stated that the negotiable instrument law must be interpreted in light of the goal of the free circulation of negotiable

---

    (d)   discharge in insolvency proceedings; and

    (e)   any other discharge of which the holder has notice when he takes the instrument.

[15] UCC §1-201(19) provides: " 'Good faith' means honesty in fact in the conduct or transaction concerned."

[16] *See* Braucher, *The Legislative History of the UCC,* 58 Colum L Rev 798, 812, 813 (1958).

[17] 296 US 27 (1935).

paper. In support, the Court cited a Supreme Court of Michigan decision. That court held that a purchaser of stolen negotiable bonds may acquire valid title as a holder in due course, even though the purchaser had received prior notice of the theft.[18]

The Uniform Commercial Code specifically states that cases like *Graham v White-Phillips Co* will not be overruled by the Code.[19] Therefore, the consumer's only hope for success is to show that the holder in due course took the paper with notice of the defense or claim.

The Code employs an objective test for notice. It provides that a person has notice of a fact when "from all the facts and circumstances known to him at the time in question he has reason to know that it exists."[20] Although the consumer would appear to benefit more from this test than from the subjective test of good faith, the consumer's chance of defeating the financier's holder in due course status is still precarious at best. For example, if the seller assigns the contract to the financier prior to the delivery date, and the consumer uses the defense of failure of delivery, then the notice argument does not help the consumer at all. Knowledge that the instrument was issued in return for an executory promise does not constitute the *notice* that will deprive the purchaser of holder in due course status.[21]

These standards will permit the consumer to win in a clear-cut case like *Financial Credit v Williams*,[22] but not in a marginal case like *Waterbury Savings Bank v Jaroszewsky*.[23] In *Financial Credit*, the consumer won because evidence showed that the financier had purchased notes from the seller at an 80 per cent discount, even though, throughout the community, newspapers had published accounts of the seller's fraudulent activity. In *Waterbury*, the consumer lost because he could not establish the financier's knowledge of more than three or four other complaints about the seller's goods at the time the financier accepted the notes.

The holder in due course doctrine thus effectively insulates the consumer's duty to pay from the seller's duty to perform. Under the traditional law dealing with these cases, the consumer usually loses.

How is such a nefarious theory justified? At its inception in the eighteenth century, the scarcity of currency required that the integrity of bills and drafts, which passed from hand to hand, be ensured. The doctrine provided this

---

[18] Merchants Natl Bank v Detroit Trust Co, 258 Mich 526, 537, 242 NW 739, 743 (1932).

[19] UCC §1-201(25) comment.

[20] UCC §1-201(25).

[21] UCC §3-304(4)(b) states:

> Knowledge of the following facts does not of itself give the purchaser notice of a defense or claim: . . .
> (b) that it was issued or negotiated in return for an executory promise or accompanied by a separate agreement, unless the purchaser has notice that a defense or claim has arisen from the terms thereof; . . .

[22] 246 Md 575, 229 A2d 712 (1967).

[23] 4 Conn Cir Ct 620, 238 A2d 446 (1967).

assurance, although today this argument is no longer valid, currency being no longer scarce. Also, originally, the doctrine protected the commercial paper market, a justification which may still have merit today. Advocates of the doctrine contend that its abolition would inhibit the flow of commerce by making financiers reluctant to advance credit to sellers. They raise the specter of a strangled market place, where only merchants with large cash flows and substantial financial resources could compete. Many also insist that the holder in due course doctrine has been a major force in making the United States the leading financial and industrial power in the world. Although these arguments have their merits, they are by no means conclusive.[24]

From the time of *Miller v Race* up to the beginning of the twentieth century, the obligors on notes and drafts were generally powerful financial institutions, such as the banks. The strength of these institutions justified the law that held them to their promise, regardless of the underlying transaction, when a good faith purchaser of the instrument is involved. With the advent of the consumer era, the consumer, not the bank, is the person who makes the promise to pay. The law must respond to this new situation by restricting the holder in due course doctrine in consumer transactions.

Also, the argument that the doctrine protects the commercial paper market is no longer persuasive. As Professor Rosenthal points out, notes signed by consumers no longer pass from hand to hand. Today, they are negotiated only once, by the seller to the lender. In the case of checks, negotiability plays almost no role, since the drawer of the check usually gets it back after payment.[25] The injustice which the holder in due course doctrine serves to the consumer is manifest, and consumer groups understandably clamor for change. Fortunately, changes have begun to occur, through court decisions, state statutes, and federal legislation.

§9.06   Decisional Law: The Doctrine of Close-Connectedness

Under traditional law, the holder in due course is protected against the buyer's claims or defenses against the seller because the holder in due course is deemed not to be party to the sale transaction between buyer and seller. Therefore, if one can show that the holder is a party to the underlying transaction, the holder will no longer be immune from the buyer's claims or defenses. As early as 1937, a New York court recognized that, in many instances,

The Finance Company [the assignee, a holder in due course] and the

---

[24] *See* Hudak & Carter, *Holder in Due Course Doctrine: Historical Perspective and Development (pt I),* 9 UCC LJ 165 (Fall 1976); Murphy, *Another Assault Upon the Citadel: Limiting the Use of Negotiable Notes and Waiver of Defense Clauses in Consumer Sales,* 29 Ohio St LJ 667 (1968).

[25] Rosenthal, *Negotiability—Who Needs It?,* 71 Colum L Rev 375 (1971).

merchant-seller are as a fact engaged in one business, like Longfellow's description of man and woman, useless one without the other. To pretend that they are separate and distinct enterprises is to draw the veil of fiction over the face of fact. . . . The Finance Company, being a de facto part of a great conditional sale commercial machine, should be no more allowed to escape from the effects of the misrepresentation of the salesman than is the merchant himself.[26]

The first case expressing the close-connectedness doctrine was *Commercial Credit Co v Childs*.[27] In this case, Childs purchased a car from Arkansas Motors, Inc. and executed a note in payment for the car. Arkansas Motors subsequently assigned the note to Commercial Credit Company. Childs refused to pay the note on Commercial Credit's request, arguing that Arkansas Motors induced him to buy the car through fraudulent misrepresentation. Commercial Credit invoked the holder in due course doctrine in an effort to repossess the car. The court declared,

We think appellant [Commercial Credit] was so closely connected with the entire transaction or with the deal, that it cannot be heard to state that it, in good faith, was an innocent purchaser of the instrument for value before maturity. It financed the deal, prepared the instrument, and on the day it was executed took an assignment of it from Arkansas Motors, Inc. Even before it was executed it prepared the written assignment thereon to itself. Rather than being a purchaser of the instrument after its execution it was to all intents and purposes a party to the agreement and instrument from the beginning.[28]

Thus, with the close-connectedness doctrine, the common law courts commence the erosion of the holder in due course. The court in *Unico v Owen*[29] resoundingly affirmed the close-connectedness doctrine three decades later. The facts of this classic case are familiar. Under a printed form contract, Universal Stereo Corporation sold to Owen 140 record albums and a stereo record player for $698. Owen made a down payment of $30. He agreed to pay the balance, which amounted to $819.72, including fees and interest, in 36 equal monthly installments. Universal delivered 12 albums at the inception of the transaction and agreed to deliver the remainder every six months until completion. The contract which Owen signed provided that

if the buyer executed a promissory note . . . in the amount of the time balance indicated, said note is not in payment thereof, but is a negotiable

---

[26] Buffalo Indus Park v De Marzio, 162 Misc 742, 744-45, 296 NYS 783, 785, 786 (NY City Civ Ct 1937).

[27] 199 Ark 1073, 137 SW2d 260 (1940).

[28] *Id* at 1077, 137 SW2d at 262.

[29] 50 NJ 101, 232 A2d 405 (1967).

instrument separate and apart from this contract, even though at the time of execution it may be temporarily attached hereto by perforation or otherwise.[30]

Owen signed the printed notes which Universal presented with the contract. Both the notes and contract contained a clause in fine print which stated that the contract could be assigned and that

> . . . the liability of the Buyer to any assignee shall be immediate and absolute and not affected by any default whatever of the Seller signing this contract . . . The Buyer further agrees not to set up any claim against such Seller as a defense, counterclaim or offset to any action by any assignee for the unpaid balance of the purchase price or for possession of the property.[31]

Universal failed to deliver the albums, and Owen's attempts to contact the company were unsuccessful. Owen therefore stopped payment on the notes. Unico, the assignee of Universal's notes, brought suit against Owen for the balance due on the notes (some $500) plus penalties and attorneys' fees.

The court first addressed the issue of whether Unico qualified as a holder in due course. If Unico did, then Owen would be prevented from using the defense of Universal's failure of consideration in refusing payment to Unico. In answering this question, the court carefully limited the scope of its holding to "the problem of consumer goods financing,"[32] as opposed to a standard business transaction.

The court indicated that, because the contract was an adhesion contract, the buyer and seller did not stand at arm's length. Even in the rare case in which the consumer did read a contract's fine print, the court pointed out that the average consumer would not understand the contract's legal jargon. The court recognized the importance, in cases involving consumer financing, of balancing the twin interests of commercial paper negotiability and consumer protection, but the court concluded that the holder of the paper "should not be permitted to isolate itself behind the fictional fence of the Negotiable Instruments Law."[33]

The court then scrutinized the relationship between Universal and Unico. As a partnership formed to finance Universal, Unico discounted up to 35 per cent of Universal's accounts receivable. Unico also held substantial control over Universal's business operation, including sales contracts and credit qualifications of Universal's customers.

The court ultimately held that Unico's connection with Universal's entire operation was too close to permit the determination that Unico acted as a good

---

[30] *Id* at 105, 232 A2d at 407.
[31] *Id* at 106, 232 A2d at 408.
[32] *Id* at 110, 232 A2d at 410.
[33] *Id* at 113, 232 A2d at 412.

faith, innocent purchaser for value. Instead, Unico had acted as a party to the agreement and from this could not be insulated. The court concluded:

> For purposes of consumer goods transactions, we hold that where the seller's performance is executory in character and when it appears from the totality of the arrangements between dealer and financier that the financier has had a substantial voice in setting the standards for the underlying transaction, or has approved the standards established by the dealer, and has agreed to take all or a predetermined or substantial quantity of the negotiable paper which is backed by such standards, the financier should be considered a participant in the original transaction and therefore not entitled to holder in due course status.[34]

Linking it to the doctrine of unconscionability under §2-302 of the Uniform Commercial Code,[35] the court also declared in dicta that the waiver of defense clause was contrary to public policy.

Other courts have followed *Unico v Owen* in affirming the close-connectedness doctrine and have refused holder in due course status to the assignee of consumer paper. These courts relied on several theories to support this conclusion.

Notice, Bad Faith

The courts in *Childs* and *Unico* employed this rationale. In *Childs*, the court stated that Commercial Credit Company "was so closely connected with the entire transaction, or with the deal, that it cannot be heard to say that it, in good faith, was an innocent purchaser of the instrument for value before maturity."[36] Similarly, in *Unico*, the New Jersey Supreme Court noted that "[t]he more the holder knows about the underlying transaction, and particularly the more he controls or participates or becomes involved in it, the less he fits the role of a good faith purchaser for value. . . ."[37]

The *Childs* court imposed upon the assignee the duty, before taking an assignment, to inquire whether fraud and misrepresentation had been used to

---

[34] *Id* at 122, 232 A2d at 417.

[35] UCC §2-302:

> (1) If the court as a matter of law finds the contract or any clause of the contract to have been unconscionable at the time it was made the court may refuse to enforce the contract, or it may enforce the remainder of the contract without the unconscionable clause, or it may so limit the application of any unconscionable clause as to avoid any unconscionable result.
> (2) When it is claimed or appears to the court that the contract or any clause thereof may be unconscionable the parties shall be afforded a reasonable opportunity to present evidence as to its commercial setting, purpose and effect to aid the court in making the determination.

[36] 199 Ark at 1077, 137 SW2d at 262.

[37] 50 NJ at 110, 232 A2d at 410.

obtain the buyer's signature.[38] Here the court appears to have abandoned the subjective test of good faith. In *Norman v Worldwide Distributors, Inc,*[39] the court used the same reasoning: "Under all the circumstances, Peoples (the assignee) was bound to inquire further into the operation of the seller of these notes, and having made no inquiry it is held as though it had knowledge of all that inquiry would have revealed."[40]

In *Mutual Finance Co v Martin,*[41] after discussing the facts of the case, the Supreme Court of Florida concluded that a connection did exist between the finance company and the seller. Therefore, "the finance company had such notice of the note's infirmity. . . ."[42] The Supreme Court of Kansas in *Kaw Valley State Bank & Trust Co v Riddle* [43] also pointed to the facts establishing the close connection between lender and seller and concluded that the lender "had reason to know" that the defense of failure of consideration existed.[44]

Other courts did not distinguish between actual knowledge, notice, or the reasonable man standard of "should have known." Instead, they concluded simply that the financier acted in bad faith. In *Gross v Appelgren,*[45] the court stated: "If the Bank did not have actual knowledge of all the fraudulent misrepresentations made by the representatives of [the seller], it most assuredly had knowledge of sufficient facts that its action in taking the instrument, amounted to bad faith."[46]

The Principal-Agent Relationship between Lender and Seller

This is another theory employed by the courts to deny the assignee holder in due course status. Under this theory, the close connection between the financier and the seller constitutes an agency relationship, with the seller acting as the financier's agent. The court in *Calvert Credit Corp v Williams* [47] adopted this approach. In this case, the consumers defaulted in their payments to the contract holder after the television sets which they had purchased proved to be defective. In refusing the finance company the right to demand payment from the consumers, the court stated:

> Appellant [the finance company] prearranged finance charges and

---

[38] 199 Ark at 1078, 137 SW2d at 262.

[39] 202 Pa Super 53, 195 A2d 115 (1963).

[40] *Id* at 59, 195 A2d at 118.

[41] 63 So 2d 649 (Fla 1953).

[42] *Id* 653.

[43] 219 Kan 550, 549 P2d 927 (1976).

[44] *Id* 556, 549 P2d at 933.

[45] 171 Colo 7, 467 P2d 789 (1970).

[46] *Id* at 19, 467 P2d at 795. For an excellent treatment of the close-connectedness doctrine, see Comment, *The Close-Connectedness Doctrine: Preserving Consumer Rights in Credit Transactions,* 33 Ark L Rev 490 (1979).

[47] 244 A2d 494 (DC 1968).

approved the "Referral Plan." It also approved each customer. Without that approval, even a customer who had signed a sales contract was unable to get a television from Interstate [the seller]. The jury could properly have concluded that appellant was so intimately involved in every step of the sales process that Interstate was, in fact, appellant's agent.[48]

The court in *Morgan v Reasor Corp*[49] used the same rationale: "As has been suggested by other courts, the gravamen of the *Commercial Credit* rule is that the seller accepts the buyer's note and extends credit, not on his own behalf, but as an agent for the finance company."[50]

Financier as the Immediate Party to the Consumer Transaction

This rationale, which preserves the consumer's claims and defenses against the financier, takes its premise from §3-305 of the Uniform Commercial Code. Section 3-305 defines the rights of the holder in due course. It states that the holder takes the instrument free from:

1. All claims to it on the part of any person
2. All defenses of any party to the instrument with whom the holder *has not dealt . . . [emphasis added]*

By finding that a close connection exists between the holder of the paper and the seller, a court may deem that, through the seller, the holder has in fact dealt with the consumer. The holder thus loses its immunity from the consumer's claims and defenses against the seller.

The court used this reasoning in *Commercial Credit Co v Childs*.[51] After enumerating the facts revealing the close cooperation between the financier and the seller, the court concluded: "Rather than being a purchaser of the instrument after its execution, it was to all intents and purposes a party to the agreement from the beginning."[52] The court in *Commercial Credit Corp v Orange County Machine Works*[53] followed the same rationale: "In a very real sense, the finance company was a moving force in the transaction from its very inception, and acted as a party to it."[54] The latter case, however, involved a commercial rather than a consumer credit transaction.

In reaching their decisions against the assignees, courts generally invoked

---

[48] *Id* 496.

[49] 69 Cal 2d 881, 447 P2d 638, 73 Cal Rptr 398 (1968).

[50] *Id* at 894, 447 P2d at 647, 73 Cal Rptr at 407; *see* Uniform Commercial Code Commentary, *Judicial and Statutory Limitations on the Rights of a "Holder in Due Course" in Consumer Transactions,* 11 BC Indus & Com L Rev 90, 100, n35 (1971).

[51] 199 Ark 1073, 137 SW 260 (1940).

[52] *Id* at 1077, 137 SW at 262.

[53] 34 Cal 2d 766, 214 P2d 819 (1950).

[54] *Id* at 771, 214 P2d at 822.

all of the above theories, rather than relying on one alone. The common factors in all these decisions were the courts' sympathy for the plight of the defrauded consumer and their conviction that the financier could bear the risk of a seller's fraud better than the consumer.

§9.07 —Appraisal of the Close-Connectedness Doctrine

The development of the close-connectedness doctrine represents a big step in the trend toward consumer protection. However, it is only a step. The doctrine offers at best a chance at episodic relief for the consumer still at the mercy of judicial discretion.[55] Skilled counsel still may manipulate the facts to avoid the appearance of any connection between the financier and the seller.[56]

The entrenchment of the holder in due course doctrine in the legal system gives it a power that many courts are reluctant to ignore. Thus, even when the facts establish a close connection between the financier and seller, the courts may still refuse to recognize it and insist on applying the holder in due course doctrine. Often, the type of consumer involved becomes important, as in the case of *Block v Ford Motor Credit Co.*[57]

In that case, Block purchased a new Ford automobile from a dealer in Baltimore, Maryland. As usual in such cases, Block signed a retail installment contract containing a waiver of defense clause. The contract provided for 36 monthly payments. The dealer then assigned the contract to the Ford Motor Credit Company (note the obvious connection). After making a few monthly payments, Block began deducting 15 per cent from each payment because the credit company had refused to assist him in having the dealer repair the car's

---

[55] Examples of cases in which the holder in due course doctrine is still upheld in consumer transactions are: Cook v Southern Credit Co, 247 Ark 981, 448 SW2d 634 (1970); Westinghouse Credit Corp v Chapman, 129 Ga App 830, 201 SE2d 686 (1973); Steelman v Associated Discount Corp, 121 Ga App 649, 175 SE2d 62 (1970); General Motors Acceptance Corp v Jett, 21 So 2d 595 (La Ct App 1970); Ford Motor Credit Corp v Williams, 225 So 2d 717 (La Ct App 1969); Securities Inv Co v Guillotte, 223 So 2d 256 (La Ct App 1969); Commercial Credit Corp v Carter, 218 So 2d 326 (La Ct App 1969); Fuller v American Aluminum Corp, 249 So 2d 410 (Miss 1971).Examples of cases in which the doctrine is not applied in consumer situations are: Vasquez v Superior Court, 4 Cal 3d 800, 484 P2d 964, 94 Cal Rptr 796 (1971); Gross v Appelgren, 171 Colo 7, 467 P2d 789 (Colo 1970); Fairfield Credit Corp v Donnelly, 158 Conn 543, 264 A2d 547 (1969); Jones v Approved Bancredit Corp, 256 A2d 739 (Del 1969); Rehurek v Chrysler Credit Corp, 262 So 2d 452 (Fla Dist Ct App 1972); Kennard v Reliance, Inc, 257 Md 654, 264 A2d 832 (Md 1970); Alcoa Credit Co v Nickerson, 43 Mass App Ct 1 (1968); General Inv Co v Angelini, 58 NJ 396, 278 A2d 193 (1971); Avco Sec Corp v Post, 42 AD2d 1055, 349 NYS2d 358 (1973); Discount Purchasing Co v Porch, 12 UCC Rep Serv 600 (Tenn Ct App 1973). *See* Rohner, *Holder in Due Course of Consumer Transactions: Requiem, Revival or Reformation?*, 60 Cornell L Rev 503, 517 (1975).

[56] *See* Countryman, *The Holder in Due Course and Other Anochronisms in Consumer Credit*, 52 Tex L Rev 1, 5 (1973).

[57] 286 A2d 228 (DC 1972).

defects. When Block ceased payment altogether, the Ford Motor Credit Company invoked the acceleration clause and sought payment through the court for the contract balance.

Ruling that Block had defaulted in payment, the trial court granted summary judgment to the credit company. The district court of appeals affirmed the decision. The court declined to apply the close-connectedness doctrine, stating that evidence failed to establish that the credit company had a vested interest in the original transaction. The court held further that the credit company's awareness of Block's complaint against the seller did not deprive it of its status as a holder in due course.

The court discounted the fact that the credit company prepared the dealer's business documents, discounted the majority of the dealer's accounts, and had allowed its name to be displayed at the dealer's place of business. In reaching its decision, the court focused instead on Block's level of education and experience. The court found that, because Block was a business executive who held a Ph.D., it could be inferred that Block understood and accepted the terms of the waiver of defense clause, even though the clause appeared on the contract in small print. Furthermore, the court observed that since the seller was still doing business, a remedy remained available to Block through an action for breach of warranty. On facts similar to the *Block* case, a Florida court found that a close connection did exist between the financier and the dealer, and that the financier was not a purchaser in good faith who was free of the buyer's defense.[58]

Also, the extent of the consumer's recovery limits the usefulness of the close-connectedness doctrine. Even when the court denies the financier the status of holder in due course, as in *Unico v Owen* and its progeny, the doctrine only relieves the consumer from further payments. In particular, the consumer cannot recover from the financier the payments already made. In other words, the doctrine can only be used as a shield, not as a sword.

These limitations of the common law doctrine of close-connectedness have led the state legislatures to enact statutes which attempt to further weaken the holder in due course doctrine in consumer transactions.

Statutory Limitations of the Holder in Due Course

§9.08 —The Uniform Commercial Code (UCC)

The UCC is not a consumer-oriented statute. The drafters intended it to apply to the professional world of commercial transactions. They viewed consumer protection as a policy decision best left to the legislatures of the respective states.

The Code, however, does pay some deference to consumer finance and protection. For example, §9-203(4), which deals with the creation of a security

---

[58] Rehurek v Chrysler Credit Corp, 262 So 2d 452 (Fla Dist Ct App 1972).

interest in goods, provides that "a transaction, although subject to this Article, is also subject to any local statute regulating small loans, retail installment sales, and the like, and in the case of conflict between the provisions of this Article and any such statute, the provisions of such statute controls." The comment to that subsection affirms that local statutes regulating consumer finance may supersede the Act.

Section 9-206 deals specifically with assignment of claims and waiver of defense clauses. Section 9-206 permits an assignee, who qualifies as a good faith purchaser, to enforce waiver of defense clauses. Except for real defenses, such a purchaser may cut off all the defenses which the debtor may assert against the assignor. Furthermore, by signing both a negotiable instrument and a security agreement, the buyer implicitly waives these claims and defenses as against the assignee.

Like §9-203(4), §9-206 subjects this rule to local statutes and decisions which establish different rules for buyers or lessees of consumer goods.[59] As Comment 2 of §9-206 explains, the UCC maintains neutrality on the question of whether consumers may execute negotiable notes or waive defenses by contractual agreement. Article 9 does provide, however, that statutes and decisions restricting waiver of defense clauses in consumer transactions do supersede the Act.

§9.09   —Nonuniform Consumer Credit Statutes

While a minority of states have adopted the Uniform Consumer Credit Code to deal with consumer financing, the majority prefer to construct their own solutions through a variety of statutory enactments. However, all have adopted one or more of the following basic approaches aimed at limiting the holder in due course doctrine:

1. The complete abolition of the holder in due course in consumer transactions
2. The prohibition of the use of negotiable instruments other than checks in consumer credit transactions
3. Giving the consumer the right to deny payment to the holder in due course after timely notification of the consumer's defense or claim against the seller

---

[59] UCC §9.206 provides:

(1) Subject to any statute or decision which establishes a different rule for buyers or lessees that he will not assert against an assignee any claim or defense which he may have against the seller or lessor is enforceable by an assignee who takes his assignment for value, in good faith and without notice of a claim or defense, except as to defenses of a type which may be asserted against a holder in due course of a negotiable instrument under the Article on Commercial Paper (Article 3). A buyer who as part of one transaction signs both a negotiable instrument and a security agreement makes such an agreement.

4. Requiring the merger into a single document of the promissory note and the contract, so that all defenses available on the contract will apply to the note[60]

All of these methods have two main goals: the elimination or restriction of the holder in due course doctrine in consumer transactions; and the prohibition or regulation of waiver of defense clauses in consumer contracts.

The Elimination or Restriction of the Holder in Due Course.

These statutes run the political gamut: from conservative to almost radical. Vermont presents a particularly simple solution. Here, the assignee who accepts an instrument issued by a consumer in connection with a contract is subject to all the defenses that would have been available to the consumer in the contract action. The statute applies to all agreements, whether they involve the sale or lease of property, the sale of services, or financial loans.[61] However, the statute does not preserve the consumer's defenses in direct loans, even though the loan qualifies as an "all in the family" loan.[62] "All in the family" loans are loans in which the financier and the dealer are closely connected.

In Rhode Island, notes taken in connection with consumer transactions must bear the legend, *nonnegotiable consumer note*. However, the violation of this law does not deprive the assignee of holder in due course status. Here again, the law insulates the *direct lender* from the consumer's defenses and claims against the seller.[63]

A number of jurisdictions have enacted statutes prohibiting the use of negotiable instruments in consumer transactions. These jurisdictions include California,[64] Delaware,[65] Hawaii,[66] Massachusetts,[67] and New York.[68]

Some of these statutes are broad enough to cover general transactions of

---

[60] Hudak & Carter, *Erosion of Holder in Due Course Doctrine (Part II)*, 9 UCC LJ 235, 258, 259 (Winter 1977).

[61] Vt Stat Ann tit 9, §2455 (1971); *see* Note, *A Case Study of the Impact of Consumer Legislation. The Elimination of Negotiability and the Cooling-Off Period*, 78 Yale LJ 618, 635 (1969); *Uniform Commercial Code Commentary, Judicial and Statutory Limitations on the Rights of a "Holder in Due Course" in Consumer Transactions*, 11 BC Indus & Com L Rev 90, 93, 99 (1969-1970).

[62] Countryman, *Holder in Due Course and Other Anachronisms in Consumer Credit*, 52 Tex L Rev 1, 78 (1973).

[63] *Cf* RI Gen Laws §6-27-5 (1985) (punishable by fine and no finance type charges available). Countryman, *supra* note 62, at 8.

[64] Cal Civ Code §1810.9 (West Supp 1968) (recently renumbered §1810.7, effective Nov 10, 1969).

[65] Del Code Ann tit 6, §4342 (Supp 1968).

[66] Haw Rev Stat §476-18(c) (1968).

[67] Mass Gen Laws Ann ch 255, §12C (West Supp 1969).

[68] NY Pers Prop Law §403(1) (McKinney 1962).

goods and services.[69] Others are more limited, applying only to sales of goods.[70]

The New York Statute, for example, prohibits the use of negotiable notes in consumer transactions involving retail installments, but makes an exception if the transaction involves "the furnishing of goods or services for repairs, alterations or improvements upon or in connection with real property."[71] In the latter case, a creditor may qualify as a holder in due course.

The Prohibition and Regulation of Waiver of Defense Clauses

The same diversity applies to statutes dealing with waiver of defense clauses. Alabama bars them altogether.[72] Maryland subjects them to time-notice requirements.[73] Hawaii retains all consumer defenses,[74] while North Carolina retains only a few.[75]

For the states such as Rhode Island, Maryland, and Vermont, which do not expressly prohibit waiver of defense clauses, but do abolish or restrict the holder in due course in consumer transactions, the question becomes: May a holder of a consumer note take it free of the consumer's defenses if the consumer waives the right to invoke them? The answer should be "no." The statutes which eliminate or restrict the holder in due course doctrine express a stated policy of consumer protection which should supersede §9-206 of the Uniform Commercial Code recognizing the enforceability of waiver of defense clauses.

These consumer-oriented statutes generally contain two loopholes which prevent the complete protection of the consumer against the assignee. First, under some of these statutes, an assignee of a consumer note, without knowledge of the note's origin or of its issuance in violation of the statute, can still qualify as a holder in due course. For example, §136(d) of the Connecticut Act provides: "A promissory note payable to order or bearer or otherwise negotiable in form issued in violation of this section may be enforced as a negotiable instrument by a holder in due course according to its terms."[76]

Second, few jurisdictions deal specifically or effectively with interlocking direct loans. While jurisdictions generally agree that the lender should not be

---

[69] Cal Civ Code §1802.5 (West Supp 1968); Del Code Ann tit 6, §4301 (Supp 1968); NY Pers Prop Law §§403(1), 401(7) (McKinney 1962).

[70] Haw Rev Stat §§476-18, 476-1 (1968); Mass Gen Laws Ann ch 255, §12C (West Supp 1969).

[71] NY Pers Prop Law §403(2) (McKinney 1962).

[72] Ala Code tit 5, §320(a) (Supp 1973).

[73] Md Ann Code art 83, §21G (1975).

[74] Haw Rev Stat §476-18(b), (d) (1968).

[75] NC Gen Stat §§25A-25(a)(b) (Supp 1974). *See* Rohner, *Holder in Due Course in Consumer Transactions: Requiem, Revival, or Reformation?*, 60 Cornell L Rev 503, 522, 523 (1975).

[76] Conn Gen Stat Ann §42-136(d) (West 1987); Conn Acts 466 (Reg Sess).

immune from the consumer's defenses and claims if the lender acts in concert with the dealer, the statutes fail to provide criteria by which the courts can determine such a connection. The Uniform Consumer Credit Code has attempted to fill these gaps on a uniform basis.

§9.10   —The Uniform Consumer Credit Code (U3C)

The Uniform Consumer Credit Code (U3C) was first promulgated in 1968 by the National Conference of Commissioners on Uniform State Laws. It was revised and strengthened in 1974 to provide more comprehensive consumer protection. As of this date, only 12 states have adopted it.[77]

The intent of the U3C drafters was ambitious. It was hoped that the enactment

> would abolish the crazy quilt, patch-work welter of prior laws on consumer credit and replace them by a single new comprehensive law providing a modern, theoretically and pragmatically consistent structure of legal regulation designed to provide an adequate volume of credit at reasonable cost under conditions fair to both consumers and creditors. Upon its enactment credit regulation within a state would no longer consist of a number of separate and uncoordinated statutes governing the activities of different types of creditors in disparate ways.[78]

The drafters' ambitious attempt did not materialize. The majority of the states failed to adopt the Uniform Consumer Credit Code. Some felt that they had already enacted statutes preserving the consumer's claims and defenses against assignees. They were, therefore, reluctant to redraft the statutes simply for sake of uniformity. Some felt that the 1968 version of the U3C did not go far enough, and, therefore, did not justify its adoption. Indeed, the problem of whether assignees of commercial paper should be allowed to take the paper free of consumer defenses and claims posed the greatest difficulty for the U3C drafters. Torn between the financing community and the consumer advocates, the drafting committee chose to "fence-straddle." This attitute miscalculated the anti-holder in due course sentiment prevailing in many states.[79] Although the 1974 revision deals more forcefully with the problem, the revision has arrived too late to persuade many legislators of the benefit of uniformity.

---

[77] These states are: Colorado, Idaho, Indiana, Iowa, Kansas, Maine, Oklahoma, South Carolina, Utah, Wisconsin, Wyoming.

[78] U3C, Prefatory Note 7A ULA 1.

[79] Rohner, *Holder in Due Course in Consumer Transactions: Requiem, Revival, or Reformation?*, 60 Cornell L Rev 503, 523 (1975).

§9.11 —The 1968 Version of the U3C

The U3C lobs a frontal attack on the holder in due course doctrine by prohibiting the use of negotiable notes in consumer transactions. Dealing with waiver of defense clauses, the U3C offers two alternatives to the states: alternative A effectively bars such clauses; alternative B preserves them to a certain extent.

Section 2-403 of the U3C provides that in a consumer credit sale or lease, other than a sale primarily for an agricultural purpose, the seller or lessor may not take any negotiable instrument other than a check as evidence of the obligation of the buyer or lessee.

Section 2-104 defines *consumer credit sale* to mean a sale of goods, services, or an interest in land in which:

1. Credit is granted by a person who regularly engages as a seller in credit transactions
2. The buyer is a person other than an organization
3. The goods, services, or interest in land are purchased primarily for a personal, family, household, or agricultural purpose
4. Either the debt is payable in installments or a credit service charge is made
5. With respect to the sale of goods or services, the amount financed does not exceed $25,000

The Act excludes credit card transactions from its scope.[80] It is obvious that the U3C's ban on the taking of consumer notes is to abolish the holder in due course in consumer transactions. What are the consequences under the Act to a person who takes a negotiable note in violation of §2-403? In most cases, such a person does not qualify as a holder in due course. Section 2-403 states that a holder does not act in good faith if the holder takes a negotiable instrument with notice that it is issued in violation of the Act. The drafters' comment to this section assumed that a ban on negotiable instruments in consumer transactions would be well known in the financial community. Therefore, professional financiers buying consumer paper from violators of the Act normally will not qualify as holders in due course.

The Act preserves the holder in due course in the rare case in which a taker does not know of the commercial paper's consumer origin, for example, if the assignee is a second, third, or subsequent assignee. Here, "the policy of favoring negotiability is upheld in order not to cast a cloud over negotiable instruments generally".[81]

Section 2-404 offers the states two alternatives in the regulation of waiver of defense clauses. Alternative A states that in a consumer credit sale or lease, other than one primarily for an agricultural purpose, the assignee is subject to

---

[80] U3C §2.104(2).
[81] U3C §2.403 Comment

all of the account debtor's claims or defenses against the assignor, notwith-standing an agreement to the contrary. The assignee's liability will not exceed the amount owed at the time the account debtor asserts the claim or defense. The account debtor may assert these rights only as a defense to a claim by the assignee. The provision therefore only renders waiver of defense clauses unenforceable against the consumer. It does not prohibit them altogether.

Alternative B is divided into three subsections. Subsection 1 abrogates waiver of defense clauses if the consumer notifies the assignee in writing of any defense or claim within three months after receiving written notification of the assignment. The assignee will be subject to the consumer's claims or defenses for the life of the contract, however, if the assignee is related to the seller or lessor.

Subsection 2 defines bad faith. A holder of consumer paper holds in bad faith if the holder has knowledge of substantial complaints by other buyers or lessees of the seller's or lessor's defective performance and its failure to remedy it after being notified of the complaints, and if the holder has notice of such complaints from the holder's course of dealing with the seller or lessor or from their records.

Subsection 3 limits the assignee's liability to the amount still owing on the contract at the time the consumer notifies the assignee of the claims or defenses.

The drafters' comment to §2-404 explains that the basis of the rule is the requirement that the consumer notify the assignee within three months of the facts giving rise to the consumer's claims or defenses. Since the consumer obviously cannot give notice within that period of claims and defenses arising afterward, §2-404 should not deprive the consumer of the right to raise these. A shortening of this period, therefore, would reduce the consumer's vulnera-bility to the assignee.

Oklahoma has adopted a version of alternative B which achieves this result. The statute permits the enforcement of waiver of defense clauses provided the assignee is not related to the assignor and has acquired the contract for value and in good faith. The assignee must notify the consumer of the assignment in writing; if, within 30 days, the assignee has received no notice of claims or defenses from the consumer, then the waiver may be enforced. Waivers are effective only with respect to claims or defenses which arise within the 30 day statutory period and for which the consumer fails to notify the assignee. Waivers are ineffective with respect to claims or defenses that arise after the 30-day period.[82]

As drafted, the 1968 U3C falls short of providing adequate protection to the consumer. First, holder in due course status still exists in consumer transac-tions. Second, waiver of defense clauses still are enforced under alternative B. The biggest loophole, however, is the Code's failure to deal with the problem of interlocking loans. Creditors may insulate themselves from consumers' claims or defenses even though creditors, sellers, or lessors are part of the same

---

[82] Okla Stat Ann tit 14A, §2-404 (West 1983).

financing enterprise.[83] The 1974 revised version attempts to close these loopholes.

§9.12 —The 1974 U3C

The 1974 U3C completely abolishes the holder in due course in consumer transactions, bans waivers of defense clauses in consumer credit contracts, and deals with interlocking loans.

The Elimination of the Holder in Due Course

Section 3-307 of the 1974 U3C abrogates the holder in due course doctrine in consumer transactions by providing that, except for an instrument primarily for an agricultural purpose, the creditor may not accept a negotiable instrument other than a check in a consumer credit sale or lease. While the 1968 Code still preserves the holder in due course status if the holder does not know of the instrument's consumer origin, the 1974 Act completely abolishes it. Now, in a consumer credit transaction, a holder may never take an instrument free of the consumer's claims and defenses against the seller or lessor, regardless of whether the holder knows of the instrument's consumer origin.

The comment to §3-307 explains this policy. It states that the harshness of denying consumers the right to raise valid defenses greatly outweighs whatever beneficial effects the holder in due course doctrine may have in promoting the flow of commercial paper. The amended version also applies to credit card transactions which were outside the scope of the 1968 U3C.

Waiver of Defense Clauses

Section 3-404 (1974) of the U3C invalidates waiver of defense clauses altogether. This section preserves consumer defenses even though the assignee may qualify as a holder in due course of an instrument issued in violation of the U3C. This section also applies to consumers who have purported to waive claims and defenses. The comment justifies the policy not only as protection for the consumer, but also to encourage financial institutions "to use discretion in dealing with sellers and lessors whose transactions give rise to an unusual percentage of consumer complaints."

Interlocking Loans

Section 3-405 (1974) protects consumers in interlocking loans by subjecting lenders closely connected to the seller to the consumer's claims and defenses arising from a sale or lease. The following criteria determine such a connection:

---

[83] *See* Uniform Commercial Code Commentary, *Judicial and Statutory Limitations on the Rights of a "Holder in Due Course" in Consumer Transactions,* 11 BC Indus & Com L Rev 90, 112 (1969-70).

1. The lender knows that the seller or lessor arranged for the extension of credit by the lender for a commission, brokerage, or referral fee
2. The lender is a person related to the seller or lessor, unless the relationship is remote or is not a factor in the transaction
3. The seller or lessor guarantees the loan or otherwise assumes the risk of loss by the lender upon the loan
4. The lender directly supplies the seller or lessor with the contract document used by the consumer to evidence the loan, and the seller or lessor has knowledge of the credit terms and participates in preparation of the document
5. The loan is conditioned upon the consumer's purchase or lease of the property or services from the particular seller or lessor, but the lender's payment of proceeds of the loan to the seller or lessor does not in itself establish that the loan was so conditioned
6. The lender, before making the consumer loan, has knowledge, or, from the lender's course of dealing with the particular seller or lessor or from records, notice, of substantial complaints by other buyers or lessees concerning the particular seller's or lessor's failure or refusal to perform contracts with them and concerning the particular seller's or lessor's failure to remedy defaults within a reasonable time after notice of the complaints

Thus, the 1974 U3C preserves the consumer's claims and defenses in interlocking loans in which the relationship between the seller and the lender does not justify separating the consumer's duty to pay from the seller's duty to perform. Although §3-405 apparently codifies the common law doctrine of close-connectedness, it defines the connection more liberally. For example, only one of the six listed situations is necessary to denote the loan as an "all in the family" loan and thereby subject the lender to the consumer's claims and defenses.

In *Central Finance Co v Stevens,*[84] a Kansas court had the opportunity to interpret §3-405. The defendant, Stevens, obtained a direct loan from Central Finance Company (CFC) to purchase a used car from Cox Motors. CFC sued to recover a deficiency judgment on the promissory note issued by the defendant. The car was used as collateral for the loan and the lender's security interest was noted on the defendant's certificate of title. The court held that neither the fact that the check was issued by the lender and made payable to both buyer and seller of the car, nor the fact that the notation of the lender's security interest was made on the buyer's certificate of title, created an "all in the family" loan. The Kansas Supreme Court noted that §3-405 intends to penalize only lenders and sellers who cooperate in an "all in the family" loan. This did not occur here.

---

[84] 221 Kan 1, 558 P2d 122 (1976).

§9.13 —Recovery under the U3C

The consumer may assert a claim or defense against the assignee only after the consumer has made a good faith attempt to obtain satisfaction from the seller or lessor. The notice of the claim or defense may be given to the assignee orally. However, if the assignee requests written confirmation, the consumer must comply with this request within 14 days. The consumer's failure to comply with the request for written confirmation renders the consumer's oral notification ineffective, and the assignee thus may cut off the consumer's claims and defenses against the seller or lessor.[85] These stipulations demand more sophistication than the average consumer generally possesses and are, therefore, difficult for most consumers to observe.

If these requirements are observed, the assignee's liability is measured at the time when "the assignee has notice of the claim or defense."[86] The U3C does not define what *notice* means. But borrowed from the Uniform Commercial Code's definition, a person has *notice of a fact* when such a person has actual knowledge of it, has received a notice or notification of it, or from all the facts and circumstances known to such person at the time in question, has reason to know that it exists.[87] If adopted, this broad definition of notice may dispose the consumer of the affirmative duty to notify the creditor when the creditor could independently acquire knowledge, or constructive knowledge, of the seller's or lessor's conduct. Furthermore, the consumer may strengthen its position against the creditor by giving notice of the claim or defense even before attempting to resolve the dispute with the seller or lessor as required.[88] Nothing in the U3C prevents this interpretation.

The U3C allows the consumer to stop payment of the amount still owing to the assignee, but does not allow the consumer to recover the amount already paid. The law thus operates as a shield only, not as a sword. In determining the amount due the assignee, payments received by the creditor after the consolidation of two or more consumer credit sales (other than open-end credit) are deemed to have been applied first to the payment on the first sale made. If they arose from sales on the same day, payments are deemed applied to the smallest sale first. With respect to open-end credit, payments are deemed applied first to the payment of finance charges in the order of their entry to the account, and then to the payment of the debts in the order in which they are entered into the account. The agreement may not limit or waive the consumer's rights so provided.[89]

---

[85] U3C §§3.404(2), .405(2)(1974).

[86] U3C §§3.403(3)(d), 404(2), 405(2) (1979).

[87] UCC §1.201(25).

[88] Rohner, *Holder in Due Course in Consumer Transactions: Requiem, Revival or Reformation?*, 60 Cornell L Rev 503, 557 (1975).

[89] U3C §3.404 (3) (1974).

§9.14   Appraisal of State Laws Dealing with Assignment of Claims

State laws lack uniformity. Only a dozen states have adopted the U3C. Even among these, great variations exist. In the other states, statutes limiting the rights of assignees of consumer contracts apply only to specific transactions, such as retail installment sales, motor vehicle financing, or motor vehicle installment sales, and not to all consumer transactions.

Additionally, while all of these statutes attempt to tie the consumer's duty to pay to the seller's or lessor's duty to perform, the methods used and the ensuing results vary greatly from state to state. Most of them, while protecting consumers against further payments, do not allow them to recover the amount already paid.

As a result of the lack of uniformity and the timidity of most of these statutes, the holder in due course is still alive in many states. What is needed is a more sweeping rule to preserve the consumer's claims and defenses against the assignee in all cases without distinguishing among motor vehicles sales, home improvement transactions, or retail sale agreements. The rule should also permit the consumer to use the consumer's claim or defense as a sword, not only as a shield. The Federal Trade Commission attempted to provide such a rule.

§9.15   The Federal Trade Commission (FTC) Rule: Purpose and Mechanics

The Federal Trade Commission (FTC) Rule was first proposed on January 21, 1971.[90] Written comments and public hearings ensued. The Rule was revised and published on January 5, 1973.[91] Further public hearings were conducted, and on November 14, 1975, the Rule was promulgated with a lengthy Statement of Basis and Purpose.[92] The Rule became effective on May 14, 1976, together with a set of Guidelines to "facilitate and encourage compliance with the Rule."[93] Three months later, the Commission issued the Statement of Enforcement Policy designed to clarify the important concept of *purchase money loan* in application of the Rule.[94]

The Rule is designed to ensure that consumer credit contracts, used in financing consumer purchases of goods and services, preserve the consumer's claims and defenses against the seller or financier. As we have seen, a seller

---

[90] 36 Fed Reg 1211 (Jan 26, 1971).

[91] 38 Fed Reg 892 (Jan 5, 1973).

[92] 40 Fed Reg 53506 (1975); 16 CFR, ch I, subch D, pt 433 (promulgated Nov 14, 1975, effective May 14, 1976). The rule is also referred to as Rule 433.

[93] Guidelines on Trade Regulation Rule Concerning Preservation of Consumers' Claims and Defenses, 41 Fed Reg 2002 (1976) [hereinafter Guidelines].

[94] 41 Fed Reg 34594 (Aug 3, 1976).

or a financier may cut off those claims and defenses using one of the following methods:

1. Use of the holder in due course doctrine through the issuance of negotiable instruments
2. Inclusion of the waiver of defense clause in the consumer contract
3. Adoption of the *direct loan* device

The Commission's Rule is directed at all of the above situations.[95]

When the seller itself extends the loan, the Rule requires the inclusion, in 10-point type, of the following notice in the text of the consumer credit contract executed with the consumer:

> **ANY HOLDER OF THIS CONSUMER CREDIT CONTRACT IS SUBJECT TO ALL CLAIMS AND DEFENSES WHICH THE DEBTOR COULD ASSERT AGAINST THE SELLER OF GOODS OR SERVICES OBTAINED PURSUANT HERETO OR WITH THE PROCEEDS HEREOF. RECOVERY HEREUNDER BY THE DEBTOR SHALL NOT EXCEED AMOUNTS PAID BY THE DEBTOR HEREUNDER.**

When the seller instead arranges a direct loan for the buyer, the Rule prohibits the seller from accepting the proceeds from the loan as payment for the sale, unless the contract between the buyer and the lender contains the following provision:

> **ANY HOLDER OF THIS CONSUMER CREDIT CONTRACT IS SUBJECT TO ALL CLAIMS AND DEFENSES WHICH THE DEBTOR COULD ASSERT AGAINST THE SELLER OF GOODS OR SERVICES OBTAINED WITH THE PROCEEDS HEREOF. RECOVERY HEREUNDER BY THE DEBTOR SHALL NOT EXCEED AMOUNTS PAID BY THE DEBTOR HEREUNDER.**

§9.16   —Transactions Subject to the Rule

The FTC Rule applies to the assignment of negotiable and non-negotiable instruments executed by the buyer for the purchase of goods or services from a seller. According to the FTC Guidelines, the notice itself, which denies holder

---

[95] Guidelines, *supra* note 93, at 20023.

in due course status to the assignee, becomes part of the contract.[96] The seller's failure to incorporate the notice in the contract constitutes an unfair and deceptive trade practice.[97]

The holder in due course status requires the existence of a negotiable instrument containing an unconditional promise. Here, the Rule attaches conditions to the promise by subjecting the promise to the debtor's claims and defenses. The note thereby loses the quality of negotiability and the holder loses the status of holder in due course. The holder becomes instead simply an assignee who possesses the same rights and duties as the assignor. In other words, when the Rule is invoked, the financier must step into the shoes of the seller vis-á-vis the consumer.

Note that the financier itself, however, is not subject to the Rule. At the time that the Rule became effective, the FTC proposed an amendment which would subject creditors to the Rule.[98] However, the Federal Trade Commission has not yet enacted this amendment, and the Rule still applies only to sellers. One reason for this omission is that the FTC lacks jurisdiction over banks regulated by the Federal Reserve Board.[99]

The Rule not only deprives the financier of protection offered by the holder in due course status, but it also prevents the financier from shielding itself behind the waiver of defense clause often inserted in the credit contract. By expressly preserving the consumer's claims and defenses against the financier, the FTC notice renders such a waiver, if it exists, ineffective.

Furthermore, when a connection exists between the lender and the seller, the Rule prohibits the seller from taking the proceeds of a direct loan if the contract does not contain the required notice.[100] The Rule thus applies only when there is a close connection between the lender and the seller. Conversely, if there is no connection between the lender and the seller, the Rule does not apply. We will see later how the FTC establishes the connection which brings the transaction within the Rule's scope.

The Rule does not extend to nonconsumer transactions. It applies only to *consumer credit* as the term is defined in the Federal Truth in Lending Act and Regulation Z.[101] This definition excludes transactions that qualify as consumer transactions, but which exceed $25,000. It excludes public utility services and consumer leases if the lease does not amount to a disguised sale.[102] The Rule does not cover credit card transactions.[103]

---

[96] Guidelines on Trade Regulation Rule Concerning Preservation of Consumers' Claims and Defenses, 41 Fed Reg 20022, 20023 (1976) [hereinafter Guidelines].

[97] §433.2, 40 Fed Reg 53530 (Nov 14, 1975).

[98] 40 Fed Reg 53520 (Nov 14, 1975).

[99] 15 USC §§45(a)(2), §57a(f)(1).

[100] 16 CFR §433.2; 12 CFR §226.1.

[101] 15 USC §1603(3); 12 CFR §226.3(b); Guidelines, *supra* note 96, at 20024.

[102] 15 USC §1603(4); Guidelines, *supra* note 96, at 20024.

[103] 16 CFR §433.3; Guidelines, *supra* note 96, at 20024.

§9.17 —Persons Protected by the Rule

The FTC Rule protects only "a natural person who seeks to acquire goods and services for personal, family, or household use."[104] Therefore, a lawyer who borrows money to purchase a word processor for use in the lawyer's office would not be covered by the Rule. The FTC finds that business people and corporations are capable of fending for themselves and therefore do not need protection under the Rule.[105] In cases where the goods are used for both professional and personal purposes, such as a doctor's car, then the primary use most likely would determine the application of the Rule.[106]

In *Jefferson Bank & Trust Co v Stamatiou*,[107] the Supreme Court of Louisiana has given a new twist to the term *consumer credit contract*. In that case, the defendant, Christos G. Stamatiou, purchased a truck from Key Dodge, Inc. (Dodge). At the time of the purchase, the defendant executed a contract and a promissory note in the same document. The defendant's signature appeared twice on the document, once following the contract entitled "Sales and Chattel Mortgage" and once following the promissory note. The promissory note contained an unconditional promise to pay $10,774.44 on prescribed terms. The contract contained the FTC Notice and a "Disclosure Statement" which stated "Buyer acknowledges that the Promissory Note secured by Sale and Chattel Mortgage will be assigned to Jefferson Bank, as assignee and creditor within the meaning of the Federal Truth in Lending Act." Key Dodge assigned the contract to the plaintiff, Jefferson Bank and Trust Co. (Bank).

When the purchased truck developed mechanical problems, the defendant stopped payment. The Bank filed action against the defendant for the unpaid balance on the note. The defendant answered the suit, seeking the rescission of the sale and the return of the amount paid.

The Bank invoked its status as a holder in due course, arguing that the FTC Rule did not apply to the present case because the defendant used the truck in his business, rather than for his personal use. Therefore, the contract between Dodge and the defendant was not a *consumer credit contract* subject to the Rule. The trial court and the court of appeals agreed with the Bank.

The Louisiana Supreme Court reversed the decision. Referring to the provisions of the Louisiana Civil Code, the court held that the contract including the FTC Notice acted as the law between the parties. The defendant had the right to rely on the notice, albeit mistakenly included. The court stated,

> That the parties to the contract mistakenly asserted that it was a consumer credit contract . . . is of little consequence. . . . The assignee/holder was put on notice that all defenses were available to the buyer against him at

---

[104] 16 CFR §433.1(b) (1985); Guidelines, on Trade Regulation Rule Concerning Preservation of Consumer's Claims and Defenses, 41 Fed Reg 2022, 20024 (1976).

[105] *See generally Statement of Basis and Purpose,* 40 Fed Reg 53509 (Nov 14, 1975).

[106] We follow UCC §9-109, comment 2.

[107] 384 So 2d 388 (La 1980).

the time he acquired the instrument. In looking at the face of the instrument, plaintiff could not have expected to be a holder in due course, and is not entitled to be so treated.[108]

In vain, the plaintiff argued that the promissory note should be treated separately from the sale and chattel mortgage which includes the FTC Notice. The court simply said that one could not "alter the effects of the contractual undertaking by the simple expedient of physically separating the promissory note from the rest of the contract."[109]

Not all sellers are subject to the Rule. Only sellers who, in the ordinary course of business, sell goods or services to consumers are subject to the Rule.[110] Thus, if the seller is one's professor or student, the Rule does not apply. The Rule also requires that the creditor or lender be a professional. A *creditor* is defined as "a person who, in the ordinary course of business, lends purchase money or finances the purchase of goods or services . . . on a deferred payment basis."[111] Thus, the Rule has no application if Daddy finances the sale of Sonny's consumer item.

§9.18 —Financing a Sale

The Rule applies only when a credit is granted under the form of *financing a sale* or a *purchase money loan*. These terms are used in the Truth in Lending Act[112] and Regulation Z.[113] *Financing a sale* means extending credit to a consumer. The term includes situations in which a merchant "extends credit to a buyer and takes a written credit contract from the buyer, in connection with an affected transaction."[114] Credit card transactions are excluded from this definition.[115] Also excluded are those writings that do not constitute a contract under local, state, or other applicable law.[116] The Guidelines cite, as an example, a casual notation which would not be assignable.[117]

The Rule does apply when there is a *series of sales* on open credit or closed credit pursuant to a master consumer credit arrangement. If more than one writing is issued, the notice need appear once and incorporation by reference

---

[108] *Id* 391.

[109] *Id* 392.

[110] 16 CFR §433.1(j).

[111] 16 CFR §433.1(c).

[112] 15 USC §1601 *et seq.*

[113] *Truth in Lending Regulation,* 12 CFR §226.1.

[114] Guidelines on Trade Regulation Rule Concerning Preservation of Consumer's Claims and Defenses, 41 Fed Reg 20022, 20024 (1976).

[115] *Id.*

[116] *Id.*

[117] *Id.*

in the other credit documents would satisfy the Rule.[118] The only requirement is that both the consumer and holder be put on notice of their respective rights and duties.[119]

§9.19 —Interlocking Loans and the FTC Rule

While the Guidelines are clear when the seller itself finances the sale, they are somewhat ambiguous about the Rule's application to the proceeds of a direct loan which the consumer obtains from the lender. To trigger the operation of the Rule, there must be a sufficient connection between the lender and seller. This connection occurs in a *purchase money loan*.

The Rule defines a *purchase money loan* as:

> a cash advance which is received by a consumer in return for a "Finance Charge" within the meaning of the Truth in Lending Act and Regulation Z, which is applied, in whole or substantial part, to a purchase of goods or services from a seller who, 1) refers consumers to the creditor or 2) is affiliated with the creditor by common control, contract, or business arrangement.[120]

The term *purchase money loan* must be read in the light of the Commission's Statement of Basis and Purpose. The goal of the Rule is to avoid the situation in which the seller imposes the risk of its misconduct on the consumer by arranging credit terms which insulate the creditor from the consumer's claims and defenses against the seller.[121] The consumer's claims and defenses must be preserved when the seller arranges financing for its customers through referrals to direct lenders, or in cases in which close affiliation exists between the seller and the direct lender. This again expresses the common law doctrine of close-connectedness, which treats sellers and direct lenders as one single entity

Three questions must be examined here: When does a loan becomes a purchase money loan? What constitutes a referral? What constitutes an affiliation?

§9.20 —Purchase Money Loan

The test of a purchase money loan is whether the loan is applied in "whole or substantial part to a specific purchase."[122] This test excludes loans obtained

---

[118] *Id.*

[119] *Id.*

[120] 16 CFR §433.1(d)(1).

[121] Guidelines on Trade Regulation Rule Concerning Preservation of Consumer's Claims and Defenses, 41 Fed Reg 20022, 20024 (May 10, 1976).

[122] Guidelines on Trade Regulation Rule Concerning Preservation of Consumers' Claims and Defenses, 41 Fed Reg 20022, 20025 (May 10, 1976).

and used by the consumer to acquire goods or services from different sellers. The Rule therefore applies only to those loans used exclusively to buy goods or services from a single seller.[123] Most open-end loan agreements are therefore excluded. However, the drafters of the Rule raise the possibility that an open-end credit agreement arranged by a lender who is affiliated with the seller could be used as a device to evade the Rule. For instance, the affiliated lender may extend an open-end credit, but may advance an amount just sufficient to pay for a particular purchase from the seller. Thereafter, the lender would close the line of credit and advance no more funds to the consumer. The FTC Staff notes that, in such a case, the substance rather than the form of the transaction would govern, and the Rule would apply.[124]

A question arises concerning the requirement that the loan be applied in *whole or substantial part* to a specific purchase. What constitutes a *substantial* part? The drafters of the Rule admit that the term "creates a slight area of uncertainty."[125] They justify this uncertainty as necessary to compensate for the loophole that would exist if the Rule simply required that the proceeds of the loan be used entirely for a particular purchase. Here, lenders trying to avoid the Rule would simply advance the consumer a few extra dollars. Again, substance rather than form would govern.[126]

Besides the destination of the loan, the term *purchase money loan* requires that a certain relationship exist between the direct lender and the seller. The seller must either *refer* the consumer to the lender, be *affiliated* with the lender, or both.

§9.21 —Referrals

When the seller *refers* consumers to the creditor, the Rule prohibits the seller from accepting the proceeds of a *purchase money loan,* unless the loan contract contains the required FTC notice.[127] A seller *refers* consumers to the creditor when the seller acts as a conduit for financing by directing the consumer to a particular lender.[128]

The Guidelines draw the distinction, albeit vaguely, between the seller's active referral and the passive transmittal of information.[129] Active referral occurs when the seller regularly names or recommends a particular credit outlet, or when a seller helps a buyer prepare the lender's credit documents.

---

[123] *Id.*

[124] *Id.*

[125] *Id.*

[126] *Id.*

[127] 16 CFR §433(1)(d).

[128] Guidelines on Trade Regulation Rule Concerning Preservation of Consumer's Claims and Defenses, 41 Fed Reg 20022, 20025 (May 10, 1976) [hereinafter Guidelines].

[129] *Id.*

No definite number of referrals, however, is specified for the Rule to apply. But once a referral relationship exists, all subsequent transactions involving the same seller and lender are subject to the Rule, even though some of the loans are not the result of a referral.[130]

The FTC staff requires several conditions for a referral to exist:

1. The conduct of the seller and creditor must manifest a cooperative or concerted effort to channel the consumer to the particular lender. If the seller only suggests credit sources, the Rule will not be invoked. If the seller and lender do work together to effect the consumer's loan, then the prescribed FTC Notice must appear in the loan contract.
2. The cooperation between seller and lender must exist on a continuing basis. Occasional referrals do not trigger the Rule
3. The Rule does not require that the seller and lender give formal consideration. Mutual benefit to the seller's and lender's respective businesses is sufficient[131]

§9.22   —Affiliation

The Rule requires a seller who accepts the proceeds of a consumer loan to ensure that the notice appears in the loan contract if the seller "is affiliated with the creditor by common control, contract, or business arrangement."[132]

Common control exists when creditor and seller are part of the same business entity, such as when the two are owned by the same holding company or by the same individuals. Common control also exists when one company is a subsidiary of the other, as well as when the creditor and seller are under common control relating to retail sales financing.[133]

A *contract* is "any oral or written agreement, formal or informal, between a creditor and a seller, which contemplates or provides for cooperative or concerted activity in connection with the sale of goods or services to consumers or the financing thereof."[134]

A *business arrangement* is "any understanding, procedure, course of dealing, or arrangement, formal or informal, between a creditor and a seller, in connection with the sale of goods or services to consumers or the financing thereof.[135]

The FTC staff provides the following examples of *affiliation:*

---

[130] Statement of Enforcement Policy, 41 Fed Reg 34594, 34596 (Aug 3, 1976); Guidelines, *supra* note 128, at 20026.

[131] Statement of Enforcement Policy, 41 Fed Reg 34596 (Aug 3, 1976).

[132] 16 CFR §433.1(d)(2).

[133] Statement of Enforcement Policy, 41 Fed Reg 34595 (Aug 3, 1976).

[134] 16 CFR §433.1(f).

[135] 16 CFR §433.1(g).

1. Maintenance of loan application forms in the office of the seller
2. Seller agrees with creditor to prepare loan documents
3. Creditor's referrals of customers to a sales outlet
4. Payment of consideration to a seller for furnishing loan customers or to a creditor for furnishing sales prospects
5. The assignment of indirect paper or the referral of loan customers to a creditor
6. Active credit participation in a sales program
7. Joint advertising efforts
8. An agreement to purchase paper on an indirect basis

Referral and *affiliation* both indicate cooperation between seller and lender for financing the consumer's transaction. But the two tests are somewhat distinguishable. *Affiliation* contemplates a pre-existing agreement between seller and lender, such as situations in which lender and seller are part of the same business entity or in which a pre-existing formal or informal contractual or business arrangement exists between the two in a concerted effort to provide consumer financing.

Referral does not contemplate any such pre-existing relationship, but simply situations in which "the lender and seller cooperate to channel purchases on a continuing basis." This course of conduct evidences a de facto or implied relationship between the lender and seller.[136] Conversely, when no such cooperation or concerted activity is present, the Rule does not apply.

Affiliation and *referral* are not intended to be read separately; they are coextensive in their impact.[137] The Commission gives eight examples to illustrate the application of *referral* and *affiliation* standards:

1. The seller has an agreement with a creditor to maintain loan application forms in the seller's office. When a buyer requests financing, the seller assists the buyer in filling out the forms. This relationship constitutes an affiliation and the Notice must be included in the consumer credit contract
2. A seller regularly sends customers to a particular creditor. The creditor, in turn, agrees to provide a favorable financing arrangement for the seller's inventory or directly or indirectly provides some other consideration. The seller and lender are *affiliated*. The Notice must be included in the consumer credit contract
3. A seller regularly sends customers to a particular creditor. The creditor agrees that as long as the seller continues to refer customers, their loan applications will be processed or approved on an expedited basis when the borrower meets certain lending criteria, but before a full credit check is completed. The Notice must be included

---

[136] Statement of Enforcement Policy, 41 Fed Reg 34595 (Aug 3, 1976).
[137] *Id.*

4. A seller routinely suggests that customers in need of credit go to a particular source or sources of financing. While the creditor is aware that seller is sending customers, the creditor does not provide any tacit or explicit *quid pro quo*, and seller and financier have no relationship that would constitute an affiliation and do not otherwise cooperate except insofar as may be necessary to arrange payment, perfect a security interest, or otherwise finalize the transaction. The Notice is not required

5. A buyer asks a seller for credit information. The seller suggests a creditor, calls up the creditor to determine whether the creditor will lend money to the particular buyer, and then sends the buyer to the creditor. Seller and creditor have no agreement, formal or informal, to refer customers. A referral relationship would be created if the channeling occurs on a continuing basis

6. A buyer asks a seller for credit sources. Seller provides a list of lenders in the area and provides information on the availability of credit from them as an accommodation to customers. The seller does not contact a creditor to arrange credit for the customer, nor does the seller have any other business arrangement or affiliation with the creditors in this respect. The notice is not required

7. A seller has a referral or affiliation relationship with a creditor. A buyer, on his or her own, goes to the creditor to obtain a loan to purchase an item from seller. The notice must be included

8. Seller has for years referred customers to a particular financial institution pursuant to an arrangement with the creditor. He now desires to end the relationship. He stops the referrals and notifies the creditor that he no longer will refer buyers. The referral relationship has been terminated[138]

§9.23   —Excluded Transactions

As the Statement of Basis and Purpose issued with the Rule indicates, the Rule applies whenever credit is arranged or secured in connection with a continuing relationship between a seller and a creditor. The seller and creditor must be viewed as *joint venturers*.[139] Conversely, if the loan does not qualify as an "all in the family loan," it is outside the scope of the Rule. In particular, business relationships that do not bear directly on the financing of consumer sales are excluded from the Rule.

Commercial financing, such as factoring of accounts receivable, maintaining a commercial checking account, commercial leasing, or other similar business arrangements, do not invoke the Rule. The mere fact that the lender issues a

---

[138] Statement of Enforcement Policy, 41 Fed Reg 34596 (Aug 3, 1976).
[139] Statement of Basis and Purpose, 40 Fed Reg 53524 (Nov 14, 1975).

check both to the seller and the buyer, or that the lender and seller confer over a particular transaction, is outside the scope of the Rule.[140]

The seller is not subject to liability if the seller accepts the proceeds of the purchase money loan without the required Notice when the seller has no reason to believe that the seller is receiving the proceeds of a purchase money loan. It is specifically provided that the Rule does not require that the seller interrogate the buyer to determine the source of the proceeds.[141]

The FTC staff gives the following examples to illustrate how the standard should apply:

1. A buyer arrives in the seller's showroom with a joint proceeds check or a bank draft drawn on a bank affiliated with the seller. The seller is on notice to inquire as to whether the notice was included. This is because, as the comment points out, a joint proceeds check provides actual knowledge that a purchase money loan is involved. A bank draft places a seller on notice that the instrument is probably the proceeds of a purchase money loan

2. A buyer pays for a seller's product or service with cash or a personal check. There is no duty to inquire

3. A buyer pays $5,000 for an automobile with a personal check drawn on the bank that purchases seller's contracts. Buyer states that he or she obtained a signature loan from that bank to pay for it. Seller must determine if the Notice was inserted

4. Seller determines that the money the buyer uses to purchase a product are the proceeds of a purchase money loan. The seller asks the buyer whether the Notice has been included in the consumer credit contract. The buyer refuses to answer or incorrectly states that the Notice was included. The seller must communicate with the creditor[142]

§9.24 —Enforcement of the Rule

FTC Enforcement

If the merchant fails to include the FTC notice on the consumer credit contract, what are the consequences of that omission? Originally, §5 of the Federal Trade Commission Act merely gave the FTC the power to ban "unfair or deceptive acts or practices."[143] The merchant's omission of the Notice qualified as such.[144] Subsequently, however, the Act was amended[145] and the

---

[140] Statement of Enforcement Policy, 41 Fed Reg 34595 (Aug 3, 1976).

[141] *Id* 34596.

[142] *Id* 34597.

[143] 15 USC §45(a)(6).

[144] 16 CFR §433.2.

[145] This was achieved by the passage of Title II of the Magnuson-Moss legislation, entitled the Federal Trade Commission Improvement Act. 15 USC §57(a).

FTC has been empowered to impose sanctions as well as monetary penalties on violators of the FTC's regulations.[146] The FTC may impose a $10,000 fine per day per violation on merchants who fail to include the required Notice in their credit sales contracts or who accept the proceeds of a purchase money loan which excludes the Notice. Direct lenders are not covered by the Rule.[147] However, a professional lender may still not qualify as a holder in due course by taking a consumer contract without the required Notice under the applicable state law. Such a lender may be deemed to be acting in bad faith or with notice of the FTC requirement and therefore cannot cut off the consumer's claims and defenses.[148]

Private Enforcement

It is not clear whether consumers have a private legal action against the seller for violation of the Rule. *Guernsey v Rich Plan for the Midwest*[149] accords that right to individual consumers. In *Guernsey,* a seller of frozen food engaged in certain fraudulent practices violating the FTC Act. Two consumers took legal action against the seller for injunctive relief and compensatory and punitive damages. The defendant claimed that the FTC Act itself contains no provision for private enforcement because the Commission had original jurisdiction over the acts complained of. The *Guernsey* court invoked the ultimate purpose of the Act, which is to protect consumers, and noted the caseload before the FTC. The court denied the motion to dismiss because:

> There is no legislative intent that the Federal Trade Commission was to have "exclusive" jurisdiction. To infer that once the Federal Trade Commission has entered a case and enforced compliance with the Act, that subsequent private consumer actions would frustrate the purposes of the Act would deny consumers who were victimized by further violations any recovery.[150]

So far, the *Guernsey* court may be the only court to accord the consumer such private legal action.

Prior to *Guernsey,* the courts had invariably held that no private actions could be implied from the FTC Act. *Holloway v Bristol-Meyers Corp*[151] resoundingly denied such an action on the ground that private enforcement would pose problems for the FTC's enforcement activities and would be inconsistent with

---

[146] 15 USC §45 (1)(m) (Supp V 1975).

[147] *See* Comment, *Let the Holder Beware! Problematic Analysis of the FTC Holder in Due Course Rule,* 27 Case W Res L Rev 977, 995 (1977).

[148] *See* Garner & Dunham, *FTC Rule 433 and the Uniform Commercial Code: An Analysis of Current Lender Status,* 43 Mo L Rev 199, 227-29 (1978).

[149] 408 F Supp 582 (ND Ind 1976).

[150] *Id* 588.

[151] 485 F2d 986 (DC Cir 1973).

the congressional intent that only an agency with expertise in commercial practices could proceed against violators of the FTC Act.

More recently, in *Saporita v Delco Corp,*[152] the New York Supreme Court reinterated *Holloway* and stated that only the Commission may enforce the provisions of the FTC Act and that consumers and the members of the public may not bring suit to enforce its provisions.[153]

§9.25 —Consumer's Recovery under the Rule

The Rule operates both as a shield and, within limitations, as a sword. As a shield, the Rule allows the consumer to assert, by way of claim or defense, a right not to pay all or part of the outstanding balance still owing the creditor under the contract. As a sword, the Rule entitles the consumer to an affirmative recovery of the amounts, including down payments, already paid, but not more. The Notice expresses this by the phrase, "Recovery hereunder by the debtor shall be limited to amounts paid by the debtor hereunder."[154]

Thus, the Rule allows the consumer to: sue to refuse any further payment under the contract and to recover the amounts already paid; and defend in a creditor action to collect the unpaid balance.

The limitation on affirmative recovery applies only to recovery under the Rule. It does not negate any other rights that the consumer may have under local, state, or other federal law.[155] *Saporita v Delco Corp*[156] is an illustration of this principle.

In that case, Mr. and Mrs. Saporita contracted with the Delco Corporation to resurface the exterior of their Brooklyn home. The contract price was $4,665, and $4,600 was financed by Delco. Upon completion of the work, Delco assigned the plaintiff's contract to Dartmouth Plan, Inc. (Dartmouth). Subsequently, Dartmouth reassigned the contract to National Bank of North America (Bank).

After the plaintiffs had paid $779.62, they found that Delco had performed the resurfacing job negligently. As a result, "their exterior walls were blistered and discolored."[157] The codefendants, Dartmouth and the Bank, argued that under the FTC Rule, their respective liabilities were limited to $779.62, the amounts paid by the debtor. However, the newly amended New York Personal Property Law provides a limitation on the creditor's liability different from that provided by the FTC Rule. Under this law, the assignee's liability "*shall not exceed*

---

[152] 104 Misc 2d 527, 428 NYS2d 581 (NY Sup Ct 1980).

[153] *Id* 584.

[154] 16 CFR §433.2 (1985); Guidelines on Trade Regulation Rule Concerning Preservation of Consumer's Claims and Defenses, 41 Fed Reg 20022, 20023 (1976) [hereinafter Guidelines].

[155] Guidelines, *supra* note 154, at 20023.

[156] 104 Misc 2d 527, 428 NYS2d 581 (NY Sup Ct 1980).

[157] *Id* 528, 428 NYS2d at 583.

the amount owing to the assignee at the time the claim or defense is asserted against the assignee"[158] (emphasis in court's opinion).

As the court remarked, under certain circumstances, a buyer would want to invoke the New York law over the FTC Rule, for example, when a greater amount is owed than has been paid. In the present case, the FTC Rule would allow a recovery of $779.62 (amount paid in), but the New York law would yield $4,864.64, the amount still due on the contract. (The plaintiffs here, however, were limited to $779.62, because the transaction took place before the New York law, which originally had allowed a recovery similar to that accorded by the FTC Rule, was amended to yield a greater recovery.)

Local, state, or other federal laws are all the more important since the FTC Rule does not create new claims or defenses. What constitutes a *claim* or *defense* has no special meaning under the Rule, but is determined by appropriate statutes, rules, and decisions in each jurisdiction.[159] For example, if the consumer buys a product and the seller disclaims any warranty by using terms such as *as is* or *with all faults,* and such disclaimers are effective under the applicable state law, the Rule would give the consumer no claim against the creditor should the product turn out to be defective. Appropriate statutes of limitations also apply. If state law provides that the consumer's right to sue for breach of warranty is extinct after a certain period, the FTC Rule would give the consumer no right against the creditor after such a period.

But once state law or other applicable rules or statutes recognize the consumer's claims and defenses, the Rule does apply to all such claims and defenses connected with the transaction, whether in tort or in contract.[160] Thus, if the consumer has a tort claim against the seller that would deny the seller's right to further payment or allow the consumer an affirmative recovery of the amount paid in, the Rule preserves the same consumer's claim or defense against the creditor. The creditor, however, is not liable for any recovery which exceeds the amount paid in. Additionally, the creditor's liability is limited only to claims or defenses arising out of the financed transaction and not to claims and defenses arising out of a separate transaction.[161]

---

[158] *Id* 529, 428 NYS2d at 583.
[159] Guidelines, *supra* note 154, at 20024.
[160] *Id.*
[161] *Id.*

10

Debt Collection and Consumer Protection

§10.01   Introduction

Usually debtors repay their debts on time. Why do some get into trouble? A study of debtors in default gave a breakdown of the major reasons for debtor default. For the most part, the debtor alone is responsible for default; yet, in some cases, the creditor is implicated. Among the reasons imputed to the debtor, the foremost is the debtor's loss of income resulting from a negative change in status—loss of employment, illness, marital instability (divorce). Other causes imputable to the debtor are overextension and irresponsibility. In this era of extensive credit and consumer borrowing, many debtors simply "bite off more than they can chew" and are unable to pay their debts. Considerable effort has been taken to reduce the hardship that the debtor experiences from unemployment or illness; however, unemployment benefits, sick leave and, as a last resort, welfare only help the debtor meet the minimum needs of existence, not pay consumer debts.

Among the reasons imputed to the creditor for causing the debtor to default, the most frequent is creditor fraud or deception which induces the debtor to misunderstand the payment schedule. This, however, is much less frequent than the debtor's mishaps.[1]

Debt collection abuse by the creditor or by a third party is a serious and widespread practice. Independent debt collection agencies are even more inclined to engage in unscrupulous practices because, unlike the creditor, their sole purpose is to collect the debt, not to provide other services, and not to seek to maintain goodwill.

It is somewhat surprising that the problem was widespread and well-known, yet, in a great number of states, there was no significant legislation to protect the debtor. For this reason, Congress stepped in and enacted legislation, such as the Fair Debt Collection Practices Act[2] and the Restrictions on Garnishment Act,[3] to protect the consumer. In this chapter, we will examine the status of the consumer with respect to debt collection under state and federal law.

§10.02   Default Defined

Debt collection problems result when the debtor defaults. Default usually means the failure to pay a debt or installment at the due date. Under the

---

[1] See D. Capovitz, Consumers in Trouble: A Study of Debtors in Default (1974).

[2] 15 USC §1692 et seq.

[3] 15 USC §§1671-1677.

common law and the Uniform Commercial Code, a creditor may act as if there was a default and accelerate the payment even before the due date. Section 1-208 of the UCC provides that "one party or his successor in interest may accelerate payment or performance or require collateral or additional collateral at will or when he deems himself insecure." A creditor often includes this *acceleration clause* in contracts for sale or credit, in time commercial paper, or in security transactions. Although UCC §1-208 specifies that the creditor can accelerate at will only if the creditor, in good faith, believes that the prospect of payment is impaired, this does not significantly help the debtor, because the Code places the burden of proving bad faith on the debtor. In *Sheppard Federal Credit Union v Palmer*,[4] an Air Force lieutenant informed the lender that he intended to resign from the Air Force. The lender repossessed the lieutenant's car, deeming itself to be insecure. The lieutenant continued to make timely payments and sued the lender. The trial court held for the lieutenant, finding that the lender failed to prove that it had acted in good faith. The Fifth Circuit reversed, holding that the burden was on the plaintiff to prove bad faith, adding that mere error alone does not show unreasonableness or bad faith.

A recent decision of the Montana Supreme Court took a more consumer-oriented view of the acceleration clause. In *First National Bank v Twombly*,[5] a bank orally promised the debtor that it would refinance a debt, but when the debtor requested refinancing, the bank refused. The debtor then informed the bank that he would be unable to make payment when due. The bank used this complaint as a ground for insecurity and, without notice, set off the debtor's account with the bank resulting in a number of bounced checks. The court acknowledged that UCC §1-208 allows the creditor to accelerate at will, but only in good faith. The court found a lack of good faith in the present case because the bank did not live up to its oral promise. The court remanded the case to determine whether punitive damages were appropriate.

Default may mean anything that the loan or credit agreement defines as default, not necessarily only the failure to pay. Typically, for instance, if the consumer sells goods subject to the creditor's interest, the agreement may define this act as a default that authorizes the creditor to take the steps necessary to collect the debt. Another example of default defined by agreement is the debtor's moving the property subject to the creditor's interest to another jurisdiction without informing the creditor, if the agreement forbids this. In other cases, default is what the parties, generally the creditor, says. One may imagine, in an unequal bargaining power situation, the possibility of abuse that may arise through an expansive definition of the term *default*. Default gives rise to creditors' remedies afforded by state law, or in the appropriate case, by federal law.

---

[4] 408 F2d 1369 (5th Cir 1969).
[5] 689 P2d 1226, 39 UCC Rep Serv (Callaghan) 1192 (Mont 1984).

§10.03   Debt Collection under State Law

Upon default, the creditor may have recourse to all remedies provided by state law. Among them are: execution on the debtor's property, garnishment, enforcement of the creditor's security interest in the debtor's property, and even imprisonment of the debtor. Self-help measures, even including the use of misrepresentations and deceits to repossess the property subject to the creditor's interest, are also permitted. The only condition of self-help measures is that there be no breach of the peace.[6] Trespass is not considered to be a breach of the peace in most instances unless a specific statute says so.[7]

Nearly 40 states have enacted statutes patterned after the Federal Fair Debt Collection Practices Act, which we will discuss later, to regulate debt collection practices of creditors or third-party collectors. In those states that have no such statutes, abusive debt collection practices may fall under the relevant provisions of consumer protection statutes such as the Uniform Consumer Credit Code or the "little FTC Acts" prohibiting unfair and deceptive acts or practices.[8]

§10.04   Seizing the Debtor's Property: Execution and Garnishment

Upon default, the creditor may commence an action and pursue it to a judgment. In many jurisdictions, the judgment becomes an automatic lien on the debtor's real estate in the county where the judgment is obtained. Only three states, Alabama,[9] Georgia,[10] and Mississippi,[11] allow automatic liens on both real and personal property. In most states, judgment by itself does not enforce the creditor's interest in the debtor's personal property. The creditor must take further steps, such as obtaining a writ of execution from the clerk of the court, to allow the creditor to seize and sell the property. In the case of land, the land can be sold through foreclosure proceedings, or, in some cases, a writ of execution is required. The law in this area varies according to jurisdiction. Generally, the common law does not include any special provisions for the plight of the consumer.

The creditor may obtain a lien on the debtor's property even before judgment is rendered. New York, for instance, permits prejudgment garnishments if the debtor is about to depart the state or is a nonresident.[12] Like execution, garnishment proceedings vary from state to state. In a typical garnishment proceeding, the writ is directed not to the debtor, but to a person

---

[6] UCC §9-503.

[7] *See* U3C §5.112 (1974).

[8] P. Rasor, Consumer Finance Law 563 (1985).

[9] Ala Code §6-9-211 (1975).

[10] Ga Code Ann §24-608 (1986 & Supp 1987).

[11] Miss Code Ann §11-7-191 (1972).

[12] NY Civ Prac Law §6201 (McKinney 1980).

who owes money to the debtor or who holds property belonging to the debtor. Wage garnishments are the most common and contoversial form of debt collection.

The most important decision dealing with garnishment of wages was the Supreme Court's in *Sniadach v Family Finance Corp.*[13] In that case, the Court struck down a Wisconsin statute which did not require any hearing on the merits before the garnishment proceedings even though *in personam* jurisdiction could be obtained. The court stated that such garnishment was a taking of property without due process. Justice Douglas emphasized that "wages were a specialized type of property."[14] Many questions, however, were left unanswered. The Court did not clarify what type of hearing would comply with the constitutional requirement—two-party hearing, full trial, or ex parte hearing? *Sniadach* involved a prejudgment garnishment; does it cover postgarnishment as well? What about other types of garnishment besides wage garnishment? Does *Sniadach* apply?

The opinion also suggests that prejudgment garnishment "may well meet the requirements of due process in extraordinary situations,"[15] but what situations would be extraordinary? The only thing that is clear is that, under *Sniadach*, unrestricted garnishment could violate due process. The specifics are unclear. They remain unclear in the cases that followed *Sniadach*, including *Fuentes v Shevin*,[16] *Mitchell v WT Grant Co*,[17] and *North Georgia Furnishings, Inc v Di Chem, Inc*,[18]

Fuentes v Shevin extended the *Sniadach* due process requirement to property other than wages and to prejudgment proceedings other than garnishment. In this case, the property was consumer goods involved in a replevin proceeding. The Court held the Florida and Pennsylvania prejudgment replevin statutes to be unconstitutional. The Court required notice and hearing prior to the seizure of property, except in extraordinary situations. The *Fuentes* Court implied that *extraordinary situations* could exist upon "a showing of immediate danger that the debtor will destroy or conceal disputed goods."[19]

Justice White filed a dissenting opinion in *Fuentes* and pointed out that creditors could avoid the constitutional issue by simply providing in the security agreement that repossession may occur without notice and hearing. Justice White also noted that *Fuentes* would raise the expense of credit and make it less available to consumers.

Mitchell involved a Louisiana statute that permitted a judge to issue, without a hearing or notice, a writ of sequestration of the debtor's property. Written by Justice White, who dissented in *Fuentes*, *Mitchell* prompted some to conclude

---

[13] 395 US 337 (1969).

[14] *Id* 340.

[15] *Id* 352.

[16] 407 US 67 (1972).

[17] 416 US 600 (1974).

[18] 419 US 601 (1975).

[19] 407 US at 93.

that *Fuentes* was overruled. Justice White distinguished the Louisiana statute from the Florida and Pennsylvania statutes in *Fuentes* by pointing out that the application for prejudgment replevin was made to a judge, not to a clerk, as in *Fuentes*.

North Georgia Furnishing suggests that those who announced the death of *Fuentes* were premature. *North Georgia* involved the prejudgment garnishment of the bank account of a corporate debtor. The Georgia statute, the Court found, contained none of the seven characteristics of the Louisiana statute upheld in *Mitchell*. In finding that the Georgia statute violated the due process clause, the Court referred to *Fuentes*. But it also relied on *Mitchell*. Under the Georgia statute, a creditor needed only to file an affidavit containing conclusory allegations of right with a court clerk to obtain the garnishment order. The creditor argued that due process protection should not be extended to corporate debtors, but the Court found that the risk of irreparable injury was sufficiently great so that corporate debtors also needed protection.

While the relationship between these cases is not entirely clear, some broad conclusions may be drawn. Except in extraordinary situations, such as clear evidence of destruction of the property, due process requires notice and the opportunity for a hearing, not necessarily before a judge, but before a competent official, and subject to certain limits, prejudgment garnishment is not unconstitutional per se. Finally, the constitutional issue arises only when a state statute is involved, not where individual action is involved.

§10.05   Repossession

Except in Louisiana, state law dealing with the enforcement of security interests in the debtor's personal property is the Uniform Commercial Code. The UCC allows the creditor to take the law into the creditor's own hands through *self-help*. Section 9-503 of the UCC provides: "Unless otherwise agreed, a secured party has on default the right to take possession of the collateral. In taking possession a party may proceed without judicial process if this can be done without breach of the peace or may proceed by action."

An often controversial issue is the term *breach of the peace*, which is a condition to determine the lawfulness or unlawfulness of the creditor's self-help measures. For example, the creditor can repossess a car owned by the debtor, but subject to the creditor's security interest, by simply using a duplicate key to drive the car from the debtor's driveway. Usually, a court will find that the peace has not been breached when the debtor does not give his or her permission on the one hand, but on the other hand, fails to object. In *Williams v Ford Motor Credit Corp*,[20] the creditor repossessed the debtor's car at approximately 4:30 AM. The debtor went outside of her house trailer and shouted at the repossessor. The court held that the repossession was lawful,

---

[20] 674 F2d 717 (8th Cir 1982).

because, even though the debtor ran outside to stop the repossessor, she did not strenuously protest the action.

Trespass is also a self-help issue. The UCC has no provision forbidding trespass for repossession. The Uniform Consumer Credit Code (U3C), however, considers trespass to be unlawful per se.[21]

Self-help has been attacked as unconstitutional under the Fourteenth Amendment's due process clause. Thus far, constitutional challenges to UCC §9-503 have failed because there was no state action with the repossession.

§10.06   Imprisonment for Debt

One remembers Dickens's father being imprisoned for failing to pay his debts. Imprisonment for debts was a fixture of Roman law. In its earlier period, a creditor who had secured a judgment against the debtor had considerable rights against the debtor's person. If the judgment debt was not paid within 30 days, the creditor could detain the debtor in the creditor's private prison. The creditor might even kill the debtor or sell him or her into slavery.

The common law continued the Roman tradition, even though there was a subtle difference. Under the common law, imprisonment for failure to perform a judgment to pay was not imprisonment for debt per se, but imprisonment for contempt of court, which was a quasi-criminal offense.[22] In practice, imprisonment for debt was common. By the time of Blackstone, all the courts of common law were arresting defendants in suits pending before them by issuing a writ called *capias ad respondendum.* The writ called *capias ad satisfaciendum* allows execution of a money judgment by imprisonment.[23]

In the United States, *body execution,* or imprisonment of the debtor until satisfaction of the debt, was accepted until the 1930s, when it was declared to be cruel and unusual punishment. States now forbid imprisonment for debt, either under their constitutions, common law, or statutory law. However, certain statutes still result in imprisonment for debt. For example, a statute may cause a person to be prosecuted for writing bad checks and imprisoned. Also, a statute may provide that it is a crime to impair collateral by selling it without the creditor's permission.[24] In *United States v Bellman,*[25] a farmer was convicted under a federal statute which provides fines and imprisonment for "whoever, with intent to defraud, knowingly conceals, removes, disposes of, or converts to his own use or that of another, any property mortgaged or pledged to, or held by . . . any production credit association . . .."[26]

Some courts have used the contempt power to "seize" the debtor. *Early Used*

---

[21] U3C §5.112 (1974).

[22] *See* Ford, *Imprisonment for Debt,* 25 Mich L Rev 24, 26 (1926).

[23] *Id* 28-29.

[24] *See, e.g.,* Kan Stat Ann §21-3734 (1981).

[25] 741 F2d 1116 (8th Cir 1984).

[26] 18 USC §658.

Cars, Inc. v Province[27] illustrates this approach. In this case, the creditor (Early Used Cars, Inc) obtained a judgment against the debtor in the sum of $408.48 including interest, costs, and attorneys' fees. Upon the creditor's application, a summons was issued by the clerk's office to be served upon the debtor requiring the latter to appear before the commission in chancery to answer interrogatories concerning the debtor's estate upon which the judgment would be executed. The debtor failed to appear. The creditor then presented to the commissioner proposed writ for the debtor's arrest. The proposed writ also provided that the debtor could discharge the writ by paying the court's judgment. The commissioner had misgivings about the writ and declined to sign it.

On appeal, the Supreme Court of Virginia held that the summons served on the debtor was an official court process and, therefore, the debtor ignored it at his peril. The court pointed out that contempt leading to the debtor's imprisonment would have been based not upon the debtor's failure to pay, but upon his failure to comply with the summons. Such contempt power is often threatened to be used as leverage for debt collection, especially in child support and alimony cases. Most courts, however, seem reluctant to resort to the extreme measure of body execution to exact payment.[28]

§10.07 Disposition of the Debtor's Property

A lien on the debtor's property obtained through a judgment or a consensual security interest gives the creditor the right to dispose of the debtor's property in order to recover the credit advanced. The Uniform Commercial Code gives creditors great flexibility in disposing of the collateral, even without judicial intervention. UCC §9-504 states that a secured party "after default may sell, lease or otherwise dispose of any or all of the collateral in its then condition or following any commercially reasonable preparations or process." Two limits are placed on the creditor's rights: the debtor must be given notice; and the disposition must be commercially reasonable.

In most circumstances, the secured party must give the debtor and certain other third parties (such as the owner of the collateral, a surety, or the guarantor of the debt) reasonable notice of the disposition. The notice requirement is justified on the ground that the disposition of the collateral will effect the debtor, since the debtor, following the disposition, is entitled to any surplus, or is liable for any deficiency, unless otherwise agreed. If the disposition is made through a public sale, the notice must state the time and place of the sale. With respect to a private sale or any other type of disposition,

---

[27] 218 Va 605, 239 SE2d 98 (1977).

[28] *See* P. Rasor, Consumer Finance Law 566-70 (1985).

the notice need only state the time at which the private sale or other disposition is to be made. Usually, public sale means an auction sale.[29]

A public sale usually requires advertising and a sizeable number of bidders. For instance, in *In re Bishop*,[30] the sale was held by auction in the dealer's used car lot in a public place; however, it was not advertised, and only two persons were present. The court held that it was not a public sale, and that the purchase of the collateral by the secured party was invalid.

The secured party has discretion to choose either a public or private sale to maximize profit. Notice, whether in a public or private sale, must include a description of the collateral and the type of sale. It must be in writing and sent to the debtor and all interested parties. Usually there is no notice requirement when the goods are perishable, the goods threaten to speedily decline in value, or the goods are customarily sold under recognized markets.[31] The debtor cannot waive the notice requirement prior to default.[32]

The disposition of the collateral must also be commercially reasonable. There is no definition of *commercially reasonable*. Usually the good faith standard is used to determine whether the requirement has been met. In *Central Budget Corp v Garrett*,[33] the court stated that a commercially reasonable disposition requires a good faith effort to protect the interests of both the secured party and the debtor. Courts usually look at all the circumstances surrounding the sale: the time, manner, method, and place. Under the UCC, the fact that a better price could have been obtained at a different time or with a method of sale different from that selected by the secured party is not necessarily commercially unreasonable.[34] Furthermore, under the UCC, the burden is on the debtor to show that the sale was not concluded in a commercially reasonable manner.[35] Usually the court will scrutinize a sale more closely if the disposition of the collateral results in a deficiency for which the debtor is liable. Like the notice requirement, a prior agreement may not waive the creditor's duty to proceed in a commercially reasonable manner,[36] but the parties may determine their own standard of what constitutes *reasonable* by agreement.[37]

If the disposition is not reasonable, some courts deny the secured party the right to a deficiency altogether.[38] Other courts, however, merely reduce the right to deficiency by the difference between the amount obtained and the

---

[29] UCC §9-504 comment 1, §2-706 comment 4.

[30] 482 F2d 2381, 12 UCC Rep Serv (Callahan) 1256 (4th Cir 1973).

[31] UCC §9-504(3).

[32] UCC §9-501(3).

[33] 48 AD2d 825, 368 NYS2d 268, 17 UCC Rep Serv (Callaghan) 327 (1975).

[34] UCC §9-507(2).

[35] *Id.*

[36] UCC §9-501(3).

[37] UCC §1-203.

[38] *See* Central Budget Corp v Garrett, 48 AD2d 825, 368 NYS2d 268, 17 UCC Rep Serv (Callaghan) 327 (1975) and Nixdorf Computer Inc v Jet Forwarding Inc, 579 F2d 1175 (9th Cir 1978).

amount which should have been obtained had there been a commercially reasonable disposition.[39]

§10.08 Strict Foreclosure

The Uniform Commercial Code is not a consumer protection statute. However, there are a few provisions written with the consumer in mind. Section 9-505 on strict foreclosure is one such provision.

Strict foreclosure applies when secured creditors do not wish to go through the disposition of the collateral in order to collect the debt, but instead keep the collateral as total satisfaction of the debt. An agreement to retain the collateral in satisfaction of the debt is effective except when the collateral is consumer goods and the debtor has paid 60 per cent or more of the debt. In this instance, the debtor must consent to strict foreclosure in writing. Under the UCC, goods are consumer goods if they are used or bought for use primarily for personal, family, or household purposes.[40]

§10.09 Cumulation of Debt Collection Devices

Under the Uniform Commercial Code, a creditor may use either non-Code methods or Code methods for realizing on the collateral. Both methods are cumulative. This approach differs from pre-UCC law which required the creditor to elect the remedies.[41] Now, the Code allows a secured party to reduce its claim to judgment, foreclosure, or otherwise enforce the security interest, by any available judicial procedure.[42] However, a consumer harassed by a creditor who pursues several avenues of attack at the same time may rely on the opinion of Professors James T. White and Robert S. Summers that neither case law nor the language of the Code authorizes the "double-barrelled" approach.[43]

The UCC does not preempt other state statutes that afford the consumer more protection. Local statutes, such as small loan statutes and retail installment sales statutes, still apply. As the note under UCC §9-203(4) explains:

> This Article (9) is designed to regulate all the "security" aspects of transactions within its scope. There is, however, much regulatory legislation, particularly in the consumer field, which supplements this Article and should not be repealed by its enactment. Examples are small loan acts, retail installment selling acts and the like. Such acts may provide for licensing and rate regulation and may prescribe particular forms of

---

[39] *See* Barbour v United States, 562 F2d 1919 (10th Cir 1977).

[40] UCC §9-109(1).

[41] *See* cases cited in Annotation, *Bringing Action for Price as Waiver by Conditional Vendor of Right to Reclaim Property,* 113 ALR 653 (1938).

[42] UCC §9-501(1).

[43] J. White & R. Summer, Uniform Commercial Code §26-4, at 1093-94 (1980).

contract. Such provisions should remain in force despite the enactment of this Article. On the other hand, if a retail installment selling act contains provisions on filing, right on default, etc., such provisions should be repealed as inconsistent with this Article except that inconsistent provisions as to deficiencies, penalties, etc., in the Uniform Consumer Credit Code and other recent related legislation should remain because those statutes were drafted after the substantial enactment of the Article and with the intention of modifying certain provisions of this Article as to consumer credit.

Under the UCC, if the collateral is both real and personal property, the secured party may proceed under the UCC as to the personal property or may proceed as to both the real and personal property under state real estate law.[44] One court, however, has said that the creditor cannot proceed against the realty under state real estate law and then apply the UCC to personal property.[45] Another court had a more reasonable interpretation: that a creditor can select to apply either real estate law against both the real and personal property in one action, or, in two separate actions, apply UCC law to the personalty and real estate law to the realty.[46] In the last few years, Congress has entered the field of debt collection, enacting legislation that considerably restricts the rights of creditors with a view to protecting the consumer.

§10.10   Federal Regulation of Garnishment

The federal regulation of garnishment is the subject of Title III of the Consumer Credit Protection Act.[47] The purpose of the Act is threefold:

1. To save the consumer from predatory extensions of credit by restricting garnishment on the consumer's wages
2. To prevent the employer from dismissing the consumer-employee who is the object of a garnishment order
3. To remedy the great disparity among state laws regarding garnishment, which destroys the uniformity of federal bankruptcy law[48]

The Act does not prohibit garnishment of wages altogether, but sets forth a number of requirements and restrictions. The Act contains some key definitions which are subject to interpretation.

---

[44] UCC §9-501(4).

[45] United States Aircraft Fin Inc v Jankovich, 407 NE2d 287 (Ind Ct App 1980).

[46] State Bank v Hanson, 302 NW2d 760, 30 UCC Rep Serv (Callaghan) 1493 (ND 1981).

[47] Pub L No 90-31, 82 Stat 146 (codified as amended in scattered sections of 15 and 18 USC).

[48] 15 USC §1671(a).

Garnishment

The Act defines garnishment as "any legal or equitable procedure through which the earnings of any individual are required to be withheld for any payment of any debt."[49] Although the Act is not explicit on the subject, several courts have interpreted Title III to cover both pre- and postjudgment garnishments.[50]

Courts equally broadly interpret what constitutes a garnishment. For example, an order for the support of any person is a garnishment order under the statute. The test is only whether, pursuant to such order, the earnings of the individual are required to be withheld to meet the requirements of the order.[51] Generally, nonjudicial transactions, such as wage assignments, are not garnishments for the purpose of Title III.[52] However, an Iowa court held that wage assignment by a debtor to satisfy a child support obligation was garnishment.[53]

Earnings

Another important issue is what constitutes *earnings*. The statute defines earnings to mean "compensation paid or payable for personal services, whether denominated as wages, salary, commission, bonus, or otherwise, and includes periodic payments to a pension or retirement program."[54] The Administrator of the Wage and Hour Division of the Department of Labor has ruled that sick pay is included in earnings.[55] Also, meals and lodging provided by the employer are earnings.[56]

Generally, the courts have held that one should ignore the label given to the money due, whether it be *wages, salary, commission,* or the like. The sole criterion is whether the funds subject to garnishment in fact represent compensation for personal services.[57] Under this test, it has been held that pensions and benefits under programs of the Veterans' Administration, Social Security Administration, and county welfare departments are not earnings for purposes of Title III because they do not represent *compensation for personal services.*[58] Garnishment

---

[49] 15 USC §1672(c).

[50] *See* Hodgson v Christopher, 365 F Supp 583 (DND 1973); General Motors Acceptance Corp v Metropolitan Opera Assn, 98 Misc 2d 307, 413 NYS2d 818 (App Term 1978).

[51] Marshall v District Court for Forty-First Dist, 444 F Supp 1110 (ED Mich 1978).

[52] *See* Western v Hodgson, 494 F2d 379, 382 (4th Cir 1974).

[53] Koethe v Johnson, 328 NW2d 293 (Iowa 1982).

[54] 15 USC §1672(a).

[55] Opinion letter of Employment Standards Administrator, [1969-1973 Transfer Binder] Lab L Rep (CCH) ¶30,836 (Feb 1, 1973).

[56] *Id* ¶30,712 (Dec 9, 1970). *See* D. Rothschild & D. Carroll, Consumer Protection Reporting Service, pt Two, ch 10 (1973) (Garnishment).

[57] *See* Gary Elson Agency Inc v Muck, 509 SW2d 750 (Mo Ct App 1974).

[58] Phillips v Bartolomie, 46 Cal App 3d 346, 121 Cal Rptr 56 (1975).

from these payments, however, may also be restricted under other federal statutes.[59] Proceeds of a life insurance policy are not earnings.[60]

Disposable Earnings

Another term to be defined is *disposable earnings*. The Act defines *disposable earnings* to mean "that part of the earnings of any individual remaining after the deduction from those earnings of any amounts required by law to be withheld."[61] Courts have interpreted amounts required by law to be withheld to include deductions for social security and withholding taxes, but not amounts withheld pursuant to an order for the support of any person.[62]

§10.11—Restrictions on Garnishment

The Act imposes a maximum allowable garnishment on the weekly aggregate disposable earnings of the debtor. The garnishment may not exceed:

> (1) Twenty-five percent of the debtor's disposable earnings for that week, or
>
> (2) The amount by which the debtor's disposable earnings for the week exceed thirty times the Federal minimum hourly wage in effect at the time the earnings are payable.[63]

These limits do not apply to the following:

> 1. Garnishment pursuant to an order for the support of any person such as child support or alimony. The garnishment here could go up to 60 per cent of the debtor's disposable earnings. This 60 per cent is reduced to 50 per cent if the debtor is supporting either or both a spouse or dependent child, and the garnishment for support concerns someone else, such as a former spouse. The 50 per cent limit may be raised to 55 per cent, and the 60 per cent limit to 65 per cent, if the earnings are subject to garnishment to enforce a support order with respect to a period prior to the 12-week period which ends with the beginning of such work week[64]
>
> 2. Orders issued by federal bankruptcy courts in accordance with Chapter 13 of the Bankruptcy Code[65]

---

[59] 38 USC §3101; 42 USC §407.

[60] John Hancock Mut Life Ins Co v First Natl Bank, 393 F Supp 204 (ED Tenn 1974), *affd mem*, 516 F2d 901 (6th Cir 1975).

[61] 15 USC §1672(b).

[62] *See*, e.g., Marshall v District Court for Forty-First Dist, 444 F Supp 1110 (ED Mich 1978).

[63] 15 USC §1673(a).

[64] 15 USC §1673(b)(1)(A) and (2), (b) (2) (B).

[65] 15 USC §1673(b)(1)(B).

3. Debts due for state and federal tax[66]

Where applicable, the maximum garnishment limit applies to not one but to all the creditors' claims combined.

As an illustration, suppose the debtor's yearly salary is $12,000. Suppose the debtor's deductions are $100 for tax, $50 for social security and $20 for insurance. The debtor's monthly disposable earnings would be $850 (the $20 insurance is not included for determining disposable earnings because insurance deduction is not "required by law to be withheld").[67] The debtor's weekly disposable earnings would be $212.50. The Act limits the amount that the debtor's creditors can garnish to 25 per cent of $212.50, or $53.125. If the debtor is supporting a spouse or a child, the debtor's former spouse may garnish up to 50 per cent of $212.50, or $106.25. If the debtor is not supporting a spouse or child, the debtor can be sued for child support or alimony up to 60 per cent of $212.50, or $159.35

However, one must also take into account the requirement that the exemption also apply to an amount equal to 30 times the federal minimum wage. For example, if the minimum wage is $3.35, the amount equal to 30 times the minimum wage is $100.50. This amount is completely exempt. If the debtor's pay is $125.00 weekly, the creditor may reach only $24.50 per week ($125.00 − $100.50) which is less than 25 per cent of the weekly earnings. For the 25 per cent limit to trigger, the debtor's weekly disposable earnings would have to be at least $134.00. The Regulation to Title III, reprinted in 29 CFR §870.10, gives tables of the amounts, weekly, bimonthly, and monthly, that cannot be garnished, based on the minimum wage.

In *KoKoszka v Belford*,[68] the Supreme Court clarified the issue of whether, in the case of bankruptcy, the trustee in bankruptcy (who represents the unsecured creditors) is limited to 25 per cent of the bankrupt's income tax refund. The Supreme Court, based on the Act's legislative history, held that *earnings*, as defined in the Act, did not include tax refunds, even if they are directly traceable to earnings.[69] Therefore, there is no 25 per cent limitation as to the right of the trustee in bankruptcy, since an income tax refund is not an *exempt asset*. This illustrates that not *all* income traceable to wages is exempt.

In *Sears Roebuck v AT&G Co*,[70] the garnishee agreed with the employer to a weekly deduction of 25 per cent of his disposable income to repay prior loans from the employer. The court held that a subsequent creditor could garnish nothing because the 25 per cent limitation had been reached.

However, in *Bache Halsey Steward Shields Inc v Killop*,[71] the court held that the debtor's voluntary assignment of 25 per cent of his earnings to his employer

---

[66] 15 USC §1673(b)(1)(C).

[67] 15 USC §1672(b).

[68] 417 US 642, *reh denied*, 419 US 886 (1974).

[69] 417 US at 651.

[70] 66 Mich App 359, 239 NW2d 614 (1976).

[71] 589 F Supp 390 (ED Mich 1984).

in satisfaction of a promissory note was not a prior garnishment which precluded a subsequent garnishment, thus declining to follow *Sears Roebuck*.

Wages placed into a bank account are considered disposable income subject to the 25 per cent limit on garnishment. The California Supreme Court made it clear that a bank may not exercise its right of setoff against deposits derived from employment and disability benefits, holding that they were exempt property.[72] The issue in such cases is tracing the bank deposit to income. Title III gives no guidelines on this. One must refer to state law to determine the tracing method.

The federal statute also fails to address the problem of priority among wage garnishments if there are more than one. The Secretary of Labor, by regulation, has referred the priority issue to state law.[73] Usually child support enjoys priority over a judgment creditor's garnishment.[74]

§10.12 —Protection of Consumer from Discharge for Garnishment

Employers required by court order to garnish the employee's wages are tempted to dismiss the employee for several reasons. One may cite among them the employer's fear that the employee will have less incentive to work and therefore will be less productive, as well as the employer's desire not to be burdened with employees who are unable to manage their own financial affairs. Employers are also reluctant to have to cope with law enforcement proceedings.

The Act prohibits the discharge of any employee "by reason of the fact that his earnings have been subjected to garnishment for any one indebtedness."[75] This language means that the Act does not protect the employee subject to garnishment based on more than a single indebtedness.

What constitutes *one indebtedness* as opposed to *more than one indebtedness* is subject to interpretation. Generally, multiple garnishments from the same creditor constitute only one indebtedness, and the employer cannot discharge the employee. But if garnishments are requested by more than one creditor, there is more than one indebtedness, and the employer can discharge the employee.

Some courts, however, have broadened the scope of the prohibition by giving a liberal interpretation to the term *one single indebtedness. Brennan v Kroger Co*[76] is illustrative of this liberal attitude. On September 20, 1970, a first court order was entered directing Kroger to garnish the wages of Boyd, a Kroger employee, to satisfy a judgment claim against him. Pursuant to the

---

[72] Kroger v Wells Fargo Bank, 11 Cal 3d 352, 521 P2d 441, 113 Cal Rptr 449, (1974).

[73] 29 CFR §870.11(b)(2).

[74] *See* Donovan v Hamilton County Mun Court, 580 F Supp 554 (SD Ohio 1984).

[75] 15 USC §1674(a).

[76] 513 F2d 961 (7th Cir 1975).

order, Kroger began to withhold the maximum allowable amount from Boyd's wages. A month later, on October 22, 1970, Kroger received a second court order directing Kroger to apply the earnings of Boyd to the satisfaction of another judgment, based on a debt unrelated to the debt which gave rise to the first order. As a result, Kroger discharged the employee.

The Seventh Circuit agreed with the Secretary of Labor's contention that Kroger's dismissal of Boyd was in violation of Title III because the second order did not constitute a second subjection to garnishment since the maximum amount permitted by law was already withheld from Boyd's wages pursuant to the first order. As a result, no withholding whatever was made from Boyd's wages pursuant to the second order. As the court saw it: "By their terms, both of the orders were in the nature of continuing liens against the earnings of Boyd, and the order which was first in time was entitled to full satisfaction before any withholding could be made for the purpose of satisfying the second order."[77] Under this construction, in order for earnings to be considered subjected to garnishment, those earnings must actually be withheld. Thus, there can never be garnishment for more than one indebtedness if a single garnishment already exhausts the maximum legal amount allowed to be garnished.

The Ninth Circuit adopted the same reasoning in *Donovan v Southern California Gas Co.*[78] In this case, on May 9, 1977, the employer received a notice of garnishment for a debt the employee owed to Creditor One. Upon receipt of the notice, the employer reviewed with the employee the company's written policy regarding garnishment. On May 18, 1977, and May 27, 1977, the employer remitted the garnished earnings to Creditor One. Under the company's policy, these remittances on separate dates were counted as the employee's first and second garnishments.

On May 31, 1977, the company received a second notice of garnishment and writ of execution against the employee from Creditor Two. Under the company's policy, this constituted a third garnishment for two debts within a nine-month period and, as a consequence, the employee was required to take a two-day disciplinary lay-off. She was also warned that another garnishment within the nine-month period would result in her termination.

On June 13, 1977, the company received an order from Creditor One to release the May 9, 1977, garnishment. But six months later, the company received another notice of garnishment from the same creditor. The company reminded the employee that this notice constituted a fourth garnishment, and informed her that she was terminated. Thereupon, the employee made arrangements with Creditor One, and a week later, an order to release from Creditor One was sent to the company. The Secretary of Labor, acting on behalf of the employee, brought suit on her behalf, seeking her reinstatement and back wages.

The Ninth Circuit, citing *Brennan v Kroger,* and noting that Title III's purpose

---

[77] *Id* 962.
[78] 715 F2d 1405 (9th Cir 1983).

was to preserve an employee's job, held that the termination was improper, because garnishment did not occur until such time as earnings were actually withheld, and not at the time the employer received a legally binding garnishment notice.[79]

§10.13 —Enforcement of Federal Law on Garnishment Restrictions

An employer who willfully dismisses an employee for garnishment in violation of Title III of the Consumer Credit Protection Act is subject to a maximum $1000 fine or imprisonment up to one year or both.[80] The Secretary of Labor, acting through the Wage and Hour Division of the Department of Labor, is responsible for enforcing the Act.[81]

Title III, on its face, does not provide for private enforcement of its provisions. The question whether such private enforcement is implicit in the Act has not been determined by the Supreme Court and is still a matter of conflict between the state and federal courts. While most courts have stuck to a restrictive interpretation of §1676 of the Act, designating the Secretary of Labor as its enforcement authority,[82] some courts in recent years have allowed a private right of action on the ground that private enforcement is necessary to ensure the fulfillment of the congressional purpose of protecting the benefited class of employees against discharge for garnishment. The Court of Appeals for the Ninth Circuit began this trend in *Stewart v Travelers Corp.*[83] The Court argued that no clear congressional intent against private action was apparent, and that criminal penalties alone are insufficient to protect the discharged employee. In *Ellis v Glover & Gardner Construction Co,*[84] a district court in Tennessee followed the Ninth Circuit decision, reasoning that "it would be unreasonable to infer that Congress intended the subchapter's limited enforcement provision to be the sole remedy."[85] Accordingly, the court ordered the employer to reinstate the plaintiff and provide him with back pay in order to "make the plaintiff whole,"[86] but denied punitive damages and attorneys' fees. The court seemed to imply, however, that punitive damages

---

[79] *Id* 1406.

[80] 15 USC §1674(b).

[81] 15 USC §1676.

[82] *See* Western v Hogson, 359 F Supp 194 (SD W Va 1973), *affd,* 494 F2d 379, (4th Cir 1974) Smith v Cotton Bros Baking co, 609 F2d 738 (5th Cir, *cert denied,* 449 US 821 (1980); McCabe v City of Eureka, 500 F Supp 59 (ED Mo 1980); LeVick v Skaggs Co, 701 F2d 777 (10th Cir 1983).

[83] 503 F2d 108 (9th Cir 1974).

[84] 562 F Supp 1054 (MD Tenn 1983).

[85] *Id* 1061.

[86] *Id* 1067.

may be awarded in cases of malicious or willful discharge, and that attorneys' fees may be allowed in "extraordinary circumstances."[87]

§10.14 —Garnishment of Federal Employees' Wages

Due to the doctrine of sovereign immunity, wages of federal employees cannot be garnished. A private citizen may not sue the government without its consent. Title III of the Consumer Credit Protection Act restricting wage garnishment does not constitute a waiver of sovereign immunity. However, pursuant to §659 of Title 42, the United States has consented to garnishment and similar proceedings for the enforcement of child support and alimony legal obligations of federal employees, including members of the Armed Services. Sections 659-662 set forth the special procedure for serving a garnishment order or process upon the federal government. The Office of Personnel Management interprets and implements §659 through regulations reprinted in 5 CFR §581.101.

Section 659 has been strictly construed. It has been held that this section was not intended, and cannot be used, to make federal courts a forum for the settlement of marital disputes in which the United States is the debtor of one of the spouses.[88]

§10.15 The Fair Debt Collection Practices Act

The Fair Debt Collection Practices Act (FDCPA) was enacted on September 21, 1977, and became effective six months later on March 20, 1978.[89] The purpose of the Act was "to eliminate abusive debt collection practices by debt collectors, to insure that those debt collectors who refrain from using abusive debt collection practices, are not competitively disadvantaged, and to promote consistent state action to protect consumers against debt collection abuses."[90] Congress found that existing state and federal laws were inadequate to fully address the problem caused by debt collectors' using unfair or deceptive practices. These abuses contributed to personal bankruptcies, marital instability, loss of jobs, and invasions of individual privacy.[91]

The Federal Trade Commission (FTC) has primary authority to enforce the provisions of the Act.[92] The FDCPA does not give the FTC special powers to enact binding regulations to implement the Act. Rather, by stating that any

---

[87] Id.

[88] Kelley v Kelley, 425 F Supp 181 (WD La 1977). See 14 C. Wright, A. Miller & E. Cooper, Federal Practice and Procedure 2d §3656 (1985).

[89] The FDCPA was enacted as Title VIII of the Consumer Credit Protection Act, Pub L No 95-109, 91 Stat 874-83 (codified as amended at 15 USC §§1692-1692.

[90] 15 USC §1692(e).

[91] 15 USC §1692(a).

[92] 15 USC §16921(a).

violation of the Act constitutes an unfair or deceptive act or practice under the Federal Trade Commission Act, Congress makes available to the FTC all the functions and powers provided by the FTC Act.[93] Further, any violation of the provisions of the FDCPA is considered a violation of an FTC trade regulation rule.[94]

The FTC has promulgated *advisory opinions* which have some legal effect. The Act provides that no civil liability may apply "to any act done or omitted in good faith in conformity with any advisory opinion of the Commission, notwithstanding that after such act or omission has occurred such opinion is amended, rescinded, or determined by judicial or other authority to be invalid for any reason."[95]

The FTC has published a proposed staff commentary on the FDCPA and requested public comment.[96] The commentary seeks to combine the several hundred informal FTC staff interpretations of the FDCPA. While the commentary is not binding upon the courts, it may guide them.

§10.16   —Scope

The Act applies principally to debt collectors. Creditors are subject to the Act only in limited circumstances. The term *debt collector* means "any person who uses any instrumentality of interstate commerce or the mails in any business the principal purpose of which is the collection of any debts, or who regularly collects or attempts to collect, directly or indirectly, debts owed or due or asserted to be owed or due another."[97] The interstate commerce requirement is not really a limitation, because the Act still applies to one who regularly attempts to collect debts, even if such person does not use any instrumentality of interstate commerce. A justification of congressional action could be based on the ground stated in the declaration of the purpose of the Act that "[e]ven where abusive debt collection practices are purely intrastate in character, they nevertheless directly effect interstate commerce."[98]

The term *debt collector* does not include creditors who, directly or indirectly, try to collect their own debts. But the term does include any creditor who, in the process of collecting his own debts, uses any name other than his own which would indicate that a third person is collecting or attempting to collect such debts.[99]

Clearly, collection agencies whose main activity is to collect debts in return for a commission or pursuant to a debt assignment are the prime targets of the

---

[93] *Id.*

[94] *Id.*

[95] 15 USC §1692k(e).

[96] 51 Fed Reg 8019-29 (Mar 7, 1986).

[97] 15 USC §1692a(6).

[98] 15 USC §1692(d).

[99] 15 USC 1692a(6).

Act. These agencies are more prone to engage in abusive practices than the creditors themselves because, unlike creditors, they are not concerned with preserving their clientele or their goodwill.

For the purposes of the Act, the creditor is any person who offers or extends credit creating a debt or to whom a debt is owed, but the term does not include any person who receives an assignment of a debt in default solely for the purpose of facilitating collection of such debt for another.[100] In other words, an assignee of a debt for collection only is not a creditor under the Act. Such assignee may be a debt collector subject to the Act if it regularly collects debts for others.

A *debt* is any obligation or alleged obligation of a consumer to pay money arising out of a transaction in which the money, property, insurance, or services which are the subject of the transaction are primarily for personal, family, or household purposes, whether or not the obligation has been reduced to judgment.[101]

§10.17 —Exclusions

The following are not *debt collectors* and, therefore, are excluded from the scope of the Act.

> 1. Any officer or employee of a creditor collecting debts for the creditor in the creditor's name. In other words, the Act does not apply to *in-house* collection[102]
>
> 2. Any person acting as a debt collector for another person with whom it is related by common ownership or corporate control, but whose principal business is not debt collection[103]
>
> 3. Any federal or state officer or employee to the extent that collecting debts is in the performance of his or her duties[104]
>
> 4. Any person serving legal process in connection with the judicial enforcement of a debt[105]
>
> 5. Any nonprofit organization, such as a consumer counseling agency, assisting the consumer in the liquidation of the consumer's debt[106]
>
> 6. Any person collecting debts owed another in the capacity of a bona fide fiduciary or escrow agent for whom collection of the debt is only an incidental function or of a collector who collects a debt owed to another that was originated by the collector. For example, a seller who assigns the

---

[100] 15 USC §1692a(4).

[101] 15 USC §1691a(5).

[102] 15 USC §1962a(6)(A).

[103] 15 USC §1692a(6)(B).

[104] 15 USC §1692a(6)(C).

[105] 15 USC §1692a(6)(D).

[106] 15 USC §1692a(6)(E).

buyer's installment sales contract to a finance company with recourse, and the seller is the collector of the debt. The Act also excludes a collector of a debt which was not in default at the time it was assigned to the collector. This is to protect assignees of commercial paper. A collector who obtains the debt as a secured party in a commercial credit transaction involving the creditor is also excluded.[107]

All of the above exceptions reflects the intent of Congress not to apply the provisions of the Act to those persons who do collect debts occasionally, but for whom debt collection is not a trade by itself.

An exclusion which was the topic of much controversy, and was finally abolished by a later amendment, concerns debt collection by an attorney. Originally, the Act excluded from its scope "any attorney at law collecting a debt as an attorney on behalf of and in the name of a client."[108] In *FTC v Shaffner*,[109] an Illinois attorney admittedly devoted most of his practice to collecting debts. The FTC issued a subpoena *duces tecum* investigating the attorney's debt collection practices. The attorney contended that the FTC did not have authority, since attorneys were not covered by the Act. The Sixth Cicuit, interpreting the Act, stated that an attorney is not excluded from the Act by reason of the mere possession of a license to practice law. Congress did not intend to vest in every attorney the right to be free from investigation. Therefore, the FTC's investigative power may be used to determine whether an attorney is in fact fully acting as an attorney or in another capacity, such as a debt collector. The issue was settled when the Act was amended on July 9, 1986, to provide that any attorney who is in the business of collecting debts on behalf of, and in the name of, clients is a debt collector subject to the Act.[110]

§10.18 —Practices Prohibited

In order to understand the extent of the prohibitions, one must be familiar with the types of practices debt collectors engage in. They include the multifaceted methods used in an attempt to intimidate, threaten, and humiliate the debtor. Countless are the number of harassments and deceptive practices used. Other types of abuse relate to attempts to deny the debtor's day in court by bringing suit in a forum that is far distant from the debtor's residence or resorting to default judgments in which the debtor could not assert claims and defenses against the creditor's claims. Many default judgments occur because the consumer never actually receives service of process. The shady practice of serving process with the intent that it not reach the defendant is called *sewer service*.

---

[107] 15 USC §1692a(6)(G).

[108] 15 USC §1692a(6)(F).

[109] 626 F2d 32 (7th Cir 1980).

[110] Pub L No 99-361, 100 Stat 768 (1986).

The FDCPA does not deal with all of these problems. Other federal statutes, such as the Federal Trade Commission Act, may help to curb unfair and deceptive acts or practices.[111] State law may also provide relief, such as prosecution for perjury in the case of a creditor who swears that process had been served when, in fact, it had not. Common law theories of tort, fraud, duress, misrepresentation, and infliction of mental distress may also afford some protection to the consumer in appropriate circumstances.

Dealing specifically with the FDCPA, we may divide the practices prohibited under the Act into:

1. Practices dealing with obtaining location information about the debtor

2. Practices dealing with communications in connection with debt collection

3. Practices that constitute harassment or abuse under the Act

4. Practices defined by the Act as unfair or unconscionable

§10.19 —Obtaining Location Information

The essence of the rules is to prevent embarrassment or harm to the reputation of the consumer-debtor. Section 1692(b) of the Act requires a debt collector who seeks to locate the debtor with the help of a third party to:

1. Identify himself or herself, and state that the purpose of the contact is simply to correct or confirm location information concerning the consumer. The agent of the debt collector will identify the agent's employer only if requested

2. Not state that the consumer owes any debt

3. Not communicate with such person more than once unless requested to do so by such person, or unless the debt collector in good faith believes that the earlier information was erroneous or incomplete, and that such person now has complete location information

4. Not communicate by postcard or use stationery that identifies the debt collector as a person in the debt collection business or indicate that the communication relates to the collection of a debt

5. If the debt collector knows that the debtor is represented by an attorney, the debt collector may communicate only with the attorney unless the attorney fails to respond within a reasonable time[112]

---

[111] 15 USC §45(a)(1); *see* §§2.05-2.06.

[112] 15 USC §1692b(6).

§10.20   —Communications in Connection with Debt Collection

While the Act recognizes the legitimacy of seeking information regarding the location of the debtor, it also seeks to protect the consumer's right to privacy by prohibiting a debt collector from communicating the debtor's affairs to third parties. Unless expressly allowed by the consumer or a court, a debt collector may not communicate with any person other than the consumer, his or her attorney, a consumer reporting agency if otherwise permitted by law, the debtor's creditor, the creditor's attorney, or the debt collector's attorney.[113]

Communications with the consumer are also strictly regulated. The debt collector may not communicate with the consumer at any time or place deemed inconvenient. Absent extraordinary circumstances, the law assumes the convenient time to be after 8:00 A.M. and before 9:00 P.M.[114]

The debt collector may not communicate with the consumer at the consumer's place of employment if the debt collector has reason to know that the employer does not permit the employee to receive this kind of information on the job.[115]

If the debt collector knows the consumer is represented by an attorney, the debt collector must communicate only with the attorney, unless the latter fails to respond within a reasonable time or consents to the debt collector's direct communication with the consumer.[116]

If the consumer notifies a debt collector that he or she refuses to pay the debt or wishes that the debt collector cease further communication, the debt collector must cease all communications except to advise the consumer that no further communication will be attempted and that the consumer must expect the creditor to seek legal remedies.[117]

For purposes of communication, the term *consumer* includes the consumer's spouse, parent (if the consumer is a minor), guardian, executor, or administrator.[118]

By direct and express consent, the consumer may waive the protection afforded by the Act on communication.[119] The consumer thus, through prior consent, may allow the collector to communicate with the debtor at unusual times or places, at the place of employment, or directly with the consumer regardless of the fact that the consumer is represented by an attorney. Note that the consent must be given directly to the debt collector. A consent waiver incorporated in the original loan contract with the creditor is not an effective

---

[113] 15 USC §1692c(b).

[114] 15 USC §1692c(a)(1).

[115] 15 USC §1692c(a)(3).

[116] 15 USC §1692c(a)(2).

[117] 15 USC §1691c(c).

[118] 15 USC §1692c(d).

[119] 15 USC §1692c(a).

waiver. In other words, the waiver must be meaningful and directed to the collector, not the original lender.

§10.21 —Harassment or Abuse

A debt collector may not engage in any conduct the natural consequence of which is to harass, oppress, or abuse the consumer in connection with the collection of the debt.[120] The FDCPA gives a few examples of such conduct, but the list is not all-inclusive. Following are practices considered abusive under the Act:

1. The use or threat of violence or other criminal means to harm the physical person, reputation, or property of the consumer.[121] The violence is not required to be directed to the consumer; the Act is violated if the violence or threat of violence is directed to the consumer's children, relatives, parents, or the like. The term *physical* may be interpreted to include also mental distress[122]

2. The use of obscene or profane language or language the natural consequence of which is to abuse the hearer or reader.[123] The recipient may be connected with or related to the debtor

3. The publication of a list of consumers who allegedly refuse to pay debts. Debt collectors can only give the names to consumer reporting agencies or to a person who may legitimately receive a consumer report from a consumer reporting agency.[124] Therefore, sending a collection letter to the debtor's employer would violate the Act

4. Advertising a debt for sale in order to coerce payment.[125] Such an advertisement would embarrass the debtor and harm the debtor's reputation

5. Causing a telephone to ring, or repeatedly and continuously engaging a person in telephone conversation with the intent to annoy, abuse, or harass any person at the called number.[126] The FTC interprets *continously* to mean "making a series of telephone calls, one right after the other" and *repeatedly* to mean "calling with excessive frequency, such as six telephone calls in one hour."[127] It is generally admitted that the debt

---

[120] 15 USC §1692d.

[121] 15 USC §1692d(1).

[122] *See* Bingham v Collection Bureau, Inc, 505 F Supp 864 (DND 1981).

[123] 15 USC §1692d(2).

[124] 15 USC §1692d(3).

[125] 15 USC §1692d(4).

[126] 15 USC §1692d(5).

[127] 51 Fed Reg 8019 (Mar 1986).

collector is entitled to more than one call. Massachusetts law, for example, allows two per week at home, plus one per month at work[128]

6. The placing of telephone calls without meaningful disclosure of the caller's identity.[129] This prohibition however, must be read in conjunction with §1692b(1), which requires a debt collector seeking location information from a third party to identify himself but *not* his employer. While §1692b(1) protects the consumer's privacy, this provision (§1692d(6)) protects the consumer or the consumer's family from annoying phone calls. An FTC staff letter reconciled the two provisions by allowing a debt collector to leave with a third party a message giving the collector's name only, not the employer's name, and disclosing the latter only when the call is returned

The use of aliases is one of the issues in *Bingham v Collection Bureau, Inc.*[130] The court noted in its opinion that the practice of using aliases greatly increased the risk of overreaching when the caller could hide behind a different name. The defendant argued, on the other hand, that using an alias would protect the caller from abusive return calls and therefore was justified. The court maintained, however, that "a telephonic collecting technique which produced a substantial body of such reaction would be, for that reason, suspect."[131] Under the FTC interpretation, a consistent use of an alias is permissible if it permits identification of the caller when, for example, contacting the caller's employer. Such a use would constitute a meaningful disclosure of the caller's identity and therefore, is not violative of the Act.[132]

The list of what constitute harassing or abusive tactics under the Act is not exhaustive. A court may find other types of practices not listed in the Act equally offensive.

The standard for determining the effect of a debt collector's practice on a consumer has fluctuated between the subjective test and the objective test. In the previously cited case of *Bingham v Collection Bureau Inc*, the standard adopted was "whether it is more likely than not so that debtors on the low side of reasonable capacity who read a given notice or hear a given statement read into the message oppressiveness, falsehood or threat."[133] Similarly, in *Wright v Credit Bureau*,[134] the court adopted the standard that protects the unsophisticated.[135] On the other hand, some decisions adopted the objective standard of the reasonable consumer.[136]

---

[128] Mass Regs Code tit 940, §7.04(1)(f) (1986).

[129] 15 USC §1692d(6).

[130] 505 F Supp 864 (DND 1981).

[131] *Id* 874.

[132] 51 Fed Reg 8019 (Mar 7, 1986).

[133] 505 F Supp at 871.

[134] 555 F Supp 1005 (ND Ga 1983).

[135] *Id* 1007.

[136] *See, e.g.,* Blackwell v Professional Business Servs, 526 F Supp 535, 537 (ND Ga 1981); Bustamonte v First Fed Savs & Loan Assn, 619 F2d 360 (5th Cir 1980).

More recently, the Eleventh Circuit refined the *unsophisticated consumer* standard in a most interesting way. In *Jeter v Credit Bureau, Inc,*[137] the court wrote:

> We note that the district court applied a "reasonable consumer" standard to Jeter's claim under §1692d, a standard which we have rejected with respect to claims of misrepresentation and deception under §1692e. However, we cannot simply apply a "least sophisticated consumer" standard. Whether a consumer is more or less likely to be harassed, oppressed, or abused by certain debt collection practices does not relate solely to the consumer's relative sophistication; rather, such susceptibility might be affected by other circumstances of the consumer or by the relationship between the consumer and the debt collection agency. For example, a very intelligent and sophisticated consumer might well be susceptive to harassment, oppression, or abuse because he is poor (i.e., has limited access to the legal system), is on probation, or is otherwise at the mercy of a power relationship. . . . Thus, we hold that claims under §1692d should be viewed from the perspective of a consumer whose circumstances make his relatively more susceptible to harassment, oppression, or abuse.[138]

§10.22 —Prohibition of False, Deceptive, or Misleading Representation

Section 1692a starts with the general statement that a debt collector may not use any false, deceptive, or misleading representation or means in connection with the collection of any debt. The Act lists 16 types of prohibited conduct:

> 1. Falsely implying that the debt collector is vouched for, bonded by, or affiliated with the government, including the use of badges or uniforms. In other words, the Act prohibits the impersonating of a government official or law enforcement officer[139]
> 2. Falsely representing the character, amount, or legal status of the debt, such as neglecting to mention that the statute of limitations has expired, or that the debt was discharged in bankruptcy;[140] or representing that the debt collector is entitled to certain compensation, or that the consumer is subject to debt collection charges or fees that are in fact illegal[141]

---

[137] 760 F2d 1168 (11th Cir 1985).

[138] *Id* 1179.

[139] 15 USC §1692e(1).

[140] 15 USC §1692e(2)(A).

[141] 15 USC §1692e(2)(B).

3. Representing that a person is an attorney or that the communication comes from an attorney[142]

4. Misrepresenting or implying that nonpayment will result in arrest, imprisonment, garnishment, attachment, or the like, when such action is unlawful or unintended[143]

5. Threatening to take any action that cannot legally be taken or that is not intended to be taken.[144] Intent may be determined objectively from the debt collector's in-house procedure and practice. In *Trans World Accounts Inc v FTC*,[145] the court reaffirmed the FTC's finding of deception when the debt collector used the so-called *flat rate* collection service and threatened immediate legal action. Under the flat rate service, the debt collector sent out five or six simulated telegrams to delinquent debtors at prearranged intervals of 10 to 14 days. If the recipient of the letters did not respond to one letter in the series, the next letter was automatically sent until the series of five or six letters had run its course. Only after the flat rate series was concluded without payment would the delinquent account be transferred to the collection division to determine whether further action should be taken. Usually, it took about 90 days from the date the first letter was sent out before the debt collector even considered whether legal action should be taken against any individual debtor. The FTC, based on this internal procedure, charged that the debt collector engaged in an unfair and deceptive practice, and the court agreed

6. Falsely representing or implying that the assignment of a debt will preclude the consumer's claim or defense to payment or will cause the consumer to be subject to any practice prohibited under the Act.[146] This provision is to prevent the situation in which the debt collector threatens to transfer the debt to another collection agency, implying that the latter's methods are even more drastic

7. Misrepresenting or falsely implying that the consumer committed a crime in order to disgrace the consumer.[147] It is generally interpreted that to *disgrace* a consumer does not imply that the consumer must prove intent to disgrace[148]

8. Communicating or threatening to communicate to any person credit information which is known or which should be known to be false, including failure to communicate that a debt is disputed[149]

---

[142] 15 USC §1692e(3).

[143] 15 USC §1692e(4).

[144] 15 USC §1692e(5).

[145] 594 F2d 212 (9th Cir 1979).

[146] 15 USC §1692e(6).

[147] 15 USC §1692e(7).

[148] *See* R. Hobbs, Debt Collection Harrassment §2.4.6.9 (The Consumer Credit and Sales Legal Practice Series No 4, 1982 & Supp 1986).

[149] 15 USC §1692e(8).

9. Using or distributing written material that gives a false impression of its source, authorization, or approval, e.g., a document falsely claiming that it is approved by a court or by a government official[150]

10. Using false or deceptive means to collect or attempt to collect a debt or to collect information about a consumer[151]

11. Except for the provision dealing with communication with third parties to acquire location information, failing to disclose that a communication is for the purpose of collecting a debt constitutes a misrepresentation or deceptive practice[152]

12. Falsely representing or implying that the accounts have been transferred to an innocent purchaser for value (BFP).[153] First, this might be a misrepresentation that the debt collector had purchased the account by paying the debtor's creditor. Second, this might be a misrepresentation that the purchaser of the account will not be subject to the consumer's claims and defenses. This is a misrepresentation because, under federal and most state laws, assignees of consumer debts are still subject to the consumer's claims and defenses

13. Falsely representing or implying that the documents are legal process[154]

14. Using a business, company, or organization name other than the debt collector's business's, company's, or organization's true name[155]

15. Falsely representing or implying that the documents are not legal process forms, and the debtor does not need to respond[156]

16. Falsely representing or implying that the debt collector is employed by a credit reporting agency[157]

As can be seen, many of these provisions overlap each other or overlap with other provisions of the Act. But the general idea is that any false representation is a deceptive practice. The list may refer to a number of practices current in the trade, but does not purport to exhaust them all.

§10.23 —Prohibition of Unfair Collection Practices

The Act prohibits the use of unfair or unconscionable means to collect or attempt to collect a debt.[158] Section 1692f gives eight examples of such

---

[150] 15 USC §1691e(9).

[151] 15 USC §1691e(10).

[152] 15 USC §1692e(11).

[153] 15 USC §1692e(12).

[154] 15 USC §1692e(13).

[155] 15 USC §1692e(14).

[156] 15 USC §1692e(15).

[157] 15 USC §1692e(16).

[158] 15 USC §1692f.

practices. The law is patterned after the Federal Trade Commission Act prohibiting unfair and deceptive acts or practices.[159] The courts may rely on FTC precedents to decide whether a given practice is unfair.

The concept of *unconscionability* was first codified in the Uniform Commercial Code.[160] In the area of consumer transactions, the Uniform Consumer Credit Code extensively deals with the concept.[161] The term *unconscionable* connotes the idea that the creditor is exploiting the debtor so much so that it "shocks the conscience" of the courts. As Comment 3 of Section 5.108 of the U3C (1974) points out:

> The basic test is whether, in the light of the background and setting of the market, the needs of the particular case, and the condition of the particular parties to the conduct or contract, the conduct involved is, or the contract or clauses involved are so one-sided as to be unconscionable under the circumstances existing at the time the conduct occurs or is threatened or at the time of the making of the contract.

Under the FDCPA, the eight practices listed as unfair or unconscionable are:

1. Collecting any amount not permitted by law or agreement.[162] The amount includes interest, fees, charges, or expenses incidental to the principal obligation. If the contract is illegal, such as where the interest rate is usurious under an applicable statute, the amount, even though authorized by agreement, will be void. Any collection of a charge which is contrary to any provision of the Act will be unfair if not illegal

2. Accepting a check or other payment instrument postdated by more than five days, unless the debt collector notifies the debtor in writing of the collector's intent to deposit such check or instrument three to ten business days prior to the actual depositing of the check or instrument[163]

3. Soliciting a postdated check or instrument for the purpose of threatening or instituting criminal prosecution[164]

4. Depositing or threatening to deposit a post dated check or instrument prior to the date of such check or instrument.[165] All of the provisions dealing with postdated checks attempt to prevent debt collectors from using postdated checks to intimidate and threaten the debtor in view of the criminal bad check laws which exist in most states. Note, however, that the use of postdated checks is not prohibited *per se*, but is simply closely regulated in order to prevent abuses

---

[159] 15 USC §45.

[160] UCC §2.302.

[161] U3C §§4.106; 5.108, 6.111 (1974).

[162] 15 USC §1692f(1).

[163] 15 USC §1691f(2).

[164] 15 USC §1692f(3).

[165] 15 USC §1691f(4).

5. Using a false purpose for communication in order to impose expenses upon the debtor by concealing the true purpose of the communication.[166] An example of such expenses is a collect telephone call or a telegram fee, using a false pretense

6. Repossessing or threatening to repossess through any nonjudicial action where there is no right or intent to so proceed, or the property is exempt by law from such action[167]

7. Communicating with a consumer regarding a debt by postcard.[168] This is to protect the debtor's right to privacy

8. Using language and symbols on envelopes when communicating with the debtor which indicate that the sender is in the debt collection business.[169] Anything that would indicate that the correspondence comes from a debt collector would violate this provision, even the use of a return address on the envelope that indicates that the addressee is in the debt collection business[170]

§10.24 —Validation of Debts

In order to avoid a mistake regarding the amount or existence of a debt or the identity of the debtor, the FDCPA gives the consumer the right to require the debt collector to confirm, validate, or verify the debt.[171] This is considered to be the most significant feature of the FDCPA.

Within five days after an initial communication with the consumer concerning the collection of a debt, the debt collector must send the consumer a written notice containing:

1. The amount of the debt
2. The name of the creditor to whom the debt is owed
3. A statement that, unless the consumer, within 30 days after the receipt of the notice, disputes the validity of the debt or its amount, the debt collector will assume the debt is valid
4. A statement that, if the consumer notifies the debt collector in writing within the 30-day period that the debt, or any portion of the debt, is disputed, the debt collector will obtain a verification of the debt or a copy of a judgment against the consumer and forward it to the consumer
5. A statement that, if the consumer makes a written request within 30 days, the debt collector will provide the consumer with the name and address of the original creditor, if different from the current creditor[172]

---

[166] 15 USC §1692f(5).

[167] 15 USC §1692f(6).

[168] 15 USC §1692f(7).

[169] 15 USC §1692f(8).

[170] *See* Rutyna v Collection Accounts Terminal, Inc, 478 F Supp 980 (ND Ill 1979).

[171] 15 USC §1692g.

[172] 15 USC §1692g(b).

Pending verification of the debt, all collection must cease. Failure of a consumer to ask for verification or to dispute the validity of a debt under this section may not be construed as an admission of liability.[173]

In *Ost v Collection Bureau, Inc*,[174] the creditor did notify the debtor of the debtor's right to validation of the debt; however, the notice was printed on the back of a standard collection form in fine print. The court held that this literal compliance with the Act was insufficient.

In *Harvey v United Adjusters*,[175] the court said that the debt collector violated the Act by not informing the consumer in the verification notice that the consumer had the right to dispute a portion of the debt as well as its entire amount. Further, the notice violated the Act by requiring that the debtor provide written notification of any dispute. Therefore, it seems that the consumer may orally dispute the debt.

§10.25   —Other Rights of the Consumer

The consumer has the right, in the case of multiple debts, to allocate payment made to any particular debt. In particular, the debt collector may not apply any payment to a debt which the consumer still disputes.[176] In exercising the right of allocation, a debtor may, for instance, decide that secured debts may be paid first to protect the debtor's property subject to the security interest.

Another right is the right to a convenient forum. Venue abuse is a frequent abuse of debt collection. By agreement or otherwise, a creditor may impose on the consumer a forum which is inconvenient or inaccessible in order to force a default judgment. The FDCPA requires that any legal action concerning real property must take place where the property is located. For personal property, the debt collector must adopt the forum in the judicial district of either the place where the consumer signed the contract sued upon or the consumer's residence at the commencement of the action.[177]

Finally, §1962j of the Act protects the consumer from the debt collector's practice known as *flat-rating*. As described earlier,[178] *flat-rating* is a practice which consists of distributing forms that are intended to mislead the consumer or disguise the identity of the creditor, or to induce the debtor to believe that a person other than the creditor is participating in the debt collection when, in fact, such a person is not. In sum, this is another form of unfair and deceptive practice.

---

[173] 15 USC §1692g(c).

[174] 493 F Supp 701 (DND 1980).

[175] 509 F Supp 1218 (D Or 1981).

[176] 15 USC §1692h.

[177] 15 USC §1692i.

[178] See **§10.22** and case related to *Trans World* case.

§10.26 —Civil Liability

A private civil action is available to victimized consumers. A debt collector who violates any provision of the Act is liable to the consumer for:

1. Any actual damage sustained by the consumer as a result of the violation

2. Statutory damages not to exceed $1000 for individual action. In the case of a class action, the statutory damages may not exceed $500,000 or 1 per cent of the debt collector's net worth, whichever is less

3. The costs of the action and reasonable attorneys' fees as determined by the court. If the suit is brought by the consumer in bad faith and for purpose of harassment, the debt collector may also be awarded reasonable attorneys' fees[179]

In determining the amount of liability in an individual suit, the court will consider factors such as frequency or persistence of noncompliance, the nature of the noncompliance, and the extent to which noncompliance was intentional. In a class action, the court will consider the same factors, plus the resources of the debt collector and the number of person adversely affected.[180] Note that statutory damages may be awarded even absent a showing of actual damages. As a defense, the collector may prove that the violation was not intentional, but was a bona fide error notwithstanding the maintenance of procedures reasonably adopted to avoid such error.[181]

The plaintiff may bring the action in any appropriate United States district court without regard to the amount in controversy or in any other court of competent jurisdiction. The statute of limitations is one year from the date of violation.[182] Compliance with any advisory opinion of the FTC will protect the debt collector against any liability that may arise under the Act.[183]

§10.27 —Administrative Enforcement

The FDCPA gives the FTC full powers to enforce it, since any violation of the Act is deemed to be an unfair or deceptive act or practice under the Federal Trade Commission Act.[184] However, when the subject matter bears a close relationship to other federal agencies, these agencies may also enforce the Act.[185] Neither the FTC nor any other agency may promulgate regulations

---

[179] 15 USC §1692k(a).

[180] 15 USC §1692k(b).

[181] 15 USC §1692k(c).

[182] 15 USC §1692k(d).

[183] 15 USC §1692k(e).

[184] 15 USC §45.

[185] 15 USC §16921(a).

regarding the collection of debts by debt collectors.[186] They may only enforce the FDCPA provisions. Generally, the federal courts have been unwilling to award damages based simply on technical violation of the provisions of the Act unless these result in injury to the consumer and indicate an intent to engage in abusive practices.[187]

§10.28   —West v Costen

This case deserves special attention because it deals with most aspects of the FDCPA. Six plaintiffs filed a class action suit against a debt collection company and the individual collectors, seeking actual and statutory damages for the class. The plaintiffs alleged a pattern of illegal collection practices by the defendant. The debts that the defendants attempted to collect were dishonored checks. Plaintiffs charged the following violations: communicating with third parties concerning the collection of debts in violation of §1692c(b); threatening that criminal prosecution was pending, when such was not intended, in violation of §1692e(4) & (5); failing to comply with the notice and validation of debt under §1692g(c); collecting illegal service charges in violation of §1692f(1); and misrepresenting the amount of the debt owned in violation of §1692e(2)(A) and (B).

The court certified the class for certain counts, such as the failure to give notice and unlawful service charges, but refused to certify other issues which the court found to be more individual than common ones.

Communication with Third Parties in Connection with Debt Collection

In order to protect the consumer's privacy, the FDCPA, §1692c(b), prohibits the debt collector from communicating with third parties in connection with debt collection. In *West v Costen*,[188] a debt collector spoke with one of the plaintiffs' grandparents and uncle. The court granted summary judgment against the collector. Another collector spoke with a debtor's wife. The court denied summary judgment because with respect to communication with third parties, the FDCPA, §1692c(d), defines *consumer* to include a spouse. The court granted summary judgment against another debt collector who talked with a plaintiff's teenage daughter.

The court also decided who may sue the debt collector besides the debtor. The mother of a consumer who was contacted by the debt collector to collect her son's debt also sought recovery, citing §1692k(a), which provides that: "any debt collector who fails to comply with any provision of this title with respect to *any person* is liable to such person . . ." (emphasis added by court). The court

---

[186] 15 USC §16921(d).

[187] *See* D. Rothschild & D. Carroll, Consumer Protection Reporting Service II, The Fair Debt Collecton Practices Act, §II:8.09 (1973).

[188] West v Costen, 558 F Supp 564 (WD Va 1983).

concluded that "it would be incongruous to permit a person other than the consumer to recover for a violation of that section since the purpose of the law is to protect the consumer's privacy and employment."[189] Therefore, the mother was not permitted to recover.

Threats of Arrest

In the case of one of the plaintiffs, the debt collector sent a demand notice of payment with the annotation: "criminal warrant pending." The court did not grant summary judgment because there was some evidence that the collector knew that one of the plaintiff's creditors did have an outstanding warrant against the plaintiff.

In the case of another plaintiff, there was no evidence that either the collector or any creditor intended to have the plaintiff arrested, as the collector told the plaintiff's grandparents and uncle. Summary judgment was therefore granted in that plaintiff's favor.

Concerning another plaintiff, the collector threatened the plaintiff with arrest and imprisonment unless the dishonored check was paid. The creditor did eventually issue criminal warrants against the plaintiff, but did not intend to do so at the time of the threat. One could argue that the Act focuses on the truthfulness of the threat of the time it is made, and that whether the threat eventually materializes should be irrelevant. Nevertheless, the court denied the plaintiff summary judgment.

Validation of Debts

The FDCPA, §1692g(a), requires debt collectors to give a consumer a statement that the consumer has the right to dispute all or any portion of the debt and to require from the debt collector a validation of the debt. Pending validation, all collection efforts must cease.

In this case, there was ample evidence that the plaintiffs never received written notice of their right to verify or dispute the validity of the debt. The court granted summary judgement to the plaintiffs who were the consumer-debtors, but denied standing to two of the plaintiffs' parents.

Collection of Illegal Charges

The collectors attempted to collect a $15 service charge on each bad check regardless of its amount. This charge was not authorized by the loan agreement nor by law. The defendants argued that state law (Virginia) did not expressly prohibit such a charge. The court still held that the defendants violated §1692f(1) of the Act because "permission requires an affirmative authorization, not just indulgent silence."[190]

---

[189] *Id* 577.
[190] *Id* 582.

Misrepresentation of Debt

Since the illegal service charge was added to the amount of the bad check, and such add-on charge was not disclosed by the defendant, there was a misrepresentation of the amount of the debt. This violated §1691e(2)(A) and (B) of the Act.

Piercing the Corporate Veil

Another interesting aspect of the case was the court's eagerness to pierce the corporate veil in order to determine the identity of the debt collector. The defendant, Costen, was the president of MSF, the collection agency. His job was to obtain new accounts from merchants and retailers. As part of his compensation, Costen received 10 per cent of the amount that MSF earned from the accounts that Costen actually sold. Costen argued that he was not a debt collector, because he never personally collected or attempted to collect any debt. The court held that Costen was a debt collector, ruling that he indirectly collected the debts because of the commission that he received. Costen further argued that he did not personally violate any provision of the Act and, unlike MSF, he could not be vicariously liable for MSF's collection agents. The court pierced the corporate veil, holding that the corporate structure should not shield dominant shareholders such as Costen that conduct illegal operations. The court further said that the most important reason for disregarding MSF's corporate form was that it would be unfair to the plaintiffs not to, since MSF had ceased to do business and its assets would be insufficient to pay damages. The purpose of the Act, to eliminate collection abuses, would be frustrated if MSF's corporate structure was maintained.[191]

§10.29   In-House Debt Collectors—The FTC Credit Practices Rule

The FDCPA does not apply to in-house collectors. However, the FTC Trade Regulation Rule on Credit Practices,[192] promulgated in March, 1984, and effective March 1, 1985, contains rules to protect the consumer from abusive practices by lenders. The Rule applies only to lenders and retailers and their assignees under the jurisdiction of the FTC. This includes most finance companies, but not other types of lending institutions. But the Federal Reserve Board has promulgated a similar regulation applicable to banks under its jurisdiction, effective January 1, 1986.[193] The Federal Home Loan Bank system has also promulgated a similar rule applicable to savings and loans under its jurisdiction effective January 1, 1986.[194]

---

[191] *Id* 586.

[192] 16 CFR §§444.1-.5.

[193] 5 Consumer Credit Guide (CCH) §96,225.

[194] *Id.*

The FTC Credit Practices Rule applies only to the financing of goods or services or extensions of credit for personal, family, or household purposes.[195] The rule does not apply, for example, to real estate transactions involving consumers.

§10.30 —Practices Proscribed by the FTC Credit Practices Rule

Cognovit or Confession of Judgment

It is an unfair credit practice for a lender or retailer to receive from the consumer an obligation that constitutes or contains a cognovit or confession of judgment or any other waiver of the right to notice and opportunity to be heard in the case of suit or process.[196] The cognovit or confession of judgment is a clause in which the consumer accepts the forum in advance and agrees not to contest the suit. The advantage to the creditor is that the creditor does not have to locate the debtor, nor give the debtor notice. It is also any easy way to obtain a judgment without having to consider the debtor's claims and defenses.

Cognovit clauses are usually in fine print in adhesion contracts. Although courts are usually adverse to the clause and are willing to vacate cognovit judgments, consumers usually, if not represented by an attorney, will acquiesce to the clause. Such a clause may be vacated as an unfair act or practice.

Executory Waivers or Limitation of Exemptions from Attachments, Execution, or Other Process on the Consumer's Real or Personal Property

Unless the property is subject to a security interest executed in connection with the obligation, these waivers and limitations are forbidden.[197] This prevents the creditor from obtaining a blanket interest in all of the debtor's property. The real or personal property of low-income consumers may not represent a great value; however, a blanket security interest intimidates the debtor.

Assignment of Wages and Other Earnings

The Rule prohibits any assignment of the consumer's wages and earnings, unless: the assignment, by its terms, is revocable at will by the debtor; or the assignment is a payroll deduction plan or preauthorized plan; or the

---

[195] 16 CFR §444.1(d).
[196] 16 CFR §444.2(a)(1).
[197] 16 CFR §444.2(a)(2).

assignment applies only to wages or earnings already earned at the time of the assignment.[198]

Nonpossessory Security Interests in Household Goods

Nonpossessory security interests in household goods other than a purchase money security interest are prohibited.[199] Household goods are defined as clothing, furniture, appliances, one radio and one television, linens, china, crockery, kitchenware, and personal effects (including wedding rings) of the consumer, and of the consumer's dependents. Household goods do not include works of art, electronic entertainment equipments, antiques, or jewelry other than wedding rings.[200]

Late Charges

When collecting a debt, a creditor is prohibited from levying a delinquency charge on a payment, which payment is otherwise a full payment and is paid on time, where the only delinquency is attributable to late fees assessed in earlier payments.[201] In other words, if the consumer's payment brings the consumer's account current, except for a previous delinquency charge on a payment that was late, the creditor may not collect any additional charge. This rule is to avoid the *pyramiding* of late charges.[202]

§10.31 —State Exemption from the FTC Credit Practices Rule

Upon a state's application to the FTC, and provided that the state affords a level of protection to consumers that is at least equivalent to the FTC Rule, the state may be exempt from the Rule and free to apply state law.[203]

§10.32 —The FTC Credit Practices Rule and the Bankruptcy Code

Before the FTC Credit Practices Rule was enacted, §522(f) of the Bankruptcy Code[204] generated much litigation in the bankruptcy courts. Section 522(f) gives the debtor the power to avoid nonpossessory, nonpurchase money security interests in certain exempt property, household goods, professional tools, or professionally prescribed health aids for the debtor or dependent of

---

[198] 16 CFR §444.2(a)(3).

[199] 16 CFR §444.2(a)(4).

[200] 16 CFR §444.1(i).

[201] 16 CFR §444.4(a).

[202] FTC Staff Advisory Letter, June 21, 1985, 5 Consumer Credit Guide (CCH) §96,257.

[203] 16 CFR §444.5.

[204] 11 USC §522(f).

the debtor. The FTC Rule nullifies this provision of the Bankruptcy Code by prohibiting an interest in these goods anyway. However, §522(f) is still useful to the consumer.

First, the definition of household goods in the FTC Rule is narrow. For example, jewelry except wedding rings is not household goods under the FTC Rule, but might be under §522(f) of the Bankruptcy Code. Thus, a creditor may still have a nonpossessory, nonpurchase money security interest in the consumer's personal property under the FTC Rule, but should the debtor become bankrupt, the property might be exempt.

Second, the FTC Rule applies only to transactions entered into after March 1, 1985. Section 522(f) is useful for transactions entered into before that date.

Finally, all creditors, including banks, savings and loans, and credit unions are subject to §522(f), not only lenders and retailers subject to the FTC jurisdiction.

11 Consumer Real Estate Transactions

§11.01   Introduction

Generally, the acquisition of a home is perhaps the most important transaction in a consumer's life. Because of this, federal legislation, as well as state legislation, has been enacted for the consumer's protection. The purpose of the legislation is twofold:

1. To enable the consumer to get all the information pertinent to the transaction that the consumer is going to undertake, whether it be before or, if no obligations are imposed upon the consumer, after consummation of the transaction. This is a purpose similar to that of the Truth in Lending Act, in that both are based on the idea of disclosure

2. To prohibit certain practices deemed abusive or deceitful which result in increasing the consumer's obligations

Legislation dealing with real estate transactions abounds.[1] We discuss here only the important pieces of legislation. On the federal level, we will cover the Truth in Lending Act,[2] the Real Estate Settlement Procedures Act,[3] and the Interstate Land Sales Full Disclosure Act.[4] On the state level, we will refer mainly to the Uniform Consumer Credit Code. One should also keep in mind that the common law tort theories of negligence and strict liability, as well as the contract theories of express and implied warranties, may also apply to real estate transactions. In many states, these traditional theories have been codified in statutes to protect purchasers of new homes.

A comprehensive treatment of the laws dealing with real estate transactions is beyond the scope of this book. The intent is to provide readers with a general roadmap pointing toward the possible legal sources that govern the subject.

---

[1] For a comprehensive treatment of the federal legislation on the subject, *see* P. Barron, Federal Regulation of Real Estate (rev ed 1983).

[2] 15 USC §1601 *et seq.*

[3] 12 USC §2601.

[4] 15 USC §1701.

§11.02   The Truth in Lending Act and Real Estate Transactions

We refer our readers to Chapter 4 for a general acquaintance with the Truth in Lending Act (TILA) and Regulation Z (found at 12 CFR §226) implementing the Act. We deal here only with the particular provisions of the Act applicable to real estate credit transactions.

TILA applies to a great number of real estate credit transactions. In fact, the Act has an even broader applicability to transactions involving real estate than to those involving personal property. Under the Act, personal property transactions that exceed $25,000 are outside its scope, but TILA will apply if the lender extending the consumer credit takes a security interest in the consumer's dwelling.[5] Thus, home mortgages are generally subject to the Act.

§11.03   —Disclosures under the Truth in Lending Act

Disclosure requirements for real estate transactions are substantially the same as those applicable to non-real estate, closed-end credit transactions.

Finance Charge and Total Payments Due

Prior to the Simplification Act of 1980,[6] there was a difference between required disclosures in real estate transactions and in non-real estate transactions. Prior to Simplification, the real estate mortgage lender did not have to disclose the finance charge and total of payments, which were required in any other closed-end credit. The dispensation was justified on the ground that, to quote a member of Congress, "if the prospective purchaser had to be told the full cost of the interest and credit charges over the life of the long-term mortgage, he would be shocked at the total and run away from the deal."[7] The Simplification Act no longer makes the distinction between real estate and non-real estate credit transactions with respect to those disclosures, and now requires home mortgagees to disclose the finance charge and total of payments.[8]

Seller's Points

Prior to Simplification, the annual percentage rate (APR) included all points and discounts paid to the creditor by the seller, to the extent that they were passed on to the consumer as part of the purchase price. Now, revised Regulation Z excludes the seller's points from the finance charge, even though

---

[5] 15 USC §1603(3).

[6] 15 USC §1638(a)(6) (now repealed).

[7] 114 Cong Rec H4118 (daily ed May 22, 1963). *See* Banfield, Jr, *The Effect of Credit Regulation on Real Estate Transactions,* 25 Bus Law 508 (1970).

[8] 15 USC §1638(a)(3) and (5); 12 CFR §226.18(d) and (h).

they were passed on to the consumer, in the form of a higher sales price, for example.[9] Seller's points are charges imposed by the lender upon the seller of property for extending credit to the buyer, or for extending credit on certain terms. Seller's points are usually present in loans extended by government agencies, such as the Veterans' Administration or the Federal Housing Administration, for financing home purchases. Since government agencies are not subject to TILA, the Federal Reserve Board, for the sake of uniformity, excludes all seller's points from the finance charge. On the other hand, buyer's points, charged to the buyer by the lender, are finance charges that must be disclosed.[10]

Closing Costs

Closing costs that are bona fide and reasonable in amount are excluded from the definition of finance charge and therefore are not required to be disclosed under TILA.[11] Closing costs generally include fees for title examination, fees for preparation of deeds or similar documents, fees for notary, appraisal, and credit reports, and escrow payments for taxes, insurance, water, sewer, and the like. These closing costs, however, are the main concern of the Real Estate Settlement Procedures Act (RESPA), discussed below. Since RESPA deals with this type of disclosure, TILA's dispensation is not harmful to the consumer.

Time for Disclosure

Dealing with real estate transactions, TILA seeks to mesh its provisions with those of RESPA. When the lender takes a security interest in the consumer's dwelling, the creditor must make a good faith estimate of the items required to be disclosed in closed-end credit transactions before consummation, or must deliver them or place them in the mail no later than three business days after the creditor receives the consumer's written application, whichever is earlier.[12] This is the same time period within which a creditor subject to RESPA must provide a good faith estimate of the settlement costs.

Right of Rescission

The right of rescission is extensively discussed in §4.18. As there stated, the right of rescission applies only to credit transactions in which the creditor acquires a security interest in the consumer's principal dwelling.[13] However, the consumer has no right to rescind if the transaction is qualified as a residential mortgage transaction.[14] A residential mortgage transaction involves an enabling loan to allow the consumer to construct or acquire the consumer's

---

[9] 12 CFR §226.4(c)(5).

[10] 12 CFR §226.4(c)(5) and Official Staff Interpretation.

[11] 12 CFR §226.4(c)(7).

[12] 12 CFR §226.19(a).

[13] 15 USC §1635(a); 12 CFR §226.23(a).

[14] 15 USC §1635(e); 12 CFR §226.23(f).

principal dwelling.[15] Whenever a consumer has the right to rescind, the creditor must disclose that fact by giving the consumer two copies of a notice of the right of rescission, one of which may be used by the consumer to inform the creditor that the consumer wishes to exercise that right.[16]

§11.04 —Disclosure of the True Terms of the Legal Obligation

Regulation Z, at 12 CFR §226.17(c), requires that the disclosures reflect the terms of the legal obligation between the parties. The legal obligation is determined by applicable state law or other law. The Official Staff Interpretation of this provision gives some examples of the so-called creative mortgage financing that was devised by the ingenious home mortgage industry to encourage home purchases in a period when interest rates were high. The creative features include:

> 1. Consumer buy-downs, in which the consumer pays an amount of the loan to the creditor to reduce the amount of payment or obtain a more favorable interest rate
> 2. Split buy-downs, in which the consumer and a third party, usually the seller of the real estate, pay an amount to the creditor to reduce the interest rate
> 3. Third party buy-downs, in which a third party, usually the seller of the real estate, pays an amount to reduce the interest payment for all or a portion of the credit term
> 4. Variable rates, in which the annual percentage rate increases or decreases after consummation

Regulation Z, at 12 CFR §226.17(c), and the Official Staff Interpretation, provide elaborate rules to deal with the above instances.

The Federal Reserve Board has proposed an amendment dealing specifically with the variable rate issue.[17] Under the proposed amendment, when the transaction is secured by the consumer's principal dwelling, the lender must disclose the fact that the transaction contains a variable-rate feature and provide a statement that variable rate disclosures have been made earlier.

§11.05 —Assumption of Mortgage

The Truth in Lending Act requires that new disclosures be made when the homeowner sells the house to another consumer who assumes the mortgage.

---

[15] 15 USC §1602(w); 12 CFR §226.2(a)(24).

[16] 15 USC §1635(a); 12 CFR §226.15(b).

[17] 51 Fed Reg 42,241 (1986) (proposed amendment to 12 CFR §226.18(1) Nov 24, 1986).

However, the new disclosures must be made only if the two following conditions exist: there is a residential mortgage transaction as defined by the Act; and the creditor expressly agrees in writing that the creditor accepts the subsequent consumer as the principal obligor.

Regulation Z, at 12 CFR §226.2(a)(24), defines a residential mortgage transaction to mean a transaction in which the lender takes a security interest in the consumer's principal dwelling to finance the acquisition or initial construction of that dwelling by the consumer. To determine whether a mortgage is a residential mortgage transaction, one must look to the consumer who assumes the mortgage, and not to the original obligor. Any terms which impose duties on the subsequent consumer and which relate to the remaining obligation must be disclosed, such as the remaining balance plus any accrued charges, the finance charge, the annual percentage rate, the security interest in any of the debtor's property, the insurance charge, and the payment schedule and other similar obligations.[18]

Penalties for failure to comply with the above disclosure provisions are the same as for violations of the Truth In Lending Act discussed in §4.29.

§11.06   The Real Estate Settlement Procedures Act (RESPA)

The Real Estate Settlement Procedures Act (RESPA)[19] was passed by Congress in 1974, and amended in 1975, to deal with the consumer's plight of high settlement costs when purchasing a home. Settlement costs include, but are not limited to, costs for credit reports, attorneys' fees, appraisal fees, title examination, title insurance, recording fees, transfer taxes, and the like. Costs which are usually borne by the seller, such as commission paid to the broker and seller's points charged on certain federally guaranteed home loans, also increase the buyer's costs, because the seller usually passes these costs to the buyer.

A proposal from the Department of Housing and Urban Development (HUD) and the Veterans' Administration (VA) to issue regulations fixing maximum charges for certain settlement costs[20] was strongly opposed by the housing industry. RESPA chose the less controversial method of requiring disclosures of the settlement costs rather than price fixing. RESPA, however, is more than a disclosure statute. It also prohibits certain practices in the home mortgage industry, practices that are deemed costly to the consumer.

The purpose of RESPA is fourfold:

---

[18] 12 CFR §226.20(b).

[19] 12 USC §§2601–2616. Pub L No 93–533, 88 Stat 1724 (Dec 22, 1974) (amended Pub L No 94–205 Jan 2, 1976).

[19] 12 USC §§2601-2616. Pub L No 93-533 (Dec 22, 1974) (amended Pub L No 94-205 Jan 2, 1976).

[20] 37 Fed Reg 13185 (1972).

1. To insure effective advance disclosure to homebuyers and sellers of settlement costs

2. To eliminate kickbacks or referral fees that result in the increase of settlement costs

3. To reduce the amounts homebuyers are required to place in escrow accounts for the payment of real estate taxes and insurance

4. To modernize the local record keeping of land title information[21]

To interpret the Act and implement its purposes, HUD also enacted a set of regulations referred to as Regulation X, codified at 24 CFR §3500.

§11.07 —Scope

RESPA applies only to *federally related mortgage loans*. The Act defines the term as follows:

> the term federally related mortgage loan includes any loan (other than temporary financing such as a construction loan) which—
>
> (A) is secured by a first lien on residential real property (including individual units of condominiums and cooperatives) designed principally for the occupancy of from one to four families; and
>
> (B)(i) is made in whole or in part by any lender the deposits or accounts of which are insured by any agency of the Federal Government, or is made in whole or in part by any lender which is regulated by any agency of the Federal Government; or
>
> (ii) is made in whole or in part, or insured, guaranteed, supplemented, or assisted in any way, by the Secretary or any other officer or agency of the Federal Government or under or in connection with a housing or urban development program administered by the Secretary or a housing or related program administered by any other such officer or agency, or
>
> (iii) is intended to be sold by the originating lender to the Federal National Mortgage Association, the Government National Mortgage Association, the Federal Home Loan Mortgage Corporation, or a financial institution from which it is to be purchased by the Federal Home Loan Mortgage Corporation; or
>
> (iv) is made in whole or in part by any "creditor", as defined in section 1602(f) of Title 15, who makes or invests in residential real estate loans aggregating more than $1,000,000 per year, except that for the purpose of this chapter, the term creditor does not include any agency or instrumentality of any State.[22]

Section 1602(f) of Title 15 is part of the Truth in Lending Act, which defines

---

[21] 12 USC §2601(b).

[22] 12 USC §2602(1).

creditor as a person who regularly extends consumer credit which is payable by agreement in more than four installments or for which the payment of a finance charge is imposed. This vast definition of *federally related mortgage loan* indicates that a great number of loans secured by a first lien on residential homes are covered by the Act.

§11.08   —Exemptions

Congress grants the Secretary of HUD authority to exempt certain classes of transactions from the scope of RESPA.[23] Pursuant to that authority, Regulation X has created the following exemptions:

   1. A loan to finance the purchase or transfer of a property of 25 or more acres[24]

   2. A home improvement loan or refinancing loan. Only a loan used to finance the purchase of the property is covered[25]

   3. A loan to finance the purchase of a vacant lot, and no proceeds of the loan are used for the construction of a one- to four-family structure or for the purpose of a mobile home to be placed on the lot[26]

   4. An assumption, novation, or any transaction subject to a preexisting loan, except the conversion of a construction loan to a mortgage loan to finance the purchase of the property by the first user[27]

   5. A construction loan, except when it is used or converted to be used as a permanent loan to finance the purchase of the property by the first user[28]

   6. A permanent loan to finance the construction of a one- to four-family structure, when the lot is already owned by the borrower[29]

   7. Speculative loans, the purpose of which is to purchase property for resale[30]

   8. A land sale contract in which the legal title is not transferred to the purchaser upon execution. However, a loan to finance the acquisition of title pursuant to a land sales contract is subject to RESPA[31]

The thrust of these exceptions is to carry out the congressional intent of protecting only a bona fide home purchase by consumers who are most in need

---

[23] 12 USC §2616(a).
[24] 24 CFR §3500.5(d)(1).
[25] 24 CFR §3500.5(d)(2).
[26] 24 CFR §3500.5(d)(3).
[27] 24 CFR §3500.5(d)(4).
[28] 24 CFR §3500.5(d)(5).
[29] 24 CFR §3500.5(d)(6).
[30] 24 CFR §3500.5(d)(7).
[31] 24 CFR §3500.5(d)(8).

of federal protection and not to extend the scope of the Act to marginal or speculative real estate transactions.

§11.09 —Disclosures

Before RESPA was amended in 1975, Congress intended disclosure of specific information concerning the settlement costs along the lines of the Truth in Lending Act. Section 2605 of RESPA (repealed in 1975) required the lender to provide the prospective buyer with a complete, itemized, and precise disclosure of the settlement costs. The disclosure had to be made at least 12 days before settlement. In addition, the seller was required to disclose the record owner's name and address as well as the date the record owner had purchased the property. Furthermore, the seller had to also disclose the last selling price and the cost of any improvement to the property. Under the old Act, a lender who failed to give a timely disclosure of these items was liable for an amount equal to the greater of actual damages or $500 plus court costs and reasonable attorneys' fees.[32]

The 1975 Amendments have retained certain disclosure requirements that were under the old Act, but they have also altered the time and method of disclosure to make them more flexible. The initial disclosures designed to inform the consumer about the closing costs take three forms:

1. An informative booklet prepared by HUD which describes the settlement process, referred to as the *Special Information Booklet*[33]
2. The Good Faith Estimate (GFE) of closing costs[34]
3. The Uniform Settlement Statement.

§11.10 —The HUD *Special Information Booklet*

Regulation X requires lenders to provide a copy of the HUD *Special Information Booklet* to every person who applies for a loan in writing. The booklet must be delivered by hand or by mail to the applicant no later than three business days after the application is received.[35]

The *Special Information Booklet* contains two parts. Part 1 gives a detailed description of what is involved in a residential real estate transaction. It describes the rights and obligations of the parties under RESPA. Part II explains each settlement cost item contained in the Uniform Settlement Statement. Using a worksheet attached to the *Booklet*, the prospective buyer can

---

[32] 12 USC §2605 (repealed 1976).
[33] 24 CFR §3500.6(a).
[34] 24 CFR §3500.7(a).
[35] 24 CFR §3500.6(a).

estimate the amount of cash needed for the closing. Lenders are not authorized to make any changes to the text of the *Special Information Booklet.*[36]

§11.11 —The Good Faith Estimate of the Settlement Costs

The good faith estimate (GFE) contains the most important initial disclosures. It provides buyers with preclosing information about closing costs. The lender must provide the GFE to buyers at the same time and in the same manner it provides the *Special Information Booklet.*[37]

Instead of precise, detailed information about all the closing costs required by the preamended Act, the Amendments now call for a good faith estimate of a certain number of charges at settlement.[38] Regulation X establishes these minimum requirements for the GFE:

1. It must be clear and concise. It shall include the lender's name. It must contain the following statement in bold type:

This form does not cover all items you will be required to pay in cash at settlement, for example, for deposit in escrow for real estate taxes and insurance. You may wish to inquire as to the amounts of such other items. You may be required to pay other additional amounts at settlement.[39]

2. The GFE must use the same terminology as that in the Uniform Settlement Statement form prepared by HUD, usually referred to as *HUD-1.* Lenders are encouraged to place next to each line of the disclosure the same number used in the HUD form for the same item. For example, the number 805 is used in the HUD form for the lender's inspection fee. The lender is encouraged to place the same number next to the item *Inspection Fee* on the lender's GFE form[40]

3. If a lender requires borrowers to obtain settlement services from a particular provider, such as a law firm or title or insurance firm, the GFE statement must indicate the identity of that provider and an estimate of that charge[41]

If the lender chooses not to use a HUD-1 form, the lender may develop its own form, provided it complies with Regulation X requirements.[42]

---

[36] 24 CFR §3500.6(c).

[37] 24 CFR §3500.7(a).

[38] 24 CFR §3500.7(c).

[39] 24 CFR §3500.7(d)(1).

[40] 24 CFR §3500.7(d)(2).

[41] 24 CFR §3500.7(e).

[42] 24 CFR §3500.7(d).

§11.12   —The Uniform Settlement Statement

The Uniform Settlement Statement (HUD-1) must be used by all persons conducting settlement in every federally related mortgage loan settlement transaction.[43] Note that this duty falls upon the person conducting the settlement, not necessarily the lender. The only obligation imposed upon the lender, assuming the lender is not the person conducting settlement, is to obtain a copy of the Uniform Settlement Statement for recordkeeping purposes.[44]

The person conducting the settlement must fill out the Uniform Settlement Statement properly to reflect all the itemized charges to be paid by the borrower and the seller in connection with the settlement. All the charges that are required by the lender must be indicated on the form, whether paid at closing or outside of closing. In the latter case, they are indicated as POC (paid outside closing). POC charges not required by the lender need not be included.[45] For example, an agreement between the buyer and the buyer's attorney that the fee will be paid outside the settlement at a later date need not be shown on the statement because the fee is not a charge required by the lender.

To insure uniformity, Regulation X requires that any reproduction of the Uniform Settlement Statement must conform to the terminology, sequence, and numbering of line items on the HUD form. However, those items that are not in use locally may be deleted, except for a number of specific items enumerated in Regulation X, §3500.9(a)(3). On the other hand, charges not listed on HUD-1, but which are customary locally or pursuant to the lender's practice, may be included.[46]

The borrower may inspect the Uniform Settlement Statement during the business day immediately preceding the date of settlement, but only the information which is then known to the person conducting the settlement can be made available to the borrower.[47]

The person conducting the settlement must deliver or mail the Uniform Settlement Statement to the buyer and the seller at or before settlement.[48] The borrower may waive the right to the delivery of the completed Uniform Settlement Statement no later than at the closing, but the waiver must be in writing, and the person conducting the settlement then has the duty to deliver the statement as soon as possible after settlement.[49]

Note that the RESPA disclosure requirements do not preempt the disclosure provisions of the Truth in Lending Act. The TILA disclosures required for

---

[43] 24 CFR §3500.8(a).

[44] 24 CFR §3500.8(c).

[45] 24 CFR §3500.8(b).

[46] 24 CFR §3500.9(a)(4).

[47] 24 CFR §3500.10(a).

[48] 24 CFR §3500.10(b).

[49] 24 CFR §3500.10(c).

closed-end credit transactions do apply to residential mortgage transactions.[50]

With respect to the time of disclosure, Regulation Z, implementing TILA, provides that, in a residential mortgage transaction subject to RESPA, the creditor must make a good faith estimate of the items required to be disclosed by Regulation Z before consummation, and shall deliver or mail it to the consumer no later than three business days after the creditor receives the consumer's written application, whichever is earlier.[51] This provision is intended to mesh with the time for disclosure under RESPA.

This early disclosure of credit terms under TILA applies only to transactions which qualify both as a residential mortgage transaction as defined by Regulation Z at §226.2(a) and a federally related mortgage loan as defined by RESPA.[52] The Federal Reserve Board implementing these provisions of TILA refers to RESPA and Regulation X as well as HUD interpretations to decide whether and when a *written application* has been received. For its part, Regulation Z deems an application to be received when, through the normal channels of transmittal by mail, hand delivery, or through an intermediary agent or broker, the application reaches the creditor. The application is deemed not to be received when it simply reaches the creditor's agent or the broker.[53]

§11.13 —Penalties for Disclosure Violations

RESPA does not impose any penalties for violating the disclosure requirements of the Act. Therefore, the person conducting the settlement is not liable under the Act for failure to mail or deliver the Special Information Booklet, the good faith estimate of closing costs, or the Uniform Settlement Statement to the buyer and seller.

This absence of penalty provisions certainly dilutes the effectiveness of RESPA. It has been argued, however, that this lack of express penalty provisions under RESPA does not affect the right of individuals who have been injured by a violation of RESPA.[54] In this respect, the courts have differed on the question of whether RESPA grants a private cause of action.

The Sixth Circuit in *Vega v First Federal Savings & Loan Association*[55] adopted the view that "while the Act does not expressly provide for such a cause of action we believe, based on the legislative history, that Congress intended to create a private remedy for violations of the Act."[56]

---

[50] *See* 12 CFR §226.19 and **§4.17.**

[51] 12 CFR §226.19(a).

[52] 12 CFR §226.19(a) and Official Staff Commentary.

[53] *Id.*

[54] *See* P. Barron, Federal Regulation of Real Estate §2.02[2][f] (rev ed 1983).

[55] 622 F2d 918 (6th Cir 1980).

[56] *Id* 925 n 8.

A few courts simply refused a private right of action altogether.[57] Some other courts adopted a middle-of-the-road position. For instance, a superior court in Arizona held that "while a private right of action should be available against a primary lender who violates the spirit and letter of RESPA, there is no right of action available to persons injured by careless estimates of closing costs."[58] Thus, a right of private action is recognized by the court, but not for any violation of the disclosure provisions of the Act.

Amendments have been introduced in Congress to provide for civil and statutory penalties for violation of the disclosure requirements. The proposed amendments also called for giving HUD injunction power under RESPA.[59] These attempts at reform, however, were dropped in committee.

Remedies for violations of the RESPA disclosure requirements may be obtained through TILA, however. Furthermore, a lender's failure to disclose may constitute an unfair and deceptive practice or act proscribed by the appropriate federal and state statutes.

§11.14   —Prohibition against Kickbacks and Unearned Fees

RESPA is not simply a disclosure statute. It also prohibits certain abusive practices in the home mortgage industry which, as a result, inflate the costs of home purchase transactions without conferring upon the consumer any real benefit.[60]

The most common of the practices which could be abusive is the payment of "commissions" to brokers or lawyers for referring the borrower to a particular title insurance company or to a particular lender. Generally, the commissions are paid in return for no actual service rendered other than the referral itself. These practices result in the *reverse competition*. The provider of services, in order to attract business, is more likely to increase the referral fees rather than reduce the price of services rendered to benefit the consumer. As a result of *reverse competition*, the consumer has to pay higher costs for these services. It is to curb these practices that Congress enacted §8(a) and (b) of RESPA.[61]

---

[57] *See* Allison v Liberty Savs, 535 F Supp 828 (ND Ill 1982).

[58] Machutta v Saguaro Savs & Loan Assn, No C-392949 (Ariz Super Ct Maricopa County, Sept 18, 1980), and Stallone v Saguaro Savs & Loan Assn, No C-392948 (Ariz Super Ct Maricopa County, Sept 18, 1980), *cited in* P. Barron, *supra* note 54, at §2.02[2][f].

[59] Housing and Community Development Amendments of 1978, Pub L No 95-577, 92 Stat 2080 (codified as amended in scattered sections of 12, 15, 40 & 42 USC), *cited in* P. Barron, *supra* note 54.

[60] Senate Banking Housing and Urban Affairs Comm, Real Estate Settlement Procedures S Rep No 866, 93d Cong, 2d Sess 6546, *reprinted in* 1974 US Code Cong & Admin News 6551.

[61] 12 USC §2607 (a)-(b).

Prohibition against Kickbacks

Section 8(a) of RESPA provides:

> No person shall give, and no person shall accept any fee, kickback, or thing of value, pursuant to any agreement or understanding, oral or otherwise, that business incident to or a part of a real estate settlement service involving a federally related mortgage loan shall be referred to any person.

Pursuant to this provision, two elements must be present in order to constitute a practice prohibited by §8(a):

1. An agreement to refer business
2. A thing of value given to the referring person

First, what constitutes an agreement or understanding to refer business is not defined by the Act. But Regulation X gives the term the broadest meaning. The agreement or understanding need not be verbalized. It may be established by a practice, pattern, or course of conduct which shows that the parties understand that the transfer of the thing of value is in return for the referral of business. Regulation X presumes the existence of such an agreement or understanding when there is a repeated payment which is connected in any way with the volume or value of the business referred to the payor by the recipient.[62]

Second, a thing of value must be given to the referring party. The term *thing of value* has the broadest meaning. As RESPA defines it, the term "includes any payment, advance, funds, loans, service, or other consideration."[63] Regulation X gives some examples of things of value. The list is long and is not limitative. Things of value may be:

> monies, things, discounts, salaries, commissions, fees, duplicate payments of a charge, stock, dividends, distribution of partnership profits, credits representing monies that may be paid at a future date, special bank deposits of accounts, banking terms, special loan or loan guarantee terms, services of all types at special or free rates and sales or rentals at special prices or rates.[64]

In a word, *thing of value* covers any transfer of value regardless of the mode of transfer, direct or indirect, or of any label.

Prohibition of Unearned Fees

Section 8(b) states: "No person shall give and no person shall accept any portion, split, or percentage of any charge made or received from the rendering

---

[62] 24 CFR §3500.14(c).

[63] 12 USC §2602(2).

[64] 24 CFR §3500.14(b).

of a real estate settlement service in connection with a transaction involving a federally related mortgage loan other than for services actually performed." This section prohibits payments or other types of transfer of things of value that exceed the reasonable value of the services actually rendered. The idea seems to be that to the extent that the compensation or the payment is not related to the services actually furnished to the payor, such compensation or payment is presumed to be related to the referral per se, and as such is prohibited as a kickback under §8(a). The value of the referral itself (i.e., the additional business obtained thereby) is not to be taken into account in determining whether the payment is reasonable.[65]

Not all payments for no actual services are violative of the law. In an informal opinion given by a HUD attorney, the payment of a tip to the title searcher at closing, an apparently customary payment in New York, is not violative of RESPA. The opinion stated:

> We do not view the payment as a fee for services since it appears entirely voluntary. It is a gratuity and no services are conditioned upon its payment. While we recognize some level of compulsion may be felt by the consumer in the closing environment, this does not elevate it to a legal obligation. It seems similar to the gratuity paid at a restaurant.
>
> Even if the payment is considered a fee, we do not believe RESPA is violated. First, no referral is involved and the payment has no connection with any such referral. Second, argument could be raised that the payment is an additional part of the compensation for title services. We are informed that the salary structure of such title searchers anticipates such payments. The payments must be for referral or for no services rendered in order to violate the RESPA kickback prohibition. We would note that in the second case, the payment should appear on the Uniform Settlement Statement (HUD-1) form. Its non-inclusion would be damaging to an attempt to characterize the payment as for services rendered.[66]

The Seventh Circuit had a different opinion on that type of payment. In *United States v Gannon*,[67] the defendant, a counterman at Cook County's title registration desk, was held to violate RESPA by accepting "gratuities" of two or three dollars for recording each change of title. The defendant argued that RESPA's prohibition of kickbacks and unearned fees was intended to apply only to those payments intended as compensation for the referral of business. Here, the "gratuities" were paid for no such referral.

The court pushed that argument aside. It stated:

> Congress' aim was to stop all abusive practices that unreasonably inflate

---

[65] 24 CFR §3500.14(e).

[66] Informal Op 122 (Sept 10, 1982), *reprinted in* P. Barron, Federal Regulation of Real Estate app A2.04[3] (rev ed 1983).

[67] 684 F2d 433 (7th Cir 1981).

federally related settlement cost to the public. Although the focus of immediate Congressional concern may have been the splitting of fees between the recipient of the charge and unrelated third parties, the arrangement we view here is no less an example of an "abusive practice" or imposition of an "unearned fee", unreasonably increasing the cost of settlement services to the banks, and ultimately to the public at large.[68]

The court was of further opinion that:

a single individual *can* violate §2607(b) by receiving in his official capacity a "charge" for the rendering of settlement services, but personally keeping a portion of the charge in fact for something other than the performance of those services. In this case, appellant in his official role imposed and received a "charge" that incorporated not only a statutorily imposed segment—but also a "gratuity" that was ostensibly required by appellant in order to get the services properly performed. At the same time, because the prompt service was already due the bank employees under state law once the statutory fee was paid, the extra payment must have been accepted in fact for something "other than services actually performed."[69] [emphasis in text.]

The difficulty with the court's reasoning is that the extra payments were not in return for referring business. It seems that "gratuities" may be illegal bribes, but they do not fit the types of arrangements and payments that RESPA prohibits.

In *Mercado v Calumet Federal Law & Loan Association*,[70] the Seventh Circuit seemed to repudiate in part the liberal interpretation of §8(a) and (b) adopted in *United States v Gannon*. In *Mercado*, a mother and her son sued a lender for imposing unwarranted charges on the acceleration and refinancing of a loan. The plaintiffs contended that the lender violated RESPA under the interpretation of *Gannon* because the new charges were for real estate settlement services and were imposed for no services actually performed.

The Seventh Circuit affirmed the district court's dismissal of the complaint. The court pointed out that §8 is an antikickback statute and, therefore, requires at least two parties to share fees. The complaint did not allege any other party. The court, not very convincingly, tried to distinguish the present case from *Gannon*. In *Gannon*, the court said the gratuities involved multiple parties. Gannon received a charge for the rendering of settlement services, but kept a portion of the charge in fact for something other than the performance of the service and passed on the rest to the county. Nothing of this sort occurred in *Mercado*. The court held that in the latter case, the issue was simply a question of interpretation and enforcement of the contract between the parties, the

---

[68] *Id* 438.
[69] *Id* 438-39.
[70] 763 F2d 269 (7th Cir 1985).

plaintiffs and the bank. That issue is committed to state law and state courts. If the contract allowed acceleration and refinancing charges, then there is no demand for payment for services not rendered. If there is no such allowance, then the court will not permit such payment. The Seventh Circuit concluded that Congress did not mean, with §8 of RESPA, "to make every violation of a contract a violation of federal law too."[71]

§11.15 —Transactions Exempted from the Kickback and Unearned Fee Prohibitions

Certain payments common in the home mortgage industry would fit the description of the practices prohibited by §8 of RESPA. Take, for example, the standard brokerage arrangement. One broker lists a property, and, through the multiple listing method, another broker sells the property. The commission is split between the listing broker and the selling broker, 50-50 or 60-40, depending on the case. One could argue that the listing agent receives a payment which does not reflect the value of the services rendered. In other words, there is a payment of unearned fees.

Congress recognizes this type of practice and does not outlaw this traditional arrangement or other similar arrangements. Congress gives the Secretary of HUD the power to interpret the Act and to expand the scope of the exempted transactions.[72] The list of exemptions has lengthened considerably since 1954, when RESPA was first enacted.[73]

The Act excludes the following arrangements from the scope of the Act's prohibitions of kickbacks and unearned fees:

1. Payment of a fee to an attorney for services actually rendered[74]

2. Payment of a fee to a duly appointed agent of a title company by that company for services performed in issuing the title insurance policy[75]

3. Payment by a lender to its duly appointed agent for services actually rendered in making the loan[76]

4. Payment of a bona fide salary to any person for services actually performed and for goods or facilities actually furnished[77]

These exemptions are not truly exemptions. They are no more than a

---

[71] *Id* 272.

[72] 12 USC §2617(a).

[73] RESPA Amendments, Pub L No 94-205, 89 Stat 1157 (1976); Pub L No 98-181, tit iv, §461(b) and (c), 97 Stat 1231 (Nov 30, 1983).

[74] 12 USC §2607(c)(1)(A).

[75] 12 USC §2607(c)(1)(B).

[76] 12 USC §2607(c)(1)(C).

[77] 12 USC §2607(2).

restatement of the general rule, that fees or payments received must be for services actually rendered.

The 1975 RESPA amendments added an exemption which is more meaningful. This exemption relates to payments made pursuant to cooperative brokerage as well as referral arrangements or agreements between real estate agents and brokers.[78] These payments are not prohibited even if no services are actually performed. Note that the exemption applied only to payments between real estate agents and brokers, and so would not apply between other persons such as an attorney and a title agent.

Pursuant to the authority given by Congress, the Secretary of HUD has added two exemptions to the list:

> 1. Payment dealing with normal promotional and educational activities.[79] The giving of a thing of value for business referral is not a violation of RESPA if the thing of value is a normal promotional or educational activity. To qualify under this exemption, the parties involved must pass a three-prong test: the thing of value must consist of a normal promotional and educational activity; the giving of the thing of value must not be directly conditioned on the referral of business; and the thing of value must not be defrayed expenses that otherwise would be incurred by the referring party in the real estate settlement. Regulation X gives example of things of value that meet the test: reception by a title company, free seminars on title matters to professionals, furnishing property descriptions and names of record owners without charge to persons such as lenders, real estate brokers, or attorneys, or distribution of calenders or other promotional material of nominal value[80]
>
> 2. Waiver by a lender of the requirement that a borrower pay a prepayment penalty provided in mortgage documents, whether or not such a waiver is conditioned on the lender's receipt of a new loan application from the borrower or from a person purchasing the property from the borrower[81]

The purpose of this exemption is to encourage lenders to waive prepayment penalties, whether or not new business is obtained through such waiver.

§11.16 —Exemption of Controlled Business Arrangements

The original prohibition against kickbacks and unearned fees was considerably diluted in 1983 with the addition of a new exemption.

---

[78] 12 USC §2607(c)(3).

[79] 24 CFR §3500.14(f)(4).

[80] *Id.*

[81] 24 CFR §3500.14(f)(5).

The new exemption reads:

> [Nothing in this section shall be construed as prohibiting]:
> (4)   controlled business arrangements so long as (A) at or prior to the time of the referral a disclosure is made of the existence of such an arrangement to the person being referred and, in connection with the referral, such person is provided a written estimate of the charge or range of charges generally made by the provider to which the person is referred, except that where the lender makes the referral, this requirement may be satisfied as part of and at the time that the estimates of settlement charges required under section 2604(c) of this title are provided, (B) such person is not required to use any particular provider of settlement services, and (C) the only thing of value that is received from the arrangement, other than the payments permitted under this subsection, is a return on the ownership interest or franchise relationship.[82]

Controlled business arrangements generally encompass situations in which a person or firm refers purchasers of settlement services to a settlement service provider that is owned by the referring party. As RESPA defines:

> controlled business arrangement means an arrangement in which (A) a person who is in position to refer business incident to or as part of a real estate settlement service involving a federally related mortgage loan, or an associate of such person, has either an affiliate relationship with or a direct or beneficial ownership interest of more than one percent in a provider of settlement services; and (B) either of such persons, directly or indirectly, refers such business to that provider or affirmatively influences the selection of that provider.[83]

In a controlled business arrangement, the referring party, although it does not receive any direct payment from the referred party, does benefit through the ownership interest in the latter. The danger of such an arrangement is again the phenomenon of reverse competition which provides no incentive to reduce the price of services to the ultimate buyer. By their nature, controlled business arrangements are anticompetitive.

The 1983 RESPA amendments exempt controlled business arrangements from §8 so long as certain required disclosures are made.

First, the referring party must, at or prior to the time the referral is made, disclose to the person being referred the existence of the controlled business arrangement, a written estimate of the normal charge or range of charges made by the provider to which the person is referred, and that the person being referred is not required to use any particular provider of settlement services.

---

[82] 12 USC §2617(c)(4).
[83] 12 USC §2602(7).

Second, the only thing of value that the referring party would receive from the arrangement is a return on the ownership interest or franchise relationship.

The 1983 amendment further specifies that the following transactions are not violative of the Act's prohibition against unearned fees under §8(b):

1. Any arrangement that requires a buyer, borrower, or seller to pay for the services of an attorney, credit reporting agency, or real estate appraiser chosen by the lender to represent the lender's interest in a real estate transaction or

2. Any arrangement in which an attorney or law firm represents a client in a real estate transaction and issues or arranges for the issuance of title insurance in the transaction directly as agent or through a separate corporate title insurance agency that may be established by that attorney or law firm and operated as an adjunct to his or its law practice[84]

These exemptions reflect the success of the home mortgage industry's lobbying effort in recent years.

§11.17 —Penalties for Violations of Prohibitions on Kickbacks and Unearned Fees

Section 8(d)(1) provides that anyone who violates the kickbacks and unearned fees prohibitions shall be fined not more than $10,000 or imprisoned for not more than one year, or both.[85]

Dealing with the civil penalty, the 1983 Amendments have modified the original Act. Prior to 1983, the violator is liable to the person who bears the cost of the kickback or unearned fee in an amount equal to three times the amount of the kickback or unearned fee. The 1983 Amendment changed the treble damage to be based not on the amount of the kickback or unearned fee, but only on the amount of the charge paid for the settlement service.[86] The change may be explained by the evidence problem: it is not easy to prove the amount of kickback or unearned fee the violators received.

The 1983 Amendments added that no liability will be imposed if the violator can prove "by a preponderance of the evidence that the violation was not intentional and resulted from a bona fide error notwithstanding maintenance of reasonable procedures that are reasonably adopted to avoid such error."[87] The new Amendments also give the Secretary of HUD, the Attorney General,

---

[84] 12 USC §2607(c)(5)(i)(ii).

[85] 12 USC §2607(d)(1).

[86] 12 USC §2607(d)(2), *amended by* Pub L No 98-181, 97 Stat 1231 (effective Jan 1, 1984).

[87] 12 USC §2607(d)(3) (as amended).

and the insurance commissioner of the state the authority to bring actions to enjoin violations of §8(a) and (b).[88]

The prevailing party, not necessarily the plaintiff, is entitled to court costs and reasonable attorneys' fees.[89]

One should also remember that a contract to pay a kickback or referral fee is unenforceable under state law because it is illegal under RESPA.

§11.18   —Prohibition against Requiring a Specific Title Insurance Company

Section 9(a) of the Act provides: "No seller of property that will be purchased with the assistance of a federally related mortgage loan shall require directly or indirectly, as a condition to selling the property that title insurance covering the property be purchased by the buyer from any particular title company."[90]

This provision was written with land developers in mind. A developer usually buys a vacant lot and seeks to insure the developer's title with a title company. With a view to obtaining a low premium, the developer promises the title insurance company that it will refer all future buyers of construction erected on the land to that same title company. The arrangement is beneficial to both parties: to the developer, because the developer can get a low premium; and to the title company, because it does not have to expend any further effort or time to search the title at the time future retail buyers contract for the same services the company has already provided the land developer.

This arrangement could be a violation of §8(a) and (b), proscribing kickbacks and unearned fees, if one could prove that the land developer gets a *thing of value* in exchange for the referral. However, §9 was enacted specifically to avoid the burden of having to prove ulterior motive behind the referral.

Any seller that requires from buyers a specific title insurance company shall be liable to the buyer in an amount equal to three times all charges made for such title insurance.[91]

§11.19   —Limitations on Advance Deposits in Escrow Accounts

It is a common practice among lenders to require borrowers to open an escrow account and make advance deposits in the account to pay for anticipated charges levied upon the mortgaged property. Examples of such charges are real estate taxes, insurance premiums, water, sewer taxes, and the like. The purpose of the escrow account is to insure that the lender's interest in the property will be protected against third-party claims and other hazards, such as destruction by fire or flood.

---

[88] 12 USC §2607(d)(4) (as amended).

[89] 12 USC §2607(d)(5).

[90] 12 USC §2607(a).

[91] 12 USC §2608(b).

An escrow account with advance deposits to cover the above charges may work to the benefit of the borrower as well, if the required amounts reasonably represent the actual anticipated charges. Borrowers may have difficulty at the due date in coming up with a full payment, and the advance deposits may be a welcome form of forced savings.

However, lenders may abuse the system, and require from the borrower advance deposits which far exceed the expected payments. Some lenders may require, at the time of the settlement, deposits to cover as much as six months, one year, or even two years advance taxes and insurance premiums. This not only results in high settlement fees, but also deprives the borrower of the use of that money, and of the interest on that money, during that time.

The purpose of §10 of RESPA is to stop these abusive practices.[92] Section 10(a) limits the escrow deposits at the time of settlement. Section 10(b) limits the escrow deposits after settlement.

At settlement, §10(a) provides:

> A lender in connection with a federal related mortgage loan may not require the borrower or prospective borrower, (1) to deposit in any escrow account which may be established in connection with such loan for the purpose of assuring payment of taxes, insurance premiums, and other charges attributable to the period beginning on the last date on which each such charge would have been paid under the normal lending practice of the lender and local custom, provided that the selection of each such date constitutes prudent lending practice, and ending on the due date of its first full installment payment under the mortgage, plus one-sixth of the estimated total amount of such taxes, insurance premiums and other charges to be paid on dates, as provided above, during the ensuing twelve-month period.

An example will illustrate this formula. Suppose the closing date for the home is on June 10. Usually, the borrower is required to pay the first full installment payment under the mortgage on August 1. Suppose the real estate tax on the property is $1,200 per year, and the tax is to be paid no later than April 30 (it is the last date on which each such charge would have been paid). At settlement, the lender cannot require an advance payment in the escrow account which exceeds $500. The $500 is computed as follows:

> $100 payment for May, (the period beginning on the last date on which such charge would have been paid)
> $100 payment for June,
> $100 payment for July,
> $200 (a cushion equivalent to one-sixth of the total amount of $1,200)
> $500

---

[92] 12 USC §2609.

The $500 total is the maximum amount that the lender could require the borrower to put in the escrow account for the payment of the real estate tax.

After settlement, §10(b) provides that the lender may not require the borrower or prospective borrower:

> (2) to deposit in any such escrow account in any month beginning with the first full installment payment under the mortgage a sum (for the purpose of assuring payment of taxes, insurance premiums and other charges with respect to the property) in excess of the sum of (A) one-twelfth of the total amount of the estimated taxes, insurance premiums and other charges which are reasonably anticipated to be paid on dates during the ensuing twelve months which dates are in accordance with the normal lending practice of the lender and local custom, provided that the selection of each such date constitutes prudent lending practice, plus (B) such amount as is necessary to maintain an additional balance in such escrow account not to exceed one-sixth of the estimated total amount of such taxes, insurance premiums and other charges to be paid on dates, as provided above, during the ensuing twelve-month period: *Provided, however*, that in the event the lender determines there will be or is a deficiency he shall not be prohibited from requiring additional monthly deposits in such escrow account to avoid or eliminate such deficiency.

This provision may be explained by the fact that a lender may circumvent §10(a) on limitation of the advance deposits at settlement by requiring modest sums at this time and then increasing their amounts in the following monthly mortgage payments. Section 10(b) prevents this from happening. Section 10(b) limits monthly advance deposits in the escrow account to one-twelfth of the charges that will become due in the ensuing year. To allow the lender adequate protection against future increases of the charges, the law grants the lender a cushion that cannot exceed, for the whole year, two months' charges.

Taking the above example of $1,200 real estate tax, at the time of settlement on June 10, $500 is deposited in the escrow account. At the beginning of August, September, October, November, and December, $100 can be collected (one-twelfth of the total tax in the ensuing year).

Additionally, the law allows the lender a cushion of $200 which may be paid as a lump sum or prorated during the 12-month period. If prorated, the total monthly escrow payment for real estate tax would be $100 + $16.60 (one-twelfth of $200).

Suppose, during October, the city announces that the real estate tax for the following year will be increased from $1,200 to $1,320. Section 10(b) allows the lender to collect "an additional monthly deposit in such escrow account to avoid or eliminate such deficiency." As a result, the lender may require an additional escrow payment of $120 to cover the increase. Section 10(b) does not spell out how this extra payment will be paid. The literal reading of §10(b) seems to allow the lender two options: either collect the total amount of $120 at the November monthly mortgage payment or prorate this amount among the monthly payments until the tax is due. It seems that the spirit of the law points to the last solution.[93]

As in the case of RESPA disclosure requirements, there are no provisions imposing penalties for violations of §10, either under the Act itself or under Regulation X. The reader is referred to §11.13 for a discussion of the courts' possible approaches to this issue.

§11.20 —State Law and RESPA

States may enact statutes similar to RESPA. RESPA does not preempt such state statutes as long as they are not inconsistent with the RESPA provisions. State law is not inconsistent with RESPA if it affords equal or greater protection to the consumer.

§11.21 Interstate Land Sales Full Disclosure Act

In 1968, Congress enacted the Interstate Land Sales Full Disclosure Act[94] (ILSFDA) to protect purchasers from abuses of real estate developers. Some of those abuses are described in a House report as follows:

> [P]urchasers living in the same state where the land was located or living out of state were persuaded to buy land that they had never seen by sophisticated sales force promising that land (which might be under water or suitable only for grazing purposes) was a good investment, suitable for homesites and easily resaleable.[96]

Since 1968, the Act has been amended six times. The last amendment, in 1979, was almost a complete revision of the Act.[97]

The Secretary of HUD was given the authority to supplement and interpret the Act and to provide for exemptions via regulations.[98] Thus, in order to get a complete view of the Act and of its implementation, the practitioner must consult both the Act itself and the HUD regulations.

§11.22 —Scope

The ILSFDA is basically a disclosure act, but it is not *only* a disclosure act. It also prohibits certain practices deemed to be abusive.

---

[93] *See* P. Baron, Federal Regulation of Real Estate §2.02[5][b][ii] (rev ed 1983).

[94] 12 USC §2616.

[95] Pub L No 90-448, 82 Stat 590 (codified as amended at 15 USC §§1701-1720).

[96] HR Rep No 154, 96th Cong, 1st Sess 1, *reprinted in* 1979 US Code Cong & Admin News 2317.

[97] Pub L No 96-153, tit IV, 93 Stat 1101 (1979).

[98] 24 CFR §1700.

Parties Covered

The Act protects purchasers and lessees of land. The reason lessees are also included is because certain sales are termed as leases, whereby the lessee will have the option to buy the land and past rents are applied to the purchase price. Thus, a purchaser includes a lessee, and a developer includes a lessor. A lessee is considered a prospective purchaser. The law defines purchaser to mean "an actual or prospective purchaser or lessee of a lot."[99]

A developer means any person who, directly or indirectly, sells or leases, or offers to sell or lease, or advertises for sale or lease, any lots.[100] The Act applies to developers and their agents. The definition of *agent* is broad. "Agent means any person who represents or acts for or on behalf of, a developer in selling or leasing or offering to sell or lease any lot or lots, but shall not include an attorney at law whose representation of another person consists solely of rendering legal services."[101]

The legal issue that often arises is when a third party is considered to be the developer's *agent*. It seems that the test is participation in the developer's activities. A financial interest, without more, will not necessarily give rise to an agency relationship. For example, a corporation which simply purchases the assets of the developer is not an agent and, therefore, is not liable for the developer's improper activities. A question arises concerning the notes subscribed by purchasers in favor of the developer, and the developer's assigning those notes to a third party. Is the assignee liable for the developer's activities? If the assignee has no knowledge of the developer's improper activities, the assignee will have the status of a holder in due course and, therefore, it seems that the purchasers still have to pay, and fraud is not a defense. However, in some cases, the courts have imputed knowledge of the developer's illegal activities to the assignee in order to deny the latter the status of a holder in due course.[102]

Transactions Covered by the Act

The Act applies to developers or agents who directly or indirectly make use of any means or instruments of transportation or communication in interstate commerce, or of the mails, for the sale or lease of undeveloped, subdivided land.[103] Note the term *subdivided* land. For the Act to apply, in addition to the interstate commerce use of mail or communication, the object of the sale or lease must be part of a subdivision.

The term *subdivision* is defined by the Act as "any land which is located in any state or in a foreign country, and is divided, or is proposed to be divided

---

[99] 15 USC §1701(10); 24 CFR §1710.1.

[100] 15 USC §1701(5); 24 CFR §1710.1.

[101] 15 USC §1701(6); 24 CFR §1710.1.

[102] *See Stewart v Thornton*, 116 Ariz 107, 568 P2d 414 (1977); P. Barron, Federal Regulation of Real Estate §3.302(2)(b) (rev ed 1983).

[103] 15 USC §1703(b); 24 CFR §1710.3.

into lots, whether contiguous or not, for the purpose of sale or lease as part of a common promotional plan."[104]

A *common promotional plan* is defined as:

> [A] plan, undertaken by a single developer or a group of developers acting in concert, to offer lots for sale or lease; where land is offered for sale by a developer or group of developers acting in concert, and the land is contiguous or is known, designated, or advertised as a common unit or by a common name, the land is presumed, without regard to the number of lots covered by each individual offering, as being offered for sale or lease as part of a common promotional plan.[105]

Thus, the definition covers both situations in which the lots are contiguous, and situations in which they are not, if in both cases they are part of a common promotional plan.

Usually, the following factors will be considered in determining whether a common promotional plan exists: common ownership; similar name or identity; common sales agents; common sales facilities; common advertising; and common inventory.[106]

§11.23 —Exempted Transactions

Certain transactions are exempted completely from the scope of the Act. Some others are exempted from some provisions only. In addition, HUD has issued a number of regulatory exemptions.

Full Exemptions

The ILSFDA does not apply to the following:

> 1. Subdivisions containing fewer than 25 lots.[107] One should note that if the developer intends to develop additional lots, they will not be exempted if the total of the new lots and the lots that are sold exceeds 25
>
> 2. Sale or lease of any improved land on which there is a residential commercial condominium or industrial building or a proposed construction on the land to be constructed within two years[108]
>
> 3. Sale of evidences of indebtedness, secured by a mortgage or deed of trust on real estate[109]

---

[104] 15 USC §1701(3); 24 CFR §1710.1.

[105] 15 USC §1701(4); 24 CFR §1710.1.

[106] 44 Fed Reg 24010, 24011 (1979).

[107] 15 USC §1701(a)(1).

[108] 15 USC §1702(a)(2).

[109] 15 USC §1702(a)(3).

4. Sale of securities issued by a real estate investment trust[110]

5. Sale or lease of real estate by the government or a governmental agency[111]

6. Sales of cemetery lots[112]

7. Sales or leases of lots from builders to other builders for purpose of resale or lease.[113] However, the person who puts such lots on sale to nonprofessional purchasers or lessees would be subject to the Act

8. Sale or lease of real estate for industrial or commercial developments.[114] This exemption applies only if the following conditions are met: the real estate is owned or intended for industrial or commercial use; the purchaser or lessee is a business entity engaged in commercial or industrial business; the purchaser or lessee of such real estate is represented in the transaction by its own selected representative; the purchaser or lessee affirms in writing that it will use the real estate for its own use or will sell or lease it only for a business purpose; and a policy of title insurance is issued in connection with the transaction, and the title to the real estate is vested in the seller or lessor. The buyer may, however, waive this last condition, provided such waiver is in writing

Partial Exemptions

The Act requires entities subject to the Act to register with HUD. The disclosure requirements under the Act are very complex. Therefore, the Act exempts certain situations from some of the registration and disclosure requirements.

Partial exemptions exist for:

1. Subdivisions containing fewer than 100 lots[115]

2. Situations in which no more than 12 lots are sold or leased within a year[116]

3. Sale or lease of lots in a noncontiguous part of the subdivision which contains no more than 20 lots, provided the purchaser or lessee, or his or her spouse, has personally inspected the lot prior to the signing of the contract of purchase or lease[117]

4. Sale or lease of lots in a subdivision in which each of the lots is at least 20 acres[118]

---

[110] 15 USC §1702(a)(4).

[111] 15 USC §1702(a)(5).

[112] 15 USC §1702(a)(6).

[113] 15 USC §1702(a)(7).

[114] 15 USC §1702(a)(8).

[115] 15 USC §1702(b)(1).

[116] 15 USC §1702(b)(2).

[117] 15 USC §1702(b)(3).

[118] 15 USC §1702(b)(4).

5. Subdivisions that are subject to local regulations limiting the use of the lots exclusively to single-family residences[119]

6. Sale or lease of a lot on which a mobile home is to be erected or placed thereon as a residence, if the lot is sold to the buyer by one entity and the home is sold by another entity[120]

7. Sale or lease of real estate which is intrastate in nature and which fulfills certain conditions, to wit: the lot is free and clear of all encumbrances and claims; the purchaser or lessee has personally inspected the lot prior to sale or lease; the agreement of purchase or lease clearly gives a good faith estimate of the year of completion or the parties responsible for providing or maintaining amenities such as roads and water and sewer facilities; the agreement gives the purchaser or lessee a cooling-off period of seven days following the signing of the contract; and the purchaser or lessee has acknowledged in writing the receipt of the developer's good faith written estimate of the cost of providing electricity, water, sewer, gas, and telephone services for the lot[121]

8. Sale or lease of a lot in a subdivision containing less than 300 lots, if the buyer's or lessee's residence is within the same standard metropolitan statistical area as the subdivision, the lot is free and clear of any claims and encumbrances; on-site inspection by the purchaser or lessee has been made; a good faith estimate of the date of completion is made, together with amenities such as gas, electricity, and water; a seven-day cooling-off period is allowed to the lessee or buyer; a written acknowledgment of receipt of the developer's written statement as to existing potential rights and duties imposed on the lot owner or lessee by other lot owners or lessees; appointment of an agent in the purchaser's state of residence, together with a declaration that the developer submits to the legal jurisdiction of the state of the purchaser's or lessee's residence; and the developer delivers to the purchaser or lessee a written affirmation on a form provided by HUD that the developer has complied with all of the above requirements[122]

Regulatory Exemptions

The Act gives authority to the Secretary of HUD to issue further exemptions, but only when the amount involved is small or the public offering limited.[123] Pursuant to this authority, HUD has granted a number of regulatory exemptions. These exemptions are partial, i.e., they are applicable only to registration and disclosure requirements. Antifraud provisions of the Act still apply. Furthermore, HUD has authority to grant ad hoc exemptions when it

---

[119] 15 USC §1702(b)(5).

[120] 15 USC §1702(b)(6).

[121] 15 USC §1703(b)(7)(A).

[122] 15 USC §1702(b)(8).

[123] 15 USC §1702(c).

deems that by reason of the small amount involved, or the limited character of the public offering, the public interest is not in danger. Partial regulatory exemptions apply to:

1. Sale or lease of a lot for less than $100 if the purchaser or lessee is not required to purchase or lease more than one lot[124]

2. Lease of a lot for a term of five years or less if the terms of the lease do not obligate the lessee to renew.[125] A lease with option to purchase might or might not qualify. A request for an advisory opinion is recommended in such a case. Of course, a sale disguised as a lease is not exempt

3. Lots sold to developers.[126] The regulation assumes that professionals do not need the same protection as nonprofessionals

4. Sale or lease of a lot to a purchaser that already has a building on the adjoining lot. This allows owners to enlarge their existing property [127]

5. Lots sold to government or a government agency[128]

6. Sale of a lot to a person who has leased or maintained his or her primary residence on it for at least one year

In all of the above exemptions, the determination is made on a lot-by-lot basis. The entire subdivision need not qualify. HUD has full authority to terminate the exemptions after notification of its intention to the developer, and after affording the latter a hearing opportunity.[129]

Upon request, HUD may issue an ad hoc exemption order with regard to a subdivision that does not fulfill the eligibility requirements of the above-described partial exemptions. An exemption order, if granted, has no retroactive effect.[130] Exemption orders are issued only after the developer submits a certain amount of required information regarding: the type of sale involved, the contract used, developers' purchasers' responsibilities with respect to the amenities; a good faith estimate of the date of completion of the amenities; a statement that the purchaser may rescind the contract seven days after the contract is signed, or within a longer period if allowed under state law; a statement that the developer will deliver to the purchaser within 180 days a warranty deed that the lot is free from liens and encumbrances; a statement to the effect that the purchaser or the purchaser's spouse will make an on-site

---

[124] 24 CFR §1710.14(a)(1).
[125] 24 CFR §1710.14(a)(2).
[126] 24 CFR §1710.14(a)(3).
[127] 24 CFR §1710.14(a)(4).
[128] 24 CFR §1710.14(a)(5).
[129] 24 CFR §1710.14(b).
[130] 24 CFR §1710.16(a).

inspection prior to the signing of the contract.[131] HUD thus tries to make sure that the public interest is duly protected before granting an exemption.

As for partial regulatory exemptions, HUD may revoke ad hoc exemption orders after notification and hearing.

§11.24 —Registration and Disclosure Requirements

The disclosure requirements of the ILSFDA were patterned after the Federal Securities Act of 1933.[132] The registration with HUD of a land development sale is similar to securities registration with a public office.[133]

The ILSFDA makes it unlawful for a developer or an agent of the developer to sell a nonexempt lot by direct or indirect use of any means or instruments of transportation or communication in interstate commerce or the mails unless:

1. A statement of record is filed with HUD[134]

2. A printed property report has been furnished to a buyer before the signing of the contract or agreement[135]

3. The statement of record and the property report contain a true statement of all material facts[136]

4. Advertising and promotional material was consistent with the information required to be disclosed in the property report[137]

A consolidated statement of record is required if the developer adds lots to be sold to the lots already registered as part of a common promotional plan.[138] The statement of record must be amended if there is a change or if there is any new material fact which needs to be disclosed.

The property report that the developer has to deliver to the prospective purchaser resembles the prospectus required by the Security Act. This property report may parallel the statement of record, but need not incorporate all the documents on file.[139]

The mandatory disclosures under the Act are very complex. It is not the intent of this chapter to discuss all of these requirements.

It suffices to say that the disclosures generally contain information dealing with the financial condition of the developer, the status of the real estate title,

---

[131] 24 CFR §1710.16(b).

[132] 15 USC §77(a)-77(aa).

[133] *See* McCormack, *An Appraisal of Disclosure Regulation of Subdivided Land Sales,* 1980 Ariz St LJ 705, 708 (1980).

[134] 15 USC §1703(a)(1)(A).

[135] 15 USC §1703(a)(b)(B).

[136] 15 USC §1703(a)(1)(C).

[137] 15 USC §1703(a)(1)(D).

[138] 24 CFR §1710.22(b)(1).

[139] 15 USC §1703(a).

and information about the land subdivision, such as availability of water and other essential amenities.

The Office of Interstate Land Sale Registration (OILSR) has prepared standard forms of disclosures for the use of developers.[140]

§11.25 —Prohibition of Fraudulent Practices

As previously stated, the ILSFDA is not only a disclosure act; it deals also with the substantive issues prohibiting unlawful and misleading sale practices.

HUD regulations define sales practices as "any conduct or advertising by a developer or its agents to induce a person to buy or lease a lot."[141] The regulations implement the ILSFDA provisions on specific sales practices, but also provide standards for other sales practices, not specifically dealt with by the Act, which could be considered misleading in light of certain circumstances. Thus, there are statutory provisions and regulatory provisions dealing with unlawful sales practices. While both specifically describe conduct which would constitute unlawful sales practices, the underlying policy is to prohibit all the maneuvers and practices that are unfair and deceptive.

Following are the unlawful sales practices under the Act:

1. Employ scheme or artifice to defraud[142]

2. Obtain money or property by means of any untrue statement or omission of any material fact required to be stated in the property report.[143] As an example, the developer gives a property report that describes the lot as a lakeside property, and the developer omits to state that the lake is dry for six months of the year

3. Engage in any transaction, practice, or course of business which would operate as a fraud or deceit upon a purchaser[144]

4. Represent that roads, sewers, water, gas, or other amenities will be provided, and the developer does not at the same time give a written covenant that the developer will complete such services or amenities.[145] If there is no such covenant, the developer may not represent that it will provide the above amenities[146]

---

[140] See 24 CFR §1710, app A.

[141] 24 CFR §1715.10.

[142] 15 USC §1703(a)(2)(A).

[143] 15 USC §1703(a)(2)(B).

[144] 15 USC §1703(a)(2)(C).

[145] 15 USC §1703(a)(2)(D).

[146] 24 CFR §1715.15(e).

The HUD regulations not only refine the statutory provisions,[147] but also extend the list of prohibited activities.[148]

The following are a few examples of regulatory unlawful sales practices:

1. Giving the property report to a purchaser and burying it under so many other materials as to conceal it from the purchaser[149]

2. Inducing a purchaser to sign a contract before delivery of the property report[150]

3. Refusing to deliver a property report to a person who expresses an interest in purchasing the property[151]

4. Representing a sales inducement that the lot has good investment potential, while no evidence of that is established in writing, based on tangible facts[152]

The regulations also give examples of sales practices that are not unlawful per se, but are considered to be misleading.[153] Misleading statements usually are ambiguous value statements used in order to induce the other party to make certain inferences which do not correspond to reality. The regulations prohibit the use of certain terms unless those terms are clarified and given a precise meaning.

For instance, the developer may not use terms such as *minutes away* or *short distance,* unless the actual distance in road miles is given; nor can it use the term *waterfront property,* unless the property being sold actually fronts on a body of water.

Misleading practices are practices which are not necessarily unlawful per se, but are unlawful if they are unfairly deceptive.

§11.26 —Remedies

Right of Rescission

The purchaser has the right to rescind the contract up to two years after signing if the purchaser does not receive a property report, or if the sales contract does not contain the disclosures required by the Act.[154] This right of rescission is lost, however, if the purchaser receives a warranty deed within 180 days after the signing of the contract. One should also bear in mind the absolute seven-day cooling-off period, in which the purchaser or lessee may absolutely rescind the signed contract regardless of the disclosures that the developer or

---

[147] 24 CFR §1715.15.

[148] 24 CFR §1715.20.

[149] 24 CFR §1715.20(a).

[150] 24 CFR §1715.20(b).

[151] 24 CFR §1715.20(c).

[152] 24 CFR §1715.20(h).

[153] 24 CFR §1715.25.

[154] 15 USC §1703(d).

agent makes. The property report, as well as the contract or agreement or promissory note, must clearly state the seven-day and the two-year rights of rescission.[155] The right of rescission starts from the time of the signing of the first document if more than one document of sale or lease is used in connection with the transaction.[156]

Upon rescission, the purchaser is entitled to all money paid under the contract or agreement. In return, the purchaser must tender to the developer an instrument conveying all the purchaser's rights and interests in the lot, and the lot itself, in a condition similar to the condition in which they were conveyed to the purchaser. The developer may subtract from the amount due the purchaser any amount representing the diminution in the value of the property due to the purchaser's conduct.

Civil Liability

The ILSFDA gives a purchaser or lessee a private right of action for unlawful sales practice, through fraud, misrepresentation, or violation of the Act.[157] The court may order damages, specific performance, or any other relief it deems appropriate.[158] In addition, the plaintiff may recover court costs and a reasonable amount of attorneys' fees, as well as incidental damages, in the form of appraisal fees, and travel to and from the lot.[159]

Criminal Liability

Any person (developer or agent) who willfully violates any of the provisions of the Act, or rules and regulations, or engages in any deceptive and unlawful practice, is to be fined up to $10,000 and imprisoned up to five years, or both.[161] The Act gives the Secretary of HUD the right to enforce the Act by pursuing injunction proceedings, restraining orders, investigations, and prosecutions against any person who violates the Act and regulations.[162]

§11.27 —Relationship to State Law

The Act specifically provides that it will not preempt similar state law.[163] The only condition is that the state law or ordinance not conflict with the provisions

---

[155] 24 CFR §1710.105(c).
[156] 24 CFR §1715.1.
[157] 15 USC §1709(a).
[158] *Id.*
[159] 15 USC §1709(c).
[160] 15 USC §1709(b).
[161] 15 USC §1717.
[162] 15 USC §1714.
[163] 15 USC §1708(e).

of the Act. The Act preserves the remedies the state affords aggrieved parties even beyond those provided by the Act itself.[164]

If a state law is deemed to afford the same protection to purchasers by requiring substantially equivalent disclosures, the Secretary of HUD will certify such state law.[165]

Another requirement of the certification, besides equal protection of the purchaser or lessee, is that the state administration be sufficient to enforce the provisions adequately.[166] The statement of record in a certified state becomes the federal statement of record as to lots located in the certified state. It may even, at the Secretary's option, become the federal statement of record for lots covered which are outside the certified state.[167] As of this date, Arizona, California, Florida, and Minnesota have been certified by the Office of Interstate Land Sales of HUD.

§11.28   Real Estate Transactions under the Uniform Consumer Credit Code

In 1968, the National Conference of Commissioners on Uniform State Laws promulgated the Uniform Consumer Credit Code (U3C). The purpose of the legislation was to make uniform the consumer credit law among the states. It is believed that uniform laws in the ever-expanding consumer credit area will benefit both the consumer and the consumer credit industry.

The scope of the law is broad. The U3C covers anything from credit sales to consumer loans, including advertising, maximum charges and rates, home solicitation sales, consumer credit insurance, and debt collection. These aspects of the U3C are covered in other chapters of this book.

With respect to real estate credit transactions, the U3C coverage is marginal. Both the 1968 and 1974 versions of the U3C make the distinction between consumer credit sales and consumer loans. A consumer credit sale exists when the seller itself extends the credit. On the other hand, a consumer loan occurs when the credit is extended by a lender who engages regularly in the business of making loans. The U3C defines both consumer credit sales and consumer loans in such a way as to exclude home mortgages. Transactions involving real estate are covered by the statute only in limited situations.

Section 1.301(12)(b) of the 1974 U3C states:

> A consumer credit sale does not include: (ii) unless the sale is made subject to this Act by agreement, a sale of an interest in land if the finance charge does not exceed 12 per cent per year calculated according to the actuarial method on the assumption that the debt will be paid according

---

[164] 15 USC §1713.

[165] 15 USC §1708(a)(1) and (2)(A).

[166] 15 USC §1708(a)(1) and (2)(B).

[167] 15 USC §1708(b).

to the agreed terms and will not be paid before the end of the agreed terms.

The same language is used with respect to *consumer loans*.[168]

The drafters give the following reasons for the limited coverage of real estate transactions:

> With respect to the Act's treatment of real property transactions, the 12% cutoff was chosen as a convenient line of demarcation between two dissimilar transactions—the home mortgage and the high rate, "small loan" type of real estate loan. The exclusion of the home mortgage was made because the problems of home financing are sufficiently difficult to justify separate statutory treatment. On the other hand, the high-rate second-mortgage transaction has been a major source of consumer complaint, and merits full coverage by this Act.[169]

(In the 1968 version of the U3C, the cutoff rate is 10 per cent.)

In a word, the sale of an interest in land or a consumer loan secured by an interest in land, in which the credit service charge is 10 per cent or less (1968), or 12 per cent or less (1974), does not fall within the scope of the U3C. Since the Truth in Lending Act does not have such a distinction and still requires disclosures for all consumer credit transactions,[170] the U3C's provisions on disclosure requirements, and the consumer's remedies for violation of disclosure provisions,[171] still apply to the excluded land transactions in order to make state law conform to the disclosure requirements of federal law.[172]

Thus, apart from the disclosure requirements,[173] the U3C has little impact on the home mortgage industry per se.

§11.29   Common Law Liability in Real Estate Transactions

The rule *caveat emptor*, or *buyer beware*, was abolished fairly early with respect to the transfer of personal property, but not so with respect to transfers of real estate.[174]

As Restatement (Second) of Torts §352 (1964) states: "A vendor of land is not subject to liability for physical harm caused to his vendee or others while

---

[168] U3C §1.301(15) (1974); U3C §§2.104(2)(b) and 3.105 (1969).

[169] U3C §1.301(15) Official Comment (1974).

[170]*See* Regulation Z, 12 CFR §226.12.

[171] U3C §6.104(a) (1974).

[172] *See* Miller & Warren, *The 1974 Uniform Consumer Credit Code*, 23 Kan L Rev 619, 637 (1975).

[173] For disclosure requirements *see* U3C §§2.301-.313 (1969) and §§3.201-3.209 (1974).

[174] See **§2.01**.

upon the land after the vendee has taken possession, by any dangerous condition, whether natural or artificial, which exists at the time the vendee took possession."

The difference between personal property and real estate in this area may be explained by the great importance that earlier societies gave to land and, consequently, to the deed of conveyance of land. The law should not disturb the transfer.

However, together with the general trend of protection of the consumer, and considering that the home purchase transaction is one of the most important transactions in the consumer's life, the doctrine of *caveat emptor* has been rejected in most instances. This rejection has been achieved by court decisions and by statutes.[175]

Another reason for the rejection of *caveat emptor* is the drastic change in the homes building industry. With the advent of home developers, the building industry took on all the features of a commercial enterprise not unlike other enterprises of mass consumption.[176] Therefore, it should be subject to the same duties and obligations as imposed upon other distributors of goods and services.

Under the common law, the liability of the builder-vendor of new homes for defects in habitability and workmanship may be based on tort or on warranty.

§11.30 —Liability Based on Tort

The tort theories of negligence and strict liability have been used to impose liability on homebuilders. For instance, in *Oakes v McCarthy Co*,[177] a builder-owner was held liable for having negligently built on improperly compacted filled ground. In another California case, even the passage of three years after construction did not bar action for an accident caused by defective lattice work.[178]

The courts applied *MacPherson v Buick Motor Co*[179] on product liability of a manufacturer to recognize the liability of a builder-vendor of real property for a dangerous condition caused by negligent construction, of which the defendant had knowledge or should have had knowledge. The same theory applied to latent defects which could not be discovered by a vendee through

---

[175] See Grand, *Implied and Statutory Warranties in the Sale of Real Estate: The Demise of Caveat Emptor*, 15 Real Estate LJ 44 (1986); *see also* Annotation, *Liability of Builder-Vendor or Other Vendor of New Dwelling for Loss, Injury, or Damage Occasioned By Defective Condition Thereof*, 25 ALR3d 38-3 (& Supp 1986).

[176] See Roberts, *The Case of the Unwary Home Buyer: "The Housing Merchant Did It"*, 52 Cornell LQ 835 (1967).

[177] 267 Cal App 2d 231, 73 Cal Rptr 127 (1968); *see also* Velotta v Leo Petronzio Landscaping Inc, 69 Ohio St 2d 376, 433 NE2d 147 (1982) and Woodward v Chico Constr Co, 141 Ariz 514, 687 P2d 1269 (1984).

[178] Freeman v Mazzera, 150 Cal App 2d 61, 309 P2d 510 (1957).

[179] 217 NY 382, 111 NE 1050 (1916).

a reasonable inspection. The negligence theory may also be used to hold liable a builder-vendor for failure to disclose defective conditions that are inherently dangerous and of which the builder-vendor knew or should have known.[180]

Some courts have held the builder-vendor of new houses strictly liable for defective construction causing injury or loss, regardless of whether due care has been exercised.[181]

§11.31   —Liability Based on Warranty

Express Warranty

An express warranty may be made orally or in writing. When an oral representation is made, the problem is often to distinguish between express warranty and mere puffing or opinion. The courts tend to find an express warranty not only when the builder-vendor specifically warrants the workmanship and materials used, but also when more general statements are made by the builder-vendor, such as that the completed house sold to the vendee would be "completed right," and that the builder-vendor "took pride in his homes," and that he "watched every detail" of construction.[182]

The courts have found written warranty in contracts for sale using no express language of warranty but simply language such as the builder-vendor "agrees to have the premises ready for occupancy on or before the date of delivery of the deed with a certificate of occupancy issued by the local municipality."[183] The court held that this language, though ambiguous, meant that the builder-vendor undertook to deliver to the vendee a dwelling completed in a workmanlike fashion.

An express warranty covering the roof issued by the roof supplier was, however, imputed to the builder-vendor because of statements made by the builder's agent to the vendee regarding the existence of the express warranty on the roof.[184]

With respect to homes purchased under financing insured by the Federal Housing Administration (FHA) or the Veterans' Administration (VA), the courts have held that the one-year "Warranty of Completion of Construction in Substantial Conformity With Approved Plans and Specifications" is an express warranty giving rise to a cause of action for defective workmanship and materials.[185]

---

[180] See Greenspring Inc v Calvere, 239 So 2d 264 (Fla 1970).

[181] Kriegler v Eichler Homes Inc, 269 Cal App 2d 224, 74 Cal Rptr 749 (1969).

[182] Lincoln v Pohly, 325 SW2d 170 (Tex Civ App 1959).

[183] Id.

[184] Weeks v Slavick Builders Inc, 24 Mich App 621, 180 NW2d 503, affd, 384 Mich 257, 181 NW2d 271 (1970).

[185] Schamens v Crow, 326 So 2d 621 (La Ct App 1975).

Implied Warranty

Not until 1957, when an Ohio court[186] applied the doctrine of implied warranty to a house under construction, did the courts begin to recognize a cause of action against builders and vendors for breach of implied warranty of habitability and workmanship.

Today, the clear majority of jurisdictions recognize some form of implied warranty in the purchase of a new residence. Georgia, however, still holds to the view that the rule of *caveat emptor* applies to real estate transactions, short of fraud or misrepresentation.[187]

Besides the implied warranty of habitability, there is also the implied warranty of good workmanship, which existed prior to, and independently of, the warranty of habitability. In the first case in the English-speaking world to recognize the doctrine of implied warranty, the court extended the doctrine only to the sale of uncompleted houses. The rationale expressed by the court in dictum was that the purchase of the house in the course of construction implied the promise that the house would be built in an efficient and workmanlike manner.[188] Later, the doctrine was also applied to new homes already built. The implied warranty of workmanship and habitability is recognized by the courts and the statutes.

In rejecting the doctrine of *caveat emptor*, and in recognizing the implied warranty of habitability and workmanship, the courts generally pointed out that in most cases, the purchase of a new home is the most important transaction of a person's lifetime. The average buyer lacks the expertise necessary to make an informed decision, especially with respect to defects which are undetectable when the purchase is made. Thus, the builder-vendor owes a duty to the buyer to provide a house that is habitable and free of defects.[189]

The builder-vendor is not required, however, to sell a perfect house. The standard applied to determine whether a house is habitable is reasonableness.[190]

Application of the implied warranty of habitability is not limited to the sale of single-family residences. It applies also to a duplex, condominium unit, or cooperative apartment.[191] However, warranty of habitability does not generally apply to commercial or industrial structures.[192]

---

[186] Vanderschrier v Aaron, 103 Ohio App 340, 140 NE2d 819 (1957).

[187] Reynolds v Wilson, 121 Ga App 158, 173 SE2d 256 (1970).

[188] Miller v Cannon Hill Estates Ltd, 2 KB 113 (Div 1 Ct 1931).

[189] *See* McDonald v Mianecki, 159 NJ Super 1, 386 A2d 1325 (1978), *affd*, 79 NJ 275, 398 A2d 1283 (1979).

[190] Waggoner v Midwestern Dev Inc, 83 SD 57, 154 NW2d 808 (1967).

[191] Waits v Thorin, 411 So 2d 127 (Ala 1982) (duplex); Gable v Silver, 258 So 2d 11 (Fla Dist Ct App), *cert discharged*, 264 So 2d (Fla 1972) (condominiums), Suarez v Rivercross Tenants Corp, 107 Misc 2d 135, 438 NYS2d 164 (Sup Ct 1981) (cooperative apartments).

[192] *See* Standard v Owens, 46 NC App 388, 265 SE2d 617 (1980). *But see* Tavares v Horstman, 542 P2d 1275 (Wyo 1975) leaving open the question of whether the implied warranty of habitability could be applied to industrial or commercial property.

The residence furthermore must be new. Whether it is new or not is a question of fact. For instance, in a case in which the house was occupied for a short period of time by tenants, and then sold, the purchaser still recovered for breach of an implied warranty of habitability.[193]

§11.32   —Disclaimers of Implied Warranties

Traditionally, the disclaimer of implied warranty of habitability may be expressed by the doctrine of merger, under which all negotiations, promises, and representations prior to the contract of sale do not survive unless expressly provided for in the deed. In other words, acceptance of the deed constitutes full compliance with all the terms of the contract, and, therefore, no obligation of the builder-vendor survives the acceptance of the deed. The merger doctrine is thus both a *caveat emptor* rule and a disclaimer or warranty rule in real estate transactions.

The courts, however, do not recognize the merger doctrine when there are latent defects, reasoning that acceptance of the deed could not extend to the unknown defects that an inspection could not reveal.[194] Some other courts hold the view that acceptance extends only to the title, not to the quality of workmanship.[195]

Some courts recognize disclaimers of implied warranty for new houses if the disclaimers are valid. As a general rule, the validity standards of such disclaimers are patterned after §2-316 of the Uniform Commercial Code dealing with disclaimers and modifications of warranties for the sale of goods, discussed in §2.29. To be valid, disclaimers must be conspicuous and in writing. In *McDonald v Mobley*,[196] the court rejected the disclaimer because it was "inconspicuously printed."[197]

Some courts simply dismiss disclaimers as contrary to public policy.[198]

§11.33   —Who May Sue for Breach of Warranty

Since warranty liability is based on contract, privity is normally required. However, as in products liability cases, the courts have mitigated the privity requirements.

It is clear that the first purchaser of a new home is entitled to recover the breach of an implied warranty of habitability or workmanship. A person who inherits the residence may also have a cause of action. Some courts limit the recovery to first purchasers and their heirs only and refuse to extend it to

---

[193] Casavant v Campopiano, 114 RI 24, 327 A2d 831 (1974).
[194] *See* Worthey v Holmes, 249 Ga 104, 287 SE2d 9 (1982).
[195] Borden v Litchford, 619 SW2d 715 (Ky Ct App 1981).
[196] 555 SW2d 916 (Tex Civ App 1979).
[197] *Id* 919.
[198] Nastri v Wood Bros Homes Inc, 142 Ariz 439, 690 P2d 158 (Ct App 1984).

subsequent buyers who are not in privity with the builder-vendor. For instance, in *Brown v Fowler*,[199] the court justified the limitation by saying that to hold otherwise would make the builder-vendor the insurer of habitability of the residence. Other courts, however, permit recovery by subsequent purchasers. This policy is justified by the doctrine of latent defects (the builder is liable for improper work to a subsequent purchaser as well as to the original purchaser) [200] and by calling the privity requirement an obsolete concept in the consumer era.[201]

Generally, a subsequent purchaser may be able to recover only if there has been no substantial change in the residence since the original purchase, and the subsequent purchaser has the burden of showing that the defect is attributable to the builder-vendor.[202] Only a small minority of states give a cause of action for breach of warranty of habitability to subsequent purchasers. [203]

§11.34 —Warranty and Statutory Law

A number of states have adopted statutes that impose implied warranties of habitability and workmanship in the sale of new homes.[204]

The Maryland statute is a typical example of statutes dealing with warranty in the sale of real property.[205] The provisions on warranties are patterned after the UCC warranty provisions with respect to the sale of goods. In the Maryland Code, §10-203 provides that, unless specifically excluded or modified, in every sale of real estate, warranties are implied that the property sold is:

1. Free from faulty materials
2. Constructed according to sound engineering standards
3. Constructed in a workmanlike manner
4. Fit for habitation

Disclaimers or modifications of such implied warranties are effective except with respect to a completed improvement. The disclaimer then must be in writing and signed by the purchaser, and must set forth in detail the warranty to be excluded or modified, the consent of the purchaser, and the terms of the new agreement.[206]

The Maryland statute also provides for a statute of limitations. The action

---

[199] 279 NW2d 907 (SD 1979).

[200] Gupta v Ritter Homes Inc, 646 SW2d 168 (Tex 1983).

[201] Elden v Simmons, 631 P2d 739 (Okla 1981).

[202] Blagg v Fred Hunt Co, 272 Ark 185, 612 SW2d 321 (Ark 1981).

[203] Causes of Action §379, at 414-17 (Shepard's/McGraw-Hill, Inc 1984).

[204] *See, e.g.,* Conn Gen Stat Ann §47-116 *et seq* (1981); NJ Stat Ann §46:38-1 *et seq* (West Supp 1985); Va Code §§5-70.1 (1981); W Va Code §36B-4-113 (1985).

[205] Md Real Prop Code Ann §§10-201 to 10-205 (1981 & Supp 1986).

[206] *Id* §10-203(d).

is limited to the two-year period after the defect was discovered or should have been discovered, or within two years after the expiration of the warranty, whichever occurs first. Unless expressly provided otherwise, a warranty expires one year after the delivery of the deed or after the taking of possession by the purchaser, whichever occurs first, or in the case of a dwelling uncompleted at the time of delivery of the deed to the purchaser, then, one year after the date of completion, or the taking of possession by the purchaser, whichever comes first.

There are wide variations among the state statutes with respect to limitations of actions. Colorado, for example, has the longest period applied in breach of contract cases.[207]

Warranty given by statutes applies in most cases to new homes only.

---

[207] Colo Rev Stat §13-80-110 (1973 & Supp 1986).

Appendix A
Consumer Credit Protection Act

15 U.S.C. §§1601-1693r

Table of Sections

TITLE I. TRUTH IN LENDING ACT
(15 U.S.C. §§1601-1667e)

Table of Sections

Chapter 1. General Provisions

Chapter 1.   General Provisions

§101.   Short title

This title may be cited as the Truth in Lending Act.

§102.   Findings and declaration of purpose [15 U.S.C. §1601]

(a)   The Congress finds that economic stabilization would be enhanced and the competition among the various financial institutions and other firms engaged in the extension of consumer credit would be strengthened by the informed use of credit. The informed use of credit results from an awareness of the cost thereof by consumers. It is the purpose of this title to assure a meaningful disclosure of credit terms so that the consumer will be able to compare more readily the various credit terms available to him and avoid the uninformed use of credit, and to protect the consumer against inaccurate and unfair credit billing and credit card practices.

(b)   The Congress also finds that there has been a recent trend toward leasing automobiles and other durable goods for consumer use as an alternative to installment credit sales and that these leases have been offered without adequate cost disclosures. It is the purpose of this title to assure a meaningful disclosure of the terms of leases of personal property for personal, family, or household purposes so as to enable the lessee to compare more readily the various lease terms available to him, limit balloon payments in consumer leasing, enable comparison of lease terms with credit terms where appropriate, and to assure meaningful and accurate disclosures of lease terms in advertisements.

§103.   Definitions and rules of construction [15 U.S.C. §1602]

(a)   The definitions and rules of construction set forth in this section are applicable for the purposes of this title.

(b)   The term *"Board"* refers to the Board of Governors of the Federal Reserve System.

(c)   The term *"organization"* means a corporation, government or governmental subdivision or agency, trust, estate, partnership, cooperative, or association.

(d)   The term *"person"* means a natural person or an organization.

(e)   The term *"credit"* means the right granted by a creditor to a debtor to defer payment of debt or to incur debt and defer its payment.

(f)   The term *"creditor"* refers only to a person who both (1) regularly extends, whether in connection with loans, sales of property or services, or otherwise, consumer credit which is payable by agreement in more than four installments or for which the payment of a finance charge is or may be required; and (2) is the person to whom the debt arising from the consumer credit transaction is initially payable on the face of the evidence of indebtedness or, if there is no such evidence of indebtedness, by agreement. Notwithstanding the preceding sentence, in the case of an open end credit plan involving a credit card, the card issuer and any person who honors the credit card and offers a discount which is a finance charge are creditors. For the purposes of the requirements imposed under chapter 4 and sections 127(a)(5), 127(a)(6), 127(a)(7), 127(b)(1), 127(b)(2), 127(b)(3), 127(b)(8), and 127(b)(10) of chapter 2 of this title, the term "creditor" shall also include card issuers whether or not the amount due is payable by agreement in more than four installments or the payment of a finance charge is or may be required, and the Board shall, by regulation, apply these requirements to such card issuers, to the extent appropriate, even though the requirements are by their terms applicable only to creditors offering open end credit plans.

(g)   The term *"credit sale"* refers to any sale in which the seller is a creditor. The term includes any contract in the form of a bailment or lease if the bailee or lessee contracts to pay as compensation for use a sum substantially equivalent to or in excess of the aggregate value of the property and services involved and it is agreed that the bailee or lessee will become, or for no other or a nominal consideration has the option to become, the owner of the property upon full compliance with his obligations under the contract.

(h)   The adjective *"consumer"*, used with reference to a credit transaction, characterizes the transaction as one in which the party to whom credit is offered or extended is a natural person, and the money, property, or services which are the subject of the transaction are primarily for personal, family, or household purposes.

(i)   The term *"open end credit plan"* means a plan under which the creditor reasonably contemplates repeated transactions, which prescribes the terms of such transactions, and which provides for a finance charge which may be computed from time to time on the outstanding unpaid balance. A credit plan which is an open end credit plan within the meaning of the preceding sentence is an open end credit plan even if credit information is verified from time to time.

(j)   The term *"adequate notice"*, as used in section 133, means a printed notice to a cardholder which sets forth the pertinent facts clearly and conspicuously so that a person against whom it is to operate could reasonably be expected to have noticed it and understood its meaning. Such notice may be given to a cardholder by printing the notice on any credit card, or on each periodic statement of account, issued to the cardholder, or by any other means reasonably assuring the receipt thereof by the cardholder.

(k)   The term *"credit card"* means any card, plate, coupon book or other credit device existing for the purpose of obtaining money, property, labor, or services on credit.

(l)   The term *"accepted credit card"* means any credit card which the cardholder has requested and received or has signed or has used, or authorized another to use, for the purpose of obtaining money, property, labor, or services on credit.

(m)   The term *"cardholder"* means any person to whom a credit card is issued or any person who has agreed with the card issuer to pay obligations arising from the issuance of a credit card to another person.

(n)   The term *"card issuer"* means any person who issues a credit card, or the agent of such person with respect to such card.

(o)   The term *"unauthorized use"*, as used in section 133, means a use of a credit card by a person other than the cardholder who does not have actual, implied, or apparent authority for such use and from which the cardholder receives no benefit.

(p)   The term *"discount"* as used in section 167 means a reduction made from the regular price. The term "discount" as used in section 167 shall not mean a surcharge.

(q)   The term *"surcharge"* as used in section 103 and section 167 means any means of increasing the regular price to a cardholder which is not imposed upon customers paying by cash, check, or similar means.

(r)   The term *"State"* refers to any State, the Commonwealth of Puerto Rico, the District of Columbia, and any territory or possession of the United States.

(s)   The term *"agricultural purposes"* includes the production, harvest, exhibition, marketing, transportation, processing, or manufacture of agricultural products by a natural person who cultivates, plants, propagates, or nurtures those agricultural products, including but not limited to the acquisition of farmland, real property with a farm residence, and personal property and services used primarily in farming.

(t)   The term *"agricultural products"* includes agricultural, horticultural, viticultural, and dairy products, livestock, wildlife, poultry, bees, forest products, fish and shellfish, and any products thereof, including processed and manufactured products, and any and all products raised or produced on farms and any processed or manufactured products thereof.

(u)   The term *"material disclosures"* means the disclosure, as required by this title, of the annual percentage rate, the method of determining the finance charge and the balance upon which a finance charge will be imposed, the amount of the finance charge, the amount to be financed, the total of payments, the number and amount of payments, and the due dates or periods of payments scheduled to repay the indebtedness.

(v)   The term *"dwelling"* means a residential structure or mobile home which contains one to four family housing units, or individual units of condominiums or cooperatives.

(w)   The term *"residential mortgage transaction"* means a transaction in which a mortgage, deed of trust, purchase money security interest arising under an installment sales contract, or equivalent consensual security interest is created or retained against the consumer's dwelling to finance the acquisition or initial construction of such dwelling.

(x)   As used in this section and section 167, the term *"regular price"* means the tag or posted price charged for the property or service if a single price is tagged or posted, or the price charged for the property or service when payment is made by use of an open-end credit plan or a credit card if either (1) no price is tagged or posted, or (2) two prices are tagged or posted, one of which is charged when payment is made by use of an open-end credit plan or a credit card and the other when payment is made by use of cash, check, or similar means. For purposes of this definition, payment by check, draft, or other negotiable instrument which may result in the debiting of an open-end credit plan or a credit cardholder's open-end account shall not be considered payment made by use of the plan or the account.

(y)   Any reference to any requirement imposed under this title or any provision thereof includes reference to the regulations of the Board under this title or the provision thereof in question.

(z)   The disclosure of an amount or percentage which is greater than the amount or percentage required to be disclosed under this title does not in itself constitute a violation of this title.

§104.   Exempted transactions [15 U.S.C. §1603]

This title does not apply to the following:

(1)   Credit transactions involving extensions of credit primarily for business, commercial, or agricultural purposes, or to government or governmental agencies or instrumentalities, or to organizations.

(2)   Transactions in securities or commodities accounts by a broker-dealer registered with the Securities and Exchange Commission.

(3)   Credit transactions, other than those in which a security interest is or will be acquired in real property, or in personal property used or

expected to be used as the principal dwelling of the consumer, in which the total amount financed exceeds $25,000.

(4) Transactions under public utility tariffs, if the Board determines that a State regulatory body regulates the charges for the public utility services involved, the charges for delayed payment, and any discount allowed for early payment.

(6) Loans made, insured, or guaranteed pursuant to a program authorized by Title IV of the Higher Education Act of 1965 (20 U.S.C. 1070 et seq.).

§105. Regulations [15 U.S.C. §1604]

(a) The Board shall prescribe regulations to carry out the purposes of this title. These regulations may contain such classifications, differentiations, or other provisions, and may provide for such adjustments and exceptions for any class of transactions, as in the judgment of the Board are necessary or proper to effectuate the purposes of this title, to prevent circumvention or evasion thereof, or to facilitate compliance therewith.

(b) The Board shall publish model disclosure forms and clauses for common transactions to facilitate compliance with the disclosure requirements of this title and to aid the borrower or lessee in understanding the transaction by utilizing readily understandable language to simplify the technical nature of the disclosures. In devising such forms, the Board shall consider the use by creditors or lessors of data processing or similar automated equipment. Nothing in this title may be construed to require a creditor or lessor to use any such model form or clause prescribed by the Board under this section. A creditor or lessor shall be deemed to be in compliance with the disclosure provisions of this title with respect to other than numerical disclosures if the creditor or lessor (1) uses any appropriate model form or clause as published by the Board, or (2) uses any such model form or clause and changes it by (A) deleting any information which is not required by this title, or (B) rearranging the format, if in making such deletion or rearranging the format, the creditor or lessor does not affect the substance, clarity, or meaningful sequence of the disclosure.

(c) Model disclosure forms and clauses shall be adopted by the Board after notice duly given in the Federal Register and an opportunity for public comment in accordance with section 553 of title 5, United States Code.

(d) Any regulation of the Board, or any amendment or interpretation thereof, requiring any disclosure which differs from the disclosures previously required by this chapter, chapter 4, or chapter 5, or by any regulation of the Board promulgated thereunder shall have an effective date of that October 1 which follows by at least six months the date of promulgation, except that the Board may at its discretion take interim action by regulation, amendment, or interpretation to lengthen the period of time permitted for creditors or lessors to adjust their forms to accommodate new requirements or shorten the length of time for creditors or lessors to make such adjustments when it makes a specific finding that such action is necessary to comply with the findings of a court or to prevent unfair or deceptive disclosure practices. Notwithstanding the previous sentence, any creditor or lessor may comply with any such newly promulgated disclosure requirements prior to the effective date of the requirements.

§106. Determination of finance charge [15 U.S.C. §1605]

(a) Except as otherwise provided in this section, the amount of the finance charge in connection with any consumer credit transaction shall be determined as the sum of all charges, payable directly or indirectly by the person to whom the credit is extended, and imposed directly or indirectly by the creditor as an incident to the extension of credit. The finance charge does not include charges of a type payable in a comparable cash transaction. Examples of charges which are included in the finance charge include any of the following types of charges which are applicable.

(1) Interest, time price differential, and any amount payable under a point, discount, or other system of additional charges.

(2) Service or carrying charge.

(3) Loan fee, finder's fee, or similar charge.

(4) Fee for an investigation or credit report.

(5) Premium or other charge for any guarantee or insurance protecting the creditor against the obligor's default or other credit loss.

(b) Charges or premiums for credit life, accident, or health insurance written in connection with any consumer credit transaction shall be included in the finance charge unless

(1) the coverage of the debtor by the insurance is not a factor in the approval by the creditor of the extension of credit, and this fact is clearly disclosed in writing to the person applying for or obtaining the extension of credit; and

(2) in order to obtain the insurance in connection with the extension of credit, the person to whom the credit is extended must give specific affirmative written indication of his desire to do so after written disclosure to him of the cost thereof.

(c) Charges of premiums for insurance, written in connection with any consumer credit transaction, against loss of or damage to property or against liability arising out of the ownership or use of property, shall be included in the finance charge unless a clear and specific statement in writing is furnished by the creditor to the person to whom the credit is extended, setting forth the cost of the insurance if obtained from or through the creditor, and stating that the person to whom the credit is extended may choose the person through which the insurance is to be obtained.

(d) If any of the following items is itemized and disclosed in accordance with the regulations of the Board in connection with any transaction, then the creditor need not include that item in the computation of the finance charge with respect to that transaction:

(1) Fees and charges prescribed by law which actually are or will be paid to public officials for determining the existence of or for perfecting or releasing or satisfying any security related to the credit transaction.

(2) The premium payable for any insurance in lieu of perfecting any security interest otherwise required by the creditor in connection with the transaction, if the premium does not exceed the fees and charges described in paragraph (1) which would otherwise be payable.

(e) The following items, when charged in connection with any extension of credit secured by an interest in real property, shall not be included in the computation of the finance charge with respect to that transaction:

(1) Fees or premiums for title examination, title insurance, or similar purposes.

(2) Fees for preparation of a deed, settlement statement, or other documents.

(3) Escrows for future payments of taxes and insurance.

(4) Fees for notarizing deeds and other documents.

(5) Appraisal fees.

(6) Credit reports.

§107. Determination of annual percentage rate [15 U.S.C. §1606]

(a) The annual percentage rate applicable to any extension of consumer credit shall be determined, in accordance with the regulations of the Board,

(1) in the case of any extension of credit other than under an open end credit plan, as

(A) that nominal annual percentage rate which will yield a sum equal to the amount of the finance charge when it is applied to the unpaid balances of the amount financed, calculated according to the actuarial method of allocating payments made on a debt between the amount financed and the amount of the finance charge, pursuant to which a payment is applied first to the accumulated finance charge and the balance is applied to the unpaid amount financed; or

(B) the rate determined by any method prescribed by the Board as a method which materially simplifies computation while retaining reasonable accuracy as compared with the rate determined under subparagraph (A).

(2) in the case of any extension of credit under an open end credit plan, as the quotient (expressed as a percentage) of the total finance charge for the period to which it relates divided by the amount upon which the finance charge for that period is based, multiplied by the number of such periods in a year.

(b) Where a creditor imposes the same finance charge for balances within a specified range, the annual percentage rate shall be computed on the median balance within the range, except that if the Board determines that a rate so computed would not be meaningful, or would be materially misleading, the annual percentage rate shall be computed on such other basis as the Board may by regulation require.

(c) The disclosure of an annual percentage rate is accurate for the purpose of this title if the rate disclosed is within a tolerance not greater than one-eighth of 1 per centum more or less than the actual rate or rounded to the nearest one-fourth of 1 per centum. The Board may allow a greater tolerance to simplify compliance where irregular payments are involved.

(d) The Board may authorize the use of rate tables or charts which may provide for the disclosure of annual percentage rates which vary from the rate determined in accordance with subsection (a)(1)(A) by not more than such tolerances as the Board may allow. The Board may not allow a tolerance greater than 8 per centum of that rate except to simplify compliance where irregular payments are involved.

(e) In the case of creditors determining the annual percentage rate in a manner other than as described in subsection (d), the Board may authorize other reasonable tolerances.

§108. Administrative enforcement [15 U.S.C. §1607]

(a) Compliance with the requirements imposed under this title shall be enforced under

(1) section 8 of the Federal Deposit Insurance Act, in the case of

(A) national banks, by the Comptroller of the Currency.

(B) member banks of the Federal Reserve System (other than national banks), by the Board.

(C) banks insured by the Federal Deposit Insurance Corporation (other than members of the Federal Reserve System), by the Board of Directors of the Federal Deposit Insurance Corporation.

(2) section 5(d) of the Home Owners' Loan Act of 1933, section 407 of the National Housing Act, and sections 6(i) and 17 of the Federal Home Loan Bank Act, by the Federal Home Loan Bank Board (acting directly or through the Federal Savings and Loan Insurance Corporation), in the case of any institution subject to any of those provisions.

(3) the Federal Credit Union Act, by the Administrator of the National Credit Union Administration with respect to any Federal credit union.

(4) the Federal Aviation Act of 1958, by the Civil Aeronautics Board with respect to any air carrier or foreign air carrier subject to that Act.

(5) the Packers and Stockyards Act, 1921 (except as provided in section 406 of that Act), by the Secretary of Agriculture with respect to any activities subject to that Act.

(6) the Farm Credit Act of 1971, by the Farm Credit Administration with respect to any Federal land bank, Federal land bank association, Federal intermediate credit bank, or production credit association.

(b) For the purpose of the exercise by any agency referred to in subsection

(a) of its powers under any Act referred to in that subsection, a violation of any requirement imposed under this title shall be deemed to be a violation of a requirement imposed under that Act. In addition to its powers under any provision of law specifically referred to in subsection (a), each of the agencies referred to in that subsection may exercise, for the purpose of enforcing compliance with any requirement imposed under this title, any other authority conferred on it by law.

(c) Except to the extent that enforcement of the requirements imposed under this title is specifically committed to some other Government agency under subsection (a), the Federal Trade Commission shall enforce such requirements. For the purpose of the exercise by the Federal Trade Commission of its functions and powers under the Federal Trade Commission Act, a violation of any requirement imposed under this title shall be deemed a violation of a requirement imposed under that Act. All of the functions and powers of the Federal Trade Commission under the Federal Trade Commission Act are available to the Commission to enforce compliance by any person with the requirements imposed under this title, irrespective of whether that person is engaged in commerce or meets any other jurisdictional tests in the Federal Trade Commission Act.

(d) The authority of the Board to issue regulations under this title does not impair the authority of any other agency designated in this section to make rules respecting its own procedures in enforcing compliance with requirements imposed under this title.

(e)(1) In carrying out its enforcement activities under this section, each agency referred to in subsection (a) or (c), in cases where an annual percentage rate or finance charge was inaccurately disclosed, shall notify the creditor of such disclosure error and is authorized in accordance with the provisions of this subsection to require the creditor to make an adjustment to the account of the person to whom credit was extended, to assure that such person will not be required to pay a finance charge in excess of the finance charge actually disclosed or the dollar equivalent of the annual percentage rate actually disclosed, whichever is lower. For the purposes of this subsection, except where such disclosure error resulted from a willfull violation which was intended to mislead the person to whom credit was extended, in determining whether a disclosure error has occurred and in calculating any adjustment, (A) each agency shall apply (i) with respect to the annual percentage rate, a tolerance of one-quarter of 1 percent more or less than the actual rate, determined without regard to section 107(c) of this title, and (ii) with respect to the finance charge, a corresponding numerical tolerance as generated by the tolerance provided under this subsection for the annual percentage rate; except that (B) with respect to transactions consummated after two years following the effective date of section 608 of the Truth in Lending Simplification and Reform Act, each agency shall apply (i) for transactions that have a scheduled amortization of ten years or less, with respect to the annual percentage rate, a tolerance not to exceed one-quarter of 1 percent more or less than the actual rate, determined without regard to section 107(c) of this title, but in no event a tolerance of less than the tolerances allowed under section 107(c), (ii) for transactions that have a scheduled amortization of more than ten years, with respect to the annual percentage rate, only such tolerances as are allowed under section 107(c) of this title, and (iii) for all transactions, with respect to the finance charge, a corresponding numerical tolerance as generated by the tolerances provided under this subsection for the annual percentage rate.

(2) Each agency shall require such an adjustment when it determines that such disclosure error resulted from (A) a clear and consistent pattern or practice of violations, (B) gross negligence, or (C) a willful violation which was intended to mislead the person to whom the credit was extended. Notwithstanding the preceding sentence, except where such disclosure error resulted from a willful violation which was intended to mislead the person to whom credit was extended, an agency need not require such an adjustment if it determines that such disclosure error—

(A) resulted from an error involving the disclosure of a fee or charge that would otherwise be excludable in computing the finance charge, including but not limited to violations involving the disclosures described in sections 106(b), (c) and (d) of this title, in which event the agency may require such remedial action as it determines to be equitable, except that for transactions consummated after two years after the effective date of section 608 of the Truth in Lending Simplification and Reform Act, such an adjustment shall be ordered for violations of section 106(b);

(B) involved a disclosed amount which was 10 per centum or less of the amount that should have been disclosed and (i) in cases where the error involved a disclosed finance charge, the annual percentage rate was disclosed correctly, and (ii) in cases where the error involved a disclosed annual percentage rate, the finance charge was disclosed correctly; in which event the agency may require such adjustment as it determines to be equitable;

(C) involved a total failure to disclose either the annual percentage rate or the finance charge, in which event the agency may require such adjustment as it determines to be equitable; or

(D) resulted from any other unique circumstance involving clearly technical and nonsubstantive disclosure violations that do not adversely affect information provided to the consumer and that have not misled or otherwise deceived the consumer.

In the case of other such disclosure errors, each agency may require such an adjustment.

(3) Notwithstanding paragraph (2), no adjustment shall be ordered (A) if it would have a significantly adverse impact upon the safety or soundness of the creditor, but in any such case, the agency may require a partial adjustment in an amount which does not have such an impact except that with respect to any transaction consummated after the effective date of section 608 of the Truth in Lending Simplification and Reform Act, the agency shall require the full adjustment, but permit the creditor to make the required adjustment in partial payments over an extended period of time which the agency considers to be reasonable, (B) if the amount of the adjustment would be less than $1, except

that if more than one year has elapsed since the date of the violation, the agency may require that such amount be paid into the Treasury of the United States, or (C) except where such disclosure error resulted from a willful violation which was intended to mislead the person to whom credit was extended, in the case of an open-end credit plan, more than two years after the violation, or in the case of any other extension of credit, as follows:

(i) with respect to creditors that are subject to examination by the agencies referred to in paragraphs (1) through (3) of section 108(a) of this title, except in connection with violations arising from practices identified in the current examination and only in connection with transactions that are consummated after the date of the immediately preceding examination, except that where practices giving rise to violations identified in earlier examinations have not been corrected, adjustments for those violations shall be required in connection with transactions consummated after the date of the examination in which such practices were first identified;

(ii) with respect to creditors that are not subject to examination by such agencies, except in connection with transactions that are consummated after May 10, 1978; and

(iii) in no event after the later of (I) the expiration of the life of the credit extension, or (II) two years after the agreement to extend credit was consummated.

(4)(A) Notwithstanding any other provision of this section, an adjustment under this subsection may be required by an agency referred to in subsection (a) or (c) only by an order issued in accordance with cease and desist procedures provided by the provision of law referred to in such subsections.

(B) In the case of an agency which is not authorized to conduct cease and desist proceedings, such an order may be issued after an agency hearing on the record conducted at least thirty but not more than sixty days after notice of the alleged violation is served on the creditor. Such a hearing shall be deemed to be a hearing which is subject to the provisions of section 8(h) of the Federal Deposit Insurance Act and shall be subject to judicial review as provided therein.

(5) Except as otherwise specifically provided in this subsection and notwithstanding any provision of law referred to in subsection (a) or (c), no agency referred to in subsection (a) or (c) may require a creditor to make dollar adjustments for errors in any requirements under this title, except with regard to the requirements of section 165.

(6) A creditor shall not be subject to an order to make an adjustment, if within sixty days after discovering a disclosure error, whether pursuant to a final written examination report or through the creditor's own procedures, the creditor notifies the person concerned of the error and adjusts the account so as to assure that such person will not be required to pay a finance charge in

excess of the finance charge actually disclosed or the dollar equivalent of the annual percentage rate actually disclosed, whichever is lower.

(7) Notwithstanding the second sentence of subsection (e)(1), subsection (e)(3)(C)(i), and subsection (e)(3)(C)(ii), each agency referred to in subsection (a) or (c) shall require an adjustment for an annual percentage rate disclosure error that exceeds a tolerance of one quarter of one percent less than the actual rate, determined without regard to section 107(c) of this title, with respect to any transaction consummated between January 1, 1977, and [October 1, 1982].

§109.   Views of other agencies [15 U.S.C. §1608]

In the exercise of its functions under this title, the Board may obtain upon request the views of any other Federal agency which, in the judgment of the Board, exercises regulatory or supervisory functions with respect to any class of creditors subject to this title.

§111.   Effect on other laws [15 U.S.C. §1610]

(a)(1) Chapters 1, 2, and 3 do not annul, alter, or affect the laws of any State relating to the disclosure of information in connection with credit transactions, except to the extent that those laws are inconsistent with the provisions of this title, and then only to the extent of the inconsistency. Upon its own motion or upon the request of any creditor, State, or other interested party which is submitted in accordance with procedures prescribed in regulations of the Board, the Board shall determine whether any such inconsistency exists. If the Board determines that a State-required disclosure is inconsistent, creditors located in that State may not make disclosures using the inconsistent term or form, and shall incur no liability under the law of that State for failure to use such term or form, notwithstanding that such determination is subsequently amended, rescinded, or determined by judicial or other authority to be invalid for any reason.

(2) Upon its own motion or upon the request of any creditor, State, or other interested party which is submitted in accordance with procedures prescribed in regulations of the Board, the Board shall determine whether any disclosure required under the law of any State is substantially the same in meaning as a disclosure required under this title. If the Board determines that a State-required disclosure is substantially the same in meaning as a disclosure required by this title, then creditors located in that State may make such disclosure in compliance with such State law in lieu of the disclosure required by this title, except that the annual percentage rate and finance charge shall be disclosed as required by section 122.

(b) This title does not otherwise annul, alter or affect in any manner the meaning, scope or applicability of the laws of any State, including, but not limited to, laws relating to the types, amounts or rate of charges, or any element or elements of charges, permissible under such laws in connection with the extension or use of credit, nor does this title extend the applicability of those laws to any class of persons or transactions to which they would not otherwise apply.

(c) In any action or proceeding in any court involving a consumer credit sale, the disclosure of the annual percentage rate as required under this title in connection with that sale may not be received as evidence that the sale was a loan or any type of transaction other than a credit sale.

(d) Except as specified in sections 125, 130, and 166, this title and the regulations issued thereunder do not affect the validity or enforceability of any contract or obligation under State or Federal law.

§112.   Criminal liability for willful and knowing violation [15 U.S.C. §1611]

Whoever willfully and knowingly

(1) gives false or inaccurate information or fails to provide information which he is required to disclose under the provisions of this title or any regulation issued thereunder,

(2) uses any chart or table authorized by the Board under section 107 in such a manner as to consistently understate the annual percentage rate determined under section 107(a)(1)(A), or

(3) otherwise fails to comply with any requirement imposed under this title, shall be fined not more than $5,000 or imprisoned not more than one year, or both.

§113.   Effect on governmental agencies [15 U.S.C. §1612]

(a) Any department or agency of the United States which administers a credit program in which it extends, insures, or guarantees consumer credit and in which it provides instruments to a creditor which contain any disclosures required by this title shall, prior to the issuance or continued use of such instruments, consult with the Board to assure that such instruments comply with this title.

(b) No civil or criminal penalty provided under this title for any violation thereof may be imposed upon the United States or any department or agency thereof, or upon any State or political subdivision thereof, or any agency of any State or political subdivision.

(c) A creditor participating in a credit program administered, insured, or guaranteed by any department or agency of the United States shall not be held liable for a civil or criminal penalty under this title in any case in which the violation results from the use of an instrument required by any such department or agency.

(d) A creditor participating in a credit program administered, insured, or guaranteed by any department or agency of the United States shall not be held liable for a civil or criminal penalty under the laws of any State (other than laws determined under section 111 to be inconsistent with this title) for any technical or procedural failure, such as a failure to use a specific form, to make information available at a specific place on an instrument, or to use a specific typeface, as required by State law, which is caused by the use of an instrument required to be used by such department or agency.

§114. Reports by Board and Attorney General [15 U.S.C. §1613]

Each year the Board and the Attorney General shall, respectively, make reports to the Congress concerning the administration of their functions under this title, including such recommendations as the Board and the Attorney General, respectively, deem necessary or appropriate. In addition, each report of the Board shall include its assessment of the extent to which compliance with the requirements imposed under this title is being achieved.

Credit Transactions

§121. General requirement of disclosure [15 U.S.C. §1631]

(a) Subject to subsection (b), a creditor or lessor shall disclose to the person who is obligated on a consumer lease or a consumer credit transaction the information required under this title. In a transaction involving more than one obligor, a creditor or lessor, except in a transaction under section 125, need not disclose to more than one of such obligors if the obligor given disclosure is a primary obligor.

(b) If a transaction involves one creditor as defined in section 103(f), or one lessor as defined in section 181(3), such creditor or lessor shall make the disclosures. If a transaction involves more than one creditor or lessor, only one creditor or lessor shall be required to make the disclosures. The Board shall by regulation specify which creditor or lessor shall make the disclosures.

(c) The Board may provide by regulation that any portion of the information required to be disclosed by this title may be given in the form of estimates where the provider of such information is not in a position to know exact information.

(d) The Board shall determine whether tolerances for numerical disclosures other than the annual percentage rate are necessary to facilitate compliance with this title, and if it determines that such tolerances are necessary to facilitate compliance, it shall by regulation permit disclosures within such tolerances. The Board shall exercise its authority to permit tolerances for numerical disclosures other than the annual percentage rate so that such tolerances are narrow enough to prevent such tolerances from resulting in misleading disclosures or disclosures that circumvent the purposes of this title.

§122. Form of disclosure; additional information [15 U.S.C. §1632]

(a) Information required by this title shall be disclosed clearly and conspicuously, in accordance with regulations of the Board. The terms "annual percentage rate" and "finance charge" shall be disclosed more conspicuously than other terms, data, or information provided in connection with a transaction, except information relating to the identity of the creditor. Regulations of the Board need not require that disclosures pursuant to this title be made in the order set forth in this title and, except as otherwise provided, may permit the use of terminology different from that employed in this title if it conveys substantially the same meaning.

(b) Any creditor or lessor may supply additional information or explanation with any disclosures required under chapters 4 and 5 and, except as provided in section 128(b)(1), under this chapter.

§123. Exemption for State-regulated transactions [15 U.S.C. §1633]

The Board shall by regulation exempt from the requirements of this chapter any class of credit transactions within any State if it determines that under the law of that State that class of transactions is subject to requirements substantially similar to those imposed under this chapter, and that there is adequate provision for enforcement.

§124. Effect of subsequent occurrence [15 U.S.C. §1634]

If information disclosed in accordance with this chapter is subsequently rendered inaccurate as the result of any act, occurrence, or agreement subsequent to the delivery of the required disclosures, the inaccuracy resulting therefrom does not constitute a violation of this chapter.

§125. Right of rescission as to certain transactions [15 U.S.C. §1635]

(a) Except as otherwise provided in this section, in the case of any consumer credit transaction (including opening or increasing the credit limit for an open end credit plan) in which a security interest, including any such interest arising by operation of law, is or will be retained or acquired in any property which is used as the principal dwelling of the person to whom credit is extended, the obligor shall have the right to rescind the transaction until midnight of the third business day following the consummation of the transaction or the delivery of the information and rescission forms required under this section together with a statement containing the material disclosures required under this title, whichever is later, by notifying the creditor, in accordance with regulations of the Board, of his intention to do so. The creditor shall clearly and conspicuously disclose, in accordance with regulations of the Board, to any obligor in a transaction subject to this section the rights of the obligor under this section. The creditor shall also provide, in accordance with regulations of the Board, appropriate forms for the obligor to exercise his right to rescind any transaction subject to this section.

(b) When an obligor exercises his right to rescind under subsection (a), he is not liable for any finance or other charge, and any security interest given by the obligor, including any such interest arising by operation of law, becomes void upon such a rescission. Within 20 days after receipt of a notice of rescission, the creditor shall return to the obligor any money or property given as earnest money, downpayment, or otherwise, and shall take any action necessary or appropriate to reflect the termination of any security interest created under the transaction. If the creditor has delivered any property to the obligor, the obligor may retain possession of it. Upon the performance of the creditor's obligations under this section, the obligor shall tender the property to the creditor, except that if return of the property in kind would be impracticable or inequitable, the obligor shall tender its reasonable value. Tender shall be made at the location of the property or at the residence of the obligor, at the option of the obligor. If the creditor does not take possession of the property within 20 days after tender by the obligor, ownership of the property vests in the obligor without obligation on his part to pay for it. The procedures prescribed by this subsection shall apply except when otherwise ordered by a court.

(c) Notwithstanding any rule of evidence, written acknowledgment of receipt of any disclosures required under this title by a person to whom information, forms, and a statement is required to be given pursuant to this section does no more than create a rebuttable presumption of delivery thereof.

(d) The Board may, if it finds that such action is necessary in order to permit homeowners to meet bona fide personal financial emergencies, prescribe regulations authorizing the modification or waiver of any rights created under this section to the extent and under the circumstances set forth in those regulations.

(e)(1) This section does not apply to—

(A) a residential mortgage transaction as defined in section 103(w);

(B) a transaction which constitutes a refinancing or consolidation (with no new advances) of the principal balance then due and any accrued and unpaid finance charges of an existing extension of credit by the same creditor secured by an interest in the same property;

(C) a transaction in which an agency of a State is the creditor; or

(D) advances under a preexisting open end credit plan if a security interest has already been retained or acquired and such advances are in accordance with a previously established credit limit for such plan.

(2) The provisions of paragraph (1)(D) shall cease to be effective 3 years after the effective date of the Truth in Lending Simplification and Reform Act.

(f) An obligor's right of rescission shall expire three years after the date of consummation of the transaction or upon the sale of the property, whichever occurs first, notwithstanding the fact that the information and forms required under this section or any other disclosures required under this chapter have not been delivered to the obligor, except that if (1) any agency empowered to enforce the provisions of this title institutes a proceeding to enforce the provisions of this section within three years after the date of consummation of the transaction, (2) such agency finds a violation of section 125, and (3) the obligor's right to rescind is based in whole or in part on any matter involved in such proceeding, then the obligor's right of rescission shall expire three years after the date of consummation of the transaction or upon the earlier sale of the property, or upon the expiration of one year following the conclusion of the proceeding, or any judicial review or period for judicial review thereof, whichever is later.

(g) In any action in which it is determined that a creditor has violated this section, in addition to rescission the court may award relief under section 130 for violations of this title not relating to the right to rescind.

§127. Open end consumer credit plans [15 U.S.C. §1637]

(a) Before opening any account under an open end consumer credit plan, the creditor shall disclose to the person to whom credit is to be extended each of the following items, to the extent applicable:

(1) The conditions under which a finance charge may be imposed, including the time period (if any) within which any credit extended may be repaid without incurring a finance charge, except that the creditor may, at his election and without disclosure, impose no such finance charge if payment is received after the termination of such time period. If no such time period is provided, the creditor shall disclose such fact.

(2) The method of determining the balance upon which a finance charge will be imposed.

(3) The method of determining the amount of the finance charge, including any minimum or fixed amount imposed as a finance charge.

(4) Where one or more periodic rates may be used to compute the finance charge, each such rate, the range of balances to which it is applicable, and the corresponding nominal annual percentage rate determined by multiplying the periodic rate by the number of periods in a year.

(5) Identification of other charges which may be imposed as part of the plan, and their method of computation, in accordance with regulations of the Board.

(6) In cases where the credit is or will be secured, a statement that a security interest has been or will be taken in (A) the property purchased as part of the credit transaction, or (B) property not purchased as part of the credit transaction identified by item or type.

(7) A statement, in a form prescribed by regulations of the Board of the protection provided by sections 161 and 170 to an obligor and the creditor's

responsibilities under sections 162 and 170. With respect to one billing cycle per calendar year, at intervals of not less than six months or more than eighteen months, the creditor shall transmit such statement to each obligor to whom the creditor is required to transmit a statement pursuant to section 127(b) for such billing cycle.

(b) The creditor of any account under an open end consumer credit plan shall transmit to the obligor, for each billing cycle at the end of which there is an outstanding balance in that account or with respect to which a finance charge is imposed, a statement setting forth each of the following items to the extent applicable:

(1) The outstanding balance in the account at the beginning of the statement period.

(2) The amount and date of each extension of credit during the period, and a brief identification, on or accompanying the statement of each extension of credit in a form prescribed by the Board sufficient to enable the obligor either to identify the transaction or to relate it to copies of sales vouchers or similar instruments previously furnished, except that a creditor's failure to disclose such information in accordance with this paragraph shall not be deemed a failure to comply with this chapter or this title if (A) the creditor maintains procedures reasonably adapted to procure and provide such information, and (B) the creditor responds to and treats any inquiry for clarification or documentation as a billing error and an erroneously billed amount under section 161. In lieu of complying with the requirements of the previous sentence, in the case of any transaction in which the creditor and seller are the same person, as defined by the Board, and such person's open end credit plan has fewer than 15,000 accounts, the creditor may elect to provide only the amount and date of each extension of credit during the period and the seller's name and location where the transaction took place if (A) a brief identification of the transaction has been previously furnished, and (B) the creditor responds to and treats any inquiry for clarification or documentation as a billing error and an erroneously billed amount under section 161.

(3) The total amount credited to the account during the period.

(4) The amount of any finance charge added to the account during the period, itemized to show the amounts, if any, due to the application of percentage rates and the amount, if any, imposed as a minimum or fixed charge.

(5) Where one or more periodic rates may be used to compute the finance charge, each such rate, the range of balances to which it is applicable, and, unless the annual percentage rate (determined under section 107(a)(2)) is required to be disclosed pursuant to paragraph (6), the corresponding nominal annual percentage rate determined by multiplying the periodic rate by the number of periods in a year.

(6) Where the total finance charge exceeds 50 cents for a monthly or longer billing cycle, or the pro rata part of 50 cents for a billing cycle shorter than monthly, the total finance charge expressed as an annual percentage rate (determined under section 107(a)(2)), except that if the finance charge is the

sum of two or more products of a rate times a portion of the balance, the creditor may, in lieu of disclosing a single rate for the total charge, disclose each such rate expressed as an annual percentage rate, and the part of the balance to which it is applicable.

(7) The balance on which the finance charge was computed and a statement of how the balance was determined. If the balance is determined without first deducting all credits during the period, that fact and the amount of such payments shall also be disclosed.

(8) The outstanding balance in the account at the end of the period.

(9) The date by which or the period (if any) within which payment must be made to avoid additional finance charges, except that the creditor may, at his election and without disclosure, impose no such additional finance charge if payment is received after such date or the termination of such period.

(10) The address to be used by the creditor for the purpose of receiving billing inquiries from the obligor.

§128. Consumer credit not under open end credit plans [15 U.S.C. §1638]

(a) For each consumer credit transaction other than under an open end credit plan, the creditor shall disclose each of the following items, to the extent applicable:

(1) The identity of the creditor required to make disclosure.

(2)(A) The "amount financed", using that term, which shall be the amount of credit of which the consumer has actual use. This amount shall be computed as follows, but the computations need not be disclosed and shall not be disclosed with the disclosures conspicuously segregated in accordance with subsection (b)(1):

(i) take the principal amount of the loan or the cash price less downpayment and trade-in;

(ii) add any charges which are not part of the finance charge or of the principal amount of the loan and which are financed by the consumer, including the cost of any items excluded from the finance charge pursuant to section 106; and

(iii) subtract any charges which are part of the finance charge but which will be paid by the consumer before or at the time of the consummation of the transaction, or have been withheld from the proceeds of the credit.

(B) In conjunction with the disclosure of the amount financed, a creditor shall provide a statement of the consumer's right to obtain, upon a written request, a written itemization of the amount financed. The statement shall include spaces for a "yes" and "no" indication to be initialed by the consumer to indicate whether the consumer wants a written itemization of the amount financed. Upon receiving an affirmative indication, the creditor shall provide, at the time other disclosures are required to be furnished, a written itemization of the amount financed. For the purposes of this subparagraph, "itemization of the amount financed" means a disclosure of the following items, to the extent applicable:

(i) the amount that is or will be paid directly to the consumer;

(ii) the amount that is or will be credited to the consumer's account to discharge obligations owed to the creditor;

(iii) each amount that is or will be paid to third persons by the creditor on the consumer's behalf, together with an identification of or reference to the third person; and

(iv) the total amount of any charges described in the preceding subparagraph (A)(iii).

(3) The "finance charge", not itemized, using that term.

(4) The finance charge expressed as an "annual percentage rate", using that term. This shall not be required if the amount financed does not exceed $75 and the finance charge does not exceed $5, or if the amount financed exceeds $75 and the finance charge does not exceed $7.50.

(5) The sum of the amount financed and the finance charge, which shall be termed the "total of payments".

(6) The number, amount, and due dates or period of payments scheduled to repay the total of payments.

(7) In a sale of property or services in which the seller is the creditor required to disclose pursuant to section 121(b), the "total sale price", using that term, which shall be the total of the cash price of the property or services, additional charges, and the finance charge.

(8) Descriptive explanations of the terms "amount financed", "finance charge", "annual percentage rate", "total of payments", and "total sale price" as specified by the Board. The descriptive explanation of "total sale price" shall include reference to the amount of the downpayment.

(9) Where the credit is secured, a statement that a security interest has been taken in (A) the property which is purchased as part of the credit transaction, or (B) property not purchased as part of the credit transaction identified by item or type.

(10) Any dollar charge or percentage amount which may be imposed by a creditor solely on account of a late payment, other than a deferral or extension charge.

(11) A statement indicating whether or not the consumer is entitled to a rebate of any finance charge upon refinancing or prepayment in full pursuant to acceleration or otherwise, if the obligation involves a precomputed finance charge. A statement indicating whether or not a penalty will be imposed in those same circumstances if the obligation involves a finance charge computed from time to time by application of a rate to the unpaid principal balance.

(12) A statement that the consumer should refer to the appropriate contract document for any information such document provides about nonpayment, default, the right to accelerate the maturity of the debt, and prepayment rebates and penalties.

(13) In any residential mortgage transaction, a statement indicating whether

a subsequent purchaser or assignee of the consumer may assume the debt obligation on its original terms and conditions.

(b)(1) Except as otherwise provided in this chapter, the disclosures required under subsection (a) shall be made before the credit is extended. Except for the disclosures required by subsection (a)(1) of this section, all disclosures required under subsection (a) and any disclosure provided for in subsection (b), (c), or (d) of section 106 shall be conspicuously segregated from all other terms, data, or information provided in connection with a transaction, including any computations or itemization.

(2) In the case of a residential mortgage transaction, as defined in section 103(w), which is also subject to the Real Estate Settlement Procedures Act, good faith estimates of the disclosures required under subsection (a) shall be made in accordance with regulations of the Board under section 121(c) before the credit is extended, or shall be delivered or placed in the mail not later than three business days after the creditor receives the consumer's written application, whichever is earlier. If the disclosure statement furnished within three days of the written application contains an annual percentage rate which is subsequently rendered inaccurate within the meaning of section 107(c), the creditor shall furnish another statement at the time of settlement or consummation.

(c)(1) If a creditor receives a purchase order by mail or telephone without personal solicitation, and the cash price and the total sale price and the terms of financing, including the annual percentage rate, are set forth in the creditor's catalog or other printed material distributed to the public, then the disclosures required under subsection (a) may be made at any time not later than the date the first payment is due.

(2) If a creditor receives a request for a loan by mail or telephone without personal solicitation and the terms of financing, including the annual percentage rate for representative amounts of credit, are set forth in the creditor's printed material distributed to the public, or in the contract of loan or other printed material delivered to the obligor, then the disclosures required under subsection (a) may be made at any time not later than the date the first payment is due.

(d) If a consumer credit sale is one of a series of consumer credit sales transactions made pursuant to an agreement providing for the addition of the deferred payment price of that sale to an existing outstanding balance, and the person to whom the credit is extended has approved in writing both the annual percentage rate or rates and the method of computing the finance charge or charges, and the creditor retains no security interest in any property as to which he has received payments aggregating the amount of the sales price including any finance charges attributable thereto, then the disclosure required under subsection (a) for the particular sale may be made at any time not later than the date the first payment for that sale is due. For the purposes of this subsection, in the case of items purchased on different dates, the first purchased shall be deemed first paid for, and in the case of items purchased on the same date, the lowest priced shall be deemed first paid for.

§130. Civil liability [15 U.S.C. §1640]

(a) Except as otherwise provided in this section, any creditor who fails to comply with any requirement imposed under this chapter, including any requirement under section 125, or chapter 4 or 5 of this title with respect to any person is liable to such person in an amount equal to the sum of—

(1) any actual damage sustained by such person as a result of the failure;

(2)(A)(i) in the case of an individual action twice the amount of any finance charge in connection with the transaction, or (ii) in the case of an individual action relating to a consumer lease under chapter 5 of this title, 25 per centum of the total amount of monthly payments under the lease, except that the liability under this subparagraph shall not be less than $100 nor greater than $1,000; or

(B) in the case of a class action, such amount as the court may allow, except that as to each member of the class no minimum recovery shall be applicable, and the total recovery under this subparagraph in any class action or series of class actions arising out of the same failure to comply by the same creditor shall not be more than the lesser of $500,000 or 1 per centum of the net worth of the creditor; and

(3) in the case of any successful action to enforce the foregoing liability or in any action in which a person is determined to have a right of rescission under section 125, the costs of the action, together with a reasonable attorney's fee as determined by the court. In determining the amount of award in any class action, the court shall consider, among other relevant factors, the amount of any actual damages awarded, the frequency and persistence of failures of compliance by the creditor, the resources of the creditor, the number of persons adversely affected, and the extent to which the creditor's failure of compliance was intentional. In connection with the disclosures referred to in section 127, a creditor shall have a liability determined under paragraph (2) only for failing to comply with the requirements of section 125, section 127(a), or of paragraph (4), (5), (6), (7), (8), (9), or (10) of section 127(b) or for failing to comply with disclosure requirements under State law for any term or item which the Board has determined to be substantially the same in meaning under section 111(a)(2) as any of the terms or items referred to in section 127(a) or any of those paragraphs of section 127(b). In connection with the disclosures referred to in section 128, a creditor shall have a liability determined under paragraph (2) only for failing to comply with the requirements of section 125 or of paragraph (2) (insofar as it requires a disclosure of the "amount financed"), (3), (4), (5), (6), or (9) of section 128(a), or for failing to comply with disclosure requirements under State law for any term which the Board has determined to be substantially the same in meaning under section 111(a)(2) as any of the terms referred to in any of those paragraphs of section 128(a). With respect to any failure to make disclosures required under this chapter or chapter 4 or 5 of this title, liability shall be imposed only upon the creditor required to make disclosure, except as provided in section 131.

(b) A creditor or assignee has no liability under this section or section 108 or section 112 for any failure to comply with any requirement imposed under this chapter or chapter 5, if within sixty days after discovering an error, whether pursuant to a final written examination report or notice issued under section 108(e)(1) or through the creditor's or assignee's own procedures, and prior to the institution of an action under this section or the receipt of written notice of the error from the obligor, the creditor or assignee notifies the person concerned of the error and makes whatever adjustments in the appropriate account are necessary to assure that the person will not be required to pay an amount in excess of the charge actually disclosed, or the dollar equivalent of the annual percentage rate actually disclosed, whichever is lower.

(c) A creditor or assignee may not be held liable in any action brought under this section or section 125 for a violation of this title if the creditor or assignee shows by a preponderance of evidence that the violation was not intentional and resulted from a bona fide error notwithstanding the maintenance of procedures reasonably adapted to avoid any such error. Examples of a bona fide error include, but are not limited to, clerical, calculation, computer malfunction and programing, and printing errors, except that an error of legal judgment with respect to a person's obligations under this title is not a bona fide error.

(d) When there are multiple obligors in a consumer credit transaction or consumer lease, there shall be no more than one recovery of damages under subsection (a)(2) for a violation of this title.

(e) Any action under this section may be brought in any United States district court, or in any other court of competent jurisdiction, within one year from the date of the occurrence of the violation. This subsection does not bar a person from asserting a violation of this title in an action to collect the debt which was brought more than one year from the date of the occurrence of the violation as a matter of defense by recoupment or set-off in such action, except as otherwise provided by State law.

(f) No provision of this section, section 108(b), section 108(c), section 108(e), or section 112 imposing any liability shall apply to any act done or omitted in good faith in conformity with any rule, regulation, or interpretation thereof by the Board or in conformity with any interpretation or approval by an official or employee of the Federal Reserve System duly authorized by the Board to issue such interpretations or approvals under such procedures as the Board may prescribe therefor, notwithstanding that after such act or omission has occurred, such rule, regulation, interpretation, or approval is amended, rescinded, or determined by judicial or other authority to be invalid for any reason.

(g) The multiple failure to disclose to any person any information required under this chapter or chapter 4 or 5 of this title to be disclosed in connection with a single account under an open end consumer credit plan, other single consumer credit sale, consumer loan, consumer lease, or other extension of consumer credit, shall entitle the person to a single recovery under this section but continued failure to disclose after a recovery has been granted shall give rise to rights to additional recoveries. This subsection does not bar any remedy permitted by section 125.

(h) A person may not take any action to offset any amount for which a creditor or assignee is potentially liable to such person under subsection (a)(2) against any amount owed by such person, unless the amount of the creditor's or assignee's liability under this title has been determined by judgment of a court of competent jurisdiction in an action of which such person was a party. This subsection does not bar a consumer then in default on the obligation from asserting a violation of this title as an original action, or as a defense or counterclaim to an action to collect amounts owed by the consumer brought by a person liable under this title.

§131.   Liability of assignees [15 U.S.C. §1641]

(a) Except as otherwise specifically provided in this title, any civil action for a violation of this title or proceeding under section 108 which may be brought against a creditor may be maintained against any assignee of such creditor only if the violation for which such action or proceeding is brought is apparent on the face of the disclosure statement, except where the assignment was involuntary. For the purpose of this section, a violation apparent on the face of the disclosure statement includes, but is not limited to (1) a disclosure which can be determined to be incomplete or inaccurate from the face of the disclosure statement or other documents assigned, or (2) a disclosure which does not use the terms required to be used by this title.

(b) Except as provided in section 125(c), in any action or proceeding by or against any subsequent assignee of the original creditor without knowledge to the contrary by the assignee when he acquires the obligation, written acknowledgment of receipt by a person to whom a statement is required to be given pursuant to this title shall be conclusive proof of the delivery thereof and, except as provided in subsection (a), of compliance with this chapter. This section does not affect the rights of the obligor in any action against the original creditor.

(c) Any consumer who has the right to rescind a transaction under section 125 may rescind the transaction as against any assignee of the obligation.

§132.   Issuance of credit cards [15 U.S.C. §1642]

No credit card shall be issued except in response to a request or application therefor. This prohibition does not apply to the issuance of a credit card in renewal of, or in substitution for, an accepted credit card.

§133.   Liability of holder of credit card [15 U.S.C. §1643]

(a)(1) A cardholder shall be liable for the unauthorized use of a credit card only if—

(A) the card is an accepted credit card;

(B) the liability is not in excess of $50;

(C) the card issuer gives adequate notice to the cardholder of the potential liability;

(D) the card issuer has provided the cardholder with a description of a means by which the card issuer may be notified of loss or theft of the card, which description may be provided on the face or reverse side of the statement required by section 127(b) or on a separate notice accompanying such statement;

(E) the unauthorized use occurs before the card issuer has been notified that an unauthorized use of the credit card has occurred or may occur as the result of loss, theft, or otherwise; and

(F) the card issuer has provided a method whereby the user of such card can be identified as the person authorized to use it.

(2) For purposes of this section, a card issuer has been notified when such steps as may be reasonably required in the ordinary course of business to provide the card issuer with the pertinent information have been taken, whether or not any particular officer, employee, or agent of the card issuer does in fact receive such information.

(b) In any action by a card issuer to enforce liability for the use of a credit card, the burden of proof is upon the card issuer to show that the use was authorized or, if the use was unauthorized, then the burden of proof is upon the card issuer to show that the conditions of liability for the unauthorized use of a credit card, as set forth in subsection (a), have been met.

(c) Nothing in this section imposes liability upon a cardholder for the unauthorized use of a credit card in excess of his liability for such use under other applicable law or under any agreement with the card issuer.

(d) Except as provided in this section, a cardholder incurs no liability from the unauthorized use of a credit card.

§134. Fraudulent use of credit card [15 U.S.C. §1644]

(a) Whoever knowingly in a transaction affecting interstate or foreign commerce, uses or attempts or conspires to use any counterfeit, fictitious, altered, forged, lost, stolen, or fraudulently obtained credit card to obtain money, goods, services, or anything else of value which within any one-year period has a value aggregating $1,000 or more; or

(b) Whoever, with unlawful or fraudulent intent, transports or attempts or conspires to transport in interstate or foreign commerce a counterfeit, fictitious, altered, forged, lost, stolen, or fraudulently obtained credit card knowing the same to be counterfeit, fictitious, altered, forged, lost, stolen, or fraudulently obtained; or

(c) Whoever, with unlawful or fraudulent intent, uses any instrumentality of interstate or foreign commerce to sell or transport a counterfeit, fictitious, altered, forged, lost, stolen, or fraudulently obtained credit card knowing the same to be counterfeit, fictitious, altered, forged, lost, stolen, or fraudulently obtained; or

(d) Whoever knowingly receives, conceals, uses, or transports money, goods, services, or anything else of value (except tickets for interstate or foreign transportation) which (1) within any one-year period has a value aggregating $1,000 or more, (2) has moved in or is part of, or which constitutes interstate or foreign commerce, and (3) has been obtained with a counterfeit, fictitious, altered, forged, lost, stolen, or fraudulently obtained credit card; or

(e) Whoever knowingly receives, conceals, uses, sells, or transports in interstate or foreign commerce one or more tickets for interstate or foreign transportation, which (1) within any one-year period have a value aggregating $500 or more, and (2) have been purchased or obtained with one or more counterfeit, fictitious, altered, forged, lost, stolen, or fraudulently obtained credit cards; or

(f) Whoever in a transaction affecting interstate or foreign commerce furnishes money, property, services, or anything else of value, which within any one-year period has a value aggregating $1,000 or more, through the use of any counterfeit, fictitious, altered, forged, lost, stolen, or fraudulently obtained credit card knowing the same to be counterfeit, fictitious, altered, forged, lost, stolen, or fraudulently obtained—

shall be fined not more than $10,000 or imprisoned not more than ten years, or both.

§135.   Business credit cards [15 U.S.C. §1645]

The exemption provided by section 104(1) does not apply to the provisions of sections 132, 133, and 134, except that a card issuer and a business or other organization which provides credit cards issued by the same card issuer to ten or more of its employees may by contract agree as to liability of the business or other organization with respect to unauthorized use of such credit cards without regard to the provisions of section 133, but in no case may such business or other organization or card issuer impose liability upon any employee with respect to unauthorized use of such a credit card except in accordance with and subject to the limitations of section 133.

§136.   Dissemination of annual percentage rates [15 U.S.C. §1646]

(a) The Board shall collect, publish, and disseminate to the public, on a demonstration basis in a number of standard metropolitan statistical areas to be determined by the Board, the annual percentage rates charged for representative types of nonsale credit by creditors in such areas. For the purpose of this section, the Board is authorized to require creditors in such areas to furnish information necessary for the Board to collect, publish, and disseminate such information.

(b) The Board is authorized to enter into contracts or other arrangements with appropriate persons, organizations, or State agencies to carry out its functions under subsection (a) and to furnish financial assistance in support thereof.

Credit Advertising

§141. Catalogs and multiple-page advertisements [15 U.S.C. §1661]

For the purposes of this chapter, a catalog or other multiple-page advertisement shall be considered a single advertisement if it clearly and conspicuously displays a credit terms table on which the information required to be stated under this chapter is clearly set forth.

§142. Advertising of downpayments and installments [15 U.S.C. §1662]

No advertisement to aid, promote, or assist directly or indirectly any extension of consumer credit may state

(1) that a specific periodic consumer credit amount or installment amount can be arranged, unless the creditor usually and customarily arranges credit payments or installments for that period and in that amount.

(2) that a specified downpayment is required in connection with any extension of consumer credit, unless the creditor usually and customarily arranges downpayments in that amount.

§143. Advertising of open end credit plans [15 U.S.C. §1663]

No advertisement to aid, promote, or assist directly or indirectly the extension of consumer credit under an open end credit plan may set forth any of the specific terms of that plan unless it also clearly and conspicuously sets forth all of the following items:

(1) Any minimum or fixed amount which could be imposed.

(2) In any case in which periodic rates may be used to compute the finance charge, the periodic rates expressed as annual percentage rates.

(3) Any other term that the Board may by regulation require to be disclosed.

§144. Advertising of credit other than open end plans [15 U.S.C. §1664]

(a) Except as provided in subsection (b), this section applies to any advertisement to aid, promote, or assist directly or indirectly any consumer credit sale, loan, or other extension of credit subject to the provisions of this title, other than an open end credit plan.

(b) The provisions of this section do not apply to advertisements of residential real estate except to the extent that the Board may by regulation require.

(c) If any advertisement to which this section applies states the rate of a finance charge, the advertisement shall state the rate of that charge expressed as an annual percentage rate.

(d) If any advertisement to which this section applies states the amount of the downpayment, if any, the amount of any installment payment, the dollar amount of any finance charge, or the number of installments or the period of repayment, then the advertisement shall state all of the following items:

(1) The downpayment, if any.

(2) The terms of repayment.

(3) The rate of the finance charge expressed as an annual percentage rate.

§145. Nonliability of media [15 U.S.C. §1665]

There is no liability under this chapter on the part of any owner or personnel, as such, of any medium in which an advertisement appears or through which it is disseminated.

§146. Use of annual percentage rate in oral disclosures [15 U.S.C. §1665a]

In responding orally to any inquiry about the cost of credit, a creditor, regardless of the method used to compute finance charges, shall state rates only in terms of the annual percentage rate, except that in the case of an open end credit plan, the periodic rate also may be stated and, in the case of an other than open end credit plan where a major component of the finance charge consists of interest computed at a simple annual rate, the simple annual rate also may be stated. The Board may, by regulation, modify the requirements of this section or provide an exception from this section for a transaction or class of transactions for which the creditor cannot determine in advance the applicable annual percentage rate.

Chapter 4. Credit Billing

§161.   Correction of billing errors [15 U.S.C. §1666]

(a) If a creditor, within sixty days after having transmitted to an obligor a statement of the obligor's account in connection with an extension of consumer credit, receives at the address disclosed under section 127(b)(10) a written notice (other than notice on a payment stub or other payment medium supplied by the creditor if the creditor so stipulates with the disclosure required under section 127(a)(7) from the obligor in which the obligor—

(1) sets forth or otherwise enables the creditor to identify the name and account number (if any) of the obligor.

(2) indicates the obligor's belief that the statement contains a billing error and the amount of such billing error, and

(3) sets forth the reasons for the obligor's belief (to the extent applicable) that the statement contains a billing error,

the creditor shall, unless the obligor has, after giving such written notice and before the expiration of the time limits herein specified, agreed that the statement was correct—

(A) not later than thirty days after the receipt of the notice, send a written acknowledgment thereof to the obligor, unless the action required in subparagraph (B) is taken within such thirty-day period, and

(B) not later than two complete billing cycles of the creditor (in no event later than ninety days) after the receipt of the notice and prior to taking any action to collect the amount, or any part thereof, indicated by the obligor under paragraph (2) either—

(i) make appropriate corrections in the account of the obligor, including the crediting of any finance charges on amounts erroneously billed, and transmit to the obligor a notification of such corrections and the creditor's explanation of any change in the amount indicated by the obligor under paragraph (2) and, if any such change is made and the obligor so requests, copies of documentary evidence of the obligor's indebtedness; or

(ii) send a written explanation or clarification to the obligor, after having conducted an investigation, setting forth to the extent applicable the reasons why the creditor believes the account of the obligor was correctly shown in the statement and, upon request of the obligor, provide copies of documentary evidence of the obligor's indebtedness. In the case of a billing error where the obligor alleges that the creditor's billing statement reflects goods not delivered to the obligor or his designee in accordance with the agreement made at the time of the transaction, a creditor may not construe such amount to be correctly shown unless he determines that such goods were actually delivered, mailed, or otherwise sent to the obligor and provides the obligor with a statement of such determination.

After complying with the provisions of this subsection with respect to an alleged billing error, a creditor has no further responsibility under this section if the obligor continues to make substantially the same allegation with respect to such error.

(b) For the purpose of this section, a "billing error" consists of any of the following:

(1) A reflection on a statement of an extension of credit which was not made to the obligor or, if made, was not in the amount reflected on such statement.

(2) A reflection on a statement of an extension of credit for which the obligor requests additional clarification including documentary evidence thereof.

(3) A reflection on a statement of goods or services not accepted by the obligor or his designee or not delivered to the obligor or his designee in accordance with the agreement made at the time of a transaction.

(4) The creditor's failure to reflect properly on a statement a payment made by the obligor or a credit issued to the obligor.

(5) A computation error or similar error of an accounting nature of the creditor on a statement.

(6) Failure to transmit the statement required under section 127(b) of this Act to the last address of the obligor which has been disclosed to the creditor, unless that address was furnished less than twenty days before the end of the billing cycle for which the statement is required.

(7) Any other error described in regulations of the Board.

(c) For the purposes of this section, "action to collect the amount, or any part thereof, indicated by an obligor under paragraph (2)" does not include the sending of statements of account, which may include finance charges on amounts in dispute, to the obligor following written notice from the obligor as specified under subsection (a), if—

(1) the obligor's account is not restricted or closed because of the failure of the obligor to pay the amount indicated under paragraph (2) of subsection (a), and

(2) the creditor indicates the payment of such amount is not required pending the creditor's compliance with this section. Nothing in this section shall be construed to prohibit any action by a creditor to collect any amount which has not been indicated by the obligor to contain a billing error.

(d) Pursuant to regulations of the Board, a creditor operating an open end consumer credit plan may not, prior to the sending of the written explanation or clarification required under paragraph (B)(ii), restrict or close an account with respect to which the obligor has indicated pursuant to subsection (a) that he believes such account to contain a billing error solely because of the obligor's failure to pay the amount indicated to be in error. Nothing in this subsection shall be deemed to prohibit a creditor from applying against the credit limit on the obligor's account the amount indicated to be in error.

(e) Any creditor who fails to comply with the requirements of this section or section 162 forfeits any right to collect from the obligor the amount indicated by the obligor under paragraph (2) of subsection (a) of this section, and any finance charges thereon, except that the amount required to be forefeited under this subsection may not exceed $50.

§162. Regulation of credit reports [15 U.S.C. §1666a]

(a) After receiving a notice from an obligor as provided in section 161(a), a creditor or his agent may not directly or indirectly threaten to report to any person adversely on the obligor's credit rating or credit standing because of the obligor's failure to pay the amount indicated by the obligor under section 161(a)(2), and such amount may not be reported as delinquent to any third party until the creditor has met the requirements of section 161 and has allowed the obligor the same number of days (not less than ten) thereafter to make payment as is provided under the credit agreement with the obligor for the payment of undisputed amounts.

(b) If a creditor receives a further written notice from an obligor that an amount is still in dispute within the time allowed for payment under subsection (a) of this section, a creditor may not report to any third party that the amount of the obligor is delinquent because the obligor has failed to pay an amount which he has indicated under section 161(a)(2), unless the creditor also reports that the amount is in dispute and, at the same time, notifies the obligor of the name and address of each party to whom the creditor is reporting information concerning the delinquency.

(c) A creditor shall report any subsequent resolution of any delinquencies reported pursuant to subsection (b) to the parties to whom such delinquencies were initially reported.

§163. Length of billing period [15 U.S.C. §1666b]

(a) If an open end consumer credit plan provides a time period within which an obligor may repay any portion of the credit extended without incurring an additional finance charge, such additional finance charge may not be imposed with respect to such portion of the credit extended for the billing cycle of which such period is a part unless a statement which includes the amount upon which the finance charge for that period is based was mailed at least fourteen days prior to the date specified in the statement by which payment must be made in order to avoid imposition of that finance charge.

(b) Subsection (a) does not apply in any case where a creditor has been prevented, delayed, or hindered in making timely mailing or delivery of such periodic statement within the time period specified in such subsection because of an act of God, war, natural disaster, strike, or other excusable or justifiable cause, as determined under regulations of the Board.

§164. Prompt crediting of payments [15 U.S.C. §1666c]

Payments received from an obligor under an open end consumer credit plan by the creditor shall be posted promptly to the obligor's account as specified in regulations of the Board. Such regulation shall prevent a finance charge from being imposed on any obligor if the creditor has received the obligor's payment in readily identifiable form in the amount, manner, location, and time indicated by the creditor to avoid the imposition thereof.

§165. Treatment of credit balances [15 U.S.C. §1666d]

Whenever a credit balance in excess of $1 is created in connection with a consumer credit transaction through (1) transmittal of funds to a creditor in excess of the total balance due on an account, (2) rebates of unearned finance charges or insurance premiums, or (3) amounts otherwise owed to or held for the benefit of an obligor, the creditor shall—

(A) credit the amount of the credit balance to the consumer's account;

(B) refund any part of the amount of the remaining credit balance, upon request of the consumer; and

(C) make a good faith effort to refund to the consumer by cash, check, or money order any part of the amount of the credit balance remaining in the account for more than six months, except that no further action is required in any case in which the consumer's current location is not known by the creditor and cannot be traced through the consumer's last known address or telephone number.

§166. Prompt notification of returns [15 U.S.C. §1666e]

With respect to any sales transaction where a credit card has been used to obtain credit, where the seller is a person other than the card issuer, and where the seller accepts or allows a return of the goods or forgiveness of a debit for services which were the subject of such sale, the seller shall promptly transmit to the credit card issuer, a credit statement with respect thereto and the credit card issuer shall credit the account of the obligor for the amount of the transaction.

§167. Use of cash discounts [15 U.S.C. §1666f]

(a)(1) With respect to credit card which may be used for extensions of credit in sales transactions in which the seller is a person other than the card issuer, the card issuer may not, by contract or otherwise, prohibit any such seller from offering a discount to a cardholder to induce the cardholder to pay by cash, check, or similar means rather than use a credit card.

(2) No seller in any sales transaction may impose a surcharge on a cardholder who elects to use a credit card in lieu of payment by cash, check, or similar means.

(b) With respect to any sales transaction, any discount from the regular price offered by the seller for the purpose of inducing payment by cash, checks, or other means not involving the use of an open-end credit plan or a credit card shall not constitute a finance charge as determined under section 106 if such discount is offered to all prospective buyers and its availability is disclosed clearly and conspicuously.

§168.   Prohibition of tie-in services [15 U.S.C. §1666g]

Notwithstanding any agreement to the contrary, a card issuer may not require a seller, as a condition to participating in a credit card plan, to open an account with or procure any other service from the card issuer or its subsidiary or agent.

§169.   Prohibition of offsets [15 U.S.C. §1666h]

(a) A card issuer may not take any action to offset a cardholder's indebtedness arising in connection with a consumer credit transaction under the relevant credit card plan against funds of the cardholder held on deposit with the card issuer unless—

(1) such action was previously authorized in writing by the cardholder in accordance with a credit plan whereby the cardholder agrees periodically to pay debts incurred in his open end credit account by permitting the card issuer periodically to deduct all or a portion of such debt from the cardholder's deposit account, and

(2) such action with respect to any outstanding disputed amount not be taken by the card issuer upon request of the cardholder.

In the case of any credit card account in existence on the effective date of this section, the previous written authorization referred to in clause (1) shall not be required until the date (after such effective date) when such account is renewed, but in no case later than one year after such effective date. Such written authorization shall be deemed to exist if the card issuer has previously notified the cardholder that the use of his credit card account will subject any funds which the card issuer holds in deposit accounts of such cardholder to offset against any amounts due and payable on his credit card account which have not been paid in accordance with the tems of the agreement between the card issuer and the cardholder.

(b) This section does not alter or affect the right under State law of a card issuer to attach or otherwise levy upon funds of a cardholder held on deposit with the card issuer if that remedy is constitutionally available to creditors generally.

§170. Rights of credit card customers [15 U.S.C. §1666i]

(a) Subject to the limitation contained in subsection (b), a card issuer who has issued a credit card to a cardholder pursuant to an open end customer credit plan shall be subject to all claims (other than tort claims) and defenses arising out of any transaction in which the credit card is used as a method of payment or extension of credit if (1) the obligor has made a good faith attempt to obtain satisfactory resolution of a disagreement or problem relative to the transaction from the person honoring the credit card; (2) the amount of the initial transaction exceeds $50; and (3) the place where the initial transaction occurred was in the same State as the mailing address previously provided by the cardholder or was within 100 miles from such address, except that the limitations set forth in clauses (2) and (3) with respect to an obligor's right to assert claims and defenses against a card issuer shall not be applicable to any transaction in which the person honoring the credit card (A) is the same person as the card issuer, (B) is controlled by the card issuer, (C) is under direct or indirect common control with the card issuer, (D) is a franchised dealer in the card issuer's products or services, or (E) has obtained the order for such transaction through a mail solicitation made by or participated in by the card issuer in which the cardholder is solicited to enter into such transaction by using the credit card issued by the card issuer.

(b) The amount of claims or defenses asserted by the cardholder may not exceed the amount of credit outstanding with respect to such transaction at the time the cardholder first notifies the card issuer or the person honoring the credit card of such claim or defense. For the purpose of determining the amount of credit outstanding in the preceding sentence, payments and credits to the cardholder's account are deemed to have been applied, in the order indicated, to the payment of: (1) late charges in the order of their entry to the account; (2) finance charges in order of their entry to the account; and (3) debits to the account other than those set forth above, in the order in which each debit entry to the account was made.

§171. Relation to State laws [15 U.S.C. §1666j]

(a) This chapter does not annul, alter, or affect, or exempt any person subject to the provisions of this chapter from complying with the laws of any State with respect to credit billing practices, except to the extent that those laws are inconsistent with any provision of this chapter, and then only to the extent of the inconsistency. The Board is authorized to determine whether such inconsistencies exist. The Board may not determine that any State law is inconsistent with any provision of this chapter if the Board determines that such law gives greater protection to the consumer.

(b) The Board shall by regulation exempt from the requirements of this chapter any class of credit transactions within any State if it determines that under the law of the State that class of transactions is subject to requirements substantially similar to those imposed under this chapter or that such law gives greater protection to the consumer, and that there is adequate provision for enforcement.

(c) Notwithstanding any other provisions of this title, any discount offered under section 167(b) of this title shall not be considered a finance charge or other charge for credit under the usury laws of any State or under the laws of any State relating to disclosure of information in connection with credit transactions, or relating to the types, amounts or rates of charges, or to any element or elements of charges permissible under such laws in connection with the extension or use of credit.

Chapter 5.   Consumer Leases

§181.   Definitions [15 U.S.C. §1667]

For purposes of this chapter—

(1) The term *"consumer lease"* means a contract in the form of a lease or bailment for the use of personal property by a natural person for a period of time exceeding four months, and for a total contractual obligation not exceeding $25,000, primarily for personal, family, or household purposes, whether or not the lessee has the option to purchase or otherwise become the owner of the property at the expiration of the lease, except that such term shall not include any credit sale as defined in section 103(g). Such term does not include a lease for agricultural, business, or commercial purposes, or to a government or governmental agency or instrumentality, or to an organization.

(2) The term *"lessee"* means a natural person who leases or is offered a consumer lease.

(3) The term *"lessor"* means a person who is regularly engaged in leasing, offering to lease, or arranging to lease under a consumer lease.

(4) The term *"personal property"* means any property which is not real property under the laws of the State where situated at the time offered or otherwise made available for lease.

(5) The terms *"security"* and *"security interest"* mean any interest in property which secures payment or performance of an obligation.

§182.   Consumer lease disclosures [15 U.S.C. §1667a]

Each lessor shall give a lessee prior to the consummation of the lease a dated written statement on which the lessor and lessee are identified setting out accurately and in a clear and conspicuous manner the following information with respect to that lease, as applicable:

(1) A brief description or identification of the leased property;

(2) The amount of any payment by the lessee required at the inception of the lease;

(3) The amount paid or payable by the lessee for official fees, registration, certificate of title, or license fees or taxes;

(4) The amount of other charges payable by the lessee not included in the periodic payments, a description of the charges and that the lessee shall be liable for the differential, if any, between the anticipated fair market value of the leased property and its appraised actual value at the termination of the lease, if the lessee has such liability;

(5) A statement of the amount or method of determining the amount of any liabilities the lease imposes upon the lessee at the end of the term and whether or not the lessee has the option to purchase the leased property and at what price and time;

(6) A statement identifying all express warranties and guarantees made by the manufacturer or lessor with respect to the leased property, and identifying the party responsible for maintaining or servicing the leased property together with a description of the responsibility;

(7) A brief description of insurance provided or paid for by the lessor or required of the lessee, including the types and amounts of the coverages and costs;

(8) A description of any security interest held or to be retained by the lessor in connection with the lease and a clear identification of the property to which the security interest relates;

(9) The number, amount, and due dates or periods of payments under the lease and the total amount of such periodic payments;

(10) Where the lease provides that the lessee shall be liable for the anticipated fair market value of the property on expiration of the lease, the fair market value of the property at the inception of the lease, the aggregate cost of the lease on expiration, and the differential between them; and

(11) A statement of the conditions under which the lessee or lessor may terminate the lease prior to the end of the term and the amount or method of determining any penalty or other charge for delinquency, default, late payments, or early termination.

The disclosures required under this section may be made in the lease contract to be signed by the lessee. The Board may provide by regulation that any portion of the information required to be disclosed under this section may be given in the form of estimates where the lessor is not in a position to know exact information.

§183. Lessee's liability on expiration or termination of lease [15 U.S.C. §1667b]

(a) Where the lessee's liability on expiration of a consumer lease is based on the estimated residual value of the property such estimated residual value shall be a reasonable approximation of the anticipated actual fair market value of the property on lease expiration. There shall be a rebuttable presumption that the estimated residual value is unreasonable to the extent that the estimated residual value exceeds the actual residual value by more than three times the average payment allocable to a monthly period under the lease. In addition, where the lessee has such liability on expiration of a consumer lease there shall be a rebuttable presumption that the lessor's estimated residual value is not in good faith to the extent that the estimated residual value exceeds the actual residual value by more than three times the average payment allocable to a monthly period under the lease and such lessor shall not collect from the lessee the amount of such excess liability on expiration of a consumer lease unless the lessor brings a successful action with respect to such excess liability. In all actions, the lessor shall pay the lessee's reasonable attorney's fees. The presumptions stated in this section shall not apply to the extent the excess of estimated over actual residual value is due to physical damage to the property beyond reasonable wear and use, or to excessive use, and the lease may set standards for such wear and use if such standards are not unreasonable. Nothing in this subsection shall preclude the right of a willing lessee to make any mutually agreeable final adjustment with respect to such excess residual liability, provided such an agreement is reached after termination of the lease.

(b) Penalties or other charges for delinquency, default, or early termination may be specified in the lease but only at an amount which is reasonable in the light of the anticipated or actual harm caused by the delinquency, default, or early termination, the difficulties of proof of loss, and the inconvenience or nonfeasibility of otherwise obtaining an adequate remedy.

(c) If a lease has a residual value provision at the termination of the lease, the lessee may obtain at his expense, a professional appraisal of the leased property by an independent third party agreed to by both parties. Such appraisal shall be final and binding on the parties.

§184. Consumer lease advertising [15 U.S.C. §1667c]

(a) No advertisement to aid, promote, or assist directly or indirectly any consumer lease shall state the amount of any payment, the number of required payments, or that any or no downpayment or other payment is required at inception of the lease unless the advertisement also states clearly and conspicuously and in accordance with regulations issued by the Board each of the following items of information which is applicable:

(1) That the transaction advertised is a lease.

(2) The amount of any payment required at the inception of the lease or that no such payment is required if that is the case.

(3) The number, amounts, due dates or periods of scheduled payments, and the total of payments under the lease.

(4) That the lessee shall be liable for the differential, if any, between the anticipated fair market value of the leased property and its appraised actual value at the termination of the lease, if the lessee has such liability.

(5) A statement of the amount or method of determining the amount of any liabilities the lease imposes upon the lessee at the end of the term and whether or not the lessee has the option to purchase the leased property and at what price and time.

(b) There is no liability under this section on the part of any owner or personnel, as such, of any medium in which an advertisement appears or through which it is disseminated.

§185.   Civil liability [15 U.S.C. §1667d]

(a) Any lessor who fails to comply with any requirement imposed under section 182 or 183 of this chapter with respect to any person is liable to such person as provided in section 130.

(b) Any lessor who fails to comply with any requirement imposed under section 184 of this chapter with respect to any person who suffers actual damage from the violation is liable to such person as provided in section 130. For the purposes of this section, the term "creditor" as used in sections 130 and 131 shall include a lessor as defined in this chapter.

(c) Notwithstanding section 130(e), any action under this section may be brought in any United States district court or in any other court of competent jurisdiction. Such actions alleging a failure to disclose or otherwise comply with the requirements of this chapter shall be brought within one year of the termination of the lease agreement.

§186.   Relation to State laws [15 U.S.C. §1667e]

(a) This chapter does not annul, alter, or affect, or exempt any person subject to the provisions of this chapter from complying with, the laws of any State with respect to consumer leases, except to the extent that those laws are inconsistent with any provision of this chapter, and then only to the extent of the inconsistency. The Board is authorized to determine whether such inconsistencies exist. The Board may not determine that any State law is inconsistent with any provision of this chapter if the Board determines that such law gives greater protection and benefit to the consumer.

(b) The Board shall by regulation exempt from the requirements of this chapter any class of lease transactions with any State if it determines that under the law of that State that class of transactions is subject to requirements substantially similar to those imposed under this chapter or that such law gives greater protection and benefit to the consumer, and that there is adequate provision for enforcement.

Appendix B
Federal Reserve Board, Regulation Z, Truth In Lending

12 C.F.R. Part 226

Table of Sections

Subpart A. General

Subpart B. Open-End Credit

Subpart C. Closed-End Credit

Subpart D. Miscellaneous

Subpart A.   General

§226.1   Authority, purpose, coverage, organization, enforcement and liability

(a) *Authority.* This regulation, known as Regulation Z, is issued by the Board of Governors of the Federal Reserve System to implement the federal Truth in Lending and Fair Credit Billing Acts, which are contained in title I of the Consumer Credit Protection Act, as amended (15 USC 1601 et seq.).

(b) *Purpose.* The purpose of this regulation is to promote the informed use of consumer credit by requiring disclosures about its terms and cost. The regulation also gives consumers the right to cancel certain credit transactions that involve a lien on a consumer's principal dwelling, regulates certain credit card practices, and provides a means for fair and timely resolution of credit billing disputes. The regulation does not govern charges for consumer credit.

(c) *Coverage.* (1) In general, this regulation applies to each individual or business that offers or extends credit when four conditions are met: (i) the credit is offered or extended to consumers; (ii) the offering or extention of credit is done regularly;[1] (iii) the credit is subject to a finance charge or is payable by a written agreement in more than four installments; and (iv) the credit is primarily for personal, family, or household purposes.

(2) If a credit card is involved, however, certain provisions apply even if the credit is not subject to a finance charge, or is not payable by a written agreement in more than four installments, or if the credit card is to be used for business purposes.

---

[1] The meaning of "regularly" is explained in the definition of "creditor" in section 226.2(a).

§226.2   Definitions and rules of construction

(a) *Definitions.*   For purposes of this regulation, the following definitions apply:

(1) *"Act"* means the Truth in Lending Act (15 USC 1601 et seq.).

(2) *"Advertisement"* means a commercial message in any medium that promotes, directly or indirectly, a credit transaction.

(3) *"Arranger of credit"* means a person who regularly arranges for the extension of consumer credit[2] by another person if:

(i) A finance charge may be imposed for that credit, or the credit is payable by written agreement in more than four installments (not including a downpayment); and

(ii) The person extending the credit is not a creditor. The term does not include a person (such as a real estate broker) when arranging seller financing of a dwelling or real property.

(4) *"Billing cycle"* or *"cycle"* means the interval between the days or dates of regular periodic statements. These intervals shall be equal and no longer than a quarter of a year. An interval will be considered equal if the number of days in the cycle does not vary more than four days from the regular day or date of the periodic statement.

(5) *"Board"* means the Board of Governors of the Federal Reserve System.

(6) *"Business day"* means a day on which a creditor's offices are open to the public for carrying on substantially all of its business functions. However, for purposes of rescission under sections 226.15 and 226.23, the term means all calendar days except Sundays and the legal public holidays specified in 5 USC 6103(a), such as New Year's Day, Washington's Birthday, Memorial Day, Independence Day, Labor Day, Columbus Day, Veterans Day, Thanksgiving Day, and Christmas Day.

(7) *"Card issuer"* means a person that issues a credit card or that person's agent with respect to the card.

(8) *"Cardholder"* means a natural person to whom a credit card is issued for consumer credit purposes, or a natural person who has agreed with the card issuer to pay consumer credit obligations arising from the issuance of a credit card to another natural person. For purposes of section 226.12(a) and (b), the term includes any person to whom a credit card is issued for any purpose, including business, commercial, or agricultural use, or a person who has agreed with the card issuer to pay obligations arising from the issuance of such a credit card to another person.

(9) *"Cash price"* means the price at which a creditor, in the ordinary course of business, offers to sell for cash the property or service that is the subject of the transaction. At the creditor's option, the term may include the price of

---

[2] A person regularly arranges for the extension of consumer credit only if it arranged credit more than 25 times (or more than 5 times for transactions secured by a dwelling) in the preceding calendar year. If a person did not meet these numerical standards in the preceding calendar year, the numerical standards shall be applied to the current calendar year.

accessories, services related to the sale, service contracts and taxes and fees for license, title, and registration. The term does not include any finance charge.

(10) *"Closed-end credit"* means consumer credit other than "open-end credit" as defined in this section.

(11) *"Consumer"* means a cardholder or a natural person to whom consumer credit is offered or extended. However, for purposes of rescission under sections 226.15 and 226.23, the term also includes a natural person in whose principal dwelling a security interest is or will be retained or acquired, if that person's ownership interest in the dwelling is or will be subject to the security interest.

(12) *"Consumer credit"* means credit offered or extended to a consumer primarily for personal, family, or household purposes.

(13) *"Consummation"* means the time that a consumer becomes contractually obligated on a credit transaction.

(14) *"Credit"* means the right to defer payment of debt or to incur debt and defer its payment.

(15) *"Credit card"* means any card, plate, coupon book, or other single credit device that may be used from time to time to obtain credit.

(16) *"Credit sale"* means a sale in which the seller is a creditor. The term includes a bailment or lease (unless terminable without penalty at any time by the consumer) under which the consumer—

(i) Agrees to pay as compensation for use a sum substantially equivalent to, or in excess of, the total value of the property and services involved; and

(ii) Will become (or has the option to become), for no additional consideration or for nominal consideration, the owner of the property upon compliance with the agreement.

(17) *"Creditor"* means:

(i) A person (A) who regularly extends consumer credit[3] that is subject to a finance charge or is payable by written agreement in more than four installments (not including a downpayment), and (B) to whom the obligation is initially payable, either on the face of the note or contract, or by agreement when there is no note or contract.

(ii) An arranger of credit.

(iii) For purposes of sections 226.4(c)(8) (Discounts), 226.9(d) (Finance charge imposed at time of transaction), and 226.12(e) (Prompt notification of returns and crediting of refunds), a person that honors a credit card.

(iv) For purposes of subpart B, any card issuer that extends either open-end credit or credit that is not subject to a finance charge and is not payable by written agreement in more than four installments.

(v) For purposes of subpart B (except for the finance charge disclosures contained in sections 226.6(a) and 226.7(d) through (g) and the right of

---

[3] A person regularly extends consumer credit only if it extended credit more than 25 times (or more than 5 times for transactions secured by a dwelling) in the preceding calendar year. If a person did not meet these numerical standards in the preceding calendar year, the numerical standards shall be applied to the current calendar year.

rescission set forth in section 226.15) and subpart C, any card issuer that extends closed-end credit that is subject to a finance charge or is payable by written agreement in more than four installments.

(18) *"Downpayment"* means an amount, including the value of any property used as a trade-in paid to a seller to reduce the cash price of goods or services purchased in a credit sale transaction. A deferred portion of a downpayment may be treated as part of the downpayment if it is payable not later than the due date of the second otherwise regularly scheduled payment and is not subject to a finance charge.

(19) *"Dwelling"* means a residential structure that contains one to four units, whether or not that structure is attached to real property. The term includes an individual condominium unit, cooperative unit, mobile home, and trailer, if it is used as a residence.

(20) *"Open-end credit"* means consumer credit extended by a creditor under a plan in which-

(i) The creditor reasonably contemplates repeated transactions;

(ii) The creditor may impose a finance charge from time to time on an outstanding unpaid balance; and

(iii) The amount of credit that may be extended to the consumer during the term of the plan (up to any limit set by the creditor) is generally made available to the extent that any outstanding balance is repaid.

(21) *"Periodic rate"* means a rate of finance charge that is or may be imposed by a creditor on a balance for a day, week, month, or other subdivision of a year.

(22) *"Person"* means a natural person or an organization, including a corporation, partnership, proprietorship, association, cooperative, estate, trust, or government unit.

(23) *"Prepaid finance charge"* means any finance charge paid separately in cash or by check before or at consummation of a transaction, or withheld from the proceeds of the credit at any time.

(24) *"Residential mortgage transaction"* means a transaction in which a mortgage, deed of trust, purchase money security interest arising under an installment sales contract, or equivalent consensual security interest is created or retained in the consumer's principal dwelling to finance the acquisition or initial construction of that dwelling.

(25) *"Security interest"* means an interest in property that secures performance of a consumer credit obligation and that is recognized by state or federal law. It does not include incidental interests such as interests in proceeds, accessions, additions, fixtures, insurance proceeds (whether or not the creditor is a loss payee or beneficiary), premium rebates, or interests in after-acquired property. For purposes of disclosure under sections 226.6 and 226.18, the term does not include an interest that arises solely by operation of law.

(26) *"State"* means any state, the District of Columbia, the Commonwealth of Puerto Rico, and any territory or possession of the United States.

(b) *Rules of construction.* For purposes of this regulation, the following rules of construction apply:

(1) Where appropriate, the singular form of a word includes the plural form and plural includes singular.

(2) Where the words "obligation" and "transaction" are used in this regulation, they refer to a consumer credit obligation or transaction, depending upon the context. Where the word "credit" is used in this regulation, it means "consumer credit" unless the context clearly indicates otherwise.

(3) Unless defined in this regulation, the words used have the meanings given to them by state law or contract.

(4) Footnotes have the same legal effect as the text of the regulation.

§226.3   Exempt transactions

This regulation does not apply to the following;

(a) *Business, commercial, agricultural, or organizational credit.*[4]   (1) An extension of credit primarily for a business, commercial or agricultural purpose.

(2) An extension of credit to other than a natural person, including credit to government agencies or instrumentalities.

(b) *Credit over $25,000 not secured by real property or a dwelling.*   An extension of credit not secured by real property, or by personal property used or expected to be used as the principal dwelling of the consumer, in which the amount financed exceeds $25,000 or in which there is an express written commitment to extend credit in excess of $25,000.

(c) *Public utility credit.*   An extension of credit that involves public utility services provided through pipe, wire, other connected facilities, or radio or similar transmission (including extensions of such facilities), if the charges for service, delayed payment, or any discounts for prompt payment are filed with or regulated by any government unit. The financing of durable goods or home improvements by a public utility is not exempt.

(d) *Securities or commodities accounts.*   Transactions in securities or commodities accounts in which credit is extended by a broker-dealer registered with the Securities and Exchange Commission or the Commodity Futures Trading Commission.

(e) *Home fuel budget plans.*   An installment agreement for the purchase of home fuels in which no finance charge is imposed.

§226.4   Finance charge

(a) *Definition.*   The finance charge is the cost of consumer credit as a dollar amount. It includes any charge payable directly or indirectly by the consumer and imposed directly or indirectly by the creditor as an incident to or a

---

[4] Extensions of credit that are exempt under paragraph (a)(1) and (2) remain subject to section 226.12(a) and (b) governing the issuance of credit cards and the liability for their unauthorized use.

condition of the extension of credit. It does not include any charge of a type payable in a comparable cash transaction.

(b) *Examples of finance charges.* The finance charge includes the following types of charges, except for charges specifically excluded by paragraphs (c) through (e) of this section:

(1) Interest, time price differential, and any amount payable under an add-on or discount system of additional charges.

(2) Service, transaction, activity, and carrying charges, including any charge imposed on a checking or other transaction account to the extent that the charge exceeds the charge for a similar account without a credit feature.

(3) Points, loan fees, assumption fees, finder's fees, and similar charges.

(4) Appraisal, investigation, and credit report fees.

(5) Premiums or other charges for any guarantee or insurance protecting the creditor against the consumer's default or other credit loss.

(6) Charges imposed on a creditor by another person for purchasing or accepting a consumer's obligation, if the consumer is required to pay the charges in cash, as an addition to the obligation, or as a deduction from the proceeds of the obligation.

(7) Premiums or other charges for credit life, accident, health, or loss-of-income insurance, written in connection with a credit transaction.

(8) Premiums or other charges for insurance against loss of or damage to property, or against liability arising out of the ownership or use of property, written in connection with a credit transaction.

(9) Discounts for the purpose of inducing payment by a means other than the use of credit.

(c) *Charges excluded from the finance charge.* The following charges are not finance charges:

(1) Application fees charged to all applicants for credit, whether or not credit is actually extended.

(2) Charges for actual unanticipated late payment, for exceeding a credit limit, or for delinquency, default, or a similar occurrence.

(3) Charges imposed by a financial institution for paying items that overdraw an account, unless the payment of such items and the imposition of the charge were previously agreed upon in writing.

(4) Fees charged for participation in a credit plan, whether assessed on an annual or other periodic basis.

(5) Seller's points.

(6) Interest forfeited as a result of an interest reduction required by law on a time deposit used as security for an extension of credit.

(7) The following fees in a transaction secured by real property or in a residential mortgage transaction, if the fees are bona fide and reasonable in amount:

   (i) Fees for title examination, abstract of title, title insurance, property survey, and similar purposes.

   (ii) Fees for preparing deeds, mortgages, and reconveyance, settlement, and similar documents.

(iii) Notary, appraisal, and credit report fees.

(iv) Amounts required to be paid into escrow or trustee accounts if the amounts would not otherwise be included in the finance charge.

(8) Discounts offered to induce payment for a purchase by cash, check, or other means, as provided in section 167(b) of the act.

(d) *Insurance.* (1) Premiums for credit life, accident, health, or loss-of-income insurance may be excluded from the finance charge if the following conditions are met:

(i) The insurance coverage is not required by the creditor, and this fact is disclosed.

(ii) The premium for the initial term of insurance coverage is disclosed. If the term of insurance is less than the term of the transaction, the term of insurance also shall be disclosed. The premium may be disclosed on a unit-cost basis only in open-end credit transactions, closed-end credit transactions by mail or telephone under section 226.17(g), and certain closed-end credit transactions involving an insurance plan that limits the total amount of indebtedness subject to coverage.

(iii) The consumer signs or initials an affirmative written request for the insurance after receiving the disclosures specified in this paragraph. Any consumer in the transaction may sign or initial the request.

(2) Premiums for insurance against loss of or damage to property, or against liability arising out of the ownership or use of property,[5] may be excluded from the finance charge if the following conditions are met:

(i) The insurance coverage may be obtained from a person of the consumer's choice,[6] and this fact is disclosed.

(ii) If the coverage is obtained from or through the creditor, the premium for the initial term of insurance coverage shall be disclosed. If the term of insurance is less than the term of the transaction, the term of insurance shall also be disclosed. The premium may be disclosed on a unit-cost basis only in open-end credit transactions, closed-end credit transactions by mail or telephone under section 226.17(g), and certain closed-end credit transactions involving an insurance plan that limits the total amount of indebtedness subject to coverage.

(e) *Certain security interest charges.* If itemized and disclosed, the following charges may be excluded from the finance charge:

(1) Taxes and fees prescribed by law that actually are or will be paid to public officials for determining the existence of or for perfecting, releasing, or satisfying a security interest.

(2) The premium for insurance in lieu of perfecting a security interest to the extent that the premium does not exceed the fees described in paragraph (e)(1) of this section that otherwise would be payable.

---

[5] This includes single interest insurance if the insurer waives all right of subrogation against the consumer.

[6] A creditor may reserve the right to refuse to accept, for reasonable cause, an insurer offered by the consumer.

(f) *Prohibited offsets.*   Interest, dividends, or other income received or to be received by the consumer on deposits or investments shall not be deducted in computing the finance charge.

Subpart B.   Open-end Credit

§226.5   General disclosure requirements

(a) *Form of disclosures.*   (1) The creditor shall make the disclosures required by this subpart clearly and conspicuously in writing,[7] in a form that the consumer may keep.[8]

(2) The terms "finance charge" and "annual percentage rate," when required to be disclosed with a corresponding amount or percentage rate, shall be more conspicuous than any other required disclosure.[9]

(b) *Time of disclosures.*   (1) *Initial disclosures.*   The creditor shall furnish the initial disclosure statement required by section 226.6 before the first transaction is made under the plan.

(2) *Periodic statements.*   (i) The creditor shall mail or deliver a periodic statement as required by section 226.7 for each billing cycle at the end of which an account has a debit or credit balance of more than $1 or on which a finance charge has been imposed. A periodic statement need not be sent for an account if the creditor deems it uncollectible, or if delinquency collection proceedings have been instituted, or if furnishing the statement would violate federal law.

(ii) The creditor shall mail or deliver the periodic statement at least 14 days prior to any date or the end of any time period required to be disclosed under section 226.7(j) in order for the consumer to avoid an additional finance charge or other charge.[10] A creditor that fails to meet this requirement shall not collect any finance or other charge imposed as a result of such failure.

(c) *Basis of disclosures and use of estimates.*   Disclosures shall reflect the terms of the legal obligation between the parties. If any information necessary for accurate disclosure is unknown to the creditor, it shall make the disclosure based on the best information reasonably available and shall state clearly that the disclosure is an estimate.

(d) *Multiple creditors; multiple consumers.*   If the credit plan involves more than one creditor, only one set of disclosures shall be given, and the creditors shall

---

[7] The disclosure required by section 226.9(d) when a finance charge is imposed at the time of a transaction need not be written.

[8] The alternative summary billing rights statement provided for in section 226.9(a)(2), and the disclosures made under section 226.10(b) about payment requirements need not be in a form that the consumer can keep.

[9] The terms need not be more conspicuous when used under section 226.7(d) on periodic statements and under section 226.16 in advertisements.

[10] This timing requirement does not apply if the creditor is unable to meet the requirement because of an act of God, war, civil disorder, natural disaster, or strike.

agree among themselves which creditor must comply with the requirements that this regulation imposes on any or all of them. If there is more than one consumer, the disclosures may be made to any consumer who is primarily liable on the account. If the right of rescission under section 226.15 is applicable, however, the disclosures required by sections 226.6 and 226.15(b) shall be made to each consumer having the right to rescind.

(e) *Effect of subsequent events.* If a disclosure becomes inaccurate because of an event that occurs after the creditor mails or delivers the disclosures, the resulting inaccuracy is not a violation of this regulation, although new disclosures may be required under section 226.9(c).

§226.6 Initial disclosure statement

The creditor shall disclose to the consumer, in terminology consistent with that to be used on the periodic statement, each of the following items, to the extent applicable:

(a) *Finance charge.* The circumstances under which a finance charge will be imposed and an explanation of how it will be determined, as follows:

(1) A statement of when finance charges begin to accrue, including an explanation of whether or not any time period exists within which any credit extended may be repaid without incurring a finance charge. If such a time period is provided, a creditor may, at its option and without disclosure, impose no finance charge when payment is received after the time period's expiration.

(2) A disclosure of each periodic rate that may be used to compute the finance charge, the range of balances to which it is applicable,[11] and the corresponding annual percentage rate.[12] When different periodic rates apply to different types of transactions, the types of transactions to which the periodic rates apply shall also be disclosed.

(3) An explanation of the method used to determine the balance on which the finance charge may be computed.

(4) An explanation of how the amount of any finance charge will be determined,[13] including a description of how any finance charge other than the periodic rate will be determined.

(b) *Other charges.* The amount of any charge other than a finance charge that may be imposed as part of the plan, or an explanation of how the charge will be determined.

(c) *Security interests.* The fact that the creditor has or will acquire a security

---

[11] A creditor is not required to adjust the range of balances disclosure to reflect the balance below which only a minimum charge applies.

[12] If a creditor is offering a variable rate plan, the creditor shall also disclose: (1) the circumstances under which the rate(s) may increase; (2) any limitations on the increase; and (3) the effect(s) of an increase.

[13] If no finance charge is imposed when the outstanding balance is less than a certain amount, no disclosure is required of that fact or of the balance below which no finance charge will be imposed.

interest in the property purchased under the plan, or in other property identified by item or type.

(d) *Statement of billing rights.*   A statement that outlines the consumer's rights and the creditor's responsibilities under sections 226.12(c) and 226.13 and that is substantially similar to the statement found in appendix G.

§226.7   Periodic statement

The creditor shall furnish the consumer with a periodic statement that discloses the following items, to the extent applicable:

(a) *Previous balance.*   The account balance outstanding at the beginning of the billing cycle.

(b) *Identification of transactions.*   An identification of each credit transaction in accordance with section 226.8.

(c) *Credits.*   Any credit to the account during the billing cycle, including the amount and the date of crediting. The date need not be provided if a delay in crediting does not result in any finance or other charge.

(d) *Periodic rates.*   Each periodic rate that may be used to compute the finance charge, the range of balances to which it is applicable,[14] and the corresponding annual percentage rate.[15] If different periodic rates apply to different types of transactions, the types of transactions to which the periodic rates apply shall also be disclosed.

(e) *Balance on which finance charge computed.*   The amount of the balance to which a periodic rate was applied and an explanation of how that balance was determined. When a balance is determined without first deducting all credits and payments made during the billing cycle, that fact and the amount of the credits and payments shall be disclosed.

(f) *Amount of finance charge.*   The amount of any finance charge debited or added to the account during the billing cycle, using the term "finance charge." The components of the finance charge shall be individually itemized and identified to show the amount(s) due to the application of any periodic rates and the amount(s) of any other type of finance charge. If there is more than one periodic rate, the amount of the finance charge attributable to each rate need not be separately itemized and identified.

(g) *Annual percentage rate.*   When a finance charge is imposed during the billing cycle, the annual percentage rate(s) determined under section 226.14, using the term "annual percentage rate."

(h) *Other charges.*   The amounts, itemized and identified by type, of any charges other than finance charges debited to the account during the billing cycle.

---

[14] See footnotes 11 and 13.

[15] If a variable rate plan is involved, the creditor shall disclose the fact that the periodic rate(s) may vary.

(i) *Closing date of billing cycle; new balance.*   The closing date of the billing cycle and the account balance outstanding on that date.

(j) *Free-ride period.*   The date by which or the time period within which the new balance or any portion of the new balance must be paid to avoid additional finance charges. If such a time period is provided, a creditor may, at its option and without disclosure, impose no finance charge when payment is received after the time period's expiration.

(k) *Address for notice of billing errors.*   The address to be used for notice of billing errors. Alternatively, the address may be provided on the billing rights statement permitted by section 226.9(a)(2).

§226.8   Identification of transactions

The creditor shall identify credit transactions on or with the first periodic statement that reflects the transaction by furnishing the following information, as applicable.[16]

(a) *Sale credit.*   For each credit transaction involving the sale of property or services, the following rules shall apply:

(1) *Copy of credit document provided.*   When an actual copy of the receipt or other credit document is provided with the first periodic statement reflecting the transaction, the transaction is sufficiently identified if the amount of the transaction and either the date of the transaction or the date of debiting the transaction to the consumer's account are disclosed on the copy or on the periodic statement.

(2) *Copy of credit document not provided-creditor and seller same or related person(s).*

When the creditor and the seller are the same person or related persons, and an actual copy of the receipt or other credit document is not provided with the periodic statement, the creditor shall disclose the amount and date of the transaction, and a brief identification[17] of the property or services purchased.[18]

(3) *Copy of credit document not provided-creditor and seller not same or related*

---

[16] Failure to disclose the information required by this section shall not be deemed a failure to comply with the regulation if: (1) the creditor maintains procedures reasonably adapted to obtain and provide the information; and (2) the creditor treats an inquiry for clarification or documentation as a notice of a billing error, including correcting the account in accordance with section 226.13(e). This applies to transactions that take place outside a state, as defined in section 226.2(a), whether or not the creditor maintains procedures reasonably adapted to obtain the required information.

[17] As an alternative to the brief identification, the creditor may disclose a number or symbol that also appears on the receipt or other credit document given to the consumer, if the number or symbol reasonably identifies that transaction with that creditor, and if the creditor treats an inquiry for clarification or documentation as a notice of a billing error, including correcting the account in accordance with section 226.13(e).

[18] An identification of property or services may be replaced by the seller's name and location of the transaction when: (1) the creditor and the seller are the same person; (2) the creditor's open-end plan has fewer than 15,000 accounts; (3) the creditor provides the consumer with point-of-sale documentation for that transaction; and

person(s).   When the creditor and seller are not the same person or related persons, and an actual copy of the receipt or other credit document is not provided with the periodic statement, the creditor shall disclose the amount and date of the transaction; the seller's name; and the city, and state or foreign country where the transaction took place.[19]

(b) *Nonsale credit.*   A nonsale credit transaction is sufficiently identified if the first periodic statement reflecting the transaction discloses a brief identification of the transaction;[20] the amount of the transaction; and at least one of the following dates: the date of the transaction, the date or debiting the transaction to the consumer's account, or, if the consumer signed the credit document, the date appearing on the document. If an actual copy of the receipt or other credit document is provided and that copy shows the amount and at least one of the specified dates, the brief identification may be omitted.

§226.9   Subsequent disclosure requirements

(a) *Furnishing statement of billing rights.*

(1) *Annual statement.*   The creditor shall mail or deliver the billing rights statement required by section 226.6(d) at least once per calendar year, at intervals of not less than 6 months nor more than 18 months, either to all consumers or to each consumer entitled to receive a periodic statement under section 226.5(b)(2) for any one billing cycle.

(2) *Alternative summary statement.*   As an alternative to paragraph (a)(1) of this section, the creditor may mail or deliver, on or with each periodic statement, a statement substantially similar to that in appendix G.

(b) *Disclosures for supplemental credit devices and additional features.*   (1) If a creditor within 30 days after mailing or delivering the initial disclosures under section 226.6(a), adds a credit feature to the consumer's account or mails or delivers to the consumer a credit device for which the finance charge terms are the same as those previously disclosed, no additional disclosures are necessary. After 30 days, if the creditor adds a credit feature or furnishes a credit device (other than as a renewal, resupply, or the original issuance of a credit card) on the same finance charge terms, the creditor shall disclose, before the consumer uses the feature or device for the first time, that it is for use in obtaining credit under the terms previously disclosed.

(2) Whenever a credit feature is added or a credit device is mailed or delivered, and the finance charge terms for the feature or device differ from disclosures previously given, the disclosures required by section 226.6(a) that

---

(4) the creditor treats an inquiry for clarification or documentation as a notice oof a billing error, including correcting the account in accordance with section 226.13(e).

[19] The creditor may omit the address or provide any suitable designation that helps the consumer to identify the transaction when the transaction (1) took place at a location that is not fixed; (2) took place in the consumer's home; or (3) was a mail or telephone order.

[20] See footnote 17.

are applicable to the added feature or device shall be given before the consumer uses the feature or device for the first time.

(c) *Change in terms.*   (1) *Written notice required.*   Whenever any term required to be disclosed under section 226.6 is changed or the required minimum periodic payment is increased, the creditor shall mail or deliver written notice of the change to each consumer who may be affected. The notice shall be mailed or delivered at least 15 days prior to the effective date of the change. The 15-day timing requirement does not apply if the change has been agreed to by the consumer, or if a periodic rate or other finance charge is increased because of the consumer's delinquency or default; the notice shall be given, however, before the effective date of the change.

(2) *Notice not required.*   No notice under this section is required when the change involves late-payment charges, charges for documentary evidence, or over-the-limit charges; a reduction of any component of a finance or other charge; suspension of future credit privileges or termination of an account or plan; or when the change results from an agreement involving a court proceeding, or from the consumer's default or delinquency (other than an increase in the periodic rate or other finance charge).

(d) *Finance charge imposed at time of transaction.*   (1) Any person, other than the card issuer, who imposes a finance charge at the time of honoring a consumer's credit card, shall disclose the amount of that finance charge prior to its imposition.

(2) The card issuer, if other than the person honoring the consumer's credit card, shall have no responsibility for the disclosure required by paragraph (d)(1) of this section, and shall not consider any such charge for purposes of sections 226.6 and 226.7.

§226.10   Prompt crediting of payments

(a) *General rule.*   A creditor shall credit a payment to the consumer's account as of the date of receipt, except when a delay in crediting does not result in a finance or other charge or except as provided in paragraph (b) of this section.

(b) *Specific requirements for payments.*   If a creditor specifies, on or with the periodic statement, requirements for the consumer to follow in making payments, but accepts a payment that does not conform to the requirements, the creditor shall credit the payment within five days of receipt.

(c) *Adjustment of account.*   If a creditor fails to credit a payment, as required by paragraphs (a) or (b) of this section, in time to avoid the imposition of finance or other charges, the creditor shall adjust the consumer's account so that the charges imposed are credited to the consumer's account during the next billing cycle.

§226.11   Treatment of credit balances

When a credit balance in excess of $1 is created on a credit account (through transmittal of funds to a creditor in excess of the total balance due on an account, through rebates of unearned finance charges or insurance premiums, or through amounts otherwise owed to or held for the benefit of a consumer), the creditor shall-

(a) Credit the amount of the credit balance to the consumer's account;

(b) Refund any part of the remaining credit balance within seven business days from receipt of a written request from the consumer; and

(c) Make a good faith effort to refund to the consumer by cash, check, or money order, or credit to a deposit account of the consumer, any part of the credit balance remaining in the account for more than six months. No further action is required if the consumer's current location is not known to the creditor and cannot be traced through the consumer's last known address or telephone number.

§226.12   Special credit card provisions

(a) *Issuance of credit cards.*   Regardless of the purpose for which a credit card is to be used, including business, commercial, or agricultural use, no credit card shall be issued to any person except—

(1) In response to an oral or written request or application for the card; or

(2) As a renewal of, or substitute for, an accepted credit card.[21]

(b) *Liability of cardholder for unauthorized use.*   (1) *Limitation on amount.*   The liability of a cardholder for unauthorized use[22] of a credit card shall not exceed the lesser of $50 or the amount of money, property, labor, or services obtained by the unauthorized use before notification to the card issuer under paragraph (b)(3) of this section.

(2) *Conditions of liability.*   A cardholder shall be liable for unauthorized use of a credit card only if—

(i) The credit card is an accepted credit card;

(ii) The card issuer has provided adequate notice[23] of the cardholder's maximum potential liability and of means by which the card issuer may be

---

[21] For purposes of this section, "accepted credit card" means any credit card that a cardholder has requested or applied for and received, or has signed, used, or authorized another person to use to obtain credit. Any credit card issued as a renewal or substitute in accordance with this paragraph becomes an accepted credit card when received by the cardholder.

[22] "Unauthorized use" means the use of a credit card by a person, other than the cardholder, who does not have actual, implied, or apparent authority for such use, and from which the cardholder receives no benefit.

[23] "Adequate notice" means a printed notice to a cardholder that sets forth clearly the pertinent facts so that the cardholder may reasonably be expected to have noticed it and understood its meaning. The notice may be given by any means reasonably assuring receipt by the cardholder.

notified of loss or theft of the card. The notice shall state that the cardholder's liability shall not exceed $50 (or any lesser amount) and that the cardholder may give oral or written notification, and shall describe a means of notification (for example, a telephone number, an address, or both); and

(iii) The card issuer has provided a means to identify the cardholder on the account or the authorized user of the card.

(3) *Notification to card issuer.*   Notification to a card issuer is given when steps have been taken as may be reasonably required in the ordinary course of business to provide the card issuer with the pertinent information about the loss, theft, or possible unauthorized use of a credit card, regardless of whether any particular officer, employee, or agent of the card issuer does, in fact, receive the information. Notification may be given, at the option of the person giving it, in person, by telephone, or in writing. Notification in writing is considered given at the time of receipt or, whether or not received, at the expiration of the time ordinarily required for transmission, whichever is earlier.

(4) *Effect of other applicable law or agreement.*   If state law or an agreement between a cardholder and the card issuer imposes lesser liability than that provided in this paragraph, the lesser liability shall govern.

(5) *Business use of credit cards.*   If 10 or more credit cards are issued by one card issuer for use by the employees of an organization, this section does not prohibit the card issuer and the organization from agreeing to liability for unauthorized use without regard to this section. However, liability for unauthorized use may be imposed on an employee of the organization, by either the card issuer or the organization, only in accordance with this section.

(c) *Right of cardholder to assert claims or defenses against card issuer.*[24]   (1) *General rule.*   When a person who honors a credit card fails to resolve satisfactorily a dispute as to property or services purchased with the credit card in a consumer credit transaction, the cardholder may assert against the card issuer all claims (other than tort claims) and defenses arising out of the transaction and relating to the failure to resolve the dispute. The cardholder may withhold payment up to the amount of credit outstanding for the property or services that give rise to the dispute and any finance or other charges imposed on that amount.[25]

(2) *Adverse credit reports prohibited.*   If, in accordance with paragraph (c)(1) of

---

[24] This paragraph does not apply to the use of a check guarantee card or a debit card in connection with an overdraft credit plan, or to a check guarantee card used in connection with cash advance checks.

[25] The amount of the claim or defense that the cardholder may assert shall not exceed the amount of credit outstanding for the disputed transaction at the time the cardholder first notifies the card issuer or the person honoring the credit card of the existence of the claim or defense. To determine the amount of credit outstanding for purposes of this section, payments and other credits shall be applied to: (1) late charges in the order of entry to the account; then to (2) finance charges in the order of entry to the account; and then to (3) any other debits in the order of entry to the account. If more than one item is included in a single extension of credit, credits are to be distributed pro rata according to prices and applicable taxes.

this section, the cardholder withholds payment of the amount of credit outstanding for the disputed transaction, the card issuer shall not report that amount as delinquent until the dispute is settled or judgment is rendered.

(3) *Limitations.*   The rights stated in paragraphs (c)(1) and (2) of this section apply only if—

(i) The cardholder has made a good faith attempt to resolve the dispute with the person honoring the credit card; and

(ii) The amount of credit extended to obtain the property or services that result in the assertion of the claim or defense by the cardholder exceeds $50, and the disputed transaction occurred in the same state as the cardholder's current designated address or, if not within the same stte, within 100 miles from that address.[26]

(d) *Offsets by card issuer prohibited.*   (1) A card issuer may not take any action, either before or after termination of credit card privileges, to offset a cardholder's indebtedness arising from a consumer credit transaction under the relevant credit card plan against funds of the cardholder held on deposit with the card issuer.

(2) This paragraph does not alter or affect the right of a card issuer acting under state or federal law to do any of the following with regard to funds of a cardholder held on deposit with the card issuer if the same procedure is constitutionally available to creditors generally: obtain or enforce a consensual security interest in the funds; attach or otherwise levy upon the funds; or obtain or enforce a court order relating to the funds.

(3) This paragraph does not prohibit a plan, if authorized in writing by the cardholder, under which the card issuer may periodically deduct all or part of the cardholder's credit card debt from a deposit account held with the card issuer (subject to the limitations in section 226.13(d)(1)).

(e) *Prompt notification of returns and crediting of refunds.*   (1) When a creditor other than the card issuer accepts the return of property or forgives a debt for services that is to be reflected as a credit to the consumer's credit card account, that creditor shall, within seven business days from accepting the return or forgiving the debt, transmit a credit statement to the card issuer through the card issuer's normal channels for credit statements.

(2) The card issuer shall, within three business days from receipt of a credit statement, credit the consumer's account with the amount of the refund.

(3) If a creditor other than a card issuer routinely gives cash refunds to consumers paying in cash, the creditor shall also give credit or cash refunds to consumers using credit cards, unless it discloses at the time the transaction is consummated that credit or cash refunds for returns are not given. This

---

[26] The limitations stated in paragraph (c)(3)(ii) of this section shall not apply when the person honoring the credit card: (1) is the same person as the card issuer; (2) is controlled by the card issuer directly or indirectly; (3) is under the direct or indirect control of a third person that also directly or indirectly controls the card issuer; (4) controls the card issuer directly or indirectly; (5) is a franchised dealer in the card issuer's products or services; or (6) hs obtained the order for the disputed transaction through a mail solicitation made or participated in by the card issuer.

section does not require refunds for returns nor does it prohibit refunds in kind.

(f) *Discounts: tie-in arrangements.*   No card issuer may, by contract or otherwise—

(1) Prohibit any person who honors a credit card from offering a discount to a consumer to induce the consumer to pay by cash, check, or similar means rather than by use of a credit card or its underlying account for the purchase of property or services; or

(2) Require any person who honors the card issuer's credit card to open or maintain any account or obtain any other service not essential to the operation of the credit card plan from the card issuer or any other person, as a condition of participation in a credit card plan. If maintenance of an account for clearing purposes is determined to be essential to the operation of the credit card plan, it may be required only if no service charges or minimum balance requirements are imposed.

(g) *Relation to Electronic Fund Transfer Act and Regulation E.*   For guidance on whether Regulation Z or Regulation E applies in instances involving both credit and electronic fund transfer aspects, refer to Regulation E, 12 CFR 205.5(c) regarding issuance and 205.6(d) regarding liability for unauthorized use. On matters other than issuance and liability, this section applies to the credit aspects of combined credit/electronic fund transfer transactions, as applicable.

§226.13   Billing-error resolution[27]

(a) *Definition of billing error.*   For purposes of this section, the term "billing error" means:

(1) A reflection on or with a periodic statement of an extension of credit that is not made to the consumer or to a person who has actual, implied, or apparent authority to use the consumer's credit card or open-end credit plan.

(2) A reflection on or with a periodic statement of an extension of credit that is not identified in accordance with the requirements of sections 226.7(b) and 226.8.

(3) A reflection on or with a periodic statement of an extension of credit for property or services not accepted by the consumer or the consumer's designee, or not delivered to the consumer or the consumer's designee as agreed.

(4) A reflection on a periodic statement of the creditor's failure to credit properly a payment or other credit issued to the consumer's account.

(5) A reflection on a periodic statement of a computational or similar error of an accounting nature that is made by the creditor.

(6) A reflection on a periodic statement of an extension of credit for which

---

[27] A creditor shall not accelerate any part of the consumer's indebtedness or restrict or close a consumer's account solely because the consumer has exercised in good faith rights provided by this section. A creditor may be subject to the forfeiture penalty under section 161(e) of the act for failure to comply with any of the requirements of this section.

the consumer requests additional clarification, including documentary evidence.

(7) The creditor's failure to mail or deliver a periodic statement to the consumer's last known address if that address was received by the creditor, in writing, at least 20 days before the end of the billing cycle for which the statement was required.

(b) *Billing-error notice.*[28]   A billing-error notice is a written notice[29] from a consumer that—

(1) Is received by a creditor at the address disclosed under section 226.7(k) no later than 60 days after the creditor transmitted the first periodic statement that reflects the alleged billing error;

(2) Enables the creditor to identify the consumer's name and account number; and

(3) To the extent possible, indicates the consumer's belief and the reasons for the belief that a billing error exists, and the type, date, and amount of the error.

(c) *Time for resolution; general procedures.*

(1) The creditor shall mail or deliver written acknowledgment to the consumer within 30 days of receiving a billing-error notice, unless the creditor has complied with the appropriate resolution procedures of paragraphs (e) and (f) of this section, as applicable, within the 30-day period; and

(2) The creditor shall comply with the appropriate resolution procedures of paragraphs (e) and (f) of this section, as applicable, within two complete billing cycles (but in no event later than 90 days) after receiving a billing-error notice.

(d) *Rules pending resolution.*   Until a billing error is resolved under paragraphs (e) or (f) of this section, the following rules apply:

(1) *Consumer's right to withhold disputed amount; collection action prohibited.*   The consumer need not pay (and the creditor may not try to collect) any portion of any required payment that the consumer believes is related to the disputed amount (including related finance or other charges).[30] If the cardholder maintains a deposit account with the card issuer and has agreed to pay the credit card indebtedness by periodic deductions from the cardholder's deposit account, the card issuer shall not deduct any part of the disputed amount or

---

[28] The creditor need not comply with the requirements of paragraphs (c) through (g) of this section if the consumer concludes that no billing error occurred and voluntarily withdraws the billing-error notice.

[29] The creditor may require that the written notice not be made on the payment medium or other material accompanying the periodic statement if the creditor so stipulates in the billing rights statement required by sections 226.6(d) and 226.9(a).

[30] A creditor is not prohibited from taking action to collect any undisputed portion of the item or bill; from deducting any disputed amount and related finance or other charges from the consumer's credit limit on the account; or from reflecting a disputed amount and related finance or other charges on a periodic statement, provided that the creditor indicates on or with the periodic statement that payment of any disputed amount and related finance or other charges is not required pending the creditor's compliance with this section.

related finance or other charges if a billing error notice is received any time up to three business days before the scheduled payment date.

(2) *Adverse credit reports prohibited.*   The creditor or its agent shall not (directly or indirectly) make or threaten to make an adverse report to any person about the consumer's credit standing, or report that an amount or account is delinquent, because the consumer failed to pay the disputed amount or related finance or other charges.

(e) *Procedures if billing error occurred as asserted.*   If a creditor determines that a billing error occurred as asserted, it shall within the time limits in paragraph (c)(2) of this section—

(1) Correct the billing error and credit the consumer's account with any disputed amount and related finance or other charges, as applicable; and

(2) Mail or deliver a correction notice to the consumer.

(f) *Procedures if different billing error or no billing error occurred.*   If, after conducting a reasonable investigation,[31] a creditor determines that no billing error occurred or that a different billing error occurred from that asserted, the creditor shall within the time limits in paragraph (c)(2) of this section—

(1) Mail or deliver to the consumer an explanation that sets forth the reasons for the creditor's belief that the billing error alleged by the consumer is incorrect in whole or in part;

(2) Furnish copies of documentary evidence of the consumer's indebtedness, if the consumer so requests; and

(3) If a different billing error occurred, correct the billing error and credit the consumer's account with any disputed amount and related finance or other charges, as applicable.

(g) *Creditor's rights and duties after resolution.*   If a creditor, after complying with all of the requirements of this section, determines that a consumer owes all or part of the disputed amount and related finance or other charges, the creditor—

(1) Shall promptly notify the consumer in writing of the time when payment is due and the portion of the disputed amount and related finance or other charges that the consumer still owes;

(2) Shall allow any time period disclosed under sections 226.6(a)(1) and 226.7(j), during which the consumer can pay the amount due under paragraph (g)(1) of this section without incurring additional finance or other charges;

(3) May report an account or amount as delinquent because the amount due under paragraph (g)(1) of this section remains unpaid after the creditor has allowed any time period disclosed under sections 226.6(a)(1) and 226.7(j) or

---

[31] If a consumer submits a billing error notice alleging either the nondelivery of property or services under paragraph (a)(3) of this section or that information appearing on a periodic statement is incorrect because a person honoring the consumer's credit card has made an incorrect report to the card issuer, the creditor shall not deny the assertion unless it conducts a reasonable investigation and determines that the property or services were actually delivered, mailed, or sent as agreed or that the information was correct.

10 days (whichever is loner) during which the consumer can pay the amount; but

(4) May not report that an amount or account is delinquent because the amount due under paragraph (g)(1) of the section remains unpaid, if the creditor receives (within the time allowed for payment in paragraph (g)(3) of this section) further written notice from the consumer that any portion of the billing error is still in dispute, unless the creditor also—

(i) Promptly reports that the amount or account is in dispute;

(ii) Mails or delivers to the consumer (at the same time the report is made) a written notice of the name and address of each person to whom the creditor makes a report; and

(iii) Promptly reports any subsequent resolution of the reported delinquency to all persons to whom the creditor has made a report.

(h) *Reassertion of billing error.*   A creditor that has fully complied with the requirements of this section has no further responsibilities under this section (other than as provided in paragraph (g)(4) of this section) if a consumer reasserts substantially the same billing error.

(i) *Relation to Electronic Fund Transfer Act and Regulation E.*   If an extension of credit is incident to an electronic fund transfer, under an agreement between a consumer and a financial institution to extend credit when the consumer's account is overdrawn or to maintain a specified minimum balance in the consumer's account, the creditor shall comply with the requirements of Regulation E, 12 CFR 205.11, governing error resolution rather than those of paragraphs (a), (b), (c), (e), (f), and (h) of this section.

§226.14   Determination of annual percentage rate

(a) *General rule.*   The annual percentage rate is a measure of the cost of credit, expressed as a yearly rate. An annual percentage rate shall be considered accurate if it is not more than 1/8 of 1 percentage point above or below the annual percentage rate determined in accordance with this section.

(b) *Annual percentage rate for initial disclosures and for advertising purposes.*   Where one or more periodic rates may be used to compute the finance charge, the annual percentage rate(s) to be disclosed for purposes of sections 226.6(a)(2) and 226.16(b)(2) shall be computed by multiplying each periodic rate by the number of periods in a year.

(c) *Annual percentage rate for periodic statements.*   The annual percentage rate(s) to be disclosed for purposes of section 226.7(d) shall be computed by multiplying each periodic rate by the number of periods in a year and, for purposes of section 226.7(g), shall be determined as follows:

(1) If the finance charge is determined solely by applying one or more periodic rates, at the creditor's option, either—

(i) By multiplying each periodic rate by the number of periods in a year; or

(ii) By dividing the total finance charge for the billing cycle by the sum of the balances to which the periodic rates were applied and multiplying the quotient (expressed as a percentage) by the number of billing cycles in a year.

(2) If the finance charge imposed during the billing cycle is or includes a minimum, fixed, or other charge not due to the application of a periodic rate, other than a charge with respect to any specific transaction during the billing cycle, by dividing the total finance charge for the billing cycle by the amount of the balance(s) to which it is applicable[32] and multiplying the quotient (expressed as a percentage) by the number of billing cycles in a year.[33]

(3) If the finance charge imposed during the billing cycle is or includes a charge relating to a specific transaction during the billing cycle (even if the total finance charge also includes any other minimum, fixed, or other charge not due to the application of a periodic rate), by dividing the total finance charge imposed during the billing cycle by the total of all balances and other amounts on which a finance charge was imposed during the billing cycle without duplication, and multiplying the quotient (expressed as a percentage) by the number of billing cycles in a year,[34] except that the annual percentage rate shall not be less than the largest rate determined by multiplying each periodic rate imposed during the billing cycle by the number of periods in a year.[35]

(4) If the finance charge imposed during the billing cycle is or includes a minimum, fixed, or other charge not due to the application of a periodic rate and the total finance charge imposed during the billing cycle does not exceed 50 cents for a monthly or longer billing cycle, or the pro rata part of 50 cents for a billing cycle shorter than monthly, at the creditor's option, by multiplying each applicable periodic rate by the number of periods in a year, notwithstanding the provisions of paragraphs (c)(2) and (3) of this section.

(d) *Calculations where daily periodic rate applied.*   If the provisions of paragraphs (c)(1)(ii) or (2) of this section apply and all or a portion of the finance charge is determined by the application of one or more daily periodic rates, the annual percentage rate may be determined either—

(1) By dividing the total finance charge by the average of the daily balances and multiplying the quotient by the number of billing cycles in a year; or

(2) By dividing the total finance charge by the sum of the daily balances and multiplying the quotient by 365.

---

[32] If there is no balance to which the finance charge is applicable, an annual percentage rate cannot be determined under this section.

[33] Where the finance charge imposed during the billing cycle is or includes a loan fee, points, or similar charge that relates to the opening of the account, the amount of such charge shall not be included in the calculation of the annual percentage rate.

[34] See appendix F regarding determination of the denominator of the fraction under this paragraph.

[35] See footnote 33.

§226.15   Right of rescission

(a) *Consumer's right to rescind.*   (1)(i) Except as provided in paragraph (a)(1)(ii) of this section, in a credit plan in which a security interest is or will be retained or acquired in a consumer's principal dwelling, each consumer whose ownership interest is or will be subject to the security interest shall have the right to rescind: each credit extension made under the plan; the plan when the plan is opened; a security interest when added or increased to secure an existing plan; and the increase when a credit limit on the plan is increased.

(ii) As provided in section 125(e) of the act, the consumer does not have the right to rescind each credit extension made under the plan if such extension is made in accordance with a previously established credit limit for the plan.

(2) To exercise the right to rescind, the consumer shall notify the creditor of the rescission by mail, telegram, or other means of written communication. Notice is considered given when mailed, or when filed for telegraphic transmission, or, if sent by other means, when delivered to the creditor's designated place of business.

(3) The consumer may exercise the right to rescind until midnight of the third business day following the occurrence described in paragraph (a)(1) of this section that gave rise to the right of rescission, delivery of the notice required by paragraph (b) of this section, or delivery of all material disclosures,[36] whichever occurs last. If the required notice and material disclosures are not delivered, the right to rescind shall expire three years after the occurrence giving rise to the right of rescission, or upon transfer of all of the consumer's interest in the property, or upon sale of the property, whichever occurs first. In the case of certain administrative proceedings, the rescission period shall be extended in accordance with section 125(f) of the act.

(4) When more than one consumer has the right to rescind, the exercise of the right by one consumer shall be effective as to all consumers.

(b) *Notice of right to rescind.*   In any transaction or occurrence subject to rescission, a creditor shall deliver two copies of the notice of the right to rescind to each consumer entitled to rescind. The notice shall identify the transaction or occurrence and clearly and conspicuously disclose the following:

(1) The retention or acquisition of a security interest in the consumer's principal dwelling.

(2) The consumer's right to rescind, as described in paragraph (a)(1) of this section.

(3) How to exercise the right to rescind, with a form for that purpose, designating the address of the creditor's place of business.

(4) The effects of rescission, as described in paragraph (d) of this section.

(5) The date the rescission period expires.

---

[36] The term "material disclosures" means the information that must be provided to satisfy the requirements in section 226.6 with regard to the method of determining the finance charge and the balance upon which a finance charge will be imposed, the annual percentage rate, and the amount or method of determining the amount of any membership or participation fee that may be imposed as part of the plan.

(c) *Delay of creditor's performance.* Unless a consumer waives the right to rescind under paragraph (e) of this section, no money shall be disbursed other than in escrow, no services shall be performed, and no materials delivered until after the rescission period has expired and the creditor is reasonably satisfied that the consumer has not rescinded. A creditor does not violate this section if a third party with no knowledge of the event activating the rescission right does not delay in providing materials or services, as long as the debt incurred for those materials or services is not secured by the property subject to rescission.

(d) *Effects of rescission.* (1) When a consumer rescinds a transaction, the security interest giving rise to the right of rescission becomes void, and the consumer shall not be liable for any amount, including any finance charge.

(2) Within 20 calendar days after receipt of a notice of rescission, the creditor shall return any money or property that has been given to anyone in connection with the transaction and shall take any action necessary to reflect the termination of the security interest.

(3) If the creditor has delivered any money or property, the consumer may retain possession until the creditor has met its obligation under paragraph (d)(2) of this section. When the creditor has complied with that paragraph, the consumer shall tender the money or property to the creditor or, where the latter would be impracticable or inequitable, tender its reasonable value. At the consumer's option, tender of property may be made at the location of the property or at the consumer's residence. Tender of money must be made at the creditor's designated place of business. If the creditor does not take possession of the money or property within 20 calendar days after the consumer's tender, the consumer may keep it without further obligation.

(4) The procedures outlined in paragraphs (d)(2) and (3) of this section may be modified by court order.

(e) *Consumer's waiver of right to rescind.* The consumer may modify or waive the right to rescind if the consumer determines that the extension of credit is needed to meet a bona fide personal financial emergency. To modify or waive the right, the consumer shall give the creditor a dated written statement that describes the emergency, that specifically modifies or waives the right to rescind, and that bears the signatures of the consumers entitled to rescind. Printed forms for this purpose are prohibited.

(f) *Exempt transactions.* The right to rescind does not apply to the following:

(1) A residential mortgage transaction.

(2) A credit plan in which a state agency is a creditor.

§226.16 Advertising

(a) *Actually available terms.* If an advertisement for credit states specific credit terms, it shall state only those terms that actually are or will be arranged or offered by the creditor.

(b) *Advertisement of terms that require additional disclosures.* If any of the terms required to be disclosed under section 226.6 is set forth in an advertisement, the advertisement shall also clearly and conspicuously set forth the following:

(1) Any minimum, fixed, transaction, activity or similar charge that could be imposed.

(2) Any periodic rate that may be applied expressed as an annual percentage rate as determined under section 226.14(b). If the plan provides for a variable periodic rate, that fact shall be disclosed.

(3) Any membership or participation fee that could be imposed.

(c) *Catalogs and multiple-page advertisements.* (1) If a catalog or other multiple-page advertisement gives information in a table or schedule in sufficient detail to permit determination of the disclosures required by paragraph (b) of this section, it shall be considered a single advertisement if—

(i) The table or schedule is clearly and conspicuously set forth; and

(ii) Any statement of terms set forth in section 226.6 appearing anywhere else in the catalog or advertisement clearly refers to that page on which the table or schedule begins.

(2) A catalog or multiple-page advertisement complies with this paragraph if the table or schedule of terms includes all appropriate disclosures for a representative scale of amounts up to the level of the more commonly sold higher-priced property or services offered.

Subpart C.   Closed-end Credit

§226.17   General disclosure requirements

(a) *Form of disclosures.* (1) The creditor shall make the disclosures required by this subpart clearly and conspicuously in writing, in a form that the consumer may keep. The disclosures shall be grouped together, shall be segregated from everything else, and shall not contain any information not directly related[37] to the disclosures required under section 226.18.[38] The itemization of the amount financed under section 226.18(c)(1) must be separate from the other disclosures under that section.

(2) The terms "finance charge" and "annual percentage rate," when required to be disclosed under section 226.18(d) and (e) together with a corresponding amount or percentage rate, shall be more conspicuous than any other disclosure, except the creditor's identity under section 226.18(a).

(b) *Time of disclosures.* The creditor shall make disclosures before consummation of the transaction. In certain residential mortgage transactions, special

---

[37] The disclosures may include an acknowledgment of receipt, the date of the transaction, and the consumer's name, address, and account number.

[38] The following disclosures may be made together or separately from other required disclosures: the creditor's identity under section 226.18(a), the variable rate example under section 226.18(f)(4), insurance under section 226.18(n), and certain security interest charges under section 226.18(o).

timing requirements are set forth in section 226.19. In certain transactions involving mail or telephone orders or a series of sales, the timing of the disclosures may be delayed in accordance with paragraphs (g) and (h) of this section.

(c) *Basis of disclosures and use of estimates.*

(1) The disclosures shall reflect the terms of the legal obligation between the parties.

(2) If any information necessary for an accurate disclosure is unknown to the creditor, it shall make the disclosure based on the best information reasonably available and shall state that the disclosure is an estimate.

(3) The creditor may disregard the effects of the following in making calculations and disclosures:

(i) That payments must be collected in whole cents.

(ii) That dates of scheduled payments and advances may be changed because the scheduled date is not a business day.

(iii) That months have different numbers of days.

(iv) The occurrence of leap year.

(4) In making calculations and disclosures, the creditor may disregard any irregularity in the first period that falls within the limits described below and any payment schedule irregularity that results from the irregular first period—

(i) For transactions in which the term is less than 1 year, a first period not more than 6 days shorter or 13 days longer than a regular period;

(ii) For transactions in which the term is at least 1 year and less than 10 years, a first period not more than 11 days shorter or 21 days longer than a regular period; and

(iii) For transactions in which the term is at least 10 years, a first period shorter than or not more than 32 days longer than a regular period.

(5) If an obligation is payable on demand, the creditor shall make the disclosures based on an assumed maturity of one year. If an alternate maturity date is stated in the legal obligation between the parties, the disclosures shall be based on that date.

(6)(i) A series of advances under an agreement to extend credit up to a certain amount may be considered as one transaction.

(ii) When a multiple-advance loan to finance the construction of a dwelling may be permanently financed by the same creditor, the construction phase and the permanent phase may be treated as either one transaction or more than one transaction.

(d) *Multiple creditors; multiple consumers.* If a transaction involves more than one creditor, only one set of disclosures shall be given and the creditors shall agree among themselves which creditor must comply with the requirements that this regulation imposes on any or all of them. If there is more than one consumer, the disclosures may be made to any consumer who is primarily liable on the obligation. If the transaction is rescindable under section 226.23, however, the disclosures shall be made to each consumer who has the right to rescind.

(e) *Effect of subsequent events.* If a disclosure becomes inaccurate because of an event that occurs after the creditor delivers the required disclosures, the inaccuracy is not a violation of this regulation, although new disclosures may be required under paragraph (f) of this section, section 226.19, or section 226.20.

(f) *Early disclosures.*   If disclosures are given before the date of consummation of a transaction and a subsequent event makes them inaccurate, the creditor shall disclose the changed terms before consummation, if the annual percentage rate in the consummated transaction varies from the annual percentage rate disclosed under section 226.18(e) by more than 1/8 of 1 percentage point in a regular transaction, or more than 1/4 of 1 percentage point in an irregular transaction, as defined in section 226.22(a).

(g) *Mail or telephone orders—delay in disclosures.*   If a creditor receives a purchase order or a request for an extension of credit by mail, telephone, or any other written or electronic communication without face-to-face or direct telephone solicitation, the creditor may delay the disclosures until the due date of the first payment, if the following information for representative amounts or ranges of credit is made available in written form to the consumer or to the public before the actual purchase order or request:

(1) The cash price or the principal loan amount.

(2) The total sale price.

(3) The finance charge.

(4) The annual percentage rate, and if the rate may increase after consummation, the following disclosures:

(i) The circumstances under which the rate may increase.

(ii) Any limitations on the increase.

(iii) The effect of an increase.

(5) The terms of repayment.

(h) *Series of sales—delay in disclosures.*   If a credit sale is one of a series made under an agreement providing that subsequent sales may be added to an outstanding balance, the creditor may delay the required disclosures until the due date of the first payment for the current sale, if the following two conditions are met:

(1) The consumer has approved in writing the annual percentage rate or rates, the range of balances to which they apply, and the method of treating any unearned finance charge on an existing balance.

(2) The creditor retains no security interest in any property after the creditor has received payments equal to the cash price and any finance charge attributable to the sale of that property. For purposes of this provision, in the case of items purchased on different dates, the first purchased is deemed the first item paid for; in the case of items purchased on the same date, the lowest priced is deemed the first item paid for.

(i) *Interim student credit extensions.*   For each transaction involving an interim credit extension under a student credit program, the creditor need not make the following disclosures: the finance charge under section 226.18(d), the payment schedule under section 226.18(g), the total of payments under section 226.18(h), or the total sale price under section 226.18(j).

§226.18 Content of disclosures

For each transaction, the creditor shall disclose the following information as applicable:

(a) *Creditor.* The identity of the creditor making the disclosures.

(b) *Amount financed.* The "amount financed," using that term, and a brief description such as "the amount of credit provided to you or on your behalf." The amount financed is calculated by—

(1) Determining the principal loan amount or the cash price (subtracting any downpayment);

(2) Adding any other amounts that are financed by the creditor and are not part of the finance charge; and

(3) Subtracting any prepaid finance charge.

(c) *Itemization of amount financed.* (1) A separate written itemization of the amount financed, including:[39]

(i) The amount of any proceeds distributed directly to the consumer.

(ii) The amount credited to the consumer's account with the creditor.

(iii) Any amounts paid to other persons by the creditor on the consumer's behalf. The creditor shall identify those persons.[40]

(iv) The prepaid finance charge.

(2) The creditor need not comply with paragraph (c)(1) of this section if the creditor provides a statement that the consumer has the right to receive a written itemization of the amount financed, together with a space for the consumer to indicate whether it is desired, and the consumer does not request it.

(d) *Finance charge.* The "finance charge," using that term, and a brief description such as "the dollar amount the credit will cost you."[41]

(e) *Annual percentage rate.* The "annual percentage rate," using that term, and a brief description such as "the cost of your credit as a yearly rate."[42]

(f) *Variable rate.* If the annual percentage rate may increase after consummation, the following disclosures:[43]

(1) The circumstances under which the rate may increase.

---

[39] Good faith estimates of settlement costs provided for transactions subject to the Real Estate Settlement Procedures Act (12 USC 2601 et seq.) may be substituted for the disclosures required by paragraph (c) of this section.

[40] The following payees may be described using generic or other general terms and need not be further identified: public officials or government agencies, credit reporting agencies, appraisers, and insurance companies.

[41] The finance charge shall be considered accurate if it is not more than $5 above or below the exact finance charge in a transaction involving an amount financed of $1,000 or less, or not more than $10 above or below the exact finance charge in a transaction involving an amount financed of more than $1,000.

[42] For any transaction involving a finance charge of $5 or less on an amount financed of $75 or less, or a finance charge of $7.50 or less on an amount financed of more than $75, the creditor need not disclose the annual percentage rate.

[43] Information provided in accordance with variable rate regulations of other federal agencies may be substituted for the disclosures required by paragraph (f) of this section.

(2) Any limitations on the increase.

(3) The effect of an increase.

(4) An example of the payment terms that would result from an increase.

(g) *Payment schedule.* The number, amounts, and timing of payments scheduled to repay the obligation.

(1) In a demand obligation with no alternate maturity date, the creditor may comply with this paragraph by disclosing the due dates or payment periods of any scheduled interest payments for the first year.

(2) In a transaction in which a series of payments varies because a finance charge is applied to the unpaid principal balance, the creditor may comply with this paragraph by disclosing the following information:

(i) The dollar amounts of the largest and smallest payments in the series.

(ii) A reference to the variations in the other payments in the series.

(h) *Total of payments.* The "total of payments," using that term, and a descriptive explanation such as "the amount you will have paid when you have made all scheduled payments."[44]

(i) *Demand feature.* If the obligation has a demand feature, that fact shall be disclosed. When the disclosures are based on an assumed maturity of one year as provided in section 226.17(c)(5), that fact shall also be disclosed.

(j) *Total sale price.* In a credit sale, the "total sale price," using that term, and a descriptive explanation (including the amount of any downpayment) such as "the total price of your purchase on credit, including your downpayment of $_____." The total sale price is the sum of the cash price, the items described in paragraph (b)(2), and the finance charge disclosed under paragraph (d) of this section.

(k) *Prepayment.* (1) When an obligation includes a finance charge computed from time to time by application of a rate to the unpaid principal balance, a statement indicating whether or not a penalty may be imposed if the obligation is prepaid in full.

(2) When an obligation includes a finance charge other than the finance charge described in paragraph (k)(1) of this section, a statement indicating whether or not the consumer is entitled to a rebate of any finance charge if the obligation is prepaid in full.

(l) *Late payment.* Any dollar or percentage charge that may be imposed before maturity due to a late payment, other than a deferral or extension charge.

(m) *Security interest.* The fact that the creditor has or will acquire a security interest in the property purchased as part of the transaction, or in other property identified by item or type.

(n) *Insurance.* The items required by section 226.4(d) in order to exclude certain insurance premiums from the finance charge.

(o) *Certain security interest charges.* The disclosures required by section

---

[44] In any transaction involving a single payment, the creditor need not disclose the total of payments.

226.4(c) in order to exclude from the finance charge certain fees prescribed by law or certain premiums for insurance in lieu of perfecting a security interest.

(p) *Contract reference.*   A statement that the consumer should refer to the appropriate contract document for information about nonpayment, default, the right to accelerate the maturity of the obligation, and prepayment rebates and penalties. At the creditor's option, the statement may also include a reference to the contract for further information about security interests and, in a residential mortgage transaction, about the creditor's policy regarding assumption of the obligation.

(q) *Assumption policy.*   In a residential mortgage transaction, a statement whether or not a subsequent purchaser of the dwelling from the consumer may be permitted to assume the remaining obligation on its original terms.

(r) *Required deposit.*   If the creditor requires the consumer to maintain a deposit as a condition of the specific transaction, a statement that the annual percentage rate does not reflect the effect of the required deposit.[45]

§226.19   Certain residential mortgage transactions

(a) *Time of disclosure.*   In a residential mortgage transaction subject to the Real Estate Settlement Procedures Act (12 USC 2601 et seq.) the creditor shall make good faith estimates of the disclosures required by section 226.18 before consummation, or shall deliver or place them in the mail not later than three business days after the creditor receives the consumer's written application, whichever is earlier.

(b) *Redisclosure required.*   If the annual percentage rate in the consummated transaction varies from the annual percentage rate disclosed under section 226.18(e) by more than 1/8 of 1 percentage point in a regular transaction or more than 1/4 of 1 percentage point in an irregular transaction, as defined in section 226.22, the creditor shall disclose the changed terms no later than consummation or settlement.

§226.20   Subsequent disclosure requirements

(a) *Refinancings.*   A refinancing occurs when an existing obligation that was subject to this subpart is satisfied and replaced by a new obligation undertaken by the same consumer. A refinancing is a new transaction requiring new disclosures to the consumer. The new finance charge shall include any unearned portion of the old finance charge that is not credited to the existing obligation. The following shall not be treated as a refinancing:

(1) A renewal of a single payment obligation with no change in the original terms.

---

[45] A required deposit need not include, for example: (1) an escrow account for items such as taxes, insurance or repairs; (2) a deposit that earns not less than 5 percent per year; or (3) payments under a Morris Plan.

(2) A reduction in the annual percentage rate with a corresponding change in the payment schedule.

(3) An agreement involving a court proceeding.

(4) A change in the payment schedule or a change in collateral requirements as a result of the consumer's default or delinquency, unless the rate is increased, or the new amount financed exceeds the unpaid balance plus earned finance charge and premiums for continuation of insurance of the types described in section 226.4(d).

(5) The renewal of optional insurance purchased by the consumer and added to an existing transaction, if disclosures relating to the initial purchase were provided as required by this subpart.

(b) *Assumptions.*   An assumption occurs when a creditor expressly agrees in writing with a subsequent consumer to accept that consumer as a primary obligor on an existing residential mortgage transaction. Before the assumption occurs, the creditor shall make new disclosures to the subsequent consumer, based on the remaining obligation. If the finance charge originally imposed on the existing obligation was an add-on or discount finance charge, the creditor need only disclose:

(1) The unpaid balance of the obligation assumed.

(2) The total charges imposed by the creditor in connection with the assumption.

(3) The information required to be disclosed under section 226.18(k), (l), (m), and (n).

(4) The annual percentage rate originally imposed on the obligation.

(5) The payment schedule under section 226.18(g) and the total of payments under section 226.18(h), based on the remaining obligation.

§226.21   Treatment of credit balances

When a credit balance in excess of $1 is created in connection with a transaction (through transmittal of funds to a creditor in excess of the total balance due on an account, through rebates of unearned finance charges or insurance premiums, or through amounts otherwise owed to or held for the benefit of a consumer), the creditor shall—

(a) Credit the amount of the credit balance to the consumer's account;

(b) Refund any part of the remaining credit balance, upon the written request of the consumer; and

(c) Make a good faith effort to refund to the consumer by cash, check, or money order, or credit to a deposit account of the consumer, any part of the credit balance remaining in the account for more than 6 months, except that no further action is required if the consumer's current location is not known to the creditor and cannot be traced through the consumer's last known address or telephone number.

§226.22   Determination of annual percentage rate

(a) *Accuracy of annual percentage rate.*   (1) The annual percentage rate is a measure of the cost of credit, expressed as a yearly rate, that relates the amount and timing of value received by the consumer to the amount and timing of payments made. The annual percentage rate shall be determined in accordance with either the actuarial method or the United States Rule method. Explanations, equations and instructions for determining the annual percentage rate in accordance with the actuarial method are set forth in appendix J to this regulation.

(2) As a general rule, the annual percentage rate shall be considered accurate if it is not more than 1/8 of 1 percentage point above or below the annual percentage rate determined in accordance with paragraph (a)(1) of this section.

(3) In an irregular transaction, the annual percentage rate shall be considered accurate if it is not more than 1/4 of 1 percentage point above or below the annual percentage rate determined in accordance with paragraph (a)(1) of this section.[46]

(b) *Computation tools.*   (1) The Regulation Z Annual Percentage Rate Tables produced by the Board may be used to determine the annual percentage rate, and any rate determined from those tables in accordance with the accompanying instructions complies with the requirements of this section. Volume I of the tables applies to single-advance transactions involving up to 480 monthly payments or 104 weekly payments. It may be used for regular transactions and for transactions with any of the following irregularities: an irregular first period, an irregular first payment, and an irregular final payment. Volume II of the tables applies to transactions involving multiple advances and any type of payment or period irregularity.

(2) Creditors may use any other computation tool in determining the annual percentage rate if the rate so determined equals the rate determined in accordance with appendix J, within the degree of accuracy set forth in paragraph (a) of this section.

(c) *Single add-on rate transactions.*   If a single add-on rate is applied to all transactions with maturities up to 60 months and if all payments are equal in amount and period, a single annual percentage rate may be disclosed for all those transactions, so long as it is the highest annual percentage rate for any such transaction.

(d) *Certain transactions involving ranges of balances.*   For purposes of disclosing the annual percentage rate referred to in section 226.17(g)(4) (Mail or Telephone Orders-Dealy in Disclosures) and (h) (Series of Sales-Delay in Disclosures), if the same finance charge is imposed on all balances within a specified range of balances, the annual percentage rate computed for the

---

[46] For purposes of paragraph (a)(3) of this section, an irregular transaction is one that includes one or more of the following features: multiple advances, irregular payment periods, or irregular payment amounts (other than an irregular first period or an irregular first or final payment).

median balance may be disclosed for all the balances. However, if the annual percentage rate computed for the median balance understates the annual percentage rate computed for the lowest balance by more than 8 percent of the latter rate, the annual percentage rate shall be computed on whatever lower balance will produce an annual percentage rate that does not result in an understatement of more than 8 percent of the rate determined on the lowest balance.

§226.23   Right of rescission

(a) *Consumer's right to rescind.*   (1) In a credit transaction in which a security interest is or will be retained or acquired in a consumer's principal dwelling, each consumer whose ownership interest is or will be subject to the security interest shall have the right to rescind the transaction, except for transactions described in paragraph (f) of this section.[47]

(2) To exercise the right to rescind, the consumer shall notify the creditor of the rescission by mail, telegram or other means of written communication. Notice is considered given when mailed, when filed for telegraphic transmission or, if sent by other means, when delivered to the creditor's designated place of business.

(3) The consumer may exercise the right to rescind until midnight of the third business day following consummation, delivery of the notice required by paragraph (b) of this section, or delivery of all material disclosures,[48] whichever occurs last. If the required notice or material disclosures are not delivered, the right to rescind shall expire three years after consummation, upon transfer of all of the consumer's interest in the property, or upon sale of the property, whichever occurs first. In the case of certain administrative proceedings, the rescission period shall be extended in accordance with section 125(f) of the act.

(4) When more than one consumer in a transaction has the right to rescind, the exercise of the right by one consumer shall be effective as to all consumers.

(b) *Notice of right to rescind.*   In a transaction subject to rescission, a creditor shall deliver two copies of the notice of the right to rescind to each consumer entitled to rescind. The notice shall be on a separate document that identifies the transaction and shall clearly and conspicuously disclose the following:

(1) The retention or acquisition of a security interest in the consumer's principal dwelling.

---

[47] For purposes of this section, the addition to an existing obligation of a security interest in a consumer's principal dwelling is a transaction. The right of rescission applies only to the addition of the security interest and not the existing obligation. The creditor shall deliver the notice required by paragraph (b) of this section but need not deliver new material disclosures. Delivery of the required notice shall begin the rescission period.

[48] The term "material disclosures" means the required disclosures of the annual percentage rate, the finance charge, the amount financed, the total of payments, and the payment schedule.

(2) The consumer's right to rescind the transaction.

(3) How to exercise the right to rescind, with a form for that purpose, designating the address of the creditor's place of business.

(4) The effects of rescission, as described in paragraph (d) of this section.

(5) The date the rescission period expires.

(c) *Delay of creditor's performance.* Unless a consumer waives the right of rescission under paragraph (e) of this section, no money shall be disbursed other than in escrow, no services shall be performed and no materials delivered until the rescission period has expired and the creditor is reasonably satisfied that the consumer has not rescinded.

(d) *Effects of rescission.* (1) When a consumer rescinds a transaction, the security interest giving rise to the right of rescission becomes void and the consumer shall not be liable for any amount, including any finance charge.

(2) Within 20 calendar days after receipt of a notice of rescission, the creditor shall return any money or property that has been given to anyone in connection with the transaction and shall take any action necessary to reflect the termination of the security interest.

(3) If the creditor has delivered any money or property, the consumer may retain possession until the creditor has met its obligation under paragraph (d)(2) of this section. When the creditor has complied with that paragraph, the consumer shall tender the money or property to the creditor, or, where the latter would be impracticable or inequitable, tender its reasonable value. At the consumer's option, tender of property may be made at the location of the property or at the consumer's residence. Tender of money must be made at the creditor's designated place of business. If the creditor does not take possession of the money or property within 20 calendar days after the consumer's tender, the consumer may keep it without further obligation.

(4) The procedures outlined in paragraphs (d)(2) and (3) of this section may be modified by court order.

(e) *Consumer's waiver of right to rescind.* The consumer may modify or waive the right to rescind if the consumer determines that the extension of credit is needed to meet a bona fide personal financial emergency. To modify or waive the right, the consumer shall give the creditor a dated written statement that describes the emergency, specifically modifies or waives the right to rescind, and bears the signature of all of the consumers entitled to rescind. Printed forms for this purpose are prohibited.

(f) *Exempt transactions.* The right to rescind does not apply to the following:

(1) A residential mortgage transaction.

(2) A refinancing or consolidation by the same creditor of an extension of credit already secured by the consumer's principal dwelling. If the new amount financed exceeds the unpaid principal balance plus any earned unpaid finance charge on the existing debt, this exemption applies only to the existing debt and its security interest.

(3) A transaction in which a state agency is a creditor.

(4) An advance, other than an initial advance, in a series of advances or in a series of single-payment obligations that is treated as a single transaction

under section 226.17(c)(6), if the notice required by paragraph (b) of this section and all material disclosures have been given to the consumer.

(5) A renewal of optional insurance premiums that is not considered a refinancing under section 226.20(a)(5).

§226.24   Advertising

(a) *Actually available terms.*   If an advertisement for credit states specific credit terms, it shall state only those terms that actually are or will be arranged or offered by the creditor.

(b) *Advertisement of rate of finance charge.*   If an advertisement states a rate of finance charge, it shall state the rate as an "annual percentage rate," using that term. If the annual percentage rate may be increased after consummation, the advertisement shall state that fact. The advertisement shall not state any other rate, except that a simple annual rate or periodic rate that is applied to an unpaid balance may be stated in conjunction with, but not more conspicuously than, the annual percentage rate.

(c) *Advertisement of terms that require additional disclosures.*   (1) If any of the following terms is set forth in an advertisement, the advertisement shall meet the requirements of paragraph (c)(2) of this section:

(i) The amount or percentage of any downpayment.

(ii) The number of payments or period of repayment.

(iii) The amount of any payment.

(iv) The amount of any finance charge.

(2) An advertisement stating any of the terms in paragraph (c)(1) of this section shall state the following terms,[49] as applicable:

(i) The amount or percentage of the downpayment.

(ii) The terms of repayment.

(iii) The "annual percentage rate," using that term, and, if the rate may be increased after consummation, that fact.

(d) *Catalogs and multiple-page advertisements.*   (1) If a catalog or other multiple-page advertisement gives information in a table or schedule in sufficient detail to permit determination of the disclosures required by paragraph (c)(2) of this section, it shall be considered a single advertisement if-

(i) The table or schedule is clearly set forth; and

(ii) Any statement of the credit terms in paragraph (c)(1) of this section appearing anywhere else in the catalog or advertisement clearly refers to the page on which the table or schedule begins.

(2) A catalog or multiple-page advertisement complies with paragraph (c)(2) of this section if the table or schedule of terms includes all appropriate disclosures for a representative scale of amounts up to the level of the more commonly sold higher-priced property or services offered.

---

[49] An example of one or more typical extensions of credit with a statement of all the terms applicable to each may be used.

Subpart D.   Miscellaneous

§226.25   Record retention

(a) *General rule.*   A creditor shall retain evidence of compliance with this regulation (other than advertising requirements under sections 226.16 and 226.24) for two years after the date disclosures are required to be made or action is required to be taken. The administrative agencies responsible for enforcing the regulation may require creditors under their jurisdictions to retain records for a longer period if necessary to carry out their enforcement responsibilities under section 108 of the act.

(b) *Inspection of records.*   A creditor shall permit the agency responsible for enforcing this regulation with respect to that creditor to inspect its relevant records for compliance.

§226.26   Use of annual percentage rate in oral disclosures

(a) *Open-end credit.*   In an oral response to a consumer's inquiry about the cost of open-end credit, only the annual percentage rate or rates shall be stated, except that the periodic rate or rates also may be stated. If the annual percentage rate cannot be determined in advance because there are finance charges other than a periodic rate, the corresponding annual percentage rate shall be stated, and other cost information may be given.

(b) *Closed-end credit.*   In an oral response to a consumer's inquiry about the cost of closed-end credit, only the annual percentage rate shall be stated, except that a simple annual rate or periodic rate also may be stated if it is applied to an unpaid balance. If the annual percentage rate cannot be determined in advance, the annual percentage rate for a sample transaction shall be stated, and other cost information for the consumer's specific transaction may be given.

§226.27   Spanish language disclosures

All disclosures required by this regulation shall be made in the English language, except in the Commonwealth of Puerto Rico, where creditors may, at their option, make disclosures in the Spanish language. If Spanish disclosures are made, English disclosures shall be provided on the consumer's request, either in substitution for or in addition to the Spanish disclosures. This requirement for providing English disclosures on request shall not apply to advertisements subject to sections 226.16 and 226.24 of this regulation.

§226.28   Effect on state laws

(a) *Inconsistent disclosure requirements.*   (1) State law requirements that are inconsistent with the requirements contained in chapter 1 (General Provisions), chapter 2 (Credit Transactions), or chapter 3 (Credit Advertising) of the act and the implementing provisions of this regulation are preempted to the extent of the inconsistency. A state law is inconsistent if it requires a creditor to make disclosures or take actions that contradict the requirements of the federal law. A state law is contradictory if it requires the use of the same term to represent a different amount or a different meaning that the federal law, or if it requires the use of a term different from that required in the federal law to describe the same item. A creditor, state, or other interested party may request the Board to determine whether a state law requirement is inconsistent. After the Board determines that a state law is inconsistent, a creditor may not make disclosures using the inconsistent term or form.

(2)(i) State law requirements are inconsistent with the requirements contained in sections 161 (Correction of Billing Errors) or 162 (Regulation of Credit Reports) of the act and the implementing provisions of this regulation and are preempted if they provide rights, responsibilities, or procedures for consumers or creditors that are different from those required by the federal law. However, a state law that allows a consumer to inquire about an open-end credit account an dimposes on the creditor an obligation to respond to such inquiry after the time allowed in the federal law for the consumer to submit written notice of a billing error shall not be preempted in any situation where the time period for making written notice of a consumer's rights under such state law, the notice shall state that reliance on the longer time period available under state law may result in the loss of important right that could be preserved by acting more promptly under federal law; it shall also explain that the state law provisions apply only after expiration of the time period for submitting a proper written notice of a billing error under the federal law. If the state disclosures are made on the same side of a page as the required federal disclosures, the state disclosures shall appear under a demarcation line below the federal disclosures, and the federal disclosures shall be identified by a heading indicating that they are made in compliance with federal law.

(ii) State law requirements are inconsistent with the requirements contained in chapter 4 (Credit Billing) of the act (other than sections 161 or 162) and the implementing provisions of this regulation and are preempted if the creditor cannot comply with state law without violating federal law.

(iii) A state may request the Board to determine whether its law is inconsistent with chapter 4 of the act and its implementing provisions.

(b) *Equivalent disclosure requirements.*   If the Board determines that a disclosure required by state law (other than a requirement relating to the finance charge or annual percentage rate) is substantially the same in meaning as a disclosure required under the act of this regulation, creditors in that state may make the state disclosure in lieu of the federal disclosure. A creditor, state, or other interested party may request the Board to determine whether a state disclosure is substantially the same in meaning as a federal disclosure.

(c) *Request for determination.* The procedures under which a request for a determination may be made under this section are set forth in appendix A.

§226.29   State exemptions

(a) *General rule.* Any state may apply to the Board to exempt a class of transactions within the state from the requirements of chapter 2 (Credit Transactions) or chapter 4 (Credit Billing) of the act and the corresponding provisions of this regulation. The Board shall grant an exemption if it determines that-

(1) The state law is substantially similar to the federal law or, in the case of chapter 4, affords the consumer greater protection than the federal law; and

(2) There is adequate provision for enforcement.

(b) *Civil liability.* (1) No exemptions granted under this section shall extend to the civil liability provisions of sections 130 and 131 of the act.

(2) If an exemption has been granted, the disclosures required by the applicable state law (except any additional requirements not imposed by federal law) shall constitute the disclosures required by this act.

(c) *Applications.* The procedures under which a state may apply for an exemption under this section are set forth in appendix B.

APPENDIX F.   Annual Percentage Rate Computations for Certain Open-End Credit Plans

In determining the denominator of the fraction under section 226.14(c)(3), no amount will be used more than once when adding the sum of the balances[1] subject to periodic rates to the sum of the amounts subject to specific transaction charges. In every case, the full amount of transactions subject to specific transaction charges shall be included in the denominator. Other balances or parts of balances shall be included according to the manner of determining the balance subject to a periodic rate, as illustrated in the following examples of accounts on monthly billing cycles:

1. Previous balance—none.

A specific transaction of $100 occurs on the first day of the billing cycle. The average daily balance is $100. A specific transaction charge of 3 percent is applicable to the specific transaction. The periodic rate is 1 1/2 percent applicable to the average daily balance. The numerator is the amount of the finance charge, which is $4.50. The denominator is the amount of the transaction (which is $100), plus the amount by which the balance subject to

---

[1] Where a portion of the finance charge is determined by application of one or more daily periodic rates, the phrase "sum of the balances" shall also means the "average of daily balances."

the periodic rate exceeds the amount of the specific transactions (such excess in this case is 0), totaling $100.

The annual percentage rate is the quotient (which is 4 1/2 percent) multiplied by 12 (the number of months in a year), i.e., 54 percent.

2.   Previous balance—$100.

A specific transaction of $100 occurs at the midpoint of the billing cycle. The average daily balance is $150. A specific transaction charge of 3 percent is applicable to the specific transaction. The periodic rate is 1 1/2 percent applicable to the average daily balance. The numerator is the amount of the finance charge which is $5.25. The denominator is the amount of the transaction (which is $100), plus the amount by which the balance subject to the periodic rate exceeds the amount of the specific transaction (such excess in this case is $50), totaling $150. As explained in example 1, the annual percentage rate is 3 1/2% $\times$ 12 = 42%.

3.   If, in example 2, the periodic rate applies only to the previous balance, the numerator is $4.50 and the denominator is $200 (the amount of the transaction, $100, plus the balance subject only to the periodic rate, the $100 previous balance). As explained in example 1, the annual percentage rate is 2 1/4% $\times$ 12 = 27%.

4.   If, in example 2, the periodic rate applies only to an adjusted balance (previous balance less payments and credits) and the consumer made a payment of $50 at the midpoint of the billing cycle, the numerator is $3.75 and the denominator is $150 (the amount of the transaction, $100, plus the balance subject to the periodic rate, the $50 adjusted balance). As explained in example 1, the annual percentage rate is 2 1/2% $\times$ 12 = 30%.

5.   Previous balance—$100.

A specific transaction (check) of $100 occurs at the midpoint of the billing cycle. The average daily balance is $150. The specific transaction charge is $.25 per check. The periodic rate is 1 1/2 percent applied to the average daily balance. The numerator is the amount of the finance charge, which is $2.50 and includes the $.25 check charge and the $2.25 resulting from the application of the periodic rate. The denominator is the full amount of the specific transaction (which is $100) plus the amount by which the average daily balance exceeds the amount of the specific transaction (which in this case is $50), totaling $150. As explained in example 1, the annual percentage rate would be 1 2/3% $\times$ 12 = 20%.

6.   Previous balance—none.

A specific transaction of $100 occurs at the midpoint of the billing cycle. The average daily balance is $50. The specific transaction charge is 3 percent of the transaction amount or $3.00. The periodic rate is 1 1/2 percent per month applied to the average daily balance. The numerator is the amount of the finance charge, which is $3.75, including the $3.00 transaction charge and $.75 resulting from application of the periodic rate. The denominator is the full amount of the specific transaction ($100) plus the amount by which the balance subject to the periodic rate exceeds the amount of the transaction ($0). Where the specific transaction amount exceeds the balance subject to the periodic rate, the resulting number is considered to be zero rather than a negative number ($50 - $100 = -$50). The denominator, in this case, is $100. As explained in example 1, the annual percentage rate is 3 3/4% × 12 = 45%.

APPENDIX G.   Open-End Model Forms and Clauses

G-1.   Balance Computation Methods Model Clauses

(a) *Adjusted balance method*

We figure [a portion of] the finance charge on your account by applying the periodic rate to the "adjusted balance" of your account. We get the "adjusted balance" by taking the balance you owed at the end of the previous billing cycle and subtracting [any unpaid finance charges and] any payments and credits received during the present billing cycle.

(b) *Previous balance method*

We figure [a portion of] the finance charge on your account by applying the periodic rate to the amount you owe at the beginning of each billing cycle [minus any unpaid finance charges]. We do not subtract any payments or credits received during the billing cycle. [The amount of payments and credits to your account this billing cycle was $_____.]

(c) *Average daily balance method (excluding current transactions)*

We figure [a portion of] the finance charge on your account by applying the periodic rate to the "average daily balance" of your account (excluding current transactions). To get the "average daily balance" we take the beginning balance of your account each day and subtract any payments or credits [and any unpaid finance charges]. We do not add in any new [purchases/advances/loans]. This gives us the daily balance. Then, we add all the daily balances for the billing cycle together and divide the total by the number of days in the billing cycle. This gives us the "average daily balance."

(d) *Average daily balance method (including current transactions)*

We figure [a portion of] the finance charge on your account by applying the periodic rate to the "average daily balance" of your account (including current transactions). To get the "average daily balance" we take the beginning balance of your account each day, add any new [purchases/advances/loans], and subtract any payments or credits, [and unpaid finance charges]. This gives us the daily balance. Then, we add up all the daily balances for the billing cycle and divide the total by the number of days in the billing cycle. This gives us the "average daily balance."

G-2.   Liability for Unauthorized Use Model Clause

You may be liable for the unauthorized use of your credit card [or other term that describes the credit card]. You will not be liable for unauthorized use that occurs after you notify [name of card issuer or its designee] at [address], orally or in writing, of the loss, theft, or possible unauthorized use. In any case, your liability will not exceed [insert $50 or any lesser amount under agreement with the cardholder].

G-3.   Long-Form Billing-Error Rights Model Form

YOUR BILLING RIGHTS KEEP THIS NOTICE FOR FUTURE USE

This notice contains important information about your rights and our responsibilities under the Fair Credit Billing Act.

Notify Us In Case of Errors or Questions About Your Bill

If you think your bill is wrong, or if you need more information about a transaction on your bill, write us [on a separate sheet] at [address] [the address listed on your bill]. Write to us as soon as possible. We must hear from you no later than 60 days after we sent you the first bill on which the error or problem appeared. You can telephone us, but doing so will not preserve your rights.

In your letter, give us the following information:
- Your name and account number.
- The dollar amount of the suspected error.
- Describe the error and explain, if you can, why you believe there is an error. If you need more information, describe the item you are not sure about.

If you have authorized us to pay your credit card bill automatically from your savings or checking account, you can stop the payment on any amount you think is wrong. To stop the payment your letter must reach us three business days before the automatic payment is scheduled to occur.

Your Rights and Our Responsibilities After We Receive Your Written Notice

We must acknowledge your letter within 30 days, unless we have corrected the error by then. Within 90 days, we must either correct the error or explain why we believe the bill was correct.

After we receive your letter, we cannot try to collect any amount you question, or report you as delinquent. We can continue to bill you for the amount you question, including finance charges, and we can apply any unpaid amount against your credit limit. You do not have to pay any questioned amount while we are investigating, but you are still obligated to pay the parts of your bill that are not in question.

If we find that we made a mistake on your bill, you will not have to pay any finance charges related to any questioned amount. If we didn't make a mistake, you may have to pay finance charges, and you will have to make up any missed payments on the questioned amount. In either case, we will send you a statement of the amount you owe and the date that it is due.

If you fail to pay the amount that we think you owe, we may report you as delinquent. However, if our explanation does not satisfy you and you write to us within ten days telling us that you still refuse to pay, we must tell anyone we report you to that you have a question about your bill. And, we must tell you the name of anyone we reported you to. We must tell anyone we report you to that the matter has been settled between us when it finally is.

If we don't follow these rules, we can't collect the first $50 of the questioned amount, even if your bill was correct.

Special Rule for Credit Card Purchases

If you have a problem with the quality of property or services that you purchased with a credit card, and you have tried in good faith to correct the problem with the merchant, you may have the right not to pay the remaining amount due on the property or services. There are two limitations on this right:

(a) You must have made the purchase in your home state or, if not within your home state within 100 miles of your current mailing address; and

(b) The purchase price must have been more than $50.

These limitations do not apply if we own or operate the merchant, or if we mailed you the advertisement for the property or services.

G-4.   Alternative Billing-Error Rights Model Form
BILLING RIGHTS SUMMARY

In Case of Errors or Questions About Your Bill

If you think your bill is wrong, or if you need more information about a transaction on your bill, write us [on a separate sheet] at [address] [the address shown on your bill] as soon as possible. We must hear from you no later than 60 days after we sent you the first bill on which the error or problem appeared. You can telephone us, but doing so will not preserve your rights.

In your letter, give us the following information:

- Your name and account number.
- The dollar amount of the suspected error.
- Describe the error and explain, if you can, why you believe there is an error. If you need more information, describe the item you are unsure about.

You do not have to pay any amount in question while we are investigating, but you are still obligated to pay the parts of your bill that are not in question. While we investigate your question, we cannot report you as delinquent or take any action to collect the amount you question.

Special Rule for Credit Card Purchases

If you have a problem with the quality of goods or services that you purchased with a credit card, and you have tried in good faith to correct the problem with the merchant, you may not have to pay the remaining amount due on the goods or services. You have this protection only when the purchase price was more than $50 and the purchase was made in your home state or within 100 miles of your mailing address. (If we own or operate the merchant, or if we mailed you the advertisement for the property or services, all purchases are covered regardless of amount or location of purchase.)

G-5. Rescission Model Form (When Opening An Account)

NOTICE OF RIGHT TO CANCEL

1. Your Right to Cancel

We have agreed to establish an open-end credit account for you, and you have agreed to give us a [mortgage/lien/security interest] [on/in] your home as security for the account. You have a legal right under federal law to cancel the account, without cost, within three business days after the latest of the following events:

(1) the opening date of your account which is _____; or

(2) the date you received your Truth-in-Lending disclosures; or

(3) the date you received this notice of your right to cancel the account.

If you cancel the account, the [mortgage/lien/security interest] [on/in] your home is also cancelled. Within 20 days of receiving your notice, we must take the necessary steps to reflect the fact that the [mortgage/lien/security interest] [on/in] your home has been cancelled. We must return to you any money or property you have given to us or to anyone else in connection with the account.

You may keep any money or property we have given you until we have done the things mentioned above, but you must then offer to return the money or property. If it is impractical or unfair for you to return the property, you must offer its reasonable value. You may offer to return the property at your home or at the location of the property. Money must be returned to the address shown below. If we do not take possession of the money or property within 20 calendar days of your offer, you may keep it without further obligation.

2. How to Cancel.

If you decide to cancel the account, you may do so by notifying us, in writing, at

(creditor's name and business address).

You may use any written statement that is signed and dated by you and states your intention to cancel, or you may use this notice by dating and signing below. Keep one copy of this notice no matter how you notify us because it contains important information about your rights.

If you cancel by mail or telegram, you must send the notice no later than midnight of

(date)

(or midnight of the third business day following the latest of the three events listed above). If you send or deliver your written notice to cancel some other way, it must be delivered to the above address no later than that time.
I WISH TO CANCEL.

_____   _____

Consumer's Signature   Date

G-6. Rescission Model Form (For Each Transaction)

NOTICE OF RIGHT TO CANCEL

1. Your Right to Cancel

We have extended credit to you under your open-end credit account. This extension of credit will increase the amount you owe on your account. We already have a [mortgage/lien/security interest] [on/in] your home as security for your account. You have a legal right under federal law to cancel the extension of credit, without cost, within three business days after the latest of the following events:

(1)   the date of the additional extension of credit which is _____; or

(2)   the date you received your Truth-in-Lending disclosures; or

(3)   the date you received this notice of your right to cancel the additional extension of credit.

If you cancel the additional extension of credit, your cancellation will only apply to the additional amount and to any increase in the [mortgage/lien/

security interest] that resulted because of the additional amount. It will not affect the amount you presently owe, and it will not affect the [mortgage/lien/ security interest] we already have [on/in] your home. Within 20 calendar days after we receive your notice of cancellation, we must take the necessary steps to reflect the fact that any increase in the [mortgage/lien/security interest] [on/in] your home has been cancelled. We must also return to you any money or property you have given to us or to anyone else in connection with this extension of credit.

You may keep any money or property we have given you until we have done the things mentioned above, but you must then offer to return the money or property. If it is impractical or unfair for you to return the property, you must offer its reasonable value. You may offer to return the property at your home or at the location of the property. Money must be returned to the address shown below. If we do not take possession of the money or property within 20 calendar days of your offer, you may keep it without further obligation.

2. How to Cancel

If you decide to cancel the additional extension of credit, you may do so by notifying us, in writing, at

(creditor's name and business address).

You may use any written statement that is signed and dated by you and states your intention to cancel, or you may use this notice by dating and signing below. Keep one copy of this notice no matter how you notify us because it contains important information about your rights.

If you cancel by mail or telegram, you must send the notice no later than midnight of

(date)

(or midnight of the third business day following the latest of the three events listed above). "If you send or deliver your written notice to cancel some other way, it must be delivered to the above address no later than that time."
I WISH TO CANCEL

_____   _____
Consumer's Signature   Date

REGULATION Z

APPENDIX H.   Closed-End Model Forms and Clauses

H-1.   Credit Sale Model Form (§226.18)
H-2.   Loan Model Form (§226.18)
H-3.   Amount Financed Itemization Model Form (§226.18(c))

H-1.   Credit Sale Model Form

ANNUAL PERCENTAGE RATE The cost of your credit as a yearly rate.	FINANCE CHARGE The dollar amount the credit will cost you.	Amount Financed The amount of credit provided to you or on your behalf.	Total of Payments The amount you will have paid after you have made all payments as scheduled.	Total Sale Price The total cost of your purchases on credit, including your down-payment of $_____
%	$	$	$	$

You have the right to receive at this time an itemization of the Amount Financed.
☐ I want an itemization   ☐ I do not want an itemization

Your payment schedule will be:

Number of Payments	Amount of Payments	When Payments are Due

Insurance

Credit life insurance and credit disability insurance are not required to obtain credit, and will not be provided unless you sign and agree to pay the additional cost.

Type	Premium	Signature
Credit Life		I want credit life insurance. _____ Signature
Credit Disability		I want credit disability insurance. _____ Signature
Credit Life and Disability		I want credit life and disability insurance. _____ Signature

You may obtain property insurance from anyone you want that is acceptable to   (creditor)   If you get the insurance from   (creditor)   you will pay $_____.

Security: You are giving a security interest in:
☐ the goods or property being purchased.
☐ (brief description of other property).

Filing fees $_____   **Non-filing insurance** $_____

Late Charge: If a payment is late, you will be charged $_____/_____% of the payment.

Prepayment: If you pay off early, you
☐ may   ☐ will not   have to pay a penalty.
☐ may   ☐ will not   be entitled to a refund of part of the finance charge.

See your contract documents for any additional information about nonpayment, default, any required repayment in full before the scheduled date, and prepayment refunds and penalties.

_____
e means an estimate

H-2. Loan Model Form

ANNUAL PERCENTAGE RATE The cost of your credit as a yearly rate.	FINANCE CHARGE The dollar amount the credit will cost you.	Amount Financed The amount of credit provided to you or on your behalf.	Total of Payments The amount you will have paid after you have made all pay-ments as scheduled.
%	$	$	$

You have the right to receive at this time an itemization of the Amount Financed.
  □ I want an itemization   □ I do not want an Itemization

Your payment schedule will be:

Number of Payments	Amount of Payments	When Payments are Due

Insurance
Credit life insurance and credit disability insurance are not required to obtain credit, and will not be provided unless you sign and agree to pay the additional cost.

Type	Premium	Signature
Credit Life		I want credit life insurance. Signature
Credit Disability		I want credit disability insurance. Signature
Credit Life and Disability		I want credit life and disability insurance. Signature

You may obtain property insurance from anyone you want that is acceptable to (creditor) If you get the insurance from (creditor) you will pay $_____ .

Security: You are giving a security interest in:
  □ the goods or property being purchased.
  □ (brief description of other property).

Filing fees $_____   **Non-filing insurance** $_____

Late Charge: If a payment is late, you will be charged $_____ /_____ % of the payment.

Prepayment: If you pay off early, you
  □ may □ will not have to pay a penalty.
  □ may □ will not be entitled to a refund of part of the finance charge.

See your contract documents for any additional information about nonpayment, default, any required repayment in full before the scheduled date, and prepayment refunds and penalties.

_____
e means an estimate

H-3. Amount Financed Itemization Model Form

Itemization of the Amount Financed of $_____

    $_____ Amount given to you directly

    $_____ Amount paid on your account

Amount paid to others on your behalf

    $_____ to [public officials] [credit bureau] [appraiser] [insurance company]

    $_____ to (*name of another creditor*)

    $_____ to (*other*)

    $_____ Prepaid finance charge

H-4. Variable-Rate Model Clauses

The annual percentage rate may increase during the term of this transaction if:

[the prime interest rate of (*creditor*) increases.]

[the balance in your deposit account falls below $_____.]

[you terminate your employment with (*employer*).]

[The interest rate will not increase above _____%.]

[The maximum interest rate increase at one time will be _____%.]

[The rate will not increase more than once every (*time period*).]

Any increase will take the form of:

[higher payment amounts.]

[more payments of the same amount.]

[a larger amount due at maturity.]

Example based on the specific transaction

[If the interest rate increases by _____% in (*time period*),

[your regular payments will increase to $_____.]

[you will have to make _____ additional payments.]

[your final payment will increase to $_____.]]

Example based on a typical transaction

[If your loan were for $_____ at _____% for (*term*) and the rate increased to _____% in (*time period*),

[your regular payments would increase by $_____.]

[you would have to make _____ additional payments.]

[your final payment would increase by $_____.]]

H-5. Demand Feature Model Clauses

This obligation [is payable on demand.] [has a demand feature.] [All disclosures are based on an assumed maturity of one year.]

H-6.   Assumption Policy Model Clause

Assumption: Someone buying your house [may, subject to conditions, be allowed to] [cannot] assume the remainder of the mortgage on the original terms.

H-7.   Required Deposit Model Clause

The annual percentage rate does not take into account your required deposit.

H-8.   Rescission Model Form (General)

NOTICE OF RIGHT TO CANCEL

Your Right to Cancel

You are entering into a transaction that will result in a [mortgage/lien/security interest] [on/in] your home. You have a legal right under federal law to cancel this transaction, without cost, within three business days from whichever of the following events occurs last:

(1) the date of the transaction, which is _____; or

(2) the date you received your Truth in Lending disclosures; or

(3) the date you received this notice of your right to cancel.

If you cancel the transaction, the [mortgage/lien/security interest] is also cancelled. Within 20 calendar days after we receive your notice, we must take the steps necessary to reflect the fact that the [mortgage/lien/security interest] [on/in] your home has been cancelled, and we must return to you any money or property you have given to us or to anyone else in connection with this transaction.

You may keep any money or property we have given you until we have done the things mentioned above, but you must then offer to return the money or property. If it is impractical or unfair for you to return the property, you must offer its reasonable value. You may offer to return the property at your home or at the location of the property. Money must be returned to the address below. If we do not take possession of the money or property within 20 calendar days of your offer, you may keep it without further obligation.

How to Cancel

If you decide to cancel this transaction, you may do so by notifying us in writing, at

(creditor's name and business address).

You may use any written statement that is signed and dated by you and states your intention to cancel, or you may use this notice by dating and signing below. Keep one copy of this notice because it contains important information about your rights.

If you cancel by mail or telegram, you must send the notice no later than midnight of

(date)

(or midnight of the third business day following the latest of the three events listed above). If you send or deliver your written notice to cancel some other way, it must be delivered to the above address no later than that time.
I WISH TO CANCEL

_____   _____

Consumer's Signature   Date

APPENDIX J.   Annual Percentage Rate Computations for Closed-End Credit Transactions

(a) *Introduction.*   (1) Section Section 226.22(a) of Regulation Z provides that the annual percentage rate for other than open-end credit transactions shall be determined in accordance with either the actuarial method or the United States Rule method. This appendix contains an explanation of the actuarial method as well as equations, instructions and examples of how this method applies to single-advance and multiple-advance transactions.

(2) Under the actuarial method, at the end of each unit period (or fractional unit period) the unpaid balance of the amount financed is increased by the finance charge earned during that period and is decreased by the total payment (if any) made at the end of that period. The determination of unit periods and fractional unit periods shall be consistent with the definitions and rules in paragraphs (b)(3), (4) and (5) of this section and the general equation in paragraph (b)(8) of this section.

(3) In contrast, under the United States Rule method, at the end of each payment period, the unpaid balance of the amount financed is increased by the finance charge earned during that payment period and is decreased by the payment made at the end of that payment period. If the payment is less than the finance charge earned, the adjustment of the unpaid balance of the amount financed is postponed until the end of the next payment period. If at that time the sum of the two payments is still less than the total earned finance charge for the two payment periods, the adjustment of the unpaid balance of the amount financed is postponed still another payment period, and so forth.

(b) *Instructions and equations for the actuarial method.*   (1) *General rule.*   The annual percentage rate shall be the nominal annual percentage rate determined by multiplying the unit-period rate by the number of unit periods in a year.

(2) *Term of the transaction.*   The term of the transaction begins on the date of its consummation, except that if the finance charge or any portion of it is

earned beginning on a later date, the term begins on the later date. The term ends on the date the last payment is due, except that if an advance is scheduled after that date, the term ends on the later date. For computation purposes, the length of the term shall be equal to the time interval between any point in time on the beginning date to the same point in time on the ending date.

(3) *Definitions of time intervals.* (i) A period is the interval of time between advances or between payments and includes the interval of time between the date the finance charge begins to be earned and the date of the first advance thereafter or the date of the first payment thereafter, as applicable.

(ii) A common period is any period that occurs more than once in a transaction.

(iii) A standard interval of time is a day, week, semimonth, month, or a multiple of a week or a month up to, but not exceeding, one year.

(iv) All months shall be considered equal. Full months shall be measured from any point in time on a given date of a given month to the same point in time on the same date of another month. If a series of payments (or advances) are scheduled for the 29th or 30th of each month, the last day of February shall be used when applicable.

(4) *Unit period.* (i) In all transactions other than a single-advance, single-payment transaction, the unit period shall be that common period, not to exceed one year, that occurs most frequently in the transaction, except that—

(A) If two or more common periods occur with equal frequency, the smaller of such common periods shall be the unit period; or

(B) If there is no common period in the transaction, the unit period shall be that period which is the average of all periods rounded to the nearest whole standard interval of time. If the average is equally near two standard intervals of time, the lower shall be the unit period.

(ii) In a single-advance, single-payment transaction, the unit period shall be the term of the transaction, but shall not exceed one year.

(5) *Number of unit periods between two given dates.* (i) The number of days between two dates shall be the number of 24-hour intervals between any point in time on the first date to the same point in time on the second date.

(ii) If the unit period is a month, the number of full unit periods between two dates shall be the number of months measured back from the later date. The remaining fraction of a unit period shall be the number of days measured forward from the earlier date to the beginning of the first full unit period, divided by 30. If the unit period is a month, there are 12 unit periods per year.

(iii) If the unit period is a semimonth or a multiple of a month not exceeding 11 months, the number of days between two dates shall be 30 times the number of full months measured back from the later date, plus the number of remaining days. The number of full unit periods and the remaining fraction of a unit period shall be determined by dividing such number of days by 15 in the case of a semi-monthly unit period or by the appropriate multiple of 30 in the case of a multimonthly unit period. If the unit period is a semimonth, the number of unit periods per year shall be 24. If the number of unit periods is a multiple of a month, the number of unit periods per year shall be 12 divided by the number of months per unit period.

(iv) If the unit period is a day, a week, or a multiple of a week, the number of full unit periods and the remaining fractions of a unit period shall be determined by dividing the number of days between the two given dates by the number of days per unit period. If the unit period is a day, the number of unit periods per year shall be 365. If the unit period is a week or a multiple of a week, the number of unit periods per year shall be 52 divided by the number of weeks per unit period.

(v) If the unit period is a year, the number of full unit periods between two dates shall be the number of full years (each equal to 12 months) measured back from the later date. The remaining fraction of a unit period shall be—

(A) The remaining number of months divided by 12 if the remaining interval is equal to a whole number of months, or

(B) The remaining number of days divided by 365 if the remaining interval is *not* equal to a whole number of months,

(vi) In a single-advance, single-payment transaction in which the term is less than a year and is equal to a whole number of months, the number of unit periods in the term shall be one, and the number of unit periods per year shall be 12 divided by the number of months in the term or 365 divided by the number of days in the term.

(vii) In a single-advance, single-payment transaction in which the term is less than a year and is *not* equal to a whole number of months, the number of unit periods in the term shall be one, and the number of unit periods per year shall be 365 divided by the number of days in the term.

(6) *Percentage rate for a fraction of a unit period.*   The percentage rate of finance charge for a fraction (less than one) of a unit period shall be equal to such fraction multiplied by the percentage rate of finance charge per unit period.

(7) *Symbols.*   The symbols used to express the terms of a transaction in the equation set forth in paragraph (b)(8) of this section are defined as follows:

A_k = The amount of the kth advance.

q_k = The number of full unit periods from the beginning of the term of the transaction to the kth advance.

e_k = The fraction of a unit period in the time interval from the beginning of the term of the transaction to the kth advance.

m = The number of advances.

P_j = The amount of the jth payment.

t_j = The number of full unit periods from the beginning of the term of the transaction to the jth payment.

f_j = The fraction of a unit period in the time interval from the beginning of the term of the transaction to the jth payment.

n = The number of payments.

i = The percentage rate of finance charge per unit period, expressed as a decimal equivalent.

Symbols used in the examples shown in this appendix are defined as follows:

$$\ddot{a}_{\overline{x}} = \text{The present value of 1 per unit period}$$
for x unit periods, first payment due
immediately.

$$= 1 + \frac{1}{(1 + i)} + \frac{1}{(1 + i)^2} +$$

$$...... + \frac{1}{(1 + i)^{x-1}}$$

w = The number of unit periods per year.
I = wi × 100 = The nominal annual
percentage rate.

(8) *General equation.* The following equation sets forth the relationship among the terms of a transaction:

$$\frac{A_1}{(1 + e_1 i)(1 + i)^{q_1}} + \frac{A_2}{(1 + e_2 i)(1 + i)^{q_2}} +$$

$$... + \frac{A_m}{(1 + e_m i)(1 + i)^{q_m}} =$$

$$\frac{P_1}{(1 + f_1 i)(1 + i)^{t_1}} + \frac{P_2}{(1 + f_2 i)(1 + i)^{t_2}} +$$

$$... + \frac{Pn}{(1 + f_n i)(1 + i)^{t_n}}$$

(9) *Solution of general equation by iteration process.* (i) The general equation in paragraph (b)(8) of this section, when applied to a simple transaction in which a loan of $1000 is repaid by 36 monthly payments of $33.61 each, takes the special form:

$$A = \frac{33.61\ \ddot{a}_{\overline{36}}}{(1 + i)}$$

Step 1:

Let I_1 = estimated annual
  percentage rate =   12.50%
Evaluate expression for A,
  letting $i = I_1/(100w)$ = .010416667
Result (referred to as A') = 1004.674391

Step 2:

Let $I_2 = I_1 + .1 =$ 12.60%
Evaluate expression for A,
  letting $i + I_2/(100w)$ = .010500000
Result
  (referred to as A'')   = 1003.235366

Step 3:

Interpolate for I (annual percentage
rate):

$$I = I_1 + .1\left[\frac{(A - A')}{(A'' - A')}\right] = 12.50 +$$

$$.1\left[\frac{(1000.000000 - 1004.674391)}{(1003.235366 - 1004.674391)}\right]$$

$$= 12.82483042\%$$

Step 4:
First iteration, let I_1
  = 12.82483042% and
  repeat Steps 1, 2, and 3
  obtaining a new I =   12.82557859%
Second iteration, let I_1
  = 12.82557859% and
  repeat Steps 1, 2, and 3
  obtaining a new I =   12.82557529%

In this case, no further iterations are required to obtain the annual percentage
rate correct to two decimal places, 12.83%.

(ii) When the iteration approach is used, it is expected that calculators or computers will be programmed to carry all available decimals throughout the calculation and that enough iterations will be performed to make virtually certain that the annual percentage rate obtained, when rounded to two decimals, is correct. Annual percentage rates in the examples below were obtained by using a 10-digit programmable calculator and the iteration procedure described above.

(c) *Examples for the actuarial method.* (1) *Single-advance transaction, with or without an odd first period, and otherwise regular.* The general equation in paragraph (b)(8) of this section can be put in the following special form for this type of transaction:

$$A = \frac{1}{(1 + fi)(1 + i)^t} \; P \, \ddot{a}_{\overline{n}|}$$

Example (i): Monthly payments (regular first period):
Amount advanced (A) = $5000. Payment (P) = $230.
Number of payments (n) = 24.
Unit period = 1 month. Unit periods per year (w) = 12.
Advance, 1-10-78. First payment, 2-10-78.
From 1-10-78 through 2-10-78 = 1 unit period. (t = 1; f = 0)
Annual percentage rate
   (I) = wi = .0969 = 9.69%
Example (ii): Monthly payments (long first period):
Amount advanced (A) = $6000. Payment (P) = $200.
Number of payments (n) = 36.
Unit period = 1 month. Unit periods per year (w) = 12.
Advance, 2-10-78. First payment, 4-1-78.
From 3-1-78 through 4-1-78 = 1 unit period. (t = 1)
From 2-10-78 through 3-1-78 = 19 days. (f = 19/30)
Annual percentage rate
   (I) = wi = .1182 = 11.82%
   . . .

(2) *Single-advance transaction, with an odd first payment, with or without an odd first period, and otherwise regular.* The general equation in paragraph (b)(8) of this section can be put in the following special form for this type of transaction:

$$A = \left[\frac{1}{(1 + fi)\,(1 + i)^t} \; P_1 + \frac{P\ddot{a}\,\overline{n-1}|}{(1 + i)} \right]$$

Example (i): Monthly payments (regular first period and irregular first payment):
Amount advanced (A) = $5000. First payment (P₁) = $250.
Regular payment (P) = $230. Number of payments (n) = 24.
Unit period = 1 month. Unit periods per year (w) = 12.
Advance, 1-10-78. First payment, 2-10-78.

From 1-10-78 through 2-10-78 = 1 unit period. (t = 1; f = 0)
Annual percentage rate
  (I) = wi = .1008 = 10.08%
. . .

(3) *Single-advance transaction, with an odd final payment, with or without an odd first period, and otherwise regular.*   The general equation in paragraph (b)(8) of this section can be put in the following special form for this type of transaction:

$$A = \frac{1}{(1 + fi)\ (1 + i)^t} \left[P\ddot{a} \underset{n-1}{+} \right.$$

$$\left. \frac{P_n}{(1 + i)^{n-1}} \right]$$

Example (i): Monthly payments (regular first period and irregular final payment):
Amount advanced (A) = $5000. Regular payment (P) = $230.
Final payment (P_n) = $280. Number of payments (n) = 24.
Unit period = 1 month. Unit periods per year (w) = 12.
Advance, 1-10-78. First payment, 2-10-78.
From 1-10-78 through 2-10-78 = 1 unit period (t = 1; f = 0)
Annual percentage rate
  (I) = wi = .1050 = 10.50%
. . .

(5) *Single-advance, single-payment transaction.*   The general equation in paragraph (b)(8) of this section can be put in the special forms below for single advance, single payment transactions. Forms 1 through 3 are for the direct determination of the annual percentage rate under special conditions. Form 4 requires the use of the iteration procedure of paragraph (b)(9) of this section and can be used for all single-advance, single-payment transactions regardless of term.

Form 1—Term less than one year:

$$I = 100w \left(\frac{P}{A} - 1 \right)$$

Form 2—Term more than one year but less than two years:

$$I = \frac{50}{f} \left\{ \left[(1 + f)^2 + \right. \right.$$

$$\left. \left. 4f \left(\frac{P}{A} - 1 \right) \right]^{1/2} - (1 + f) \right\}$$

Form 3—Term equal to exactly a year or exact multiple of a year:

$$I = 100\left[\left(\frac{P}{A}\right)^{1/t} - 1\right]$$

Form 4—Special form for iteration procedure (no restriction on term):

$$A = \frac{P}{(1 + fi)\ (1 + i)^t}$$

Example (i): Single-advance, single-payment (term of less than one year, measured in days):
Amount advanced (A) = $1000. Payment (P) = $1080.
Unit period = 255 days. Unit periods per year (w) = 365/255.
Advance, 1-3-78. Payment, 9-15-78.
From 1-3-78 through 9-15-78 = 255 days. (t = 1; f = 0)
Annual percentage rate
   (I) = wi = .1145 = 11.45% (Use form 1 or 4.)
Example (ii). Single-advance, single-payment (term of less than one year, measured in exact calendar months):
Amount advanced (A) = $1000. Payment (P) = $1044.
Unit period = 6 months. Unit periods per year (w) = 2.
Advance, 7-15-78. Payment, 1-15-79.
From 7-15-78 through 1-15-79 = 6 mos. (t = 1; f = 0)
Annual percentage rate
   (I) = wi = .0880 = 8.80% (Use form 1 or 4.)
Example (iii): Single-advance, single-payment (term of more than one year but less than two years, fraction measured in exact months):
Amount advanced (A) = $1000. Payment (P) = $1135.19.
Unit period = 1 year. Unit periods per year (w) = 1.
Advance, 7-17-78. Payment, 1-17-80.
From 1-17-79 through 1-17-80 = 1 unit period. (t = 1)
From 7-17-78 through 1-17-79 = 6 mos. (f = 6/12)
Annual percentage rate
   (I) = wi = .0876 = 8.76% (Use form 2 or 4.)
Example (iv): Single-advance, single-payment (term of exactly two years):
Amount advanced (A) = $1000. Payment (P) = $1240.
Unit period = 1 year. Unit periods per year (w) = 1.
 Advance, 1-3-78. Payment, 1-3-80.
From 1-3-78 through 1-3-79 = 1 unit period. (t = 2; f = 0)
Annual percentage rate
   (I) = wi = .1136 = 11.36% (Use form 3 or 4.)

Appendix C
Federal Reserve Board, Regulation M, Consumer Leasing

12 C.F.R. Part 213

Table of Sections

---

§213.1   General provisions

(a) *Authority.*   This regulation, known as Regulation M, is issued by the Board of Governors of the Federal Reserve System to implement the consumer leasing portions of the Truth in Lending Act, which is title I of the Consumer Credit Protection Act, as amended (15 USC 1601 et seq.).

(b) *Purpose.*   The purpose of this regulation is to assure that lessees of personal property are given meaningful disclosures of lease terms, to delimit the ultimate liability of lessees in leasing personal property and to require meaningful and accurate disclosures of lease terms in advertising.

. . .

§213.2   Definitions and rules of construction

(a) *Definitions.*   For the purposes of this regulation, unless the context indicates otherwise, the following definitions apply:

(1) *"Act"* means the Truth in Lending Act (15 USC 1601 et seq.).

(2) *"Advertisement"* means any commercial message in any newspaper, magazine, leaflet, flyer or catalog, on radio, television or public address system, in direct mail literature or other printed material on any interior or exterior sign or display, in any window display, in any point-of-transaction literature or

484

price tag which is delivered or made available to a lessee or prospective lessee in any manner whatsoever.

(3) *"Agricultural purpose"* means a purpose related to the production, harvest, exhibition, marketing, transportation, processing, or manufacture of agricultural products by a natural person who cultivates, plants, propagates, or nurtures those agricultural products, including but not limited to the acquisition of personal property and services used primarily in farming. "Agricultural products" includes agricultural, horticultural, agricultural, and dairy products, livestock, wildlife, poultry, bees, forest products, fish and shellfish, and any products thereof, including processed and manufactured products, and any and all products raised or produced on farms and any processed or manufactured products thereof.

(4) *"Arrange for lease of personal property"* means to provide or offer to provide a lease which is or will be extended by another person under a business or other relationship pursuant to which the person arranging such lease:

(i) Receives or will receive a fee, compensation, or other consideration for such services; or

(ii) Has knowledge of the lease terms and participates in the preparation of the contract documents required in connection with the lease.

(5) *"Board"* refers to the Board of Governors of the Federal Reserve System.

(6) *"Consumer lease"* means a contract in the form of a bailment or lease for the use of personal property by a natural person primarily for personal, family or household purposes, for a period of time exceeding four months, for a total contractual obligation not exceeding $25,000, whether or not the lessee has the option to purchase or otherwise become the owner of the property at the expiration of the lease. It does not include a lease which meets the definition of a credit sale in Regulation Z, 12 CFR part 226.2(a), nor does it include a lease for agricultural, business or commercial purposes or one made to an organization.

(7) *"Lessee"* means a natural person who leases under, or who is offered a consumer lease.

(8) *"Lessor"* means a person who, in the ordinary course of business regularly leases, offers to lease, or arranges for the leasing of personal property under a consumer lease.

(9) *"Organization" means a corporation, trust, estate, partnership, cooperative, association, government, or governmental subdivision, agency, or instrumentality.*

(10) *"Period"* means a day, week, month, or other subdivision of a year.

(11) *"Person"* means a natural person or an organization.

(12) *"Personal property"* means any property which is not real property under the law of the state where it is located at the time it is offered or made available for lease.

(13) *"Real property"* means property which is real property under the law of the state in which it is located.

(14) *"Realized value"* means (i) the price received by the lessor for the leased property at disposition, (ii) the highest offer for disposition, or (iii) the fair market value at the end of the lease term.

(15) *"Security interest"* and *"security"* mean any interest in property which secures payment or performance of an obligation. The terms include, but are not limited to, security interests under the Uniform Commercial Code, real property mortgages, deeds of trust, and other consensual or confessed liens whether or not recorded, mechanic's, materialman's, artisan's, and other similar liens, vendor's liens in both real and personal property, any lien on property arising by operation of law, and any interest in a lease when used to secure payment or performance of an obligation.

(16) *"State"* means any state, the District of Columbia, the Commonwealth of Puerto Rico, and any territory or possession of the United States.

(17) *"Total lease obligation"* equals the total of (i) the scheduled periodic payments under the lease, (ii) any nonrefundable cash payment required of the lessee or agreed upon by the lessor and lessee or any trade-in allowance made at consummation, and (iii) the estimated value of the leased property at the end of the lease term.

(18) *"Value at consummation"* equals the cost to the lessor of the leased property including, if applicable, any increase or markup by the lessor prior to consummation.

(b) *Rules of construction.*   For purposes of this regulation, the following rules of construction apply:

(1) Unless the context indicates otherwise, "lease" shall be construed to mean "consumer lease."

(2) A transaction shall be considered consummated at the time a contractual relationship is created between the lessor and lessee, irrespective of the time of the performance of either party.

(3) Captions and catchlines are intended solely as aids to convenient reference, and no inference as to the intent of any provision may be drawn from them.

§213.3   Exempted transactions

This regulation does not apply to lease transactions of personal property which are incident to the lease of real property and which provide that (a) the lessee has no liability for the value of the property at the end of the lease term except for abnormal wear and tear, and (b) the lessee has no option to purchase the leased property.

§213.4   Disclosures

(a) *General requirements.*   (1) Any lessor shall, in accordance with this regulation and to the extent applicable, make the disclosures required by paragraph (g) of this section with respect to any consumer lease. Such disclosures shall be made clearly, conspicuously, in meaningful sequence, and in accordance with the further requirements of this section. All numerical amounts and percentages shall be stated in figures and shall be printed in not less than the equivalent of 10-point type, .075 inch computer type, or elite size typewritten numerals, or shall be legibly handwritten.

(2) Disclosures shall be made prior to the consummation of the lease on a dated written statement which identifies the lessor and the lessee, and a copy of the statement shall be given to the lessee at that time. All of the disclosures shall be made together on either (i) the contract or other instrument evidencing the lease on the same page and above the place for the lessee's signature; or (ii) a separate statement which identifies the lease transaction.

(3) In any lease of multiple items, the description required by paragraph (g)(1) of this section may be provided on a separate statement or statements which are incorporated by reference in the disclosure statement required by paragraph (a) of this section.

(4) All disclosures required to be given by this regulation shall be made in the English language except in the Commonwealth of Puerto Rico, where disclosures may be made in the Spanish language with English language disclosures provided upon the customer's request, either in substitution for the Spanish disclosures or as additional information in accordance with paragraph (b) of this section.

(b) *Additional information.*   At the lessor's option, additional information or explanations may be supplied with any disclosure required by this regulation, but none shall be stated, utilized, or placed so as to mislead or confuse the lessee or contradict, obscure, or detract attention from the information required to be disclosed. Any lessor who elects to make disclosures specified in any provision of state law which, under section 213.7 of this regulation, is inconsistent with the requirements of the act and this regulation may—

(1) Make such inconsistent disclosures on a separate paper apart from the disclosures made pursuant to this regulation; or

(2) Make such inconsistent disclosures on the same statement on which disclosures required by this regulation are made, provided:

(i) All disclosures required by this regulation appear separately and above any other disclosures,

(ii) Disclosures required by this regulation are identified by a clear and conspicuous heading indicating that they are made in compliance with federal law, and

(iii) All inconsistent disclosures appear separately and below a conspicuous demarcation line, and are identified by a clear and conspicuous heading indicating that the statements made thereafter are inconsistent with the disclosure requirements of the federal Consumer Leasing Act.

(c) *Multiple lessors; multiple lessees.*   When a transaction involves more than one lessor, only one lessor need make the disclosures required by this regulation, and the one that discloses shall be the one chosen by the lessors. When a lease involves more than one lessee, the disclosures may be made to any lessee who is primarily liable on the lease.

(d) *Unknown-information estimate.*   If, at the time disclosures must be made, an amount or other item of information required to be disclosed, or needed to determine a required disclosure, is unknown or not available to the lessor and the lessor has made a reasonable effort to ascertain it, the lessor may use an estimated amount or an approximation of the information, provided the estimate or approximation is clearly identified as such, is reasonable, is based on the best information available to the lessor, and is not used for the purpose of circumventing or evading the disclosure requirements of this regulation. Notwithstanding the requirement of this paragraph that the estimate be based on the best information available, a lessor is not precluded in a purchase option lease from understating the estimated value of the leased property at the end of the term in computing the total lease obligation as required in paragraph (g)(15)(i) of this section.

(e) *Effect of subsequent occurrence.* If information required to be disclosed in accordance with this regulation is subsequently rendered inaccurate as a result of any act, occurrence, or agreement subsequent to the delivery of the required disclosures, the inaccuracy resulting therefrom does not constitute a violation of this regulation.[1]

(f) *Leap year.* Any variance in any term required under this regulation to be disclosed, or stated in any advertisement, which occurs by reason of the addition of February 29, in each leap year, may be disregarded, and such term may be disclosed or stated without regard to such variance.

(g) *Specific disclosure requirements.* In any lease subject to this section, the following items, as applicable, shall be disclosed:

(1) A brief description of the leased property, sufficient to identify the property to the lessee and lessor.

(2) The total amount of any payment, such as a refundable security deposit paid by cash, check or similar means, advance payment, capitalized cost reduction or any trade-in allowance, appropriately identified, to be paid by the lessee at consummation of the lease.

(3) The number, amount, and due dates or periods of payments scheduled under the lease and the total amount of such periodic payments.

(4) The total amount paid or payable by the lessee during the lease term for official fees, registration, certificate of title, license fees, or taxes.

(5) The total amount of all other charges, individually itemized, payable by the lessee to the lessor, which are not included in the periodic payments. This total includes the amount of any liabilities the lease imposes upon the lessee at the end of the term, but excludes the potential difference between the estimated and realized values, required to be disclosed under paragraph (g)(13) of this section.

(6) A brief identification of insurance in connection with the lease including (i) if provided or paid for by the lessor, the types and amounts of coverages

---

[1] Such acts, occurrences, or agreements include the failure of the lessee to perform his obligations under the contract and such actions by the lessor as may be proper to protect his interests in such circumstances. Such failure may result in the liability of the lessee to pay delinquency charges, collection costs, or expenses of the lessor for perfection or acquisition of any security interest or amounts advanced by the lessor on behalf of the lessee in connection with insurance, repairs to, or preservation of leased property.

and cost to the lessee, or (ii) if not provided or paid for by the lessor, the types and amounts of coverages required of the lessee.

(7) A statement identifying any express warranties or guarantees available to the lessee made by the lessor or manufacturer with respect to the leased property.

(8) An identification of the party responsible for maintaining or servicing the leased property together with a brief description of the responsibility, and a statement of reasonable standards for wear and use, if the lessor sets such standards.

(9) A description of any security interest, other than a security deposit disclosed under paragraph (g)(2) of this section, held or to be retained by the lessor in connection with the lease and a clear identification of the property to which the security interest relates.

(10) The amount or method of determining the amount of any penalty or other charge for delinquency, default, or late payments.

(11) A statement of whether or not the lessee has the option to purchase the leased property and, if at the end of the lease term, at what price, and, if prior to the end of the lease term, at what time, and the price or method of determining the price.

(12) A statement of the conditions under which the lessee or lessor may terminate the lease prior to the end of the lease term and the amount or method of determining the amount of any penalty or other charge for early termination.

(13) A statement that the lessee shall be liable for the difference between the estimated value of the property and its realized value at early termination or the end of the lease term, if such liability exists.

(14) Where the lessee's liability at early termination or at the end of the lease term is based on the estimated value of the leased property, a statement that the lessee may obtain at the end of the lease term or at early termination, at the lessee's expense, a professional appraisal of the value which could be realized at sale of the leased property by an independent third party agreed to by the lessee and the lessor, which appraisal shall be final and binding on the parties.

(15) Where the lessee's liability at the end of the lease term is based upon the estimated value of the leased property:

(i) The value of the property at consummation of the lease, the itemized total lease obligation at the end of the lease term, and the difference between them.

(ii) That there is a rebuttable presumption that the estimated value of the leased property at the end of the lease term is unreasonable and not in good faith to the extent that it exceeds the realized value by more than three times the average payment allocable to a monthly period, and that the lessor cannot collect the amount of such excess liability unless the lessor brings a successful action in court in which the lessor pays the lessee's attorney's fees, and that this provision regarding the presumption and attorney's fees does not apply to the extent the excess of estimated value over realized value is due to unreasonable wear or use, or excessive use.

(iii) A statement that the requirements of paragraph (g)(15)(ii) of this section do not preclude the right of a willing lessee to make any mutually agreeable final adjustment regarding such excess liability.

(h) *Renegotiations or extensions.* If any existing lease is renegotiated or extended, such renegotiation or extension shall be considered a new lease subject to the disclosure requirements of this regulation, except that the requirements of this paragraph shall not apply to (1) a lease of multiple items where a new item(s) is provided or a previously leased item(s) is returned, and the average payment allocable to a monthly period is not changed by more than 25 per cent, or (2) a lease which is extended for not more than six months on a month-to-month basis or otherwise.

§213.5   Advertising

(a) *General rule.*   No advertisement to aid, promote, or assist directly or indirectly any consumer lease may state that a specific lease of any property at specific amounts or terms is available unless the lessor usually and customarily leases or will lease such property at those amounts or terms.

(b) *Catalogs and multipage advertisements.*   If a catalog or other multiple-page advertisement sets forth or gives information in sufficient detail to permit determination of the disclosures required by this section in a table or schedule of lease terms, such catalog or multiple-page advertisement shall be considered a single advertisement provided—

(1) The table or schedule and the disclosures made therein are set forth clearly and conspicuously, and

(2) Any statement of lease terms appearing in any place other than in that table or schedule of lease terms clearly and conspicuously refers to the page or pages on which that table or schedule appears, unless that statement discloses all of the lease terms required to be stated under this section.

(c) *Terms that require additional information.*   No advertisement to aid, promote, or assist directly or indirectly any consumer lease shall state the amount of any payment, the number of required payments, or that any or no downpayment or other payment is required at consummation of the lease unless the advertisement also states clearly and conspicuously each of the following items of information as applicable:

(1) That the transaction advertised is a lease.

(2) The total amount of any payment such as a security deposit or capitalized cost reduction required at the consummation of the lease, or that no such payments are required.

(3) The number, amounts, due dates or periods of scheduled payments, and the total of such payments under the lease.

(4) A statement of whether or not the lessee has the option to purchase the leased property and at what price and time. The method of determining the price may be substituted for disclosure of the price.

(5) A statement of the amount or method of determining the amount of any liabilities the lease imposes upon the lessee at the end of the term and a

statement that the lessee shall be liable for the difference, if any, between the estimated value of the leased property and its realized value at the end of the lease term, if the lessee has such liability.

(d) *Multiple-item leases; merchandise tags.* If a merchandise tag for an item normally included in a multiple-item lease sets forth information which would require additional disclosures under paragraph (c) of this section, such merchandise tag need not contain such additional disclosures, provided it clearly and conspicuously refers to a sign or display which is prominently posted in the lessor's showroom. Such sign or display shall contain a table or schedule of those items of information to be disclosed under paragraph (c) of this section.

§213.6   Preservation and inspection of evidence of compliance

(a) Evidence of compliance with the requirements imposed under this regulation, other than advertising requirements under section 213.5, shall be preserved by the lessor for a period of not less than two years after the date such disclosure is required to be made.

(b) Each lessor shall, when directed by the appropriate administrative enforcement authority designated in section 108 of the act, permit that authority or its duly authorized representative to inspect its relevant records and evidence of compliance with this regulation.

§213.7   Inconsistent state requirements

(a) *Preemption.* A state law which is similar in nature, purpose, scope, intent, effect, or requisites to a section of chapter 5 of the act is not inconsistent with the act or this regulation within the meaning of section 186(a) of the act if the lessor can comply with the state law without violating this regulation. If a lessor cannot comply with a state law without violating a provision of this regulation which implements a section of chapter 5 of the act, such state law is inconsistent with the requirements of the act and this regulation within the meaning of section 186(a) of the act and is preempted.

(b) *Procedures.* A state, through its governor, attorney general, or other appropriate official having primary enforcement or interpretative responsibilities for its consumer leasing law, may apply to the Board for a determination that the state law offers greater protection and benefit to lessees than a comparable provision(s) of chapter 5 of the act and its implementing provision(s) in this regulation, or is otherwise not inconsistent with chapter 5 of the act and this regulation, or for a determination with respect to any issues not clearly covered by paragraph (a) of this section as to the consistency or inconsistency of a state law with chapter 5 of the act or its implementing provisions in this regulation.

§213.8   Exemption of certain state-regulated transactions

(a) *Exemption for state-regulated transactions.*   In accordance with the provisions of appendix A to Regulation M, any state may make application to the Board for exemption of any class of transactions within the state from the requirements of chapter 5 of the act and the corresponding provisions of this regulation, provided that—

(1) The Board determines that under the law of that state, that class of transactions is subject to requirements substantially similar to those imposed under chapter 5 of the act and the corresponding provisions of this regulation; or the lessee is afforded greater protection and benefit than is afforded under chapter 5 of the act, and

(2) There is adequate provision for enforcement.

(b) *Procedures and criteria.*   The procedures and criteria under which a state may apply for the determination provided for in paragraph (a) of this section are set forth in appendix A to Regulation M.

(c) *Civil liability.*   In order to assure that the concurrent jurisdiction of federal and state courts created in sections 130(e) and 185(c) of the act shall continue to have substantive provisions to which such jurisdiction shall apply, and generally to aid in implementing the act with respect to any class of transactions exempted pursuant to paragraph (a) of this section and appendix A, the Board pursuant to sections 105 and 186(b) of the act hereby prescribes that—

(1) No such exemptions shall be deemed to extend to the civil liability provisions of sections 130, 131, and 185 of the act; and

(2) After an exemption has been granted, the disclosure requirements of the applicable state law shall constitute the disclosure requirements of the act, except to the extent that such state law imposes disclosure requirements not imposed by the act. Information required under such state law with the exception of those provisions which impose disclosure requirements not imposed by the act shall, accordingly, constitute a "requirement imposed" under chapter 5 of the act for the purpose of section 130(a).

APPENDIX A.   Procedures and Criteria for State Exemptions from the Consumer Leasing Act

(c) *Criteria for determination.*   The Board will consider the following criteria along with any other relevant information in making a determination whether the laws of a state impose requirements substantially similar to or provide greater protection and benefit to lessees than under chapter 5, and whether there is adequate provision for enforcement of such laws:

(1) In order for provisions of state law to be substantially similar to or provide greater protection and benefit to lessees than the provision of chapter 5, the provisions of state law shall require that

(i) Definitions and rules of construction import the same meaning and have the same application as those prescribed under section 213.2 of this regulation;

(ii) Lessors make all of the applicable disclosures required by this regulation and within the same (or more stringent) time periods as are prescribed by this regulation;

(iii) Lessors abide by obligations substantially similar to those prescribed by chapter 5, under conditions substantially similar to (or more stringent than) those prescribed in chapter 5;

(iv) Lessors abide by the same (or more stringent) prohibitions as are provided in chapter 5;

(v) Lessees need comply with no obligations or responsibilities which are more costly or burdensome as a condition of exercising any of the rights or gaining the benefits and protections in the state law which correspond to those afforded by chapter 5, than those obligations or responsibilities imposed upon lessees in chapter 5; and

(vi) Substantially similar or more favorable rights and protections are provided to lessees under conditions substantially similar to or more favorable (to lessees) than those afforded by chapter 5.

(2) In determining whether the provisions for enforcement of the state law referred to in paragraph (b)(1) of this appendix are adequate, consideration will be given to the extent to which, under the laws of the state, provision is made for

(i) Administrative enforcement, including necessary facilities, personnel and funding;

(ii) Criminal liability for willful and knowing violation with penalties substantially similar to those prescribed under section 112 of the act, except that more severe criminal penalties may be prescribed;

(iii) Civil liability for failure to comply with the provisions of the state law substantially similar to that provided under sections 130, 131 and 185(b) of the act, except that more severe civil liability penalties may be prescribed;

(iv) In leases where the lessee's liability at the end of the lease term is based on the estimated value of the leased property, a limitation on the lessee's liability at the end of the lease term substantially similar to that provided in section 183(a) of the act, and a provision requiring that penalties be reasonably substantially similar to that provided in section 183(b) of the act, except that stricter standards on end-term liability and penalty provisions may be prescribed; and

(v) A statute of limitations with respect to civil liability of substantially similar duration to that provided under section 185(c) of the act, except that a longer duration may be provided.

. . .

APPENDIX B.   Procedures and Criteria for Board Determination Regarding Preemption

(c) *Criteria for determination.*   The Board will consider the following criteria along with any other relevant information, in addition to the criteria set forth in section 213.7 of this regulation, in making a determination of whether or not state law is inconsistent with a provision of chapter 5. In order for provisions of state law to be determined to be consistent with a provision of chapter 5, the provisions of state law shall, to the extent relevant to the determination, require that—

(1) Definitions and rules of construction import the same meaning and have the same application as those prescribed by this regulation;

(2) Lessors make all of the applicable disclosures required by the corresponding provision of chapter 5 and this regulation, and within the same (or more stringent) time periods as those prescribed by this regulation;

(3) Lessors abide by obligations substantially similar to those prescribed by a provision of chapter 5 under conditions substantially similar (or more stringent) to those in chapter 5;

(4) Lessors abide by the same (or more stringent) prohibitions as are provided by chapter 5;

(5) Lessees need comply with no obligations or responsibilities which are more costly or burdensome as a condition of exercising any of the rights or gaining the benefits and protections provided in the state law, which correspond to those afforded by chapter 5, than those obligations or responsibilities imposed on lessees in chapter 5; and

(6) Lessees are to have rights and protection substantially similar to or more favorable than those provided by the corresponding provisions of chapter 5 under conditions and within time periods which are substantially similar to or more favorable (to lessees) than those prescribed by chapter 5.[5]

. . .

APPENDIX C.   Model Forms

C-1. Model Open-End or Finance Vehicle Lease Disclosures
C-2. Model Closed-End or Net Vehicle Lease Disclosures
C-3. Model Furniture Lease Disclosures [Omitted]

---

[5] A state may make a showing that in certain limited readily identifiable circumstances a law which may otherwise be inconsistent with a provision of chapter 5 is not inconsistent under the criteria set forth in paragraph (c) of this appendix. The Board may determine such state law to be consistent only under those circumstances but will make no such determination if doing so would mislead or confuse lessees.

C-1. Model Open-End or Finance Vehicle Lease Disclosure

Date _____

These disclosures are provided pursuant to the Federal Consumer Leasing Act.

1. LESSOR(S)   LESSEE(S)
   _____   _____
   _____   _____

2. Description of leased property

Year	Make	Model	Body Style	Vehicle ID #

3. (a) Initial Charges consisting of
   ☐ Capital Cost Reduction   ☐ Trade-in Allowance   ☐ _____ $_____

   (b) Other Charges Payable at Inception, consisting of
   ☐ Advance Monthly Payment of _____
   ☐ Refundable Security Deposit   ☐ Delivery Charge $_____
   ☐ Registration Fees   ☐ _____

   Total Payment Due at Inception: $_____

4. (a) Basic Monthly Payment $_____

   (b) Other Charges Payable Monthly:
   ☐ Maintenance   ☐ Registration Fees $_____
   ☐ Insurance   ☐ _____

   Total Monthly Payment. $_____

5. Term of this lease: _____
   The first monthly payment of $_____ is due on _____; _____ subsequent
   payments of $_____ on the _____ of each month thereafter.

6. Total of Basic Monthly Payments: $_____

7. Total of Other Charges Payable to Lessor:
   ☐ Disposition $_____   ☐ Maintenance $_____
   ☐ _____ $_____ $_____

8. Fees and Taxes
   Total amount you will pay during the term for official fees, registration, certificate of title, license fees
   and taxes. $_____

9. Insurance
   The following types and amounts of insurance will be acquired in connection with this lease: _____
   _____
   ☐ We (lessor) will provide the insurance coverage quoted above for a total premium cost of $_____
   ☐ You (lessee) agree to provide insurance coverage in the amounts and types indicated above. $_____

10. Estimated _____ value of the vehicle at the end of lease term: $_____
    (Your liability for this sum may be limited. See Item 14).

11. Total Lease Obligation: $_____
    (Items 3(a), 6 and 10.)
12. Initial Value of Vehicle: $_____
13. Difference: $_____
    (Item 11 less Item 12.)

14. End of Term Liability
    (a) The estimated value of the vehicle stated in Item 10 is based on a reasonable, good faith estimate of the value of the vehicle at the end of the lease term. If the actual value of the vehicle at that time is *greater* than the estimated value, you will have no further liability under this lease, except for other charges already incurred [and are entitled to a credit or refund of any surplus].
        If the actual value of the vehicle is *less* than the estimated value, you will be liable for any difference up to $_____ (3 times Item 4 (a). For any difference in excess of that amount, you will be liable only if:
        1. Excessive use or damage [as described in Item 15] [representing more than normal wear and tear] resulted in an unusually low value at the end of the term.
        2. You voluntarily agree with us after the end of the lease term to make a higher payment.
        3. The matter is not otherwise resolved and we win a lawsuit against you seeking a higher payment.
        Should we bring a lawsuit against you, we must prove that our original estimate of the value of the leased property at the end of the lease term was reasonable and was made in good faith. For example, we might prove that the actual value was less than the original estimated value, although the original estimate was reasonable, because of an unanticipated decline in value for that type of vehicle.
        Unless we prove that the excess amount owed was the result of excessive use or unreasonable wear and tear, we will pay your reasonable attorney's fees.
    (b) If you disagree with the value we assign to the vehicle, you may obtain, at your own expense, from an independent third party agreeable to both of us, a professional appraisal of the _____ value of the leased vehicle which could be realized at sale. The appraised value shall then be used as the actual value.

15. Standards for Wear and Use
The following standards are applicable for determining unreasonable or excessive wear and use of the leased vehicle

_____

16. Maintenance
[You are responsible for the following maintenance and servicing of the leased vehicle: _____

_____]

[We are responsible for the following maintenance and servicing of the leased vehicle: _____

_____]

17. Warranties:
The leased vehicle is subject to the following express warranties: _____

_____

18 Early Termination and Default
(a) You may terminate this lease before the end of the lease term under the following conditions: _____

The charge for such early termination is _____

(b) We may terminate this lease before the end of the lease term under the following conditions: _____

Upon such termination we shall be entitled to the following charge(s) for _____

(c) To the extent these charges take into account the value of the vehicle at the end of the lease term, you have the same right to a professional appraisal as that stated in Item 14(b).

19. Security Interest
We reserve a security interest of the following type in the property listed below to secure performance of your obligations under this lease: _____

_____

20. Late Payments
The charge for late payments is: _____

21. Option to Purchase
[You have an option to purchase the leased vehicle at the following times _____

If at the end of the term, the price will be $_____
If prior to the end of the term, the price will be $_____]

[You have no option to purchse the leased vehicle.]

(C6648)

Instructions for Completion of Model Open-End or Finance Vehicle Lease Disclosures

General Instructions

Completion of this form may be facilitated by reference to the following instructions. Any question to the permissibility or accuracy of a specific disclosure may be answered by reference to Regulation M, 12 CFR Part 213.

Information which is required to be disclosed may be estimated if the information is unknown or unavailable, provided that the information is clearly identified as an estimate, and the estimate is based on the best information available and is reasonable.

Any inapplicable disclosures should be deleted. This form is based on a monthly periodic payment. Any lessor whose lease contemplates a different payment period should change the form where it refers to "monthly" amounts to read "weekly" or other time period, as appropriate.

All numerical amounts must be stated in figures and shall be printed in not less than the equivalent of ten point type or elite typewritten numerals or legibly handwritten. Paragraph numbers need not be printed in ten point type or its equivalent.

Specific Instructions

Item 1.   The disclosures must be made on a written dated statement. All lessors and lessees must be identified by name. If, for example, one person arranges the lease and another person enters into the lease, both must be identified as lessors. An address may augment the identification but need not be supplied as part of the disclosure form.

Item 2.   This disclosure provides a brief description of the leased property. Lessors may include a more detailed description including, for example, special accessories. There is no requirement that a vehicle identification number for the vehicle be disclosed.

Item 3.   This disclosure shows the total amount of any initial payment the customer must make when the lease is entered into. The components of the initial payment *must* be identified and *may*, at the lessor's option, be itemized with respect to dollar amount.

This item is divided into two distinct parts. The items identified in 3(a) are those which are included in the calculation of the "Total Lease Obligation." Those which appear in 3(b) are not included in the "Total Lease Obligation." For convenient reference and to provide the customer with the total amount due at the inception of the lease, subtotals for 3(a) and 3(b) are provided as well as a combined total of 3(a) and 3(b) (shown as "Total Payment Due at Inception").

The term "Capitalized Cost Reduction" is used to indicate payment in the nature of a downpayment which reduces the value of the leased vehicle to be amortized over the term of the lease.

The "Advanced Monthly Payment" is the total of all amounts collected at the inception of the lease which are to be attributed to a monthly payment(s). For example, if the first month's rental payment is collected at the inception, the form might read "Advance Monthly Payment of the first month's rent" or a similar phrase. If the last month's payment, or any other payment in the nature of rental for a portion of the term, is collected at the inception, appropriate language should be provided to describe the components of the "Advance Monthly Payment."

Checklists are provided for both 3(a) and 3(b) to aid in identifying their components. Blank spaces and check boxes are provided to identify any other elements which are to be included in these items.

Item 4.   This item discloses the payment the lessee must make each payment period. This item is divided into two parts. The terms in 4(a) are those portions of each payment which are included in the computation of the "Total Lease Obligation." This item includes sales/use taxes paid on the periodic (monthly) payment. The terms in 4(b) are not included in the "Total Lease Obligation." For convenient reference and to provide the customer with the total amount of each payment, subtotals are provided for 4(a) and 4(b) as well as the combined total of 4(a) and 4(b) (shown as the "Total Monthly Payment"). The components of 4(a) and 4(b) may be itemized as to dollar amount.

Item 5. This item discloses the term of the lease, the date of the first periodic payment and the dates or periods of all subsequent periodic payments. The blank spaces should be filled in with the appropriate terms. For example, after the phrase "Term of this lease:" the lessor may place the words "24 months" or "April 2, 1977, through April 2, 1979" as appropriate. In the blank spaces provided after the phrase "The first monthly payment of:" should be the appropriate amount and date. The first monthly payment may be part or all of the "Advance Monthly Payment" disclosed under 3(b). The phrase "subsequent payments of" should be preceded by the appropriate number of payments and followed with the appropriate terms, such as "$100.00 on the 2d of each month thereafter."

Item 6. This item discloses the total of the basic monthly payments payable over the term of the lease. This figure is computed by multiplying the basic monthly payment from Item 4(a) by the number of subsequent payments in Item 5 and adding to the product the basic portion of the first monthly payment. This figure will be used in computing the "Total Lease Obligation."

Item 7. This item discloses the total of other charges payable to the lessor. This excludes charges for official fees, taxes, insurance and charges disclosed as totals under other items. The individual components must be identified and itemized as to amount. A blank check box is provided in order to add to the list, as necessary.

Item 8. This item discloses the total amount to be paid by the lessee during the lease term for taxes and other official fees.

Item 9. This item requires disclosure of the types and amounts of insurance coverage, with their total premium cost, if the insurance is provided by the lessor. In the alternative, only the types and amounts of coverage required of the lessee must be disclosed if the lessee provides the insurance coverage. The disclosure is to be completed by identifying the types and amounts of insurance coverage following the colon at the end of the first sentence. If the lessor is to provide the coverage the top check box should be filled in and the total premium cost indicated in the blank space provided. Otherwise the bottom check box should be filled in.

Item 10. This item provides for disclosure of the estimated value of the leased vehicle at the end of the term, an element of the "Total Lease Obligation." A blank space is provided in which to indicate whether the value shown is, for example, "retail" or "wholesale" value.

Items 11, 12 and 13. These items provide for disclosure of the difference between the "Total Lease Obligation" and the vehicle's value at the inception of the lease. The definition of "Total Lease Obligation" is the sum of any initial charges (Item 3(a)), the total of basic monthly payments (Item 6) and the estimated value of the property at the end of the term (Item 10). The "Total Lease Obligation" does not include items such as refundable security deposits and insurance premiums.

Item 14. This item provides disclosures with respect to the lessee's liability at the end of the lease term. The bracketed phrase in the second sentence is appropriate only where the lessee will be given any surplus resulting from the disposition. The lessor may, in Item 14(a)1, reference the standards set forth in Item 15, if the lessor set such standards. If the lessor does not set standards for wear and use, the second bracketed phrase should be used. Item 14(b) discloses the lessee's right to an independent appraisal. The blank space in Item 14(b) is provided to indicate whether the value of the appraisal should be, for example, "wholesale" or "retail." This item should be consistent with the type of value used in Item 10.

Item 15.   This item discloses reasonable standards for wear and use established by the lessor. The lessor is permitted but not required to set such standards. Therefore, the disclosure may be omitted by lessors who do not set standards for wear and use.

Item 16.   This item provides for disclosure of the maintenance and servicing responsibilities of the parties. These responsibilities may be allocated either to the lessor or to the lessee, or may be divided between them.

Item 17.   This item discloses all express warranties on the leased property made by the manufacturer or lessor and available to the lessee. A brief identification of the warranty must be supplied. A reference to the standard manufacturer's warranty, for example, would suffice.

Item 18.   This item discloses the conditions under which the lessee may terminate the lease prior to the end of the lease term. It also discloses the amount or method of determining the amount of the charge which the lessee must pay for early termination. This item should disclose the conditions under which the lessor may terminate the lease prior to the end of the term, such as default. This item should also be used to disclose the amount or method of determining the amount of any default charges. The charges or method of determining the charges for early termination by the lessor other than for lessee's default should be separately specified in this item.

Item 19.   This disclosure of the security taken must include, in the space provided, a brief identification of the types of security interests and an identification of the property covered by each.

Item 20.   This disclosure indicates the amount or method of determining the amount of any charges for late payment.

Item 21.   This item provides alternative disclosures covering the several options a lessor may offer to a lessee to purchase the leased property. A lessor should use the disclosures applicable to the lease plan used. For example, if no option to purchase is offered, only the last sentence of the item should be used. If the lessor offers an option to purchase, the times at which it may be exercised must be supplied. The price must be disclosed for an option exercised at the end of the term and the price or method of computing the price for an option exercised during the lease term must be supplied.

C-2. Model Closed-End or Net Vehicle Lease Disclosures

Instructions for Completion of Model Closed-End or Net Vehicle Lease Disclosures

---

Date _____

These disclosures are provided pursuant to the Federal Consumer Leasing Act.

1. LESSOR(S) _____   LESSEE(S) _____

2. Description of leased property

Year	Make	Model	Body Style	Vehicle ID #

3. Total Payment Due at Inception:
   ☐ Capitalized Cost Reduction   ☐ Delivery Charge
   ☐ Trade-in Allowance   ☐ Registration Fees
   ☐ Advance Monthly Payment of _____
   ☐ Refundable Security Deposit   ☐ _____ $_____

4. Term of this lease:
   The first monthly payment of $_____ is due on _____; ____ subsequent payments of $_____ on the _____ of each month thereafter.

5. Total of Monthly Payment: $_____

6. Total of Monthly Payments: $_____

7. Total of Other Charges Payable to Lessor:
   ☐ Disposition $_____   ☐ Maintenance $_____
   ☐ _____ $_____ $_____

8. Fees and Taxes
   Total amount you will pay during the term for official fees, registration, certificate of title, license fees and taxes. $_____

9. Insurance
   The following types and amounts of insurance will be acquired in connection with this lease:

   ☐ We (lessor) will provide the insurance coverage quoted above for a total premium cost of $_____
   ☐ You (lessee) agree to provide insurance coverage in the amounts and types indicated above. $_____

10. Standards for Wear and Use
    The following standards are applicable for determining unreasonable or excessive wear and use of the leased vehicle:
    _____

11. Maintenance
    [You are responsible for the following maintenance and servicing of the leased vehicle: _____]

    [We are responsible for the following maintenance and servicing of the leased vehicle: _____]

12. Warranties
The leased vehicle is subject to the following express warranties: _____
_____
_____

13. Early Termination and Default
(a) You may terminate this lease before the end of the lease term under the following conditions: _____
_____

The charge for such early termination is: _____
_____

(b) We may terminate this lease before the end of the lease term under the following conditions: _____
_____
_____

Upon such termination we shall be entitled to the following charge(s) for _____
_____
_____

(c) To the extent that these charges take into account the value of the vehicle at the end of the lease term, if you disagree with the value we assign to the vehicle, you may obtain at your own expense, from an independent third party agreeable to both of us, a professional appraisal of the _____ value of the leased vehicle which could be realized at sale. The appraised value shall then be used as the actual value.

14. Security Interest
We reserve a security interest of the following type in the property listed below to secure performance of your obligations under this lease: _____
_____
_____

15. Late Payments
The charge for late payments is: _____
_____

16. Lessee's Options to Purchase
[You have an option to purchase the leased vehicle at the following times: _____

If at the end of the term, the price will be $_____
If prior to the end of the term, the price will be $_____]

[You have no option to purchase the leased vehicle.]

[C6650]

General Instructions

Completion of this form may be facilitated by reference to the following instructions. Any question as to the permissibility or accuracy of a specific disclosure may be answered by reference to Regulation M, 12 CFR Part 213.

Information which is required to be disclosed may be estimated if the information is unknown or unavailable, provided that the information is clearly identified as an estimate and the estimate is based on the best information available and is reasonable.

Any inapplicable disclosures should be deleted. This form is based on a monthly periodic payment. Any lessor whose lease contemplates a different payment period should change the form where it refers to "monthly" amounts to read "weekly" or other time period, as appropriate. All numerical amounts must be stated in figures and shall be printed in not less than the equivalent of ten point type or elite typewritten numerals or legibly handwritten. Paragraph numbers need not be printed in ten point type or its equivalent.

Specific Instructions

Item 1. The disclosures must be made on a written dated statement. All lessors and lessees must be identified by name. If, for example, one person arranges the lease and another person enters into the lease, both must be identified as lessors. An address may augment the identification but need not be supplied as part of the disclosure form.

Item 2. This disclosure provides a brief description of the leased property. Lessors may include a more detailed description including, for example, special accessories. There is no requirement that a vehicle identification number for the vehicle be disclosed.

Item 3. This disclosure shows the total amount of any initial payment the customer must make when the lease is entered into. The components of the initial payment *must* be identified and *may*, at the lessor's option, be itemized with respect to dollar amount.

The term "Capitalized Cost Reduction" is used to indicate a payment in the nature of a downpayment which reduces the value of the leased vehicle to be amortized over the term of the lease.

The "Advance Monthly Payment" is the total of all amounts collected at the inception of the lease which are to be attributed to a monthly payment(s). For example, if the first month's rental payment is collected at the inception, the form might read "Advance Monthly Payment" of the first month's rent" or a similar phrase. If the last month's payment, or any other payment in the nature of rental for a portion of the term, is collected at the inception, appropriate language should be provided to describe the components of the "Advance Monthly Payment."

Checklists are provided to aid in identifying the components. Blank spaces and check boxes are provided to identify any other elements which are to be included in this item.

Item 4. This item discloses the term of the lease, the date of the first periodic payment and the dates or periods of all subsequent periodic payments. The blank spaces should be filled in with the appropriate terms. For example, after the phrase "Term of this lease:" the lessor may place the words "24 months" or "April 2, 1977, through April 2, 1979," as appropriate. In the blank spaces provided after the phrase "The first monthly payment of:" should be the appropriate amount and date. The first monthly payment may be part or all of the "Advance Monthly Payment" disclosed under Item 3. The phrase "subsequent payments of" should be preceded by the appropriate number of payments and followed with the appropriate terms, such as "$100.00 on the 2d of each month thereafter."

Item 5. This item discloses the payment the lessee must make each payment period. The component parts of the "Total Monthly Payment" may but need not be identified and itemized as to amount.

Item 6. This item discloses the total of the monthly payments payable over the term of the lease. This figure is computed by multiplying the monthly payment from Item 5 by the number of subsequent payments in Item 4 and adding the first monthly payment to the product.

Item 7. This item discloses the total of other charges payable to the lessor. This excludes charges for official fees, taxes, insurance and charges disclosed as totals under other items. The individual components must be identified and itemized as to amount. A blank check box is provided in order to add to the list, as necessary.

Item 8.   This item discloses the total amount to be paid by the lessee during the lease term for taxes and other official fees.

Item 9.   This item requires disclosure of the types and amounts of insurance coverage, with their total premium cost, if the insurance is provided by the lessor. In the alternative, only the types and amounts of coverage required of the lessee must be disclosed if the lessee provides the insurance coverage. The disclosure is to be completed by identifying the types and amounts of insurance coverage following the colon at the end of the first sentence. If the lessor is to provide the coverage the top check box should be filled in and the total premium cost indicated in the blank space provided. Otherwise the bottom check box should be filled in.

Item 10.   This item discloses reasonable standards for wear and use established by the lessor. The lessor is permitted but not required to set such standards. Therefore, the disclosure may be omitted by lessors who do not set standards for wear and use.

Item 11.   This item provides for disclosure of the maintenance and servicing responsibilities of the parties. These responsibilities may be allocated either to the lessor or to the lessee, or may be divided between them.

Item 12.   This item discloses all express warranties on the leased property made by the manufacturer or lessor and available to the lessee. A brief identification of the warranty must be supplied. A reference to the standard manufacturer's warranty, for example, would suffice.

Item 13.   This item discloses the conditions under which the lessee may terminate the lease prior to the end of the lease term. It also discloses the amount or method of determining the amount of the charge which the lessee must pay for early termination. This item should disclose the conditions under which the lessor may terminate the lease prior to the end of the term, such as default. This item should also be used to disclose the amount or method of determining the amount of any default charges. The charges or method of determining the charges for early termination by the lessor other than for lessee's default should be separately specified in this item. The blank space in 13(c) is provided to indicate whether the appraisal should be, for example, "retail" or "wholesale."

Item 14.   This disclosure of the security taken must include, in the space provided, a brief identification of the types of security interests and an identification of the property covered by each.

Item 15.   This disclosure indicates the amount or method of determining the amount of any charges for late payment.

Item 16.   This item provides alternative disclosures covering the several options a lessor may offer to a lessee to purchase the leased property. A lessor should use the disclosures applicable to the leased plan used. For example, if no option to purchase is offered, only the last sentence of the item should be used. If the lessor offers an option to purchase, the times at which it may be exercised must be supplied. The price must be disclosed for an option exercised at the end of the term and the price or method of computing the price for an option exercised during the lease term must be supplied.

Appendix D
Title III. Restriction on Garnishment

(15 U.S.C. §§1671-1677)

Table of Sections

---

§301. Findings [15 U.S.C. §1671]

(a) The Congress finds:

(1) The unrestricted garnishment of compensation due for personal services encourages the making of predatory extensions of credit. Such extensions of credit divert money into excessive credit payments and thereby hinder the production and flow of goods in interstate commerce.

(2) The application of garnishment as a creditors' remedy frequently results in loss of employment by the debtor, and the resulting disruption of employment, production, and consumption constitutes a substantial burden on interstate commerce.

(3) The great disparities among the laws of the several States relating to garnishment have, in effect, destroyed the uniformity of the bankruptcy laws and frustrated the purposes thereof in many areas of the country.

(b) On the basis of the findings stated in subsection (a) of this section, the Congress determines that the provisions of this title are necessary and proper for the purpose of carrying into execution the powers of the Congress to regulate commerce and to establish uniform bankruptcy laws.

§302. Definitions [15 U.S.C. §1672]

For the purposes of this title:

(a) The term "earnings" means compensation paid or payable for personal services, whether denominated as wages, salary, commission, bonus, or otherwise, and includes periodic payments pursuant to a pension or retirement program.

(b) The term "disposable earnings" means that part of the earnings of any

505

individual remaining after the deduction from those earnings of any amounts required by law to be withheld.

(c) The term "garnishment" means any legal or equitable procedure through which the earnings of any individual are required to be withheld for payment of any debt.

§303.   Restriction on garnishment [15 U.S.C. §1673]

(a) Except as provided in subsection (b) of this section and in section 305, the maximum part of the aggregate disposable earnings of an individual for any workweek which is subjected to garnishment may not exceed

(1) 25 per centum of his disposable earnings for that week, or

(2) the amount by which his disposable earnings for that week exceed thirty times the Federal minimum hourly wage prescribed by section 6(a)(1) of the Fair Labor Standards Act of 1938 in effect at the time the earnings are payable,

whichever is less. In the case of earnings for any pay period other than a week, the Secretary of Labor shall be regulation prescribe a multiple of the Federal minimum hourly wage equivalent in effect to that set forth in paragraph (2).

(b)(1) The restrictions of subsection (a) of this section do not apply in the case of

(A) any order for the support of any person issued by a court of competent jurisdiction or in accordance with an administrative procedure, which is established by State law, which affords substantial due process, and which is subject to judicial review.

(B) any order of any court of the United States having jurisdiction over cases under chapter 13 of Title 11.

(C) any debt due for any State or Federal tax.

(2) The maximum part of the aggregate disposable earnings of an individual for any workweek which is subject to garnishment to enforce any order for the support of any person shall not exceed—

(A) where such individual is supporting his spouse or dependent child (other than a spouse or child with respect to whose support such order is used), 50 per centum of such individual's disposable earnings for that week; and

(B) where such individual is not supporting such a spouse or dependent child described in clause (A), 60 per centum of such individual's disposable earnings for that week;

except that, with respect to the disposable earnings of any individual for any workweek, the 50 per centum specified in clause (A) shall be deemed to be 55 per centum and the 60 per centum specified in clause (B) shall be deemed to be 65 per centum, if and to the extent that such earnings are subject to garnishment to enforce a support order with respect to a period which is prior to the twelve-week period which ends with the beginning of such workweek.

(C) No court of the United States or any State, and no State (or officer or agency thereof), may make, execute, or enforce any order or process in violation of this section.

§304. Restriction on discharge from employment by reason of garnishment [15 U.S.C. §1674]

(a) No employer may discharge any employee by reason of the fact that his earnings have been subjected to garnishment for any one indebtedness.

(b) Whoever willfully violates subsection (a) of this section shall be fined not more than $1,000, or imprisoned not more than one year, or both.

§305. Exemption for State-regulated garnishment [15 U.S.C. §1675]

The Secretary of Labor may be regulation exempt from the provisions of section 303(a) and (b)(2) of this title garnishments issued under the laws of any State if he determines that the laws of that State provide restrictions on garnishment which are substantially similar to those provided in section 303(a) and (b)(2).

§306. Enforcement by Secretary of Labor [15 U.S.C. §1676]

The Secretary of Labor, acting through the Wage and Hour Division of the Department of Labor, shall enforce the provisions of this title.

§307. Effect on State laws [15 U.S.C. §1677]

This title does not annul, alter, or affect, or exempt any person from complying with, the laws of any State

(1) prohibiting garnishments or providing for more limited garnishments than are allowed under this title, or

(2) prohibiting the discharge of any employee by reason of the fact that his earnings have been subjected to garnishment for more than one indebtedness.

APPENDIX E
Title VI. Fair Credit Reporting Act

(15 U.S.C. §§1681-1681t)

Table of Sections

---

§601. Short title

This title may be cited as the Fair Credit Reporting Act.

§602. Findings and purpose [15 U.S.C. §1681]

(a) The Congress makes the following findings:

(1) The banking system is dependent upon fair and accurate credit reporting. Inaccurate credit reports directly impair the efficiency of the banking system, and unfair credit reporting methods undermine the public confidence which is essential to the continued functioning of the banking system.

(2) An elaborate mechanism has been developed for investigating and

evaluating the credit worthiness, credit standing, credit capacity, character, and general reputation of consumers.

(3) Consumer reporting agencies have assumed a vital role in assembling and evaluating consumer credit and other information on consumers.

(4) There is a need to insurance that consumer reporting agencies exercise their grave responsibilities with fairness, impartiality, and a respect for the consumer's right to privacy.

(b) It is the purpose of this title to require that consumer reporting agencies adopt reasonable procedures for meeting the needs of commerce for consumer credit, personnel, insurance, and other information in a manner which is fair and equitable to the consumer, with regard to the confidentiality, accuracy, relevancy, and proper utilization of such information in accordance with the requirements of this title.

§603.   Definitions and rules of construction [15 U.S.C. §1681a]

(a) Definitions and rules of construction set forth in this section are applicable for the purposes of this title.

(b) The term "person" means any individual, partnership, corporation, trust, estate, cooperative, association, government or governmental subdivision or agency, or other entity.

(c) The term "consumer" means an individual.

(d) The term "consumer report" means any written, oral, or other communication of any information by a consumer reporting agency bearing on a consumer's credit worthiness, credit standing, credit capacity, character, general reputation, personal characteristics, or mode of living which is used or expected to be used or collected in whole or in part for the purpose of serving as a factor in establishing the consumer's eligibility for (1) credit or insurance to be used primarily for personal, family, or household purposes, or (2) employment purposes, or (3) other purposes authorized under section 604. The term does not include (A) any report containing information solely as to transactions or experiences between the consumer and the person making the report; (B) any authorization or approval of a specific extension of credit directly or indirectly by the issuer of a credit card or similar device; or (C) any report in which a person who has been requested by a third party to make a specific extension of credit directly or indirectly to a consumer conveys his decision with respect to such request, if the third party advises the consumer of the name and address of the person to whom the request was made and such person makes the disclosures to the consumer required under section 615.

(e) The term "investigative consumer report" means a consumer report or portion thereof in which information on a consumer's character, general reputation, personal characteristics, or mode of living is obtained through personal interviews with neighbors, friends, or associates of the consumer reported on or with others with whom he is acquainted or who may have knowledge concerning any such items of information. However, such information shall not include specific factual information on a consumer's credit record obtained directly from a creditor of the consumer or from a consumer reporting agency when such information was obtained directly from a creditor of the consumer or from the consumer.

(f) The term "consumer reporting agency" means any person which, for monetary fees, dues, or on a cooperative nonprofit basis, regularly engages in whole or in part in the practice of assembling or evaluating consumer credit information or other information on consumers for the purpose of furnishing consumer reports to third parties, and which uses any means or facility of interstate commerce for the purpose of preparing or furnishing consumer reports.

(g) The term "file", when used in connection with information on any consumer, means all of the information on that consumer recorded and retained by a consumer reporting agency regardless of how the information is stored.

(h) The term "employment purposes" when used in connection with a consumer report means a report used for the purpose of evaluating a consumer for employment, promotion, reassignment or retention as an employee.

(i) The term "medical information" means information or records obtained, with the consent of the individual to whom it relates, from licensed physicians or medical practitioners, hospitals, clinics, or other medical or medically related facilities.

§604. Permissible purposes of reports [15 U.S.C. §1681b]

A consumer reporting agency may furnish a consumer report under the following circumstances and no other:

(1) In response to the order of a court having jurisdiction to issue such an order.

(2) In accordance with the written instructions of the consumer to whom it relates.

(3) To a person which it has reason to believe—

(A) intends to use the information in connection with a credit transaction involving the consumer on whom the information is to be furnished and involving the extension of credit to, or review or collection of an account of, the consumer; or

(B) intends to use the information for employment purposes; or

(C) intends to use the information in connection with the underwriting of insurance involving the consumer; or

(D) intends to use the information in connection with a determination of the consumer's eligibility for a license or other benefit granted by a governmental instrumentality required by law to consider an applicant's financial responsibility or status; or

(E) otherwise has a legitimate business need for the information in connection with a business transaction involving the consumer.

§605. Obsolete information [15 U.S.C. §1681c]

(a Except as authorized under subsection (b) of this section, no consumer reporting agency may make any consumer report containing any of the following items of information:

(1) Cases under Title 11 or under the Bankruptcy Act that, from the date of entry of the order for relief or the date of adjudication, as the case may be, antedate the report by more than 10 years.

(2) Suits and judgments which, from date of entry, antedate the report by more than seven years or until the governing statute of limitations has expired, whichever is the longer period.

(3) Paid tax liens which, from date of payment, antedate the report by more than seven years.

(4) Accounts placed for collection or charged to profit and loss which antedate the report by more than seven years.

(5) Records of arrest, indictment, or conviction of crime which, from date of disposition, release, or parole, antedate the report by more than seven years.

(6) Any other adverse item of information which antedates the report by more than seven years.

(b) The provisions of subsection (a) of this section are not applicable in the case of any consumer credit report to be used in connection with—

(1) a credit transaction involving, or which may reasonably be expected to involve, a principal amount of $50,000 or more;

(2) the underwriting of life insurance involving, or which may reasonably be expected to involve, a face amount of $50,000 or more; or

(3) the employment of any individual at an annual salary which equals, or which may reasonably be expected to equal $20,000, or more.

§606. Disclosure of investigative consumer reports [15 U.S.C. §1681d]

(a) A person may not procure or cause to be prepared an investigative consumer report on any consumer unless—

(1) it is clearly and accurately disclosed to the consumer that an investigative consumer report including information as to his character, general reputation, personal characteristics, and mode of living, whichever are applicable, may be made, and such disclosure (A) is made in a writing mailed, or otherwise delivered, to the consumer, not later than three days after the date on which the report was first requested, and (B) includes a statement informing the consumer of his right to request the additional disclosures provided for under subsection (b) of this section; or

(2) the report is to be used for employment purposes for which the consumer has not specifically applied.

(b) Any person who procures or causes to be prepared an investigative consumer report on any consumer shall, upon written request made by the consumer within a reasonable period of time after the receipt by him of the disclosure required by subsection (a)(1) of this section, make a complete and accurate disclosure of the nature and scope of the investigation requested. This disclosure shall be made in a writing mailed, or otherwise delivered, to the consumer not later than five days after the date on which the request for such disclosure was received from the consumer or such report was first requested, whichever is the later.

(c) No person may be held liable for any violation of subsection (a) or (b) of this section if he shows by a preponderance of the evidence that at the time of the violation he maintained reasonable procedures to assure compliance with subsection (a) or (b) of this section.

§607. Compliance procedures [15 U.S.C. §1681e]

(a) Every consumer reporting agency shall maintain reasonable procedures designed to avoid violations of section 1681c of this title and to limit the furnishing of consumer reports to the purposes listed under section 1681b of this title. These procedures shall require that prospective users of the information identify themselves, certify the purposes for which the information is sought, and certify that the information will be used for no other purpose. Every consumer reporting agency shall make a reasonable effort to verify the identity of a new prospective user and the uses certified by such prospective user prior to furnishing such user a consumer report. No consumer reporting agency may furnish a consumer report to any person if it has reasonable grounds for believing that the consumer report will not be used for a purpose listed in section 604.

(b) Whenever a consumer reporting agency prepares a consumer report it shall follow reasonable procedures to assure maximum possible accuracy of the information concerning the individual about whom the report relates.

§608. Disclosures to governmental agencies [15 U.S.C. §1681f]

Notwithstanding the provisions of section 604, a consumer reporting agency may furnish identifying information respecting any consumer, limited to his name, address, former addresses, places of employment, or former places of employment, to a governmental agency.

§609. Disclosures to consumers [15 U.S.C. §1681g]

(a) Every consumer reporting agency shall, upon request and proper identification of any consumer, clearly and accurately disclose to the consumer:

(1) The nature and substance of all information (except medical information) in its files on the consumer at the time of the request.

(2) The sources of the information; except that the sources of information

acquired solely for use in preparing an investigative consumer report and actually used for no other purpose need not be disclosed: *Provided*, That in the event an action is brought under this subchapter, such sources shall be available to the plaintiff under appropriate discovery procedures in the court in which the action is brought.

(3) The recipients of any consumer report on the consumer which it has furnished—

(A) for employment purposes within the two-year period preceding the request, and

(B) for any other purpose within the six-month period preceding the request.

(b) The requirements of subsection (a) of this section respecting the disclosure of sources of information and the recipients of consumer reports do not apply to information received or consumer reports furnished prior to the effective date of this subchapter except to the extent that the matter involved is contained in the files of the consumer reporting agency on that date.

§610. Conditions of disclosure to consumers [15 U.S.C. §1681h]

(a) A consumer reporting agency shall make the disclosures required under section 609 during normal business hours and on reasonable notice.

(b) The disclosures required under section 609 shall be made to the consumer—

(1) in person if he appears in person and furnishes proper identification; or

(2) by telephone if he has made a written request, with proper identification, for telephone disclosure and the toll charge, if any, for the telephone call is prepaid by or charged directly to the consumer.

(c) Any consumer reporting agency shall provide trained personnel to explain to the consumer any information furnished to him pursuant to section 609.

(d) The consumer shall be permitted to be accompanied by one other person of his choosing, who shall furnish reasonable identification. A consumer reporting agency may require the consumer to furnish a written statement granting permission to the consumer reporting agency to discuss the consumer's file in such person's presence.

(e) Except as provided in sections 616 and 617, no consumer may bring any action or proceeding in the nature of defamation, invasion of privacy, or negligence with respect to the reporting of information against any consumer reporting agency, any user of information, or any person who furnishes information to a consumer reporting agency, based on information disclosed pursuant to section 609, 610, or 615, except as to false information furnished with malice or willful intent to injure such consumer.

§611.   Procedure in case of disputed accuracy [15 U.S.C. §1681i]

(a) If the completeness or accuracy of any item of information contained in his file is disputed by a consumer, and such dispute is directly conveyed to the consumer reporting agency by the consumer, the consumer reporting agency shall within a reasonable period of time reinvestigate and record the current status of that information unless it has reasonable grounds to believe that the dispute by the consumer is frivolous or irrelevant. If after such reinvestigation such information is found to be inaccurate or can no longer be verified, the consumer reporting agency shall promptly delete such information. The presence of contradictory information in the consumer's file does not in and of itself constitute reasonable grounds for believing the dispute is frivolous or irrelevant.

(b) If the reinvestigation does not resolve the dispute, the consumer may file a brief statement setting forth the nature of the dispute. The consumer reporting agency may limit such statements to not more than one hundred words if it provides the consumer with assistance in writing a clear summary of the dispute.

(c) Whenever a statement of a dispute is filed, unless there is reasonable grounds to believe that it is frivolous or irrelevant, the consumer reporting agency shall, in any subsequent consumer report containing the information in question, clearly note that it is disputed by the consumer and provide either the consumer's statement or a clear and accurate codification or summary thereof.

(d) Following any deletion of information which is found to be inaccurate or whose accuracy can no longer be verified or any notation as to disputed information, the consumer reporting agency shall, at the request of the consumer, furnish notification that the item has been deleted or the statement codification or summary pursuant to subsection (b) or (c) of this section to any person specifically designated by the consumer who has within two years prior thereto received a consumer report for employment purposes, or within six months prior thereto received a consumer report for any other purpose, which contained the deleted or disputed information. The consumer reporting agency shall clearly and conspicuously disclose to the consumer his rights to make such a request. Such disclosure shall be made at or prior to the time the information is deleted or the consumer's statement regarding the disputed information is received.

§612.   Charges for certain disclosures [15 U.S.C. §1681j]

A consumer reporting agency shall make all disclosures pursuant to section 609 and furnish all consumer reports pursuant to section 611d without charge to the consumer if, within thirty days after receipt by such consumer of a notification pursuant to section 615 of this title or notification from a debt collection agency affiliated with such consumer reporting agency stating that the consumer's credit rating may be or has been adversely affected, the consumer makes a request under section 609 or 611(d). Otherwise, the consumer reporting agency may impose a reasonable charge on the consumer for making disclosure to such consumer pursuant to section 609, the charge for which shall be indicated to the consumer prior to making disclosure; and for furnishing notifications, statements, summaries, or codifications to persons designated by the consumer pursuant to section 611(d), the charge for which shall be indicated to the consumer prior to furnishing such information and shall not exceed the charge that the consumer reporting agency would impose on each designated receipient for a consumer report except that no charge may be made for notifying such persons of the deletion of information which is found to be inaccurate or which can no longer be verified.

§613. Public record information for employment purposes [15 U.S.C. §1681k]

A consumer reporting agency which furnishes a consumer report for employment purposes and which for that purpose compiles and reports items of information on consumers which are matters of public record and are likely to have an adverse effect upon a consumer's ability to obtain employment shall—

(1) at the time such public record information is reported to the user of such consumer report, notify the consumer of the fact that public record information is being reported by the consumer reporting agency, together with the name and address of the person to whom such information is being reported; or

(2) maintain strict procedures designed to insure that whenever public record information which is likely to have an adverse effect on a consumer's ability to obtain employment is reported it is complete and up to date. For purposes of this paragraph, items of public record relating to arrests, indictments, convictions, suits, tax liens, and outstanding judgments shall be considered up to date if the current public record status of the item at the time of the report is reported.

§614. Restrictions on investigative consumer reports [15 U.S.C. §1681

Whenever a consumer reporting agency prepares an investigative consumer report, no adverse information in the consumer report (other than information which is a matter of public record) may be included in a subsequent consumer report unless such adverse information has been verified in the process of making such subsequent consumer report, or the adverse information was received within the three-month period preceding the date the subsequent report is furnished.

§615.   Requirements on users of consumer reports [15 U.S.C. §1681m]

(a) Whenever credit or insurance for personal, family, or household purposes, or employment involving a consumer is denied or the charge for such credit or insurance is increased either wholly or partly because of information contained in a consumer report from a consumer reporting agency, the user of the consumer report shall so advise the consumer against whom such adverse action has been taken and supply the name and address of the consumer reporting agency making the report.

(b) Whenever credit for personal, family, or household purposes involving a consumer is denied or the charge for such credit is increased either wholly or partly because of information obtained from a person other than a consumer reporting agency bearing upon the consumer's credit worthiness, credit standing, credit capacity, character, general reputation, personal characteristics, or mode of living, the user of such information shall, within a reasonable period of time, upon the consumer's written request for the reasons for such adverse action received within sixty days after learning of such adverse action, disclose the nature of the information to the consumer. The user of such information shall clearly and accurately disclose to the consumer his right to make such written request at the time such adverse action is communicated to the consumer.

(c) No person shall be held liable for any violation of this section if he shows a preponderance of the evidence that at the time of the alleged violation he maintained reasonable procedures to assure compliance with the provisions of subsections (a) and (b) of this section.

§616.   Civil liability for willful noncompliance [15 U.S.C. §1681n]

Any consumer reporting agency or user of information which willfully fails to comply with any requirement imposed under this title with respect to any consumer is liable to that consumer in an amount equal to the sum of—

(1) any actual damages sustained by the consumer as a result of the failure;

(2) such amount of punitive damages as the court may allow; and

(3) in the case of any successful action to enforce any liability under this section, the costs of the action together with reasonable attorney's fees as determined by the court.

§617.   Civil liability for negligent noncompliance [15 U.S.C. §1681o]

Any consumer reporting agency or user of information which is negligent in failing to comply with any requirement imposed under this title with respect to any consumer is liable to that consumer in an amount equal to the sum of—

(1) any actual damage sustained by the consumer as a result of the failure;

(2) in the case of any successful action to enforce any liability under this section, the costs of the action together with reasonable attorney's fees as determined by the court.

§618. Jurisdiction of courts; limitation of actions [15 U.S.C. §1681p]

An action to enforce any liability created under this title may be brought in any appropriate United States district court without regard to the amount in controversy, or in any other court of competent jurisdiction, within two years from the date on which the liability arises, except that where a defendant has materially and willfully misrepresented any information required under this title to be disclosed to an individual and the information so misrepresented is material to the establishment of the defendant's liability to that individual under this title, the action may be brought at any time within two years after discovery by the individual of the misrepresentation.

§619. Obtaining information under false pretenses [15 U.S.C. §1681q]

Any person who knowingly and willfully obtains information on a consumer from a consumer reporting agency under false pretenses shall be fined nor more than $5,000 or imprisoned not more than one year, or both.

§620. Unauthorized disclosures by officers or employees [15 U.S.C. §1681r]

Any officer or employee of a consumer reporting agency who knowingly and willfully provides information concerning an individual from the agency's files to a person not authorized to receive that information shall be fined not more than $5,000 or imprisoned not more than one year, or both.

§621. Administrative enforcement [15 U.S.C. §1681s]

(a) Compliance with the requirements imposed under this title shall be enforced under the Federal Trade Commission Act by the Federal Trade Commission with respect to consumer reporting agencies and all other persons subject thereto, except to the extent that enforcement of the requirements imposed under this title is specifically committed to some other government agency under subsection (b) hereof. For the purpose of the exercise by the Federal Trade Commission of its functions and powers under the Federal Trade Commission Act, a violation of any requirement or prohibition imposed under this title shall constitute an unfair or deceptive act or practice in commerce in violation of section 5(a) of the Federal Trade Commission Act and shall be subject to enforcement by the Federal Trade Commission under section 5(b) thereof with respect to any consumer reporting agency or person subject to enforcement by the Federal Trade Commission pursuant to this subsection, irrespective of whether that person is engaged in commerce or meets any other jurisdictional tests in the Federal Trade Commission Act. The Federal Trade Commission shall have such procedural, investigative, and enforcement powers, including the power to issue procedural rules in enforcing compliance with the requirements imposed under this title and to require the filing of reports, the production of documents, and the appearance of witnesses as though the applicable terms and conditions of the Federal Trade Commission Act were part of this title. Any person violating any of the provisions of this title shall be subject to the penalties and entitled to the privileges and immunities provided in the Federal Trade Commission Act as though the applicable terms and provisions thereof were part of this title.

(b) Compliance with the requirements imposed under this title with respect to consumer reporting agencies and persons who use consumer reports from such agencies shall be enforced under—

(1) section 8 of the Federal Deposit Insurance Act, in the case of:

(A) national banks, by the Comptroller of the Currency;

(B) member banks of the Federal Reserve System (other than national banks), by the Federal Reserve Board; and

(C) banks insured by the Federal Deposit Insurance Corporation (other than members of the Federal Reserve System), by the Board of Directors of the Federal Deposit Insurance Corporation.

(2) section 5(d) of the Home Owners Loan Act of 1933, section 407 of the National Housing Act, and sections 6(i) and 17 of the Federal Home Loan Bank Act, by the Federal Home Loan Bank Board (acting directly or through the Federal Savings and Loan Insurance Corporation), in the case of any institution subject to any of those provisions;

(3) the Federal Credit Union Act, by the Administrator of the National Credit Union Administration with respect to any Federal credit union;

(4) the Acts to regulate commerce, by the Interstate Commerce Commission with respect to any common carrier subject to those Acts;

(5) the Federal Aviation Act of 1958, by the Civil Aeronautics Board with respect to any air carrier or foreign air carrier subject to that Act; and

(6) the Packers and Stockyards Act, 1921 (except as provided in section 406 of that Act), by the Secretary of Agriculture with respect to any activities subject to that Act.

(c) For the purpose of the exercise by any agency referred to in subsection (b) of this section of its powers under any Act referred to in that subsection, a violation of any requirement imposed under this title shall be deemed to be a violation of a requirement imposed under that Act. In addition to its powers under any provision of law specifically referred to in subsection (b) of this section, each of the agencies referred to in that subsection may exercise, for the purpose of enforcing compliance with any requirement imposed under this title any other authority conferred on it by law.

§622.   Relation to State laws [15 U.S.C. §1681t]

This title does not annul, alter, affect, or exempt any person subject to the provisions of this subchapter from complying with the laws of any State with respect to the collection, distribution, or use of any information on consumers, except to the extent that those laws are inconsistent with any provision of this title and then only to the extent of the inconsistency.

Appendix F
Title VII. Equal Credit Opportunity Act

(15 U.S.C. §§1691-161f)

Table of Sections

---

§701. Prohibited discrimination; reasons for adverse action [15 U.S.C. §1691]

(a) It shall be unlawful for any creditor to discriminate against any applicant, with respect to any aspect of a credit transaction—

(1) on the basis of race, color, religion, national origin, sex or marital status, or age (provided the applicant has the capacity to contract);

(2) because all or part of the applicant's income derives from any public assistance program; or

(3) because the applicant has in good faith exercised any right under this chapter.

(b) It shall not constitute discrimination for purposes of this title for a creditor—

(1) to make an inquiry of marital status if such inquiry is for the purpose of ascertaining the creditor's rights and remedies applicable to the particular extension of credit and not to discriminate in a determination of credit-worthiness;

(2) to make an inquiry of the applicant's age or of whether the applicant's income derives from any public assistance program if such inquiry is for the purpose of determining the amount and probable continuance of income levels, credit history, or other pertinent element of credit-worthiness as provided in regulations of the Board;

(3) to use any empirically derived credit system which considers age if such system is demonstrably and statistically sound in accordance with regulations

520

of the Board, except that in the operation of such system the age of an elderly applicant may not be assigned a negative factor or value; or

(4) to make an inquiry or to consider the age of an elderly applicant when the age of such applicant is to be used by the creditor in the extension of credit in favor of such applicant.

(c) It is not a violation of this section for a creditor to refuse to extend credit offered pursuant to—

(1) any credit assistance program expressly authorized by law for an economically disadvantaged class of persons;

(2) any credit assistance program administered by a nonprofit organization for its members or an economically disadvantaged class of persons; or

(3) any special purpose credit program offered by a profit-making organization to meet special social needs which meets standards prescribed in regulations by the Board;

if such refusal is required by or made pursuant to such program.

(d)(1) Within thirty days (or such longer reasonable time as specified in regulations of the Board for any class of credit transaction) after receipt of a completed application for credit, a creditor shall notify the applicant of its action on the application.

(2) Each applicant against whom adverse action is taken shall be entitled to a statement of reasons for such action from the creditor. A creditor satisfies this obligation by—

(A) providing statements of reasons in writing as a matter of course to applicants against whom adverse action is taken; or

(B) giving written notification of adverse action which discloses (i) the applicant's right to a statement of reasons within thirty days after receipt by the creditor of a request made within sixty days after such notification, and (ii) the identity of the person or office from which such statement may be obtained. Such statement may be given orally if the written notification advises the applicant of his right to have the statement of reasons confirmed in writing on written request.

(3) A statement of reasons meets the requirements of this section only if it contains the specific reasons for the adverse action taken.

(4) Where a creditor has been requested by a third party to make a specific extension of credit directly or indirectly to an applicant, the notification and statement of reasons required by this subsection may be made directly by such creditor, or indirectly through the third party, provided in either case that the identity of the creditor is disclosed.

(5) The requirements of paragraph (2), (3), or (4) may be satisfied by verbal statements or notifications in the case of any creditor who did not act on more than one hundred and fifty applications during the calender year preceding the calender year in which the adverse action is taken, as determined under regulations of the Board.

(6) For purposes of this subsection, the term "adverse action" means a denial or revocation of credit, a change in the terms of an existing credit arrangement, or a refusal to grant credit in substantially the amount or on

substantially the terms requested. Such term does not include a refusal to extend additional credit under an existing credit arrangement where the applicant is delinquent or otherwise in default, or where such additional credit would exceed a previously established credit limit.

§702.   Definitions [15 U.S.C. §1691a]

(a) The definitions and rules of construction set forth in this section are applicable for the purposes of this title.

(b) The term "applicant" means any person who applies to a creditor directly for an extension, renewal, or continuation of credit, or applies to a creditor indirectly by use of an existing credit plan for an amount exceeding a previously established credit limit.

(c) The term "Board" refers to the Board of Governors of the Federal Reserve System.

(d) The term "credit" means the right granted by a creditor to a debtor to defer payment of debt or to incur debts and defer its payment or to purchase property or services and defer payment therefor.

(e) The term "creditor" means any person who regularly extends, renews, or continues credit; any person who regularly arranges for the extension, renewal, or continuation of credit; or any assignee of an original creditor who participates in the decision to extend, renew, or continue credit.

(f) The term "person" means a natural person, a corporation, government or governmental subdivision or agency, trust, estate, partnership, cooperative, or association.

(g) Any reference to any requirement imposed under this title or any provision thereof includes reference to the regulations of the Board under this title or the provision thereof in question.

§703.   Regulations [15 U.S.C. §1691b]

(a) The Board shall prescribe regulations to carry out the purposes of this title. These regulations may contain but are not limited to such classifications, differentiation, or other provision, and may provide for such adjustments and exceptions for any class of transactions, as in the judgment of the Board are necessary or proper to effectuate the purposes of this title, to prevent circumvention or evasion thereof, or to facilitate or substantiate compliance therewith. In particular, such regulations may exempt from one or more of the provisions of this subchapter any class of transactions not primarily for personal, family, or household purposes, if the Board makes an express finding that the application of such provision or provisions would not contribute substantially to carrying out the purposes of this title. Such regulations shall be prescribed as soon as possible after the date of enactment of this Act, but in no event later than the effective date of this Act.

(b) The Board shall establish a Consumer Advisory Council to advise and consult with it in the exercise of its functions under the Consumer Credit Protection Act and to advise and consult with it concerning other consumer related matters it may place before the Council. In appointing the members of the Council, the Board shall seek to achieve a fair representation of the interests of creditors and consumers. The Council shall meet from time to time at the call of the Board. Members of the Council who are not regular full-time employees of the United States shall, while attending meetings of such Council, be entitled to receive compensation at a rate fixed by the Board, but not exceeding $100 per day, including travel time. Such members may be allowed travel expenses, including transportation and subsistence, while away from their homes or regular place of business.

§704. Administrative enforcement [15 U.S.C. §1691c]

(a) Compliance with the requirements imposed under this title shall be enforced under:

(1) Section 8 of the Federal Deposit Insurance Act, in the case of—

(A) national banks, by the Comptroller of the Currency,

(B) member banks of the Federal Reserve System (other than national banks), by the Board,

(C) banks insured by the Federal Deposit Insurance Corporation (other than members of the Federal Reserve System), by the Board of Directors of the Federal Deposit Insurance Corporation.

(2) Section 5(d) of the Home Owners' Loan Act of 1933, section 407 of National Housing Act, and sections 6(i) and 17 of the Federal Home Loan Bank Act, by the Federal Home Loan Bank Board (acting directly or through the Federal Savings and Loan Insurance Corporation), in the case of any institution subject to any of those provisions.

(3) The Federal Credit Union Act, by the Administrator of the National Credit Union Administration with respect to any Federal Credit Union.

(4) The Acts to regulate commerce, by the Interstate Commerce Commission with respect to any common carrier subject to those Acts.

(5) The Federal Aviation Act of 1958, by the Civil Aeronautics Board with respect to any air carrier or foreign air carrier subject to that Act.

(6) The Packers and Stockyards Act, 1921 (except as provided in section 406 of that Act), by the Secretary of Agriculture with respect to any activities subject to that Act.

(7) The Farm Credit Act of 1971, by the Farm Credit Administration with respect to any Federal land bank, Federal land bank association, Federal intermediate credit bank, and production credit association;

(8) The Securities Exchange Act of 1934, by the Securities and Exchange Commission with respect to brokers and dealers; and

(9) The Small Business Investment Act of 1958, by the Small Business Administration, with respect to small business investment companies.

(b) For the purpose of the exercise by any agency referred to in subsection

(a) of this section of its powers under any Act referred to in that subsection, a violation of any requirement imposed under this title shall be deemed to be a violation of a requirement imposed under that Act. In addition to its powers under any provision of law specifically referred to in subsection (a) of this section, each of the agencies referred to in that subsection may exercise for the purpose of enforcing compliance with any requirement imposed under this title, any other authority conferred on it by law. The exercise of the authorities of any of the agencies referred to in subsection (a) of this section for the purpose of enforcing compliance with any requirement imposed under this title shall in no way preclude the exercise of such authorities for the purpose of enforcing compliance with any other provision of law not relating to the prohibition of discrimination on the basis of sex or marital status with respect to any aspect of a credit transaction.

(c) Except to the extent that enforcement of the requirements imposed under this title is specifically committed to some other Government agency under subsection (a) of this section, the Federal Trade Commission shall enforce such requirements. For the purpose of the exercise by the Federal Trade Commission of its functions and powers under the Federal Trade Commission Act, of its functions and powers under the Federal Trade Commission Act, a violation of any requirement imposed under this title shall be deemed a violation of a requirement imposed under that Act. All of the functions and powers of the Federal Trade Commission under the Federal Trade Commission Act are available to the Commission to enforce compliance by any person with the requirements imposed under this title, irrespective of whether that person is engaged in commerce or meets any other jurisdictional tests in the Federal Trade Commission Act, including the power to enforce any Federal Reserve Board regulation promulgated under this title in the same manner as if the violation had been a violation of a Federal Trade Commission trade regulation rule.

(d) The authority of the Board to issue regulations under this title does not impair the authority of any other agency designated in this section to make rules respecting its own procedures in enforcing compliance with requirements imposed under this title.

§705. Relation to State laws [15 U.S.C. §1691d]

(a) A request for the signature of both parties to a marriage for the purpose of creating a valid lien, passing clear title, waiving inchoate rights to property, or assigning earnings, shall not constitute discrimination under this title: *Provided, however,* That this provision shall not be construed to permit a creditor to take sex or marital status into account in connection with the evaluation of creditworthiness of any applicant.

(b) Consideration or application of State property laws directly or indirectly affecting creditworthiness shall not constitute discrimination for purposes of this title.

(c) Any provision of State law which prohibits the separate extension of consumer credit to each party to a marriage shall not apply in any case where each party to a marriage voluntarily applies for separate credit from the same creditor: *Provided,* That in any case where such a State law is so preempted, each party to the marriage shall be solely responsible for the debt so contracted.

(d) When each party to a marriage separately and voluntarily applies for and obtains separate credit accounts with the same creditor, those accounts shall not be aggregated or otherwise combined for purposes of determining permissible finance charges or permissible loan ceilings under the laws of any State or of the United States.

(e) Where the same act or omission constitutes a violation of this title and of applicable State law, a person aggrieved by such conduct may bring a legal action to recover monetary damages either under this title or under such State law, but not both. This election of remedies shall not apply to court actions in which the relief sought does not include monetary damages or to administrative actions.

(f) This title does not annul, alter, or affect, or exempt any person subject to the provisions of this title from complying with, the laws of any State with respect to credit discrimination, except to the extent that those laws are inconsistent with any provision of this title, and then only to the extent of the inconsistency. The Board is authorized to determine whether such inconsistencies exist. The Board may not determine that any State law is inconsistent with any provision of this title if the Board determines that such law gives greater protection to the applicant.

(g) The Board shall by regulation exempt from the requirements of sections 701 and 702 any class of credit transactions within any State if it determines that under the law of that State that class of transactions is subject to requirements substantially similar to those imposed under this title or that such law gives greater protection to the applicant, and that there is adequate provision for enforcement. Failure to comply with any requirement of such State law in any transaction so exempted shall constitute a violation of this title for the purposes of section 706.

§706. Civil liability [15 U.S.C. §1691e]

(a) Any creditor who fails to comply with any requirement imposed under this title shall be liable to the aggrieved applicant for any actual damages sustained by such applicant acting either in an individual capacity or as a member of a class.

(b) Any creditor, other than a government or governmental subdivision or agency, who fails to comply with any requirement imposed under this title shall be liable to the aggrieved applicant for punitive damages in an amount not greater than $10,000, in addition to any actual damages provided in subsection (a) of this section, except that in the case of a class action the total recovery under this subsection shall not exceed the lesser of $500,000 or 1 per centum of the net worth of the creditor. In determining the amount of such damages in any action, the court shall consider, among other relevant factors, the amount of any actual damages awarded, the frequency and persistance of failures of compliance by the creditor, the resources of the creditor, the number of persons adversely affected, and the extent to which the creditor's failure of compliance was intentional.

(c) Upon application by an aggrieved applicant, the appropriate United States district court or any other court of competent jurisdiction may grant such equitable and declaratory relief as is necessary to enforce the requirements imposed under this title.

(d) In the case of any successful action under subsection (a), (b), or (c) of this section, the costs of the action, together with a reasonable attorney's fee as determined by the court, shall be added to any damages awarded by the court under such subsection.

(e) No provision of this title imposing liability shall apply to any act done or omitted in good faith in conformity with any official rule, regulation, or interpretation thereof by the Board or in conformity with any interpretation or approval by an official or employee of the Federal Reserve System duly authorized by the Board to issue such interpretations or approvals under such procedures as the Board may prescribe therefor, notwithstanding that after such act or omission has occurred, such rule, regulation, interpretation, or approval is amended, rescinded, or determined by judicial or other authority to be invalid for any reason.

(f) Any action under this section may be brought in the appropriate United States district court without regard to the amount in controversy, or in any other court of competent jurisdiction. No such action shall be brought later than two years from the date of the occurrence of the violation, except that—

(1) whenever any agency having responsibility for administrative enforcement under section 704 commences an enforcement proceeding within two years from the date of the occurrence of the violation,

(2) whenever the Attorney General commences a civil action under this section within two years from the date of the occurrence of the violation, then any applicant who has been a victim of the discrimination which is the subject of such proceeding or civil action may bring an action under this section not later than one year after the commencement of that proceeding or action.

(g) The agencies having responsibility for administrative enforcement under section 704, if unable to obtain compliance with section 701, are authorized to refer the matter to the Attorney General with a recommendation that an appropriate civil action be instituted.

(h) When a matter is referred to the Attorney General pursuant to subsection (g) of this section, or whenever he has reason to believe that one or more creditors are engaged in a pattern or practice in violation of this title, the Attorney General may bring a civil action in any appropriate United States district court for such relief as may be appropriate, including injunctive relief.

(i) No person aggrieved by a violation of this title and by a violation of section 805 of the Civil Rights Act of 1968 shall recover under this title and section 812 of the Civil Rights Act of 1968 if such violation is based on the same transaction.

(j) Nothing in this title shall be construed to prohibit the discovery of a creditor's credit granting standards under appropriate discovery procedures in the court or agency in which an action or proceeding is brought.

§707. Annual reports to Congress [15 U.S.C. §1691f]

Each year, the Board and the Attorney General shall, respectively, make reports to the Congress concerning the administration of their functions under this title, including such recommendations as the Board and the Attorney General, respectively deem necessary or appropriate. In addition, each report of the Board shall include its assessment of the extent to which compliance with the requirements of this title is being achieved, and a summary of the enforcement actions taken by each of the agencies assigned administrative enforcement responsibilities under section 704.

§709. Short title

This title may be cited as the "Equal Credit Opportunity Act."

Appendix G
Federal Reserve Board, Regulation B, Equal Credit Opportunity

12 C.F.R. Part 202

Table of Sections

§202.1 Authority, scope, enforcement, penalties and liabilities, interpretations

(a) *Authority and scope.* This part comprises the regulations issued by the Board of Governors of the Federal Reserve System pursuant to Title VII (Equal Credit Opportunity Act) of the Consumer Credit Protection Act, as amended (15 U.S.C. 1601 et seq.). Except as otherwise provided herein, this part applies to all persons who are creditors, as defined in §202.2(1).

. . .

(d) *Issuance of staff interpretations.* (1) Unofficial staff interpretations will be issued at the staff's discretion where the protection of section 706(e) of the Act is neither requested nor required, or where a rapid response is necessary.

(2)(i) Official staff interpretations will be issued at the discretion of designated officials. No such interpretation will be issued approving creditors' forms or statements. . . .

(4) Pursuant to section 706(e) of the Act, the Board has designated the Director and other officials of the Division of Consumer Affairs as officials "duly authorized" to issue, at their discretion, official staff interpretations of this part.

§202.2 Definitions and rules of construction

For the purposes of this part, unless the context indicates otherwise, the following definitions and rules of construction shall apply:[2]

(a) *Account* means an extension of credit. When employed in relation to an account, the word *use* refers only to open end credit.

(b) *Act* means the Equal Credit Opportunity Act (Title VII of the Consumer Credit Protection Act).

(c) *Adverse action.* (1) For the purposes of notification of action taken, statement of reasons for denial, and record retention, the term means:

(i) A refusal to grant credit in substantially the amount or on substantially the terms requested by an applicant unless the creditor offers to grant credit other than in substantially the amount or on substantially the terms requested by the applicant and the applicant uses or expressly accepts the credit offered; or

(ii) A termination of an account or an unfavorable change in the terms of an account that does not affect all or a substantial portion of a classification of a creditor's accounts; or

(iii) A refusal to increase the amount of credit available to an applicant when the applicant requests an increase in accordance with procedures established by the creditor for the type of credit involved.

(2) The term does not include:

---

[2] Note that some of the definitions in this part are not identical to those in 12 CFR Part 226 (Regulation Z).

(i) A change in the terms of an account expressly agreed to by an applicant; or

(ii) Any action or forbearance relating to an account taken in connection with inactivity, default, or delinquency as to that account; or

(iii) A refusal or failure to authorize an account transaction at a point of sale or loan, except when the refusal is a termination or an unfavorable change in the terms of an account that does not affect all or a substantial portion of a classification of the creditor's accounts or when the refusal is a denial of an application to increase the amount of credit available under the account; or

(iv) A refusal to extend credit because applicable law prohibits the creditor from extending the credit requested; or

(v) A refusal to extend credit because the creditor does not offer the type of credit or credit plan requested.

(3) An action that falls within the definition of both paragraphs (c)(1) and (c)(2) of this section shall be governed by the provisions of paragraph (c)(2) of this section.

(d) *Age* refers only to natural persons and means the number of fully elapsed years from the date of an applicant's birth.

(e) *Applicant* means any person who requests or who has received an extension of credit from a creditor, and includes any person who is or may be contractually liable regarding an extension of credit other than a guarantor, surety, endorser, or similar party.

(f) *Application* means an oral or written request for an extension of credit that is made in accordance with procedures established by a creditor for the type of credit requested. The term does not include the use of an account or line of credit to obtain an amount of credit that does not exceed a previously established credit limit. A *completed application for credit* means an application in connection with which a creditor has received all the information that the creditor regularly obtains and considers in evaluating applications for the amount and type of credit requested (including, but not limited to, credit reports, any additional information requested from the applicant, and any approvals or reports by governmental agencies or other persons that are necessary to guarantee, insure, or provide security for the credit or collateral); provided however, that the creditor has exercised reasonable diligence in obtaining such information. Where an application is incomplete respecting matters that the applicant can complete, a creditor shall make a reasonable effort to notify the applicant of the incompleteness and shall allow the applicant a reasonable opportunity to complete the application.

(g) *Board* means the Board of Governors of the Federal Reserve System.

(h) *Consumer credit* means credit extended to a natural person in which the money, property, or service that is the subject of the transaction is primarily for personal, family, or household purposes.

(i) *Contractually liable* means expressly obligated to repay all debts arising on an account by reason of an agreement to that effect.

(j) *Credit* means the right granted by a creditor to an applicant to defer payment of a debt, incur debt and defer its payment, or purchase property or services and defer payment therefore.

(k) *Credit card* means any card, plate, coupon book, or other single credit device existing for the purpose of being used from time to time upon presentation to obtain money, property, or services on credit.

(l) *Creditor* means a person who, in the ordinary course of business, regularly participates in the decision of whether or not to extend credit. The term includes a creditor's assignee, transferee, or subrogee who so participates. For purposes of §§202.4 and 202.5(a), the term also includes a person who, in the ordinary course of business, regularly refers applicants or prospective applicants to creditors, or selects or offers to select creditors to whom requests for credit may be made. A person is not a creditor regarding any violation of the Act or this part committed by another creditor unless the person knew or had reasonable notice of the act, policy, or practice that constituted the violation before its involvement with the credit transaction. The term does not include a person whose only participation in a credit transaction involves honoring a credit card.

(m) *Credit transaction* means every aspect of an applicant's dealings with a creditor regarding an application for, or an existing extension of, credit including, but not limited to, information requirements; investigation procedures; standards of creditworthiness; terms of credit; furnishing of credit information; revocation, alteration, or termination of credit; and collection procedures.

(n) *Discriminate against an applicant* means to treat an applicant less favorably than other applicants.

(o) *Elderly* means an age of 62 or older.

(p) *Empirically derived credit system.* (1) The term means a credit scoring system that evaluates an applicant's creditworthiness primarily by allocating points (or by using a comparable basis for assigning weights) to key attributes describing the applicant and other aspects of the transaction. In such a system, the points (or weights) assigned to each attribute, and hence the entire score:

(i) Are derived from an empirical comparison of sample groups or the population of creditworthy and non-creditworthy applicants of a creditor who applied for credit within a reasonable preceding period of time; and

(ii) Determine, alone or in conjunction with an evaluation of additional information about the applicant, whether an applicant is deemed creditworthy.

(2) *A demonstrably and statistically sound, empirically derived credit system* is a system:

(i) In which the date used to develop the system, if not the complete population consisting of all applicants, are obtained from the applicant file by using appropriate sampling principles;

(ii) Which is developed for the purpose of predicting the creditworthiness of applicants with respect to the legitimate business interests of the creditor utilizing the system, including, but not limited to, minimizing bad debt losses and operating expenses in accordance with the creditor's business judgment;

(iii) Which, upon validation using appropriate statistical principles, separates creditworthy and non-creditworthy applicants at a statistically significant rate; and

(iv) Which is periodically revalidated as to its predictive ability by the use of appropriate statistical principles and is adjusted as necessary to maintain its predictive ability.

(3) A creditor may use a demonstrably and statistically sound, empirically derived credit system obtained from another person or may obtain credit experience from which such a system may be developed. Any such system must satisfy the tests set forth in paragraphs (p)(1) and (2) of this section; provided that, if a creditor is unable during the development process to validate the system based on its own credit experience in accordance with paragraph (p)(2)(iii) of this section, then the system must be validated when sufficient credit experience becomes available. A system that fails this validity test shall henceforth be deemed not to be a demonstrably and statistically sound, empirically derived credit system for that creditor.

(q) *Extend credit and extension of credit* mean the granting of credit in any form and include, but are not limited to, credit granted in addition to any existing credit or credit limit; credit granted pursuant to an open end credit plan; the refinancing or other renewal of credit, including the issuance of a new credit card in place of an expiring credit card or in substitution for an existing credit card; the consolidation of two or more obligations; or the continuance of existing credit without any special effort to collect at or after maturity.

(r) *Good faith* means honesty in fact in the conduct or transaction.

(s) *Inadvertent error* means a mechanical, electronic, or clerical error that a creditor demonstrates was not intentional and occurred notwithstanding the maintenance of procedures reasonably adapted to avoid any such error.

(t) *Judgmental system of evaluating applicants* means any system for evaluating the creditworthiness of an applicant other than a demonstrably and statistically sound, empirically derived credit system.

(u) *Marital status* means the state of being unmarried, married, or separated, as defined by applicable State law. For the purposes of this part, the term "unmarried" includes persons who are single, divorced, or widowed.

(v) *Negative factor or value,* in relation to the age of elderly applicants, means utilizing a factor, value, or weight that is less favorable regarding elderly applicants than the creditor's experience warrants or is less favorable than the factor, value, or weight assigned to the class of applicants that are not classified as elderly applicants and are most favored by a creditor on the basis of age.

(w) *Open end credit* means credit extended pursuant to a plan under which a creditor may permit an applicant to make purchases or obtain loan from time to time directly from the creditor or indirectly by use of a credit card, check, or other device as the plan may provide. The term does not include negotiated advances under an open end real estate mortgage or a letter of credit.

(x) *Person* means a natural person, corporation, government or governmental subdivision or agency, trust, estate, partnership, cooperative, or association.

(y) *Pertinent element of creditworthiness,* in relation to a judgmental system of evaluating applicants, means any information about applicants that a creditor obtains and considers and that has a demonstrable relationship to a determination of creditworthiness.

(z) *Prohibited basis* means race, color, religion, national origin, sex, marital status, or age (provided that the applicant has the capacity to enter into a binding contract); the fact that all or part of the applicant's income derives from any public assistance program, or the fact that the applicant has in good faith exercised any right under the Consumer Credit Protection Act[3] or any State law upon which an exemption has been granted by the Board.

(aa) *Public assistance program* means any Federal, State, or local governmental assistance program that provides a continuing, periodic income supplement, whether premised on entitlement or need. The term includes, but is not limited to, Aid to Families with Dependent Children, food stamps, rent and mortgage supplement or assistance programs, Social Security and Supplemental Security Income, and unemployment compensation.

(bb) *State* means any State, the District of Columbia, the Commonwealth of Puerto Rico, or any territory or possession of the United States.

(cc) Captions and catchlines are intended solely as aids to convenient reference, and no inference as to the substance of any provision of this part may be drawn from them.

(dd) Footnotes shall have the same legal effect as the text of the regulation, whether they are explanatory or illustrative in nature.

§202.3 Special treatment for certain classes of transactions

(a) *Classes of transactions afforded special treatment.* Pursuant to section 703(a) of the Act, the following classes of transactions are afforded specialized treatment:

(1) Extensions of credit relating to transactions under public utility tariffs involving services provided through pipe, wire, or other connected facilities if

---

[3] The first clause of the definition is not limited to characteristics of the applicant. Therefore, "prohibited basis" as used in this part refers not only to the race, color, religion, national origin, sex, marital status, or age of an applicant (or of partners or officers of an applicant), but refers also to the characteristics of individuals with whom an applicant deals. This means, for example, that, under the general rule stated in §202.4, a creditor may not discriminate against a non-Jewish applicant because of that person's business dealings with Jews, or discriminate against an applicant because of the characteristics of persons to whom the extension of credit relates (e.g., the prospective tenants in an apartment complex to be constructed with the proceeds of the credit requested), or because of the characteristics of other individuals residing in the neighborhood where the property offered as collateral is located. A creditor may take into account, however, any applicable law, regulation, or executive order restricting dealings with citizens or governments of other countries or imposing limitations regarding credit extended for their use.

The second clause is limited to an applicant's receipt of public assistance income and to an applicant's good faith exercise of rights under the Consumer Credit Protection Act or applicable State law.

the charges for such public utility services, the charges for delayed payment, and any discount allowed for early payment are filed with, or reviewed or regulated by, an agency of the Federal Government, a State, or a political subdivision thereof;

(2) Extensions of credit subject to regulation under section 7 of the Securities Exchange Act of 1934 or extensions of credit by a broker or dealer subject to regulation as a broker or dealer under the Securities Exchange Act of 1934;

(3) Extensions of incidental consumer credit, other than of the types described in paragraph (a)(1) and (2) of this section:

(i) That are not made pursuant to the terms of a credit card account;

(ii) On which no finance charge as defined in §226.4 of this Title (Regulation Z, 12 CFR 226.4) is or may be imposed; and

(iii) That are not payable by agreement in more than four installments;

(4) Extensions of credit primarily for business or commercial purposes, including extensions of credit primarily for agricultural purposes, but excluding extensions of credit of the types described in paragraphs (a)(1) and (2) of this section; and

(5) Extensions of credit made to goverments or governmental subdivisions, agencies, or instrumentalities.

(b) *Public utilities credit.* The following provisions of this part shall not apply to extensions of credit of the type described in paragraph (a)(1) of this section:

(1) Section 202.5(d)(1) concerning information about marital status;

(2) Section 202.10 relating to furnishing of credit information; and

(3) Section 202.12(b) relating to record retention.

(c) *Securities credit.* The following provisions of this part shall not apply to extensions of credit of the type described in paragraph (a)(2) of this section:

(1) Section 202.5(c) concerning information about a spouse or former spouse;

(2) Section 202.5(d)(1) concerning information about marital status;

(3) Section 202.5(d)(3) concerning information about the sex of an applicant;

(4) Section 202.7(b) relating to designation of name, but only to the extent necessary to prevent violation of rules regarding an account in which a broker or dealer has an interest, or rules necessitating the aggregation of accounts of spouses for the purpose of determining controlling interests, beneficial interests, beneficial ownership, or purchase limitations and restrictions;

(5) Section 202.7(c) relating to action concerning open end accounts, but only to the extent the action taken is on the basis of a change of name or marital status;

(6) Section 202.7(d) relating to signatures of a spouse or other person;

(7) Section 202.10 relating to furnishing of credit information; and

(8) Section 202.12(b) relating to record retention.

(d) *Incidental credit.* The following provisions of this part shall not apply to extensions of credit of the type described in paragraph (a)(3) of this section:

(1) Section 202.5(c) concerning information about a spouse or former spouse;

(2) Section 202.5(d)(1) concerning information about marital status;

(3) Section 202.5(d)(2) concerning information about income derived from alimony, child support, or separate maintenance payments;

(4) Section 202.5(d)(3) concerning information about the sex of an applicant to the extent necessary for medical records or similar purposes;

(5) Section 202.7(d) relating to signatures of a spouse or other person;

(6) Section 202.9 relating to notifications;

(7) Section 202.10 relating to furnishing of credit information; and

(8) Section 202.12(b) relating to record retention.

(e) *Business credit.* The following provisions of this part shall not apply to extensions of credit of the type described in paragraph (a)(4) of this section:

(1) Section 202.5(d)(1) concerning information about marital status;

(2) Section 202.9 relating to notifications, unless an applicant, within 30 days after oral or written notification that adverse action has been taken, requests in writing the reasons for such action;

(3) Section 202.10 relating to furnishing of credit information; and

(4) Section 202.12(b) relating to record retention, unless an applicant, within 90 days after adverse action has been taken, requests in writing that the records relating to the application be retained.

(f) *Governmental credit.* Except for §202.1 relating to authority, scope, enforcement, penalties and liabilities, and interpretation, §202.2 relating to definitions and rules of construction, this section, §202.4 relating to the general rule prohibiting discrimination, §202.6(a) relating to the use of information, §202.11 relating to State laws, and §202.12(a) relating to the retention of prohibited information, the provisions of this part shall not apply to extensions of credit of the type described in paragraph (a)(5) of this section.

§202.4   General rules prohibiting discrimination

A creditor shall not discriminate against an applicant on a prohibited basis regarding any aspect of a credit transaction.

§202.5   Rules concerning applications

(a) *Discouraging applications.* A creditor shall not make any oral or written statement, in advertising or otherwise, to applicants or prospective applicants that would discourage on a prohibited basis a reasonable person from making or pursuing an application.

(b) *General rules concerning requests for information.* (1) Except as otherwise provided in this section, a creditor may request any information in connection with an application.[4]

---

[4] This subsection is not intended to limit or abrogate any Federal or State law

(2) Notwithsanding any other provision of this section, a creditor shall request an applicant's race/national origin, sex, and marital status as required in §202.13 (information for monitoring purposes). In addition, a creditor may obtain such information as may be required by a regulation, order, or agreement issued by, or entered into with, a court or an enforcement agency (including the Attorney General or a similar State official) to monitor or enforce compliance with the Act, this part, or other Federal or State statute or regulation.

(3) The provisions of this section limiting permissible information requests are subject to the provisions of §202.7(e) regarding insurance and §202.8(c) and (d) regarding special purpose credit programs.

(c) *Information about a spouse or former spouse.* (1) Except as permitted in this subsection, a creditor may not request any information concerning the spouse or former spouse of an applicant.

(2) A creditor may request any information concerning an applicant's spouse (or former spouse under paragraph (c)(2)(v) of this section) that may be requested about the applicant if:

(i) The spouse will be permitted to use the account; or

(ii) The spouse will be contractually liable upon the account; or

(iii) The applicant is relying on the spouse's income as a basis for repayment of the creidt requested; or

(iv) The applicant resides in a community property State or property upon which the applicant is relying as a basis for repayment of the credit requested is located in such a State; or

(v) The applicant is relying on alimony, child support, or separate maintenance payments from a spouse or former spouse as a basis for repayment of the credit requested.

(3) A creditor may request an applicant to list any account upon which the applicant is liable and to provide the name and address in which such account is carried. A creditor may also ask the names in which an applicant has previously received credit.

(d) *Information a creditor may not request.* (1) If an applicant applies for an individual, unsecured account, a creditor shall not request the applicant's marital status, unless the applicant resides in a community property State or property upon which the applicant is relying as a basis for repayment of the credit requested is located in such a State.[5] Where an application is for other

---

regarding privacy, privileged information, credit reporting limitations, or similar restrictions on obtainable information. Furthermore, permission to request information should not be confused with how it may be utilized, which is governed by §202.6 (rules concerning evaluations of applications).

[5] This provision does not preclude requesting relevant information that may indirectly disclose marital status, such as asking about liability to pay alimony, child support, or separate maintenance; the source of income to be used as a basis for the repayment of the credit requested, which may disclose that it is a spouse's income; whether any obligation disclosed by the applicant has a co-obligor, which may disclose that the co-obligor is a spouse or former spouse; or the ownership of assets, which may

than individual, unsecured credit, a creditor may request an applicant's marital status. Only the terms "married," "unmarried," and "separated" shall be used, and a creditor may explain that the category "unmarried" includes single, divorced, and widowed persons.

(2) A creditor shall not inquire whether any income stated in an application is derived from alimony, child support, or separate maintenance payments, unless the creditor appropriately discloses to the applicant that such income need not be revealed if the applicant does not desire the creditor to consider such income in determining the applicant's creditworthiness. Since a general inquiry about income, without further specification, may lead an applicant to list alimony, child support, or separate maintenance payments, a creditor shall provide an appropriate notice to an applicant before inquiring about the source of an applicant's income, unless the terms of the inquiry (such as an inquiry about salary, wages, investment income, or similarly specified income) tend to preclude the unintentional disclosure of alimony, child support, or separate maintenance payments.

(3) A creditor shall not request the sex of an applicant. An applicant may be requested to designate a title on an application form (such as Ms., Miss, Mr., or Mrs.) if the form appropriately discloses that the designation of such a title is optional. An application form shall otherwise use only terms that are neutral as to sex.

(4) A creditor shall not request information about birth control practices, intentions concerning the bearing or rearing of children, or capability to bear children. This does not preclude a creditor from inquiring about the number and ages of an applicant's dependents or about dependent-related financial obligations or expenditures, provided such information is requested without regard to sex, marital status, or any other prohibited basis.

(5) A creditor shall not request the race, color, religion, or national origin of an applicant or any other person in connection with a credit transaction. A creditor may inquire, however, as to an applicant's permanent residence and immigration status.

(e) *Application forms.* A creditor need not use written applications. If a creditor chooses to use written forms, it may design its own, use forms prepared by another person, or use the appropriate model application forms contained in Appendix B. If a creditor chooses to use an Appendix B form, it may change the form:

(1) By asking for additional information not prohibited by this section;

(2) By deleting any information request; or

(3) By rearranging the format without modifying the substance of the inquiries; provided that in each of these three instances the appropriate notices regarding the optional nature of courtesy titles, the option to disclose alimony, child support, or separate maintenance, and the limitation concerning marital

---

disclose the interest of a spouse, when such assets are relied upon in extending the credit. Such inquiries are allowed by the general rule of subparagraph (b)(1) of this section.

status inquiries are included in the appropriate places if the items to which they relate appear on the creditor's form. If a creditor uses an appropriate Appendix B model form or to the extent that it modifies such a form in accordance with the provisions of clauses (2) or (3) of the preceding sentence or the instructions to Appendix B, that creditor shall be deemed to be acting in compliance with the provisions of paragraphs (c) and (d) of this section.

§202.6   Rules concerning evaluation of applications

(a) *General rule concerning use of information.* Except as otherwise provided in the Act and this part, a creditor may consider in evaluating an application any information that the creditor obtains, so long as the information is not used to discriminate against an applicant on a prohibited basis.[7]

(b) *Specific rules concerning use of information.* (1) Except as provided in the Act and this part, a creditor shall not take a prohibited basis into account in any system of evaluating the creditworthiness of applicants.[8]

(2)(i) Except as permitted in this section, a creditor shall not take into account an applicant's age [*Provided,* That the applicant has the capacity to enter into a binding contract) or whether an applicant's income derives from any public assistance program.

(ii) In a demonstrably and statistically sound, empirically derived credit system, a creditor may use an applicant's age as a predictive variable, provided that the age of an elderly applicant is not assigned a negative factor or value.

(iii) In a judgmental system of evaluating creditworthiness, a creditor may consider an applicant's age or whether an applicant's income derives from any public assistance program only for the purpose of determining a pertinent element of creditworthiness.[9]

---

[7] The legislative history of the Act indicates that the Congress intended an "effects test" concept, as outlined in the employment field by the Supreme Court in the cases of Griggs v. Duke Power Co., 401 U.S. 424 (1971), and Albemarle Paper Co. v. Moody, 422 U.S. 405 (1975), to be applicable to a creditor's determination of creditworthiness. See Senate Report to accompany H.R. 6516, No. 94-589, pp. 4-5; House Report to accompany H.R. 6516, N. 94-210, p. 5.

[8] This provision does not prevent a creditor from considering the marital status of an applicant or the source of an applicant's income for the purpose of ascertaining the creditor's rights and remedies applicable to the particular extension of credit and not to discriminate in a determination of creditworthiness. Furthermore, a prohibited basis may be considered in accordance with §202.8 (special purpose credit programs).

[9] Concerning income derived from a public assistance program, a creditor may consider, for example, the length of time an applicant has been receiving such income; whether an applicant intends to continue to reside in the jurisdiction in relation to residency requirements for benefits; and the status of an applicant's dependents to ascertain whether benefits that the applicant is presently receiving will continue.

Concerning age, a creditor may consider, for example, the occupation and length of time to retirement of an applicant to ascertain whether the applicant's income (including retirement income, as applicable) will support the extension of credit until its maturity;

(iv) In any system of evaluating creditworthiness, a creditor may consider the age of an elderly applicant when such age is to be used to favor the elderly applicant in extending credit.

(3) A creditor shall not use, in evaluating the creditworthiness of an applicant, assumptions or aggregate statistics relating to the likelihood that any group of persons will bear or rear children or, for that reason, will receive diminished or interrupted income in the future.

(4) A creditor shall not take into account the existence of a telephone listing in the name of an applicant for consumer credit. A creditor may take into account the existence of a telephone in the residence of such an applicant.

(5) A creditor shall not discount or exclude from consideration the income of an applicant or the spouse of the applicant because of a prohibited basis or because the income is derived from part-time employment or from an annuity, pension, or other retirement benefit; but a creditor may consider the amount and probable continuance of any income in evaluating an applicant's creditworthiness. Where an applicant relies on alimony, child support, or separate maintenance payments in applying for credit, a creditor shall consider such payments as income to the extent that they are likely to be consistently made. Factors that a creditor may consider in determining the likelihood of consistent payments include, but are not limited to, whether the payments are received pursuant to a written agreement or court decree; the length of time that the payments have been received; the regularity of receipt; the availability of procedures to compel payment; and the creditworthiness of the payor, including the credit history of the payor where available to the creditor under the Fair Credit Reporting Act or other applicable laws.

(6) To the extent that a creditor considers credit history in evaluating the creditworthiness of similarly qualified applicants for a similar type and amount of credit, in evaluating an applicant's creditworthiness, a creditor shall consider (unless the failure to consider results from an inadvertent error):

(i) The credit history, when available, of accounts designated as accounts that the applicant and a spouse are permitted to use or for which both are contractually liable;

(ii) On the applicant's request, any information that the applicant may present tending to indicate that the credit history being considered by the creditor does not accurately reflect the applicant's creditworthiness; and

(iii) On the applicant's request, the credit history, when available, of any account reported in the name of the applicant's spouse or former spouse that

---

or the adequacy of any security offered if the duration of the credit extension will exceed the life expectancy of the applicant. An elderly applicant might not qualify for a five-percent down, 30-year mortgage loan because the duration of the loan exceeds the applicant's life expectancy and the cost of realizing on the collateral might exceed the applicant's equity. The same applicant might qualify with a larger downpayment and a shorter loan maturity. A creditor could also consider an applicant's age, for example to assess the significance of the applicant's length of employment or residence (a young applicant may have just entered the job market; an elderly applicant may recently have retired and moved from a long-time residence).

the applicant can demonstrate accurately reflects the applicant creditworthiness.

(7) A creditor may consider whether an applicant is a permanent resident of the United States, the applicant's immigration status, and such additional information as may be necessary to ascertain its rights and remedies regarding repayment.

(c) *State property laws.* A creditor's consideration or application of State property laws directly or indirectly affecting creditworthiness shall not constitute unlawful discrimination for the purposes of the Act or this part.

§202.7   Rules concerning extensions of credit

(a) *Individual accounts.* A creditor shall not refuse to grant an individual account to a creditworthy applicant on the basis of sex, marital status, or any other prohibited basis.

(b) *Designation of name.* A creditor shall not prohibit an applicant from opening or maintaining an account in a birth-given first name and a surname that is the applicant's birth-given surname, the spouse's surname, or a combined surname.

(c) *Action concerning existing open end accounts.* (1) In the absence of evidence of inability or unwillingness to repay, a creditor shall not take any of the following actions regarding an applicant who is contractually liable on an existing open end account on the basis of the applicant's reaching a certain age or retiring, or on the basis of a change in the applicant's name or marital status:

　(i) Require a reapplication; or
　(ii) Change the terms of the account; or
　(iii) Terminate the account.

(2) A creditor may require a reapplication regarding an open end account on the basis of a change in an applicant's marital status where the credit granted was based on income earned by the applicant's spouse if the applicant's income alone at the time of the original application would not support the amount of credit currently extended.

(d) *Signature of spouse or other person.* (1) Except as provided in this subsection, a creditor shall not require the signature of an applicant's spouse or other person, other than a joint applicant, on any credit instrument if the applicant qualifies under the creditor's standards of creditworthiness for the amount and terms of the credit requested.

(2) If an applicant requests unsecured credit and relies in part upon property to establish creditworthiness, a creditor may consider State law; the form of ownership of the property; its susceptibility to attachment, execution, severance, and partition; and other factors that may affect the value to the creditor of the applicant's interest in the property. If necessary to satisfy the creditor's standards of creditworthiness, the creditor may require the signature of the applicant's spouse or other person on any instrument necessary, or reasonably believed by the creditor to be necessary, under applicable State law to make the property relied upon available to satisfy the debt in the event of default.

(3) If a married applicant requests unsecured credit and resides in a community property State or if the property upon which the applicant is relying is located in such a State, a creditor may require the signature of the spouse on any instrument necessary, or reasonably believed by the creditor to be necessary, under applicable State law to make the community property available to satisfy the debt in the event of default if:

(i) Applicable State law denied the applicant power to manage or control sufficient community property to qualify for the amount of credit requested under the creditor's standards of creditworthiness; and

(ii) The applicant does not have sufficient separate property to qualify for the amount of credit requested without regard to community property.

(4) If an applicant requests secured credit, a creditor may require the signature of the applicant's spouse or other person on any instrument necessary, or reasonably believed by the creditor to be necessary, under applicable State law to make the property being offered as security available to satisfy the debt in the event of default, for example, any instrument to create a valid lien, pass clear title, waive inchoate rights, or assign earnings.

(5) If, under a creditor's standards of creditworthiness, the personal liability of an additional party is necessary to support the extension of the credit requested,[10] a creditor may request that the applicant obtain a co-signer, guarantor, or the like. The applicant's spouse may serve as an additional party, but a creditor shall not require that the spouse be the additional party. For the purposes of paragraph (d) of this section, a creditor shall not impose requirements upon an additional party that the creditor may not impose upon an applicant.

(e) *Insurance.* Differentiation in the availability, rates, and terms on which credit-related casualty insurance or credit life, health, accident, or disability insurance is offered or provided to an applicant shall not constitute a violation of the Act or this part; but a creditor shall not refuse to extend credit and shall not terminate an account because credit life, health, accident, or disability insurance is not available on the basis of the applicant's age. Notwithstanding any other provision of this part, information about the age, sex, or marital status of an applicant may be requested in an application for insurance.

§202.8 Special purpose credit programs

(a) *Standards for programs.* Subject to the provisions of paragraph (b) of this section, the Act and this part are not violated if a creditor refuses to extend credit to the applicant solely because the applicant does not qualify under the special requirements that define eligibility for the following types of special purpose credit programs:

---

[10] If an applicant requests individual credit relying on the separate income of another person, a creditor may require the signature of the other person to make the income available to pay the debt.

(1) Any credit assistance program expressly authorized by Federal or State law for the benefit of an economically disadvantaged class of persons; or

(2) Any credit assistance program offered by a not-for-profit organization, as defined under section 501(c) of the Internal Revenue Code of 1954, as amended, for the benefit of its members or for the benefit of an economically disadvantaged class of persons; or

(3) Any special purpose credit program offered by a for-profit organization or in which such an organization participates to meet special social needs, provided that:

(i) The program is established and administered pursuant to a written plan that (A) identifies the class or classes of persons that the program is designed to benefit and (B) sets forth the procedures and standards for extending credit pursuant to the program; and

(ii) The program is established and administered to extend credit to a class of persons who, pursuant to the customary standards of creditworthiness used by the organization extending the credit, either probably would not receive such credit or probably would receive it on less favorable terms than are ordinarily available to other applicants applying to the organization for a similar type and amount of credit.

(b) *Applicability of other rules.* (1) All of the provisions of this part shall apply to each of the special purpose credit programs described in paragraph (a) of this section to the extent that those provisions are not inconsistent with the provisions of this section.

(2) A program described in paragraphs (a)(2) or (a)(3) of this section shall qualify as a special purpose credit program under paragraph (a) of this section only if it was established and is administered so as not to discriminate against an applicant on the basis of race, color, religion, national origin, sex, marital status, age (*Provided,* That the applicant has the capacity to enter into a binding contract), income derived from a public assistance program, or good faith exercise of any right under the Consumer Credit Protection Act or any State law upon which an exemption has been granted therefrom by the Board; except that all program participants may be required to share one or more of those characteristics so long as the program was not established and is not administered with the purpose of evading the requirments of the Act or this part.

(c) *Special rule concerning requests and use of information.* If all participants in a special purpose credit program described in paragraph (a) of this section are or will be required to possess one or more common characteristics relating to race, color, religion, national origin, sex, marital status, age, or receipt of income from a public assistance program and if the special purpose credit program otherwise satisfies the requirements of paragraph (a) of this section, then, notwithstanding the prohibitions of §§202.5 and 202.6, the creditor may request of an applicant and may consider, in determining eligibility for such program, information regarding the common characteristics required for eligibility. In such circumstances, the solicitation and consideration of that information shall not constitute unlawful discrimination for the purposes of the Act or this part.

(d) *Special rule in the case of financial need.* If financial need is or will be one of the criteria for the extension of credit under a special purpose credit program described in paragraph (a) of this section, then, notwithstanding the prohibitions of §§202.5 and 202.6, the creditor may request and consider, in determining eligibility for such program, information regarding an applicant's marital status, income from alimony, child support, or separate maintenance, and the spouse's financial resources. In addition, notwithstanding the prohibitions of §202.7(d), a creditor may obtain the signature of an applicant's spouse or other person on an application or credit instrument relating to a special purpose program if required by Federal or State law. In such circumstances, the solicitation and consideration of that information and the obtaining of a required signature shall not constitute unlawful discrimination for the purposes of the Act or this part.

§202.9 Notifications

(a) *Notification of action taken, ECOA notice, and statement of specific reasons*—(1) *Notification of action taken.* A creditor shall notify an applicant of action taken within:

(i) 30 days after receiving a completed application concerning the creditor's approval of, or adverse action regarding, the application (notification of approval may be expressed by implication, where, for example, the applicant receives a credit card, money, property, or services in accordance with the application);

(ii) 30 days after taking adverse action on an uncompleted application;

(iii) 30 days after taking adverse action regarding an existing account; and

(iv) 90 days after the creditor has notified the applicant of an offer to grant credit other than in substantially the amount or on substantially the terms requested by the applicant if the applicant during those 90 days has not expressly accepted or used the credit offered.

(2) *Content of notification.* Any notification given to an applicant against whom adverse action taken shall be in writing and shall contain: a statement of the action taken; a statement of the provisions of section 701(a) of the Act; the name and address of the Federal agency that administers compliance concerning the creditor giving the notification; and

(i) A statement of specific reasons for the action taken; or

(ii) A disclosure of the applicant's right to a statement of reasons within 30 days after receipt by the creditor of a request made within 60 days of such notification, the disclosure to include the name, address, and telephone number of the person or office from which the statement of reasons can be obtained. If the creditor chooses to provide the statement of reasons orally, the notification shall also include a disclosure of the applicant's right to have any oral statement of reasons confirmed in writing within 30 days after a written request for confirmation is received by the creditor.

(3) *Multiple applicants.* If there is more than one applicant, the notification need only be given to one of them, but must be given to the primary applicant where one is readily apparent.

(4) *Multiple creditors.* If a transaction involves more than one creditor and the applicant expressly accepts or uses the credit offered, this section does not require notification of adverse action by any creditor. If a transaction involves more than one creditor and either no credit is offered or the applicant does not expressly accept or use any credit offered, then each creditor taking adverse action must comply with this section. The required notification may be provided indirectly through a third party, which may be one of the creditors, provided that the identify of each creditor taking adverse action is disclosed. Whenever the notification is to be provided through a third party, a creditor shall not be liable for any act or omission of the third party that constitutes a violation of this section if the creditor accurately and in a timely manner provided the third party with the information necessary for the notification and was maintaining procedures reasonably adapted to avoid any such violation.

(b) *Form of ECOA notice and statement of specific reasons*—(1) *ECOA notice.* A creditor satisfies the requirements of paragraph (a)(2) of this section regarding a statement of the provisions of section 701(a) of the Act and the name and address of the appropriate Federal enforcement agency if it provides the following notice, or one that is substantially similar:

> The Federal Equal Credit Opportunity Act prohibits creditors from discriminating against credit applicants on the basis of race, color, religion, national origin, sex, marital status, age (provided that the applicant has the capacity to enter into a binding contract); because all or part of the applicant's income derives from any public assistance program; or because the applicant has in good faith exercised any right under the Consumer Credit Protection Act. The Federal agency that administers compliance with this law concerning this creditor is (name and address as specified by the appropriate agency listed in Appendix A).

The sample notice printed above may be modified immediately following the required references to the Federal Act and enforcement agency to include references to any similar State statute or regulation and to a State enforcement agency.

(2) *Statement of specific reasons.* A statement of reasons for adverse action shall be sufficient if it is specific and indicates the principal reason(s) for the adverse action. A creditor may formulate its own statement of reasons in checklist or letter form or may use all or a portion of the sample form printed below, which, if properly completed, satisfies the requirements of paragraph (a)(2)(i) of this section. Statements that the adverse action was based on the creditor's internal standards or policies or that the applicant failed to achieve the qualifying score on the creditor's credit scoring system are insufficient.

STATEMENT OF CREDIT DENIAL, TERMINATION, OR CHANGE

Date _____

Applicant's Name: _____

Applicant's Address: _____

Description of Account, Transaction, or Requested Credit:

_____

_____

Description of Adverse Action Taken:

_____

_____

PRINCIPAL REASON(S) FOR ADVERSE ACTION CONCERNING CREDIT

☐ Credit application incomplete
☐ Insufficient credit references
☐ Unable to verify credit references
☐ Temporary or irregular employment
☐ Unable to verify employment
☐ Length of employment
☐ Insuficient income
☐ Excessive obligations
☐ Unable to verify income
☐ Inadequate collateral
☐ We do not grant credit to any applicant on the terms and conditions you request.
☐ Too short a period of residence
☐ Temporary residence
☐ Unable to verify residence
☐ No credit file
☐ Insufficient credit file
☐ Delinquent credit obligations
☐ Garnishment, attachment, foreclosure, repossession, or suit
☐ Bankruptcy
☐ Other specify:_____

DISCLOSURE OF USE OF INFORMATION OBTAINED FROM AN OUTSIDE SOURCE

☐ Disclosure inapplicable
☐ Information obtained in a report from a consumer reporting agency
Name: _____

_____

Street Address: _____

_____

Phone: _____

☐ Information obtained from an outside source other than a consumer reporting agency. Under the Fair Credit Reporting Act, you have the right to make a written request, within 60 days of receipt of this notice, for disclosure of the nature of the adverse information.

Creditor's name: _____

Creditor's address: _____

_____

Creditor's telephone number: _____

[Add ECOA Notice]

(3) *Other information.* The notification required by paragraph (a)(1) of this section may include other information so long as it does not detract from the required content. This notification also may be combined with any disclosures required under other titles of the Consumer Credit Protection Act or any other law, provided that all requirements for clarity and placement are satisfied; and it may appear on either or both sides of the paper if there is a clear reference on the front to any information on the back.

(c) *Oral notifications.* The applicable requirements of this section are satisfied by oral notifications (including statements of specific reasons) in the case of any creditor that did not receive more than 150 applications during the calendar year immediately preceding the calendar year in which the notification of adverse action is to be given to a particular applicant.

(d) *Withdrawn applications.* Where an applicant submits an application and the parties contemplate that the applicant will inquire about its status, if the creditor approves the application and the applicant has not inquired within 30 days after applying, then the creditor may treat the application as withdrawn and need not comply with paragraph (a)(1) of this section.

(e) *Failure of compliance.* A failure to comply with this section shall not constitute a violation when caused by an inadvertent error; provided that, on discovering the error, the creditor corrects it as soon as possible and commences compliance with the requirements of this section.

(f) *Notification.* A creditor notifies an applicant when a writing addressed to the applicant is delivered or mailed to the applicant's last known address or, in the case of an oral notification, when the creditor communicates with the applicants.

§202.10   Furnishing of credit information

(a) *Accounts established on or after June 1, 1977.* (1) For every account established on or after June 1, 1977, a creditor that furnishes credit information shall:

(i) Determine whether an account offered by the creditor is one that an applicant's spouse is permitted to use or upon which the spouses are contractually liable other than as guarantors, sureties, endorsers, or similar parties; and

(ii) Designate any such account to reflect the fact of participation of both spouses,[11]

(2) Except as provided in paragraph (a)(3) of this section, if a creditor furnishes credit information concerning an account designated under this section (or designated prior to the effective date of this part) to a consumer reporting agency, it shall furnish the information in a manner that will enable the agency to provide access to the information in the name of each spouse.

(3) If a creditor furnishes credit information concerning an account designated under this section (or designated prior to the effective date of this part) in response to an inquiry regarding a particular applicant, it shall furnish the information in the name of the spouse about whom such information is requested.[12]

(b) *Accounts established prior to June 1, 1977.* For every account established prior to and in existence on June 1, 1977, a creditor that furnishes credit information shall either:

(1) Not later than June 1, 1977

(i) Determine whether the account is one that an applicant's spouse, if any, is permitted to use or upon which the spouses are contractually liable other than as guarantors, sureties, endorsers, or similar parties;

(ii) Designate any such account to reflect the fact of participation of both spouses:[13] and

(iii) Comply with the reporting requirements of paragraphs (a)(2) and (a)(3) of this section; or

(2) Mail or deliver to all applicants, or all married applicants, in whose name an account is carried on the creditor's records one copy of the notice set forth below.[14] The notice may be mailed with a billing statement or other mailing. All such notices shall be mailed or delivered by October 1, 1977. As to open end accounts, this requirement may be satisfied by mailing one notice at any time prior to October 2, 1977, regarding each account for which a billing statement is sent between June 1 and October 1, 1977. The notice may be supplemented as necessary to permit identification of the account by the creditor or by a consumer reporting agency. A creditor need only send notices relating to those accounts on which it lacks the information necessary to make the proper designation regarding participation or contractual liability.

---

[11] A creditor need not distinguish between participation as a user or as a contractually liable party.

[12] If a creditor learns that new parties have undertaken payment on an account, then the subsequent history of the account shall be furnished in the names of the new parties and need not continue to be furnished in the names of the former parties.

[13] See footnote 11.

[14] A creditor may delete the references to the "use" of an account when providing notices regarding closed end accounts.

NOTICE
CREDIT HISTORY FOR MARRIED PERSONS

The Federal Equal Credit Opportunity Act prohibits credit discrimination on the basis of race, color, religion, national origin, sex, marital status, age (provided that a person has the capacity to enter into a binding contract); because all or part of a person's income derives from any public assistance program; or because a person in good faith has exercised any right under the Federal Consumer Credit Protection Act. Regulations under the Act give married persons the right to have credit information included in credit reports in the name of both the wife and the husband if both use or are responsible for the account. This right was created, in part, to insure that credit histories will be available to women who become divorced or widowed.

If your account with us is one that both husband and wife signed for or is an account that is being used by one of you who did not sign, then you are entitled to have us report credit information relating to the account in both your names. If you choose to have credit information concerning your account with us reported in both your names, please complete and sign the statement below and return it to us.

Federal regulations provide that signing your name below will not change your or your spouse's legal liability on the account. Your signature will only request that credit information be reported in both your names.

If you do not complete and return the form below, we will continue to report your credit history in the same way that we do now.

When you furnish credit information on this account, please report all information concerning the account in both our names.

_____

Account number

_____

Print or type name

_____

Print or type name

_____

Signature of either spouse

(c) *Requests to change manner in which information is reported.* Within 90 days after receipt of a properly completed request to change the manner in which information is reported to consumer reporting agencies and others regarding an account described in paragraph (b) of this section a creditor shall designate the account to reflect the fact of participation of both spouses. When furnishing information concerning any such account, the creditor shall comply with the reporting requirements of subparagraphs (a)(2) and (a)(3) of this section. The signature of an applicant or the applicant's spouse on a request to change the manner in which information concerning an account is furnished shall not alter the legal liability of either spouse upon the account or require the creditor to change the name in which the account is carried.

(d) *Inadvertent errors.* A failure to comply with this section shall not constitute a violation when caused by an inadvertent error; *Provided,* That, on discovering the error the creditor corrects it as soon as possible and commences compliance with the requirements of this section.

§202.11   Relation to State law

(a) *Inconsistent State laws.* Except as otherwise provided in this section, this part alters, affects, or preempts only those State laws that are inconsistent with this part and then only to the extent of the inconsistency. A state law is not inconsistent with this part if it is more protective of an applicant.

(b) *Preempted provisions of State law.* (1) State law is deemed to be inconsistent with the requirements of the Act and this part and less protective of an applicant within the meaning of section 705(f) of the Act to the extent that such law:

(i) Requires or permits a practice or act prohibited by the Act or this part;

(ii) Prohibits the individual extension of consumer credit to both parties to a marriage if each spouse individually and voluntarily applies for such credit;

(iii) Prohibits inquiries or collection of data required to comply with the Act or this part;

(iv) Prohibits asking age or considering age in a demonstrably and statistically sound, empirically derived credit system, to determine a pertinent element of creditworthiness, or to favor an elderly applicant; or

(v) Prohibits inquiries necessary to establish or administer a special purpose credit program as defined by §202.8.

(2) A determination as to whether a State law is inconsistent with the requirements of the Act and this part will be made only in response to a request for a formal Board interpretation. All requests for such interpretations, in addition to meeting the requirements of §202.1(d), shall comply with the applicable provisions of subsections (b)(1) and (2) of Supplement I. Notice of the interpretation shall be provided as specified in subsection (e)(1) of Supplement I, but the interpretation shall be effective in accordance with §202.1. The interpretation shall be subject to revocation or modification at any time, as provided in subsection (g)(4) of Supplement I.

(c) *Finance charges and loan ceilings.* If married applicants voluntarily apply for and obtain individual accounts with the same creditor, the accounts shall not be aggregated or otherwise combined for purposes of determining permissible finance charges or permissible loan ceilings under any Federal or State law. Permissible loan ceiling laws shall be construed to permit each spouse to become individually liable up to the amount of the loan ceilings, less the amount for which the applicant is jointly liable.[16]

(d) *State and Federal laws not affected.* This section does not alter or annul any provision of State property laws, laws relating to the disposition of decedents' estates, or Federal or State banking regulations directed only towards insuring the solvency of financial institutions.

(e) *Exemption for State regulated transactions.* (1) In accordance with the provisions of Supplement I to this part, any State may apply to the Board for an exemption from the requirements of sections 701 and 702 of the Act and the corresponding provisions of this part for any class of credit transactions within the State. The Board will grant such an exemption if:

(i) The Board determines that, under the law of that State, that class of credit transactions is subject to requirements substantially similar to those imposed under sections 701 and 702 of the Act and the corresponding provisions of this part, or that applicants are afforded greater protection than is afforded under Sections 701 and 702 of the Act and the corresponding provisions of this part; and

(ii) There is adequate provision for State enforcement.

(2) In order to assure that the concurrent jurisdiction of Federal and State courts created in section 706(f) of the Act will continue to have substantive provisions to which such jurisdiction shall apply; to allow Federal enforcement agencies to retain their authority regarding any class of credit transactions exempted pursuant to paragraph (e)(1) of this section and Supplement I; and, generally, to aid in implementing the Act:

(i) No such exemption shall be deemed to extend to the civil liability provisions of section 706 or the administrative enforcement provisions of section 704 of the Act; and

(ii) After an exemption has been granted, the requirements of the applicable State law shall constitute the requirements of the Act and this part, except to the extent such State law imposes requirements not imposed by the Act or this part.

(3) Exemptions granted by the Board to particular classes of credit transactions within specified States will be set forth in Supplement II to this part.

§202.12   Record retention

(a) *Retention of prohibited information.* Retention in a creditor's files of any information, the use of which in evaluating applications is prohibited by the Act or this part, shall not constitute a violation of the Act or this part where such information was obtained:

---

[16] For example, in a State with a permissible loan ceiling of $1,000, if a married couple were jointly liable for unpaid debt in the amount of $250, each spouse could subsequently become individually liable for $750.

(1) From any source prior to March 23, 1977;[17] or

(2) At any time from consumer reporting agencies; or

(3) At any time from any applicant or others without the specific request of the creditor; or

(4) At any time as required to monitor compliance with the Act and this part or other Federal or State statutes or regulations.

(b) *Preservation of records.* (1) for 25 months after the date that a creditor notifies an applicant of action taken on an application, the creditor shall retain as to that application in original form or a copy thereof.[18]

(i) Any application form that it receives, any information required to be obtained concerning characteristics of an applicant to monitor compliance with the Act and this part or other similar law, and any other written or recorded information used in evaluating the application and not return to the applicant at the applicant's request;

(ii) A copy of the following documents if furnished to the applicant in written form (or, if furnished orally, any notation or memorandum with respect thereto made by the creditor):

(A) The notification of action taken; and

(B) The statement of specific reasons for adverse action; and

(iii) Any written statement submitted by the applicant alleging a violation of the Act or this part.

(2) For 25 months after the date that a creditor notifies an applicant of adverse action regarding an account, other than in connection with an application, the creditor shall retain as to that account, in original form or a copy thereof:

(i) Any written or recorded information concerning such adverse action; and

(ii) Any written statement submitted by the applicant alleging a violation of the Act or this part.

(3) In addition to the requirements of paragraphs (b)(1) and (2), of this section, any creditor that has actual notice that it is under investigation or is subject to an enforcement proceeding for an alleged violation of the Act or this part by an enforcement agency charged with monitoring that creditor's compliance with the Act and this part, or that has been served with notice of an action filed pursuant to section 706 of the Act and §202.1(b) or (c) of this part, shall retain the information required in paragraphs (b)(1) and (2) of this section until final disposition of the matter, unless an earlier time is allowed by order of the agency or court.

(4) In any transaction involving more than one creditor, any creditor not

---

[17] Pursuant to the October 28, 1975 version of Regulation B, the applicable date for sex and marital status information is June 30, 1976.

[18] "A copy thereof" includes carbon copies, photocopies, microfilm or microfiche copies or copies produced by any accurate information retrieval system. A creditor who uses a computerized or mechanized system need not keep a written copy of a document if it can regenerate the precise text of the document upon request.

required to comply with §202.9 (notifications) shall retain for the time period specified in paragraph (b) of this section all written or recorded information in its possession concerning the applicant, including a notation of action taken in connection with any adverse action.

(c) *Failure of compliance.* A failure to comply with this section shall not constitute a violation when caused by an inadvertent error.

§202.13   Information for monitoring purposes

(a) *Scope and information requested.* (1) For the purpose of monitoring compliance with the provisions of the Act and this part, any creditor that receives an application for consumer credit relating to the purchase of residential real property, where the extension of credit is to be secured by a lien on such property, shall request as part of any written application for such credit the following information regarding the applicant and joint applicant (if any):

(i) Race/national origin, using the categories American Indian or Alaskan Native; Asian or Pacific Islander; Black; White; Hispanic; Other (Specify);

(ii) Sex;

(iii) Marital status, using the categories married, unmarried, and separated; and

(iv) Age.

(2) "Residential real property" means improved real property used or intended to be used for residential purposes, including single family homes, dwellings for from two to four families, and individual units of condominiums and cooperatives.

(b) *Method of obtaining information.* Questions regarding race/national origin, sex, marital status, and age may be listed at the creditor's option, either on the application form or on a separate form that refers to the application.

(c) *Disclosure to applicant and joint applicant.* The applicant and joint applicant (if any) shall be informed that the information regarding race/national origin, sex, marital status, and age is being requested by the Federal government for the purpose of monitoring compliance with Federal anti-discrimination statutes and that those statutes prohibit creditors from discriminating against applicants on those bases. The applicant and joint applicant shall be asked, but not required, to supply the requested information. If the applicant or joint applicant chooses not to provide the information or any part of it, that fact shall be noted on the form on which the information is obtained.

(d) *Substitute monitoring program.* Any monitoring program required by an agency charged with administrative enforcement under section 704 of the Act may be substituted for the requirements contained in paragraphs (a), (b) and (c) of this section.

Appendix H
Title VIII. Fair Debt Collection Practices Act

(15 U.S.C. §§1692-1692m)

Table of Sections

§801. Short title

This title may be cited as the "Fair Debt Collection Practices Act."

§802. Findings and purpose [15 U.S.C. §1692]

(a) There is abundant evidence of the use of abusive, deceptive, and unfair debt collection practices by many debt collectors. Abusive debt collection practices contribute to the number of personal bankruptcies, to marital instability, to the loss of jobs, and to invasions of individual privacy.

(b) Existing laws and procedures for redressing these injuries are inadequate to protect consumers.

(c) Means other than misrepresentation or other abusive debt collection practices are available for the effective collection of debts.

(d) Abusive debt collection practices are carried on to a substantial extent in interstate commerce and through means and instrumentalities of such commerce. Even where abusive debt collection prac-tices are purely intrastate in character, they nevertheless directly affect interstate commerce.

(e) It is the purpose of this title to eliminate abusive debt collection practices by debt collectors, to insure that those debt collectors who refrain from using abusive debt collection practices are not competitively disadvantaged, and to promote consistent State action to protect consumers against debt collection abuses.

§803. Definitions [15 U.S.C. §1692a]

As used in this title—

(1) The term "Commission" means the Federal Trade Commission.

(2) The term "communication" means the conveying of information regarding a debt directly or indirectly to any person through any medium.

(3) The term "consumer" means any natural person obligated or allegedly obligated to pay any debt.

(4) The term "creditor" means any person who offers or extends credit creating a debt or to whom a debt is owed, but such term does not include any person to the extent that he receives an assignment or transfer of a debt in default solely for the purpose of facilitating collection of such debt for another.

(5) The term "debt" means any obligation or alleged obligation of a consumer to pay money arising out of a transaction in which the money, property, insurance, or services which are the subject of the transaction are primarily for personal, family, or household purposes, whether or not such obligation has been reduced to judgment.

(6) The term "debt collector" means any person who uses any instrumentality of interstate commerce or the mails in any business the principal purpose of which is the collection of any debts, or who regularly collects or attempts to collect, directly or indirectly, debts owed or due or asserted to be owed or due another. Notwithstanding the exclusion provided by clause (G) of the last sentence of this paragraph, the term includes any creditor who, in the process of collecting his own debts, uses any name other than his own which would indicate that a third person is collecting or attempting to collect such debts. For the purpose of section 808(6), such term also includes any person who uses any instrumentality of interstate commerce or the mails in any business the principal purpose of which is the enforcement of security interests. The term does not include—

(A) any officer or employee of a creditor while, in the name of the creditor, collecting debts for such creditor;

(B) any person while acting as a debt collector for another person, both of whom are related by common ownership or affiliated by corporate control, if the person acting as a debt collector does so only for persons to whom it is so related or affiliated and if the principal business of such person is not the collection of debts;

(C) any officer or employee of the United States or any State to the extent that collecting or attempting to collect any debt is in the performance of his official duties;

(D) any person while serving or attempting to serve legal process on any other person in connection with the judicial enforcement of any debt;

(E) any nonprofit organization which, at the request of consumers, performs bona fide consumer credit counseling and assists consumers in the liquidation of their debts by receiving payments from such consumers and distributing such amounts to creditor;

(F) any attorney-at-law collecting a debt as an attorney on behalf of and in the name of a client; and

(G) any person collecting or attempting to collect any debt owed or due or asserted to be owed or due another to the extent such activity (i) is incidental to a bona fide fiduciary obligation or a bona fide escrow arrangement; (ii) concerns a debt which was originated by such person; (iii) concerns a debt which was not in default at the time it was obtained by such person; or (iv) concerns a debt obtained by such person as a secured party in a commercial credit transaction involving the creditor.

(7) The term "location information" means a consumer's place of abode and his telephone number at such place, or his place of employment.

(8) The term "State" means any State, territory, or possession of the United States, the District of Columbia, the Commonwealth of Puerto Rico, or any political subdivision of any of the foregoing.

§804. Acquisition of location information [15 U.S.C. §1692b]

Any debt collector communicating with any person other than the consumer for the purpose of acquiring location information about the consumer shall—

(1) identify himself, state that he is confirming or correcting location information concerning the consumer, and, only if expressly requested, identify his employer;

(2) not state that such consumer owes any debt;

(3) not communicate with any such person more than once unless requested to do so by such person or unless the debt collector reasonably believes that the earlier response of such person is erroneous or incomplete and that such person now has correct or complete location information;

(4) not communicate by post card;

(5) not use any language or symbol on any envelope or in the contents of any communication effected by the mails or telegram that indicates that the debt collector is in the debt collection business or that the communication relates to the collection of a debt; and

(6) after the debt collector knows the consumer is represented by an attorney with regard to the subject debt and has knowledge of, or can readily ascertain, such attorney's name and address, not communicate with any person other than that attorney, unless the attorney fails to respond within a reasonable period of time to communication from the debt collector.

§805. Communication in connection with debt collection [15 U.S.C. §1692c]

(a) Communication with the consumer generally—Without the prior consent of the consumer given directly to the debt collector or the express permission of a court of competent jurisdiction, a debt collector may not communicate with a consumer in connection with the collection of any debt—

(1) at any unusual time or place or a time or place known or which should be known to be inconvenient to the consumer. In the absence of knowledge of circumstances to the contrary, a debt collector shall assume that the convenient time for communicating with a consumer is after 8 o'clock antimeridian and before 9 o'clock postmeridian, local time at the consumer's location;

(2) if the debt collector knows the consumer is represented by an attorney with respect to such debt and has knowledge of, or can readily ascertain, such attorney's name and address, unless the attorney fails to respond within a reasonable period of time to a communication from the debt collector or unless the attorney consents to direct communication with the consumer; or

(3) at the consumer's place of employment if the debt collector knows or has reason to know that the consumer's employer prohibits the consumer from receiving such communication.

(b) Communication with third parties—Except as provided in section 804, without the prior consent of the consumer given directly to the debt collector, or the express permission of a court of competent jurisdiction, or as reasonably necessary to effectuate a postjudgment judicial remedy, a debt collector may not communicate, in connection with the collection of any debt, with any person other than the consumer, his attorney, a consumer reporting agency if otherwise permitted by law, the creditor, the attorney of the creditor, or the attorney of the debt collector.

(c) Ceasing communication—If a consumer notifies a debt collector in writing that the consumer refuses to pay a debt or that the consumer wishes the debt collector to cease further communication with the consumer, the debt collector shall not communicate further with the consumer with respect to such debt, except—

(1) to advise the consumer that the debt collector's further efforts are being terminated;

(2) to notify the consumer that the debt collector or creditor may invoke specified remedies which are ordinarily invoked by such debt collector or creditor; or

(3) where applicable, to notify the consumer that the debt collector or creditor intends to invoke a specified remedy.

If such notice from the consumer is made by mail, notification shall be complete upon receipt.

(d) For the purpose of this section, the term "consumer" includes the consumer's spouse, parent (if the consumer is a minor), guardian, executor, or administrator.

§806. Harassment or abuse [15 U.S.C. §1692d]

A debt collector may not engage in any conduct the natural consequence of which is to harass, oppress, or abuse any person in connection with the collection of a debt. Without limiting the general application of the foregoing, the following conduct is a violation of this section:

(1) The use or threat of use of violence or other criminal means to harm the physical person, reputation, or property of any person.

(2) The use of obscene or profane language or language the natural consequence of which is to abuse the hearer or reader.

(3) The publication of a list of consumers who allegedly refuse to pay debts, except to a consumer reporting agency or to persons meeting the requirements of section 603(f) or 604(3) of this Act.

(4) The advertisement for sale of any debt to coerce payment of the debt.

(5) Causing a telephone to ring or engaging any person in telephone conversation repeatedly or continuously with intent to annoy, abuse, or harass any person at the called number.

(6) Except as provided in section 804, the placement of telephone calls without meaningful disclosure of the caller's identity.

§807. False or misleading representations [15 U.S.C. §1692e]

A debt collector may not use any false, deceptive, or misleading representation or means in connection with the collection of any debt. Without limiting the general application of the foregoing, the following conduct is a violation of this section:

(1) The false representation or implication that the debt collector is vouched for, bonded by, or affiliated with the United States or any State, including the use of any badge, uniform, or facsimile thereof.

(2) The false representation of—

(A) the character, amount, or legal status of any debt; or

(B) any services rendered or compensation which may be lawfully received by any debt collector for the collection of a debt.

(3) The false representation or implication that any individual is an attorney or that any communication is from an attorney.

(4) The representation or implication that nonpayment of any debt will result in the arrest or imprisonment of any person or the seizure, garnishment, attachment, or sale of any property or wages of any person unless such action is lawful and the debt collector or creditor intends to take such action.

(5) The threat to take any action that cannot legally be taken or that is not intended to be taken.

(6) The false representation or implication that a sale, referral, or other transfer of any interest in a debt shall cause the consumer to—

(A) lose any claim or defense to payment of the debt; or

(B) become subject to any practice prohibited by this subchapter.

(7) The false representation or implication that the consumer committed any crime or other conduct in order to disgrace the consumer.

(8) Communicating or threatening to communicate to any person credit information which is known or which should be known to be false, including the failure to communicate that a disputed debt is disputed.

(9) The use or distribution of any written communication which simulates or is falsely represented to be a document authorized, issued, or approved by any court, official, or agency of the United States or any State, or which creates a false impression as to its source, authorization or approval.

(10) The use of any false representation or deceptive means to collect or attempt to collect any debt or to obtain information concerning a consumer.

(11) Except as otherwise provided for communications to acquire location information under section 1692b of this title, the failure to disclose clearly in all communications made to collect a debt or to obtain information about a consumer, that the debt collector is attempting to collect a debt and that any information obtained will be used for that purpose.

(12) The false representation or implication that accounts have been turned over to innocent purchasers for value.

(13) The false representation or implication that documents are legal process.

(14) The use of any business, company, or organization name other than the true name of the debt collector's business, company, or organization.

(15) The false representation or implication that documents are not legal process forms or do not require action by the consumer.

(16) The false representation or implication that a debt collector operates or is employed by a consumer reporting agency as defined by section 603(f) of this Act.

§808.   Unfair practices [15 U.S.C. §1692f]

A debt collector may not use unfair or unconscionable means to collect or attempt to collect any debt. Without limiting the general application of the foregoing, the following conduct is a violation of this section:

(1) The collection of any amount (including any interest, fee, charge, or expense incidental to the principal obligation) unless such amount is expressly authorized by the agreement creating the debt or permitted by law.

(2) The acceptance by a debt collector from any person of a check or other payment instrument postdated by more than five days unless such person is notified in writing of the debt collector's intent to deposit such check or instrument not more than ten nor less than three business days prior to such deposit.

(3) The solicitation by a debt collector of any postdated check or other postdated payment instrument for the purpose of threatening or instituting criminal prosecution.

(4) Depositing or threatening to deposit any postdated check or other postdated payment instrument prior to the date on such check or instrument.

(5) Causing charges to be made to any person for communications by concealment of the true purpose of the communication. Such charges include, but are not limited to, collect telephone calls and telegram fees.

(6) Taking or threatening to take any nonjudicial action to effect dispossession or disablement of property if—

(A) there is no present right to possession of the property claimed as collateral through an enforceable security interest;

(B) there is no present intention to take possession of the property; or

(C) the property is exempt by law from such dispossession or disablement.

(7) Communicating with a consumer regarding a debt by post card.

(8) Using any language or symbol, other than the debt collector's address, on any envelope when communicating with a consumer by use of the mails or by telegram, except that a debt collector may use his business name if such name does not indicate that he is in the debt collection business.

§809. Validation of debts [15 U.S.C. §1692g]

(a) Within five days after the initial communication with a consumer in connection with the collection of any debt, a debt collector shall, unless the following information is contained in the initial communication or the consumer has paid the debt, send the consumer a written notice containing—

(1) the amount of the debt;

(2) the name of the creditor to whom the debt is owed;

(3) a statement that unless the consumer, within thirty days after receipt of the notice, disputes the validity of the debt, or any portion thereof, the debt will be assumed to be valid by the debt collector;

(4) a statement that if the consumer notifies the debt collector in writing within the thirty-day period that the debt, or any portion thereof, is disputed, the debt collector will obtain verification of the debt or a copy of a judgment against the consumer and a copy of such verification or judgment will be mailed to the consumer by the debt collector; and

(5) a statement that, upon the consumer's written request within the thirty-day period, the debt collector will provide the consumer with the name and address of the original creditor, if different from the current creditor.

(b) If the consumer notifies the debt collector in writing within the thirty-day period described in subsection (a) of this section that the debt, or any portion thereof, is disputed, or that the consumer requests the name and address of the original creditor, the debt collector shall cease collection of the debt, or any disputed portion thereof, until the debt collector obtains verification of the debt or a copy of a judgment, or the name and address of the original creditor, and a copy of such verification or judgment, or name and address of the original creditor, is mailed to the consumer by the debt collector.

(c) The failure of a consumer to dispute the validity of a debt under this section may not be construed by any court as an admission of liability by the consumer.

§810. Multiple debts [15 U.S.C. §1692h]

If any consumer owes multiple debts and makes any single payment to any debt collector with respect to such debts, such debt collector may not apply such payment to any debt which is disputed by the consumer and, where applicable, shall apply such payment in accordance with the consumer's directions.

§811. Legal actions by debt collectors [15 U.S.C. §1692i]

(a) Any debt collector who brings any legal action on a debt against any consumer shall—

(1) in the case of an action to enforce an interest in real property securing the consumer's obligation, bring such action only in a judicial district or similar legal entity in which such real property is located; or

(2) in the case of an action not described in paragraph (1), bring such action only in the judicial district or similar legal entity—

(A) in which such consumer signed the contract sued upon; or

(B) in which such consumer resides at the commencement of the action.

(b) Nothing in this subchapter shall be construed to authorize the bringing of legal actions by debt collectors.

§812. Furnishing certain deceptive forms [15 U.S.C. §1692j]

(a) It is unlawful to design, compile, and furnish any form knowing that such form would be used to create the false belief in a consumer that a person other than the creditor of such consumer is participating in the collection of or in an attempt to collect a debt such consumer allegedly owes such creditor, when in fact such person is not so participating.

(b) Any person who violates this section shall be liable to the same extent and in the same manner as a debt collector is liable under section 813 for failure to comply with a provision of this title.

§813. Civil liability [15 U.S.C. §1692k]

(a) Except as otherwise provided by this section, any debt collector who fails to comply with any provision of this title with respect to any person is liable to such person in an amount equal to the sum of—

(1) any actual damage sustained by such person as a result of such failure;

(2)(A) in the case of any action by an individual, such additional damages as the court may allow, but not exceeding $1,000; or

(B) in the case of a class action, (i) such amount for each named plaintiff as could be recovered under subparagraph (A), and (ii) such amount as the court may allow for all other class members, without regard to a minimum individual recovery, not to exceed the lesser of $500,000 or 1 per centum of the net worth of the debt collector; and

(3) in the case of any successful action to enforce the foregoing liability, the cost of the action, together with a reasonable attorney's fee as determined by the court. On a finding by the court that an action under this section was brought in bad faith and for the purpose of harassment, the court may award to the defendant attorney's fees reasonable in relation to the work expended and costs.

(b) In determining the amount of liability in any action under subsection (a) of this section, the court shall consider, amoung other relevant factors—

(1) in any individual action under subsection (a)(2)(A) of this section, the frequency and persistence of noncompliance by the debt collector, the nature of such noncompliance, and the extent to which such noncompliance was intentional; or

(2) in any class action under subsection (a)(2)(B) of this section, the frequency and persistence of noncompliance by the debt collector, the nature of such noncompliance, the resources of the debt collector, the number of persons adversely affected, and the extent to which the debt collector's noncompliance was intentional.

(c) A debt collector may not be held liable in any action brought under this title if the debt collector shows by a preponderance of evidence that the violation was not intentional and resulted from a bona fide error notwithstanding the maintenance of procedures reasonably adapted to avoid any such error.

(d) An action to enforce any liability created by this title may be brought in any appropriate United States district court without regard to the amount in controversy, or in any other court of competent jurisdiction, within one year from the date on which the violation occurs.

(e) No provision of this section imposing any liability shall apply to any act done or omitted in good faith in conformity with any advisory opinion of the Commission, notwithstanding that after such act or omission has occurred, such opinion is amended, rescinded, or determined by judicial or other authority to be invalid for any reason.

§814. Administrative enforcement [15 U.S.C. §1692l]

(a) Compliance with this title shall be enforced by the Commission, except to the extent that enforcement of the requirements imposed under this title is specifically committed to another agency under subsection (b) of this section. For purpose of the exercise by the Commission of its functions and powers under the Federal Trade Commission Act, a violation of this title shall be deemed an unfair or deceptive act or practice in violation of that Act. All of the functions and powers of the Commission under the Federal Trade Commission Act are available to the Commission to enforce compliance by any person with this title, irrespective of whether that person is engaged in commerce or meets any other jurisdictional tests in the Federal Trade Commission Act, including the power to enforce the provisions of this title in the same manner as if the violation had been a violation of a Federal Trade Commission trade regulation rule.

(b) Compliance with any requirements imposed under this title shall be enforced under—

(1) section 8 of Federal Deposit Insurance Act, in the case of—

(A) national banks, by the Comptroller of the Currency;

(B) member banks of the Federal Reserve System (other than national banks), by the Federal Reserve Board; and

(C) banks the deposits or accounts of which are insured by the Federal Deposit Insurance Corporation (other than members of the Federal Reserve System), by the Board of Directors of the Federal Deposit Insurance Corporation;

(2) section 5(d) of the Home Owners Loan Act of 1933, section 407 of the National Housing Act, and sections 6(i) and 17 of the Federal Home Loan Bank Act, by the Federal Home Loan Bank Board (acting directly or through the Federal Savings and Loan Insurance Corporation), in the case of any institution subject to any of those provisions;

(3) the Federal Credit Union Act, by the Administrator of the National Credit Union Administration with respect to any Federal credit union;

(4) the Acts to regulate commerce, by the Interstate Commerce Commission with respect to any common carrier subject to those Acts;

(5) the Federal Aviation Act of 1958, by the Civil Aeronautics Board with respect to any air carrier or any foreign air carrier subject to that Act; and

(6) the Packers and Stockyards Act, 1921 (except as provided in section 406 of that Act), by the Secretary of Agriculture with respect to any activities subject to that Act.

(c) For the purpose of the exercise by any agency referred to in subsection (b) of this section of its powers under any Act referred to in that subsection, a violation of any requirement imposed under this title shall be deemed to be a violation of a requirement imposed under that Act. In addition to its powers under any provision of law specifically referred to in subsection (b) of this section, each of the agencies referred to in that subsection may exercise, for the purpose of enforcing compliance with any requirement imposed under this title any other authority conferred on it by law, except as provided in subsection (d) of this section.

(d) Neither the Commission nor any other agency referred to in subsection (b) of this section may promulgate trade regulation rules or other regulations with respect to the collection of debts by debt collectors as defined in this title.

§815.   Reports to Congress by the Commission [15 U.S.C. §1692m]

(a) Not later than one year after the effective date of this subchapter and at one-year intervals thereafter, the Commission shall make reports to the

Congress concerning the administration of its functions under this subchapter, including such recommendations as the Commission deems necessary or appropriate. In addition, each report of the Commission shall include its assessment of the extent to which compliance with this title is being achieved and a summary of the enforcement actions taken by the Commission under section 814.

(b) In the exercise of its functions under this title, the Commission may obtain upon request the views of any other Federal agency which exercises enforcement functions under section 814.

§816.   Relation to State laws [15 U.S.C. §1692n]

This title does not annul, alter, or affect, or exempt any person subject to the provisions of this title from complying with the laws of any State with respect to debt collection practices, except to the extent that those laws are inconsistent with any provision of this title, and then only to the extent of the inconsistency. For purposes of this section, a State law is not inconsistent with this title if the protection such law affords any consumer is greater than the protection provided by this title.

§817.   Exemption for State regulation [15 U.S.C. §1692o]

The Commission shall by regulation exempt from the requirements of this title any class of debt collection practices within any State if the Commission determines that under the law of that State that class of debt collection practices is subject to requirements substantially similar to those imposed by this title, and that there is adequate provision for enforcement.

Appendix I
Title IX. Electronic Fund Transfer Act

(15 U.S.C. §§1693-1963r)

Table of Sections

---

§901. Short title

This Act may be cited as the "Electronic Fund Transfer Act."

§902. Findings and purpose [15 U.S.C. §1693]

(a) The Congress finds that the use of electronic systems to transfer funds provides the potential for substantial benefits to consumers. However, due to the unique characteristics of such systems, the application of existing consumer protection legislation is unclear, leaving the rights and liabilities of consumers, financial institutions, and intermediaries in electronic fund transfers undefined.

(b) It is the purpose of this title to provide a basic framework establishing the rights, liabilities, and responsibilities of participants in electronic fund transfer systems. The primary objective of this title, however, is the provision of individual consumer rights.

§903. Definitions [15 U.S.C. §1693a]

As used in this title—

(1) the term "accepted card or other means of access" means a card, code, or other means of access to a consumer's account for the purpose of initiating electronic fund transfers when the person to whom such card or other means of access was issued has requested and received or has signed or has used, or authorized another to use, such card or other means of access for the purpose of transferring money between accounts or obtaining money, property, labor, or services;

(2) the term "account" means a demand deposit, savings deposit, or other asset account (other than an occasional or incidental credit balance in an open end credit plan as defined in section 103(i) of this Act), as described in regulations of the Board, established primarily for personal, family, or household purposes, but such term does not include an account held by a financial institution pursuant to a bona fide trust agreement;

(3) the term "Board" means the Board of Governors of the Federal Reserve System;

(4) the term "business day" means any day on which the offices of the consumer's financial institution involved in an electronic fund transfer are open to the public for carrying on substantially all of its business functions;

(5) the term "consumer" means a natural person;

(6) the term "electronic fund transfer" means any transfer of funds, other than a transaction originated by check, draft, or similar paper instrument, which is initiated through an electronic terminal, telephonic instrument, or computer or magnetic tape so as to order, instruct, or authorize a financial institution to debit or credit an account. Such term includes, but is not limited to, point-of-sale transfers, automated teller machine transactions, direct deposits or withdrawals of funds, and transfers initiated by telephone. Such term does not include—

(A) any check guarantee or authorization service which does not directly result in a debit or credit to a consumer's account:

(B) any transfer of funds, other than those processed by automated clearinghouse, made by a financial institution on behalf of a consumer by means of a service that transfers funds held at either Federal Reserve banks or other depository institutions and which is not designed primarily to transfer funds on behalf of a consumer;

(C) any transaction the primary purpose of which is the purchase or sale of securities or commodities through a broker-dealer registered with or regulated by the Securities and Exchange Commission;

(D) any automatic transfer from a savings account to a demand deposit account pursuant to an agreement between a consumer and a financial institution for the purpose of covering an overdraft or maintaining an agreed upon minimum balance in the consumer's demand deposit account; or

(E) any transfer of funds which is initiated by a telephone conversation between a consumer and an officer or employee of a financial institution which is not pursuant to a prearranged plan and under which periodic or recurring transfers are not contemplated;

as determined under regulations of the Board;

(7) the term "electronic terminal" means an electronic device, other than a telephone operated by a consumer, through which a consumer may initiate an electronic fund transfer. Such term includes, but is not limited to, point-of-sale terminals, automated teller machines, and cash dispensing machines;

(8) the term "financial institution" means a State or National bank, a State or Federal savings and loan association, a mutual savings bank, a State or Federal Credit union, or any other person who, directly or indirectly, holds an account belonging to a consumer;

(9) the term "preauthorized electronic fund transfer" means an electronic fund transfer authorized in advance to recur at substantially regular intervals;

(10) the term "State" means any State, territory, or possession of the United States, the District of Columbia, the Commonwealth of Puerto Rico, or any political subdivision of any of the foregoing; and

(11) the term "unauthorized electronic fund transfer" means an electronic fund transfer from a consumer's account initiated by a person other than the consumer without actual authority to initiate such transfer and from which the consumer receives no benefit, but the term does not include any electronic fund transfer (A) initiated by a person other than the consumer who was furnished with the card, code, or other means of access to such consumer's account by such consumer, unless the consumer has notified the financial institution involved that transfers by such other person are no longer authorized, (B) initiated with fraudulent intent by the consumer or any person acting in concert with the consumer, or (C) which constitutes an error committed by a financial institution.

§904.   Regulations [15 U.S.C. §1693b]

(a) The Board shall prescribe regulations to carry out the purposes of this title. In prescribing such regulations, the Board shall:

(1) consult with the other agencies referred to in section 917 and take into account, and allow for, the continuing evolution of electronic banking services and the technology utilized in such services,

(2) prepare an analysis of economic impact which considers the costs and benefits to financial institutions, consumers, and other users of electronic fund transfers, including the extent to which additional documentation, reports, records, or other paper work would be required, and the effects upon competition in the provision of electronic banking services among large and small financial institutions and the availability of such services to different classes of consumers, particularly low income consumers,

(3) to the extent practicable, the Board shall demonstrate that the consumer protections of the proposed regulations outweigh the compliance costs imposed upon consumers and financial institutions, and

(4) any proposed regulations and accompanying analyses shall be sent promptly to Congress by the Board.

(b) The Board shall issue model clauses for optional use by financial institutions to facilitate compliance with the disclosure requirements of section 905 and to aid consumers in understanding the rights and responsibilities of participants in electronic fund transfers by utilizing readily understandable language. Such model clauses shall be adopted after notice duly given in the Federal Register and opportunity for public comment in accordance with section 553 of Title 5. With respect to the disclosures required by section 905(a)(3) and (4), the Board shall take account of variations in the services and charges under different electronic fund transfer systems and, as appropriate, shall issue alternative model clauses for disclosure of these differing account terms.

(c) Regulations prescribed hereunder may contain such classifications, differentiations, or other provisions, and may provide for such adjustments and exceptions for any class of electronic fund transfers, as in the judgment of the Board are necessary or proper to effectuate the purposes of this title, to prevent circumvention or evasion thereof, or to facilitate compliance therewith. The Board shall by regulation modify the requirements imposed by this title on small financial institutions if the Board determines that such modifications are necessary to alleviate any undue compliance burden on small financial institutions and such modifications are consistent with the purpose and objective of this title.

(d) In the event that electronic fund transfer services are made available to consumers by a person other than a financial institution holding a consumer's account, the Board shall by regulation assure that the disclosures, protections, responsibilities, and remedies created by this title are made applicable to such persons and services.

§905. Terms and conditions of transfers [15 U.S.C. §1693c]

(a) The terms and conditions of electronic fund transfers involving a consumer's account shall be disclosed at the time the consumer contracts for an electronic fund transfer service, in accordance with regulations of the Board. Such disclosures shall be in readily understandable language and shall include, to the extent applicable—

(1) the consumer's liability for unauthorized electronic fund transfers and, at the financial institution's option, notice of the advisability of prompt reporting of any loss, theft, or unauthorized use of a card, code, or other means of access;

(2) the telephone number and address of the person or office to be notified

in the event the consumer believes that an unauthorized electronic fund transfer has been or may be effected;

(3) the type and nature of electronic fund transfers which the consumer may initiate, including any limitations on the frequency or dollar amount of such transfers, except that the details of such limitations need not be disclosed if their confidentiality is necessary to maintain the security of an electronic fund transfer system, as determined by the Board;

(4) any charges for electronic fund transfers or for the right to make such transfers;

(5) the consumer's right to stop payment of a preauthorized electronic fund transfer and the procedure to initiate such a stop payment order;

(6) the consumer's right to receive documentation of electronic fund transfers under section 906;

(7) a summary, in a form prescribed by regulations of the Board, of the error resolution provisions of section 908 and the consumer's rights thereunder. The financial institution shall thereafter transmit such summary at least once per calendar year;

(8) the financial institution's liability to the consumer under section 910; and

(9) under what circumstances the financial institution will in the ordinary course of business disclose information concerning the consumer's account to third persons.

(b) A financial institution shall notify a consumer in writing at least twenty-one days prior to the effective date of any change in any term or condition of the consumer's account required to be disclosed under subsection (a) of this section if such change would result in greater cost or liability for such consumer or decreased access to the consumer's account. A financial institution may, however, implement a change in the terms or conditions of an account without prior notice when such change is immediately necessary to maintain or restore the security of an electronic fund transfer system or a consumer's account. Subject to subsection (a)(3) of this section, the Board shall require subsequent notification if such a change is made permanent.

(c) For any account of a consumer made accessible to electronic fund transfers prior to the effective date of this title, the information required to be disclosed to the consumer under subsection (a) of this section shall be disclosed not later than the earlier of—

(1) the first periodic statement required by section 906(c) after the effective date of this title; or

(2) thirty days after the effective date of this title.

§906.   Documentation of transfers; periodic statements [15 U.S.C. §1693d]

(a) For each electronic fund transfer initiated by a consumer from an electronic terminal, the financial institution holding such consumer's account shall, directly or indirectly, at the time the transfer is initiated, make available to the consumer written documentation of such transfer. The documentation shall clearly set forth to the extent applicable—

(1) the amount involved and date the transfer is initiated;

(2) the type of transfer;

(3) the identity of the consumer's account with the financial institution from which or to which funds are transferred;

(4) the identity of any third party to whom or from whom funds are transferred; and

(5) the location or identification of the electronic terminal involved.

(b) For a consumer's account which is scheduled to be credited by a preauthorized electronic fund transfer from the same payor at least once in each successive sixty-day period, except where the payor provides positive notice of the transfer to the consumer, the financial institution shall elect to provide promptly either positive notice to the consumer when the credit is made as scheduled, or negative notice to the consumer when the credit is not made as scheduled, in accordance with regulations of the Board. The means of notice elected shall be disclosed to the consumer in accordance with section 905.

(c) A financial institution shall provide each consumer with a periodic statement for each account of such consumer that may be accessed by means of an electronic fund transfer. Except as provided in subsections (d) and (e) of this section, such statement shall be provided at least monthly for each monthly or shorter cycle in which an electronic fund transfer affecting the account has occurred, or every three months, whichever is more frequent. The statement, which may include information regarding transactions other than electronic fund transfers, shall clearly set forth—

(1) with regard to each electronic fund transfer during the period, the information described in subsection (a) of this section, which may be provided on an accompanying document;

(2) the amount of any fee or charge assessed by the financial institution during the period for electronic fund transfers or for account maintenance;

(3) the balances in the consumer's account at the beginning of the period and at the close of the period; and

(4) the address and telephone number to be used by the financial institution for the purpose of receiving any statement inquiry or notice of account error from the consumer. Such address and telephone number shall be preceded by the caption "Direct Inquiries To:" or other similar language indicating that the address and number are to be used for such inquiries or notices.

(d) In the case of a consumer's passbook account which may not be accessed by electronic fund transfers other than preauthorized electronic fund transfers crediting the account, a financial institution may, in lieu of complying with the requirements of subsection (c) of this section, upon presentation of the passbook provide the consumer in writing with the amount and date of each such transfer involving the account since the passbook was last presented.

(e) In the case of a consumer's account, other than a passbook account, which may not be accessed by electronic fund transfers other than preauthorized electronic fund transfers crediting the account, the financial institution may provide a periodic statment on a quarterly basis which otherwise complies with the requirements of subsection (c) of this section.

(f) In any action involving a consumer, any documentation required by this section to be given to the consumer which indicates that an electronic fund transfer was made to another person shall be admissible as evidence of such transfer and shall constitute prima facie proof that such transfer was made.

§907. Preauthorized transfers [15 U.S.C. §1693e]

(a) A preauthorized electronic fund transfer from a consumer's account may be authorized by the consumer only in writing, and a copy of such authorization shall be provided to the consumer when made. A consumer may stop payment of a preauthorized electronic fund transfer by notifying the financial institution orally or in writing at any time up to three business days preceding the scheduled date of such transfer. The financial institution may require written confirmation to be provided to it within fourteen days of an oral notification if, when the oral notification is made, the consumer is advised of such requirement and the address to which such confirmation should be sent.

(b) In the case of preauthorized transfers from a consumer's account to the same person which may vary in amount, the financial institution or designated payee shall, prior to each transfer, provide reasonable advance notice to the consumer, in accordance with regulations of the Board, of the amount to be transferred and the scheduled date of the transfer.

§908. Error resolution [15 U.S.C. §1693f]

(a) If a financial institution, within sixty days after having transmitted to a consumer documentation pursuant to section 906(a), (c), or (d) or notification pursuant to section 906(b), receives oral or written notice in which the consumer—

(1) sets forth or otherwise enables the financial institution to identify the name and account number of the consumer;

(2) indicates the consumer's belief that the documentation, or, in the case of notification pursuant to section 906(b), the consumer's account, contains an error and the amount of such error; and

(3) sets forth the reasons for the consumer's belief (where applicable) that an error has occurred,

the financial institution shall investigate the alleged error, determine whether an error has occurred, and report or mail the results of such investigation and determination to the consumer within ten business days. The financial institution may require written confirmation to be provided to it within ten business days of an oral notification of error if, when the oral notification is made, the consumer is advised of such requirement and the address to which such confirmation should be sent. A financial institution which requires written confirmation in accordance with the previous sentence need not provisionally recredit a consumer's account in accordance with subsection (c) of this section, nor shall the financial institution be liable under subsection (e) of this section if the written confirmation is not received within the ten-day period referred to in the previous sentence.

(b) If the financial institution determines that an error did occur, it shall promptly, but in no event more than one business day after such determination, correct the error, subject to section 909, including the crediting of interest where applicable.

(c) If a financial institution receives notice of an error in the manner and within the time period specified in subsection (a) of this section, it may, in lieu of the requirements of subsections (a) and (b) of this section, within ten business days after receiving such notice provisionally recredit the consumer's account for the amount alleged to be in error, subject to section 909, including interest where applicable, pending the conclusion of its investigation and its determination of whether an error has occurred. Such investigation shall be concluded not later than forty-five days after receipt of notice of the error. During the pendency of the investigation, the consumer shall have full use of the funds provisionally recredited.

(d) If the financial institution determines after its investigation pursuant to subsection (a) or (c) of this section that an error did not occur, it shall deliver or mail to the consumer an explanation of its findings within 3 business days after the conclusion of its investigation, and upon request of the consumer promptly deliver or mail to the consumer reproductions of all documents which the financial institution relied on to conclude that such error did not occur. The financial institution shall include notice of the right to request reproductions with the explanation of its findings.

(e) If in any action under section 915, the court finds that—

(1) the financial institution did not provisionally recredit a consumer's account within the ten-day period specified in subsection (c) of this section, and the financial institution (A) did not make a good faith investigation of the alleged error, or (B) did not have a reasonable basis for believing that the consumer's account was not in error; or

(2) the financial institution knowingly and willfully concluded that the consumer's account was not in error when such conclusion could not reasonably have been drawn from the evidence available to the financial institution at the time of its investigation,

then the consumer shall be entitled to treble damages determined under section 915(a)(1).

(f) For the purpose of this section, an error consists of—

(1) an unauthorized electronic fund transfer;

(2) an incorrect electronic fund transfer from or to the consumer's account;

(3) the omission from a periodic statement of an electronic fund transfer affecting the consumer's account which should have been included;

(4) a computational error by the financial institution;

(5) the consumer's receipt of an incorrect amount of money from an electronic terminal;

(6) a consumer's request for additional information or clarification concerning an electronic fund transfer or any documentation required by this title; or

(7) any other error described in regulations of the Board.

§909. Consumer liability for unauthorized transfers [15 U.S.C. §1693g]

(a) A consumer shall be liable for any unauthorized electronic fund transfer involving the account of such consumer only if the card or other means of access utilized for such transfer was an accepted card or other means of access and if the issuer of such card, code, or other means of access has provided a means whereby the user of such card, code, or other means of access can be identified as the person authorized to use it, such as by signature, photograph, or fingerprint or by electronic or mechanical confirmation. In no event, however, shall a consumer's liability for an unauthorized transfer exceed the lesser of—

(1) $50; or

(2) the amount of money or value of property or services obtained in such unauthorized electronic fund transfer prior to the time the financial institution is notified of, or otherwise becomes aware of, circumstances which lead to the reasonable belief that an unauthorized electronic fund transfer involving the consumer's account has been or may be effected. Notice under this paragraph is sufficient when such steps have been taken as may be reasonably required in the ordinary course of business to provide the financial institution with the pertinent information, whether or not any particular officer, employee, or agent of the financial institution does in fact receive such information.

Notwithstanding the foregoing, reimbursement need not be made to the consumer for losses the financial institution establishes would not have occurred but for the failure of the consumer to report within sixty days of transmittal of the statement (or in extenuating circumstances such an extended travel or hospitalization, within a reasonable time under the circumstances) any unauthorized electronic fund transfer or account error which appears on the periodic statement provided to the consumer under section 906. In addition, reimbursement need not be made to the consumer for losses which the financial institution establishes would not have occurred but for the failure of the consumer to report any loss or theft of a card or other means of access within two business days after the consumer learns of the loss or theft (or in extenuating circumstances such as extended travel or hospitalization, within a longer period which is reasonable under the circumstances), but the consumer's liability under this subsection in any such case may not exceed a total of $500, or the amount of unauthorized electronic fund transfers which occur following the close of two business days (or such longer period) after the consumer learns of the loss or theft but prior to notice to the financial institution under this subsection, whichever is less.

(b) In any action which involves a consumer's liability for an unauthorized electronic fund transfer, the burden of proof is upon the financial institution to show that the electronic fund transfer was authorized or, if the electronic fund transfer was unauthorized, then the burden of proof is upon the financial institution to establish that the conditions of liability set forth in subsection (a) of this section have been met, and, if the transfer was initiated after the effective date of section 905, that the disclosures required to be made to the consumer under section 905(a)(1) and (2) were in fact made in accordance with such section.

(c) In the event of a transaction which involves both an unauthorized electronic fund transfer and an extension of credit as defined in section 103(e) of this Act pursuant to an agreement between the consumer and the financial institution to extend such credit to the consumer in the event the consumer's account is overdrawn, the limitation on the consumer's liability for such transaction shall be determined solely in accordance with this section.

(d) Nothing in this section imposes liability upon a consumer for an unauthorized electronic fund transfer in excess of his liability for such a transfer under other applicable law or under any agreement with the consumer's financial institution.

(e) Except as provided in this section, a consumer incurs no liability from an unauthorized electronic fund transfer.

§910. Liability of financial institutions [15 U.S.C. §1693h]

(a) Subject to subsections (b) and (c) of this section, a financial institution shall be liable to a consumer for all damages proximately caused by—

(1) the financial institution's failure to make an electronic fund transfer, in accordance with the terms and conditions of an account, in the correct amount or in a timely manner when properly instructed to do so by the consumer, except where—

(A) the consumer's account has insufficient funds;

(B) the funds are subject to legal process or other encumbrance restricting such transfer;

(C) such transfer would exceed an established credit limit;

(D) an electronic terminal has insufficient cash to complete the transaction; or

(E) as otherwise provided in regulations of the Board;

(2) the financial institution's failure to make an electronic fund transfer due to insufficient funds when the financial institution failed to credit, in accordance with the terms and conditions of an account, a deposit of funds to

the consumer's account which would have provided sufficient funds to make the transfer, and

(3) the financial institution's failure to stop payment of a preauthorized transfer from a consumer's account when instructed to do so in accordance with the terms and conditions of the account.

(b) A financial institution shall not be liable under subsection (a)(1) or (2) of this section if the financial institution shows by a preponderance of the evidence that its action or failure to act resulted from—

(1) an act of God or other circumstance beyond its control, that it exercised reasonable care to prevent such an occurrence, and that it exercised such diligence as the circumstances required; or

(2) a technical malfunction which was known to the consumer at the time he attempted to initiate an electronic fund transfer or, in the case of a preauthorized transfer, at the time such transfer should have occurred.

(c) In the case of a failure described in subsection (a) of this section which was not intentional and which resulted from a bona fide error, notwithstanding the maintenance of procedures reasonably adapted to avoid any such error, the financial institution shall be liable for actual damages proved.

§911.   Issuance of cards or other means of access [15 U.S.C. §1693i]

(a) No person may issue to a consumer any card, code, or other means of access to such consumer's account for the purpose of initiating an electronic fund transfer other than—

(1) in response to a request or application therefor; or

(2) as a renewal of, or in substitution for, an accepted card, code, or other means of access, whether issued by the initial issuer or a successor.

(b) Notwithstanding the provisions of subsection (a) of this section, a person may distribute to a consumer on an unsolicited basis a card, code, or other means of access for use in initiating an electronic fund transfer from such consumer's account, if—

(1) such card, code, or other means of access is not validated;

(2) such distribution is accompanied by a complete disclosure, in accordance with section 905, of the consumer's rights and liabilities which will apply if such card, code, or other means of access is validated;

(3) such distribution is accompanied by a clear explanation, in accordance with regulations of the Board, that such card, code, or other means of access is not validated and how the consumer may dispose of such code, card, or other means of access if validation is not desired; and

(4) such card, code, or other means of access is validated only in response to a request or application from the consumer, upon verification of the consumer's identity.

(c) For the purpose of subsection (b) of this section, a card, code, or other means of access is validated when it may be used to initiate an electronic fund transfer.

§912.   Suspension of obligations [15 U.S.C. §1693j]

If a system malfunction prevents the effectuation of an electronic fund transfer initiated by a consumer to another person, and such other person has agreed to accept payment by such means, the consumer's obligation to the other person shall be suspended until the malfunction is corrected and the electronic fund transfer may be completed, unless such other person has subsequently, by written request, demanded payment by means other than an electronic fund transfer.

§913.   Compulsory use of electronic fund transfers [15 U.S.C. §1693k]

No person may—

(1) condition the extension of credit to a consumer on such consumer's repayment by means of preauthorized electronic fund transfers; or

(2) require a consumer to establish an account for receipt of electronic fund transfers with a particular financial institution as a condition of employment or receipt of a government benefit.

§914.   Waiver of rights [15 U.S.C. §1693*l*]

No writing or other agreement between a consumer and any other person may contain any provision which constitutes a waiver of any right conferred or cause of action created by this title. Nothing in this section prohibits, however, any writing or other agreement which grants to a consumer a more extensive right or remedy or greater protection than contained in this title or a waiver given in settlement of a dispute or action.

§915.   Civil liability [15 U.S.C. §1693m]

(a) Except as otherwise provided by this section and section 910, any person who fails to comply with any provision of this title with respect to any consumer, except for an error resolved in accordance with section 908, if liable to such consumer in an amount equal to the sum of—

(1) any actual damage sustained by such consumer as a result of such failure;

(2)(A) in the case of an individual action, an amount not less than $100 nor greater than $1,000; or

(B) in the case of a class action, such amount as the court may allow, except that (i) as to each member of the class no minimum recovery shall be applicable, and (ii) the total recovery under this subparagraph in any class action or series of class actions arising out of the same failure to comply by the same person shall not be more than the lesser of $500,000 or 1 per centum of the net worth of the defendant; and

(3) in the case of any successful action to enforce the foregoing liability, the costs of the action, together with a reasonable attorney's fee as determined by the court.

(b) In determining the amount of liability in any action under subsection (a) of this section, the court shall consider, among other relevant factors—

(1) in any individual action under subsection (a)(2)(A) of this section, the frequency and persistence of noncompliance, the nature of such noncompliance, and the extent to which the noncompliance was intentional; or

(2) in any class action under subsection (a)(2)(B) of this section, the frequency and persistence of noncompliance, the nature of such noncompliance, the resources of the defendant, the number of persons adversely affected, and the extent to which the noncompliance was intentional.

(c) Except as provided in section 910, a person may not be held liable in any action brought under this section for a violation of this title if the person shows by a preponderance of evidence that the violation was not intentional and resulted from a bona fide error notwithstanding the maintenance of procedures reasonably adapted to avoid any such error.

(d) No provision of this section or section 916 imposing any liability shall apply to—

(1) any act done or omitted in good faith in conformity with any rule, regulation, or interpretation thereof by the Board or in conformity with any interepretation or approval by an official or employee of the Federal Reserve System duly authorized by the Board to issue such interpretations or approvals under such procedures as the Board may prescribe therefor; or

(2) any failure to make disclosure in proper form if a financial institution utilized as appropriate model clause issued by the Board,

notwithstanding that after such act, omission, or failure has occurred, such rule, regulation, approval, or model clause is amended, rescinded, or determined by judicial or other authority to be invalid for any reason.

(e) A person has no liability under this section for any failure to comply with any requirement under this title if, prior to the institution of an action under this section, the person notifies the consumer concerned of the failure, complies with the requirements of this title, and makes an appropriate adjustment to the consumer's account and pays actual damages or, where applicable, damages in accordance with section 910.

(f) On a finding by the court that an unsuccessful action under this section was brought in bad faith or for purposes of harassment, the court shall award to the defendant attorney's fees reasonable in relation to the work expended and costs.

(g) Without regard to the amount in controversy, any action under this section may be brought in any United States district court, or in any other court of competent jurisdiction, within one year from the date of the occurrence of the violation.

§916. Criminal liability [15 U.S.C. §1693n]

(a) Whoever knowingly and willfully—

(1) gives false or inacurrate information or fails to provide information which he is required to disclose by this title or any regulation issued thereunder; or

(2) otherwise fails to comply with any provision of this title;

shall be fined not more than $5,000 or imprisoned not more than one year, or both.

(b) Whoever—

(1) knowingly, in a transaction affecting interstate or foreign commerce, uses or attempts or conspires to use any counterfeit, fictitious, altered, forged, lost, stolen, or fraudulently obtained debit instrument to obtain money, goods, services, or anything else of value which within any one-year period has a value aggregating $1,000 or more; or

(2) with unlawful or fraudulent intent, transports or attempts or conspires to transport in interstate or foreign commerce a counterfeit, fictitious, altered, forged, lost, stolen, or fraudulently obtained debit instrument knowing the same to be counterfeit, fictitious, altered, forged, lost, stolen, or fraudulently obtained; or

(3) with unlawful or fraudulent intent, uses any instrumentality of interstate or foreign commerce to sell or transport a counterfeit, fictitious, altered, forged, lost, stolen, or fraudulently obtained debit instrument knowing the same to be counterfeit, fictitious, altered, forged, lost, stolen, or fraudulently obtained; or

(4) knowingly receives, conceals, uses, or transports money, goods, services, or anything else of value (except tickets for interstate or foreign transportation) which (A) within any one-year period has a value aggregating $1,000 or more, (B) has moved in or is part of, or which constitutes interstate or foreign commerce, and (C) has been obtained with a counterfeit, fictitious, altered, forged, lost, stolen, or fraudulently obtained debit instrument; or

(5) knowingly receives, conceals, uses, sells, or transports in interstate or foreign commerce one or more tickets for interstate or foreign transportation, which (A) within any one-year period have a value aggregating $500 or more, and (B) have been purchased or obtained with one or more counterfeit, fictitious, altered, forged, lost, stolen, or fraudulently obtained debit instrument; or

(6) in a transaction affecting interstate or foreign commerce, furnishes money, property, services, or anything else of value, which within any one-year period has a value aggregating $1,000 or more, through the use of any counterfeit, fictitious, altered, forged, lost, stolen, or fraudulently obtained debit instrument knowing the same to be counterfeit, fictitious, altered, forged, lost, stolen, or fraudulently obtained shall be fined not more than $10,000 or imprisoned not more than ten years, or both.

(c) As used in this section, the term "debit instrument" means a card, code, or other device, other than a check, draft, or similar paper instrument, by the use of which a person may initiate an electronic fund transfer.

§917. Administrative enforcement [15 U.S.C. §1693*o*]

(a) Compliance with the requirements imposed under this title shall be enforced under—

(1) section 8 of the Federal Deposit Insurance Act, in the case of—

(A) national banks, by the Comptroller of the Currency;

(B) member banks of the Federal Reserve System (other than national banks), by the Board;

(C) banks insured by the Federal Deposit Insurance Corporation (other than members of the Federal Reserve System), by the Board of Directors of the Federal Deposit Insurance Corporation;

(2) section 5(d) of the Home Owners' Loan Act of 1933, section 407 of the National Housing Act, and sections 6(i) and 17 of the Federal Home Loan Bank Act, by the Federal Home Loan Bank Board (acting directly or through the Federal Savings and Loan Insurance Corporation), in the case of any institution subject to any of those provisions;

(3) the Federal Credit Union Act, by the Administrator of the National Credit Union Administration with respect to any Federal credit union;

(4) the Federal Aviation Act of 1958, by the Civil Aeronautics Board, with respect to any air carrier or foreign air carrier subject to that Act; and

(5) the Securities Exchange Act of 1934, by the Securities and Exchange Commission, with respect to any broker or dealer subject to that Act.

(b) For the purpose of the exercise by any agency referred to in subsection (a) of this section of its powers under any Act referred to in that subsection, a violation of any requirement imposed under this title shall be deemed to be a violation of a requirement imposed under that Act. In addition to its powers under any provision of law specifically referred to in subsection (a) of this section, each of the agencies referred to in that subsection may exercise, for the purpose of enforcing compliance with any requirement imposed under this title, any other authority conferred on it by law.

(c) Except to the extent that enforcement of the requirements imposed under this title is specifically committed to some other Government agency under subsection (a) of this section, the Federal Trade Commission shall enforce such requirements. For the purpose of the exercise by the Federal Trade Commission of its functions and powers under the Federal Trade Commission Act, a violation of any requirement imposed under this title shall be deemed a violation of a requirement imposed under that Act. All of the functions and powers of the Federal Trade Commission under the Federal Trade Commission Act are available to the Commission to enforce compliance by any person subject to the jurisdiction of the Commission with the requirements imposed under this title, irrespective of whether that person is engaged in commerce or meets any other jurisdictional tests in the Federal Trade Commission Act.

§918.   Reports to Congress [15 U.S.aC. §1693p]

(a) Not later than twelve months after the effective date of this subchapter and at one-year intervals thereafter, the Board and the Attorney General shall, respectively, make reports to the Congress concerning the administration of their functions under this title, including such recommendations as the Board and the Attorney General, respectively, deem necessary or appropriate. In addition, each report of the Board shall include its assessment of the extent to which compliance with this title is being achieved, and a summary of the enforcement actions taken under section 917. In such report, the Board shall particularly address the effects of this title on the costs and benefits to financial institutions and consumers, on competition, on the introduction of new technology, on the operations of financial institutions, and on the adequacy of consumer protection. The report of the Attorney General shall also contain an analysis of the impact of this title on the operation, workload, and efficiency of the Federal courts.

(b) In the exercise of its functions under this title, the Board may obtain upon request the views of any other Federal agency which, in the judgment of the Board, exercises regulatory or supervisory functions with respect to any class of persons subject to this title.

§919.   Relation to State laws [15 U.S.C. §1693q]

This title does not annul, alter, or affect the laws of any State relating to electronic fund transfers, except to the extent that those laws are inconsistent with the provisions of this title, and then only to the extent of the inconsistency. A State law is not inconsistent with this title if the protection such law affords any consumer is greater than the protection afforded by this title. The Board shall, upon its own motion or upon the request of any financial institution, State, or other interested party, submitted in accordance with procedures prescribed in regulations of the Board, determine whether a State requirement is inconsistent or affords greater protection. If the Board determines that a State requirement is inconsistent, financial institutions shall incur no liability under the law of that State for a good faith failure to comply with that law, notwithstanding that such determination is subsequently amended, rescinded, or determined by judicial or other authority to be invalid for any reason. This title does not extend the applicability of any such law to any class of persons or transactions to which it would not otherwise apply.

§920.   Exemption for State regulation [15 U.S.C. §1693r]

The Board shall by regulation exempt from the requirements of this title any class of electronic fund transfers within any State if the Board determines that under the law of that State that class of electronic fund transfers is subject to requirements substantially similar to those imposed by this title, and that there is adequate provision for enforcement.

Appendix J
Federal Reserve Board, Regulation E, Electronic Fund Transfers

12 C.F.R. Part 205

Table of Sections

---

§205.1 Authority, purpose, and scope

(a) *Authority.* This regulation, issued by the Board of Governors of the Federal Reserve System, implements Title IX (Electronic Fund Transfer Act) of the Consumer Credit Protection Act, as amended (15 U.S.C. 1601 et seq.).

(b) *Purpose and Scope.* In November 1978, the Congress enacted the Electronic Fund Transfer Act. The Congress found that the use of electronic systems to transfer funds provides the potential for substantial benefits to consumers, but that the unique characteristics of these systems make the application of existing consumer protection laws unclear, leaving the rights and liabilities of users of electronic fund transfer systems undefined. The Act establishes the basic rights, liabilities, and responsibilities of consumers who use electronic money transfer services and of financial institutions that offer these services. This regulation is intended to carry out the purposes of the Act, including, primarily, the protection of individual consumers engaging in electronic transfers. Except as otherwise provided, this regulation applies to all persons who are financial institutions as defined in §205.2(i).

§205.2   Definitions and rules of construction

For the purposes of this regulation, the following definitions apply, unless the context indicates otherwise:

(a)(1) "Access device" means a card, code, or other means of access to a consumer's account, or any combination thereof, that may be used by the consumer for the purpose of initiating electronic fund transfers.

(2) An access device becomes an "accepted access device" when the consumer to whom the access device was issued:

(i) Requests and receives, or signs, or uses, or authorizes another to use, the access device for the purpose of transferring money between accounts or obtaining money, property, labor or services;

(ii) Requests validation of an access device issued on an unsolicited basis; or

(iii) Receives an access device issued in renewal of, or in substitution for, an accepted access device, whether such access device is issued by the initial financial institution or a successor.

(b) "Account" means a demand deposit (checking), savings, or other consumer asset account (other than an occasional or incidental credit balance in a credit plan) held either directly or indirectly by a financial institution and established primarily for personal, family, or household purposes.

(c) "Act" means the Electronic Fund Transfer Act (Title IX of the Consumer Credit Protection Act, 15 U.S.C. 1601 et seq.).

(d) "Business day" means any day on which the offices of the consumer's financial institution are open to the public for carrying on substantially all business functions.

(e) "Consumer" means a natural person.

(f) "Credit" means the right granted by a financial institution to a consumer to defer payment of debt, incur debt and defer its payment, or purchase property or services and defer payment therefor.

(g) "Electronic fund transfer" means any transfer of funds, other than a transaction originated by check, draft, or similar paper instrument, that is initiated through an electronic terminal, telephone, or computer or magnetic tape for the purpose of ordering, instructing, or authorizing a financial institution to debit or credit an account. The term includes, but is not limited to, point-of-sale transfers, automated teller machine transfers, direct deposits or withdrawals of funds, and transfers initiated by telephone. The term does not include payments made by check, draft, or similar paper instrument at an electronic terminal.

(h) "Electronic terminal" means an electronic device, other than a telephone operated by a consumer, through which a consumer may initiate an electronic fund transfer. The term includes, but is not limited to, point-of-sale terminals, automated teller machines, and cash dispensing machines.

(i) "Financial institution" means a State or National bank, a State or Federal savings and loan association, a State or Federal mutual savings bank, a State or Federal credit union, or any other person who, directly or indirectly, holds an account belonging to a consumer. The term also includes any person who issues an access device and agrees with a consumer to provide electronic fund transfer services.

(j) "Preauthorized electronic fund transfer" means an electronic fund transfer authorized in advance to recur at substantially regular intervals.

(k) "State" means any State, territory or possession of the United States, the District of Columbia, the Commonwealth of Puerto Rico, or any political subdivision of any of the above.

(*l*) "Unauthorized electronic fund transfer" means an electronic fund transfer from a consumer's account initiated by a person other than the consumer without actual authority to initiate the transfer and from which the consumer receives no benefit. The term does not include any electronic fund transfer (1) initiated by a person who was furnished with the access device to the consumer's account by the consumer, unless the consumer has notified the financial institution involved that transfers by that person are no longer authorized, (2) initiated with fraudulent intent by the consumer or any person acting in concert with the consumer, or (3) that is initiated by the financial institution or its employee.

(m) Footnotes have the same legal effect as the text of the regulation.

§205.3   Exemptions

This Act and this regulation do not apply to the following:

(a) *Check guarantee or authorization services.*   Any service that guarantees payment or authorizes acceptance of a check, draft, or similar paper instrument and that does not directly result in a debit or credit to a consumer's account.

(b) *Wire transfers.*   Any wire transfer of funds for a consumer through the Federal Reserve Communications System or other similar network that is used primarily for transfers between financial institutions or between businesses.

(c) *Certain securities or commodities transfers.*   Any transfer the primary purpose of which is the purchase or sale of securities or commodities regulated by the Securities and Exchange Commission or the Commodity Futures Trading Commission.

(d) *Certain automatic transfers.*   Any transfer under an agreement between a consumer and a financial institution which provides that the institution will initiate individual transfers without a specific request from the consumer.

(1) Between a consumer's accounts within the financial institution, such as a transfer from a checking account to a savings account;

(2) Into a consumer's account by the financial institution, such as the crediting of interest to a savings account;[1a]

[1a.] The financial institution remains subject to section 913 of the act regarding

(3) From a consumer's account to an account of the financial institution, such as a loan payment;[1a] or

(4) From a consumer's account to an account of another consumer, within the financial institution, who is a member of the transferor's family.

(e) *Certain telephone-initiated transfers.* Any transfer of funds that (1) is initiated by a telephone conversation between a consumer and an officer or employee of a financial institution and (2) is not under a telephone bill-payment or other prearranged plan or agreement in which periodic or recurring transfers are contemplated.

(f) *Trust accounts.* Any trust account held by a financial institution under a bona fide trust agreement.

(g) *Preauthorized transfers to small financial institutions.* (1) Any preauthorized transfer to or from an account if the assets of the account-holding financial institution are $25 million or less on December 31.[1a]

(2) If the account-holding financial institution's assets subsequently exceed $25 million, the institution's exemption for this class of transfers shall terminate one year from the end of the calendar year in which the assets exceed $25 million.

§205.4 Special requirements

(a) *Services offered by two or more financial institutions.* Two or more financial institutions that jointly provide electronic fund transfer services may contract among themselves to comply with the requirements that this regulation imposes on any or all of them. When making disclosures under §§205.7 and 205.8, a financial institution that provides electronic fund transfer services under an agreement with other financial institutions need make only those disclosures which are within its knowledge and the purview of its relationship with the consumer for whom it holds on account.

(b) *Multiple accounts and account holders.* (1) If a consumer holds two or more accounts at a financial institution, the institution may combine the disclosures required by the regulation into one statement (for example, the financial institution may mail or deliver a single periodic statement or annual error resolution notice to a consumer for multiple accounts held by that consumer at that institution).

(2) If two or more consumers hold a joint account from or to which electronic fund transfers can be made, the financial institution need provide only one set of the disclosures required by the regulation for each account.

(c) *Additional information; disclosures required by other laws.* At the financial institution's option, additional information or disclosures required by other

---

compulsory use of electronic fund transfers. A financial institution may, however, require the automatic repayment of credit that is extended under an overdraft credit plan or that is extended to maintain a specified minimum balance in the consumer's account. Financial institutions also remain subject to sections 915 and 916 regarding civil and criminal liability.

laws (for example, Truth in Lending disclosures) may be combined with the disclosures required by this regulation.

§205.5   Issuance of access devices

(a) *General rule.*   A financial institution may issue an access device to a consumer only:

(1) In response to an oral or written request or application for the device;[1b] or

(2) As a renewal of, or in substitution for, an accepted access device, whether issued by the initial financial institution or a successor.

(3) As a renewal of, or in substitution for, an access device issued before February 8, 1979 (other than an accepted access device, which can be renewed or substituted under paragraph (a)(2) of this section), provided that the disclosures set forth in §§205.7(a)(1), (2), and (3) accompany the renewal or substitute device; except that for a renewal or substitution that occurs before July 1, 1979, the disclosures may be sent within a reasonable time after the renewal or substitute device is issued.

(b) *Exception.*   Notwithstanding the provisions of paragraph (a)(1) of this section, a financial institution may distribute an access device to a consumer on an unsolicited basis if:

(1) The access device is not validated;

(2) The distribution is accompanied by a complete disclosure, in accordance with §205.7(a), of the consumer's rights and liabilities that will apply if the access device is validated;

(3) The distribution is accompanied by a clear explanation that the access device is not validated and how the consumer may dispose of the access device if validation is not desired; and

(4) The access device is validated only in response to the consumer's oral or written request or application for validation and after verification of the consumer's identity by any reasonable means, such as by photograph, fingerprint, personal visit, or signature comparison. An access device is considered validated when a financial institution has performed all procedures necessary to enable a consumer to use it to initiate an electronic fund transfer.

(c) *Relation to Truth in Lending.*   (1) The Act and this regulation govern

(i) Issuance of access devices;

(ii) Addition to an accepted credit card, as defined in 12 CFR 226.2(a) (Regulation Z), of the capability to initiate electronic fund transfers; and

(iii) Issuance of access devices that permit credit extensions only under a preexisting agreement between a consumer and a financial institution to

---

[1b.] In the case of a joint account, a financial institution may issue an access device to each account holder for whom the requesting holder specifically requests an access device.

extend the credit when the consumer's account is overdrawn or to maintain a specified minimum balance in the consumer's account.

(2) The Truth in Lending Act (15 U.S.C. 1601 et seq.) and 12 CFR Part 226 (Regulation Z), which prohibit the unsolicited issuance of credit cards, govern

(i) Issuance of credit cards as defined in 12 CFR 226.2(r);

(ii) Addition of a credit feature to an accepted access device; and

(iii) Issuance of credit cards that are also access devices, except as provided in paragraph (c)(1)(iii) of this section.

§205.6   Liability of consumer for unauthorized transfers

(a) *General rule.*   A consumer is liable, within the limitations described in paragraph (b) of this section, for unauthorized electronic fund transfers involving the consumer's account only if:

(1) The access device used for the unauthorized transfers is an accepted access device;

(2) The financial institution has provided a means (such as by signature, photograph, fingerprint, or electronic or mechanical confirmation) to identify the consumer to whom the access device was issued; and

(3) The financial institution has provided the following information, in writing, to the consumer:

(i) A summary of the consumer's liability under this section, or under other applicable law or agreement, for unauthorized electronic fund tranfers and, at the financial institution's option, notice of the advisability of promptly reporting loss or theft of the access device or unauthorized transfers.

(ii) The telephone number and address of the person or office to be notified in the event the consumer believes that an unauthorized electronic fund transfer has been or may be made.

(iii) The financial institution's business day, as determined under §205.2(d), unless applicable State law or an agreement between the consumer and the financial institution sets a liability limit not greater than $50.

(b) *Limitations on amount of liability.*   The amount of a consumer's liability for an unauthorized electronic fund transfer or a series of related unauthorized transfers shall not exceed $50 or the amount of unauthorized transfers that occur before notice to the financial institution under paragraph (c) of this section, whichever is less, unless one or both of the following exceptions apply:

(1) If the consumer fails to notify the financial institution within 2 business days after learning of the loss or theft of the access device, the consumer's liability shall not exceed the lesser of $500 or the sum of

(i) $50 or the amount of unauthorized electronic fund transfers that occur before the close of the 2 business days, whichever is less, and

(ii) the amount of unauthorized electronic fund transfers that the financial institution establishes would not have occurred but for the failure of the consumer to notify the institution within 2 business days after the consumer learns of the loss or theft of the access device, and that occur after the close of 2 business days and before notice to the financial institution.

(2) If the consumer fails to report within 60 days of transmittal of the periodic statement any unauthorized electronic fund transfer that appears on the statement, the consumer's liability shall not exceed the sum of

(i) The lesser of $50 or the amount of unauthorized electronic fund transfers that appear on the periodic statement or that occur during the 60-day period, and

(ii) The amount of unauthorized electronic fund transfers that occur after the close of the 60 days and before notice to the financial institution and that the financial institution establishes would not have occurred but for the failure of the consumer to notify the financial institution within that time.

(3) Paragraphs (b)(1) and (2) of this section may both apply in some circumstances. Paragraph (b)(1) shall determine the consumer's liability for any unauthorized transfers that appear on the periodic statement and occur before the close of the 60-day period, and paragraph (b)(2)(ii) shall determine liability for transfers that occur after the close of the 60-day period.

(4) If a delay in notifying the financial institution was due to extenuating circumstances, such as extended travel or hospitalization, the time periods specified above shall be extended to a reasonable time.

(5) If applicable State law or an agreement between the consumer and financial institution imposes lesser liability than that provided in paragraph (b) of this section, the consumer's liability shall not exceed that imposed under that law or agreement.

(c) *Notice to financial institution.*   For purposes of this section, notice to a financial institution is given when a consumer takes such steps as are reasonably necessary to provide the financial institution with the pertinent information, whether or not any particular officer, employee, or agent of the financial institution does in fact receive the information. Notice in writing is considered given at the time the consumer deposits the notice in the mail or delivers the notice for transmission by any other usual means to the financial institution. Notice in writing is considered given at the time of receipt or, whether or not received, at the expiration of the time ordinarily required for transmission, whichever is earlier. Notice is also considered given when the financial institution becomes aware of circumstances that lead to the reasonable belief that an unauthorized electronic fund transfer involving the consumer's account has been or may be made.

(d) *Relation to Truth in Lending.*   (1) consumer's liability for an unauthorized electronic fund transfer shall be determined solely in accordance with this section if the electronic fund transfer

(i) Was initiated by use of an access device that is also a credit card as defined in 12 CFR 226.2(r), or

(ii) Involves an extension of credit under an agreement between a consumer and a financial institution to extend the credit when the consumer's account is overdrawn or to maintain a specified minimum balance in the consumer's account.

(2) A consumer's liability for unauthorized use of a credit card that is also an access device but that does not involve an electronic fund transfer shall be determined solely in accordance with the Truth in Lending Act and 12 CFR Part 226 (Regulation Z).

§205.7 Initial disclosure of terms and conditions

(a) *Content of disclosures.* At the time a consumer contracts for an electronic fund transfer service or before the first electronic fund transfer is made involving a consumer's account, a financial institution shall disclose to the consumer, in a readily understandable written statement that the consumer may retain, the following terms and conditions of the electronic fund transfer service, as applicable:

(1) A summary of the consumer's liability under §205.6, or other applicable law or agreement, for unauthorized electronic fund transfers and, at the financial institution's option, the advisability of promptly reporting loss or theft of the access device or unauthorized transfers.

(2) The telephone number and address of the person or office to be notified when the consumer believes that an unauthorized electronic fund transfer has been or may be made.

(3) The financial institution's business days, as determined under §205.2(d).

(4) The type of electronic fund transfers that the consumer may make and any limitations on the frequency and dollar amount of transfers. The details of the limitations need not be disclosed if their confidentiality is essential to maintain the security of the electronic fund transfer system.

(5) Any charges for electronic fund transfers or for the right to make transfers.

(6) A summary of the consumer's right to receive documentation of electronic fund transfers, as provided in §§205.9, 205.10(a), and 205.10(d).

(7) A summary of the consumer's right to stop payment of a preauthorized electronic fund transfer and the procedure for initiating a stop-payment order, as provided in §205.10(c).

(8) A summary of the financial institution's liability to the consumer for its failure to make or to stop certain transfers under §910 of the Act.

(9) The circumstances under which the financial institution in the ordinary course of business will disclose information to third parties concerning the consumer's account.

(10) A notice that is substantially similar to the following notice concerning error resolution procedures and the consumer's rights under them:

IN CASE OF ERRORS OR QUESTIONS ABOUT YOUR ELECTRONIC TRANSFERS

Telephone us at [insert phone number]

or

Write us at [insert address]

as soon as you can, if you think your statement or receipt is wrong or if you need more information about a transfer listed on the statement or receipt. We must hear from you no later than 60 days after we sent you the FIRST statement on which the problem or error appeared.

(1) Tell us your name and account number (if any).

(2) Describe the error or the transfer you are unsure about, and explain as clearly as you can why you believe it is an error or why you need more information.

(3) Tell us the dollar amount of the suspected error.

If you tell us orally, we may require that you send us your complaint or question in writing within 10 business days.

We will tell you the results of our investigation within 10 business days after we hear from you and will correct any error promptly. If we need more time, however, we may take up to 45 days to investigate your complaint or question. If we decide to do this, we will recredit your account within 10 business days for the amount you think is in error, so that you will have the use of the money during the time it takes us to complete our investigation. If we ask you to put your complaint or question in writing and we do not receive it within 10 business days, we may not recredit your account.

If we decide that there was no error, we will send you a written explanation within 3 business days after we finish our investigation. You may ask for copies of the documents that we used in our investigation.

(b) *Timing of disclosures for accounts in existence on May 10, 1980.* A financial institution shall mail or deliver to the consumer the information required by paragraph (a) of this section on or before June 9, 1980, or with the first periodic statement required by §205.9(b) after May 10, 1980, whichever is earlier, for any account that is open on May 10, and

(1) From or to which electronic fund transfers were made prior to May 10, 1980;

(2) With respect to which a contract for such transfers was entered into between a consumer and a financial institution; or

(3) For which an access device was issued to a consumer.

§205.8 Change in terms; error resolution notice

(a) *Change in terms.*   A financial institution shall mail or deliver a written notice to the consumer at least 21 days before the effective date of any change in a term or condition required to be disclosed under §205.7(a) if the change would result in increased fees or charges, increased liability for the consumer, fewer types of available electronic fund transfers, or stricter limitations on the frequency or dollar amounts of transfers. Prior notice need not be given where an immediate change in terms or conditions is necessary to maintain or restore the security of an electronic fund transfer system or account. However, if a change required to be disclosed under this paragraph is to be made permanent, the financial institution shall provide written notice of the change to the consumer on or with the next regularly scheduled periodic statement or within 30 days, unless disclosure would jeopardize the security of the system or account. However, if such a change is to be made permanent, the financial institution shall provide written notice of the change to the consumer on or with the next regularly scheduled periodic statement or within 30 days, unless disclosure would jeopardize the security of the system or account.

(b) *Error resolution notice.*　For each account from or to which electronic fund transfers can be made, a financial institution shall mail or deliver to the consumer, at least once each calendar year, the notice set forth in §205.7(a)(10). Alternatively, a financial institution may mail or deliver a notice that is substantially similar to the following notice in or with each periodic statement required by §205.9(b):

IN CASE OF ERRORS OR QUESTIONS ABOUT YOUR ELECTRONIC TRANSFERS

Telephone us at [insert telephone number]

or

Write us at [insert address]

as soon as you can, if you think your statement or receipt is wrong or if you need more information about a transfer on the statement or receipt. We must hear from you no later than 60 days after we sent you the FIRST statement on which the error or problem appeared.

(1) Tell us your name and account number (if any).

(2) Describe the error or the transfer you are unsure about, and explain as clearly as you can why you believe there is an error or why you need more information.

(3) Tell us the dollar amount of the suspected error.

We will investigate your complaint and will correct any error promptly. If we take more than 10 business days to do this, we will recredit your account for the amount you think is in error, so that you will have use of the money during the time it takes us to complete our investigation.

§205.9　Documentation of transfers

(a) *Receipts at electronic terminals.*　At the time an electronic fund transfer is initiated at an electronic terminal by a consumer, the financial institution shall make available[2] to the consumer a written receipt of the transfer(s) that clearly sets forth the following information, as applicable:

(1) The amount of the transfer. A charge for the transfer may be included in this amount if the terminal is owned or operated by a person other than the financial institution holding the consumer's account, provided the amount of the charge is disclosed on the receipt and on a sign posted on or at the terminal.

(2) The calendar date the consumer initiated the transfer.

(3) The type of transfer and the type of the consumer's account(s)[3] to or from which funds are transferred, such as "withdrawal from checking," "transfer from savings to checking," or "payment from savings." These descriptions may be used for transfers to or from accounts that are similar in function to checking accounts (such as share draft or negotiable order of withdrawal accounts) or to savings accounts (such as share accounts). Codes may be used only if they are explained elsewhere on the receipt.

(4) A number or code that uniquely identifies the consumer initiating the transfer, the consumer's account(s), or the access device used to initiate the transfer.

(5) The location (in a form prescribed by paragraph (b)(1)(iv) of this section) of the terminal at which the transfer was initiated or an identification (such as a code or terminal number).

(6) The name of any third party to or from whom funds are transferred; a code may be used only if it is explained elsewhere on the receipt. This requirement does not apply if the name is provided by the consumer in a form that the electronic terminal cannot duplicate on the receipt.

(b) *Periodic statements.* For any account to or from which electronic fund transfers can be made, the financial institution shall mail or deliver a statement for each monthly or shorter cycle in which an electronic fund transfer has occurred, but at least a quarterly statement if no transfer has occurred. The statement shall include the following, as applicable:

(1) For each electronic fund transfer occurring during the cycle,[4]

(i) The amount of the transfer. If a transfer charge was added at the time of initiation by the owner or operator of an electronic terminal in accordance with paragraph (a)(1) of this section, that charge may be included in the amount of the transfer.

---

[2] A financial institution may arrange for a third party, such as a merchant to make the receipt available.

[3] If more than one account of the same type may be accessed by a single access device, the accounts must be uniquely identified unless the terminal is incapable of such identification and was purchased or ordered by the financial institution prior to February 6, 1980. In a point-of-sale transfer, the type of account need not be identified if the access device used may access only one account at point of sale. The type of account need not be identified if the access device may access only one account at that terminal.

[4] The information required by paragraph (b)(1) of this section may be provided on accompanying documents. Codes explained on the statement or on accompanying documents are acceptable.

(ii) The date the transfer was credited or debited to the consumer's account.

(iii) The type of transfer and the type of the consumer's account(s) to or from which funds were transferred.

(iv) For each transfer initiated by the consumer at an electronic terminal[4a], the location that appeared on the receipt or, if an identification (such as a code or terminal number) was used, that identification and one of the following descriptions of the terminal's location:

(A) The address, including number and street (the number may be omitted if the street alone uniquely identifies the terminal location) or intersection, city, and state or foreign country;[5]

(B) A generally accepted name for a specific location (such as a branch of the financial institution, a shopping center, or an airport), city, and state or foreign country;[6] or

(C) The name of the entity at whose place of business the terminal is located or which owns or operates the terminal (such as the financial institution[7] or the seller of goods or services), city, and state or foreign country.[8]

(v) The name of any third party to or from whom funds were transferred.[9]

(2) The number(s) of the consumer's account(s) for which the statement is issued.

(3) The total amount of any fees or charges, other than a finance charge under 12 CFR 226.7(b)(1)(iv), assessed against the account during the statement period for electronic fund transfers or the right to make such transfers, or for account maintenance.

(4) The balances in the consumer's account(s) at the beginning and at the close of the statement period.

(5) The address and telephone number to be used for inquiry or notice of errors, preceded by "Direct Inquiries To:" or similar language. Alternatively,

---

[4a.] A financial institution need not identify the terminal location for deposits of cash, checks, drafts, or similar paper instruments at electronic terminals.

[5.] The city and state may be omitted if all the terminals owned or operated by the financial institution providing the statement (or by the system in which it participates) are located in the same city. The state may be omitted if all the terminals owned or operated by the financial institution providing the statement (or by the system in which it participates) are located in that state. The state may also be omitted for transfers occurring at terminals within 50 miles of the financial institution's main office.

[6.] See footnote 5.

[7.] If the financial institution providing the statement owns or operates terminals at more than one location, it shall describe the location of its electronic terminals by use of paragraphs (b)(1)(iv)(A) or (B) of this section.

[8.] See footnote 5.

[9.] A financial institution need not identify third parties whose names appear on checks, drafts, or similar paper instruments deposited to the consumer's account at an electronic terminal.

the address and telephone number may be provided on the notice of error resolution procedures set forth in §205.8(b).

(6) If the financial institution uses the notice procedure set forth in §205.10(a)(1)(iii), the telephone number the consumer may call to ascertain whether a preauthorized transfer to the consumer's account has occurred.

(c) *Documentation for certain passbook accounts.* In the case of a consumer's passbook account which may not be accessed by any electronic fund transfers other than preauthorized transfers to the account,[9a] the financial institution may, in lieu of complying with paragraph (b) of this section, upon presentation of the consumer's passbook, provide the consumer with documentation by entering in the passbook or on a separate document the amount and date of each electronic fund transfer made since the passbook was last presented.

(d) *Periodic statements for certain non-passbook accounts.* If a consumer's account other than a passbook account may not be accessed by any electronic fund transfers other than preauthorized transfers to the account,[9a] the financial institution need provide the periodic statement required by paragraph (b) of this section only quarterly.

(e) *Use of abbreviations.* A financial institution may use commonly accepted or readily understandable abbreviations in complying with the documentation requirements of this section.

(f) *Receipt requirements for certain cash-dispensing terminals.* The failure of a financial institution to comply with the requirement of paragraph (a) of this section that a receipt be made available to the consumer at the time an electronic fund transfer is initiated at an electronic terminal shall not constitute a violation of the Act or this regulation, provided:

(1) The transfer occurs at an electronic terminal that:

(i) Does not permit transfers other than cash withdrawals by the consumer,

(ii) Cannot make a receipt available to the consumer at the time the transfer is initiated,

(iii) Cannot be modified to provide a receipt at that time, and

(iv) Was purchased or ordered by the financial institution prior to February 6, 1980; and

(2) The financial institution mails or delivers a written receipt to the consumer that complies with the other requirements of paragraph (a) of this section on the next business day following the transfer.

(g) *Delayed effective date for certain periodic statement requirements.* The failure of a financial institution to describe an electronic fund transfer in accordance with the requirements of paragraphs (b)(1)(iv) and (v) of this section shall not constitute a violation of the Act or this regulation unless the transfer occurs on or after August 10, 1980, if, when a transfer involves a payment to another person, the financial institution, upon the consumer's request, and without

---

[9a.] Accounts that also are accessible by the intra-institutional transfers described in paragraph (h) of this section may continue to be documented in accordance with paragraph (c) or (d) of this section.

charge, promptly provides the consumer with proof that such a payment was made.

(h) *Periodic statements for certain intra-institutional transfers.* A financial institution need not provide the periodic statement required by paragraph (b) of this section for an account accessed only by electronic fund transfers initiated by the consumer to or from another account of the consumer for which the financial institution documents transfers in compliance with paragraph (b) of this section.

(i) *Documentation for foreign-initiated transfers.* Failure to provide the terminal receipt and periodic statement required by paragraphs (a) and (b) of this section for a particular electronic fund transfer shall not be deemed a failure to comply with this regulation, if:

(1) the transfer is not initiated in a state as defined in §205.2(k); and

(2) in accordance with §205.11, the financial institution treats an inquiry for clarification or documentation as a notice of error and corrects the error.

§205.10 Preauthorized transfers

(a) *Preauthorized transfers to a consumer's account.* (1) Where a consumer's account is scheduled to be credited by a preauthorized electronic fund transfer from the same payor at least once every 60 days, except where the payor provides positive notice to the consumer that the transfer has been initiated, the financial institution shall provide notice by one of the following means:

(i) The institution shall transmit oral or written notice to the consumer, within 2 business days after the transfer, that the transfer occurred;

(ii) The institution shall transmit oral or written notice to the consumer, within 2 business days after the date on which the transfer was scheduled to occur, that the transfer did not occur; or

(iii) The institution shall provide a readily available telephone line that the consumer may call to ascertain whether or not the transfer occurred, and shall disclose the telephone number on the initial disclosures required by §205.7 and on each periodic statement.

(2) A financial institution that receives a preauthorized transfer of the type described in paragraph (a)(1) of this section shall credit the amount of the transfer as of the day the funds for the transfer are received.

(b) *Preauthorized transfers from a consumer's account; written authorization.* Preauthorized electronic fund transfers from a consumer's account may be authorized by the consumer only in writing, and a copy of the authorization shall be provided to the consumer by the party that obtains the authorization from the consumer.

(c) *Consumer's right to stop payment.* A consumer may stop payment of a preauthorized electronic fund transfer from the consumer's account by notifying the financial institution orally or in writing at any time up to 3 business days before the scheduled date of the transfer. The financial institution may require written confirmation of the stop-payment order to be made within 14 days of an oral notification if, when the oral notification is made, the requirement is disclosed to the consumer together with the address to which confirmation should be sent. If written confirmation has been required by the financial institution, the oral stop-payment order shall cease to be binding 14 days after it has been made.

(d) *Notice of transfers varying in amount.*   Where a preauthorized electronic fund transfer from the consumer's account varies in amount from the previous transfer relating to the same authorization, or the preauthorized amount, the financial institution or the designated payee shall mail or deliver, at least 10 days before the scheduled transfer date, a written notice of the amount and scheduled date of the transfer. If the financial institution or designated payee informs the consumer of the right to receive notice of all varying transfers, the consumer may elect to receive notice only when a transfer does not fall within a specified range of amounts or, alternatively, only when a transfer differs from the most recent transfer by more than an agreed-upon amount.

§205.11   Procedures for resolving errors

(a) *Definition of error.*   For purposes of this section, the term "error" means:

(1) A unauthorized electronic fund transfer;

(2) An incorrect electronic fund transfer to or from the consumer's account;

(3) The omission from a periodic statement of an electronic fund transfer to or from the consumer's account that should have been included;

(4) A computational or bookkeeping error made by the financial institution relating to an electronic fund transfer;

(5) The consumer's receipt of an incorrect amount of money from an electronic terminal;

(6) An electronic fund transfer not identified in accordance with the requirements of §§205.9 or 205.10(a); or

(7) A consumer's request for any documentation required by §§205.9 or 205.10(a), or for additional information or clarification concerning an electronic fund transfer. This includes any request for documentation, information, or clarification in order to assert an error within the meaning of paragraphs (a)(1) through (6) of this section. It does not include a routine inquiry about the balance in the consumer's account or a request for duplicate copies of documentation or other information that is made only for tax or other recordkeeping purposes.

(b) *Notice of error from consumer.*   (1) A notice of an error is an oral or written notice from the consumer that

(i) Is received by the financial institution[10] no later than 60 days after the institution

---

[10.] A financial institution may require the consumer to give notice only at the telephone number or address disclosed by the institution, provided the institution maintains reasonable procedures to refer the consumer to the specified telephone number or address if the consumer attempts to give notice to the institution in a different manner.

(A) Transmitted a periodic statement or provided documentation under §205.9(c) on which the alleged error is first reflected; or

(B) Transmitted additional information, clarification, or documentation described in paragraph (a)(7) of this section that was initially requested in accordance with paragraph (b)(1)(i)(A) of this section;

(ii) Enables the financial institution to identify the consumer's name and account number; and

(iii) Except for errors described in paragraph (a)(7) of this section, indicates the consumer's belief, and the reasons for that belief, that an error exists in the consumer's account or is reflected on documentation required by §§205.9 or 205.10(a), and indicates to the extent possible the type, the date, and the amount of the error.

(2) A financial institution may require a written confirmation to be received within 10 business days of an oral notice if, when the oral notice is given, the consumer is advised of the requirement and of the address to which confirmation must be sent.

(c) *Investigation of errors.* (1) After receiving a notice of an error, the financial institution shall promptly investigate the alleged error, determine whether an error occurred, and transmit the results of its investigation and determination to the consumer within 10 business days.

(2) As an alternative to the 10-business-day requirement of paragraph (c)(1) of this section, the financial institution shall investigate the alleged error and determine whether an error occurred, promptly but in no event later than 45 calendar days after receiving a notice of an error, and shall transmit the results of its investigation and determination to the consumer, provided

(i) The financial institution provisionally recredits the consumer's account in the amount of the alleged error (including interest where applicable) within 10 business days after receiving the notice of error. If the financial institution has a reasonable basis for believing that an unauthorized electronic fund transfer may have occurred and that it has satisfied the requirements of §205.6(a), it may withhold a maximum of $50 from the amount recredited;

(ii) The financial institution, promptly but no later than 2 business days after the provisional recrediting, orally reports or mails or delivers notice to the consumer of the amount and date of the recrediting and of the fact that the consumer will have full use of the funds pending the determination of whether an error occurred;

(iii) The financial institution gives the consumer full use of the funds provisionally recredited during the investigation; and

(iv) If the financial institution determines that no error occurred and debits the account, the institution gives notice of the debiting and continues to honor certain items as required by paragraph (f)(2) of this section.

(3) A financial institution that requires but does not receive timely written confirmation of oral notice of an error shall comply with all requirements of this section except that it need not provisionally recredit the consumer's acocunt.

(4) If a notice of an error involves an electronic fund transfer that was not initiated in a state as defined in §205.2(k), the applicable time periods for action in subsections (c), (e), and (f) shall be 20 business days in place of 10 business days, and 90 calendar days in place of 45 calendar days.

(d) *Extent of required investigation.*   (1) A financial institution complies with its duty to investigate, correct, and report its determination regarding an error described in paragraph (a)(7) of this section by transmitting the requested information, clarification, or documentation within the time limits set forth in paragraph (c) of this section. If the institution has provisionally recredited the consumer's account in accordance with paragraph (c)(2) of this section, it may debit the amount upon transmitting the requested information, clarification, or documentation.

(2) Except in the case of services covered by §205.14, a financial institution's review of its own records regarding an alleged error will satisfy its investigation responsibilities under paragraph (c) of this section if the alleged error concerns a transfer to or from a third party and there is no agreement between the financial institution and the third party[11] regarding the type of electronic fund transfer alleged in the error.

(3) A financial institution may make, without investigation, a final correction to a consumer's account in the amount or manner alleged by the consumer to be in error, but must comply with all other applicable requirements of this section.

(e) *Procedures after financial institution determines that error occurred.*   If the financial institution determines that an error occurred, it shall

(1) Promptly, but no later than 1 business day after its determination, correct the error (subject to the liability provisions of §§205.6(a) and (b)), including, where applicable, the crediting of interest and the refunding of any fees or charges imposed, and

(2) Promptly, but in any event within the 10-business-day or 45-day time limits, orally report or mail or deliver to the consumer notice of the correction and, if applicable, notice that a provisional credit has been made final.[12]

(f) *Procedures after financial institution determines that no error occurred.*   If the financial institution determines that no error occurred or that an error occurred in a different manner or amount from that described by the consumer,

(1) The financial institution shall mail or deliver to the consumer a written explanation of its findings within 3 business days after concluding its investigation, but in no event later than 10 business days after receiving notice

---

[11.] Institutions do not have an agreement for purposes of paragraph (d)(2) of this section solely because they participate in transactions under the federal recurring payments program, or that are cleared through an automated or other clearing house or similar arrangement for the clearing and settlement of fund transfers generally, or because they agree to be bound by the rules of such arrangements. An agreement that a third party will honor an access device is an agreement for purposes of this paragraph.

[12.] This notice requirement may be satisfied by a notice on a periodic statement that is mailed or delivered within the 10-business-day or 45-day time limits and that clearly identifies the correction to the consumer's account.

of the error if the institution is proceeding under paragraph (c)(1) of this section. The explanation shall include notice of the consumer's right to request the documents upon which the institution relied in making its determination.

(2) Upon debiting a provisionally recredited amount, the financial institution

(i) Shall orally report or mail or deliver notice to the consumer of the date and amount of the debiting and the fact that the financial institution will honor checks, drafts, or similar paper instruments payable to third parties, and preauthorized transfers from the consumer's account (using the provisionally recredited funds) for 5 business days after transmittal of the notice.

(ii) Shall honor checks, drafts, or similar paper instruments payable to third parties and preauthorized transfers from the consumer's account (without charge to the consumer as a result of an overdraft) for 5 business days after transmittal of the notice. The institution need only honor items that it would have paid if the provisionally recredited funds had not been debited.

(3) Upon the consumer's request, the financial institution shall promptly mail or deliver to the consumer copies of the documents on which it relied in making its determination.

(g) *Withdrawal of notice of error.*   The financial institution has no further error resolution responsibilities as to a consumer's assertion of an error if the consumer concludes that no error did in fact occur and voluntarily withdraws the notice.

(h) *Reassertion of error.*   A financial institution that has fully complied with the requirements of this section with respect to an error has no further responsibilities under this section if the consumer subsequently reasserts the same error, regardless of the manner in which it is reasserted. This paragraph does not preclude the assertion of an error defined in paragraphs (a)(1) through (6) of this section following the assertion of an error described in paragraph (a)(7) of this section regarding the same electronic fund transfer.

(i) *Relation to Truth in Lending.*   Where an electronic fund transfer also involves an extension of credit under an agreement between a consumer and a financial institution to extend credit when the consumer's account is overdrawn or to maintain a specified minimum balance in the consumer's account, the financial institution shall comply with the requirements of this section rather than those of 12 CFR 226.2(j), 226.2(cc), and 226.14(a) governing error resolution.

§205.12   Relation to state law

(a) *Preemption of inconsistent state laws.*   The Board shall determine, upon the request of any state, financial institution, or other interested party, whether the Act and this regulation preempt state laws relating to electronic fund transfers. Only those state laws that are inconsistent with the Act and this regulation shall be preempted and then only to the extent of the inconsistency. A state law is not inconsistent with the Act and this regulation if it is more protective of a consumer.

(b) *Standards for preemption.*   The following are examples of the standards the Board will apply in determining whether a state law, or a provision of that law, is inconsistent with the Act and this regulation. Inconsistency may exist when state law:

(1) Requiers or permits a practice or act prohibited by the Act or this regulation;

(2) Provides for consumer liability for unauthorized electronic fund transfers which exceeds that imposed by the Act and this regulation;

(3) Provides for longer time periods than the Act and this regulation for investigation and correction of errors alleged by a consumer, or fails to provide for the recrediting of the consumer's account during the institution's investigation of errors as set forth in §205.11(c); or

(4) Provides for initial disclosures, periodic statements, or receipts that are different in content from that required by the Act and this regulation except to the extent that the disclosures relate to rights granted to consumers by the state law and not by the Act or this regulation.

(c) *Procedures for preemption.*   Any request for a determination shall include the following:

(1) A copy of the full text of the state law in question, including any regulatory implementation or judicial interpretation of that law;

(2) A comparison of the provisions of state law with the corresponding provisions in the Act and this regulation, together with a discussion of reasons why specific provisions of state law are either consistent or inconsistent with corresponding sections of the Act and this regulation; and

(3) A comparison of the civil and criminal liability for violation of state law with the provisions of sections 915 and 916(a) of the Act.

(d) *Exemption for state-regulated transfers.*   (1) Any state may apply to the Board for an exemption from the requirements of the Act and the corresponding provisions of this regulation for any class of electronic fund transfers within the state. The Board will grant such an exemption if the Board determines that:

(i) Under the law of the state that class of electronic fund transfers is subject to requirements substantially similar to those imposed by the Act and the corresponding provisions of this regulation, and

(ii) There is adequate provision for state enforcement.

(2) To assure that the federal and state courts will continue to have concurrent jurisdiction, and to aid in implementing the Act:

(i) No exemption shall extend to the civil liability provisions of section 915 of the Act; and

(ii) After an exemption has been granted, for the purposes of section 915 of the Act, the requirements of the applicable state law shall constitute the requirements of the Act and this regulation, except to the extent the state law imposes requirements not imposed by the Act or this regulation.

§205.13 Administrative enforcement

(a) *Enforcement by Federal agencies.* (1) Administrative enforcement of the Act and this regulation for certain financial institutions is assigned to the Comptroller of the Currency, Board of Governors of the Federal Reserve System, Board of Directors of the Federal Deposit Insurance Corporation, Federal Home Loan Bank Board (acting directly or through the Federal Savings and Loan Insurance Corporation), National Credit Union Administration Board, Secretary of Transportation, and Securities and Exchange Commission.

(2) Except to the extent that administrative enforcement is specifically committed to other authorities, compliance with the requirments imposed under the Act and this regulation is enforced by the Federal Trade Commission.

(b) *Issuance of staff interpretations.* (1) Unofficial staff interpretations are issued at the staff's discretion where the protection of section 915(d) of the Act is neither requested nor required, or where a repaid response is necessary.

(2)(i) Official staff interpretations are issued at the discretion of designated officials. No interpretations will be issued approving financial institutions' forms or statements . . . .

(4) Pursuant to section 915(d) of the Act, the Board has designated the Director and other officials of the Division of Consumer and Community Affairs as officials "duly authorized" to issue, at their discretion, official staff interpretations of this regulation.

(c) *Record retention.* (1) Evidence of compliance with the requirements imposed by the Act and this regulation shall be preserved by any person subject to the Act and this regulation for a period of not less than 2 years. Records may be stored by use of microfiche, microfilm, magnetic tape, or other methods capable of accurately retaining and reproducing information.

(2) Any person subject to the Act and this regulation that has actual notice that it is being investigated or is subject to an enforcement proceeding by an agency charged with monitoring that person's compliance with the Act and this regulation, or that has been served with notice of an action filed under section 910, 915, or 916(a) of the Act, shall retain the information required in paragraph (c)(1) of this section that pertains to the action or proceeding until final disposition of the matter, unless an earlier time is allowed by order of the agency or court.

§205.14 Services offered by financial institutions not holding consumer's account

(a) *Compliance by service-providing institution.* Except as provided in this section, where a financial institution issues an access device to a consumer to be used for initiating electronic fund transfers to or from the consumer's account held by another financial institution, and the service-providing institution does not have an agreement with the account-holding institution regarding the service, the service-providing institution shall comply with all requirements of the Act and this regulation that relate to the service or the electronic fund transfers made by the consumer under the service. For this purpose, the following special rules shall apply:

(1) Section 205.6 shall require the service-providing institution to reimburse the consumer for unauthorized electronic fund transfers in excess of the limits set by that section.

(2) Sections 205.7, 205.8, and 205.9 shall require the service-providing institution to provide those disclosures and documentation that are within its knowledge and the purview of its relationship with the consumer.

(3) Section 205.11(b)(1)(i) shall require the service-providing institution to extend by a reasonable time the time periods within which notice of an error must be received if a delay in notifying the service-providing institution was due to the fact that the consumer initially notified or attempted to notify the account-holding institution.

(4) Sections 205.11(c)(2)(i) and (e)(1) shall require the service-providing institution to transfer funds, in the appropriate amount and within the applicable time period, to the consumer's account at the account-holding institution.

(5) Section 205.11(c)(2)(ii) shall require the service-providing institution to disclose the date on which it initiates a transfer to effect the provisional recredit.

(6) Section 205.11(f)(2) shall require the service-providing institution to notify the account-holding institution of the date until which the account-holding institution must honor any debit to the account as required by §205.11(f)(2). If an overdraft results, the service-providing institution shall promptly reimburse the account-holding institution in the amount of the overdraft.

(b) *Compliance by account-holding institution.*   An account-holding institution described in paragraph (a) of this section need not comply with the requirements of the Act and this regulation with respect to electronic fund transfers to or from the consumer's account made by the service-providing institution, except that the account holding institution shall comply with §205.11 by

(1) Promptly providing, upon the request of the service-providing institution information or copies of documents required for the purpose of investigating alleged errors or furnishing copies of documents to the consumer; and

(2) Honoring debits to the account in accordance with §205.11(f)(2).

(c) *Definition of agreement.*   For purposes of this section, an agreement between the service-providing and the account-holding institutions regarding the electronic fund transfer service refers to a specific agreement(s) among institutions (or among institutions and another person that participates in the operation of the service) which sets forth the rights and obligations of the institutions with respect to a service involving the issuance of an access device to the consumer. Institutions do not have such an agreement solely because they participate in transactions that are cleared through an automated or other clearing house or similar arrangement for the clearing and settlement of fund transfers generally, or because they agree to be bound by the rules of such an arrangement.

APPENDIX A.   Model Disclosure Clauses

This appendix contains model disclosure clauses for optional use by financial institutions to facilitate compliance with the disclosure requirements of sections 205.5(a)(3), (b)(2), and (b)(3), 205.6(a)(3), and 205.7. Section 915(d)(2) of the Act provides that use of these clauses in conjunction with other requirements of the regulation will protect financial institutions from liability under sections 915 and 916 of the Act to the extent that the clauses accurately reflect the institutions' electronic fund transfer services.

Financial institutions need not use any of the clauses, but may use clauses of their own design in conjunction with the model clauses. The inapplicable words or portions of phrases in parentheses should be deleted. The underscored catchlines are not part of the clauses and should not be used as such. Financial institutions may make alterations, substitutions, or additions in the clauses in order to reflect the services offered, such as technical changes (e.g., substitution of a trade name for the word "card," deletion of inapplicable services, or substitution of lesser liability limits in section A(2)). Sections A(3) and A(9) include references to a telephone number and address. Where two or more of these clauses are used in a disclosure, the telephone number and address need not be repeated if referenced.

SECTION A(1)—DISCLOSURE THAT ACCESS DEVICE IS NOT VALIDATED AND HOW TO DISPOSE OF DEVICE IF VALIDATION IS NOT DESIRED (§205.5(b)(3))

(a) *Accounts using cards.*   You cannot use the enclosed card to transfer money into or out of your account until we have validated it. If you do not want to use the card, please (destroy it at once by cutting it in half).

FINANCIAL INSTITUTION MAY ADD VALIDATION INSTRUCTIONS HERE

(b) *Accounts using codes.*   You cannot use the enclosed code to transfer money into or out of your account until we have validated it. If you do not want to use the code, please (destroy this notice at once).

FINANCIAL INSTITUTION MAY ADD VALIDATION INSTRUCTIONS HERE

SECTION A(2)—DISCLOSURE OF CONSUMER'S LIABILITY FOR UNAUTHORIZED TRANSFERS AND OPTIONAL DISCLOSURE OF ADVISABILITY OF PROMPT REPORTING (§205.7(a)(1))

(a) *Liability disclosure.*   (Tell us AT ONCE if you believe your (card) (code) has been lost or stolen. Telephoning is the best way of keeping your possible losses down. You could lose all the money in your account (plus your maximum overdraft line of credit). If you tell us within 2 business days, you can lose no more than $50 if someone used your (card) (code) without your permission.)

(If you believe your (card) (code) has been lost or stolen, and you tell us within 2 business days after you learn of the loss or theft, you can lose no more than $50 if someone uses your (card) (code) without your permission).

If you do NOT tell us within 2 business days after you learn of the loss or theft of your (card) (code), and we can prove we could have stopped someone from using your (card) (code) without your permission if you had told us, you could lose as much as $500.

Also, if your statement shows transfers that you did not make, tell us at once. If you do not tell us within 60 days after the statement was mailed to you, you may not get back any money you lost after the 60 days if we can prove that we could have stopped someone from taking the money if you had told us in time.

If a good reason (such as a long trip or a hospital stay) kept you from telling us, we will extend the time period.

SECTION A(3)—DISCLOSURE OF TELEPHONE NUMBER AND ADDRESS TO BE NOTIFIED IN EVENT OF UNAUTHORIZED TRANSFER (§205.7(a)(2))

(a) *Address and telephone number.* If you believe your (card) (code) has been lost or stolen or that someone has transferred or may transfer money from your account without your permission, call:

_____

[Telephone number]

_____

or write:

_____

[Name of person or office to be notified]

_____

[Address]

SECTION A(4)—DISCLOSURE OF WHAT CONSTITUTES BUSINESS DAY OF INSTITUTION (§205.7(a)(3))

(a) *Business day disclosure.* Our business days are (Monday through Friday) (Monday through Saturday) (any day including Saturdays and Sundays). Holidays are (not) included.

SECTION A(5)—DISCLOSURE OF TYPES OF AVAILABLE TRANSFERS AND LIMITS ON TRANSFERS (§205.7(a)(4))

(a) *Account access.* You may use your (card) (code) to (1) withdraw cash from your (checking) (or) (savings) account.

(2) Make deposits to your (checking) (or) (savings) account.

(3) Transfer funds between your checking and savings accounts whenever you request.

(4) Pay for purchases at places that have agreed to accept the (card) (code).

(5) Pay bills directly (by telephone) from your (checking) (or) (savings) account in the amounts and on the days you request.

Some of these services may not be available at all terminals.

(b) *Limitations on frequency of transfers.*

(1) You may make only [insert number, e.g., 3] cash withdrawals from our terminals each [insert time period, e.g., week].

(2) You can use your telephone bill-payment service to pay [insert number] bills each ([insert time period]) (telephone call).

(3) You can use our point-of-sale transfer service for [insert number] transactions each [insert time period].

(4) For security reasons, there are (other) limits on the number of transfers you can make using our (terminals) (telephone bill-payment service) (point-of-sale transfer service).

(c) *Limitations on dollar amounts of transfers.*

(1) You may withdraw up to [insert dollar amount] from our terminals each ([insert time period]) (time you use the (card) (code)).

(2) You may buy up to [insert dollar amount] worth of goods or services each ([insert time period]) (time you use the (card) (code)) in our point-of-sale transfer service.

SECTION A(6)—DISCLOSURE OF CHARGES FOR TRANSFERS OF RIGHT TO MAKE TRANSFERS (§205.7(a)(5))

(a) *Per transfer charge.*   We will charge you [insert dollar amount] for each transfer you make using our (automated teller machines) (telephone bill-payment service) (point-of-sale transfer service).

(b) *Fixed charge.*   We will charge you [insert dollar amount] each [insert time period] for our (automated teller machine service) (telephone bill-payment service) (point-of-sale transfer service).

(c) *Average or minimum balance charge.*   We will only charge you for using our (automated teller machines) (telephone bill-payment service) (point-of-sale transfer service) if the (average) (minimum) balance in your (checking account) (savings account) (accounts) falls below [insert dollar amount]. If it does, we will charge you [insert dollar amount] each (transfer) ([insert time period]).

SECTION A(7)—DISCLOSURE OF ACCOUNT INFORMATION TO THIRD PARTIES (§205.7(a)(9))

(a) *Account information disclosure.*   We will disclose information to third parties about your account or the transfers you make: (1) Where it is necessary for completing transfers, or

(2) In order to verify the existence and condition of your account for a third party, such as a credit bureau or merchant, or

(3) In order to comply with government agency or court orders, or

(4) If you give us your written permission.

SECTION A(8)—DISCLOSURE OF RIGHT TO RECEIVE DOCUMENTATION OF TRANSFERS (§205.7(a)(6))

(a) *Terminal transfers.*   You can get a receipt at the time you make any transfer to or from your account using one of our (automated teller machines) (or) (point-of-sale terminals).

(b) *Preauthorized credits.*   If you have arranged to have direct deposits made to your account at least once every 60 days from the same person or company.

(we will let you know if the deposit is (not) made.)

(the person or company making the deposit will tell you every time they send us the money.)

(you can call us at (insert telephone number) to find out whether or not the deposit has been made.)

(c) *Periodic statements.*   You will get a (monthly) (quarterly) account statement (unless there are no transfers in a particular month. In any case you will get the statement at least quarterly).

(d) *Passbook account where the only possible electronic fund transfers are preauthorized credits.*   If you bring your passbook to us, we will record any electronic deposits that were made to your account since the last time you brought in your passbook.

SECTION A(9)—DISCLOSURE OF RIGHT TO STOP PAYMENT OF PREAUTHORIZED TRANSFERS, PROCEDURE FOR DOING SO, RIGHT TO RECEIVE NOTICE OF VARYING AMOUNTS, AND FINANCIAL INSTITUTION'S LIABILITY FOR FAILURE TO STOP PAYMENT (§205.7(a)(6), (7), and (8))

(a) *Right to stop payment and procedure for doing so.*   If you have told us in advance to make regular payments out of your account, you can stop any of these payments. Here's how:

Call us at (insert telephone number), or write us at (insert address), in time for us to receive your request 3 business days or more before the payment is scheduled to be made. If you call, we may also require you to put your request in writing and get it to us within 14 days after you call. (We will charge you (insert amount) for each stop-payment order you give).

(b) *Notice of varying amounts.*   If these regular payments may vary in amount, (we) (the person you are going to pay) will tell you, 10 days before each payment, when it will be made and how much it will be. (You may choose instead to get this notice only when the payment would differ by more than a certain amount from the previous payment, or when the amount would fall outside certain limits that you set.)

(c) *Liability for failure to stop payment of preauthorized transfer.*   If you order us to stop one of these payments 3 business days or more before the transfer is scheduled, and we do not do so, we will be liable for your losses or damages.

SECTION A(10)—DISCLOSURE OF FINANCIAL INSTITUTION'S LIABILITY FOR FAILURE TO MAKE TRANSFERS (§205.7(a)(8))

(a) *Liability for failure to make transfers.*   If we do not complete a transfer to or from your account on time or in the correct amount according to our agreement with you, we will be liable for your losses or damages. However, there are some exceptions. We will not be liable, for instance:

- If, through no fault of ours, you do not have enough money in your account to make the transfer.
- If the transfer would go over the credit limit on your overdraft line.
- If the automated teller machine where you are making the transfer does not have enough cash.
- If the (terminal) (system) was not working properly and you knew about the breakdown when you started the transfer.
- If circumstances beyond our control (such as fire or flood) prevent the transfer, despite reasonable precautions that we have taken.
- There may be other exceptions stated in our agreement with you.

Appendix K
Magnuson-Moss Warranty Act
15 U.S.C. §§2301-2312

Table of Sections

---

§101. Definitions [15 U.S.C. §2301]

For the purposes of this title:

(1) The term "consumer product" means any tangible personal property which is distributed in commerce and which is normally used for personal, family, or household purposes (including any such property intended to be attached to or installed in any real property without regard to whether it is so attached or installed).

(2) The term "Commission" means the Federal Trade Commission.

(3) The term "consumer" means a buyer (other than for purposes of resale) of any consumer product, any person to whom such product is transferred during the duration of an implied or written warranty (or service contract) applicable to the product, and any other person who is entitled by the terms of such warranty (or service contract) or under applicable State law to enforce against the warrantor (or service contractor) the obligations of the warranty (or service contract).

(4) The term "supplier" means any person engaged in the business of making a consumer product directly or indirectly available to consumers.

(5) The term "warrantor" means any supplier or other person who gives or offers to give a written warranty or who is or may be obligated under an implied warranty.

(6) The term "written warranty" means—

(A) any written affirmation of fact or written promise made in connection with the sale of a consumer product by a supplier to a buyer which relates to the nature of the material or workmanship and affirms or promises that such material or workmanship is defect free or will meet a specified level of performance over a specified period of time, or

(B) any undertaking in writing in connection with the sale by a supplier of a consumer product to refund, repair, replace, or take other remedial action with respect to such product in the event that such product fails to meet the specifications set forth in the undertaking,

which written affirmation, promise, or undertaking becomes part of the basis of the bargain between a supplier and a buyer for purposes other than resale of such product.

(7) The term "implied warranty" means an implied warranty arising under State law (as modified by sections 108 and 104(a)) in connection with the sale by a supplier of a consumer product.

(8) The term "service contract" means a contract in writing to perform, over a fixed period of time or for a specified duration, services relating to the maintenance or repair (or both) of a consumer product.

(9) The term "reasonable and necessary maintenance" consists of those operations (A) which the consumer reasonably can be expected to perform or have performed and (B) which are necessary to keep any consumer product performing its intended function and operating at a reasonable level of performance.

(10) The term "remedy" means whichever of the following actions the warrantor elects:

(A) repair,

(B) replacement, or

(C) refund;

except that the warrantor may not elect refund unless (i) the warrantor is unable to provide replacement and repair is not commercially practicable or cannot be timely made, or (ii) the consumer is willing to accept such refund.

(11) The term "replacement" means furnishing a new consumer product which is identical or reasonably equivalent to the warranted consumer product.

(12) The term "refund" means refunding the actual purchase price (less reasonable depreciation based on actual use where permitted by rules of the Commission).

(13) The term "distributed in commerce" means sold in commerce, introduced or delivered for introduction into commerce, or held for sale or distribution after introduction into commerce.

(14) The term "commerce" means trade, traffic, commerce, or transportation—

(A) between a place in a State and any place outside thereof, or

(B) which affects trade, traffic, commerce, or transportation described in subparagraph (A).

(15) The term "State" means a State, the District of Columbia, the Commonwealth of Puerto Rico, the Virgin Islands, Guam, the Canal Zone, or

American Samoa. The term "State law" includes a law of the United States applicable only to the District of Columbia or only to a territory or possession of the United States; and the term "Federal law" excludes any State law.

§102. Warranty provisions [15 U.S.C. §2302]

(a) In order to improve the adequacy of information available to consumers, prevent deception, and improve competition in the marketing of consumer products, any warrantor warranting a consumer product to a consumer by means of a written warranty shall, to the extent required by rules of the Commission, fully and conspicuously disclose in simply and readily understood language the terms and conditions of such warranty. Such rules may require inclusion in the written warranty of any of the following items among others:

(1) The clear identification of the names and addresses of the warrantors.

(2) The identity of the party or parties to whom the warranty is extended.

(3) The products or parts covered.

(4) A statement of what the warrantor will do in the event of a defect, malfunction, or failure to conform with such written warranty—at whose expense—and for what period of time.

(5) A statement of what the consumer must do and expenses he must bear.

(6) Exceptions and exclusions from the terms of the warranty.

(7) The step-by-step procedure which the consumer should take in order to obtain performance of any obligation under the warranty, including the identification of any person or class of persons authorized to perform the obligations set forth in the warranty.

(8) Information respecting the availability of any informal dispute settlement procedure offered by the warrantor and a recital, where the warranty so provides, that the purchaser may be required to resort to such procedure before pursuing any legal remedies in the courts.

(9) A brief, general description of the legal remedies available to the consumer.

(10) The time at which the warrantor will perform any obligations under the warranty.

(11) The period of time within which, after notice of a defect, malfunction, or failure to conform with the warranty, the warrantor will perform any obligations under the warranty.

(12) The characteristics or properties of the products, or parts thereof, that are not covered by the warranty.

(13) The elements of the warranty in words or phrases which would not mislead a reasonable, average consumer as to the nature or scope of the warranty.

(b)(1)(A) The Commission shall prescribe rules requiring that the terms of any written warranty on a consumer product be made available to the consumer (or prospective consumer) prior to the sale of the product to him.

(B) The Commission may prescribe rules for determining the manner and form in which information with respect to any written warranty of a consumer product shall be clearly and conspicuously presented or displayed so as not to mislead the reasonable, average consumer, when such information is contained in advertising, labeling, point-of-sale material, or other representations in writing.

(2) Nothing in this [Act] (other than paragraph (3) of this subsection) shall be deemed to authorize the Commission to prescribe the duration of written warranties given or to require that a consumer product or any of its components be warranted.

(3) The Commission may prescribe rules for extending the period of time a written warranty or service contract is in effect to correspond with any period of time in excess of a reasonable period (not less than 10 days) during which the consumer is deprived of the use of such consumer product by reason of failure of the product to conform with the written warranty or by reason of the failure of the warrantor (or service contractor) to carry out such warranty (or service contract) within the period specified in the warranty (or service contract).

(c) No warrantor of a consumer product may condition his written or implied warranty of such product on the consumer's using, in connection with such product, any article or service (other than article or service provided without charge under the terms of the warranty) which is identified by brand, trade, or corporate name; except that the prohibition of this subsection may be waived by the Commission if—

(1) the warrantor satisfies the Commission that the warranted product will function properly only if the article or service so identified is used in connection with the warranted product, and

(2) the Commission finds that such a waiver is in the public interest.

The Commission shall identify in the Federal Register, and permit public comment on, all applications for waiver of the prohibition of this subsection, and shall publish in the Federal Register its disposition of any such application, including the reasons therefor.

(d) The Commission may be rule devise detailed substantive warranty provisions which warrantors may incorporate by reference in their warranties.

(e) The provisions of this section apply only to warranties which pertain to consumer products actually costing the consumer more than $5.

§103. Designation of warranties [15 U.S.C. §2303]

(a) Any warrantor warranting a consumer product by means of a written warranty shall clearly and conspicuously designate such warranty in the following manner, unless exempted from doing so by the Commission pursuant to subsection (c) of this section:

(1) If the written warranty meets the Federal minimum standards for warranty set forth in section 104 of this Act, then it shall be conspicuously designated a "full (statement of duration) warranty".

(2) If the written warranty does not meet the Federal minimum standards

for warranty set forth in section 104 of thsi Act, then it shall be conspicuously designed a "limited warranty".

(b) Sections 102, 103 and 104 shall not apply to statements or representations which are similar to expressions of general policy concerning customer satisfaction and which are not subject to any specific limitations.

(c) In addition to exercising the authority pertaining to disclosure granted in section 102 of this Act, the Commission may by rule determine when a written warranty does not have to be designated either "full (statement of duration)" or "limited" in accordance with this section.

(d) The provisions of subsections (a) and (c) of this section apply only to warranties which pertain to consumer products actually costing the consumer more than $10 and which are not designated "full (statement of duration) warranties".

§104. Federal minimum standards for warranty [15 U.S.C. §2304]

(a) In order for a warrantor warranting a consumer product by means of a written warranty to meet the Federal minimum standards for warranty—

(1) such warrantor must as a minimum remedy such consumer product within a reasonable time and without charge, in the case of a defect, malfunction, or failure to conform with such written warranty;

(2) notwithstanding section 108(b), such warrantor may not impose any limitation on the duration of any implied warranty on the product;

(3) such warrantor may not exclude or limit consequential damages for breach of any written or implied warranty on such product, unless such exclusion or limitation conspicuously appears on the face of the warranty; and

(4) if the product (or a component part thereof) contains a defect or malfunction after a reasonable number of attempts by the warrantor to remedy defects or malfunctions in such product, such warrantor must permit the consumer or elect either a refund for, or replacement without charge of, such product or part (as the case may be). The Commission may by rule specify for purposes of this paragraph, what constitutes a reasonable number of attempts to remedy particular kinds of defects or malfunctions under different circumstances. If the warrantor replaces a component part of a consumer product, such replacement shall include installing the part in the product without charge.

(b)(1) In fulfilling the duties under subsection (a) of this section respecting a written warranty, the warrantor shall not impose any duty other than notification upon any consumer as a condition of securing remedy of any consumer product which malfunctions, is defective, or does not conform to the written warranty unless the warrantor has demonstrated in a rulemaking proceeding, or can demonstrate in an administrative or judicial enforcement proceeding (including private enforcement), or in an informal dispute settlement proceeding, that such a duty is reasonable.

(2) Notwithstanding paragraph (1), a warrantor may require, as a condition

to replacement of, or refund for, any consumer product under subsection (a) of this section, that such consumer product shall be made available to the warrantor free and clear of liens, and other encumbrances, except as otherwise provided by rule or order of the Commission in cases in which such a requirement would not be practicable.

(3) The Commission may, by rule define in detail the duties set forth in subsection (a) of this section and the applicability of such duties to warrantors of different categories of consumer products with "full (statement of duration)" warranties.

(4) The duties under subsection (a) of this section extend from the warrantor to each person who is a consumer with respect to the consumer product.

(c) The performance of the duties under subsection (a) of this section shall not be required of the warrantor if he can show that the defect, malfunction, or failure of any warranted consumer product to conform with a written warranty, was caused by damage (not resulting from defect or malfunction) while in the possession of the consumer, or unreasonable use (including failure to provide reasonable and necessary maintenance).

(d) For purposes of this section and of section 102(c), the term "without charge" means that the warrantor may not assess the consumer for any costs the warrantor or his representatives incur in connection with the required remedy of a warranted consumer product. An obligation under subsection (a)(1)(A) of this section to remedy without charge does not necessarily require the warrantor to compensate the consumer for incidental expenses; however, if any incidental expenses are incurred because the remedy is not made within a reasonable time or because the warrantor imposed an unreasonable duty upon the consumer as a condition of securing remedy, then the consumer shall be entitled to recover reasonable incidental expenses which are so incurred in any action against the warrantor.

(e) If a supplier designates a warranty applicable to a consumer product as a "full (statement of duration)" warranty, then the warranty on such product shall, for purposes of any action under section 110(d) or under any State law, be deemed to incorporate at least the minimum requirements of this section and rules prescribed under this section.

§105. Full and limited warranting of a consumer product (15 U.S.C. §2305]

Nothing in this [Act] shall prohibit the selling of a consumer product which has both full and limited warranties if such warranties are clearly and conspicuously differentiated.

§106. Service contracts [15 U.S.C. §2306]

(a) The Commission may prescribe by rule the manner and form in which the terms and conditions of service contracts shall be fully, clearly, and conspicuously disclosed.

(b) Nothing in this [Act] shall be construed to prevent a supplier or warrantor from entering into a service contract with the consumer in addition to or in lieu of a written warranty if such contract fully, clearly, and conspicuously discloses its terms and conditions in simple and readily understood language.

§107.   Designation of representatives [15 U.S.C. §2307]

Nothing in this [Act] shall be construed to prevent any warrantor from designating representatives to perform duties under the written or implied warranty: *Provided,* That such warrantor shall make reasonable arrangements for compensation of such designated representatives, but no such designation shall relieve the warrantor of his direct responsibilities to the consumer or make the representative a cowarrantor.

§108.   Limitation on disclaimer of implied warranties [15 U.S.C. §2308]

(a) No supplier may disclaim or modify (except as provided in subsection (b) of this section) any implied warranty to a consumer with respect to such consumer product if (1) such supplier makes any written warranty to the consumer with respect to such consumer product, or (2) at the time of sale, or within 90 days thereafter, such supplier enters into a service contract with the consumer which applies to such consumer product.

(b) For purposes of this [Act] (other than section 104(a)(2)), implied warranties may be limited in duration to the duration of a written warranty of reasonable duration, if such limitation is conscionable and is set forth in clear and unmistakable language and prominently displayed on the face of the warranty.

(c) A disclaimer, modification, or limitation made in violation of this section shall be ineffective for purposes of this [Act] and State law.

§109.   Commission rules [15 U.S.C. §2309]

(a) Any rule prescribed under this [Act] shall be prescribed in accordance with section 553 of Title 5; except that the Commission shall give interested persons an opportunity for oral presentations of data, views, and arguments, in addition to written submissions. A transcript shall be kept of any oral presentation. Any such rule shall be subject to judicial review under section 18(e) of the Federal Trade Commission Act in the same manner as rules prescribed under section 18(a)(1)(B) of such Act, except that section 18(e)(3)(B) of such Act shall not apply.

(b) The Commission shall initiate within one year after January 4, 1975, a rulemaking proceeding dealing with warranties and warranty practices in connection with the sale of used motor vehicles; and, to the extent necessary to supplement the protections offered the consumer by this [Act] shall prescribe rules dealing with such warranties and practices. In prescribing rules under this subsection, the Commission may exercise any authority it may have under this [Act], or other law, and in addition it may require disclosure that a used motor vehicle is sold without any warranty and specify the form and content of such disclosure.

§110. Remedies [15 U.S.C. §2310]

(a)(1) Congress hereby declares it to be its policy to encourage warrantors to establish procedures whereby consumer disputes are fairly and expeditiously settled through informal dispute settlement mechanisms.

(2) The Commission shall prescribe rules setting forth minimum requirements for any informal dispute settlement procedure which is incorporated into the terms of a written warranty to which any provision of this [Act] applies. Such rules shall provide for participation in such procedure by independent or governmental entities.

(3) One or more warrantors may establish an informal dispute settlement procedure which meets the requirements of the Commission's rules under paragraph (2). If—

(A) a warrantor establishes such a procedure,

(B) such procedure, and its implementation, meets the requirements of such rules, and

(C) he incorporates in a written warranty a requirement that the consumer resort to such procedure before pursuing any legal remedy under this section respecting such warranty,

then (i) the consumer may not commence a civil action (other than a class action) under subsection (d) of this section unless he initially resorts to such procedure; and (ii) a class of consumers may not proceed in a class action under subsection (d) of this section except to the extent the court determines necessary to establish the representative capacity of the named plaintiffs, unless the named plaintiffs (upon notifying the defendant that they are named plaintiffs in a class action with respect to a warranty obligation) initially resort to such procedure. In the case of such a class action which is brought in a district court of the United States, the representative capacity of the named plaintiffs shall be established in the application of rule 23 of the Federal Rules of Civil Procedure. In any civil action arising out of a warranty obligation and relating to a matter considered in such a procedure, any decision in such procedure shall be admissible in evidence.

(4) The Commission on its own initiative may, or upon written complaint filed by any interested person shall, review the bona fide operation of any dispute settlement procedure resort to which is stated in a written warranty to be a prerequisite to pursuing a legal remedy under this section. If the

Commission finds that such procedure or its implementation fails to comply with the requirements of the rules under paragraph (2), the Commission may take appropriate remedial action under any authority it may have under this chapter or any other provision of law.

(5) Until rules under paragraph (2) take effect, this subsection shall not affect the validity of any informal dispute settlement procedure respecting consumer warranties, but in any action under subsection (d) of this section, the court may invalidate any such procedure if it finds that such procedure is unfair.

(b) It shall be a violation of section 5(a)(1) of the Federal Trade Commission Act for any person to fail to comply with any requirement imposed on such person by this [Act] (or a rule thereunder) or to violate any prohibition contained in this [Act] (or a rule thereunder).

(c)(1) The district courts of the United States shall have jurisdiction of any action brought by the Attorney General (in his capacity as such), or by the Commission by any of its attorneys designated by it for such purpose, to restrain (A) any warrantor from making a deceptive warranty with respect to a consumer product, or (B) any person from failing to comply with any requirement imposed on such person by or pursuant to this [Act] or from violating any prohibition contained in this [Act]. Upon proper showing that, weighing the equities and considering the Commission's or Attorney General's likelihood of ultimate success, such action would be in the public interest and after notice to the defendant, a temporary restraining order or preliminary injunction may be granted without bond. In the case of an action brought by the Commission, if a complaint under section 5 of the Federal Trade Commission Act is not filed within such period (not exceeding 10 days) as may be specified by the court after the issuance of the temporary restraining order or preliminary injunction, the order or injunction shall be dissolved by the court and be of no further force and effect. Any suit shall be brought in the district in which such person resides or transacts business. Whenever it appears to the court that the ends of justice require that other persons should be parties in the action, the court may cause them to be summoned whether or not they reside in the district in which the court is held, and to that end process may be served in any district.

(2) For the purposes of this subsection, the term "deceptive warranty" means (A) a written warranty which (i) contains an affirmation, promise, description, or representation which is either false or fraudulent, or which, in light of all of the circumstances, would mislead a reasonable individual exercising due care; or (ii) fails to contain information which is necessary in light of all of the circumstances, to make the warranty not misleading to a reasonable individual exercising due care; or (B) a written warranty created by the use of such terms as "guaranty" or "warranty", if the terms and conditions of such warranty so limit its scope and application as to deceive a reasonable individual.

(d)(1) Subject to subsections (a)(3) and (e) of this section, a consumer who is damaged by the failure of a supplier, warrantor, or service contractor to comply with any obligation under this [Act], or under a written warranty, implied warranty, or service contract, may bring suit for damages and other legal and equitable relief—

(A) in any court of competent jurisdiction in any State or the District of Columbia; or

(B) in an appropriate district court of the United States, subject to paragraph (3) of this subsection.

(2) If a consumer finally prevails in any action brought under paragraph (1) of this subsection, he may be allowed by the court to recover as part of the judgment a sum equal to the aggregate amount of cost and expenses (including attorneys' fees based on actual time expended) determined by the court to have been reasonably incurred by the plaintiff for or in connection with the commencement and prosecution of such action, unless the court in its discretion shall determine that such an award of attorneys' fees would be inappropriate.

(3) No claim shall be cognizable in a suit brought under paragraph (1)(B) of this subsection—

(A) if the amount in controversy of any individual claim is less than the sum or value of $25;

(B) if the amount in controversy is less than the sum or value of $50,000 (exclusive of interest and costs) computed on the basis of all claims to be determined in this suit; or

(C) if the action is brought as a class action, and the number of named plaintiffs is less than one hundred.

(e) No action (other than a class action or an action respecting a warranty to which subsection (a)(3) of this section applies) may be brought under subsection (d) of this section for failure to comply with any obligation under any written or implied warranty or service contract, and a class of consumers may not proceed in a class action under such subsection with respect to such a failure except to the extent the court determines necessary to establish the representative capacity of the named plaintiffs, unless the person obligated under the warranty or service contract is afforded a reasonable opportunity to cure such failure to comply. In the case of such a class action (other than a class action representing a warranty to which subsection (a)(3) of this section applies) brought under subsection (d) of this section for breach of any written or implied warranty or service contract, such reasonable opportunity shall be afforded by the named plaintiffs and they shall at that time notify the defendant that they are acting on behalf of the class. In the case of such a class action which is brought in a district court of the United States, the representative capacity of the named plaintiffs shall be established in the application of rule 23 of the Federal Rules of Civil Procedure.

(f) For purposes of this section, only the warrantor actually making a written affirmation of fact, promise, or undertaking shall be deemed to have created a written warranty, and any rights arising thereunder may be enforced under this section only against such warrantor and no other person.

§111.   Effect on other laws [15 U.S.C. §2311]

(a)(1) Nothing contained in this [Act] shall be construed to repeal, invalidate, or supersede the Federal Trade Commission Act or any statute defined therein as an Antitrust Act.

(2) Nothing in this [Act] shall be construed to repeal, invalidate, or supersede the Federal Seed Act and nothing in this [Act] shall apply to seed for planting.

(b)(1) Nothing in this [Act] shall invalidate or restrict any right or remedy of any consumer under State law or any other Federal law.

(2) Nothing in this [Act] (other than sections 108 and 104(a)(2) and (4)) shall (A) affect the liability of, or impose liability on, any person for personal jury, or (B) supersede any provision of State law regarding consequential damages for injury to the person or other injury.

(c)(1) Except as provided in subsection (b) of this section and in paragraph (2) of this subsection, a State requirement—

(A) which relates to labeling or disclosure with respect to written warranties or performance thereunder;

(B) which is within the scope of an applicable requirement of sections 102, 103, and 104 (and rules implementing such sections), and

(C) which is not identical to a requirement of section 102, 103, or 104 (or a rule thereunder),

shall not be applicable to written warranties complying with such sections (or rules thereunder).

(2) If, upon application of an appropriate State agency, the Commission determines (pursuant to rules issued in accordance with section 109) that any requirement of such State covering any transaction to which this [Act] applies (A) affords protection to consumers greater than the requirements of this [Act] and (B) does not unduly burden interstate commerce, then such State requirement shall be applicable (notwithstanding the provisions of paragraph (1) of this subsection) to the extent specified in such determination for so long as the State administers and enforces effectively any such greater requirement.

(d) This chapter (other than section 102(c)) shall be inapplicable to any written warranty the making or content of which is otherwise governed by Federal law. If only a portion of a written warranty is so governed by Federal law, the remaining portion shall be subject to this [Act].

§112.   Effective dates [15 U.S.C. 2312]

(a) Except as provided in subsection (b) of this section, this [Act] shall take effect 6 months after January 4, 1975, but shall not apply to consumer products manufactured prior to such date.

Appendix L
Federal Trade Commission Rules, Regulations, Statements And Interpretations Under The Magnuson-Moss Warranty Act

16 C.F.R. Parts 700-703

PART 700. INTERPRETATIONS OF MAGNUSON-MOSS WARRANTY ACT

Table of Sections

§700.1   Products covered

(a) The Act applies to written warranties or tangible personal property which is normally used for personal, family, or household purposes. This definition includes property which is intended to be attached to or installed in any real property without regard to whether it is so attached or installed. This means that a product is a "consumer product" if the use of that type of product is not uncommon. The percentage of sales or the use to which a product is put by any individual buyer is not determinative. For example, products such as automobiles and typewriters which are used for both personal and commercial purposes come within the definition of consumer product. Where it is unclear whether a particular product is covered under the definition of consumer product, any ambiguity will be resolved in favor of coverage.

(b) Agricultural products such as farm machinery, structures and implements used in the business or occupation of farming are not covered by the Act where their personal, family, or household use is uncommon. However, those agricultural products normally used for personal or household gardening

617

(for example, to produce goods for personal consumption, and not for resale) are consumer products under the Act.

(c) The definition of "Consumer product" limits the applicability of the Act to personal property, "including any such property intended to be attached to or installed in any real property without regard to whether it is so attached or installed." This provision brings under the Act separate items of equipment attached to real property, such as air conditioners, furnaces, and water heaters.

(d) The coverage of separate items of equipment attached to real property includes, but is not limited to, appliances and other thermal, mechanical, and electrical equipment. (It does not extend to the wiring, plumbing, ducts, and other items which are integral component parts of the structure.) State law would classify many such products as fixtures to, and therefore a part of, realty. The statutory definition is designed to being such products under the Act regardless of whether they may be considered fixtures under state law.

(e) The coverage of building materials which are not separate items of equipment is based on the nature of the purchase transaction. An analysis of the transaction will determine whether the goods are real or personal property. The numerous products which go into the construction of a consumer dwelling are all consumer products when sold "over the counter," as by hardware and building supply retailers. This is also true where a consumer contracts for the purchase of such materials in connection with the improvement, repair, or modification of a home (for example, paneling, dropped ceilings, siding, roofing, storm windows, remodeling). However, where such products are at the time of sale integrated into the structure of a dwelling they are not consumer products as they cannot be practically distinguished from realty. Thus, for example, the beams, wallboard, wiring, plumbing, windows, roofing, and other structural components of a dwelling are not consumer products when they are sold as part of real estate covered by a written warranty.

(f) In the case where a consumer contracts with a builder to construct a home, a substantial addition to a home, or other realty (such as a garage or an in-ground swimming pool) the building materials to be used are not consumer products. Although the materials are separately identifiable at the time the contract is made, it is the intention of the parties to contract for the construction of realty which will integrate the component materials. Of course, as noted above, any separate items of equipment to be attached to such realty are consumer products under the Act.

(g) Certain provisions of the Act apply only to products actually costing the consumer more than a specified amount. Section 103 applies to consumer products actually costing the consumer more than $10, excluding tax. The $10 minimum will be interpreted to include multiple-packaged items which may individually sell for less than $10, but which have been packaged in a manner that does not permit breaking the package to purchase an item or items at a price less than $10. Thus, a written warranty on a dozen items packaged and priced for sale at $12 must be designated, even though identical items may be offered in smaller quantities at under $10. This interpretation applies in the same manner to the minimum dollar limits in section 102 and rules promulgated under that section.

(h) Warranties on replacement parts and components used to repair consumer products are covered; warranties on services are not covered. Therefore, warranties which apply solely to a repairer's workmanship in performing repairs are not subject to the Act. Where a written agreement warrants both the parts provided to effect a repair and the workmanship in making that repair, the warranty must comply with the Act and the rules thereunder.

(i) The Act covers written warranties on consumer products "distributed in commerce" as that term is defined in section 101(3). Thus, by its terms the Act arguably applies to products exported to foreign jurisdictions. However, the public interest would not be served by the use of Commission resources to enforce the Act with respect to such products. Moreover, the legislative intent to apply the requirements of the Act to such products is not sufficiently clear to justify such an extraordinary result. The Commission does not contemplate the enforcement of the Act with respect to consumer products exported to foreign jurisdictions. Products exported for sale at military post exchanges remain subject to the same enforcement standards as products sold within the United States, its territories and possessions.

§700.2 Date of manufacture

Section 112 of the Act provides that the Act shall apply only to those consumer products manufactured after July 4, 1975. When a consumer purchases repair of a consumer product the date of manufacture of any replacement parts used is the measuring date for determining coverage under the Act. The date of manufacture of the consumer product being repaired is in this instance not relevant. Where a consumer purchases or obtains on an exchange basis a rebuilt consumer product, the date that the rebuilding process is completed determines the Act's applicability.

§700.3 Written warranty

(a) The Act imposes specific duties and liabilities on suppliers who offer written warranties on consumer products. Certain representations, such as energy efficiency ratings for electrical appliances, care labeling of wearing apparal, and other product information disclosures may be express warranties under the Uniform Commercial Code. However, these disclosures alone are not written warranties under this Act. Section 101(6) provides that a written affirmation of fact or a written promise of a specified level of performance must relate to a specified period of time in order to be considered a "written warranty."[1] A product information disclosure without a specified time period

---

[1] A "written warranty" is also created by a written affirmation of fact or a written

to which the disclosure relates is therefore not a written warranty. In addition, section 111(d) exempts from the Act (except section 102(c)) any written warranty the making or content of which is required by federal law. The Commission encourages the disclosure of product information which is not deceptive and which may benefit consumers, and will not construe the Act to impede information disclosure in product advertising or labeling.

(b) Certain terms, or conditions, of sale of a consumer product may not be "written warranties" as that term is defined in section 101(6), and should not be offered or described in a manner that may deceive consumers as to their enforceability under the Act. For example, a seller of consumer products may give consumers an unconditional right to revoke acceptance of goods within a certain number of days after delivery without regard to defects or failure to meet a specified level of performance. Or a seller may permit consumers to return products for any reason for credit toward purchase of another item. Such terms of sale taken alone are not written warranties under the Act. Therefore, suppliers should avoid any characterization of such terms of sale as warranties. The use of such terms as "free trial period" and "trade-in credit policy" in this regard would be appropriate. Furthermore, such terms of sale should be stated separately from any written warranty. Of course, the offering and performance of such terms of sale remain subject to section 5 of the Federal Trade Commission Act, 15 U.S.C. 45.

(c) The Magnuson-Moss Warranty Act generally applies to written warranties covering consumer products. Many consumer products are covered by warranties which are neither intended for, nor enforceable by, consumers. A common example is a warranty given by a component supplier to a manufacturer of consumer products. (The manufacturer may, in turn, warrant these components to consumers.) The component supplier's warranty is generally given solely to the product manufacturer, and is neither intended to be conveyed to the consumer nor brought to the consumer's attention in connection with the sale. Such warranties are not subject to the Act, since a written warranty under section 101(6) of the Act must become "part of the basis of the bargain between a supplier and a buyer for purposes other than resale." However, the Act applies to a component supplier's warranty in writing which is given to the consumer. An example is a supplier's written warranty to the consumer covering a refrigerator that is sold installed in a boat or recreational vehicle. The supplier of the refrigerator relies on the boat or vehicle assembler to convey the written agreement to the consumer. In this case, the supplier's written warranty is to a consumer, and is covered by the Act.

---

promise that the product is defect free, or by a written undertaking of remedial action within the meaning of section 101(6)(B).

§700.4 Parties "Actually making" a written warranty

Section 110(f) of the Act provides that only the supplier "actually making" a written warranty is liable for purposes of FTC and private enforcement of the Act. A supplier who does no more than distribute or sell a consumer product covered by a written warranty offered by another person or business and which identifies that person or business as the warrantor is not liable for failure of the written warranty to comply with the Act or rules thereunder. However, other actions and written and oral representations of such a supplier in connection with the offer or sale of a warranted product may obligate that supplier under the Act. If under state law the supplier is deemed to have "adopted" the written affirmation of fact, promise, or undertaking, the supplier is also obligated under the Act. Suppliers are advised to consult state law to determine those actions and representations which may make them co-warrantors, and therefore obligated under the warranty of the other person or business.

§700.5 Expressions of general policy

(a) Under section 103(b), statements or representations of general policy concerning customer satisfaction which are not subject to any specific limitation need not be designated as full or limited warranties, and are exempt from the requirements of sections 102, 103, and 104 of the Act and rules thereunder. However, such statements remain subject to the enforcement provisions of section 110 of the Act, and to section 5 of the Federal Trade Commission Act, 15 U.S.C. 45.

(b) The section 103(b) exemption applies only to general policies, not to those which are limited to specific consumer products manufactured or sold by the supplier offering such a policy. In addition, to qualify for an exemption under section 103(b) such policies may not be subject to any specific limitations. For example, policies which have an express limitation of duration or a limitation of the amount to be refunded are not exempted. This does not preclude the imposition of reasonable limitations based on the circumstances in each instance a consumer seeks to invoke such an agreement. For instance, a warrantor may refuse to honor such an expression of policy where a consumer has used a product for 10 years without previously expressing any specific disatisfaction with the product. Such a refusal would not be a specific limitation under this provision.

§700.6 Designation of warranties

(a) Section 103 of the Act provides that written warranties on consumer products manufactured after July 4, 1975, and actually costing the consumer more than $10, excluding tax, must be designated either "Full (statement of duration) Warranty" or "Limited Warranty". Warranties may include a statement of duration in a limited warranty designation. The designation or designations should appear clearly and conspicuously as a caption, or prominent title, clearly separated from the text of the warranty. The full (statement of duration) warranty and limited warranty are the exclusive designations permitted under the Act, unless a specific exception is created by rule.

(b) Section 104(b)(4) states that "the duties under subsection (a) (of section 104) extend from the warrantor to each person who is a consumer with respect to the consumer product." Section 101(3) defines a consumer as "a buyer (other than for purposes of resale) of any consumer product, any person to whom such product is transferred during the duration of an implied or written warranty (or service contract) applicable to the product. . . ." Therefore, a full warranty may not expressly restrict the warranty rights of a transferee during its stated duration. However, where the duration of a full warranty is defined solely in terms of first purchaser ownership there can be no violation of section 104(b)(4), since the duration of the warranty expires, by definition, at the time of transfer. No rights of a subsequent transferee are cut off as there is no transfer of ownership "during the duration of (any) warranty." Thus, these provisions do not preclude the offering of a full warranty with its duration determined exclusively by the period during which the first purchaser owns the product, or uses it in conjunction with another product. For example, an automotive battery or muffler warranty may be designated as "full warranty for as long as you own your car." Because this type of warranty leads the consumer to believe that proof of purchase is not needed so long as he or she owns the product a duty to furnish documentary proof may not be reasonably imposed on the consumer under this type of warranty. The burden is on the warrantor to prove that a particular claimant under this type of warranty is not the original purchaser or owner of the product. Warrantors or their designated agents may, however, ask consumers to state or affirm that they are the first purchasers of the product.

§700.7   Use of warranty registration cards

(a) Under section 104(b)(1) of the Act a warrantor offering a full warranty may not impose on consumers any duty other than notification of a defect as a condition of securing remedy of the defect or malfunction, unless such additional duty can be demonstrated by the warrantor to be reasonable. Warrantors have in the past stipulated the return of a "warranty registration" or similar card. By "warranty registration card" the Commission means a card which must be returned by the consumer shortly after purchase of the product and which is stipulated or implied in the warranty to be a condition precedent to warranty coverage and performance.

(b) A requirement that the consumer return a warranty registration card or a similar notice as a condition of performance under a full warranty is an unreasonable duty. Thus, a provision such as, "This warranty is void unless the warranty registration card is returned to the warrantor" is not permissible in a full warranty, nor is it permissible to imply such a condition in a full warranty.

(c) This does not prohibit the use of such registration cards where a warrantor suggests use of the card as one possible means of proof of the date the product was purchased. For example, it is permissible to provide in a full warranty that a consumer may fill out and return a card to place on file proof of the date the product was purchased. Any such suggestion to the consumer must include notice that failure to return the card will not affect rights under the warranty, so long as the consumer can show in a reasonable manner the date the product was purchased. Nor does this interpretation prohibit a seller from obtaining from purchasers at the time of sale information requested by the warrantor.

§700.8   Warrantor's decision as final

A warrantor shall not indicate in any written warranty or service contract either directly or indirectly that the decision of the warrantor, service contractor, or any designated third party is final or binding in any dispute concerning the warranty or service contract. Nor shall a warrantor or service contractor state that it alone shall determine what is a defect under the agreement. Such statements are deceptive since section 110(d) of the Act gives state and federal courts jurisdiction over suits for breach of warranty and service contract.

§700.9   Duty to install under a full warranty

Under section 104(a)(1) of the Act, the remedy under a full warranty must be provided to the consumer without charge. If the warranted product has utility only when installed, a full warranty must provide such installment without charge regardless of whether or not the consumer originally paid for installation by the warrantor or his agent. However, this does not preclude the warrantor from imposing on the consumer a duty to remove, return, or reinstall where such duty can be demonstrated by the warrantor to meet the standard of reasonableness under section 104(b)(1).

§700.10   Section 102(c)

(a) Section 102(c) prohibits tying arrangements that condition coverage under a written warranty on the consumer's use of an article or service identified by brand, trade, or corporate name unless that article or service is provided without charge to the consumer.

(b) Under a limited warranty that provides only for replacement of defective parts and no portion of labor charges, section 102(c) prohibits a condition that the consumer use only service (labor) identified by the warrantor to install the replacement parts. A warrantor or his designated representative may not provide parts under the warranty in a manner which impedes or precludes the choice by the consumer of the person or business to perform necessary labor to install such parts.

(c) No warrantor may condition the continued validity of a warranty on the use of only authorized repair service and/or authorized replacement parts for non-warranty service and maintenance. For example, provisions such as, "this warranty is void if service is performed by anyone other than an authorized 'ABC' dealer and all replacement parts must be genuine 'ABC' parts, and the like, are prohibited where the service or parts are not covered by the warranty. These provisions violate the Act in two ways. First, they violate the section 102(c) ban against tying arrangements. Second, such provisions are deceptive under section 110 of the Act, because a warrantor cannot, as a matter of law, avoid liability under a written warranty where a defect is unrelated to the use by a consumer of "unauthorized" articles or service. This does not preclude a warrantor from expressly excluding liability for defects or damage caused by such "unauthorized" articles or service; nor does it preclude the warrantor from denying liability where the warrantor can demonstrate that the defect or damage was so caused.

§700.11 Written warranty, service contract, and insurance distinguished for purposes of compliance under the Act

(a) The Act recognizes two types of agreements which may provide similar coverage of consumer products, the written warranty, and the service contract. In addition, other agreements may meet the statutory definitions of either "written warranty" or "service contract," but are sold and regulated under state law as contracts of insurance. One example is the automobile breakdown insurance policies sold in many jurisdictions and regulated by the state as a form of casualty insurance. The McCarran-Ferguson Act, 15 U.S.C. 1011 et seq., precludes jurisdiction under federal law over "the business of insurance" to the extent an agreement is regulated by state law as insurance. Thus, such agreements are subject to the Magnuson-Moss Warranty Act only to the extent they are not regulated in a particular state as the business of insurance.

(b) "Written warranty" and "service contract" are defined in sections 101(6) and 101(8) of the Act, respectively. A written warranty must be "part of the basis of the bargain." This means that it must be conveyed at the time of sale of the consumer product and the consumer must not give any consideration beyond the purchase price of the consumer product in order to benefit from the agreement. It is not a requirement of the Act that an agreement obligate a supplier of the consumer product to a written warranty, but merely that it be part of the basis of the bargain between a supplier and a consumer. This contemplates written warranties by third-party non-suppliers.

(c) A service contract under the Act must meet the definitions of section 101(8). An agreement which would meet the definition of written warranty in section 101(6)(A) or (B) but for its failure to satisfy the basis of the bargain test is a service contract. For example, an agreement which calls for some consideration in addition to the purchase price of the consumer product, or which is entered into at some date after the purchase of the consumer product to which it applies, is a service contract. An agreement which relates only to the performance of maintenance and/or inspection services and which is not an undertaking, promise, or affirmation with respect to a specified level of performance, or that the product is free of defects in materials or workmanship, is a service contract. An agreement to perform periodic cleaning and inspection of a product over a specified period of time, even when offered at the time of sale and without charge to the consumer, is an example of such a service contract.

Part 701. Disclosure of Written Consumer Product Warranty Terms and Conditions

Table of Sections

---

§701.1   Definitions

(a) "The Act" means the Magnuson-Moss Warranty Federal Trade Commission Improvement Act, 15 U.S.C. 2301, et seq.

(b) "Consumer product" means any tangible personal property which is distributed in commerce and which is normally used for personal, family, or household purposes (including any such property intended to be attached to or installed in any real property without regard to whether it is so attached or installed). Products which are purchased solely for commercial or industrial use are excluded solely for purposes of this Part.

(c) "Written warranty" means:

(1) Any written affirmation of fact or written promise made in connection with the sale of a consumer product by a supplier to a buyer which relates to the nature of the material or workmanship and affirms or promises that such material or workmanship is defect free or will meet a specified level of performance over a specified period of time, or

(2) Any undertaking in writing in connection with the sale by a supplier of a consumer product to refund, repair, replace, or take other remedial action with respect to such product in the event that such product fails to meet the specifications set forth in the undertaking, which written affirmation, promise or undertaking becomes part of the basis of the bargain between a supplier and a buyer for purposes other than resale of such product.

(d) "Implied warranty" means an implied warranty arising under State law (as modified by secs. 104(a) and 108 of the Act) in connection with the sale by a supplier of a consumer product.

(e) "Remedy" means whichever of the following actions the warrantor elects:

(1) Repair,

(2) Replacement, or

(3) Refund; except that the warrantor may not elect refund unless: (i) The warrantor is unable to provide replacement and repair is not commercially practicable or cannot be timely made, or

(ii) The consumer is willing to accept such refund.

(f) "Supplier" means any person engaged in the business of making a consumer product directly or indirectly available to consumers.

(g) "Warrantor" means any supplier or other person who gives or offers to give a written warranty.

(h) "Consumer" means a buyer (other than for purposes of resale or use in the ordinary course of the buyer's business) of any consumer product, any person to whom such product is transferred during the duration of an implied or written warranty applicable to the product, and any other such person who is entitled by the terms of such warranty or under applicable State law to enforce against the warrantor the obligations of the warranty.

(i) "On the face of the warranty" means:

(1) Where the warranty is a single sheet with printing on both sides of the sheet or where the warranty is comprised of more than one sheet, the page on which the warranty text begins;

(2) Where the warranty is included as part of a larger document, such as a use and care manual, the page in such document on which the warranty text begins.

§701.2 Scope

The regulations in this part establish requirements for warrantors for disclosing the terms and conditions of written warranties on consumer products actually costing the consumer more than $15.00.

§701.3 Written warranty terms

(a) Any warrantor warranting to a consumer by means of a written warranty a consumer product actually costing the consumer more than $15.00 shall clearly and conspicuously disclose in a single document in simple and readily understood language, the following items of information:

(1) The identity of the party or parties to whom the written warranty is extended, if the enforceability of the written warranty is limited to the original consumer purchaser or is otherwise limited to persons other than every consumer owner during the terms of the warranty;

(2) A clear description and identification of products, or parts, or characteristics, or components or properties covered by and where necessary for clarification, excluded from the warranty;

(3) A statement of what the warrantor will do in the event of a defect, malfunction or failure to conform with the written warranty, including the items or services the warrantor will pay for or provide, and, where necessary for clarification, those which the warrantor will not pay for or provide;

(4) The point in time or event on which the warranty term commences, if different from the purchase date, and the time period or other measurement of warranty duration;

(5) A step-by-step explanation of the procedure which the consumer should

follow in order to obtain performance of any warranty obligation, including the persons or class of persons authorized to perform warranty obligations. This includes the name(s) of the warrantor(s), together with: The mailing address(es) of the warrantor(s), and/or the name or title and the address of any employee or department of the warrantor responsible for the performance of warranty obligations, and/or a telephone number which consumers may use without charge to obtain information on warranty performance;

(6) Information respecting the availability of any informal dispute settlement mechanism elected by the warrantor in compliance with Part 703 of this subchapter;

(7) Any limitations on the duration of implied warranties, disclosed on the face of the warranty as provided in Section 108 of the Act, accompanied by the following statement:

Some states do not allow limitations on how long an implied warranty lasts, so the above limitation may not apply to you.

(8) Any exclusions of or limitations on relief such as incidental or consequential damages, accompanied by the following statement, which may be combined with the statement required in paragraph (a)(7) of this section:

Some states do not allow the exclusion or limitation of incidental or consequential damages, so the above limitation or exclusion may not apply to you.

(9) A statement in the following language:

This warranty gives you specific legal rights, and you may also have other rights which vary from state to state.

(b) Paragraphs (a)(1) through (9) of this section shall not be applicable with respect to statements of general policy on emblems, seals or insignas issued by third parties promising replacement or refund if a consumer product is defective, which statements contain no representation or assurance of the quality or performance characteristics of the product; provided that (1) the disclosures required by paragraphs (a)(1) through (9) of this section are published by such third parties in each issue of a publication with a general circulation, and (2) such disclosures are provided free of charge to any consumer upon written request.

§701.4   Owner registration cards

When a warrantor employs any card such as an owner's registration card, a warranty registration card, or the like, and the return of such card is a condition precedent to warranty coverage and performance, the warrantor shall disclose this fact in the warranty. If the return of such card reasonably appears to be a condition precedent to warranty coverage and performance, but is not such a condition, that fact shall be disclosed in the warranty.

Part 702. Pre-Sale Availability of Written Warranty Terms

Table of Sections

§702.1 Definitions

(a) "The Act" means the Magnuson-Moss Warranty Federal Trade Commission Improvement Act, 15 U.S.C. 2301, et seq.

(b) "Consumer product" means any tangible personal property which is distributed in commerce and which is normally used for personal, family, or household purposes (including any such property intended to be attached to or installed in any real property without regard to whether it is so attached or installed). Products which are purchased solely for commercial or industrial use are excluded solely for purposes of this part.

(c) "Written warranty" means:

(1) Any written affirmation of fact or written promise made in connection with the sale of a consumer product by a supplier to a buyer which relates to the nature of the material or workmanship and affirms or promises that such material or workmanship is defect free or will meet a specified level of performance over a specified period of time, or

(2) Any undertaking in writing in connection with the sale by a supplier of a consumer product to refund, repair, replace, or take other remedial action with respect to such product in the event that such product fails to meet the specifications set forth in the undertaking, which written affirmation, promise or undertaking becomes part of the basis of the bargain between a supplier and a buyer for purposes other than resale of such product.

(d) "Warrantor" means any supplier or other person who gives or offers to give a written warranty.

(e) "Seller" means any person who sells or offers for sale for purposes other than resale or use in the ordinary course of the buyer's business any consumer product.

(f) "Supplier" means any person engaged in the business of making a consumer product directly or indirectly available to consumers.

(g) "Binder" means a locking binder, note book, or similar system which will provide the consumer with convenient access to copies of product warranties.

§702.2 Scope

The regulations in this part establish requirements for sellers and warrantors for making the terms of any written warranty on a consumer product available to the consumer prior to sale.

§702.3   Pre-sale availability of written warranty terms

The following requirements apply to consumer products actually costing the consumer more than $15.00:

(a) *Duties of the seller.*   Except as provided in paragraphs (c) through (d) of this section, the seller of a consumer product with a written warranty shall:

(1) Make available for the prospective buyer's review, prior to sale, the text of such written warranty by the use of one or more of the following means:

(i) Clearly and conspicuously displaying the text of the written warranty in close conjunction to each warranted product; and/or

(ii) Maintaining a binder or series of binders which contain(s) copies of the warranties for the products sold in each department in which any consumer product with a written warranty is offered for sale. Such binder(s) shall be maintained in each such department, or in a location which provides the prospective buyer with ready access to such binder(s), and shall be prominently entitled "Warranties" or other similar title which clearly identifies the binder(s). Such binder(s) shall be indexed according to product or warrantor and shall be maintained up to date when new warranted products or models or new warranties for existing products are introduced into the store or department by substituting superseding warranties and by adding new warranties as appropriate. The seller shall either:

(A) Display such binder(s) in a manner reasonably calculated to elicit the prospective buyer's attention; or

(B) Make the binders available to prospective buyers on request, and place signs reasonably calculated to elicit the prospective buyer's attention in prominent locations in the store or department advising such prospective buyers of the availability of the binders, including instructions for obtaining access; and/or

(iii) Displaying the package of any consumer product on which the text of the written warranty is disclosed, in a manner such that the warranty is clearly visible to prospective buyers at the point of sale; and/or

(iv) Placing in close proximity to the warranted consumer product a notice which discloses the text of the written warranty, in a manner which clearly identifies to prospective buyers the product to which the notice applies;

(2) Not remove or obscure any warranty disclosure materials provided by a warrantor, except:

(i) Where such removal is necessary for store window displays, fashion shows, or picture taking; or

(ii) Where the seller otherwise, through means provided for in paragraph (a)(1) of this section, makes the terms of the warranty information available to the consumer.

(b) *Duties of the warrantor.*   (1) A warrantor who gives a written warranty warranting to a consumer a consumer product actually costing the consumer more than $15.00 shall:

(i) Provide sellers with warranty materials necessary for such seller to comply with the requirements set forth in paragraph (a) of this section, by the use of one or more by the following means:

(A) Providing a copy of the written warranty with every warranted consumer product; and/or

(B) Providing a tag, sign, sticker, label, decal or other attachment to the product, which contains the full text of the written warranty; and/or

(C) Printing on or otherwise attaching the text of the written warranty to the package, carton, or other container if that package, carton or other container is normally used for display purposes. If the warrantor elects this option a copy of the written warranty must also accompany the warranted product; and/or

(D) Providing a notice, sign, or poster disclosing the text of a consumer product warranty. If the warrantor elects this option, a copy of the written warranty must also accompany each warranted product.

(ii) Provide catalog, mail order, and door-to-door sellers with copies of written warranties necessary for such sellers to comply with the requirements set forth in paragraphs (c) and (d) of this section.

(2) Paragraph (a)(1) of this section shall not be applicable with respect to statements of general policy on emblems, seals or insignias issued by third parties promising replacement or refund if a consumer product is defective which statements contain no representation or assurance of the quality or performance characteristics of the product; provided that (i) the disclosures required by §701.3(a)(1) through (9) of this part are published by such third parties in each issue of a publication with a general circulation, and (ii) such disclosures are provided free of charge to any consumer upon written request.

(c) *Catalog and Mail Order Sales.* (1) For purposes of this paragraph:

(i) "Catalog or mail order sales", means any offer for sale, or any solicitation for an order for a consumer product with a written warranty, which includes instructions for ordering the product which do not required a personal visit to the seller's establishment.

(ii) "Close conjunction" means on the page containing the description of the warranted product, or on the page facing that page.

(2) Any seller who offers for sale to consumers consumer products with written warranties by means of a catalog or mail order solicitation shall:

(i) Clearly and conspicuously disclose in such catalog or solicitation in close conjunction to the description of warranted product, or in an information section of the catalog or solicitation clearly referenced, including a page number, in close conjunction to the description of the warranted product, *either:*

(A) The full text of the written warranty; or

(B) That the written warranty can be obtained free upon specific written request, and the address where such warranty can be obtained. If this option is elected, such seller shall promptly provide a copy of any written warranty requested by the consumer.

(d) *Door-to-door sales.* (1) For purposes of this paragraph:

(i) "Door-to-door sales" means a sale of consumer products in which the seller or his representative personally solicits the sale, including those in response to or following an invitation by a buyer, and the buyer's agreement to offer to purchase is made at a place other than the place of business of the seller.

(ii) "Prospective buyer" means an individual solicited by a door-to-door seller to buy a consumer product who indicates sufficient interest in that consumer product or maintains sufficient contact with the seller for the seller reasonably to conclude that the person solicited is considering purchasing the product.

(2) Any seller who offers for sale to consumers consumer products with written warranties by means of door-to-door sales shall, prior to the consummation of the sale, disclose the fact that the sales representative has copies of the warranties for the warranted products being offered for sale, which may be inspected by the prospective buyer at any time during the sales presentation. Such disclosure shall be made orally and shall be included in any written materials shown to prospective buyers.

Part 703. Informal Dispute Settlement Procedures

Table of Sections

§703.1   Definitions

(a) "The Act" means the Magnuson-Moss Warranty—Federal Trade Commission Improvement Act, 15 U.S.C. 2301, *et seq.*

(b) "Consumer product" means any tangible personal property which is distributed in commerce and which is normally used for personal, family, or household purposes (including any such property intended to be attached to or installed in any real property without regard to whether it is so attached or installed).

(c) "Written warranty" means:

(1) Any written affirmation of fact or written promise made in connection with the sale of a consumer product by a supplier to a buyer which relates to the nature of the material or workmanship and affirms or promises that such material or workmanship is defect free or will meet a specified level of performance over a specified period of time, or

(2) Any undertaking in writing in connection with the sale by a supplier of a consumer product to refund, repair, replace, or take other remedial action with respect to such product in the event that such product fails to meet the specifications set forth in the undertaking, which written affirmation, promise or undertaking becomes part of the basis of the bargain between a supplier and a buyer for purposes other than resale of such product.

(d) "Warrantor" means any person who gives or offers to give a written warranty which incorporates an informal dispute settlement mechanism.

(e) "Mechanism" means an informal dispute settlement procedure which is incorporated into the terms of a written warranty to which any provision of Title I of the Act applies, as provided in Section 110 of the Act.

(f) "Members" means the person or persons within a Mechanism actually deciding disputes.

(g) "Consumer" means a buyer (other than for purposes of resale) of any consumer product, any person to whom such product is transferred during the duration of a written warranty applicable to the product, and any other person who is entitled by the terms of such warranty or under applicable state law to enforce against the warrantor the obligations of the warranty.

(h) "On the face of the warranty" means:

(1) If the warranty is a single sheet with printing on both sides of the sheet, or if the warranty is comprised of more than one sheet, the page on which the warranty text begins;

(2) If the warranty is included as part of a longer document, such as a use and care manual, the page in such document on which the warranty text begins.

§703.2   Duties of warrantor

(a) The warrantor shall not incorporate into the terms of a written warranty a Mechanism that fails to comply with the requirements contained in §§703.3-703.8 of this part. This paragraph shall not prohibit a warrantor from incorporating into the terms of a written warranty the step-by-step procedure which the consumer should take in order to obtain performance of any obligation under the warranty as described in section 102(a)(7) of the Act and required by Part 701 of this subchapter.

(b) The warrantor shall disclose clearly and conspicuously at least the following information on the face of the written warranty:

(1) A statement of the availability of the informal dispute settlement mechanism;

(2) The name and address of the Mechanism, or the name and a telephone number of the Mechanism which consumers may use without charge;

(3) A statement of any requirement that the consumer resort to the Mechanism before exercising rights or seeking remedies created by Title I of the Act; together with the disclosure that if a consumer chooses to seek redress by pursuing rights and remedies not created by Title I of the Act, resort to the Mechanism would not be required by any provision of the Act; and

(4) A statement, if applicable, indicating where further information on the Mechanism can be found in materials accompanying the product, as provided in §703.2(c) of this section.

(c) The warrantor shall include in the written warranty or in a separate section of materials accompanying the product, the following information:

(1) Either (i) a form addressed to the Mechanism containing spaces requesting the information which the Mechanism may require for prompt resolution of warranty disputes; or (ii) a telephone number of the Mechanism which consumers may use without charge;

(2) The name and address of the Mechanism;

(3) A brief description of Mechanism procedures;

(4) The time limits adhered to by the Mechanism; and

(5) The types of information which the Mechanism may require for prompt resolution of warranty disputes.

(d) The warrantor shall take steps reasonably calculated to make consumers aware of the Mechanism's existence at the time consumers experience warranty disputes. Nothing contained in paragraphs (b), (c), or (d) of this section shall limit the warrantor's option to encourage consumers to seek redress directly from the warrantor as long as the warrantor does not expressly require consumers to seek redress directly from the warrantor. The warrantor shall proceed fairly and expeditiously to attempt to resolve all disputes submitted directly to the warrantor.

(e) Whenever a dispute is submitted directly to the warrantor, the warrantor shall, within a reasonable time, decide whether, and to what extent, it will satisfy the consumer, and inform the consumer of its decision. In its notification to the consumer of its decision, the warrantor shall include the information required in §703.2(b) and (c) of this section.

(f) The warrantor shall: (1) Respond fully and promptly to reasonable requests by the Mechanism for information relating to disputes;

(2) Upon notification of any decision of the Mechanism that would require action on the part of the warrantor, immediately notify the Mechanism whether, and to what extent, warrantor will abide by the decision; and

(3) Perform any obligations it has agreed to.

(g) The warrantor shall act in good faith in determining whether, and to what extent, it will abide by a Mechanism decision.

(h) The warrantor shall comply with any reasonable requirements imposed by the Mechanism to fairly and expeditiously resolve warranty disputes.

Minimum Requirements of the Mechanism

§703.3 Mechanism organization

(a) The Mechanism shall be funded and competently staffed at a level sufficient to ensure fair and expeditious resolution of all disputes, and shall not charge consumers any fee for use of the Mechanism.

(b) The warrantor and the sponsor of the Mechanism (if other than the warrantor) shall take all steps necessary to ensure that the Mechanism, and its members and staff, are sufficiently insulated from the warrantor and the sponsor, so that the decisions of the members and the performance of the staff are not influenced by either the warrantor or the sponsor. Necessary steps shall include, at a minimum, committing funds in advance, basing personal decisions solely on merit, and not assigning conflicting warrantor or sponsor duties to Mechanism staff persons.

(c) The Mechanism shall impose any other reasonable requirements necessary to ensure that the members and staff act fairly and expeditiously in each dispute.

§703.4   Qualification of members

(a) No member deciding a dispute shall be: (1) A party to the dispute, or an employee or agent of a party other than for purposes of deciding disputes; or

(2) A person who is or may become a party in any legal action, including but not limited to class actions, relating to the product or complaint in dispute, or an employee or agent of such person other than for purposes of deciding disputes. For purposes of this paragraph (a) a person shall not be considered a "party" solely because he or she acquires or owns an interest in a party solely for investment, and the acquisition or ownership of an interest which is offered to the general public shall be prima facie evidence of its acquisition or ownership solely for investment.

(b) When one or two members are deciding a dispute, all shall be persons having no direct involvement in the manufacture, distribution, sale or service of any product. When three or more members are deciding a dispute, at least two-thirds shall be persons having no direct involvement in the manufacture, distribution, sale or service of any product. "Direct involvement" shall not include acquiring or owning an interest solely for investment, and the acquisition or ownership of an interest which is offered to the general public shall be prima facie evidence of its acquisition or ownership solely for investment. Nothing contained in this section shall prevent the members from consulting with any persons knowledgeable in the technical, commercial or other areas relating to the product which is the subject of the dispute.

(c) Members shall be persons interested in the fair and expeditious settlement of consumer disputes.

§703.5   Operation of the Mechanism

(a) The Mechanism shall establish written operating procedures which shall include at least those items specified in paragraphs (b) through (j) of this section. Copies of the written procedures shall be made available to any person upon request.

(b) Upon notification of a dispute, the Mechanism shall immediately inform both the warrantor and the consumer of receipt of the dispute.

(c) The Mechanism shall investigate, gather and organize all information necessary for a fair and expeditious decision in each dispute. When any evidence gathered by or submitted to the Mechanism raises issues relating to the number of repair attempts, the length of repair periods, the possibility of unreaonableness use of the product, or any other issues relevant in light of Title I of the Act (or rules thereudner), including issues relating to consequential damages, or any other remedy under the Act (or rules thereunder), the Mechanism shall investigate these issues. When information which will or may be used in the decision, submitted by one party, or a consultant under §703.4(b) of this part, or any other source tends to contradict facts submitted by the other party, the Mechanism shall clearly, accurately, and completely disclose to both parties the contradictory information (and its source) and shall provide both parties an opportunity to explain or rebut the information and to submit additional materials. The Mechanism shall not require any information not reasonably necessary to decide the dispute.

(d) If the dispute has not been settled, the Mechanism shall, as expeditiously as possible but at least within 40 days of notification of the dispute, except as provided in paragraph (e) of this section:

(1) Render a fair decision based on the information gathered as described in paragraph (c) of this section, and on any information submitted at an oral presentation which conforms to the requirements of paragraph (f) of this section (A decision shall include any remedies appropriate under the circumstances, including repair, replacement, refund, reimbursement for expenses, compensation for damages, and any other remedies available under the written warranty or the Act (or rules thereunder); and a decision shall state a specified reasonable time for performance);

(2) Disclosure to the warrantor its decision and the reasons therefor;

(3) If the decision would require action on the part of the warrantor, determine whether, and to what extent, warrantor will abide by its decision; and

(4) Disclose to the consumer its decision, the reasons therefor, warrantor's intended actions (if the decision would require action on the part of the warrantor), and the information described in paragraph (g) of this section. For purposes of this paragraph (d) a dispute shall be deemed settled when the Mechanism has ascertained from the consumer that:

(i) The dispute has been settled to the consumer's satisfaction; and (ii) the settlement contains a specified reasonable time for performance.

(e) The Mechanism may delay the performance of its duties under paragraph (d) of this section beyond the 40 day time limit;

(1) Where the period of delay is due solely to failure of a consumer to provide promptly his or her name and address, brand name and model number of the product involved, and a statement as to the nature of the defect or other complaint; or

(2) For a 7 day period in those cases where the consumer has made no attempt to seek redress directly from the warrantor.

(f) The Mechanism may allow an oral presentation by a party to a dispute (or a party's respresentative) only if: (1) Both warrantor and consumer expressly agree to the presentation;

(2) Prior to agreement the Mechanism fully discloses to the consumer the following information:

(i) That the presentation by either party will take place only if both parties so agree, but that if they agree, and one party fails to appear at the agreed upon time and place, the presentation by the other party may still be allowed;

(ii) That the members will decide the dispute whether or not an oral presentation is made;

(iii) The proposed date, time and place for the presentation; and

(iv) A brief description of what will occur at the presentation including, if applicable, parties' rights to bring witnesses and/or counsel; and

(3) Each party has the right to be present during the other party's oral presentation. Nothing contained in this paragraph (b) of this section shall preclude the Mechanism from allowing an oral presentation by one party, if the other party fails to appear at the agreed upon time and place, as long as all of the requirements of this paragraph have been satisfied.

(g) The Mechanism shall inform the consumer, at the time of disclosure required in paragraph (d) of this section that:

(1) If he or she is dissatisfied with its decision or warrantor's intended actions, or eventual performance, legal remedies, including use of small claims court, may be pursued;

(2) The Mechanism's decision is admissible in evidence as provided in section 110(a)(3) of the Act; and

(3) The consumer may obtain, at reasonable cost, copies of all Mechanism records relating to the consumer's dispute.

(h) If the warrantor has agreed to perform any obligations, either as part of a settlement agreed to after notification to the Mechanism of the dispute or as a result of a decision under paragraph (d) of this section, the Mechanism shall ascertain from the consumer within 10 working days of the date for performance whether performance has occurred.

(i) A requirement that a consumer resort to the Mechanism prior to commencement of an action under section 110(d) of the Act shall be satisfied 40 days after notification to the Mechanism of the dispute or when the Mechanism completes all of its duties under paragraph (d) of this section, whichever occurs sooner. Except that, if the Mechanism delays performance of its paragraph (d) of this section duties as allowed by paragraph (e) of this section, the requirement that the consumer initially resort to the Mechanism shall not be satisfied until the period of delay allowed by paragraph (e) of this section has ended.

(j) Decisions of the Mechanism shall not be legally binding on any person. However, the warrantor shall act in good faith, as provided in §703.2(g) of this part. In any civil action arising out of a warranty obligation and relating to a matter considered by the Mechanism, any decision of the Mechanism shall be admissible in evidence, as provided in section 110(a)(3) of the Act.

§703.6   Recordkeeping

(a) The Mechanism shall maintain records on each dispute referred to it which shall include:

(1) Name, address and telephone number of the consumer;

(2) Name, address, telephone number and contact person of the warrantor;

(3) Brand name and model number of the product involved;

(4) The date of receipt of the dispute and the date of disclosure to the consumer of the decision;

(5) All letters or other written documents submitted by either party;

(6) All other evidence collected by the Mechanism relating to the dispute, including summaries of relevant and material portions of telephone calls and meetings between the Mechanism and any other person (including consultants described in §703.4(b) of this part);

(7) A summary of any relevant and material information presented by either party at an oral presentation;

(8) The decision of the members including information as to date, time and place of meeting, and the identity of members voting; or information on any other resolution;

(9) A copy of the disclosure to the parties of the decision;

(10) A statement of the warrantor's intended action(s);

(11) Copies of follow-up letters (or summaries of relevant and material portions of follow-up telephone calls) to the consumer, and responses thereto; and

(12) Any other documents and communications (or summaries of relevant and material portions of oral communications) relating to the dispute.

(b) The Mechanism shall maintain an index of each warrantor's disputes grouped under brand name and subgrouped under product model.

(c) The Mechanism shall maintain an index for each warrantor as will show:

(1) All disputes in which the warrantor has promised some performance (either by settlement or in response to a Mechanism decision) and has failed to comply; and

(2) All disputes in which the warrantor has refused to abide by a Mechanism decision.

(d) The Mechanism shall maintain an index as will show all disputes delayed beyond 40 days.

(e) The Mechanism shall compile semi-annually and maintain statistics which show the number and percent of disputes in each of the following categories:

(1) Resolved by staff of the Mechanism and warrantor has complied;

(2) Resolved by staff of the Mechanism, time for compliance has occurred, and warrantor has not complied;

(3) Resolved by staff of the Mechanism and time for compliance has not yet occurred;

(4) Decided by members and warrantor has complied;

(5) Decided by members, time for compliance has occurred, and warrantor has not complied;

(6) Decided by members and time for compliance has not yet occurred;

(7) Decided by members adverse to the consumer;

(8) No jurisdiction;

(9) Decision delayed beyond 40 days under §703.5(e)(1) of this part;

(10) Decision delayed beyond 40 days under §703.5(e)(2) of this part;

(11) Decision delayed beyond 40 days for any other reason; and

(12) Pending decision.

(f) The Mechanism shall retain all records specified in paragraphs (a) through (e) of this section for at least 4 years after final disposition of the dispute.

§703.7 Audits

(a) The Mechanism shall have an audit conducted at least annually, to determine whether the Mechanism and its implementation are in compliance with this part. All records of the Mechanism required to be kept under §703.6 of this part shall be available for audit.

(b) Each audit provided for in paragraph (a) of this section shall include at a minimum the following;

(1) Evaluation of warrantors' efforts to make consumers aware of the Mechanism's existence as required in §703.2(d) of this part;

(2) Review of the indexes maintained pursuant to §703.6(b), (c), and (d) of this part; and

(3) Analysis of a random sample of disputes handled by the Mechanism to determine the following:

(i) Adequacy of the Mechanism's complaint and other forms, investigation, mediation and follow-up efforts, and other aspects of complaint handling; and

(ii) Accuracy of the Mechanism's statistical compilations under §703.6(e) of this part. (For purposes of this subparagraph "analysis" shall include oral or written contract with the consumers involved in each of the disputes in the random sample).

(c) A report of each audit under this section shall be submitted to the Federal Trade Commission, and shall be made available to any person at reasonable cost. The Mechanism may direct its auditor to delete names of parties to disputes, and identity of products involved, from the audit report.

(d) Auditors shall be selected by the Mechanism. No auditor may be involved with the Mechanism as a warrantor, sponsor or member, or employee or agent thereof, other than for purposes of the audit.

§703.8 Openness of records and proceedings

(a) The statistical summaries specified in §703.6(e) of this part shall be available to any person for inspection and copying.

(b) Except as provided under paragraphs (a) and (e) of this section, and paragraph (c) of §703.7 of this part, all records of the Mechanism may be kept confidential, or made available only on such terms and conditions, or in such form, as the Mechanism shall permit.

(c) The policy of the Mechanism with respect to records made available at the Mechanism's option shall be set out in the procedures under §703.5(a) of this part; the policy shall be applied uniformly to all requests for access to or copies of such records.

(d) Meetings of the members to hear and decide disputes shall be open to observers on reasonable and nondiscriminatory terms. The identity of the parties and products involved in disputes need not be disclosed at meetings.

(e) Upon request the Mechanism shall provide to either party to a dispute:

(1) Access to all records relating to the dispute; and

(2) Copies of any records relating to the dispute, at reasonable cost.

(f) The Mechanism shall make available to any person upon request, information relating to the qualifications of Mechanism staff and members.

Appendix M
Federal Trade Commission Act

15 U.S.C. §§41-58

Table of Sections

§1. Federal Trade Commission established; membership; vacancies; seal [15 U.S.C. §41]

A commission is created and established, to be known as the Federal Trade Commission (hereinafter referred to as the Commission), which shall be composed of five Commissioners, who shall be appointed by the President, by and with the advice and consent of the Senate. Not more than three of the Commissioners shall be members of the same political party. . . .

§4. Definitions [15 U.S.C. §44]

The words defined in this section shall have the following meaning when found in this subchapter, to wit:

"Commerce" means commerce among the several States or with foreign nations, or in any Territory of the United States or in the District of Columbia, or between any such Territory and another, or between any such Territory and any State or foreign nation, or between the District of Columbia and any State or Territory or foreign nation.

§5. Unfair methods of competition unlawful; prevention by Commission [15 U.S.C. §45]

(a) Declaration of unlawfulness; power to prohibit unfair practices

(1) Unfair methods of competition in or affecting commerce, and unfair or deceptive acts or practices in or affecting commerce, are declared unlawful.

(2) The Commission is empowered and directed to prevent persons, partnerships, or corporations, except banks, savings and loan institutions described in section 18(f)(3), common carriers subject to the Acts to regulate commerce, air carriers and foreign air carriers subject to the Federal Aviation Act of 1958, and persons, partnerships, or corporations insofar as they are subject to the Packers and Stockyards Act, 1921, except as provided in section 406(b) of said Act, from using unfair methods of competition in or affecting commerce and unfair or deceptive acts or practices in or affecting commerce.

(b) Proceeding by Commission; modifying and setting aside orders

Whenever the Commission shall have reason to believe that any such person, partnership, or corporation has been or is using any unfair method of competition or unfair or deceptive act or practice in or affecting commerce, and if it shall appear to the Commission that a proceeding by it in respect thereof would be to the interest of the public, it shall issue and serve upon such person, partnership, or corporation a complaint stating its charges in that respect and containing a notice of a hearing upon a day and at a place therein fixed at least thirty days after the service of said complaint. The person, partnership, or corporation so complained of shall have the right to appear at the place and time so fixed and show cause why an order should not be entered by the Commission requiring such person, partnership, or corporation to cease and desist from the violation of the law so charged in said complaint. Any person, partnership, or corporation may make application, and upon good cause shown may be allowed by the Commission to intervene and appear in said proceeding by counsel or in person. The testimony in any such proceeding shall be reduced to writing and filed in the office of the Commission. If upon such hearing the Commission shall be of the opinion that the method of competition or the act or practice in question is prohibited by this Act, it shall make a report in writing in which it shall state its findings as to the facts and shall issue and cause to be served on such person, partnership, or corporation an order requiring such person, partnership, or corporation to cease and desist from using such method of competition or such act or practice. Until the expiration of the time allowed for filing a petition for review, if no such petition has been duly filed within such time then until the record in the proceeding has been filed in a court of appeals of the United States, as hereinafter provided, the Commission may at any time, upon such notice and in such manner as it shall deem proper, modify or set aside, in whole or in part, any report or any order made or issued by it under this section. After the expiration of the time allowed for filing a petition for review, if no such petition has been duly filed within such time, the Commission may at any time, after notice and opportunity for hearing, reopen and alter, modify, or set aside, in whole or in part any report or order made or issued by it under this section, whenever in the opinion of the Commission conditions of fact or of law have so changed as to require such action or if the public interest shall so require, except that (1) the said person, partnership, or corporation may, within sixty days after service upon him or it of said report or order entered after such a reopening, obtain a review thereof in the appropriate court of appeals of the United States, in the manner provided in subsection (c) of this section; and (2) in the case of an order, the Commission shall reopen any such order to consider whether such order (including any affirmative relief provision contained in such order) should be altered, modified, or set aside, in whole or in part, if the person, partnership, or corporation involved files a request with the Commission which makes a satisfactory showing that changed conditions of law or fact require such order to be altered, modified, or set aside, in whole or in part. The Commission shall determine whether to alter, modify, or set aside any order of the Commission in response to a request made by a person, partnership, or corporation under paragraph (2) not later than 120 days after the date of the filing of such request.

(c) **Review of order; rehearing**

Any person, partnership, or corporation required by an order of the Commission to cease and desist from using any method of competition or act or practice may obtain a review of such order in the court of appeals of the United States, within any circuit where the method of competition or the act or practice in question was used or where such person, partnership, or corporation resides or carries on business, by filing in the court, within sixty days from the date of the service of such order, a written petition praying that the order of the Commission be set aside. A copy of such petition shall be forthwith transmitted by the clerk of the court to the Commission, and thereupon the Commission shall file in the court the record in the proceeding, as provided in section 2112 of title 28. Upon such filing of the petition the court shall have jurisdiction of the proceeding and of the question determined therein concurrently with the Commission until the filing of the record and shall have power to make and enter a decree affirming, modifying, or setting aside the order of the Commission, and enforcing the same to the extent that such order is affirmed and to issue such writs as are ancillary to its jurisdiction or are necessary in its judgment to prevent injury to the public or to competitors pendente lite. The findings of the Commission as to the facts, if supported by evidence, shall be conclusive. To the extent that the order of the Commission is affirmed, the court shall thereupon issue its own order commanding obedience to the terms of such order of the Commission. If either party shall apply to the court for leave to adduce additional evidence, and shall show to the satisfaction of the court that such additional evidence is material and that there were reasonable grounds for the failure to adduce such evidence in the proceeding before the Commission, the court may order such additional evidence to be taken before the Commission and to be adduced upon the hearing in such manner and upon such terms and conditions as to the court may seem proper. The Commission may modify its findings as to the facts, or make new findings, by reason of the additional evidence so taken, and it shall file such modified or new findings, which, if supported by evidence, shall be conclusive, and its recommendation, if any, for the modification or setting aside of its original order, with the return of such additional evidence. The judgment and decree of the court shall be final, except that the same shall be subject to review by the Supreme Court upon certiorari, as provided in section 1254 of title 28.

(d) Jurisdiction of court

Upon the filing of the record with it the jurisdiction of the court of appeals of the United States to affirm, enforce, modify, or set aside orders of the Commission shall be exclusive.

(e) Precedence of proceedings; exemption from liability

Such proceedings in the court of appeals shall be given precedence over other cases pending therein, and shall be in every way expedited. . . .

(l) Penalty for violation of order; injunctions and other appropriate equitable relief

Any person, partnership, or corporation who violates an order of the Commission after it has become final, and while such order is in effect, shall forfeit and pay to the United States a civil penalty of not more than $10,000 for each violation, which shall accrue to the United States and may be recovered in a civil action brought by the Attorney General of the United States. Each separate violation of such an order shall be a separate offense, except that in a case of a violation through continuing failure to obey or neglect to obey a final order of the Commission, each day of continuance of such failure or neglect shall be deemed a separate offense. In such actions, the United States district courts are empowered to grant mandatory injunctions and such other and further equitable relief as they deem appropriate in the enforcement of such final orders of the Commission.

(m) Civil actions for recovery of penalties for knowing violations of rules and cease and desist orders respecting unfair or deceptive acts or practices; jurisdiction; maximum amount of penalties; continuing violations; de novo determinations; compromise or settlement procedure

(1)(A) The Commission may commence a civil action to recover a civil penalty in a district court of the United States against any person, partnership, or corporation which violates any rule under this Act respecting unfair or deceptive acts or practices (other than an interpretive rule or a rule violation of which the Commission has provided is not an unfair or deceptive act or practice in violation of subsection (a)(1) of this section) with actual knowledge or knowledge fairly implied on the basis of objective circumstances that such act is unfair or deceptive and is prohibited by such rule. In such action, such person, partnership, or corporation shall be liable for a civil penalty of not more than $10,000 for each violation.

(B) If the Commission determines in a proceeding under subsection (b) of this section that any act or practice is unfair or deceptive, and issues a final cease and desist order with respect to such act or practice, then the Commission may commence a civil action to obtain a civil penalty in a district court of the United States against any person, partnership, or corporation which engages in such act or practice—

(1) after such cease and desist order becomes final (whether or not such person, partnership, or corporation was subject to such cease and desist order), and

(2) with actual knowledge that such act or practice is unfair or deceptive and is unlawful under subsection (a)(1) of this section.

In such action, such person, partnership, or corporation shall be liable for a civil penalty of not more than $10,000 for each violation.

(C) In the case of a violation through continuing failure to comply with a rule or with subsection (a)(1) of this section, each day of continuance of such failure shall be treated as a separate violation, for purposes of subparagraphs (A) and (B). In determining the amount of such a civil penalty, the court shall take into account the degree of culpability, any history of prior such conduct, ability to pay, effect on ability to continue to do business, and such other matters as justice may require.

(2) If the cease and desist order establishing that the act or practice is unfair or deceptive was not issued against the defendant in a civil penalty action under paragraph (1)(B) the issues of fact in such action against such defendant shall be tried de novo.

(3) The Commission may compromise or settle any action for a civil penalty if such compromise or settlement is accompanied by a public statement of its reasons and is approved by the court.

§6. Additional powers of Commission [15 U.S.C. §46]

The Commission shall also have power—

(a) Investigation of persons, partnerships, or corporations

To gather and compile information concerning, and to investigate from time to time the organization, business, conduct, practices, and management of any person, partnership, or corporation engaged in or whose business affects commerce, excepting banks, savings and loan institutions described in section 18(f)(3), and common carriers subject to the Act to regulate commerce, and its relation to other persons, partnerships, and corporations.

(b) Reports of persons, partnerships, and corporations

To require, by general or special orders, persons, partnerships, and corporations, engaged in or whose business affects commerce, excepting banks, savings and loan institutions described in section 18(f)(3), and common carriers subject to the Act to regulate commerce, or any class of them, or any of them, respectively, to file with the Commission in such form as the Commission may prescribe annual or special, or both annual and special, reports or answers in writing to specific questions, furnishing to the Commission such information as it may require as to the organization, business, conduct, practices, management, and relation to other corporations, partnerships, and individuals of the respective persons, partnerships, and corporations filing such reports or answers in writing. Such reports and answers shall be made under oath, or otherwise, as the Commission may prescribe, and shall be filed with the Commission within such reasonable period as the Commission may prescribe, unless additional time be granted in any case by the Commission.

(f) Publication of information; reports

To make public from time to time such portions of the information obtained by it hereunder as are in the public interest; and to make annual and special reports to the Congress and to submit therewith recommendations for additional legislation; and to provide for the publication of its reports and decisions in such form and manner as may be best adapted for public information and use: *Provided,* That the Commission shall not have any authority to make public any trade secret or any commercial or financial information which is obtained from any person and which is privileged or confidential, . . .

(g) Classification of corporations; regulations

From time to time classify corporations and (except as provided in section 18(a)(2)) to make rules and regulations for the purpose of carrying out the provisions of this Act.

Provided, That the exception of "banks, savings and loan institutions described in section 18(f)(3), and common carriers subject to the Act to regulate commerce" from the Commission's powers defined in clauses (a) and (b) of this section, shall not be construed to limit the Commission's authority to gather and compile information, to investigate, or to require reports or answers from, any person, partnership, or corporation to the extent that such action is necessary to the investigation of any person, partnership, or corporation, group of persons, partnerships, or corporations, or industry which is not engaged or is engaged only incidentally in banking, in business as a savings and loan institution, or in business as a common carrier subject to the Act to regulate commerce.

The Commission shall establish a plan designed to substantially reduce burdens imposed upon small businesses as a result of requirements established by the Commission under clause (b) relating to the filing of quarterly financial reports. Such plan shall (1) be established after consultation with small businesses and persons who use the information contained in such quarterly financial reports; (2) provide for a reduction of the number of small businesses required to file such quarterly financial reports; and (3) make revisions in the forms used for such quarterly financial reports for the purpose of reducing the complexity of such forms. . . .

Nothing in this section (other than the provisions of clause (c) and clause (d)) shall apply to the business of insurance, except that the Commission shall have authority to conduct studies and prepare reports relating to the business of insurance. The Commission may exercise such authority only upon receiving a request which is agreed to by a majority of the members of the Committee on Commerce, Science, and Transportation of the Senate or the Committee on Energy and Commerce of the House of Representatives. The authority to conduct any such study shall expire at the end of the Congress during which the request for such study was made.

§8. Information and assistance from departments [15 U.S.C. §48]

The several departments and bureaus of the Government when directed by the President shall furnish the Commission, upon its request, all records, papers, and information in their possession relating to any corporation subject to any of the provisions of this Act, and shall detail from time to time such officials and employees to the Commission as he may direct.

§9. Documentary evidence; depositions; witnesses [15 U.S.C. §49]

For the purposes of this Act the Commission, or its duly authorized agent or agents, shall at all reasonable times have access to, for the purpose of examination, and the right to copy any documentary evidence of any person, partnership, or corporation being investigated or proceeded against; and the Commission shall have power to require by subpoena the attendance and testimony of witnesses and the production of all such documentary evidence relating to any matter under investigation. Any member of the Commission may sign subpoenas, and members of the examiners of the Commission may administer oaths and affirmations, examine witnesses, and receive evidence.

Such attendance of witnesses, and the production of such documentary evidence, may be required from any place in the United States, at any designated place of hearing. And in case of disobedience to a subpoena the

Commission may invoke the aid of any court of the United States in requiring the attendance and testimony of witnesses and the production of documentary evidence.

Any of the district courts of the United States within the jurisdiction of which such inquiry is carried on may, in case of contumacy or refusal to obey a subpoena issued to any person, partnership, or corporation issue an order requiring such person, partnership, or corporation to appear before the Commission, or to produce documentary evidence if so ordered, or to give evidence touching the matter in question; and any failure to obey such order of the court may be punished by such court as a contempt thereof.

Upon the application of the Attorney General of the United States, at the request of the Commission, the district courts of the United States shall have jurisdiction to issue writs of mandamus commanding any person, partnership, or corporation to comply with the provisions of this Act or any order of the Commission made in pursuance thereof.

The Commission may order testimony to be taken by deposition in any proceeding or investigation pending under this Act at any stage of such proceeding or investigation. Such depositions may be taken before any person designated by the Commission and having power to administer oaths. Such testimony shall be reduced to writing by the person taking the deposition, or under his direction, and shall then be subscribed by the deponent. Any person may be compelled to appear and depose and to produce documentary evidence in the same manner as witnesses may be compelled to appear and testify and produce documentary evidence before the Commission as hereinbefore provided.

Witnesses summoned before the Commission shall be paid the same fees and mileage that are paid witnesses in the courts of the United States and witnesses whose depositions are taken and the persons taking the same shall severally be entitled to the same fees as are paid for like services in the courts of the United States.

§10. Offenses and penalties [15 U.S.C. §50]

Any person who shall neglect or refuse to attend and testify, or to answer any lawful inquiry or to produce any documentary evidence, if in his power to do so, in obedience to an order of a district court of the United States directing compliance with the subpoena or lawful requirement of the Commission, shall be guilty of an offense and upon conviction thereof by a court of competent jurisdiction shall be punished by a fine of not less than $1,000 nor more than $5,000, or by imprisonment for not more than one year, or by both such fine and imprisonment.

Any person who shall willfully make, or cause to be made, any false entry or statement of fact in any report required to be made under this Act, or who shall willfully make, or cause to be made, any false entry in any account, record, or memorandum kept by any person, partnership, or corporation subject to this Act, or who shall willfully neglect or fail to make, or to cause to be made, full, true, and correct entries in such accounts, records, or memoranda of all facts and transactions appertaining to the business of such person, partnership, or corporation, or who shall willfully remove out of the jurisdiction of the United States, or willfully mutilate, alter, or by any other means falsify any documentary evidence of such person, partnership, or corporation, or who shall willfully refuse to submit to the Commission or to any of its authorized agents, for the purpose of inspection and taking copies, any documentary evidence of such person, partnership, or corporation in his possession or within his control, shall be deemed guilty of an offense against the United States, and shall be subject, upon conviction in any court of the United States of competent jurisdiction, to a fine of not less than $1,000 nor more than $5,000, or to imprisonment for a term of not more than three years, or to both such fine and imprisonment.

§11. Effect on other statutory provisions [15 U.S.C. §51]

Nothing contained in this Act shall be construed to prevent or interfere with the enforcement of the provisions of the antitrust Acts or the Acts to regulate commerce, nor shall anything contained in this Act be construed to alter, modify, or repeal the said antitrust Acts or the Acts to regulate commerce or any part or parts thereof.

§12. Dissemination of false advertisements [15 U.S.C. §52]

(a) Unlawfulness

It shall be unlawful for any person, partnership, or corporation to disseminate, or cause to be disseminated, any false advertisement—

(1) By United States mails, or in having an effect upon commerce, by any means, for the purpose of inducing, or which is likely to induce, directly or indirectly the purchase of food, drugs, devices, or cosmetics; or

(2) By any means, for the purpose of inducing, or which is likely to induce, directly or indirectly, the purchase in or having an effect upon commerce, of food, drugs, devices, or cosmetics.

(b) Unfair or deceptive act or practice

The dissemination or the causing to be disseminated of any false advertisement within the provisions of subsection (a) of this section shall be an unfair or deceptive act or practice in or affecting commerce within the meaning of section 5.

§13. False advertisements; injunctions and restraining orders [15 U.S.C. §53]

(a) Power of Commission; jurisdiction of courts

Whenever the Commission has reason to believe—

(1) that any person, partnership, or corporation is engaged in, or is about to engage in, the dissemination or the causing of the dissemination of any advertisement in violation of section 12, and

(2) that the enjoining thereof pending the issuance of a complaint by the Commission under section 5, and until such complaint is dismissed by the Commission or set aside by the court on review, or the order of the Commission to cease and desist made thereon has become final within the meaning of section 5, would be to the interest of the public.

the Commission by any of its attorneys designated by it for such purpose may bring suit in a district court of the United States or in the United States court of any Territory, to enjoin the dissemination or the causing of the dissemination of such advertisement. Upon proper showing a temporary injunction or restraining order shall be granted without bond. Any such suit shall be brought in the district in which such person, partnership, or corporation resides or transacts business.

(b) Temporary restraining orders; preliminary injunctions
Whenever the Commission has reason to believe—

(1) that any person, partnership, or corporation is violating, or is about to violate, any provision of law enforced by the Federal Trade Commission, and

(2) that the enjoining thereof pending the issuance of a complaint by the Commission and until such complaint is dismissed by the Commission or set aside by the court on review, or until the order of the Commission made thereon has become final, would be in the interest of the public—

the Commission by any of its attorneys designated by it for such purpose may bring suit in a district court of the United States to enjoin any such act or practice. Upon a proper showing that, weighing the equities and considering the Commission's likelihood of ultimate success, such action would be in the public interest, and after notice to the defendant, a temporary restraining order or a preliminary injunction may be granted without bond: *Provided, however,* That if a complaint is not filed within such period (not exceeding 20 days) as may be specified by the court after issuance of the temporary restraining order or preliminary injunction, the order or injunction shall be dissolved by the court and be of no further force and effect: *Provided further,* That in proper cases the Commission may seek, and after proper proof, the court may issue, a permanent injunction. Any such suit shall be brought in the district in which such person, partnership, or corporation resides or transacts business.

(c) Exception of periodical publications
Whenever it appears to the satisfaction of the court in the case of a newspaper, magazine, periodical, or other publication, published at regular intervals—

(1) that restraining the dissemination of a false advertisement in any particular issue of such publication would delay the delivery of such issue after the regular time therefor, and

(2) that such delay would be due to the method by which the manufacture and distribution of such publication is customarily conducted by the

publisher in accordance with sound business practice, and not to any method or device adopted for the evasion of this section or to prevent or delay the issuance of an injunction or restraining order with respect to such false advertisement or any other advertisement,
the court shall exclude such issue from the operation of the restraining order or injunction.

§14.   False advertisements; penalties [15 U.S.C. §54]

(a) Imposition of penalties

Any person, partnership, or corporation who violates any provision of section 12(a) shall, if the use of the commodity advertised may be injurious to health because of results from such use under the conditions prescribed in the advertisement thereof, or under such conditions as are customary or usual, or if such violation is with intent to defraud or mislead, be guilty of a misdemeanor, and upon conviction shall be punished by a fine of not more than $5,000 or by imprisonment for not more than six months, or by both such fine and imprisonment; except that if the conviction is for a violation committed after a first conviction of such person, partnership, or corporation, for any violation of such section, punishment shall be by a fine of not more than $10,000 or by imprisonment for not more than one year, or by both such fine and imprisonment: *Provided,* That for the purposes of this section meats and meat food products duly inspected, marked, and labeled in accordance with rules and regulations issued under the Meat Inspection Act shall be conclusively presumed not injurious to health at the time the same leave official "establishments."

(b) Exception of advertising medium or agency

No publisher, radio-broadcast licensee, or agency or medium for the dissemination of advertising, except the manufacturer, packer, distributor, or seller of the commodity to which the false advertisement relates, shall be liable under this section by reason of the dissemination by him of any false advertisement, unless he has refused, on the request of the Commission, to furnish the Commission the name and post-office address of the manufacturer, packer, distributor, seller, or advertising agency, residing in the United States, who caused him to disseminate such advertisement. No advertising agency shall be liable under this section by reason of the causing by it of the dissemination of any false advertisement, unless it has refused, on the request of the Commission, to furnish the Commission the name and post-office address of the manufacturer, packer, distributor, or seller, residing in the United States, who caused it to cause the dissemination of such advertisement.

§15.   Additional definitions [15 U.S.C. §55]

For the purposes of sections 12, 13, and 14—

(a) False advertisement

(1) The term "false advertisement" means an advertisement, other than labeling, which is misleading in a material respect; and in determining whether any advertisement is misleading there shall be taken into account (among other things) not only representations made or suggested by statement, word, design, device, sound, or any combination thereof, but also the extent to which the advertisement fails to reveal facts material in the light of such representations or material with respect to consequences which may result from the use of the commodity to which the advertisement relates under the conditions prescribed in said advertisement, or under such conditions as are customary or usual. No advertisement of a drug shall be deemed to be false if it is disseminated only to members of the medical profession, contains no false representation of a material fact, and includes, or is accompanied in each instance by truthful disclosure of, the formula showing quantitatively each ingredient of such drug.

(2) In the case of oleomargarine or margarine an advertisment shall be deemed misleading in a material respect if in such advertisement representations are made or suggested by statement, word, grade designation, design, device, symbol, sound, or any combination thereof, that such oleomargarine or margarine is a dairy product, except that nothing contained herein shall prevent a truthful, accurate, and full statement in any such advertisement of all the ingredients contained in such oleomargarine or margarine.

(b) Food

The term "food" means (1) articles used for food or drink for man or other animals, (2) chewing gum, and (3) articles used for components of any such article.

(c) Drug

The term "drug" means (1) articles recognized in the official United States Pharmacopoeia, official Homoeopathic Pharmacopoeia of the United States, or official National Formulary, or any supplement to any of them; and (2) articles intended for use in the diagnosis, cure, mitigation, treatment, or prevention of disease in man or other animals; and (3) articles (other than food) intended to affect the structure or any function of the body of man or other animals; and (4) articles intended for use as a component of any article specified in clause (1), (2), or (3); but does not include devices or their components, parts, or accessories.

(d) Device

The term "device" (except when used in subsection (a) of this section) means an instrument, apparatus, implement, machine, contrivance, implant, in vitro reagent, or other similar or related article, including any component, part, or accessory, which is—

    (1) recognized in the official National Formulary, or the United States Pharmacopeia, or any supplement to them,

    (2) intended for use in the diagnosis of disease or other conditions, or in the cure, mitigation, treatment, or prevention of disease, in man or other animals, or

(3) intended to affect the structure or any function of the body of man or other animals, and

which does not achieve any of its principal intended purposes through chemical action within or on the body of man or other animals and which is not dependent upon being metabolized for the achievement of any of its principal intended purposes.

(e) Cosmetic

The term "cosmetic" means (1) articles to be rubbed, poured, sprinkled, or sprayed on, introduced into, or otherwise applied to the human body or any part thereof intended for cleansing, beautifying, promoting attractiveness, or altering the appearance, and (2) articles intended for use as a component of any such article; except that such term shall not include soap.

(f) Oleomargarine or margarine

For the purposes of this section and section 407 of the Food, Drug, and Cosmetic Act, the term "oleomargarine" or "margarine" includes—

(1) all substances, mixtures, and compounds known as oleomargarine or margarine;

(2) all substances, mixtures, and compounds which have a consistence similar to that of butter and which contain any edible oils or fats other than milk fat if made in imitation or semblance of butter.

§16.   Commencement, defense, intervention and supervision of litigation and appeal by Commission or Attorney General; procedure for exercise of authority to litigate or appeal; certification by Commission to Attorney General for criminal proceedings [15 U.S.C. §56]

(a)(1) Except as otherwise provided in paragraph (2) or (3), if—

(A) before commencing, defending, or intervening in, any civil action involving this Act (including an action to collect a civil penalty) which the Commission, or the Attorney General on behalf of the Commission, is authorized to commence, defend, or intervene in, the Commission gives written notification and undertakes to consult with the Attorney General with respect to such action; and

(B) the Attorney General fails within 45 days after receipt of such notification to commence, defend, or intervene in, such action;

the Commission may commence, defend, or intervene in, and supervise the litigation or, such action and any appeal of such action in its own name by any of its attorneys designated by it for such purpose.

(2) Except as otherwise provided in paragraph (3), in any civil action—

(A) under section 13 (relating to injunctive relief);

(B) under section 19 (relating to consumer redress);

(C) to obtain judicial review of a rule prescribed by the Commission, or a cease and desist order issued under section 5; or

(D) under the second paragraph of section 9 (relating to enforcement of a subpoena) and under the fourth paragraph of such section (relating to compliance with section 6);

the Commission shall have exclusive authority to commence or defend, and supervise the litigation of, such action and any appeal of such action in its own name by any of its attorneys designated by it for such purpose, unless the Commission authorizes the Attorney General to do so. The Commission shall inform the Attorney General of the exercise of such authority and such exercise shall not preclude the Attorney General from intervening on behalf of the United States in such action and any appeal of such action as may be otherwise provided by law.

(3)(A) If the Commission makes a written request to the Attorney General, within the 10-day period which begins on the date of the entry of the judgment in any civil action in which the Commission represented itself pursuant to paragraph (1) or (2), to represent itself through any of its attorneys designated by it for such purpose before the Supreme Court in such action, it may do so, if—

(i) the Attorney General concurs with such request; or

(ii) the Attorney General, within the 60-day period which begins on the date of the entry of such judgment—

(a) refuses to appeal or file a petition for writ of certiorari with respect to such civil action, in which case he shall give written notification to the Commission of the reasons for such refusal within such 60-day period; or

(b) the Attorney General fails to take any action with respect to the Commission's request.

(B) In any case where the Attorney General represents the Commission before the Supreme Court in any civil action in which the Commission represented itself pursuant to paragraph (1) or (2), the Attorney General may not agree to any settlement, compromise, or dismissal of such action, or confess error in the Supreme Court with respect to such action, unless the Commission concurs.

(C) For purposes of this paragraph (with respect to representation before the Supreme Court), the term "Attorney General" includes the Solicitor General.

(4) If, prior to the expiration of the 45-day period specified in paragraph (1) of this section or a 60-day period specified in paragraph (3), any right of the Commission to commence, defend, or intervene in, any such action or appeal may be extinguished due to any procedural requirement of any court with respect to the time in which any pleadings, notice of appeal, or other acts pertaining to such action or appeal may be taken, the Attorney General shall have one-half of the time required to comply with any such procedural requirement of the court (including any extension of such time granted by the court) for the purpose of commencing, defending, or intervening in the civil action pursuant to paragraph (1) or for the purpose of refusing to appeal or

file a petition for writ of certiorari and the written notification or failing to take any action pursuant to paragraph 3(A)(ii).

(5) The provisions of this subsection shall apply notwithstanding chapter 31 of title 28, or any other provision of law.

(b) Whenever the Commission has reason to believe that any person, partnership, or corporation is liable for a criminal penalty under this Act, the Commission shall certify the facts to the Attorney General, whose duty it shall be to cause appropriate criminal proceedings to be brought.

§17.   Separability clause [15 U.S.C. §57]

If any provision of this Act, or the application thereof to any person, partnership, or corporation, or circumstance, is held invalid, the remainder of this Act, and the application of such provisions to any other person, partnership, corporation, or circumstance, shall not be affected thereby.

§18.   Unfair or deceptive acts or practices rulemaking proceedings [15 U.S.C. §57a]

(a) Authority of Commission to prescribe rules and general statements of policy

(1) Except as provided in subsection (i) of this section, the Commission may prescribe—

(A) interpretive rules and general statements of policy with respect to unfair or deceptive acts or practices in or affecting commerce (within the meaning of section 5(a)(1)), and

(B) rules which define with specificity acts or practices which are unfair or deceptive acts or practices in or affecting commerce (within the meaning of section 5(a)(1)), except that the Commission shall not develop or promulgate any trade rule or regulation with regard to the regulation of the development and utilization of the standards and certification activities pursuant to this section. Rules under this subparagraph may include requirements prescribed for the purpose of preventing such acts or practices.

(2) The Commission shall have no authority under this Act, other than its authority under this section, to prescribe any rule with respect to unfair or deceptive acts or practices in or affecting commerce (within the meaning of section 5(a)(1)). The preceding sentence shall not affect any authority of the Commission to prescribe rules (including interpretive rules), and general statements of policy, with respect to unfair methods of competition in or affecting commerce.

(b) Procedures applicable

(1) When prescribing a rule under subsection (a)(1)(B) of this section, the Commission shall proceed in accordance with section 553 of title 5 (without regard to any reference in such section to sections 556 and 557 of such title), and shall also (A) publish a notice of proposed rulemaking stating with

particularity the text of the rule, including any alternatives, which the Commission proposes to promulgate, and the reason for the proposed rule; (B) allow interested persons to submit written data, views, and arguments, and make all such submissions publicly available; (C) provide an opportunity for an informal hearing in accordance with subsection (c) of this section; and (D) promulgate, if appropriate, a final rule based on the matter in the rulemaking record (as defined in subsection (e)(1)(B) of this section), together with a statement of basis and purpose.

(2)(A) Prior to the publication of any notice of proposed rulemaking pursuant to paragraph (1)(A), the Commission shall publish an advance notice of proposed rulemaking in the Federal Register. Such advance notice shall—

(i) contain a brief description of the area of inquiry under consideration, the objectives which the Commission seeks to achieve, and possible regulatory alternatives under consideration by the Commission; and

(ii) invite the response of interested parties with respect to such proposed rulemaking, including any suggestions or alternative methods for achieving such objectives.

(B) The Commission shall submit such advance notice of proposed rulemaking to the Committee on Commerce, Science, and Transportation of the Senate and to the Committee on Energy and Commerce of the House of Representatives. The Commission may use such additional mechanisms as the Commission considers useful to obtain suggestions regarding the content of the area of inquiry before the publication of a general notice of proposed rulemaking under paragraph (1)(A).

(C) The Commission shall, 30 days before the publication of a notice of proposed rulemaking pursuant to paragraph (1)(A), submit such notice to the Committee on Commerce, Science, and Transportation of the Senate and to the Committee on Energy and Commerce of the House of Representatives.

(c) Informal hearing procedure

The Commission shall conduct any informal hearings required by subsection (b)(1)(C) of this section in accordance with the following procedure:

(1)(A) The Commission shall provide for the conduct of proceedings under this subsection by hearing officers who shall perform their functions in accordance with the requirements of this subsection.

(B) The officer who presides over the rulemaking proceedings shall be responsible to a chief presiding officer who shall not be responsible to any other officer or employee of the Commission. The officer who presides over the rulemaking proceeding shall make a recommended decision based upon the findings and conclusions of such officer as to all relevant and material evidence, except that such recommended decision may be made by another officer if the officer who presided over the proceeding is no longer available to the Commission.

(C) Except as required for the disposition of ex parte matters as authorized by law, no presiding officer shall consult any person or party with respect to any fact in issue unless such officer gives notice and opportunity for all parties to participate.

(2) Subject to paragraph (3) of this subsection, an interested person is entitled—

(A) to present his position orally or by documentary submission (or both), and

(B) if the Commission determines that there are disputed issues of material fact it is necessary to resolve, to present such rebuttal submissions and to conduct (or have conducted under paragraph (3)(B)) such cross-examination of persons as the Commission determines (i) to be appropriate, and (ii) to be required for a full and true disclosure with respect to such issues.

(3) The Commission may prescribe such rules and make such rulings concerning proceedings in such hearings as may tend to avoid unnecessary costs or delay. Such rules or rulings may include (A) imposition of reasonable time limits on each interested person's oral presentations, and (B) requirements that any cross-examination to which a person may be entitled under paragraph (2) be conducted by the Commission on behalf of that person in such manner as the Commission determines (i) to be appropriate, and (ii) to be required for a full and true disclosure with respect to disputed issues of material fact.

(4)(A) Except as provided in subparagraph (B), if a group of persons each of whom under paragraphs (2) and (3) would be entitled to conduct (or have conducted) cross-examination and who are determined by the Commission to have the same or similar interests in the proceeding cannot agree upon a single representative of such interests for purposes of cross-examination, the Commission may make rules and rulings (i) limiting the representation of such interest, for such purposes, and (ii) governing the manner in which such cross-examination shall be limited.

(B) When any person who is a member of a group with respect to which the Commission has made a determination under subparagraph (A) is unable to agree upon group representation with the other members of the group, then such person shall not be denied under the authority of subparagraph (A) the opportunity to conduct (or have conducted) cross-examination as to issues affecting his particular interests if (i) he satisfies the Commission that he has made a reasonable and good faith effort to reach agreement upon group representation with the other members of the group and (ii) the Commission determines that there are substantial and relevant issues which are not adequately presented by the group representative.

(5) A verbatim transcript shall be taken of any oral presentation, and cross-examination, in an informal hearing to which this subsection applies. Such transcript shall be available to the public.

(d) Statement of basis and purpose accompanying rule; "Commission" defined; judicial review of amendment or repeal of rule; violation of rules

(1) The Commission's statement of basis and purpose to accompany a rule promulgated under subsection (a)(1)(B) of this section shall include (A) a statement as to the prevalence of the acts or practices treated by the rule; (B) a statement as to the manner and context in which such acts or practices are

unfair or deceptive; and (C) a statement as to the economic effect of the rule, taking into account the effect on small business and consumers.

(2)(A) The term "Commission" as used in this subsection and subsections (b) and (c) of this section includes any person authorized to act in behalf of the Commission in any part of the rulemaking proceeding.

(B) A substantive amendment to, or repeal of, a rule promulgated under subsection (a)(1)(B) of this section shall be prescribed, and subject to judicial review, in the same manner as a rule prescribed under such subsection. An exemption under subsection (g) of this section shall not be treated as an amendment or repeal of a rule.

(3) When any rule under subsection (a)(1)(B) of this section takes effect a subsequent violation thereof shall constitute an unfair or deceptive act or practice in violation of section 5(a)(1), unless the Commission otherwise expressly provides in such rule.

(e) Judicial review; petition; jurisdiction and venue; rulemaking record; additional submissions and presentations; scope of review and relief; review by Supreme Court; additional remedies

(1)(A) Not later than 60 days after a rule is promulgated under subsection (a)(1)(B) of this section by the Commission, any interested person (including a consumer or consumer organization) may file a petition, in the United States Court of Appeals for the District of Columbia circuit or for the circuit in which such person resides or has his principal place of business, for judicial review of such rule. Copies of the petition shall be forthwith transmitted by the clerk of the court to the Commission or other officer designated by it for that purpose. The provisions of section 2112 of title 28 shall apply to the filing of the rulemaking record of proceedings on which the Commission based its rule and to the transfer of proceedings in the courts of appeals.

(B) For purposes of this section, the term "rulemaking record" means the rule, its statement of basis and purpose, the transcript required by subsection (c)(5) of this section, any written submissions, and any other information which the Commission considers relevant to such rule.

(5) . . . The contents and adequacy of any statement required by subsection (b)(1)(D) of this section shall not be subject to judicial review in any respect.

(f) Unfair or deceptive acts or practices by banks or savings and loan institutions; promulgation of regulations by Board of Governors of Federal Reserve System and by Federal Home Loan Bank Board; agency enforcement and compliance proceedings; violations; power of other Federal agencies unaffected; reporting requirements

(1) In order to prevent unfair or deceptive acts or practices in or affecting commerce (including acts or practices which are unfair or deceptive to consumers) by banks or savings and loan institutions described in paragraph (3), each agency specified in paragraph (2) or (3) of this subsection shall establish a separate division of consumer affairs which shall receive and take appropriate action upon complaints with respect to such acts or practices by banks or savings and loan institutions described in paragraph (3) subject to its jurisdiction. The Board of Governors of the Federal Reserve System (with

respect to banks) and the Federal Home Loan Bank Board (with respect to savings and loan institutions described in paragraph (3)) shall prescribe regulations to carry out the purposes of this section, including regulations defining with specificity such unfair or deceptive acts or practices, and containing requirements prescribed for the purpose of preventing such acts or practices. Whenever the Commission prescribes a rule under subsection (a)(1)(B) of this section, then within 60 days after such rule takes effect such Board shall promulgate substantially similar regulations prohibiting acts or practices of banks or savings and loan institutions described in paragraph (3), as the case may be, which are substantially similar to those prohibited by rules of the Commission and which impose substantially similar requirements, unless (A) either such Board finds that such acts or practices of banks or savings and loan institutions described in paragraph (3), as the case may be, are not unfair or deceptive, or (B) the Board of Governors of the Federal Reserve System finds that implementation of similar regulations with respect to banks would seriously conflict with essential monetary and payments systems policies of such Board, and publishes any such finding, and the reasons therefor, in the Federal Register.

(2) Compliance with regulations prescribed under this subsection shall be enforced under section 8 of the Federal Deposit Insurance Act, in the case of—

(A) national banks and banks operating under the code of law for the District of Columbia, by the division of consumer affairs established by the Comptroller of the Currency;

(B) member banks of the Federal Reserve System (other than banks referred to in subparagraph (A)), by the division of consumer affairs established by the Board of Governors of the Federal Reserve System; and

(C) banks insured by the Federal Deposit Insurance Corporation (other than banks referred to in subparagraph (A) or (B)), by the division of consumer affairs established by the Board of Directors of the Federal Deposit Insurance Corporation.

(3) Compliance with regulations prescribed under this subsection shall be enforced under section 5 of the Home Owners' Loan Act of 1933 (12 U.S.C. 1464) with respect to Federal savings and loan association, section 407 of the National Housing Act (12 U.S.C. 1730) with respect to insured institutions, and sections 6(i) and 17 of the Federal Home Loan Bank Act (12 U.S.C. 1426(i), 1437) with respect to savings and loan institutions which are members of a Federal Home Loan Bank, by a division of consumer affairs to be established by the Federal Home Loan Bank Board pursuant to the Federal Home Loan Bank Act.

(4) For the purpose of the exercise by any agency referred to in paragraph (2) of its powers under any Act referred to in that paragraph, a violation of any regulation prescribed under this subsection shall be deemed to be a violation of a requirement imposed under that Act. In addition to its powers under any provision of law specifically referred to in paragraph (2), each of the agencies referred to in that paragraph may exercise, for the purpose of enforcing

compliance with any regulation prescribed under this subsection, any other authority conferred on it by law.

(5) The authority of the Board of Governors of the Federal Reserve System to issue regulations under this subsection does not impair the authority of any other agency designated in this subsection to make rules respecting its own procedures in enforcing compliance with regulations prescribed under this subsection.

(6) Each agency exercising authority under this subsection shall transmit to the Congress each year a detailed report on its activities under this paragraph during the preceding calendar year.

(g) Exemptions and stays from application of rules; procedures

(1) Any person to whom a rule under subsection (a)(1)(B) of this section applies may petition the Commission for an exemption from such rule.

(2) If, on its own motion or on the basis of a petition under paragraph (1), the Commission finds that the application of a rule prescribed under subsection (a)(1)(B) of this section to any person or class of persons is not necessary to prevent the unfair or deceptive act or practice to which the rule relates, the Commission may exempt such person or class from all or part of such rule. Section 553 of title 5 shall apply to action under this paragraph.

(3) Neither the pendency of a proceeding under this subsection respecting an exemption from a rule, nor the pendency of judicial proceedings to review the Commission's action or failure to act under this subsection, shall stay the applicability of such rule under subsection (a)(1)(B) of this section.

(h) Compensation for attorney fees, expert witness fees, etc., incurred by persons in rulemaking proceedings; limitation on amount; establishment of small business outreach program.

(1) The Commission may, pursuant to rules prescribed by it, provide compensation for reasonable attorneys fees, expert witness fees, and other costs of participating in a rulemaking proceeding under this section to any person (A) who has, or represents, an interest (i) which would not otherwise be adequately represented in such proceeding, and (ii) representation of which is necessary for a fair determination of the rulemaking proceeding taken as a whole, and (B) who is unable effectively to participate in such proceeding because such person cannot afford to pay costs of making oral presentations, conducting cross-examination, and making rebuttal submissions in such proceeding.

(2) The Commission shall reserve an amount equal to 25 percent of the amount appropriated for the payment of compensation under this subsection for any fiscal year for use in accordance with this paragraph. Such reserved amount shall be available solely for the payment of compensation to persons who either (A) would be regulated by the proposed rule involved; or (b) represent persons who would be so regulated. Any portion of such reserved amount which is not used for the payment of compensation to such persons under this paragraph shall revert to the Treasury of the United States.

(3) The amount of compensation which may be paid to any person under this subsection in connection with the participation by such person in any

particular rulemaking proceeding under this section may not exceed $75,000. The aggregate amount of compensation paid under this subsection in any fiscal year to any person for all rulemaking proceedings in which such person participates during such fiscal year may not exceed $50,000.

(4) The aggregate amount of compensation paid to all persons in any fiscal year under this subsection may not exceed $750,000.

(5) The Commission, in connection with the administration of this subsection pursuant to rules prescribed by the Commission under paragraph (1), shall establish a small business outreach program. Such program shall—

(A) solicit public comment from small businesses whose views otherwise would not be adequately represented, in order to ensure a fair determination in rulemaking proceedings under this section; and

(B) encourage the participation of small businesses in the compensation program administered by the Commission under this subsection by disseminating to small businesses information which explains the procedures and requirements applicable to the receipt of compensation under such program.

(i) Restriction on rulemaking authority of Commission respecting children's advertising proceedings pending on May 28, 1980

The Commission shall not have any authority to promulgate any rule in the children's advertising proceeding pending on May 28, 1980, or in any substantially similar proceeding on the basis of a determination by the Commission that such advertising constitutes an unfair act or practice in or affecting commerce.

(j) Meetings with outside parties

(1) For purposes of this subsection, the term "outside party" means any person other than (A) a Commissioner; (B) an officer or employee of the Commission; or (C) any person who has entered into a contract or any other agreement or arrangement with the Commission to provide any goods or services (including consulting services) to the Commission.

(2) Not later than 60 days after May 28, 1980, the Commission shall publish a proposed rule, and not later than 180 days after May 28, 1980, the Commission shall promulgate a final rule, which shall authorize the Commission or any Commissioner to meet with any outside party concerning any rulemaking proceeding of the Commission. Such rule shall provide that—

(A) notice of any such meeting shall be included in any weekly calendar prepared by the Commission; and

(B) a verbatim record or a summary of any such meeting, or of any communication relating to any such meeting, shall be kept, made available to the public, and included in the rulemaking record.

(k) Communications by investigative personnel with staff of Commission concerning matters outside rulemaking record prohibited

Not later than 60 days after May 28, 1980, the Commission shall publish a proposed rule, and not later than 180 days after May 28, 1980, the Commission shall promulgate a final rule, which shall prohibit any officer, employee, or agent of the Commission with any investigative responsibility or other responsibility relating to any rulemaking proceeding within any operating bureau of the Commission, from communicating or causing to be communicated to any Commissioner or to the personal staff of any Commissioner any fact which is relevant to the merits of such proceeding and which is not on the rulemaking record of such proceeding, unless such communication is made available to the public and is included in the rulemaking record. The provisions of this subsection shall not apply to any communication to the extent such communication is required for the disposition of ex parte matters as authorized by law.

§19. Civil actions for violations of rules and cease and desist orders respecting unfair or deceptive acts or practices [15 U.S.C. §57b]

(a) Suits by Commission against persons, partnerships, or corporations; jurisdiction; relief for dishonest or fraudulent acts

(1) If any person, partnership, or corporation violates any rule under this Act respecting unfair or deceptive acts or practices (other than an interpretive rule, or a rule violation of which the Commission has provided is not an unfair or deceptive act or practice in violation of section 5(a)), then the Commission may commence a civil action against such person, partnership, or corporation for relief under subsection (b) of this section in a United States district court or in any court of competent jurisdiction of a State.

(2) If any person, partnership, or corporation engages in any unfair or deceptive act or practice (within the meaning of section 5(a)(1)) with respect to which the Commission has issued a final cease and desist order which is applicable to such person, partnership, or corporation, then the Commission may commence a civil action against such person, partnership, or corporation in a United States district court or in any court of competent jurisdiction of a State. If the Commission satisfies the court that the act or practice to which the cease and desist order relates is one which a reasonable man would have known under the circumstances was dishonest or fraudulent, the court may grant relief under subsection (b) of this section.

(b) Nature of relief available

The court in an action under subsection (a) of this section shall have jurisdiction to grant such relief as the court finds necessary to redress injury to consumers or other persons, partnerships, and corporations resulting from the rule violation or the unfair or deceptive act or practice, as the case may be. Such relief may include, but shall not be limited to, rescission or reformation of contracts, the refund of money or return of property, the payment of damages, and public notification respecting the rule violation or the unfair or deceptive act or practice, as the case may be; except that nothing in this subsection is intended to authorize the imposition of any exemplary or punitive damages.

(c) Conclusiveness of findings of Commission in cease and desist proceedings; notice of judicial proceedings to injured persons, etc.

(1) If (A) a cease and desist order issued under section 5(b) has become final under section 5g with respect to any person's, partnership's, or corporation's rule violation or unfair or deceptive act or practice, and (B) an action under this section is brought with respect to such person's, partnership's, or corporation's rule violation or act or practice, then the findings of the Commission as to the material facts in the proceeding under section 5(b) with respect to such person's, partnership's, or corporation's rule violation or act or practice, shall be conclusive unless (i) the terms of such cease and desist order expressly provide that the Commission's findings shall not be conclusive, or (ii) the order became final by reason of section 5(g)(1), in which case such finding shall be conclusive if supported by evidence.

(2) The court shall cause notice of an action under this section to be given in a manner which is reasonably calculated, under all of the circumstances, to apprise the persons, partnerships, and corporations allegedly injured by the defendant's rule violation or act or practice of the pendency of such action. Such notice may, in the discretion of the court, be given by publication.

(d) Time for bringing of actions

No action may be brought by the Commission under this section more than 3 years after the rule violation to which an action under subsection (a)(1) of this section relates, or the unfair or deceptive act or practice to which an action under subsection (a)(2) of this section relates; except that if a cease and desist order with respect to any person's, partnership's, or corporation's rule violation or unfair or deceptive act or practice has become final and such order was issued in a proceeding under section 5(b) which was commenced not later than 3 years after the rule violation or act or practice occurred, a civil action may be commenced under this section against such person, partnership, or corporation at any time before the expiration of one year after such order becomes final.

(e) Availability of additional Federal or State remedies; other authority of Commission unaffected

Remedies provided in this section are in addition to, and not in lieu of, any other remedy or right of action provided by State or Federal law. Nothing in this section shall be construed to affect any authority of the Commission under any other provision of law.

§20. Civil investigative demands [15 U.S.C. §57b-1]

(a) Definitions

For purposes of this section:

(1) The terms "civil investigative demand" and "demand" mean any demand issued by the Commission under subsection (c)(1) of this section.

(2) The term "Commission investigation" means any inquiry conducted by a Commission investigator for the purpose of ascertaining whether any person

is or has been engaged in any unfair or deceptive acts or practices in or affecting commerce (within the meaning of section 5(a)(1)).

(3) The term "Commission investigator" means any attorney or investigator employed by the Commission who is charged with the duty of enforcing or carrying into effect any provisions relating to unfair or deceptive acts or practices in or affecting commerce (within the meaning of section 5(a)(1)).

(4) The term "custodian" means the custodian or any deputy custodian designated under section 21(b)(2)(A).

(5) The term "documentary material" includes the original or any copy of any book, record, report, memorandum, paper, communication, tabulation, chart, or other document.

(6) The term "person" means any natural person, partnership, corporation, association, or other legal entity, including any person acting under color or authority of State law.

(7) The term "violation" means any act or omission constituting an unfair or deceptive act or practice in or affecting commerce (within the meaning of section 5(a)(1)).

(b) Actions conducted by Commission respecting unfair or deceptive acts or practices in or affecting commerce

For the purpose of investigations performed pursuant to this section with respect to unfair or deceptive acts or practices in or affecting commerce (within the meaning of section 5(a)(1)); all actions of the Commission taken under section 6 and section 9 shall be conducted pursuant to subsection (c) of this section.

(c) Issuance of demand; contents; service; verified return; sworn certificates; answers; taking of oral testimony

(1) Whenever the Commission has reason to believe that any person may be in possession, custody, or control of any documentary material, or may have any information, relevant to unfair or deceptive acts or practices in or affecting commerce (within the meaning of section 5(a)(1)), the Commission may, before the institution of any proceedings under this Act, issue in writing, and cause to be served upon such person, a civil investigative demand requiring such person to produce such documentary material for inspection and copying or reproduction, to file written reports or answers to questions, to give oral testimony concerning documentary material or other information, or to furnish any combination of such material, answers, or testimony.

(2) Each civil investigative demand shall state the nature of the conduct constituting the alleged violation which is under investigation and the provision of law applicable to such violation.

(3) Each civil investigative demand for the production of documentary material shall—

(A) describe each class of documentary material to be produced under the demand with such definiteness and certainty as to permit such material to be fairly identified;

(B) prescribe a return date or dates which will provide a reasonable period of time within which the material so demanded may be assembled and made available for inspection and copying or reproduction; and

(C) identify the custodian to whom such material shall be made available.

(4) Each civil investigative demand for written reports or answers to questions shall—

(A) propound with definiteness and certainty the reports to be produced or the questions to be answered;

(B) prescribe a date or dates at which time written reports or answers to questions shall be submitted; and

(C) identify the custodian to whom such reports or answers shall be submitted.

(d) Procedures for demand material

Materials received as a result of a civil investigative demand shall be subject to the procedures established in section 21.

(e) Petition for enforcement

Whenever any person fails to comply with any civil investigative demand duly served upon him under this section, or whenever satisfactory copying or reproduction of material requested pursuant to the demand cannot be accomplished and such person refuses to surrender such material, the Commission, through such officers or attorneys as it may designate, may file, in the district court of the United States for any judicial district in which such person resides, is found, or transacts business, and serve upon such person, a petition for an order of such court for the enforcement of this section. All process of any court to which application may be made as provided in this subsection may be served in any judicial district.

(h) Jurisdiction of court

Whenever any petition is filed in any district court of the United States under this section, such court shall have jurisdiction to hear and determine the matter so presented, and to enter such order or orders as may be required to carry into effect the provisions of this section. Any final order so entered shall be subject to appeal pursuant to section 1291 of title 28. Any disobedience of any final order entered under this section by any court shall be punished as a contempt of such court.

(i) Commission authority to issue subpoenas or make demand for information

Notwithstanding any other provision of law, the Commission shall have no authority to issue a subpoena or make a demand for information, under authority of this Act or any other provision of law, unless such subpoena or demand for information is signed by a Commissioner acting pursuant to a Commission resolution. The Commission shall not delegate the power conferred by this section to sign subpoenas or demands for information to any other person.

(j) Applicability of this section

The provisions of this section shall not—

(1) apply to any proceeding under section 5(b); or

(2) apply to or affect the jurisdiction, duties, or powers of any agency of the

Federal Government, other than the Commission, regardless of whether such jurisdiction, duties, or powers are derived in whole or in part, by reference to this Act.

§21. Confidentiality [15 U.S.C. §57b-2]

(a) Definitions

For purposes of this section:

(1) The term "material" means documentary material, written reports or answers to questions, and transcripts of oral testimony.

(2) The term "Federal agency" has the meaning given it in section 552(e) of title 5.

(b) Procedures respecting documents or transcripts of oral testimony received pursuant to compulsory process or investigation

(1) With respect to any document or transcript of oral testimony received by the Commission pursuant to compulsory process in an investigation, a purpose of which is to determine whether any person may have violated any provision of the laws administered by the Commission, the procedures established in paragraph (2) through paragraph (7) shall apply.

(2)(A) The Commission shall designate a duly authorized agent to serve as custodian of documentary material, or written reports or answers to questions, and transcripts of oral testimony, and such additional duly authorized agents as the Commission shall determine from time to time to be necessary to serve as deputies to the custodian.

(3)(A) The custodian to whom any documentary material, written reports or answers to questions, and transcripts of oral testimony are delivered shall take physical possession of such material, reports or answers, and transcripts, and shall be responsible for the use made of such material, reports or answers, and transcripts, and for the return of material, pursuant to the requirements of this section.

(C) Except as otherwise provided in this section, while in the possession of the custodian, no documentary material, reports or answers to questions, and transcripts of oral testimony shall be available for examination by any individual other than a duly authorized officer or employee of the Commission without the consent of the person who produced the material or transcripts. Nothing in this section is intended to prevent disclosure to either House of the Congress or to any committee or subcommittee of the Congress, except that the Commission immediately shall notify the owner or provider of any such information of a request for information designated as confidential by the owner or provider.

(4) Whenever the Commission has instituted a proceeding against a person, partnership, or corporation, the custodian may deliver to any officer or employee of the Commission documentary material, written reports or answers to questions, and transcripts of oral testimony for official use in connection with such proceeding. Upon the completion of the proceeding, the officer or

employee shall return to the custodian any such material so delivered which has not been received into the record of the proceeding.

(5) If any documentary material, written reports or answers to questions, and transcripts of oral testimony have been produced in the course of any investigation by any person pursuant to compulsory process and—

(A) any proceeding arising out of the investigation has been completed; or

(B) no proceeding in which the material may be used has been commenced within a reasonable time after completion of the examination and analysis of all such material and other information assembled in the course of the investigation;

then the custodian shall, upon written request of the person who produced the material, return to the person any such material which has not been received into the record of any such proceeding (other than copies of such material made by the custodian pursuant to paragraph (3)(B)).

(6) The custodian of any documentary material, written reports or answers to questions, and transcripts of oral testimony may deliver to any officers or employees of appropriate Federal law enforcement agencies, in response to a written request, copies of such material for use in connection with an investigation or proceeding under the jurisdiction of any such agency. Such materials shall not be made available to any such agency until the custodian received certification of any officer of such agency that such information will be maintained in confidence and will be used only for official law enforcement purposes. Such documentary material, written reports or answers to questions, and transcripts of oral testimony may be used by any officer or employee of such agency only in such manner and subject to such conditions as apply to the Commission under this section. The custodian may make such materials available to any State law enforcement agency upon the prior certification of any officer of such agency that such information will be maintained in confidence and will be used only for official law enforcement purposes.

(d) Particular disclosures allowed

(1) The provisions of subsection (c) of this section shall not be construed to prohibit—

(A) the disclosure of information to either House of the Congress or to any committee or subcommittee of the Congress, except that the Commission immediately shall notify the owner or provider of any such information of a request for information designated as confidential by the owner or provider;

(B) the disclosure of the results of any investigation or study carried out or prepared by the Commission, except that no information shall be identified nor shall information be disclosed in such a manner as to disclose a trade secret of any person supplying the trade secret, or to disclose any commercial or financial information which is obtained from any person and which is privileged or confidential;

(C) the disclosure of relevant and material information in Commission adjudicative proceedings or in judicial proceedings to which the Commission is a party; or

(D) the disclosure to a Federal agency of disaggregated information obtained in accordance with section 3512 of title 44, except that the recipient agency shall use such disaggregated information for economic, statistical, or policymaking purposes only, and shall not disclose such information in an individually identifiable form.

(2) Any disclosure of relevant and material information in Commission adjudicative proceedings or in judicial proceedings to which the Commission is a party shall be governed by the rules of the Commission for adjudicative proceedings or by court rules or orders, except that the rules of the Commission shall not be amended in a manner inconsistent with the purposes of this section.

(e) Effect on other statutory provisions limiting disclosure

Nothing in this section shall supersede any statutory provision which expressly prohibits or limits particular disclosures by the Commission, or which authorizes disclosures to any other Federal agency.

(f) Exemption from disclosure

Any material which is received by the Commission in any investigation, a purpose of which is to determine whether any person may have violated any provision of the laws administered by the Commission, and which is provided pursuant to any compulsory process under this subchapter or which is provided voluntarily in place of such compulsory process shall be exempt from disclosure under section 552 of title 5.

§22.   Rulemaking process [15 U.S.C. §57b-3]

(a) Definitions

For purposes of this section:

(1) The term "rule" means any rule promulgated by the Commission under section 6 or section 18, except that such term does not include interpretive rules, rules involving Commission management or personnel, general statements of policy, or rules relating to Commission organization, procedure, or practice. Such term does not include any amendment to a rule unless the Commission—

(A) estimates that such amendment will have an annual effect on the national economy of $100,000,000 or more;

(B) estimates that such amendment will cause a substantial change in the cost or price of goods or services which are used extensively by particular industries, which are supplied extensively in particular geographic regions, or which are required in significant quantities by the Federal Government, or by State or local governments; or

(C) otherwise determines that such amendment will have a significant impact upon persons subject to regulation under such amendment and upon consumers.

(2) The term "rulemaking" means any Commission process for formulating or amending a rule.

(b) Notice of proposed rulemaking; regulatory analysis; contents; issuance

(1) In any case in which the Commission publishes notice of a proposed rulemaking, the Commission shall issue a preliminary regulatory analysis relating to the proposed rule involved. Each preliminary regulatory analysis shall contain—

(A) a concise statement of the need for, and the objectives of, the proposed rule;

(B) a description of any reasonable alternatives to the proposed rule which may accomplish the stated objective of the rule in a manner consistent with applicable law; and

(C) for the proposed rule, and for each of the alternatives described in the analysis, a preliminary analysis of the projected benefits and any adverse economic effects and any other effects, and of the effectiveness of the proposed rule and each alternative in meeting the stated objectives of the proposed rule.

(2) In any case in which the Commission promulgates a final rule, the Commission shall issue a final regulatory analysis relating to the final rule. Each final regulatory analysis shall contain—

(A) a concise statement of the need for, and the objectives of, the final rule;

(B) a description of any alternatives to the final rule which were considered by the Commission;

(C) an analysis of the projected benefits and any adverse economic effects and any other effects of the final rule;

(D) an explanation of the reasons for the determination of the Commission that the final rule will attain its objectives in a manner consistent with applicable law and the reasons the particular alternative was chosen; and

(E) a summary of any significant issues raised by the comments submitted during the public comment period in response to the preliminary regulatory analysis, and a summary of the assessment by the Commission of such issues.

(3)(A) In order to avoid duplication or waste, the Commission is authorized to—

(i) consider a series of closely related rules as one rule for purposes of this subsection; and

(ii) whenever appropriate, incorporate any data or analysis contained in a regulatory analysis issued under this subsection in the statement of basis and purpose to accompany any rule promulgated under section 18(a)(1)(B), and incorporate by reference in any preliminary or final regulatory analysis information contained in a notice of proposed rulemaking or a statement of basis and purpose.

(B) The Commission shall include, in each notice of proposed rulemaking and in each publication of a final rule, a statement of the manner in which the public may obtain copies of the preliminary and final regulatory analyses. The

Commission may charge a reasonable fee for the copying and mailing of regulatory analyses. The regulatory analyses shall be furnished without charge or at a reduced charge if the Commission determines that waiver or reduction of the fee is in the public interest because furnishing the information primarily benefits the general public.

(4) The Commission is authorized to delay the completion of any of the requirements established in this subsection by publishing in the Federal Register, not later than the date of publication of the final rule involved, a finding that the final rule is being promulgated in response to an emergency which makes timely compliance with the provision of this subsection impracticable. Such publication shall include a statement of the reasons for such finding.

(5) The requirements of this subsection shall not be construed to alter in any manner the substantive standards applicable to any action by the Commission, or the procedural standards otherwise applicable to such action.

(c) Judicial review

(1) The contents and adequacy of any regulatory analysis prepared or issued by the Commission under this section, including the adequacy of any procedure involved in such preparation or issuance, shall not be subject to any judicial review in any court, except that a court, upon review of a rule pursuant to section 18(e) may set aside such rule if the Commission has failed entirely to prepare a regulatory analysis.

(2) Except as specified in paragraph (1), no Commission action may be invalidated, remanded, or otherwise affected by any court on account of any failure to comply with the requirements of this section.

(3) The provisions of this subsection do not alter the substantive or procedural standards otherwise applicable to judicial review of any action by the Commission.

(d) Regulatory agenda; contents; publication dates in Federal Register

(1) The Commission shall publish at least semiannually a regulatory agenda. Each regulatory agenda shall contain a list of rules which the Commission intends to propose or promulgate during the 12-month period following the publication of the agenda. On the first Monday in October of each year, the Commission shall publish in the Federal Register a schedule showing the dates during the current fiscal year on which the semiannual regulatory agenda of the Commission will be published.

(2) For each rule listed in a regulatory agenda, the Commission shall—

(A) describe the rule;

(B) state the objectives of and the legal basis for the rule; and

(C) specify any dates established or anticipated by the Commission for taking action, including dates for advance notice of proposed rulemaking, notices of proposed rulemaking, and final action by the Commission.

(3) Each regulatory agenda shall state the name, office address, and office telephone number of the Commission officer or employee responsible for responding to any inquiry relating to each rule instead.

(4) The Commission shall not propose or promulgate a rule which was not

listed on a regulatory agenda unless the Commission publishes with the rule an explanation of the reasons the rule was omitted from such agenda.

§23.   Good faith reliance on actions of Board of Governors [15 U.S.C. §57b-4]

(a) Board of Governors defined

For purposes of this section, the term "Board of Governors" means the Board of Governors of the Federal Reserve System.

(b) Use as defense

Notwithstanding any other provision of law, if—

(1) any person, partnership, or corporation engages in any conduct or practice which allegedly constitutes a violation of any Federal law with respect to which the Board of Governors of the Federal Reserve System has rulemaking authority; and

(2) such person, partnership, or corporation engaged in such conduct or practice in good faith reliance upon, and in conformity with, any rule, regulation, statement of interpretation, or statement of approval prescribed or issued by the Board of Governors under such Federal law;

then such good faith reliance shall constitute a defense in any administrative or judicial proceeding commenced against such person, partnership, or corporation by the Commission under this Act or in any administrative or judicial proceeding commenced against such person, partnership, or corporation by the Attorney General of the United States, upon request made by the Commission, under any provision of law.

(c) Applicability of subsection (b)

The provisions of subsection (b) of this section shall apply regardless of whether any rule, regulation, statement of interpretation, or statement of approval prescribed or issued by the Board of Governors is amended, rescinded, or held to be invalid by judicial authority or any other authority after a person, partnership, or corporation has engaged in any conduct or practice in good faith reliance upon, and in conformity with, such rule, regulation, statement of interpretation, or statement of approval.

(d) Request for issuance of statement or interpretation concerning conduct or practice

If, in any case in which—

(1) the Board of Governors has rulemaking authority with respect to any Federal law; and

(2) the Commission is authorized to enforce the requirements of such Federal Law;

any person, partnership, or corporation submits a request to the Board of Governors for the issuance of any statement of interpretation or statement of approval relating to any conduct or practice of such person, partnership, or corporation which may be subject to the requirements of such Federal law, then the Board of Governors shall dispose of such request as soon as practicable after the receipt of such request.

§25.   Short title [15 U.S.C. §58]

This Act may be cited as the "Federal Trade Commission Act."

15 U.S.C. §57a-1.   Congressional review of rules

(a) Promulgation of final rule by Commission; submittal to Congress; effective date

(1) The Federal Trade Commission, after promulgating a final rule, shall submit such final rule to the Congress for review in accordance with this section. Such final rule shall be delivered to each House of the Congress on the same date and to each House of the Congress while it is in session. Such final rule shall be referred to the Committee on Commerce, Science, and Transportation of the Senate and to the Committee on Energy and Commerce of the House, respectively.

(2) Any such final rule shall become effective in accordance with its terms unless, before the end of the period of 90 calendar days of continuous session after the date such final rule is submitted to the Congress, both Houses of the Congress adopt a concurrent resolution disapproving such final rule.

(b) Congressional authority; disapproval of final rule by concurrent resolution; motion to discharge; appeals; approval of concurrent resolution

(1) The provisions of this subsection are enacted by the Congress—

(A) as an exercise of the rulemaking power of the Senate and the House of Representatives, respectively, and as such they are deemed a part of the rules of each House, respectively, but applicable only with respect to the procedure to be followed in that House in the case of concurrent resolutions which are subject to this section, and such provisions supersede other rules only to the extent that they are inconsistent with such other rules; and

(B) with full recognition of the constitutional right of either House to change the rules (so far as relating to the procedure of that House) at any time, in the same manner and to the same extent as in the case of any other rule of that House.

(2)(A) Any concurrent resolution disapproving a final rule of the Commission shall, upon introduction or receipt from the other House of the Congress, be referred immediately by the presiding officer of such House to the Committee on Commerce, Science, and Transportation of the Senate or to the Committee on Energy and Commerce of the House, as the case may be.

(B) If a committee to which a concurrent resolution is referred does not report such concurrent resolution before the end of the period of 75 calendar days of continuous session of the Congress after the referral of such resolution to the Committee on Commerce, Science, and Transportation of the Senate or to the Committee on Energy and Commerce of the House, as the case may be, under subsection (a)(1) of this section, it shall be in order to move to discharge any such committee from further consideration of such concurrent resolution.

(C)(i) A motion to discharge in the Senate may be made only by a Member favoring the concurrent resolution, shall be privileged (except that it may not be made after the committee has reported a concurrent resolution with respect to the same final rule of the Commission), and debate on such motion shall be limited to not more than 1 hour, to be divided equally between those favoring and those opposing the motion. An amendment to the motion shall not be in order, and it shall not be in order to move to reconsider the vote by which the motion was agreed to or disagreed to. If the motion to discharge is agreed to or disagreed to, the motion may not be renewed, nor may another motion to discharge the committee be made with respect to any other concurrent resolution with respect to the same final rule of the Commission.

(ii) A motion to discharge in the House may be made by presentation in writing to the Clerk. The motion may be called up only if the motion has been signed by one-fifth of the Members of the House. The motion is highly privileged (except that it may not be made after the committee has reported a concurrent resolution of disapproval with respect to the same rule). Debate on such motion shall be limited to not more than 1 hour, the time to be divided equally between those favoring and those opposing the motion. An amendment to the motion is not in order, and it is not in order to move to reconsider the vote by which the motion is agreed to or disagreed to.

(3)(A) When a committee has reported, or has been discharged from further consideration of, a concurrent resolution, it shall be at any time thereafter in order (even though a previous motion to the same effect has been disagreed to) to move to proceed to the consideration of the concurrent resolution. The motion shall be privileged in the Senate and highly privileged in the House of Representatives, and shall not be debatable. An amendment to the motion shall not be in order, and it shall not be in order to move to reconsider the vote by which the motion was agreed to or disagreed to.

(B) Debate on the concurrent resolution shall be limited to not more than 10 hours, which shall be divided equally between those favoring and those opposing such concurrent resolution. A motion further to limit debate shall not be debatable. An amendment to, or motion to recommit, the concurrent resolution shall not be in order, and it shall not be in order to move to reconsider the vote by which such concurrent resolution was agreed to or disagreed to.

(4) Appeals from the decision of the Chair relating to the application of the rules of the Senate or the House of Representatives, as the case may be, to the procedure relating to a concurrent resolution shall be decided without debate.

(5) Notwithstanding any other provision of this subsection, if a House has approved a concurrent resolution with respect to any final rule of the Commission, then it shall not be in order to consider in such House any other concurrent resolution with respect to the same final rule.

(c) Promulgation of final rule in accordance with congressional disapproval; submittal to Congress

(1) If a final rule of the Commission is disapproved by the Congress under subsection (a)(2) of this section, then the Commission may promulgate a final rule which relates to the same acts or practices as the final rule disapproved by the Congress in accordance with this subsection. Shall final rule—

(A) shall be based upon—

(i) the rulemaking record of the final rule disapproved by the Congress; or

(ii) such rulemaking record and the record established in supplemental rulemaking proceedings conducted by the Commission in accordance with section 553 of title 5, in any case in which the Commission determines that it is necessary to supplement the existing rulemaking record; and

(B) may contain such changes as the Commission considers necessary or appropriate.

(2) The Commission, after promulgating a final rule under this subsection, shall submit the final rule to the Congress in accordance with subsection (a)(1) of this section.

(d) Effect of congressional inaction on, or rejection of, a concurrent resolution of disapproval

Congressional inaction on, or rejection of, a concurrent resolution of disapproval under this section shall not be construed as an expression of approval of the final rule involved, and shall not be construed to create any presumption of validity with respect to such final rule.

(e) Preparation of report by Comptroller General respecting congressional review of rules; submittal to Congress

(1) The Comptroller General shall prepare a report which examines the review of Commission rules under this section. Such report shall—

(A) list the final rules submitted to the Congress by the Commission during the period in which this section is in effect;

(B) list the final rules disapproved by the Congress under subsection (a)(2) of this section;

(C) specify the number of instances in which the Commission promulgates a final rule in accordance with subsection (c) of this section; and

(D) include an analysis of any impact which the provisions of this section have had upon the decisionmaking and rulemaking processes of the Commission.

(2) The Comptroller General shall submit the report required in paragraph (1) to the Congress before the end of fiscal year 1982.

(f) Actions in district court of the United States

(1) Any interested party may institute such actions in the appropriate district court of the United States, including actions for declaratory judgment, as may be appropriate to construe the constitutionality of any provision of this section. The district court immediately shall certify all questions of the constitutionality of this section to the United States court of appeals for the circuit involved, which shall hear the matter sitting en banc.

(2) Notwithstanding any other provision of law, any decision on a matter certified under paragraph (1) shall be reviewable by appeal directly to the Supreme Court of the United States. Such appeal shall be brought not later than 20 days after the decision of the court of appeals.

(3) It shall be the duty of the court of appeals and of the Supreme Court of the United States to advance on the docket and to expedite to the greatest possible extent the disposition of any matter certified under paragraph (1).

(g) Congressional adjournments

(1) For purposes of this section—

(A) continuity of session is broken only by an adjournment sine die; and

(B) days on which either House is not in session because of an adjournment of more than 5 days to a day certain are excluded in the computation of the periods specified in subsection (a)(2) of this section and subsection (b) of this section.

(2) If an adjournment sine die of the Congress occurs after the Commission has submitted a final rule under subsection (a)(1) of this section, but such adjournment occurs—

(A) before the end of the period specified in subsection (a)(2) of this section; and

(B) before any action necessary to disapprove the final rule is completed under subsection (a)(2) of this section;

then the Commission shall be required to resubmit the final rule involved at the beginning of the next regular session of the Congress. The period specified in subsection (a)(2) of this section shall begin on the date of such resubmission.

(h) Definitions

For purposes of this section:

(1) The term "Commission" means the Federal Trade Commission.

(2) The term "concurrent resolution" means a concurrent resolution the matter after the resolving clause of which is as follows: "That the Congress disapproves the final rule promulgated by the Federal Trade Commission dealing with the matter of _____, which final rule was submitted to the Congress on _____.". (The blank spaces shall be filled appropriately.)

(3) The term "rule" means any rule promulgated by the Commission pursuant to the Federal Trade Commission Act (15 U.S.C. 41 et seq.), other than any rule promulgated under section 18(a)(1)(A) of such Act (15 U.S.C. 57a(a)(1)(A)).

Appendix N
Cooling-Off Period for Door-to-Door Sales

§429.1 The Rule

In connection with any door-to-door sale, it constitutes an unfair and deceptive act or practice for any seller to:

(a) Fail to furnish the buyer with a fully completed receipt or copy of any contract pertaining to such sale at the time of its execution, which is in the same language, e.g., Spanish, as that principally used in the oral sales presentation and which shows the date of the transaction and contains the name and address of the seller, and in immediate proximity to the space reserved in the contract for the signature of the buyer or on the front page of the receipt if a contract is not used and in bold face type of a minimum size of 10 points, a statement is substantially the following form:

"You, the buyer, may cancel this transaction at any time prior to midnight of the third business day after the date of this transaction. See the attached notice of cancellation form for an explanation of this right."

(b) Fail to furnish each buyer, at the time he signs the door-to-door sales contract or otherwise agrees to buy consumer goods or services from the seller, a completed form in duplicate, captioned "NOTICE OF CANCELLATION", which shall be attached to the contract or receipt and easily detachable, and which shall contain in ten point bold face type the following information and statements in the same language, e.g., Spanish, as that used in the contract:

NOTICE OF CANCELLATION

[enter date of transaction]

_____
(Date)

YOU MAY CANCEL THIS TRANSACTION, WITHOUT ANY PENALTY OR OBLIGATION, WITHIN THREE BUSINESS DAYS FROM THE ABOVE DATE.

IF YOU CANCEL, ANY PROPERTY TRADED IN, ANY PAYMENTS MADE BY YOU UNDER THE CONTRACT OR SALE, AND ANY NEGOTIABLE INSTRUMENT EXECUTED BY YOU WILL BE RETURNED WITHIN 10 BUSINESS DAYS FOLLOWING RECEIPT BY THE SELLER OF YOUR CANCELLATION NOTICE, AND ANY SECURITY INTEREST ARISING OUT OF THE TRANSACTION WILL BE CANCELED.

IF YOU CANCEL, YOU MUST MAKE AVAILABLE TO THE SELLER AT YOUR RESIDENCE, IN SUBSTANTIALLY AS GOOD CONDITION AS WHEN RECEIVED, ANY GOODS DELIVERED TO YOU UNDER THIS CONTRACT OR SALE; OR YOU MAY IF YOU WISH, COMPLY WITH THE

INSTRUCTIONS OF THE SELLER REGARDING THE RETURN SHIP-
MENT OF THE GOODS AT THE SELLER'S EXPENSE AND RISK.

IF YOU DO MAKE THE GOODS AVAILABLE TO THE SELLER AND
THE SELLER DOES NOT PICK THEM UP WITHIN 20 DAYS OF THE
DATE OF YOUR NOTICE OF CANCELLATION, YOU MAY RETAIN OR
DISPOSE OF THE GOODS WITHOUT ANY FURTHER OBLIGATION. IF
YOU FAIL TO MAKE THE GOODS AVAILABLE TO THE SELLER, OR IF
YOU AGREE TO RETURN THE GOODS TO THE SELLER AND FAIL TO
DO SO, THEN YOU REMAIN LIABLE FOR PERFORMANCE OF ALL
OBLIGATIONS UNDER THE CONTRACT.

TO CANCEL THIS TRANSACTION, MAIL OR DELIVER A SIGNED AND
DATED COPY OF THIS CANCELLATION NOTICE OR ANY OTHER
WRITTEN NOTICE, OR SEND A TELEGRAM, TO [Name of seller], AT
[address of seller's place of business] NOT LATER THAN MIDNIGHT OF
_____ (date).

I HEREBY CANCEL THIS TRANSACTION.

(Date) _____

_____

(Buyer's signature)

(c) Fail, before furnishing copies of the "Notice of Cancellation" to the
buyer, to complete both copies by entering the name of the seller, the address
of the seller's place of business, the date of the transaction, and the date, not
earlier than the third business day following the date of the transaction, by
which the buyer may give notice of cancellation.

(d) Include in any door-to-door contract or receipt any confession of
judgment or any waiver of any of the rights to which the buyer is entitled under
this section including specifically his right to cancel the sale in accordance with
the provisions of this section.

(e) Fail to inform each buyer orally, at the time he signs the contract or
purchases the goods or services, of his right to cancel.

(f) Misrepresent in any manner the buyer's right to cancel.

(g) Fail or refuse to honor any valid notice of cancellation by a buyer and
within 10 business days after the receipt of such notice, to: (i) Refund all
payments made under the contract or sale; (ii) return any goods or property
traded in, in substantially as good condition as when received by the seller;
(iii) cancel and return any negotiable instrument executed by the buyer in
connection with the contract or sale and take any action necessary or
appropriate to terminate promptly any security interest created in the
transaction.

(h) Negotiate, transfer, sell, or assign any note or other evidence of
indebtedness to a finance company or other third party prior to midnight of
the fifth business day following the day the contract was signed or the goods
or services were purchased.

(i) Fail, within 10 business days of receipt of the buyer's notice of cancellation, to notify him whether the seller intends to repossess or to abandon any shipped or delivered goods.

Note 1: *Definitions.* For the purposes of this section the following definitions shall apply:

(a) *Door-to-Door Sale*—A sale, lease, or rental of consumer goods or services with a purchase price of $25 or more, whether under single or multiple contracts, in which the seller or his representative personally solicits the sale, including those in response to or following an invitation by the buyer, and the buyer's agreement or offer to purchase is made at a place other than the place of business of the seller. The term "door-to-door sale" does not include a transaction:

(1) Made pursuant to prior negotiations in the course of a visit by the buyer to a retail business establishment having a fixed permanent location where the goods are exhibited or the services are offered for sale on a continuing basis; or

(2) In which the consumer is accorded the right of recision by the provisions of the Consumer Credit Protection Act (15 U.S.C. 1635) or regulations issued pursuant thereto; or

(3) In which the buyer has initiated the contact and the goods or services are needed to meet a bona fide immediate personal emergency of the buyer, and the buyer furnishes the seller with a separate dated and signed personal statement in the buyer's handwriting describing the situation requiring immediate remedy and expressly acknowledging and waiving the right to cancel the sale within 3 business days; or

(4) Conducted and consummated entirely by mail or telephone; and without any other contact between the buyer and the seller or its representative prior to delivery of the goods or performance of the services; or

(5) In which the buyer has initiated the contact and specifically requested the seller to visit his home for the purpose of repairing or performing maintenance upon the buyer's personal property. If in the course of such a visit, the seller sells the buyer the right to receive additional services or goods other than replacement parts necessarily used in performing the maintenance or in making the repairs, the sale of those additional goods or services would not fall within this exclusion; or

(6) Pertaining to the sale or rental of real property, to the sale of insurance or to the sale of securities or commodities by a broker-dealer registered with the Securities and Exchange Commission.

(b) *Consumer Goods or Services*—Goods or services purchased, leased, or rented primarily for personal, family, or household purposes, including courses of instruction or training regardless of the purpose for which they are taken.

(c) *Seller*—Any person, partnership, corporation, or association engaged in the door-to-door sale of consumer goods or services.

(d) *Place of Business*—The main or permanent branch office or local address of a seller.

(e) *Purchase Price*—The total price paid or to be paid for the consumer goods or services, including all interest and service charges.

(f) *Business Day*—Any calendar day except Sunday, or the following business holidays:

New Year's Day, Washington's Birthday, Memorial Day, Independence Day, Labor Day, Columbus Day, Veterans' Day, Thanksgiving Day, and Christmas Day.

Note 2: *Effect on State Laws and Municipal Ordinances.*

(a) The Commission is cognizant of the significant burden imposed upon door-to-door sellers by the various and often inconsistent State laws which provide the buyer with the right to cancel door-to-door sales transactions. However, it does not believe that this constitutes sufficient justification for preempting all of the provisions of such laws or of the ordinances of the political subdivisions of the various States. The Record in the proceedings supports the view that the joint and coordinated efforts of both the Commission and State and local officials are required to insure that a consumer who has purchased from a door-to-door seller something he does not want, does not need, or cannot afford, is accorded a unilateral right to rescind, without penalty, his agreement to purchase the goods or services.

(b) This section will not be construed to annul, or exempt any seller from complying with the laws of any State, or with the ordinances of political subdivisions thereof, regulating door-to-door sales, except to the extent that such laws or ordinances, if they permit door-to-door selling, are directly inconsistent with the provisions of this section. Such laws or ordinances which do not accord the buyer, with respect to the particular transaction, a right to cancel a door-to-door sale which is substantially the same or greater than that provided in this section, or which permit the imposition of any fee or penalty on the buyer for the exercise of such right, or which do not provide for giving the buyer notice of his right to cancel the transaction in substantially the same form and manner provided for in this section, are among those which will be considered directly inconsistent.

Appendix O
Preservation of Consumers' Claims and Defenses

16 C.F.R. Part 433

§433.1 Definitions

(a) *Person.* An individual, corporation, or any other business organization.

(b) *Consumer.* A natural person who seeks or acquires goods or services for personal, family, or household use.

(c) *Creditor.* A person who, in the ordinary course of business, lends purchase money or finances the sale of goods or services to consumers on a deferred payment basis; *Provided,* such person is not acting, for the purposes of a particular transaction, in the capacity of a credit card issuer.

(d) *Purchase money loan.* A cash advance which is received by a consumer in return for a "Finance Charge" within the meaning of the Truth in Lending Act and Regulation Z, which is applied, in whole or substantial part, to a purchase of goods or services from a seller who (1) refers consumers to the creditor or (2) is affiliated with the creditor by common control, contract, or business arrangement.

(e) *Financing a sale.* Extending credit to a consumer in connection with a "Credit Sale" within the meaning of the Truth in Lending Act and Regulation Z.

(f) *Contract.* Any oral or written agreement, formal or informal, between a creditor and a seller, which contemplates or provides for cooperative or concerted activity in connection with the sale of goods or services to consumers or the financing thereof.

(g) *Business arrangement.* Any understanding, procedure, course of dealing, or arrangement, formal or informal, between a creditor and a seller, in connection with the sale of goods or services to consumers or the financing thereof.

(h) *Credit card issuer.* A person who extends to cardholders the right to use a credit card in connection with purchases of goods or services.

(i) *Consumer credit contract.* Any instrument which evidences or embodies a debt arising from a "Purchase Money Loan" transaction or a "financed sale" as defined in paragraphs (d) and (e) of this section.

(j) *Seller.* A person who, in the ordinary course of business, sells or leases goods or services to consumers.

§433.2 Preservation of consumers' claims and defenses, unfair or deceptive acts or practices

In connection with any sale or lease of goods or services to consumers, in or affecting commerce as "commerce" is defined in the Federal Trade Commission Act, it is an unfair or deceptive act or practice within the meaning of Section 5 of that Act for a seller, directly or indirectly, to:

(a) Take or receive a consumer credit contract which fails to contain the following provision in at least ten point, bold face, type:

NOTICE

ANY HOLDER OF THIS CONSUMER CREDIT CONTRACT IS SUBJECT TO ALL CLAIMS AND DEFENSES WHICH THE DEBTOR COULD ASSERT AGAINST THE SELLER OF GOODS OR SERVICES OBTAINED PURSUANT HERETO OR WITH THE PROCEEDS HEREOF. RECOVERY HEREUNDER BY THE DEBTOR SHALL NOT EXCEED AMOUNTS PAID BY THE DEBTOR HEREUNDER.

or,

(b) Accept, as full or partial payment for such sale or lease, the proceeds of any purchase money loan (as purchase money loan is defined herein), unless any consumer credit contract made in connection with such purchase money loan contains the following provision in at least ten point, bold face, type:

NOTICE

ANY HOLDER OF THIS CONSUMER CREDIT CONTRACT IS SUBJECT TO ALL CLAIMS AND DEFENSES WHICH THE DEBTOR COULD ASSERT AGAINST THE SELLER OF GOODS OR SERVICES OBTAINED WITH THE PROCEEDS HEREOF. RECOVERY HEREUNDER BY THE DEBTOR SHALL NOT EXCEED AMOUNTS PAID BY THE DEBTOR HEREUNDER.

§433.3 Exemption of sellers taking or receiving open end consumer credit contracts before November 1, 1977 from requirements of §433.2(a)

(a) Any seller who has taken or received an open end consumer credit contract before November 1, 1977, shall be exempt from the requirements of 16 CFR Part 433 with respect to such contract provided the contract does not cut off consumers' claims and defenses.

(b) *Definitions.* The following definitions apply to this exemption:

(1) All pertinent definitions contained in 16 CFR 433.1.

(2) Open end consumer credit contract: a consumer credit contract pursuant to which "open end credit" is extended.

(3) "Open end credit": consumer credit extended on an account pursuant to a plan under which a creditor may permit an applicant to make purchases or make loans, from time to time, directly from the creditor or indirectly by use of a credit card, check, or other device, as the plan may provide. The term does not include negotiated advances under an open-end real estate mortgage or a letter of credit.

(4) Contract which does not cut off consumers' claims and defenses: a consumer credit contract which does not constitute or contain a negotiable instrument, or contain any waiver, limitation, term, or condition which has the effect of limiting a consumer's right to assert against any holder of the contract all legally sufficient claims and defenses which the consumer could assert against the seller of goods or services purchased pursuant to the contract.

Appendix P
Credit Practices

CREDIT PRACTICES

Sec.
444.1   Definitions.
444.2   Unfair credit practices.
444.3   Unfair or deceptive cosigner practices.
444.4   Late charges.
444.5   State exemptions.

AUTHORITY: Sec. 18(a), 88 Stat. 2193, as amended 93 Stat. 95 (15 U.S.C. 57a); 80 Stat. 383, as amended, 81 Stat. 54 (5 U.S.C. 552).

SOURCE: 49 FR 7789, Mar. 1, 1984, unless otherwise noted.

§444.1   Definitions.

(a) *Lender.*   A person who engages in the business of lending money to consumers within the jurisdiction of the Federal Trade Commission.

(b) *Retail installment seller.*   A person who sells goods or services to consumers on a deferred payment basis or pursuant to a lease-purchase arrangement within the jurisdiction of the Federal Trade Commission.

(c) *Person.*   An individual, corporation, or other business organization.

(d) *Consumer.*   A natural person who seeks or acquires goods, services, or money for personal, family, or household use.

(e) *Obligation.*   An agreement between a consumer and a lender or retail installment seller.

(f) *Creditor.*   A lender or a retail installment seller.

(g) *Debt.*   Money that is due or alleged to be due from one to another.

(h) *Earnings.*   Compensation paid or payable to an individual or for his or her account for personal services rendered or to be rendered by him or her, whether denominated as wages, salary, commission, bonus, or otherwise, including periodic payments pursuant to a pension, retirement, or disability program.

(i) *Household goods.*   Clothing, furniture, appliances, one radio and one television, linens, china, crockery, kitchenware, and personal effects (including wedding rings) of the consumer and his or her dependents, provided that the following are not included within the scope of the term "household goods":

(1) Works of art;

(2) Electronic entertainment equipment (except one television and one radio);

(3) Items acquired as antiques; and

(4) Jewelry (except wedding rings).

(j) *Antique.*   Any item over one hundred years of age, including such items that have been repaired or renovated without changing their original form or character.

(k) *Cosigner.*   A natural person who renders himself or herself liable for the obligation of another person without compensation. The term shall include any person whose signature is requested as a condition to granting credit to another person, or as a condition for forbearance on collection of another person's obligation that is in default. The term shall not include a spouse whose signature is required on a credit obligation to perfect a security interest pursuant to State law. A person who does not receive goods, services, or money in return for a credit obligation does not receive compensation within the meaning of this definition. A person is a cosigner within the meaning of this definition whether or not he or she is designated as such on a credit obligation.

§444.2   Unfair credit practices.

(a) In connection with the extension of credit to consumers in or affecting commerce, as commerce is defined in the Federal Trade Commission Act, it is an unfair act or practice within the meaning of Section 5 of that Act for a lender or retail installment seller directly or indirectly to take or receive from a consumer an obligation that:

(1) Constitutes or contains a cognovit or confession of judgment (for purposes other than executory process in the State of Louisiana), warrant of attorney, or other waiver of the right to notice and the opportunity to be heard in the event of suit or process thereon.

(2) Constitutes or contains an executory waiver or a limitation of exemption from attachment, execution, or other process on real or personal property held, owned by, or due to the consumer, unless the waiver applies solely to property subject to a security interest executed in connection with the obligation.

(3) Constitutes or contains an assignment of wages or other earnings unless:

(i) The assignment by its terms is revocable at the will of the debtor, or

(ii) The assignment is a payroll deduction plan or preauthorized payment plan, commencing at the time of the transaction, in which the consumer authorizes a series of wage deductions as a method of making each payment, or

(iii) The assignment applies only to wages or other earnings already earned at the time of the assignment.

(4) Constitutes or contains a nonpossessory security interest in household goods other than a purchase money security interest.

§444.3   Unfair or deceptive cosigner practices.

(a) In connection with the extension of credit to consumers in or affecting commerce, as commerce is defined in the Federal Trade Commission Act, it is:

(1) A deceptive act or practice within the meaning of section 5 of that Act

for a lender or retail installment seller, directly or indirectly, to misrepresent the nature or extent of cosigner liability to any person.

(2) An unfair act or practice within the meaning of section 5 of that Act for a lender or retail installment seller, directly or indirectly, to obligate a cosigner unless the cosigner is informed prior to becoming obligated, which in the case of open end credit shall mean prior to the time that the agreement creating the cosigner's liability for future charges is executed, of the nature of his or her liability as cosigner.

(b) Any lender or retail installment seller who complies with the preventive requirements in paragraph (c) of this section does not violate paragraph (a) of this section.

(c) To prevent these unfair or deceptive acts or practices, a disclosure, consisting of a separate document that shall contain the following statement and no other, shall be given to the cosigner prior to becoming obligated, which in the case of open end credit shall mean prior to the time that the agreement creating the cosigner's liability for future charges is executed:

NOTICE TO COSIGNER

You are being asked to guarantee this debt. Think carefully before you do. If the borrower doesn't pay the debt, you will have to. Be sure you can afford to pay if you have to, and that you want to accept this responsibility.

You may have to pay up to the full amount of the debt if the borrower does not pay. You may also have to pay late fees or collection costs, which increase this amount.

The creditor can collect this debt from you without first trying to collect from the borrower. The creditor can use the same collection methods against you that can be used against the borrower, such as suing you, garnishing your wages, etc. If this debt is ever in default, that fact may become a part of *your* credit record.

This notice is not the contract that makes you liable for the debt.

§444.4   Late charges.

(a) In connection with collecting a debt arising out of an extension of credit to a consumer in or affecting commerce, as commerce is defined in the Federal Trade Commission Act, it is an unfair act or practice within the meaning of section 5 of that Act for a creditor, directly or indirectly, to levy or collect any delinquency charge on a payment, which payment is otherwise a full payment for the applicable period and is paid on its due date or within an applicable grace period, when the only delinquency is attributable to late fee(s) or delinquency charge(s) assessed on earlier installment(s).

(b) For purposes of this section, "collecting a debt" means any activity other than the use of judicial process that is intended to bring about or does bring about repayment of all or part of a consumer debt.

§444.5 State exemptions.

(a) If, upon application to the Federal Trade Commission by an appropriate State agency, the Federal Trade Commission determines that:

(1) There is a State requirement or prohibition in effect that applies to any transaction to which a provision of this rule applies; and

(2) The State requirement or prohibition affords a level of protection to consumers that is substantially equivalent to, or greater than, the protection afforded by this rule;

Then that provision of the rule will not be in effect in that State to the extent specified by the Federal Trade Commission in its determination, for as long as the State administers and enforces the State requirement or prohibition effectively.

Appendix Q
National Bank Act

§85.   Any association may take, receive, reserve, and charge on any loan or discount made, or upon any notes, bills of exchange, or other evidences of debt, interest at the rate allowed by the laws of the State, Territory, or District where the bank is located, or at a rate of 1 per centum in excess of the discount rate on ninety-day commercial paper in effect at the Federal reserve bank in the Federal reserve district where the bank is located, whichever may be the greater, and no more, except that where by the laws of any State a different rate is limited for banks organized under State laws, the rate so limited shall be allowed for associations organized or existing in any such State under this chapter. When no rate is fixed by the laws of the State, or Territory, or District, the bank may take, receive, reserve, or charge a rate not exceeding 7 per centum, or 1 per centum in excess of the discount rate on ninety-day commercial paper in effect at the Federal reserve bank in the Federal reserve district where the bank is located, whichever may be the greater, and such interest may be taken in advance, reckoning the days for which the note, bill, or other evidence of debt has to run. The maximum amount of interest or discount to be charged at a branch of an association located outside of the States of the United States and the District of Columbia shall be at the rate allowed by the laws of the country, territory, dependency, province, dominion, insular possession, or other political subdivision where the branch is located. And the purchase, discount, or sale of a bona fide bill of exchange, payable at another place than the place of such purchase, discount, or sale, at not more than the current rate of exchange for sight drafts in addition to the interest, shall not be considered as taking or receiving a greater rate of interest.

§86.   The taking, receiving, reserving, or charging a rate of interest greater than is allowed by section 85 of this title, when knowingly done, shall be deemed a forfeiture of the entire interest which the note, bill, or other evidence of debt carries with it, or which has been agreed to be paid thereon. In case the greater rate of interest has been paid, the person by whom it has been paid, or his legal representatives, may recover back, in an action in the nature of an action of debt, twice the amount of the interest thus paid from the association taking or receiving the same: *Provided,* That such action is commenced within two years from the time the usurious transaction occurred.

DEPOSITORY INSTITUTIONS DEREGULATION AND MONETARY CONTROL ACT OF 1980 P.L. 96-221

§501.   [12 U.S.C. §1735f-7 note]

(a)(1) The provisions of the constitution or law of any State expressly limiting the rate or amount of interest, discount points, finance charges, or other charges which may be charged, taken, received, or reserved shall not apply to any loan, mortgage, credit sale, or advance which is—

(A) secured by a first lien on residential real property, by a first lien on all stock allocated to a dwelling unit in a residential cooperative housing corporation, or by a first lien on a residential manufactured home;

(B) made after March 31, 1980; and

(C) described in section 527(b) of the National Housing Act (12 U.S.C. 1735f-5(b)), . . .

(2)(A) The provisions of the constitution or law of any State expressly limiting the rate or amount of interest which may be charged, taken, received, or reserved shall not apply to any deposit or account held by, or other obligation of a depository institution.

(b)(1) Except as provided in paragraphs (2) and (3), the provisions of subsection (a)(1) shall apply to any loan, mortgage, credit sale, or advance made in any State on or after April 1, 1980.

(2) Except as provided in paragraph (3), the provisions of subsection (a)(1) shall not apply to any loan, mortgage, credit sale, or advance made in any State after the date (on or after April 1, 1980, and before April 1, 1983) on which such State adopts a law or certifies that the voters of such State have voted in favor of any provision, constitutional or otherwise, which states explicitly and by its terms that such State does not want the provisions of subsection (a)(1) to apply with respect to loans, mortgages, credit sales, and advances made in such State.

(3) In any case in which a State takes an action described in paragraph (2), the provisions of subsection (a)(1) shall continue to apply to—

(A) any loan, mortgage, credit sale, or advance which is made after the date such action was taken pursuant to a commitment therefor which was entered during the period beginning on April 1, 1980, and ending on the date on which such State takes action; and

(B) any loan, mortgage, or advance which is a rollover of a loan, mortgage, or advance, as described in regulations of the Federal Home Loan Bank Board, which was made or committed to be made during the period beginning on April 1, 1980, and ending on the date on which such State takes any action described in paragraph (2).

(4) At any time after the date of enactment of this Act, any State may adopt a provision of law placing limitations on discount points or such other charges on any loan, mortgage, credit sale, or advance described in subsection (a)(1).

(c) The provisions of subsection (a)(1) shall not apply to a loan, mortgage, credit sale, or advance which is secured by a first lien on a residential manufactured home unless the terms and conditions relating to such loan, mortgage, credit sale, or advance comply with consumer protection provisions specified in regulations prescribed by the Federal Home Loan Bank Board. Such regulations shall—

(1) include consumer protection provisions with respect to balloon payments, prepayment penalties, late charges, and deferral fees;

(2) require a 30-day notice prior to instituting any action leading to repossession or foreclosure (except in the case of abandonment or other extreme circumstances);

(3) require that upon prepayment in full, the debtor shall be entitled to a refund of the unearned portion of the precomputed finance charge in an amount not less than the amount which would be calculated by the actuarial method, except that the debtor shall not be entitled to a refund which is less than $1; and

(4) include such other provisions as the Federal Home Loan Bank Board may prescribe after a finding that additional protections are required.

(d) The provisions of subsection (c) shall not apply to a loan, mortgage, credit sale, or advance secured by a first lien on a residential manufactured home until regulations required to be issued pursuant to paragraphs (1), (2), and (3) of subsection (c) take effect, except that the provisions of subsection (c) shall apply in the case of such a loan, mortgage, credit sale, or advance made prior to the date on which such regulations take effect if the loan, mortgage, credit sale, or advance includes a precomputed finance charge and does not provide that, upon prepayment in full, the refund of the unearned portion of the precomputed finance charge is in an amount not less [than] the amount which would be calculated by the actuarial method, except that the debtor shall not be entitled to a refund which is less than $1. The Federal Home Loan Bank Board shall issue regulations pursuant to the provisions of paragraphs (1), (2), and (3) of subsection (c) that shall take effect prospectively not less than 30 days after publication in the Federal Register and not later than 120 days from the date of enactment of this Act.

(e) For the purpose of this section—

(1) a "prepayment" occurs upon—

(A) the refinancing or consolidation of the indebtedness;

(B) the actual prepayment of the indebtedness by the consumer whether voluntarily or following acceleration of the payment obligation by the creditor; or

(C) the entry of a judgment for the indebtedness in favor of the creditor;

(2) the term "actuarial method" means the method of allocating payments made on a debt between the outstanding balance of the obligation and the precomputed finance charge pursuant to which a payment is applied first to the accrued precomputed finance charge and any remainder is subtracted from, or any deficiency is added to, the outstanding balance of the obligation;

(3) the term "precomputed finance charge" means interest or a time price differential within the meaning of sections 106(a)(1) and (2) of the Truth in

Lending Act (15 U.S.C. 1605 (a)(1) and (2)) as computed by an add-on or discount method; and

(4) the term "residential manufactured home" means a mobile home as defined in section 603(6) of the National Mobile Home Construction and Safety Standards Act of 1974 which is used as a residence.

(f) The Federal Home Loan Bank Board is authorized to issue rules and regulations and to publish interpretations governing the implementation of this section.

(g) This section takes effect on April 1, 1980.

Appendix R
Credit Insurance Act

§1. Purpose

The purpose of this Act is to promote the public welfare by regulating credit life insurance and credit accident and health insurance. Nothing in this Act is intended to prohibit or discourage reasonable competition. The provisions of this Act shall be liberally construed.

§2. Scope and Definitions

A. Citation and Scope

(1) This Act may be cited as "The Model Act for the Regulation of Credit Life Insurance and Credit Accident and Health Insurance."

(2) All life insurance and all accident and health insurance in connection with loans or other credit transactions shall be subject to the provisions of this Act, except such insurance in connection with a loan or other credit transaction of more than ten years duration; nor shall insurance be subject to the provisions of this Act where the issuance of such insurance is an isolated transaction on the part of the insurer not related to an agreement or a plan for insuring debtors of the creditor.

B. Definitions

For the purpose of this Act:

(1) "Credit life insurance" means insurance on the life of a debtor pursuant to or in connection with a specific loan or other credit transaction;

(2) "Credit accident and health insurance" means insurance on a debtor to provide indemnity for payments becoming due on a specific loan or other credit transaction while the debtor is disabled as defined in the policy;

(3) "Creditor" means the lender of money or vendor or lessor of goods, services, or property, rights or privileges, for which payment is arranged through a credit transaction, or any successor to the right, title or interest of any such lender, vendor, or lessor, and an affiliate, associate or subsidiary of any of them or any director, officer or employee of any of them or any other person in any way associated with any of them;

(4) "Debtor" means a borrower of money or a purchaser or lessee of goods, services, property, rights or privileges for which payment is arranged through a credit transaction;

(5) "Indebtedness" means the total amount payable by a debtor to a creditor in connection with a loan or other credit transaction;

(6) "Commissioner" means (Insurance Supervisory Authority of the State).

692

§3. Forms of Credit Life Insurance and Credit Accident and Health Insurance

Credit life insurance and credit accident and health insurance shall be issued only in the following forms:

A. Individual policies of life insurance issued to debtors on the term plan;

B. Individual policies of accident and health insurance issued to debtors on a term plan or disability benefit provisions in individual policies of credit life insurance;

C. Group policies of life insurance issued to creditors providing insurance upon the lives of debtors on the term plan;

D. Group policies of accident and health insurance issued to creditors on a term plan insuring debtors or disability benefit provisions in group credit life insurance policies to provide such coverage.

§4. Amount of Credit Life Insurance and Credit Accident and Health Insurance

A. Credit Life Insurance

(1) The initial amount of credit life insurance shall not exceed the total amount repayable under the contract of indebtedness and, where an indebtedness is repayable in substantially equal installments, the amount of insurance shall at no time exceed the scheduled or actual amount of unpaid indebtedness, whichever is greater.

Note: If desired the following provisions may be added as subsection (2) and (3).

(2) Notwithstanding the provisions of the above paragraph, insurance on agricultural credit transaction commitments, not exceeding one year in duration may be written up to the amount of the loan commitment, on a nondecreasing or level term plan.

(3) Notwithstanding the provisions of paragraph A(1) of this or any other subsection, insurance on educational credit transaction commitments may be written for the amount of the portion of such commitment that has not been advanced by the creditor.

B. Credit Accident and Health Insurance

The total amount of periodic indemnity payable by credit accident and health insurance in the event of disability, as defined in the policy, shall not exceed the aggregate of the periodic scheduled unpaid installments of the indebtedness; and the amount of each periodic indemnity payment shall not exceed the original indebtedness divided by the number of periodic installments.

§5.   Term of Credit Life Insurance and Credit Accident and Health Insurance

The term of any credit life insurance or credit accident and health insurance shall, subject to acceptance by the insurer, commence on the date when the debtor becomes obligated to the creditor, except that, where a group policy provides coverage with respect to existing obligations, the insurance on a debtor with respect to such indebtedness shall commence on the effective date of the policy. Where evidence of insurability is required and such evidence is furnished more than thirty (30) days after the date when the debtor becomes obligated to the creditor, the term of the insurance may commence on the date on which the insurance company determines the evidence to be satisfactory, and in such event there shall be an appropriate refund or adjustment of any charge to the debtor for insurance. The term of such insurance shall not extend more than fifteen days beyond the scheduled maturity date of the indebtedness except when extended without additional cost to the debtor. If the indebtedness is discharged due to renewal or refinancing prior to the scheduled maturity date, the insurance in force shall be terminated before any new insurance may be issued in connection with the renewed or refinanced indebtedness. In all cases of termination prior to scheduled maturity, a refund shall be paid or credited as provided in Section 8.

§6.   Provisions of Policies and Certificates of Insurance: Disclosure to Debtors

A. All credit life insurance and credit accident and health insurance shall be evidenced by an individual policy, or in the case of group insurance by a certificate of insurance, which individual policy or group certificate of insurance shall be delivered tot he debtor.

B. Each individual policy or group certificate of credit life insurance, and/or credit accident and health insurance shall, in addition to other requirements of law, set forth the name and home office address of the insurer, the name or names of the debtor or in the case of a certificate under a group policy, the identity by name or otherwise of the debtor, the premium or amount of payment, if any, by the debtor separately for credit life insurance and credit accident and health insurance, a description of the coverage including the amount and term thereof, and any exceptions, limitations and restrictions, and shall state that the benefits shall be paid to the creditor to reduce or extinguish the unpaid indebtedness and, wherever the amount of insurance may exceed the unpaid indebtedness, that any such excess shall be payable to a beneficiary, other than the creditor, named by the debtor or to his estate.

C. Said individual policy or group certificate of insurance shall be delivered to the insured debtor at the time the indebtedness is incurred except as hereinafter provided.

D. If said individual policy or group certificate of insurance is not delivered to the debtor at the time the indebtedness is incurred, a copy of the application for such policy or a notice of proposed insurance, signed by the debtor and setting forth the name and home office address of the insurer, the name or names of the debtor, the premium or amount of payment by the debtor, if any, separately for credit life insurance and credit accident and health insurance, the amount, term and a brief description of the coverage provided, shall be delivered to the debtor at the time such indebtedness is incurred. The copy of the application for, or notice of proposed insurance, shall also refer exclusively to insurance coverage, and shall be separate and apart from the loan, sale or other credit statement of account, instrument or agreement, unless the information required by this subsection is prominently set forth therein. Upon acceptance of the insurance by the insurer and within thirty (30) days of the date upon which the indebtedness is incurred, the insurer shall cause the individual policy or group certificates of insurance to be delivered to the debtor. Said application or notice of proposed insurance shall state that upon acceptance by the insurer, the insurance shall become effective as provided in Section 5.

L. If the named insurer does not accept the risk, then and in such event the debtor shall receive a policy or certificate of insurance setting forth the name and home office address of the substituted insurer and the amount of the premium to be charged, and if the amount of premium is less than that set forth in the notice of proposed insurance an appropriate refund shall be made.

§7.   Filing, Approval and Withdrawal of Forms

A. All policies, certificates of insurance, notices of proposed insurance, applications for insurance, endorsements and riders delivered or issued for delivery in this State and the schedules of premium rates pertaining thereto shall be filed with the Commissioner.

B. The Commissioner shall within thirty (30) days after the filing of any such policies, certificates of insurance, notices of proposed insurance, applications for insurance, endorsements and riders, disapprove any such form if the benefits provided therein are not reasonable in relation to the premium charge, or if it contains provisions which are unjust, unfair, inequitable, misleading, deceptive or encourage misrepresentation of the coverage, or are contrary to any provision of the Insurance Code or of any rule or regulation promulgated thereunder.

C. If the Commissioner notifies the insurer that the form is disapproved, it is unlawful thereafter for such insurer to issue or use such form. In such notice, the Commissioner shall specify the reason for his disapproval and state that a hearing will be granted within twenty (20) days after request in writing by the insurer. No such policy, certificate of insurance, notice of proposed insurance, nor any application, endorsement or rider, shall be issued or used until the expiration of thirty (30) days after it has been so filed, unless the Commissioner shall give his prior written approval thereto.

D. The Commissioner may, at any time after a hearing held not less than twenty (20) days after written notice to the insurer, withdraw his approval of any such form on any ground set forth in subsection B above. The written notice of such hearing shall state the reason for the proposed withdrawal.

E. It is not lawful for the insurer to issue such forms or use them after the effective date of such withdrawal.

F. If a group policy of credit life insurance or credit accident and health insurance

(i) has been delivered in this State before the effective date of this Act, or

(ii) has been or is delivered in another State before or after the effective date of this Act,

the insurer shall be required to file only the group certificate and notice of proposed insurance delivered or issued for delivery in this State as specified in subsections B and D of Section 6 of this Act and such forms shall be approved by the Commissioner if they conform with the requirements specified in said subsections and if the schedules of premium rates applicable to the insurance evidenced by such certificate or notice are not in excess of the insurer's schedules of premium rates filed with the Commissioner; provided, however, the premium rate in effect on existing group policies may be continued until the first policy anniversary date following the date this Act becomes operative as provided in Section 12.

G. Any order or final determination of the Commissioner under the provisions of this section shall be subject to judicial review.

§8.   Premiums and Refunds

A. Any insurer may revise its schedules of premium rates from time to time, and shall file such revised schedules with the Commissioner. No insurer shall issue any credit life insurance policy or credit accident and health insurance policy for which the premium rate exceeds that determined by the schedules of such insurer as then on file with the Commissioner.

B. Each individual policy, or group certificate shall provide that in the event of termination of the insurance prior to the scheduled maturity date of the indebtedness, any refund of an amount paid by the debtor for insurance shall be paid or credited promptly to the person entitled thereto; provided, however, that the Commissioner shall prescribe a minimum refund and no refund which would be less than such minimum need be made. The formula to be used in computing such refund shall be filed with and approved by the Commissioner.

C. If a creditor requires a debtor to make any payment for credit life insurance or credit accident and health insurance and an individual policy or group certificate of insurance is not issued, the creditor shall immediately give written notice to such debtor and shall promptly make an appropriate credit to the account.

D. The amount charged to a debtor for any credit life or credit health and accident insurance shall not exceed the premiums charged by the insurer, as computed at the time the charge to the debtor is determined.

Note: Where a state prohibits payments for insurance by the debtor in connection with credit transactions, the following paragraph may be included.

E. Nothing in this Act shall be construed to authorize any payments for insurance now prohibited under any statute, or rule thereunder, governing credit transactions.

§9.   Issuance of Policies

All policies of credit life insurance and credit accident and health insurance shall be delivered or issued for delivery in this state only by an insurer authorized to do an insurance business therein, and shall be issued only through holders of licenses or authorizations issued by the Commissioner.

§10.   Claims

A. All claims shall be promptly reported to the insurer or its designated claim representative, and the insurer shall maintain adequate claim files. All claims shall be settled as soon as possible and in accordance with the terms of the insurance contract.

B. All claims shall be paid either by draft drawn upon the insurer or by check of the insurer to the order of the claimant to whom payment of the claim is due pursuant to the policy provisions, or upon direction of such claimant to one specified.

C. No plan or arrangement shall be used whereby any person, firm or corporation other than the insurer or its designated claim representative shall be authorized to settle or adjust claims. The creditor shall not be designated as claim representative for the insurer in adjusting claims; provided, that a group policyholder may, by arrangement with the group insurer, draw drafts or checks in payment of claims due to the group policyholder subject to audit and review by the insurer.

§11.   Existing Insurance—Choice of Insurer

When credit life insurance or credit accident and health insurance is required as additional security for any indebtedness, the debtor shall, upon request to the creditor, have the option of furnishing the required amount of insurance through existing policies of insurance owned or controlled by him or of procuring and furnishing the required coverage through any insurer authorized to transact an insurance business within this state.

§12.   Enforcement

The Commissioner may, after notice and hearing, issue such rules and regulations as he deems appropriate for the supervision of this Act. Whenever the Commissioner finds that there has been a violation of this Act or any rules or regulations issued pursuant thereto, and after written notice thereof and hearing given to the insurer or other person authorized or licensed by the Commissioner, he shall set forth the details of his findings together with an order for compliance by a specified date. Such order shall be binding on the insurer and other person authorized or licensed by the Commissioner on the date specified unless sooner withdrawn by the Commissioner or a stay thereof has been ordered by a court of competent jurisdiction. The provisions of Sections 5, 6, 7 and 8 of this Act shall not be operative until ninety (90) days after the effective date of this Act, and the Commissioner in his discretion may extend by not more than an additional ninety (90) days the initial period within which the provisions of said sections shall not be operative.

§13. Judicial Review

Any party to the proceeding affected by an order of the Commissioner shall be entitled to judicial review by following the procedure set forth in (insert applicable section).

§14. Penalties

In addition to any other penalty provided by law, any person, firm or corporation which violates an order of the Commissioner after it has become final, and while such order is in effect, shall, upon proof thereof to the satisfaction of the court, forfeit and pay to the State of (insert state) a sum not to exceed $250.00 which may be recovered in a civil action, except that if such violation is found to be willful, the amount of such penalty shall be a sum not to exceed $1,000.00. The Commissioner, in his discretion, may revoke or suspend the license or certificate of authority of the person, firm or corporation guilty of such violation. Such order for suspension or revocation shall be upon notice and hearing, and shall be subject to judicial review as provided in Section 13 of this Act.

§15. Separability Provision

If any provision of this Act, or the application of such provision to any person or circumstances, shall be held invalid, the remainder of the Act, and the application of such provision to any person or circumstances other than those as to which it is held invalid, shall not be affected thereby.

Appendix S
Real Estate Settlement Procedures Act of 1974
Public Law 93-533, December 22, 1974
As Amended by Public Law 94-205, January 2, 1976

An Act

88 STAT. 1724

Real Estate Settlements Procedures Act of 1974. 12 USC 2601 note.

To further the national housing goal of encouraging homeownership by regulating certain lending practices and closing and settlement procedures in federally related mortgage transactions to the end that unnecessary costs and difficulties of purchasing housing are minimized, and for other purposes.

Be it enacted by the Senate and House of Representatives of the United States of America in Congress assembled,

SHORT TITLE

SECTION 1. This Act may be cited as the "Real Estate Settlement Procedures Act of 1974".

FINDINGS AND PURPOSE

12 USC 2601.   SEC 2. (a) The Congress finds that significant reforms in the real estate settlement process are needed to insure that consumers throughout the Nation are provided with greater and more timely information on the nature and costs of the settlement process and are protected from unnecessarily high settlement charges caused by certain abusive practices that have developed in some areas of the country. The Congress also finds that it has been over two years since the Secretary of Housing and Urban Development and the Administrator of Veterans' Affairs submitted their joint report to the Congress on "Mortgage Settlement Costs" and that the time has come for the recommendations for Federal legislative action made in that report to be implemented.

(b) It is the purpose of this Act to effect certain changes in the settlement process for residential real estate that will result—

(1) in more effective advance disclosure to home buyers and sellers of settlement costs;

(2) in the elimination of kickbacks or referral fees that tend

---

*Material contained in brackets was repealed by the RESPA Amendments. Meterial underlined was added by the RESPA Amendments.

to increase unnecessarily the costs of certain settlement services;

(3) in a reduction in the amounts home buyers are required to place in escrow accounts established to insure the payment of real estate taxes and insurance; and

(4) in significant reform and modernization of local recordkeeping of land title information.

DEFINITIONS

12 USC 2602.   **SEC 3.** For purposes of this Act—

(1) the term "federally related mortgage loan" includes any loan *other than temporary financing such as a construction loan*) which—

(A) is secured by *a first lien on* residential real property (including individual units of condominiums and cooperatives) designed principally for the occupancy of from one to four families; and

(B) (i) is made in whole or in part by any lender the deposits or accounts of which are insured by any agency of the Federal Government, or is made in whole or in part by any lender which is regulated by any agency of the Federal Government; or

(ii) is made in whole or in part, or insured, guaranteed, supplemented, or assisted in any way, by the Secretary or any other officer or agency of the Federal Government or under or in connection with a housing or urban development program administered by the Secretary or a housing or related program administered by any other such officer or agency; or

(iii) [is eligible for purchase by] *is intended to be sold by the originating lender to* the Federal National Mortgage Association, the Government National Mortgage Association, [or] the Federal Home Loan Mortgage Corporation, or [from any] *a* financial institution from which it [could] *is to* be purchased by the Federal Home Loan Mortgage Corporation; or

(iv) is made in whole or in part by any "creditor", as defined in section 103(f) of the Consumer Credit Protection Act (15 U.S.C. 1602(f)), who makes or invests in residential real estate loans aggregating more than $1,000,000 per year, *except that for the purpose of this Act, the term "creditor" does not include any agency or instrumentality of any State;*

(2) the term "thing of value" includes any payment, advance, funds, loan, service, or other consideration;

(3) the term "settlement services" includes any service

provided in connection with a real estate settlement including, but not limited to, the following: title searches, title examinations, the provision of title certificates, title insurance, services rendered by an attorney, the preparation of documents, property surveys, the rendering of credit reports or appraisals, pest and fungus inspections, services rendered by a real estate agent or broker, and the handling of the processing, and closing or settlement;

(4) the term "title company" means any institution which is qualified to issue title insurance, directly or through its agents, and also refers to any duly authorized agent of a title company;

(5) the term "person" includes individuals, corporations, associations, partnerships, and trusts; and

(6) the term "Secretary" means the Secretary of Housing and Urban Development.

UNIFORM SETTLEMENT STATEMENT

12 USC 2603.   **SEC. 4. (a)** The Secretary, in consultation with the Administrator of Veterans' Affairs, the Federal Deposit Insurance Corporation, and the Federal Home Loan Bank Board, shall develop and prescribe a standard form for the statement of settlement costs which shall be used (with such [minimum] variations as may be necessary to reflect [unavoidable] differences in legal and administrative requirements or practices in different areas of the country) as the standard real estate settlement form in all transactions in the United States which involve federally related mortgage loans. Such form shall conspicuously and clearly itemize all charges imposed upon the borrower and all charges imposed upon the seller in connection with the settlement and shall indicate whether any title insurance premium included in such charges covers or insures the lender's interest in the property, the borrower's interest, or both. [Such form shall include all information and data required to be provided for such transactions under the Truth in Lending Act and the regulations issued thereunder by the Federal Reserve Board, and may be used in satisfaction of the disclosure requirements of that Act, and shall also include provision for execution of the waiver allowed by section 6(c).]

The Secretary may, by regulation, permit the deletion from the form prescribed under this section of items which are not, under local laws or customs, applicable in any locality, except that such regulation shall require that the numerical code prescribed by the Secretary be retained in forms to be used in all localities. Nothing in this section may be construed to require that that part of the standard form which relates to the borrower's transaction be furnished to the seller, or to require that that part of the standard form which relates to the seller be furnished to the borrower.

(b) The form prescribed under this section shall be completed and made available for inspection by the borrower at or before settlement by the person conducting the settlement, except that (1) the Secretary may exempt from the requirements of this section settlements occurring in localities where the final settlement statement is not customarily provided at or before the date of settlement, or settlements where such requirements are impractical and (2) the borrower may, in accordance with regulations of the Secretary, waive his right to have the form made available at such time.

SPECIAL INFORMATION BOOKLETS

12 USC 2604. **SEC. 5. (a)** The Secretary shall prepare and distribute booklets to help persons borrowing money to finance the purchase of residential real estate better to understand the nature and costs of real estate settlement services. The Secretary shall distribute such booklets to all lenders which make federally related mortgage loans.

(b) Each booklet shall be in such form and detail as the Secretary shall prescribe and, in addition to such other information as the Secretary may provide, shall include in clear and concise language—

(1) a description and explanation of the nature and purpose of each cost incident to a real estate settlement;

(2) an explanation and sample of the standard real estate settlement form developed and prescribed under section 4;

(3) a description and explanation of the nature and purpose of escrow accounts when used in connection with loans secured by residential real estate;

(4) an explanation of the choices available to buyers of residential real estate in selecting persons to provide necessary services incident to a real estate settlement; and

(5) an explanation of the unfair practices and unreasonable or unnecessary charges to be avoided by the prospective buyer with respect to a real estate settlement.

Such booklets shall take into consideration differences in real estate settlement procedures which may exist among the several States and territories of the United States and among separate political subdivisions within the same State and territory.

(c) Each lender shall include with the booklet a good faith estimate of the amount or range of charges for specific settlement services the

borrower is likely to incur in connection with the settlement as prescribed by the Secretary.

[(c)] (*d*) Each lender referred to in subsection (a) shall provide the booklet described in such subsection to each person from whom it receives [an application] *or for whom it prepares a written application* to borrow money to finance the purchase of residential real estate. Such booklet shall be provided at the time of receipt *or preparation* of such application.

[(d)] (*e*) Booklets may be printed and distributed by lenders if their form and content are approved by the Secretary as meeting the requirements of subsection (b) of this section.

12 USC 2605.   [**SEC. 6. (a)** Any lender agreeing to make a federally related mortgage loan shall provide or cause to be provided to the prospective borrower, to the prospective seller, and to any officer or agency of the Federal Government proposing to insure, guarantee, supplement, or assist such loan, at the time of the loan commitment, but in no case later than twelve calendar days prior to settlement, upon the standard real estate settlement form developed and prescribed under section 4, or upon a form developed and prescribed by the Secretary specifically for the purposes of this section, and in accordance with regulations prescribed by the Secretary, an itemized disclosure in writing of each charge arising in connection with such settlement. For the purposes of complying with this section, it shall be the duty of the lender agreeing to make the loan to obtain or cause to be obtained from persons who provide or will provide services in connection with such settlement the amount of each charge they intend to make. In the event the exact amount of any such charge is not available, a good faith estimate of such charge may be provided.

[(b) If any lender fails to provide a prospective borrower or seller with the disclosure as required by subsection (a), it shall be liable to such borrower or seller, as the case may be, in an amount equal to—

[(1) the actual damages involved or $500, whichever is greater, and

[(2) in the case of any successful action to enforce the foregoing liability, the court costs of the action together with a reasonable attorney's fee as determined by the court; except that a lender may not be held liable for a violation in any action brought under this subsection if it shows by a preponderance of the evidence that the violation was not intentional and resulted from a bona fide error notwithstanding the maintenance of procedures adopted to avoid any such error.

15 USC 1631.
12 USC 2606.

[(c) The provisions of subsection (a) shall be deemed to be satisfied with respect to a borrower or seller in connection with any settlement involving a federally related mortgage loan if the disclosure required by subsection (a) is provided at any time prior to settlement and the prospective borrower or seller, as the case may be, executes, under terms and conditions prescribed by regulations to be issued by the Secretary after consultation with the appropriate Federal agencies, a waiver of the requirement that the disclosure be provided at least twelve calendar days prior to such settlement. In issuing such regulations, the Secretary shall take into account the need to protect the borrower's and the seller's right to a timely disclosure.

[(d) With respect to any particular transaction involving a federally related mortgage loan, no borrower shall maintain an action or separate actions against any lender under both the provisions of this section and the provisions of section 130 of the Consumer Credit Protection Act (15 U.S.C. 1640).

[(e) The provisions of this Act shall supersede the provisions of section 121(c) of the Consumer Credit Protection Act insofar as the latter applies to federally related mortgage loans as defined in this Act.]

DISCLOSURE OF PREVIOUS SELLING PRICE OF EXISTING REAL PROPERTY

[SEC. 7. (a) No lender shall make any commitment for a federally related mortgage loan on a residence on which construction has been completed more than twelve months prior to the date of such commitment unless it has confirmed that the following information has been disclosed in writing by the seller or his agent to the buyer—

[(1) the name and address of the present owner of the property being sold;

[(2) the date the property was acquired by the present owner (the year only if the property was acquired more than two years previously); and

[(3) if the seller has not owned the property for at least two years prior to the date of the loan application and has not used the property as a place of residence, the date and purchase price of the last arm's length transfer of the property, a list of any subsequent improvements made to the property (excluding maintenance repairs) and the cost of such improvements.

[(b) the obligations imposed upon a lender by this section shall be deemed satisfied and a commitment for a federally related mortgage loan may thereafter be made if the lender receives a copy of the written statement provided by the seller to the buyer supplying the information required by subsection (a).

[(c) Whoever knowingly and willfully provides false information under this section or otherwise willfully fails to comply with its requirements shall be fined not more than $10,000 or imprisoned for not more than one year, or both.]

PROHIBITION AGAINST KICKBACKS AND UNEARNED FEES

12 USC 2607.   **SEC. 8.** (a) No person shall give and no person shall accept any fee, kickback, or thing of value pursuant to any agreement or understanding, oral or otherwise, that business incident to or a part of a real estate settlement service involving a federally related mortgage loan shall be referred to any person.

(b) No person shall give and no person shall accept any portion, split, or percentage of any charge made or received for the rendering of a real estate settlement service in connection with a transaction involving a federally related mortgage loan other than for services actually performed.

(c) Nothing in this section shall be construed as prohibiting (1) the payment of a fee (A) to attorneys at law for services actually rendered or (B) by a title company to its duly appointed agent for services actually performed in the issuance of a policy of title insurance or (C) by a lender to its duly appointed agent for services actually performed in the making of a loan, [or] (2) the payment to any person of a bona fide salary or compensation or other payment for goods or facilities actually furnished or for services actually performed, *or (3) payments pursuant to cooperative brokerage arrangements between real estate agents, and referral arrangements or agreements between real estate agents and brokers, or (4) such other payments or classes of payments or other transfers as are specified in regulations prescribed by the Secretary, after consultation with the Attorney General, the Administrator of Veterans' Affairs, the Federal Home Loan Bank Board, the Federal Deposit Insurance Corporation, the Board of Governors of the Federal Reserve System, and the Secretary of Agriculture.*

(d)(1) Any person or persons who violate the provisions of this section shall be fined not more than $10,000 or imprisoned for not more than one year, or both.

(2) In addition to the penalties provided by paragraph (1) of this subsection, any person or persons who violate the provisions of subsection (a) shall be jointly and severally liable to the person or persons whose business has been referred in an amount equal to three times the value or amount of the fee or thing of value, and any person or persons who violate the provisions of subsection (b) shall be jointly and severally liable to the person or persons charged for the settlement services

involved in an amount equal to three times the amount of the portion, split, or percentage. In any successful action to enforce the liability under this paragraph, the court may award the court costs of the action together with a reasonable attorney's fee as determined by the court.

TITLE COMPANIES

12 USC 2608.   **SEC. 9. (a)** No seller of property that will be purchased with the assistance of a federally related mortgage loan shall require directly or indirectly, as a condition to selling the property, that title insurance covering the property be purchased by the buyer from any particular title company.

(b) Any seller who violates the provisions of subsection (a) shall be liable to the buyer in an amount equal to three times all charges made for such title insurance.

[LIMITATION ON REQUIREMENT OF ADVANCE DEPOSITS IN ESCROW ACCOUNTS]

[SEC. 10. No lender, in connection with a federally related mortgage loan, shall require the borrower or prospective borrower—

[(1) to deposit in any escrow account which may be established in connection with such loan for the purpose of assuring payment of taxes and insurance premiums with respect to the property, prior to or upon the date of settlement, an aggregate sum (for such purpose) in excess of—

(A) in any jurisdiction where such taxes and insurance premiums are postpaid, the total amount of such taxes and insurance premiums which will actually be due and payable on the date of settlement and the pro rata portion thereof which has accrued, or

[(B) in any jurisdiction where such taxes and insurance premiums are prepaid, a pro rata portion of the estimated taxes and insurance premiums corresponding to the number of months from the last date of payment to the date of settlement,

plus one-twelfth of the estimated total amount of such taxes and insurance premiums which will become due and payable during the twelve-month period beginning on the date of settlement; or

[(2) to deposit in any such escrow account in any month beginning after the date of settlement a sum (for the purpose of assuring payment of taxes and insurance premiums with respect to the property) in excess of one-twelfth of the total amount of the estimated taxes and insurance premiums which will become due and payable during the twelve-month period beginning on the first day of such month, except that in the event the lender determines there will be a deficiency on the due date he shall not be prohibited from requiring additional monthly deposits in such escrow account of pro rata portions of the deficiency corresponding to the number of months from the date of the lender's determination of such deficiency to the date upon which such taxes and insurance premiums become due and payable.]

ESCROW ACCOUNTS

12 USC 2609.   **SEC. 10.** *A lender, in connection with a federally related mortgage loan, may not require the borrower or prospective borrower—*

(1) to deposit in any escrow account which may be established in connection with such loan for the purpose of assuring payment of taxes, insurance premiums, or other charges with respect to the property, in connection with the settlement, an aggregate sum (for such purpose) in excess of a sum that will be sufficient to pay such taxes, insurance premiums and other charges attributable to the period beginning on the last date on which each such charge would have been paid under the normal lending practice of the lender and local custom, provided that the selection of each such date constitutes prudent lending practice, and ending on the due date of its first full installment payment under the mortgage, plus one-sixth of the estimated total amount of such taxes, insurance premiums and other charges to be paid on dates, as provided above, during the ensuing twelve-month period; or

(2) to deposit in any such escrow account in any month beginning with the first full installment payment under the mortgage a sum (for the purpose of assuring payment of taxes, insurance premiums and other charges which are reasonably anticipated to be paid on dates during the ensuing twelve months which dates are in accordance with the normal lending practice of the lender and local custom, provided that the selection of each such date constitutes prudent lending practice, plus (B) such amount as is necessary to maintain an additional balance in such escrow account not to exceed one-sixth of the estimated total amount of such taxes, insurance premiums and other charges to be paid on dates, as provided above, during the ensuing twelve-month period. Provided, however, That in the event the lender determines there will be or is a deficiency he shall not be prohibited from requiring additional monthly deposits in such escrow account to avoid or eliminate such deficiency.

LIMITATIONS AND DISCLOSURES WITH RESPECT TO CERTAIN FEDERALLY RELATED MORTGAGE LOANS

SEC. 11. (a) The federal Deposit Insurance Act is amended by adding at the end thereof the following new section:

12 USC 1831b. "SEC. 25. (a) No insured bank, or mutual savings or cooperative bank which is not an insured bank, shall make any federally related mortgage loan to any agent, trustee, nominee, or other person acting in a fiduciary capacity without the prior condition that the identity of the person receiving the beneficial interest of such loan shall at all times be revealed to the bank. At the request of the Corporation, the bank shall report to the Corporation on the identity of such person and the nature and amount of the loan, discount, or other extension of credit.

"(b) In addition to other available remedies, this section may be enforced with respect to mutual savings and cooperative banks which are not insured banks in accordance with section 8 of this Act, and for such purpose such mutual savings and cooperative banks shall be held and considered to be State nonmember insured banks and the appropriate Federal agency with respect to such mutual savings and cooperative banks shall be the Federal Deposit Insurance Corporation."

(b) Title IV of the National Housing Act is amended by adding at the end thereof the following new section:

12 USC 1730f. "SEC. 413. No insured institution shall make any federally related mortgage loan to any agent, trustee, nominee, or other person acting in a fiduciary capacity without the prior condition that the identity of the person receiving the beneficial interest of such loan shall at all times be revealed to the institution. At the request of the Federal Home Loan Bank Board, the insured institution shall report to the Board on the identity of such person and the nature and amount of the loan".

12 USC 1730f. note.   (c) The Federal Deposit Insurance Corporation or the Federal Home Loan Bank Board as appropriate may by regulation exempt classes or types of transactions from the provisions added by this section if the Corporation or the Board determines that the purposes of such provisions would not be advanced materially by their application to such transactions.

FEE FOR PREPARATION OF TRUTH-IN-LENDING AND UNIFORM SETTLEMENT STATEMENTS

12 USC 2610.
16 USC 1601
note.   SEC. 12. No fee shall be imposed or charge made upon any other person (as a part of settlement costs or otherwise) by a lender in connection with a federally related mortgage loan made by it (or a loan for the purchase of a mobile home), for or on account of the preparation and submission by such lender of the statement or statements required (in connection with such loan) by sections 4 and 6 of this Act or by the Truth in Lending Act.

ESTABLISHMENT ON DEMONSTRATION BASIS OF LAND PARCEL RECORDATION SYSTEM

12 USC 2611.   SEC. 13. The Secretary shall establish and place in operation on a demonstration basis, in representative political subdivisions (selected by him) in various areas of the United States, a model system or systems for the recordation of land title information in a manner and form calculated to facilitate and simplify land transfers and mortgage transactions and reduce the cost thereof, with a view to the possible development (utilizing the information and experience gained under this section) of a nationally uniform system of land parcel recordation.

REPORT OF THE SECRETARY ON NECESSITY FOR FURTHER CONGRESSIONAL ACTION

Report to Congress.
12 USC 2612.   SEC. 14. (a) The Secretary, after consultation with the Administrator of Veterans' Affairs, the Federal Deposit Insurance Corporation, and the Federal Home Loan Bank Board, and after such study, investigation, and hearings (at which representatives of consumers groups shall be allowed to testify) as he deems appropriate, shall, not less than three years nor more than five years from the effective date of this Act, report to the Congress on whether, in view of the implementation of the provisions of this Act imposing certain requirements and prohibiting certain practices in connection with real estate settlements, there is any necessity for further legislation in this area.

Report to Congress.   (b) If the Secretary concludes that there is necessity for further legislation, he shall report to the Congress on the specific practices or problems that should be the subject of such legislation and the corrective measures that need to be taken. In addition, the Secretary shall include in his report

(1) recommendations on the desirability of requiring lenders of federally related mortgage loans to bear the costs of particular real estate settlement services that would otherwise be paid for by borrowers;

(2) recommendations on whether Federal regulation of the charges for real estate settlement services in federally related mortgage transactions is necessary and desirable, and, if he concludes that such regulation is necessary and desirable, a description and analysis of the regulatory scheme he believes Congress should adopt; and

(3) recommendations on the ways in which the Federal Government can assist and encourage local governments to modernize their methods for the recordation of land title information, including the feasibility of providing financial

assistance or incentives to local governments that seek to adopt one of the model systems developed by the Secretary in accordance with the provisions of section 13 of this Act.

DEMONSTRATION TO DETERMINE FEASIBILITY OF INCLUDING STATEMENTS OF SETTLEMENT COSTS IN SPECIAL INFORMATION BOOKLETS

12 USC 2613.
Report to
Congress.

SEC. 15. The Secretary shall, on a demonstration basis in selected housing market areas, have prepared and included in the special information booklets required to be furnished under section 5 of this Act, statements of the range of costs for specific settlement services in such areas. Not later than June 30, 1976, the Secretary shall transmit to the Congress a full report on the demonstration conducted under this section. Such report shall contain the Secretary's assessment of the feasibility of preparing and including settlement cost range statements for all housing market areas in the special information booklets for such areas.

JURISDICTION OF COURTS

12 USC 2614.

SEC. 16. Any action to recover damages pursuant to the provisions of section 6, 8, or 9 may be brought in the United States district court for the district in which the property involved is located, or in any other court of competent jurisdiction, within one year from the date of the occurrence of the violation.

VALIDITY OF CONTRACTS AND LIENS

12 USC 2615.

SEC. 17. Nothing in this Act shall affect the validity or enforceability of any sale or contract for the sale of real property or any loan, loan agreement, mortgage, or lien made or arising in connection with a federally related mortgage loan.

RELATION TO STATE LAWS

12 USC 2616.

SEC. 18. [(a)] This Act does not annul, alter, or affect, or exempt any person subject to the provisions of this Act from complying with, the laws of any State with respect to settlement practices, except to the extent that those laws are inconsistent with any provision of this Act, and then only to the extent of the inconsistency. The Secretary is authorized to determine whether such inconsistencies exist. The Secretary may not determine that any State law is inconsistent with any provision of this Act if the Secretary determines that such law gives greater protection to the consumer. In making these determinations the Secretary shall consult with the appropriate Federal agencies.

[(b) No provision of this Act or of the laws of any State imposing any liability shall apply to any act done or omitted in good faith in conformity with any rule, regulation, or interpretation thereof by the Secretary, notwithstanding that after such act or omission has occurred, such rule, regulation, or interpretation is amended, rescinded, or determined by judicial or other authority to be invalid for any reason.]

AUTHORITY OF THE SECRETARY

SEC. 19. (a) The Secretary is authorized to prescribe such rules and regulations, to make such interpretations, and to grant such reasonable exemptions for classes of transactions, as may be necessary to achieve the purposes of this Act.

(b) No provision of this Act or the laws of any State imposing any liability shall apply to any act done or omitted in good faith in conformity with any rule, regulation, or interpretation thereof by the Secretary or the Attorney General, notwithstanding that after such act or omission has occurred, such rule, regulation, or interpretation is amended, rescinded, or determined by judicial or other authority to be invalid for any reason.

EFFECTIVE DATE

12 USC 2617.   SEC. [19] *20.* The provisions of this Act, and the amendments made thereby, shall become effective one hundred and eighty days after the date of the enactment of this Act.

A2.02   Text of Regulation X

[1]   Regulation X Effective June 30, 1976

Title 24—Housing and Urban Development

CHAPTER XX—OFFICE OF ASSISTANT SECRETARY FOR CONSUMER AFFAIRS AND REGULATORY FUNCTIONS, DEPARTMENT OF HOUSING AND URBAN DEVELOPMENT

[Docket No. R-76-394]

PART 3500—REAL ESTATE SETTLEMENT PROCEDURES ACT

The Real Estate Settlement Procedures Act Amendments of 1975 (herein the "RESPA Amendments"), signed into law January 2, 1976 (Pub. L. 94-205), made significant changes in the Real Estate Settlement Procedures Act of 1974 (RESPA), (Pub. L. 93-533), 12 U.S.C. 2601, et seq. The RESPA Amendments repealed the original requirements of advance disclosure (section 6), the disclosure of the previous selling price (section 7) and the Truth-in-Lending provisions of section 4. In their place lenders are required to provide borrowers, at time of loan application, good faith estimates of settlement costs. Persons conducting settlement are required to provide borrowers with an opportunity to inspect their settlement statements one day prior to settlement. The RESPA Amendments authorized the suspension, until June 30, 1976, of the RESPA provisions dealing with advance inspection of the Uniform Settlement Statement, use of the Special Information Booklet and the provision for good faith estimates, to allow for orderly implementation and public comment on these provisions.

On January 9, 1976, regulations were issued under this part (41 FR 1672) to conform Regulation X to the RESPA Amendments. These regulations are now superseded by the following Regulation X effective June 30, 1976.

On March 29, 1976 (41 FR 13032) the Department issued a notice of proposed rule-making with respect to the Real Estate Settlement Procedures Act. This proposal would implement the entire RESPA program including certain suspended provisions, and would make various technical and editorial changes.

Over 240 comments were received and the Department is now issuing a final rule which adopt various changes to the proposed regulations. These changes are set forth hereinafter. Most of these changes are in response to comment, however the Department is making certain other modifications at its own initiative. Of the technical changes being made hereby, of principal note is the recodification of these RESPA regulations under 24 CFR Chapter XX. In the time since the first RESPA regulations were issued, the Department has established a new Assistant Secretary for Consumer Affairs and Regulatory Functions to whom responsibility for the program has been delegated, 41 FR 19365. Since parts 0-199 are reserved under Subtitle VIII to the use of the Secretary, these RESPA regulations should properly now be incorporated in Chapter XX and are therefore being recodified in that Chapter as Part 3500.

SUMMARY OF RESPA PROVISIONS

General. While many comments submitted indicated general acceptance of RESPA requirements, there were numerous specific comments directed at improving or deleting particular sections. Only a few commenters called for the outright repeal of RESPA on the grounds that these provisions would not assist consumers, but would create unnecessary work for lenders and additional costs to consumers. Many commenters felt that lenders should be given considerable flexibility in implementing RESPA provisions because of the wide variations of settlement procedures between localities. The regulations have been amended to achieve flexibility.

Coverage.   Coverage of RESPA and Regulation X has been restricted to first mortgage loans secured by 1-4 family residential properties made by a federally regulated or insured lender (see §3500.5). Included in the definition of a "federally related mortgage loan" is the refinancing of land sales contracts where the proceeds of the loan are used to finance the acquisition of legal title pursuant to the land sales contract. Otherwise, if legal title is not transferred to the purchaser upon execution of the contract the transaction is not covered by the regulations. Loans eligible for but not intended to be sold by the originating lender to the Federal National Mortgage Association (FNMA), Government National Mortgage Association (GNMA), or the Federal Home Loan Mortgage Corporation (FHLMC), or to a financial institution from which it is to be purchased by FHLMC are exempt. Also exempt are all construction loans, assumptions, novations, and sales or transfers subject to a preexisting loan (except as noted in §3500.5(d) (4, 5 & 6) of the regulations).

Reliance upon Rule, Regulation, or Interpretation.   The Secretary is authorized by section 19 of RESPA to prescribe such rules, regulations and interpretations as are necessary to achieve the purposes of RESPA. Any act done or omitted in good faith in conformity with such rules, regulations or interpretations will not result in liability under the Act or state law. Rules, regulations or interpretations have been defined to include Regulation X, the Uniform Settlement Statement (HUD-1) and Appendices to Regulation X. A number of commenters suggested that this definition be extended to written statements from the Secretary, General Counsel, and Assistant Secretary for Consumer Affairs and Regulatory Functions. Where a question arises as to the application of a provision (except for Section 8 of RESPA and related issues), to a specific fact situation, the Assistant Secretary for Consumer Affairs and Regulatory Functions may issue a written response. Such response, however, would not constitute an "interpretation" pursuant to Section 19 of RESPA. Where the situation is a product of state law or otherwise likely to recur, the Secretary may issue a binding interpretative ruling by appending said ruling to Regulation X and by publication of the letter of interpretation in the FEDERAL REGISTER.

Special Information Booklet and Good Faith Estimates.   The proposed regulations required the lender to provide the borrower with a Special Information Booklet no later than one day after the lender receives or prepares a written mortgage loan application on an application form or forms normally used by that lender. A number of commenters indicated that it would be extremely difficult to provide the good faith estimates within one business day of receipt where the application is received by an agent who normally would not provide such estimates. The Department has modified the proposed regulations to meet this concern by allowing up to three business days after loan application. The intent of the regulations is to provide the good faith estimates as soon as possible.

The proposed regulations of March 29 provided for inclusion in the Special Information Booklet of information where the lender required use of a particular provider or three or less providers for a particular service.

The regulations published for effect instead require a statement as part of the good faith estimates where the lender requires a particular provider to be used. The revised requirement only applies where one provider is required to be used by the lender, and only requires identification of the provider and a statement whether the provider has a business relationship with the lender. There is no requirement to describe the business relationship. Numerous comments were received objecting to the proposed requirement for a statement whether other providers would provide the service at a lower cost. That requirement has been deleted.

In such cases, the lender is required to base the estimate of the charge on the lender's knowledge of charges imposed by the selected provider. These requirements, which are contained in Section 3500.7(b) and (e), are issued pursuant to RESPA Section 5(c). It should be noted that House Report No. 94-667 regarding the RESPA amendments stated at page 5: "Where the lender will arrange to have a settlement service provided by a particular provider, the prospective borrower should be so informed and the estimates given should reflect the lender's knowledge of the cost of that service."

Form of Good Faith Estimates. Section 5(c) of RESPA requires that the lender provide the borrower with the booklet and a good faith estimate of the amount or range for each charge for specific settlement services that the borrower is likely to incur in connection with the settlement. In the March 29th proposed rules, good faith estimates were required for a subset of settlement charges. Comment was made to the effect that estimates for charges computed on the basis of the actual date of settlement (reserves and prepaid items) could not be provided. Based on public comments, Regulation X was revised to require that lenders provide good faith estimates for all settlement services reported in Section L of the Uniform Settlement Statement except item 903 and series 1000 (Reserves Deposited with Lender). With respect to item 901 (Prepaid Interest) and 902 (Prepaid Mortgage Insurance Premium) the lender is required to state the maximum amount which can be collected at settlement. The lender's reserve requirements were not included in the required disclosure because the date of settlement and other variables are not usually within the lender's knowledge at time of loan application and represented a considerable origination burden.

The techniques used to develop the good faith estimates for either approach have not been specified in the regulations and are left to the lender. The Department recognizes that there are several ways of arriving at good faith estimates and the regulations do not restrict lenders to any specific approach. However, under Section 3500.7(b), the estimate of the amount or range of cost must bear a reasonable relationship to the borrower's ultimate cost for each settlement charge.

Uniform Settlement Statement (HUD-1). The regulation now permits lenders substantial flexibility in reproducing HUD-1 with adjustments to the form to allow for variations in settlement services between localities. The regulations provide that where the blank lines on HUD-1 are not adequate to take care of local insertions, additional spaces may be added without HUD approval. Also the previous restrictions on distances between lines and the size of the page have been removed. This means that space or lines may be added vertically and horizontally where the space on the HUD-1 is inadequate. This will permit, for example, listing pay-offs of prior liens and the time periods involved in prorations. In addition, the regulations do not restrict type size or style and do not require that local insertions appear in a different style of type. Finally, it is no longer necessary for information concerning sellers costs to be included on the buyer's copy of HUD-1 and vice versa.

Numerous comments were received indicating the need for additional space on the form for the inclusion of customary recitals and information used locally in real estate settlement. The regulations now provide that an additional page may be attached to HUD-1 for this purpose or, if space on the form permits, this information may be added at the end of the form.

Several comments indicated a need for signature lines other than after line 1400 of the form. The final regulations do not restrict the place of signature lines on the form. A few commenters suggested that the HUD-1 not be changed from its original format due to the cost of modifying their computer programs. The changes reflected in the revision of the form are based on experience gained from both manual and computer use of the form. The greater flexibility allowed in the final regulations to simplify the design of the form for computer application should minimize extensive reprogramming.

All settlement service charges are to be included in Section L of the HUD-1 except charges for services which (1) are not required by the Lender and (2) are paid for separately outside of settlement. When the lender requires the borrower to secure a settlement service and it is paid outside of settlement, the charge is to be included in Section L and noted as a charge paid outside of settlement.

Many comments requested that the authority to exhaust supplies of the original HUD-1 be extended to all persons conducting settlement as well as lenders. the regulations have been modified to permit this. The form has also been modified to cover situations where the lender is not the person conducting settlement. The person conducting the settlement is required to provide the lender with a copy which contains both buyer and seller information. The lender is required to retain this copy for two years, and, if a copy is required by HUD or another Federal agency, a legible reproduction of this copy may be used.

In enacting the RESPA Amendments, Congress concluded that there were certain RESPA transactions for which use of the Uniform Settlement Statement should not be required. The final regulations exempt from the use of HUD-1, RESPA transactions in which the borrower is not required to pay any settlement charges or adjustments. Also exempted are transactions in which the total amount the borrower is required to pay at settlement is a fixed amount and the borrower is so informed at the time of loan application.

Section 4 of RESPA now requires (1) that the Uniform Settlement Statement be completed and delivered at or before settlement by the person conducting settlement and (2) that on the business day before settlement, the borrower, upon request, be allowed to inspect such Uniform Settlement Statement information as the person conducting settlement has available. HUD was given the authority to exempt from this provision those settlement transactions occurring in localities where the Uniform Settlement Statement is not customarily provided at or before the date of settlement or where meeting this requirement is impractical. Numerous comments were received requesting an exemption. The Department decided not to provide blanket exemptions by jurisdiction as proposed in the March 29 proposed rules because this would result in inequities to borrowers. Exemptions tied to the specific types of transactions were considered more appropriate. The regulations, §3500.10(d), exempt those particular settlement transactions where the borrower (or the borrower's agent) does not attend the settlement or where the person conducting settlement does not require a meeting. This is intended to cover the "escrow" type closings and special situations where the borrower or borrower's agent traditionally is not present at the settlement. When a transaction qualifies under this exemption, the person conducting settlement is required to mail to both the borrower and the seller the Uniform Settlement Statement as soon as practicable after settlement.

Prohibition Against Kickbacks and Unearned Fees.   The proposed rules of March 29 contained regulations pertaining to kickbacks and unearned fees. Most changes in these regulations were limited to clarifying language. A change from the proposed rules is contained in §3500.14(d) which clarifies the Department's intention that a payment of a thing of value pursuant to an agreement or understanding that settlement will be referred is a violation of Section 8. Two new fact-comment situations, No. 9 and No. 10, were added to Appendix B to respond to industry practices developed partially in response to the Section 8 prohibitions.

Distribution of Revised Booklet and Form.   The Department expects that lenders will use regular sources of supplies to secure copies of the Special Information Booklet and HUD-1. Recognizing that regular sources may not have these documents before June 30, the Department intends to provide each lender (supervised by the Federal Home Loan Bank Board, Federal Reserve Board, Federal Deposit Insurance Corporation, Comptroller of the Currency, National Credit Union Administration or HUD) a copy of the final booklet. This copy will be mailed to the lender by the appropriate supervising agency. Lenders will be authorized to duplicate copies for distribution to loan applicants. Lenders who are not supervised by the before mentioned agencies, and who need a copy of the Special Information Booklet and HUD-1, can submit a request to the Assistant Secretary for Consumer Affairs and Regulatory Functions (including a self-addressed label). A copy of both the booklet and the form will be sent. The address is Suite 4100, Attention: RESPA, Department of Housing and Urban Development, 451 7th Street SW., Washington, D.C. 20410.

A finding of inapplicability of section 102(2)(C) of the National Environmental Policy Act of 1969 has been made with respect to this rule, in accordance with HUD Handbook Section 1300.1 A similar finding of inapplicability, as required by OMB circular A-107, has been made with respect to potential inflation impact of the rule. Copies of these findings are available during regular business hours for public inspection in the Office of the Rules Docket Clerk, Office of the Secretary, Room 10141, Department of Housing and Urban Development, 451 7th Street, SW., Washington, D.C.

Accordingly, Subtitle B of Title 24 is amended by adopting a new Part 3500-Real Estate Settlement Procedures to read as follows:

AUTHORITY: Real Estate Settlement Procedures Act of 1974, Pub. L. 93-533 (12 U.S.C. 2601 et seq.), Real Estate Settlement Procedures Act Amendments of 1975 (Pub. L. 94-205).

§3500.1   Authority, scope and purpose.

This part, which may be referred to as Regulation X, comprises the regulations issued by the Secretary of Housing and Urban Development pursuant to the Real Estate Settlement Procedures Act of 1974 (Pub. L. 93-533), 12 U.S.C. 2061, et seq., as amended by the Real Estate Settlement Procedures Act Amendments of 1975 (Pub. L. 94-205) herein "RESPA".

§3500.2   Definitions.

(a) "Date of Settlement" means the date on which the documents creating the security interest in real property become effective as between the borrower and the Lender, except that in the conversion of a construction loan to a permanent security interest in real property to finance purchase by a first user,

Date of Settlement shall be the date on which title is transferred as between seller and buyer not subject to revocation by seller or buyer.

(b) "Federally Related Mortgage Loan" is defined in §3500.5.

(c) "Lender" means the secured creditor or creditors named as such in the debt obligation and document creating the lien or other security interest.

(d) "Mortgaged Property" means the real property covered by the Federally Related Mortgage Loan, or the cooperative unit with respect to which stock is pledged to secure the Federally Related Mortgage Loan.

(e) "Person" means any individual, corporation, partnership, trust, association or other entity.

(f) "RESPA" means the Real Estate Settlement Procedures Act of 1974 (Pub. L. 93-533), U.S.C. 2601 et seq., as amended by the Real Estate Settlement Procedures Act Amendments of 1975 (Pub. L. 94-205).

(g) "Secretary" means the Secretary of Housing and Urban Development or any official delegated the authority of the Secretary with respect to RESPA.

(h) "State" means any State of the United States, the District of Columbia, the Commonwealth of Puerto Rico, and any territory or possession of the United States.

§35.03   No delegation of authority to HUD Field Offices.

No authority granted to the Secretary under RESPA has been delegated to HUD Regional Offices, HUD Area Offices or HUD Insuring Offices. Any questions or suggestions from the public regarding RESPA should be directed to the Office of Consumer Affairs and Regulatory Functions, Attention: RESPA, Department of Housing and Urban Development, Room 4100, 451 7th Street, SW., Washington, D.C. 20410.

§3500.4   Reliance upon rule, regulation or interpretation by HUD.

(a) Section 19(b) of RESPA provides:

"No provision of this Act or the laws of any State imposing any liability shall apply to any act done or omitted in good faith in conformity with any rule, regulation, or interpretation thereof by the Secretary or the Attorney General, notwithstanding that after such act or omission has occurred, such rule, regulation, or interpretation is amended, rescinded, or determined by judicial or other authority to be invalid for any reason."

(b) For purposes of Section 19(b) of RESPA only the following constitute a "rule, regulation, or interpretation therof by the Secretary":

(1) The Uniform Settlement Statement, HUD-1, and HUD instructions set forth in Appendix A; and

(2) All other provisions, Appendices and Amendments thereto contained in

this part, but not including any document referred to in this part except to the extent such document is set forth in this part.

(c) A "rule, regulation, or interpretation thereof by the Secretary" for purposes of section 19(b) of RESPA shall not include the Special Information Booklet prescribed by the Secretary or any other statement or issuance, whether oral or written, by an officer or representative of HUD, letter or memorandum by the Secretary, General Counsel, any Assistant Secretary or other officer or employee of HUD, preamble to a regulation or other issuance of HUD, report to Congress, pleading, affidavit or other document in litigation, pamphlet, handbook, guide, telegraphic communication, explanation, instructions to forms, speech or other material of any nature which is not specifically included in paragraph (b) of this section.

§3500.5   Coverage of RESPA.

(a) *Applicability.*   RESPA and this part as applicable to all Federally Related Mortgage Loans.

(b) *Definition of Federally Related Mortgage Loan.*   "Federally Related Mortgage Loan" means a loan which is not made to finance an exempt transaction specified in subsection (d), below, and which meets all of the following four requirements:

(1) The proceeds of the loan are used in whole or in part to finance the purchase by the borrower, or other transfer of legal title of the Mortgaged Property. Execution of an instrument creating a security interest is not considered to be a transfer of legal title for purposes of this part;

(2) The loan is secured by a first lien or other first security interest covering real estate, including a fee simple, life estate, remainder interest, ground lease or other long-term leasehold estate:

(i) Upon which there is located a structure designed principally for the occupancy of from 1 to 4 families; or

(ii) Upon which there is located a mobile home; or

(iii) Upon which a structure designed principally for the occupancy of from 1 to 4 families is to be constructed using proceeds of the loan; or

(iv) Upon which there will be placed a mobile home to be purchased using proceeds of the loan; or

(v) Which is a condominium unit (or a first lien covering a cooperative unit) designed principally for the occupancy of from 1 to 4 families;

(3) The Mortgaged Property is located in a State; and

(4) The loan (i) is made by a Lender meeting the requirements of paragraph (c), below, or (ii) is made in whole or in part, or insured, guaranteed, supplemented, or assisted in any way, by the Secretary or other officer or agency of the Federal Government, or (iii) is made in connection with a housing or urban development program administered by the Secretary or other agency of the Federal Government, or (iv) is intended to be sold by the originating lender to the Federal National Mortgage Association (FNMA), the Government National Mortgage Association (GNMA), or the Federal Home

Loan Mortgage Corporation (FHLMC), or to a financial institution which intends to sell the mortgage to FHLMC.

(c) A Lender is within paragraph (b)(4)(i) if it is:

(1) A lending institution the deposits or accounts of which are insured by the Federal Savings and Loan Corporation (FSLIC), the Federal Deposit Insurance Corporation (FDIC) or any other agency of the Federal Government.

(2) A lending institution which is regulated by the Federal Home Loan Bank Board or any other agency of the Federal Government, or

(3) A "creditor", as defined in section 103(f) of the Consumer Credit Protection Act (15 U.S.C. 1602(f)), who makes or invests in residential real estate loans aggregating more than $1,000,000 in either the calendar year in which the Date of Settlement of the Federally Related Mortgage Loan in question occurs or the calendar year prior thereto, except that the term "creditor" does not include any agency or instrumentality of any state. Section 103(f) of the Consumer Credit Protection Act defines "creditor" as follows:

". . . The term 'creditor' refers only to creditors who regularly extend, or arrange for the extension of, credit which is payable by agreement in more than four installments or for which the payment of a finance charge is or may be required, whether in connection with loans, sales of property or services, or otherwise."

(d) *Exempt transactions.* This part shall not apply to:

(1) A loan to finance the purchase or transfer of a property of 25 or more acres;

(2) A home improvement loan, loan to refinance, or other loan where the proceeds are not used to finance the purchase or transfer of legal title to the property;

(3) A loan to finance the purchase or transfer of a vacant lot, where no proceeds of the loan are to be used for the construction of a 1 to 4 family residential structure or for the purchase of a mobile home to be placed on the lot;

(4) An assumption, novation, or sale or transfer subject to a pre-existing loan, except that the use of or conversion of a construction loan to a permanent mortgage loan to finance purchase by the first user;

(5) A construction loan, except where the construction loan is used as or converted to a permanent loan to finance purchase by the first user;

(6) A permanent loan the proceeds of which will be used to finance the construction of a 1 to 4 family structure, where the lot is already owned by the borrower or borrowers;

(7) A loan to finance the purchase of a property where the primary purpose of the purchase is for resale; or

(8) Execution of a land sales contract or installment land contract where the legal title is not transferred to the purchaser upon execution. However, a loan to finance the acquisition of title pursuant to a land sales contract is a Federally Related Mortgage Loan.

§3500.6   Special Information Booklet at time of loan application.

(a) *Lender to provide information booklet.* The Lender shall provide a copy of the Special Information Booklet currently prescribed by the Secretary, together with the Good Faith Estimates of closing costs required under Section 3500.7, to every person from whom the Lender receives or for whom it prepares a written application on an application form or forms normally used by the Lender for a Federally Related Mortgage Loan. Where more than one individual applies for a loan, the Lender is in compliance with this requirement if the Lender supplies a copy of the Special Information Booklet to one of the individuals applying. The Lender shall supply the Special* Booklet by delivering it or placing it in the mail to the applicant on the day the application is received not later than three business days after the application is received. The Lender shall supply the Good Faith Estimates by delivering or placing* the mail or not later than three business days after the application is received. [The Lender shall complete the Equal Credit Opportunity Notice, located on the inside rear cover of the Special Information Booklet, in accordance with Regulation B, 12 CFR 202.4(d) of the Federal Reserve Board.]

(b) *Printing and duplication.* The Secretary may from time to time revise the Special Information Booklet. The Special Information Booklet may be printed or reproduced in any form, provided that no change is made, other than as provided under subsection (c) below. The Special Information Booklet may not be made a part of a larger document for purposes of distribution under RESPA and this section. Any color, size and quality of paper, type of print, and method of reproduction may be used so long as the booklet is clearly legible and easily readable.

(c) *Permissible changes.* No changes to, deletions from or additions to the foreword and text of the Special Information Booklet currently prescribed by the Secretary shall be made other than those specified below or any others approved in writing by the Secretary.

(1) The cover of the booklet may be in any form and may contain any drawings, pictures, of artwork, provided that the words "settlement costs" are used in the title. Names, addresses and telephone numbers of the Lender or others and similar information may appear on the cover, but no discussion of the matters covered in the booklet shall appear on the cover.

(2) The Special Information Booklet may be translated into other languages.

§3500.7   Good faith estimates of settlement services.

(a) *Lender to provide Good Faith Estimates with information booklet at time of loan application.* The Lender shall provide the Good Faith Estimates required

---

* The material contained in brackets was deleted by the April 13, 1977 Amendment.

under this section to every person to whom it must provide a copy of the Special Information Booklet under §3500.6 of this part. Time of provision is set forth in §3500.6(a).

(b) *Good Faith Estimate.* The Lender shall provide a good faith estimate, as a dollar amount or range, of each charge for a settlement service which the borrower is likely to incur. Each such good faith estimate must bear a reasonable relationship to the charge a borrower is likely to be required to pay at settlement, and must be based upon experience in the locality or area in which the Mortgaged Property is located.

As to each charge with respect to which the Lender requires a particular settlement service provider to be used, the Lender shall make its good faith estimate based upon the Lender's knowledge of the amounts charged by such provider.

(c) *Settlement Services for which Good Faith Estimates are required.* The Lender is required to provide the loan applicant with a Good Faith Estimate for each settlement charge which will be listed in Section L (except item 903 and series 1000 of Section L) of the Uniform Settlement Statement which the Lender anticipates that the borrower will pay at settlement based upon the Lender's general experience as to which party normally pays each charge in the locality.

*(d) *Form of Good Faith Estimates.* The Lender may provide the loan applicant with the required Good Faith Estimates on any form, including Section L, of the Uniform Settlement Statement, which the Lender determines to use, if the following requirements are met:

(1) The form must be clear and concise. It shall include the Lender's name. The form shall set forth in bold type the following or a substantially equivalent statement:

"This form does not cover all items you will be required to pay in cash at settlement, for example, deposit in escrow for real estate taxes and insurance. You may wish to inquire as to the amounts of such other items."
You may be required to pay other additional amounts at settlement

(2) The terminology shall be identical, so far as practicable, to the terms used in the Uniform Settlement Statement (HUD-1) or the terms which will be inserted in blank spaces in the Uniform Settlement Statement. Lenders are encouraged, but are not required, to set forth the items numbers for each item which appears in the Uniform Settlement Statement (HUD-1).

(3) Additional information relating to a stated item may be provided. Charges which may be grouped together pursuant to the instructions of the Uniform Settlement Statement may be grouped in this disclosure. For example, the amount for several title charges (listed as lines 1101-1106 of the Uniform Settlement Statement) may, in some jurisdictions, customarily be included in an attorney's fee (listed as line 1107).

(e) *Description of Lender's requirements on selection of providers.* Where the Lender requires that a particular provider (or affiliated group of providers, such as a law firm) be used to provide legal services, title examination services or title insurance or to conduct settlement and requires the borrower to pay all or a portion of the cost of such services (regardless of the interests represented by the provider), the Lender is required to include as part of the Good Faith Estimate, a statement which clearly designates the corresponding estimated charges, and states:

(1) The name, address and telephone number of each provider designated by the Lender, the services which would be rendered by such provider, and the fact that Lender's estimate is based upon the charges of the designated provider; and

(2) A statement whether or not each such provider has a business relationship with the Lender.

(f) As to each Federally Related Mortgage Loan which is exempt from the use of the Uniform Settlement Statement by reason of Section 3500.8(d) of this part, the lender shall keep an accurate record for two years of the itemized list of the settlement services provided, the exact charge, if any, which is to be imposed at settlement, and the subparagraph (Section 3500.8(d)(1) or (d)(2) under which the exemption is granted. With respect to a transaction which is exempt under Section 3500.8(d)(2), the lender shall deliver or place in the mail to the borrower not later than three business days after loan application a statement of the amount of the fixed charge and a statement of the settlement services and other items covered by such charge.

§3500.8 Use of Uniform Settlement Statement Form.

(a) *Use of HUD-1.* As required by section 4 of RESPA, the Uniform Settlement Statement (HUD-1, set forth in Appendix A) shall be used by the person conducting settlement in every Federally Related Mortgage Loan settlement transaction whether or not such person is the Lender. Persons conducting settlements may exhaust supplies of the original HUD-1 which are in stock at the time these regulations take effect.

(b) *Charges to be stated.* The Uniform Settlement Statement, HUD-1, shall be completed to itemize all charges to be paid by the borrower and the seller in connection with the settlement, except those charges not imposed upon the borrower or seller by the Lender and which the borrower or seller contract to pay for separately outside of the settlement. Charges which are required by the Lender but paid outside of closing shall be included on the statement but marked "P.O.C.", as provided in the general instructions to the form. Lines and columns which relate to the borrower's transaction may be deleted from the copy of the form which will be furnished to the seller and lines and columns which relate to the seller's transaction may be deleted from the copy of the form which will be furnished to the borrower.

(c) *Recordkeeping.* The person conducting the settlement shall provide the Lender with a copy of each settlement statement (both borrower's and seller's copies, where different) required to be prepared pursuant to section 4 of RESPA. The Lender shall retain the settlement statement for two years after the date of settlement unless the Lender disposes of its interest in the mortgage and does not service the mortgage. The Lender may permit its copy of the settlement statement to be delivered to the owner or servicer of the mortgage as a part of the transfer of the loan file. If copy of the settlement statement is required to be submitted to the Secretary or other Federal agency, a legible reproduction of the copy retained by the Lender may be used to meet this requirement.

(d) *RESPA Transactions exempt from the use of the Uniform Settlement Statement.*

(1) Transactions in which the borrower is not required to pay any settlement charges or adjustments.

(2) Transactions in which the borrower is required to pay a fixed amount for all charges imposed at settlement and the borrower is informed of the fixed amount at the time of loan application.

§3500.9 Printing and duplication of Uniform Settlement Statement Form.

(a) *Permissible changes.*   The Uniform Settlement Statement form, HUD-1, may be reproduced with the following permissible changes and insertions:

(1) The person reproducing the form may insert in Section A its business name and/or logotype and may rearrange, but not delete, the other information which appears in Section A.

(2) The name, address and other information regarding the Lender and settlement agent (person conducting settlement), respectively, may be printed in Sections F and H.

(3) Reproduction of HUD-1 must conform to the terminology, sequence and numbering of line items as presented in lines 100-1400 which are not used locally or in connection with mortgages by the Lender may be deleted, except for the following: Lines 100, 120, 200, 220, 300, 301, 302, 303, 400, 420, 500, 520, 600, 601, 602, 603, 700, 800, 900, 1000, 1100, 1200, 1300, and 1400. The form may be correspondingly shortened. The number of a deleted item shall not be used for a substitute or new item, but the number of a blank space on HUD-1 may be used for a substitute or new item.

(4) Charges not listed on HUD-1 but which are customary locally or pursuant to the Lender's practice may be inserted in blank spaces; or where existing blank spaces on HUD-1 are insufficient, additional lines and spaces may be added and numbered in sequence with HUD-1 spaces.

(5) The following variations in layout and format are within the discretion of persons reducing HUD-1 and do not require prior HUD approval: size of pages; tint or color of pages; size and style of type or print; vertical spacing between lines or provision for additional horizontal space on lines (for example, to provide sufficient space for recording time periods used in prorations); printing of HUD-1 contents on separate pages, on the front and back of a single page, or on one continuous page; use of multi-copy tear-out sets; printing on rolls for computer purposes: reorganization of Sections B through I where necessary to accommodate computer printing; placement on the form* the HUD number but not the OMB approval number, neither of which in any case may be deleted from the form.

(6) The borrower's information and the seller's information may be provided on separate pages.

(7) Signature lines may be added.

(8) The form may be translated into any other language.

(9) An additional page may be attached to HUD-1 for the purpose of including customary recitals and information used locally in real estate settlements, for example, breakdown of payoff figures; a breakdown of mortgagor's total monthly mortgage payments; check disbursements; a statement indicating receipt of funds; applicable special stipulations between buyer and seller; and the date funds are transferred. If space permits, such information may be added at the end of HUD-1.

(b) Any other deviation in the form is only permissible upon receipt of written approval of the Secretary. A request to the Secretary for approval may be submitted in writing to the Assistant Secretary for Consumer Affairs and Regulatory Functions, Attention: RESPA, Room 4100, 451 7th Street, SW., Washington, D.C. 20410, stating the reasons why the applicant believes such deviation is needed. Prior to receiving such approval, the prescribed form must be used.

§3500.10   One day advance inspection of Uniform Settlement Statement; delivery.

(a) *Inspection one day prior to settlement.*   Except as provided in paragraph (d), upon the request of the borrower, the person conducting the settlement shall permit the borrower to inspect the Uniform Settlement Statement, completed to set forth those items which are known to such person at the time of inspection, during the business day immediately preceding the Date of Settlement.

(b) *Delivery.*   The Uniform Settlement Statement shall be delivered or mailed to the borrower and the seller or their agents at or before settlement, except as provided in paragraphs (c) and (d).

(c) *Waiver.*   The borrower may waive the right to delivery of the completed Uniform Settlement Statement no later than at settlement by executing a written waiver at or before settlement. In such case, the completed Uniform Settlement Statement shall be mailed or delivered to the borrower and seller as soon as practicable after settlement.

(d) *Exempt transactions.*   Where the borrower or the borrower's agent does not attend the settlement or where the person conducting settlement does not require a meeting of the parties for that purpose, the transaction shall be exempt from the requirements of paragraphs (a) and (b) above, except that the Uniform Settlement Statement shall be delivered as soon as practicable after settlement.

§3500.11   Mailing.

The provisions of this part requiring or permitting mailing of settlement statements or other documents shall be deemed to be satisfied by placing the document in the mail (whether or not received by the addressee) addressed to the addresses stated in the loan application or in other information submitted to or obtained by Lender at the time of loan application, or submitted to or obtained by the Lender or person conducting settlement, except that a revised address shall be used where the Lender or such other person has been expressly informed in writing of a change of address.

§3500.12   No fee.

As provided in section 12 of RESPA, no fee shall be imposed or charge made upon any other person, as a part of settlement costs or otherwise, by a Lender in connection with or on account of the preparation and distribution of the statement required by section 4 of RESPA (Uniform Settlement Statement) or by the Truth in Lending Act.

§3500.13   Relation to State laws.

Section 18 of RESPA provides:

This Act does not annul, alter, or affect or exempt any person subject to the provisions of this Act from complying with the laws of any State with respect to settlement practices, except to the extent that those laws are inconsistent with any provision of this Act, and then only to the extent of the inconsistency. The Secretary is authorized to determine whether such inconsistencies exist. The Secretary may not determine that any State law is inconsistent with any provision of this Act if the Secretary determines that such law gives greater protection to the consumer. In making these determinations the Secretary shall consult with the appropriate Federal agencies.

A determination by the Secretary that such an inconsistency exists shall be made, after consultation with appropriate Federal agencies, by publication of a notice in the FEDERAL REGISTER.

§3500.14   Prohibition against kickbacks and unearned fees.

(a) *Statutory prohibitions.*   Section 8 of RESPA provides:

(a) No person shall give and no person shall accept any fee, kickback, or thing of value pursuant to any agreement or understanding, oral or otherwise, that business incident to or a part of a real estate settlement service involving a federally related mortgage loan shall be referred to any person.

(b) No person shall give and no person shall accept any portion, split, or percentage of any charge made or received for the rendering of a real estate settlement service in connection with a transaction involving a federally related mortgage loan other than for services actually performed.

(c) Nothing in this section shall be construed as prohibiting (1) the payment of a fee (A) to attorneys at law for services actually rendered or (B) by a title company to its duly appointed agent for services actually performed in the issuance of a policy of title insurance or (C) by a lender to its duly appointed agent for services actually performed in the making of a loan, (2) the payment to any person of a bona fide salary or compensation of other payment for goods or facilities actually furnished or for services actually performed,

or (3) payments pursuant to cooperative brokerage and referral arrangements or agreements between real estate agents and brokers, or (4) such other payments or classes of payments or other transfers as are specified in regulations prescribed by the Secretary, after consultation with the Attorney General, the Administrator of Veterans' Affairs, the Federal Home Loan Bank Board, the Federal Deposit Insurance Corporation, the Board of Governors of the Federal Reserve System, and the Secretary of Agriculture.

(d)(1) Any person or persons who violate the provisions of this section shall be fined not more than $10,000 or imprisoned for not more than one year, or both

(2) In addition to the penalties provided by paragraph (1) of this subsection, any person or persons who violate the provisions of subsection (a) shall be jointly and severally liable to the person or persons whose business has been referred in an amount equal to three times the value or amount of the fee or thing of value, and any person or persons who violate the provisions of subsection (b) shall be jointly and severally liable to the person or persons charged for the settlement services involved in an amount equal to three times the amount of the portion, split, or percentage. In any successful action to enforce the liability under this paragraph, the court may award the court costs of the action together with a reasonable attorney's fee as determined by the court.

(b) *Thing of value.*   "Thing of value" is broadly defined by section 3(2) of RESPA to include any payment, advance, fund, loan, service, or other consideration. Under section 8 of RESPA, a thing of value may be provided either directly or indirectly to the person referring settlement business and can take many forms including, but not limited to, monies, things, discounts, salaries, commissions, fees, duplicate payments of a charge, stock, dividends, distributions of partnership profits, credits representing monies that may be paid at a future date, special bank deposits or accounts, banking terms, special loan or loan guarantee terms, services of all types at special or free rates, and sales or rentals at special prices or rates.

(c) *Agreement or understanding.*   An agreement or understanding for the referral of settlement business need not be verbalized but may be established by a practice, pattern or course of conduct pursuant to which the payor and recipient of the thing of value understand that the payment is in return for the referral of business. A payment that is made repeatedly and is connected to any way with the volume or value of the business referred to the payor by the recipient is presumptively pursuant to an agreement or understanding.

(d) *Payment of thing of value for referral of business.*   Any person who gives and any person who receives any fee, kickback or thing of value that represents compensation for the referral of business incident to or a part of a real estate settlement service is in violation of section 8 of RESPA. The fact that the payment of the thing of value does not result in an increase in the charge made for the settlement service by the payor in the particular transaction is irrelevant in determining whether the payment is prohibited.

(e) *Payment for goods or services actually rendered.*   The payment and receipt of a thing of value that bears a reasonable relationship to the value of the goods or services received by the person or company making the payment is not prohibited by RESPA section 8. To the extent the thing of value is in excess of the reasonable value of the goods provided or services performed, the excess is not for services actually rendered and may be considered a kickback or referral fee proscribed by RESPA section 8. The value of the referral itself (i.e., the additional business obtained thereby) is not to be taken into account in determining whether the payment is reasonable.

(f) *Exemptions.*   The following are not proscribed by RESPA section 8:

(1) The payment of a fee (a) to attorneys at law for services actually rendered, or (b) by a title company to its duly appointed agent for services actually performed in the issuance of a policy of title insurance, or (c) by a Lender to its duly appointed agent for services actually performed in the making of a loan.

(2) The payment to any person of a bona fide salary, compensation or other payment for goods or facilities actually furnished or for services actually performed.

(3) Payments pursuant to cooperative brokerage and referral arrangements or agreements between real estate agents and brokers.

(4) Normal promotional and educational activities not directly conditioned on the referral of business and that do not involve the defraying of expenses that otherwise would be incurred by persons in a position to refer settlement business, such as a reception by a title company, free seminars on title matters to professionals, furnishing property descriptions and names of record owners without charge to persons such as Lenders, real estate brokers or attorneys or distribution of calendars and other promotional material of nominal value.

(5) The waiver by a Lender of the requirement that a borrower pay a prepayment penalty provided in mortgage documents, whether or not such waiver is conditioned upon receipt by the Lender of a loan application from, or the making of a loan to, such borrower or a person purchasing a property from such borrower. This exemption is established pursuant to authority to establish exemptions from Section 8 of RESPA; and is not applicable by analogy to any category of cases other than waiver of prepayment penalties.

(g) *Examples of violations under section 8.*   The following are examples of violations under section 8 and are applicable by analogy to other providers of settlement services in addition to those specified in the examples:

(1) A title company pays a portion of the title insurance premium to a person who performs no services for the title company other than placing an application with the title company.

(2) A title company gives a discount or allowance for the prompt payment of a title insurance premium or other charge for a settlement service to a real estate agent, attorney or lender as a rebate for the placement of business with such title company.

(3) An attorney gives a portion of his fees to another attorney, a Lender or a real estate agent who only referred a prospective client to the attorney.

(4) A title company pays a "commission" to a corporation that is wholly owned by one or more Lenders, even though such corporation performs no substantial services on behalf of the title company.

Appendix A—Instructions for Completing Uniform Settlement Statement (HUD-1)

The following are instructions for completing sections A through L of the Uniform Settlement Statement HUD-1, required under section 4 of RESPA and called Regulation X. This form is to be used as a uniform statement of actual costs and adjustments to be given to the parties in connection with the settlement. The instructions for completion of the form are primarily for the benefit of the persons who prepare the statements and need not be transmitted to the parties as an integral part of the form. Refer to Regulation X of the Department of Housing and Urban Development (24 CFR Part 3500) to determine if the Uniform Settlement Statement is legally required to be used in a particular mortgage loan transaction. There is no objection of the use of the form in transactions in which its use is not legally required.

GENERAL INSTRUCTIONS

Information and amounts may be filled in by typewriter, hand printing, computer printing, or any other method producing clear and legible results. Copies of the form sent to the borrower and the seller may be carbon copies or other clear legible copies. Refer to Regulation X regarding rules applicable to printing of the form. An additional page may be attached to HUD-1 for the purpose of including customary recitals and information used locally in real estate settlements, for example, a breakdown of payoff figures; a breakdown of mortgagor's total monthly mortgage payments; check disbursements; a statement indicating receipt of funds; applicable special stipulations between buyer and seller; and the date funds are transferred. The reverse side of the form may be used instead of an additional sheet.

Where charges are paid outside of the settlement (normally by separate check), but are included in the requirements of §3500.8(b), they shall be stated with the notation "P.O.C." (Paid outside closing) and shall not be included in computing totals. In accordance with §3500.8(b), charges not imposed upon the borrower or seller by the Lender and which borrower or seller contract to pay for separately outside of the settlement, need not be entered on HUD-1.

Instructions for completing the individual items on the form follow. Where no instructions are given, the item is thought to be self-explanatory.

Section A. The Lender, title company, other firm, or other person conducting settlement and preparing the form may insert its name and/or logotype in Section A.

Section B. Check appropriate loan type and complete the remaining items as applicable.

Sections D and E. Fill in the names and current mailing addresses and zip codes of the borrower and the seller. Where there is more than one buyer or seller, the name and address of one is sufficient.

Section G. The street address of the secured property, should be given. If there is no street address, a brief legal description or other location of the property should be inserted. In all cases give the zip code of the property.

Section H. Fill in name, address, and zip code of settlement agent; address and zip code of "place of settlement."

Section J. Summary of Borrower's Transaction. The borrower may be given a copy of the form which does not contain the information filled in under "Summary of Seller's Transaction" (Section K, Series 400, 500, and 600 items).

Lines 104 and 105 are for additional amounts owed by the buyer. For example, the balance in the seller's reserve account held by the Lender, if assigned to the buyer in a loan assumption case, will be entered here. These lines will also be used when a tenant in the property being sold has not yet paid his rent, which the buyer will collect, for a period of time prior to the settlement. The seller will be credited on lines 404-405.

Lines 106 through 112 are for items which the seller had paid in advance, and for which the buyer must therefore reimburse the seller. Examples of items for which adjustments will be made may include taxes and assessments paid in advance for an entire year or other period, when settlement occurs prior to the expiration of the year or other period for which they were paid. Additional examples include flood and hazard insurance premiums, if the buyer is being substituted as an insured under the same policy; mortgage insurance in loan assumption cases; planned unit development or condominium association assessments paid in advance; fuel or other supplies on hand, purchased by the seller, which the buyer will use when buyer takes possession of the property; and ground rent paid in advance.

Line 203 is used for cases in which the buyer is assuming or taking title subject to an existing loan or lien on the property.

Lines 204-209 may be used in cases in which the seller has taken a trade-in or other property from the buyer in part payment for the property being sold. They may also be used in cases in which a seller (typically a builder) is making an "allowance" to the buyer for carpets or drapes which the buyer is to purchase on his own. Such an allowance should also be entered on lines 506 to 509.

Lines 210 through 219 are for items which have not yet been paid, and which the buyer is expected to pay, but which are attributable in part to a period of time prior to the settlement. In jurisdictions in which taxes are paid late in the tax year, most cases will show the proration of taxes in these lines. Other examples include utilities used but not paid for by the seller, rent collected in advance by the seller from a tenant for a period extending beyond the settlement date, and interest on loan assumptions.

Line 303 may indicate either the cash required from the borrower at settlement (the usual case in a purchase transaction) or cash payable to the borrower at settlement (if, for example, the buyer's earnest money deposit exceeded his cash obligations in the transaction). The appropriate box should be checked.

Section K. Summary of Seller's Transaction. The seller may be given a copy of the form which does not contain the information filled in under "Summary of Borrower's Transaction" (Section J, Series 100, 200, and 300 items).

Instructions for the use of lines 106-112, above, apply also to lines 406 to 412.

Line 501 If the seller's real estate broker has received and holds an earnest money deposit which exceeds the commission owed to him, and if he will tender the excess deposit directly to the seller, rather than through the settlement agent, the amount of excess deposit should be entered on line 501.

Line 503 is used if the purchaser is assuming or taking title subject to existing liens which are to be deducted from sales price.

Line 506 through 509 may be used to list additional liens which must be paid off through the settlement to clear title to the property. They may also be used to indicate funds to be held by the settlement agent for the payment of water, fuel, or other utility bills which cannot be prorated between the parties at settlement because the amounts used by the seller prior to settlement are not yet known.

Instructions for the use of lines 510 through 519 are the same as those for lines 210 to 219 above.

Section L. Settlement Charges. For all items except those paid to and retained by the Lender, the name of the person or firm receiving the payment should be shown. The column which relates to the borrower's transaction may be deleted from the copy of the form which will be furnished to the seller and the column which relates to the seller's transaction may be deleted from the copy of the form which will be furnished to the borrower.

Line 700. If the sales commission paid by the seller is based on a percentage of the purchase price, enter the purchase price, the percentage, and the dollar amount of the total commission paid by the seller.

Lines 701-702 are to be used to state the split of the commission where the person conducting the settlement disburses portions of the commission to two or more agents.

Lines 703. If the broker is retaining a part of the earnest money deposit to apply towards his commission, include in lines 703 only that part of the commission being disbursed at settlement.

Line 704 may be used for additional charges made by the sales agent, or for a sales commission charged to the buyer, which will be disbursed by the settlement agent.

Line 801. Enter the fee charged by the Lender for processing or originating the loan. If this fee is computed as a percentage of the loan amount, enter the percentage in the blank indicated.

Line 802. Enter the loan discount charged by the lender, and, if it is computed as a percentage of the loan amount, enter the percentage in the blank indicated.

Line 803. Enter appraisal fees, if there is a charge separate from the origination fee. The VA or FHA appraisal fee is included on line 806.

Line 805 is used only for inspections by the lender or his personnel. Charges for other pest or structural inspections, required by Regulation X to be stated, should be entered in lines 1301-1305.

Line 806 should be used for a VA appraisal fee, FHA application fee (which covers the cost of appraisal for the agency as well), or a fee required by a private mortgage insurance company.

Line 807 is provided for convenience in using the form for loan assumption transactions.

Line 901. If interest is collected at settlement for a part of a month or other period between settlement and the date from which interest will be collected with the first regular monthly payment, enter that amount here. If such interest is not collected until the first regular monthly payment, no entry should be made on line 901.

Lines 1000-1006. This series is used for amounts collected by the Lender from the borrower and held in an account for the future payment of the obligations listed as they fall due. In many jurisdictions this is referred to as an "escrow," "impound," or "trust" account. In addition to the items listed, some Lenders may require reserves for flood insurance, condominium owners association assessments, etc.

Lines 1100-1113. In many jurisdictions the same person (for example, an attorney or a title insurance company) performs several of the services listed in this series and makes a single undifferentiated charge for such services. In such cases, enter the overall fee on line 1107 (for attorneys), or line 1108 (for title companies), and enter on that line the item numbers of the services listed which are covered in the overall fee. If this is done, no amounts should be entered for the individual items which are covered by the overall fee.

Line 1101. Enter here the fee of the person or firm conducting the settlement. In some jurisdictions this is termed a closing or escrow fee. If two or more persons or firms make charges in connection with the same transaction, enter total charges in the appropriate columns, and indicate the breakdown of charges on the line after the word "to."

Lines 1102 and 1103. In some jurisdictions the same person (for example, an attorney) both searches the title (that is, performs the necessary research in the records) and examines title (that is, makes a determination as to what matters affect title, and provides a title report or opinion). If such a person charges only one fee for both services, it should be entered on line 1103. If separate persons perform these tasks, or if separate charges are made for searching and examination, they should be listed separately.

Line 1105. Enter charges for preparation of deeds, mortgages, notes, etc. If more than one person receives a fee for such work in the same transaction, show the total paid in the appropriate column and the individual charges on the line following the word "to."

Lines 1108-1110. Enter the total charge for title insurance (except for the cost of the title binder) on line 1108. Enter on lines 1109 and 1110 the individual charges for the Lender's and owner's policies. Note that these charges are not carried over into the borrower's and seller's columns, since to do so would result in a duplication of the amount in line 1108. If a combination Lender's/owner's policy is available show this amount as an additional entry on line 1109 and 1110.

Lines 1111-1113. These lines are for the entry of other title charges not already itemized. Examples in some jurisdictions would include a fee to a private tax service, a fee to a county tax collector for a tax certificate, and a fee to a public title registrar for a certificate of title under a Torrens Act. Show the Lender's attorney's fee if any on lines 1111-1113.

Lines 1303-1305. Enter on these lines any other settlement charges not referrable to the categories listed above on the form, which are required to be stated by Regulation X. Examples may include structural inspections of pre-sale inspection of heating, plumbing, or electrical equipment. These inspection charges may include a fee for insurance or warranty coverage.

Line 1400. Enter the total settlement charges paid from borrower's funds and seller's funds. These totals are also entered on lines 103 and 502, respectively, in sections J and K.

Form Approved
OMB NO. 63-R-1501

A.	B. TYPE OF LOAN
U.S. DEPARTMENT OF HOUSING AND URBAN DEVELOPMENT SETTLEMENT STATEMENT	1. ☐ FHA 2. ☐ FmHA 3. ☐ CONV. UNINS. 4. ☐ VA 5. ☐ CONV. INS.
	6. File Number: 7. Loan Number:
	8. Mortage Insurance Case Number:

C. NOTE: *This form is furnished to give you a statement of actual settlement costs. Amounts paid to and by the settlement agent are shown. Items marked "(p.o.c.)" were paid outside the closing; they are shown here for informational purposes and are not included in the totals.*

D. NAME OF BORROWER:	E. NAME OF SELLER:	F. NAME OF LENDER:
G. PROPERTY LOCATION:	H. SETTLEMENT AGENT: PLACE OF SETTLEMENT:	I. SETTLEMENT DATE:

J. SUMMARY OF BORROWER'S TRANSACTION		K. SUMMARY OF SELLER'S TRANSACTION	
100. GROSS AMOUNT DUE FROM BORROWER		**400. GROSS AMOUNT DUE TO SELLER:**	
101. Contract sales price		401. Contract sales price	
102. Personal property		402. Personal property	
103. Settlement charges to borrower *(line 1400)*		403.	
104.		404.	
105.		405.	
Adjustments for items paid by seller in advance		*Adjustments for items paid by seller in advance*	
106. City/town taxes to		406. City/town taxes to	
107. County taxes to		407. County taxes to	
108. Assessments to		408. Assessments to	
109.		409.	
110.		410.	
111.		411.	
112.		412.	
120. GROSS AMOUNT DUE FROM BORROWER		**420. GROSS AMOUNT DUE TO SELLER**	
200. AMOUNTS PAID BY OR IN BEHALF OF BORROWER:		**500. REDUCTIONS IN AMOUNT DUE TO SELLER:**	
201. Deposit or earnest money		501. Excess deposit *(see instructions)*	
202. Principal amount of new loan(s)		502. Settlement charges to seller *(line 1400)*	
203. Existing loan(s) taken subject to		503. Existing loan(s) taken subject to	
204.		504. Payoff of first mortgage loan	
205.		505. Payoff of second mortgage loan	
206.		506.	
207.		507.	
208.		508.	
209.		509.	
Adjustments for items unpaid by seller		*Adjustments for items unpaid by seller*	
210. City/town taxes to		510. City/town taxes to	
211. County taxes to		511. County taxes to	
212. Assessments to		512. Assessments to	
213.		513.	
214.		514.	
215.		515.	
216.		516.	
217.		517.	
218.		518.	
219.		519.	
220. TOTAL PAID BY/FOR BORROWER		**520. TOTAL REDUCTION AMOUNT DUE SELLER**	
300. CASH AT SETTLEMENT FROM/TO BORROWER		**600. CASH AT SETTLEMENT FROM/TO SELLER**	
301. Gross amount due from borrower *(line 120)*		601. Gross amount due to seller *(line 420)*	
302. Less amounts paid by/for borrower *(line 220)*	( )	602. Less reductions in amount due seller *(line 520)*	( )
303. CASH (☐ FROM) (☐TO) BORROWER		**603. CASH (☐ FROM) (☐TO) SELLER**	

Previous Edition is Obsolete

HUD-1 (5-76)

L. SETTLEMENT CHARGES	PAID FROM BORROWER'S FUNDS AT SETTLEMENT	PAID FROM SELLER'S FUNDS AT SETTLEMENT
700. TOTAL SALES/BROKER'S COMMISSION based on price $		
Division of Commission (line 700) as follows:		
701. $ to		
702. $ to		
703. Commission paid at Settlement		
704.		
800. ITEMS PAYABLE IN CONNECTION WITH LOAN		
801. Loan Origination Fee %		
802. Loan Discount %		
803. Appraisal Fee to		
804. Credit Report to		
805. Lender's Inspection Fee		
806. Mortgage Insurance Application Fee to		
807. Assumption Fee		
808.		
809.		
810.		
811.		
900. ITEMS REQUIRED BY LENDER TO BE PAID IN ADVANCE		
901. Interest from to @ $ day		
902. Mortgage Insurance Premium for months to		
903. Hazard Insurance Premium for years to		
904. years to		
905.		
1000. RESERVES DEPOSITED WITH LENDER		
1001. Hazard insurance months@ $ per month		
1002. Mortgage insurance months@ $ per month		
1003. City property taxes months@ $ per month		
1004. County property taxes months@ $ per month		
1005. Annual assessments months@ $ per month		
1006. months@ $ per month		
1007. months@ $ per month		
1008. months@ $ per month		
1100. TITLE CHARGES		
1101. Settlement or closing fee to		
1102. Abstract or title search to		
1103. Title examination to		
1104. Title insurance binder to		
1105. Document preparation to		
1106. Notary fees to		
1107. Attorney's fees to		
(includes above items numbers:)		
1108. Title insurance to		
(includes above items numbers:)		
1109. Lender's coverage $		
1110. Owner's coverage $		
1111.		
1112.		
1113.		
1200. GOVERNMENT RECORDING AND TRANSFER CHARGES		
1201. Recording fees Deed $ Mortgage $ Releases $		
1202. City/county tax/stamps Deed $ Mortgage $		
1203. State tax/stamps Deed $ Mortgage $		
1204.		
1205.		
1300. ADDITIONAL SETTLEMENT CHARGES		
1301. Survey to		
1302. Pest inspection to		
1303.		
1304.		
1305.		
1400. TOTAL SETTLEMENT CHARGES (enter on lines 103, Section J and 502, Section K)		

HUD-1 (5-76)

Cases

A

Ackerley v Credit Bureau, Inc, 385 F Supp 658 (DC Wyo 1974) §3.23

Albemarle Paper Co v Moody, 422 US 405 (1975) §3.32

Alcoa Credit Co v Nickerson, 43 Mass App Ct 1 (1968) §9.07

Alexander v Moore & Assocs, Inc, 553 F Supp 948 (D Haw 1982) §3.19

Allison v Liberty Savs, 535 F Supp 828 (ND Ill 1982) §11.13

American Airlines Inc v Remis Indus, Inc, 494 F2d 196 (2d Cir 1974) §7.09

American Express Co v Koerner, 452 US 233 (1981) §7.18

American Natl Bank & Trust Co v Haroco, Inc, 473 US 606 (1985) §5.33

Anderson v United Fin Co, 666 F2d 1274 (9th Cir 1982) §3.40

Anthony v Community Loan & Inv Corp, 559 F2d 1363 (5th Cir 1977) §6.06

Aquino v Public Fin Consumer Discount Co, 606 F Supp 504 (ED Pa 1985) §§4.28, 4.30

Attorney Gen v Equitable Trust Co, 294 Md 385, 450 A2d 1273 (1982) §5.12

Avco Sec Corp v Post, 42 AD2d 1055, 349 NYS2d 358 (1973) §9.07

Avenell v Westinghouse Elec Corp, 41 Ohio App 2d 150, 324 NE2d 583 (1974) §2.31

B

Bache Halsey Steward Shields Inc v Killop, 589 F Supp 390 (ED Mich 1984) §10.11

Bank of Louisville Royal v Sims, 435 SW2d 57, 7 UCC Rep Serv (Callaghan) 234 (Ky 1968) §8.27

Barbour v United States, 562 F2d 19 (10th Cir 1977) §10.07

Barker v Retail Credit Co, 8 Wis 2d 664, 100 NW2d 391 (1960) §3.16

Barnett v Chrysler Corp, 434 F Supp 1167 (D Neb 1977) §2.44

737

Y

Statutes

State Statutes

Uniform Commercial Code

Uniform Consumer Credit Code

Regulations

Index

WEST V COSTEN
Fair Debt Collection Practices Act
§10.28